To
Miss Yemisi Khalidson

From
The Library of GrandMa & GrandPa Elebute

Happy New Year!
January 2011.

A HISTORY OF THE YORUBA PEOPLE

To the Pathfinders

Samuel Johnson
Saburi O. Biobaku
Jacob F. Ade Ajayi
Isaac Adeagbo Akinjogbin

A HISTORY OF THE YORUBA PEOPLE

S. Adebanji Akintoye

Published by Amalion Publishing 2010

Amalion Publishing
BP 5637 Dakar-Fann
Dakar CP 00004
Senegal

www.amalion.net

Copyright © S. Adebanji Akintoye 2010

ISBN 978-2-35926-005-2 HB

ISBN 978-2-35926-006-9 PB

Cover designed by Mkuki Bgoya

Printed and bound in the United Kingdom by CPI Antony Rowe, Wiltshire

All rights reserved. No part of this publication may be reproduced, transmitted, or stored in a retrieval system, in any form or by any means, without permission in writing from Amalion Publishing, nor be otherwise circulated in any form of binding or cover than that in which it is published.

Contents

	Preface	vii
	Acknowledgements	x
1.	The Beginnings	1
2.	The Development of Early Yoruba Society	17
3.	Before Oduduwa: Ife in the Ninth to Tenth Century	43
4.	The Revolution in Ife: Tenth to Eleventh Century	55
5.	The Primacy of Ife: Eleventh to Fifteenth Century	71
6.	Traditions of Kingdom Founders	87
7.	The Kingdoms of Yorubaland	97
8.	The Politics of Kingdom Rule	119
9.	The Kingdoms and the Economy: Part I	155
10.	The Kingdoms and the Economy: Part II	179
11.	The Frontier Effect	205
12.	The Great Oyo Empire	229
13.	The Fall of the Oyo Empire	261
14.	Yorubaland in the Nineteenth Century: The Wars of Change	291
15.	Yorubaland in the Nineteenth Century: Other Agencies of Change	333
16.	The Yoruba Diaspora	365
17.	The Politics of the Twentieth Century	387
18.	The Social Transformations in the Twentieth Century	429

Notes	453
Bibliography	468
Index	479

Maps

1. Yorubaland	86
2. Yorubaland and frontier kingdoms in the western Sudan	208
3. Oyo Empire at its greatest extent (c. 1780)	228
4. Early Christian missions in Nigeria	332
5. Nigeria's regional structure, 1955	400
6. Nigeria's state structure, 1967	412
7. Nigeria's state structure, 1995	424

Preface

My objective in writing this book is to place in the hands of the Yoruba people, in the hands of students of Yoruba and African history, and in the hands of the general reader, a lucid account of Yoruba history, using the products of the latest research on the subject. Writing such an account has been far from easy. The volume of research on the subject is large and continually growing, and many partly unresolved issues of fact and interpretation litter the field. Therefore, the urge for me to write an account addressed only to academic historians, my own colleagues, has been very difficult to overcome. I can only hope that I have overcome it to some extent (by, among other things, trimming down on the more difficult controversies as well as on complex cross-referencing and footnoting that might distract the general reader); and that the volume that has hereby resulted goes a long way to fulfill my objective.

With a population variously estimated at between thirty and forty million, the Yoruba are perhaps the largest single ethnic group, or nationality, in Black Africa. Moreover, their history is one of the most researched and analyzed of any people in Africa. For this latter fact there are various reasons, of which one is the traditional structure (and the consequent historical consciousness) of Yoruba society, another is the high level of literacy among the Yoruba people today, and yet another is the growing importance of Yoruba Studies in the overall spectrum of African and Black Studies. The Yoruba were the most urbanized people in the history of the tropical African forestlands, having largely lived in walled cities and towns since as early as the eleventh or twelfth century. In those towns and cities they evolved a sophisticated monarchical system of government, whose governing elites established detailed institutions and processes for preserving society's history and passing it on – a circumstance that has both encouraged and facilitated the study of Yoruba history in our times. Then, since the beginning of the twentieth century, the Yoruba have invested more in education than any other African people and, by the end of the twentieth century, were widely regarded as the most literate people in Africa. A significant consequence of this growing literacy has been that much indigenous effort has gone into the writing of Yoruba history. Venturing into written reconstruction of the past began as soon as there were some literate Yoruba in the nineteenth century; then it flowered vigorously in the course of the twentieth century; and it has been augmented by contributions from many professional historians, indigenous and foreign. Finally, to black people in general, and especially to the people of the Black African Diaspora in the Americas (in the United States, Brazil, Central America, Cuba, Haiti, Trinidad, and other parts of the West Indies), a knowledge of Yoruba history has been growing in importance. This is not merely because of the size of the Yoruba population, but also because of the high level of civilization attained by the Yoruba people in the past, the growing knowledge of Yoruba contributions to Black cultures in the New World, and the continued dynamism of Yoruba civilization in modern times – all of which have attracted increasing interest into Yoruba research.

The present book is an attempt by a student and teacher of Yoruba and African history to synthesize for popular education the data that has become available to us on Yoruba history at the beginning of the twenty-first century. It is a product of my life-long participation in the development of Yoruba and African History Studies – in universities in Africa and the United States. I offer it in the humble hope that it will contribute something to the growing knowledge of Yoruba history in particular and the history of Africa and black people in general, that it will provoke further interest in Yoruba and African history, and, above all, that it will increase the Yoruba people's love of, and romance with, their impressive and fascinating heritage.

Because most of the Yoruba people have lived in the modern country of Nigeria since the beginning of European imperialist rule over Africa in the early twentieth century, there now exists a tendency to write of the Yoruba as if they are entirely a Nigerian people – to the dismay of those who are now citizens of the Republics of Benin and Togo. The Yoruba people and country are split by two international boundaries, and while the largest portion is to be found in Nigeria, some substantial parts are to be found in Benin and Togo. This book presents a history of all Yoruba people.

Finally, I have added a somewhat novel dimension to the perspective of this work. As professor of African History at the Obafemi Awolowo University, Ile-Ife, Nigeria, in the 1960s and 1970s, I designed and taught an introductory course in African-American History, and, during a sabbatical in the United States, I worked with others to establish an African and African-American Studies Program at the University of South Florida in Tampa, Florida. Later, when I served as Director of the Institute of African Studies at the Obafemi Awolowo University in the late 1970s, we initiated some programs on the African Diaspora in the Americas as an integral part of our multi-disciplinary approach to African Studies. All these stemmed from my belief that a study of the experience of Africans transplanted to the Americas in the era of the Atlantic slave trade needs to be seen by scholars and peoples of Africa as a part of the African experience in general. In recent years, happily, considerable advances have been made worldwide in the study of the African Diaspora in the Americas. Since the 1990s, that study has moved beyond the computing of the numbers of Africans transported to the Americas, and beyond the impact of American slavery on enslaved Africans; it has deepened to include studies of the contributions of transplanted African heritages to the evolution of African-American and American cultures. In the context of this deeper approach, much light has been thrown on the contribution of the Yoruba heritage in particular to the development of the cultures of the African Diaspora in the Americas. People of Yoruba descent, and the heritage of Yoruba civilization, constitute a very significant component of African-American cultures in most parts of the Americas. Therefore, I have ventured to include a short chapter on the history of the Yoruba Diaspora in the Americas in this book to highlight the unavoidable continuity between the history of Africa and the history of the African Diaspora, in the hope that the Yoruba people in the West African homeland will become more actively interested in the history of their people across the Atlantic, and in the hope that black people in the Americas will become more proactive in searching and proudly interacting with their African roots and heritage.

December 2008.

Acknowledgements

I started to sketch the outline of this book in 1978 in the Department of History, Obafemi Awolowo University, Nigeria, at a time when colleagues in that department, in collaboration with other departments, were working on a research project focused on a systematic collection of Yoruba oral traditions. I finally completed the writing in retirement in the United States from early 2006 to the end of 2007, utilizing my research notes spanning four decades as well as the rich spread of research work by many historians, now available in monographs, composite books, professional journal articles, and unpublished papers and theses. First and foremost, therefore, I acknowledge my indebtedness to the Department of History at Obafemi Awolowo University and to my colleagues in that department, among whom it was always easy to think great thoughts and dream great dreams. Among these colleagues, I must highlight for special mention Dr. Adeagbo Akinjogbin, for many years chair of our department and pioneer of many of our joint research programs; and my friend, Dr. Charles Arnade, for years Chair of International Studies at the University of South Florida, Tampa, Florida, who worked with us at Ife as Visiting Professor in the 1970s and became very helpful in the development of my efforts in African-American and American History.

I wrote the manuscript of this book, as I did my earlier books, in longhand – and that means that I received a lot of help from my close friends in word processing on computer. While thanking all for their invaluable assistance, I must express particular gratitude to Mr. Oluremi Oyeyemi, a Nigerian journalist now living in exile in the United States, for his intense interest in, and unflagging encouragement of, this work.

Throughout the months that I worked on completing this book, my wife, Fehintola, and our sons enthusiastically supported and encouraged me, and took turns to read parts of my draft. I am grateful for their loving support.

This book represents, for me, the final harvest of my career of studies in Yoruba history. For that reason, I hereby acknowledge the contributions to my academic career by the men who, in my undergraduate years at the University College, Ibadan, Nigeria, in the late 1950s, first ignited my interest in the

Acknowledgements

study of African history – my professors Kenneth Dike, J. F. Ade Ajayi, Abdullahi Smith, J. D. Omer-Cooper and A. B. Aderibigbe. Of these, Professor Ajayi went on to supervise my graduate studies, showing great understanding of and patience with my other wide interests, and continuing ever after as my mentor and friend.

In the course of the past two years, I have depended on my favorite local library, Indian Valley Public Library, Telford, Pennsylvania, for a heavy program of inter-library loans. I am very grateful to the staff of this wonderful institution for always making their services promptly and smoothly available to me.

I am very grateful to the following historians of African and Yoruba History for kindly reading my manuscript and offering important comments and suggestions: Dr. J. F. Ade Ajayi (Emeritus Professor of History, University of Ibadan, Nigeria), Dr. Elisee Soumonni (Professor of History, Department of African History and Archaeology, National University of Benin at Abomey-Calavi, Benin Republic, now retired), Dr. R. C. C. Law (Professor of African History, Stirling University, Stirling, Scotland), Dr. Toyin Falola (the Frances Higginbotham Nalle Centennial Professor in History, University of Texas at Austin, Texas), Dr. Funso Afolayan (Associate Professor of History and African Studies, University of New Hampshire, Durham, New Hampshire), and Dr. Adebayo Oyebade (Professor of History, Tennessee State University, Nashville, Tennessee). I also thank Dr. Elisee Soumonni for his assistance with some of the materials relating to the history of the Yoruba of Benin Republic, Dr. Dele Agbede of the Department of Agriculture, State of Maryland, for his help with some of the maps, Dr. Yiwola Awoyale of the Linguistic Data Consortium, University of Pennsylvania, Philadelphia, and Dr. Mayowa Ogedemgbe of the Department of African Studies, Temple University, Philadelphia, for their assistance with the Yoruba orthography employed in this book.

Finally, I give glory to God for all the help I have received while working to complete this book, and for the health and strength to bring it to this successful conclusion.

December 2008.

Photo credits

Agence France Presse Photos: #28, 31 & 32.

Atanda, J. A., *An Introduction to Yoruba History*, Ibadan University Press, 1980: #20 & 22.

CMS Yoruba Mission Papers, National Archives, Ibadan, Nigeria: #27.

Dirk Bakker and the National Commission for Museum and Monuments, Ife, Nigeria in Tom Phillips, ed., *Africa: The Art of a Continent,* London, Prestel Verlag, 1999: #2 & 3.

Henry Drewal, John Pemberton and Rowland Abiodun, *Yoruba: Nine Centuries of African Art and Thought,* NY, Center for African Art, in association with Harry N. Abrams, Inc., 1999, pp. 193–4: #8.

Elisee Soumonni: #16.

Getty Images: #29 & 30.

Institut Fondamental d'Afrique Noir, Université Cheikh Anta Diop, Dakar, Senegal: #1, 4, 5, 6, 7a, 7b, 9, 10, 11, 12, 13, 14, 15, 17, 18, 21, 23, 24, 25, 26, 28, 33, & 34.

John Pemberton III in Rowland Abiodun, Ulli Beier, and John Pemberton, *Cloth Only Wears to Shreds: Yoruba Textiles and Photographs from the Beier Collection,* Mead Art Museum, Amherst College, Massachusetts, 2004, p. 35: #19.

1

The Beginnings

The Yoruba have some remarkable graphic myths of creation and of origins. The most widely known Yoruba myth has it that at the beginning of time, when the whole surface of the earth was one watery matter, Olodumare (also known as Olorun, "king of heaven") sent down some heavenly beings to create solid land, as well as plant life and animal life, on the earth. Bringing with them some quantity of earth, one chicken and one palm nut, they came down by a chain and landed on the spot that is now known as Ife in the heart of Yorubaland. They poured the earth onto the water, and thus created a small piece of solid land. They then set the chicken on the land, and as the chicken scratched at it with its claws, the small piece of dry land spread – and continued to spread until all the continents and islands of the world came into existence. The heavenly beings sowed the palm nut, and it sprouted and grew as the beginning of plant life in the world. The heavenly beings themselves became the progenitors of the human race. The place where all this began was named Ife – that is, "the source of the spreading". The Yoruba believe, then, that theirs is the first race of humans, and that all human life and civilization originated in their country.

One version of this myth supplies names to the heavenly beings that came down to establish life at Ife. The leader appointed by Olodumare to head the expedition was, according to this version, Obatala. Along the way, however, Obatala got drunk and fell into a stupor, and Oduduwa took over and completed the mission, and thus became the father of the Yoruba people – and of all the people of the world.

This body of myths is very strongly held among the Yoruba people, and its influence pervades all areas of their culture. The historian who embarks on studying, or writing about, the very beginnings of the history of the Yoruba as a people must start with an examination of those myths. The first Europeans to enter Yorubaland in the nineteenth century encountered it everywhere. For instance, the first Christian missionary to visit Ife in the 1850s (David Hinderer) was told, after he had finished preaching the Christian gospel to a large crowd at the palace of Ife, that all religion originated from Ife, and that what he had preached was no more than one of the versions that had evolved later in a distant part of the world. David Hinderer wrote:

> Ife is famous as being the seat of idolatry; all the multiple idols of this part of the country are said to emanate from the town; from there the sun and moon rises [sic] where they are buried in the ground, and all people of this country and even white men spring from the town.[1]

In 1882, Rev. Samuel Johnson, an Anglican missionary and son of Yoruba freed slaves who had returned to Yorubaland from Sierra Leone, was told by the chiefs of the city of Ibadan that Ife was "the place where all nations of the earth have sprung from."[2] In 1886, British agents visiting the Yoruba interior were told by the Alaafin of Oyo that "the Ifes…were the fathers of all and all people came from Ife…"; by the chiefs of Ife, at Isoya where they and their people were camped, outside the ruins of their city, that the Ife people were "the fathers of all tribes", and that if they continued longer in a camp and unable to resettle their ancient city of Ile-Ife, "the whole world would spoil, as they were the priests of the deities who ruled the world"; and by the Seriki of the Ijebu, Chief Ogunsigun, that "Even the English king can be shown the spot at Ile-Ife from where his ancestors went out". Henry Higgins, the leading British agent in this 1886 mission, summed up his information about Ife as follows:

> There are all manner of legends as to the wonders to be seen at Ile-Ife.… The Ifes call themselves the conservators of the world and the oldest of mankind and boast that all crowned personages in the world, including the white man's sovereign, went out originally from Ile-Ife, and it was curious the deference with which other tribes treat them although they are at war with them… and as every one was supposed to be a descendant of the Ifes, they looked upon all strangers who visited their town in the light of pilgrims who came, as they put it, "to make their house good", that is to pay reverence to departed ancestors.[3]

To the historian, discerning the meanings and implications of these myths is important. Of the implications, the most obvious would seem to be that the Yoruba people believe that they originated in their present homeland and have always lived there. Since, however, it is known from other evidence than myths that the earliest ancestors of all the peoples of West Africa came into that region from other parts of Africa, the Yoruba belief can only mean that the Yoruba have lived so long in their present homeland that they can no longer remember originally coming into it from elsewhere. Indeed, available archaeological evidence strongly indicates that the Yoruba are one of the oldest peoples in the tropical forests of the West African region.

As for the introduction of the names of Obatala and Oduduwa into these creation myths, there seems no doubt that what we have here is a conflation of very ancient myths with later known facts at some point in Yoruba history. As will be seen in subsequent chapters, Obatala and Oduduwa were not mythical, heavenly beings; they were humans – humans who played very significant roles in a great era of Yoruba history. Without doubt, what happened was that the contemporaries or successors of Obatala and Oduduwa added these two names to myths that had existed probably very long before their time, in an attempt to accord Oduduwa in particular the very high position he deserved in the transformation of Yoruba civilization in the most significant era in early Yoruba history.

Furthermore, the myths appear to represent a statement of a very important fact of Yoruba history – namely, the extensive penetration, from quite early times, of Yoruba people and Yoruba culture into the lands of their non-Yoruba neighbors, and the considerable impact of Yoruba culture in much of the West African sub-region. More will be said on this subject of interfertilization of Yoruba and neighboring cultures in subsequent chapters. Suffice it to say here that, as far as is known, Yoruba culture exerted so much influence on, and absorbed such inputs from, so many neighbors (the Edo and related peoples, the Aja, the Bariba, the Nupe, etc.) and drew so many so close to itself (in family structure, trade practices, language, religion, political system and traditions) that the Yoruba people apparently came to perceive their country as the source of civilization – and ultimately of the human societies which created observable variations in civilization – and evolved myths that gave meaning and support to that perception. It is significant that some of the neighbors of the Yoruba in fact subscribed to parts of the Yoruba myths.

The above, then, is the little that a study of Yoruba history can, as at this point in the task, discern from the people's powerful and influential myths of creation and of origins. From these myths of gods and heavenly beings, the historian, for a reconstruction of the earliest beginnings of Yoruba history, must begin to look into the available evidence of the earliest activities of humans. Thankfully, there is a wealth of such historical data in the oral traditions, institutions, rituals, festivals and folklore of the Yoruba people. Traditional Yoruba family structures, and monarchical and chieftaincy systems, attached enormous importance from early times to the preservation of traditions from generation to generation, since title to political and other significant positions, as well as to land, was based, to an extraordinary degree, on ancestry and history as preserved in the traditions. Reenactment rituals accompany various phases and stages of the Yoruba political system, and old centers and practices of worship preserve treasures of group memory. Yoruba people's varied and vast culture of poetry, songs, chants and collection of folk wisdom, offer extensive insights into the group's past. All these have greatly helped – and encouraged – the study of Yoruba history in our times.

Much help has also come from sciences in the course of the twentieth century. One such science is archaeology – the study of prehistoric cultures through the excavation and analysis of their material remains. Another is linguistics – especially its application to the study of the prehistoric origins and development of the languages of peoples.

Since historical information available through archaeology and linguistics goes much farther back in time than the information available through the traditions and other aspects of Yoruba culture, it makes sense to start with the archaeological and linguistic record. Archaeological excavations have been carried out in almost all regions of the Yoruba homeland – at Ife, Ifetedo and Asejire in central Yorubaland, at Iwo Eleru and Itaogbolu (both near Akure) and Owo in the Yoruba eastern provinces, at Apa near Badagry on the southwest coast, at Mejiro near the ruins of Oyo-Ile in the far northwest, at Itaakpe in the Ife-Jumu area in the extreme northeast. Excavations done in other parts of Nigeria, and indeed in other parts of Africa, also help to illuminate the early history of the Yoruba people.[4]

According to available archaeological evidence, the earliest humans lived in the broad country comprising Eastern Africa in an era estimated to be between one and three million years ago. Archaeologists are mostly of the opinion that humans spread out from the area of the Rift Valley in Eastern Africa, to Northern Africa, and from Northern Africa to Western Africa, slowly over hundreds of thousands of years. Evidence of human existence in the area now known as Nigeria dates to about 40,000 years ago – that is, about 38000 BC. By about this date, Middle Stone Age groups of humans roamed parts of the Middle Niger Valley in what is now Nigeria. Using tools and other implements made of stone (and perhaps also wood, bones and shells), these early people made their living by gathering food in the forests, by hunting animals for meat, and by fishing. If food was plentiful in a forest area, a group might stay there for a while, and then move on again.

Archaeologists believe that in those very early times when human groups came gradually into the West African region from the Northern African subcontinent, the region now known as the Sahara Desert was not yet a desert but a country of various types of grassland where many rivers and streams flowed. The total number of humans coming into West Africa was small; and their stone tools were primitive and improved very slowly. By about 10000 BC, humans in West Africa were making greatly improved stone tools and implements, in the era which archaeologists now call the Late Stone Age. While Early Stone Age and Middle Stone Age tools had consisted of crudely trimmed flakes and pebbles as well as bi-facial core-axes and chisels, Late Stone Age tools consisted of microliths (that is, small, finely chipped and finely ground stone tools) and ground axes. Some of the microliths were very probably mounted on wooden or bone handles to produce spears, arrows and other types of tools – all for hunting, cutting, digging and scraping. At some late period in the Late Stone Age, from about 5000 BC, people began to make pots from clay (for fetching and holding water) – a very important technological advance.

But the most important progress made during the Late Stone Age was the discovery, some time starting from roughly 4000 BC, of agriculture – that is, the domestication of crops and animals. With this discovery, people slowly changed from being wanderers to settlers – the first real, solid, steps in the creation of human culture and civilization.

Among archaeologists, there is a debate over how people in West Africa came to the knowledge of agriculture. Did they make the discovery by themselves or was it brought entirely to them by groups of people migrating into West Africa from other parts of Africa where agriculture was already being practiced? Did West Africans domesticate any crops or animals, or were all their crops and animals domesticated in other regions of Africa and then brought to West Africa by generations of early immigrants?[5]

Some archaeologists believe that people in West Africa did not domesticate any crops or animals, but received all their crops (yams, grains, legumes, etc.) and domestic animals (goats, sheep, cows, horses, etc.) from outside sources. But other archaeologists now question that opinion, and suggest that while they did receive some domesticated crops and animals from the outside, some crops were also locally domesticated in West Africa. Since none of the domestic animals (goats, sheep, cows, asses, horses, etc.) were, in their wild state, native to West Africa, it seems certain that they were domesticated in other places and later introduced to West Africa. Similarly, many types of yams were domesticated in other places and then brought to West Africa. Certain types, however, appear to have been native to the area now known as Southern Nigeria in West Africa. These include the yam types known as *Diascoria latifolia* and *Diascoria cayenensis* – including the various types that the Yoruba people call *ewura*. These types of yam would seem to have been domesticated in Southern Nigeria, including Yorubaland, and to have remained more or less restricted to the area. What this suggests is that there was a local yam culture in Yorubaland before, or side by side with, the coming of many other species of yams that were domesticated in other places – some of them across the African continent even from as far as Asia. Also, the two kolanut species – *Cola nitida* (*gooro*) and *Cola acuminata* (*obi abata*) were domesticated locally in the West African forests. Some grains (such as millets) would seem also to have been native to the West African grasslands and to have been domesticated there. Finally, there is general agreement that the expansion of the oil palm to virtually all parts of West Africa was the result of the growth of agriculture. The oil palm is native to West Africa, but according to available archaeological and other evidence, before the growth of agriculture in West Africa, it formed only a small part of the vegetation. By nature, the oil palm tends to spread quickly only in places where agricultural activity has made the forests less dense – that is, it followed the expansion of farming. West African farmers, therefore, were responsible for creating the conditions that led to the spread of the oil palm until it became the most important tree crop in almost all parts of the West African forest and savannah lands.

In time, yam tubers and the products of the palm tree became the most important food sources for humans in the tropical forest regions of West Africa, supplemented over time with some grains, beans, vegetables and, much later, plantains and coco-yams. Oils and fats from the oil-palm fruit were the most important food items from the palm tree. But it also became the source of many other valuables – edible nuts, an alcoholic beverage now known as palm-wine (*emu*), various types of domestic fuels, and even materials for building shelters. It is not surprising, therefore, that the palm tree and some of its products became very important in the religion, divination and rituals of many West African peoples (including the Yoruba) from early times.

All over the world, whenever the Agricultural Revolution started in an area, its greatest effect was to transform people from wanderers to settlers. Instead of wandering to collect food from fruits of the wild vegetation and to hunt animals, they gradually settled down to take care of their crops and domestic animals. In that way, humans began to set up their first permanent abodes. In West Africa, the first such homes were no doubt established in no more than caves, rock and the man-made shelters.

During the later stages of the Late Stone Age, as farming turned wandering folks into settlers (from about 4000 BC), the scattered spread of farming people living in the West African region slowly began to get differentiated into related clusters and groups speaking proto-languages consisting of dialects that were related to one another. Available linguistic evidence indicates that many such groups and clusters slowly formed on the banks of the Middle Niger, mostly in the area of the Niger–Benue confluence and above it. This linguistic evidence suggests that the Yoruba, Igala, Edo, Idoma, Ebira, Nupe, Kakanda, Gbagyi and Igbo belonged to a cluster of languages, now called Kwa sub-group of languages by modern scholars, belonging to a larger family of languages now called the Niger-Congo (or Nigritic) family of languages. The small cluster was concentrated roughly around the Niger–Benue confluence. Over thousands of years, the groups in this cluster slowly separated as they developed distinctive characteristics, probably the last language groups to separate being the Igala and Yoruba. One study suggests that the proto-Yoruba and proto-Nupe language sub-families seem to have migrated from a little further up the Niger, slowly expanding towards the confluence, and that during that process each finally became differentiated from a mother language group.[6]

The clear implication of all this is that the origin of the Yoruba people as a linguistic and ethnic group belongs in the process of slow differentiation of proto-groups which occurred in the Middle Niger and around the Niger–Benue confluence, beginning about 4000 BC and continuing for thousands of years. It is, therefore, in this area that we must find the first home of the Yoruba as one people – the area close to the Niger–Benue confluence and further up the Niger, where the southern Nupe and the far northeastern Yoruba groups – the Yagba, Jumu, Ikiri, Oworo, Owe, and Bunu (now collectively called the Okun Yoruba by some scholars) – and the northernmost Igbomina, live today.

From that original center, the Yoruba group spread out, over many centuries, towards the south and the west. As they came into these forests, they found small groups of people who had been there for a very long time, first as wandering folks, and later as farming folks. Archaeological excavations at a rock shelter at Iwo Eleru near Akure, and another site at Ifetedo to the northwest of Iwo Eleru, have yielded valuable information about these earlier inhabitants. The human bones found at Iwo Eleru, dated to about 7000 BC, are the oldest human remains found yet in the whole of West Africa. Altogether, the evidence found at Iwo Eleru and Ifetedo indicates that the earliest of these people had arrived in this forest country as early as about 10000–9000 BC. They were scattered farming folks by the time the Yoruba elements began to arrive, and they were ultimately absorbed into the spreading Yoruba culture group.[7]

As the Yoruba were spreading out, there came a time when some slightly faster rate of migration from the Northern African region brought somewhat increased numbers of people from that region into West Africa. From about 5000 BC, the Sahara region of Northern Africa had begun to dry up as a result of some climatic changes in that belt of the world. As the region very slowly turned to desert, the peoples living there migrated out, some eastwards to the area of the Nile Valley, others southwards into West Africa, forming a somewhat bigger flow of immigrants than before. From sometime probably after 3000 BC, this bigger flow of immigration began to speed up the growth of human populations in West Africa in general. It seems probable that these fairly large migrations are responsible for the persistence of traditions of a "northern" origin among many peoples of West Africa. Those of these immigrants who came into what was then becoming Yorubaland were absorbed into the evolving Yoruba culture group.

The Yoruba continued to spread southwards and westwards. Southwards they ultimately reached the Atlantic coast. According to archaeological evidence, human settlers who were probably part of the Yoruba had reached the area of modern Badagry by about 1000 BC. Westwards, they continued to expand until their westernmost elements occupied territories in the areas that are now the Republics of Benin and Togo.

The Yoruba had gradually evolved as a group of many small fragments; each of the fragments spoke some dialect of the evolving common Yoruba language. Thousands of years followed the initial emergence of the Yoruba as a group, and their many mutually intelligible dialects remained more or less clearly distinct, and ultimately came to define the internal differentiations that constituted the Yoruba subgroups that we have today – the Oyo, Ijebu, Ekiti, Ijesa, Ife, Ondo, Egba, Ibarapa, Egbado, Akoko, Owo, Ikale, Ilaje, Itsekiri, Awori, Ketu, Sabe, Ifonyin, Idasa, Popo, Ife (also known as the Ana, and found today in Togo Republic), Ahori, Itsha, Mahi, Igbomina, Ibolo, Owe, Oworo, Jumu, Bunu, Yagba, Gbede, Ikiri – some large and some small. As pointed out earlier, some scholars of the Yoruba people have suggested the collective name "Okun Yoruba" for the small Yoruba subgroups living in the area of the far northeastern Yorubaland close to the Niger–Benue confluence – namely, the Owe, Oworo, Jumu, Bunu, Yagba, and Ikiri. The name was coined from the common occurrence of "okun" in the mode of greetings by all these subgroups. In this book, that collective name is used whenever such a usage is deemed to serve the purpose of brevity. For clarity also, the Ife subgroup in today's Togo Republic will sometimes be identified as the Western Ife.

As the Yoruba spread and settled into their country, each particular subgroup inhabited a particular region. In the extreme northeastern region, close to the Niger–Benue confluence, lived about seven small subgroups – the Owe, Oworo, Gbede, Jumu, Ikiri, Bunu and Yagba. To the west of these, in the Yoruba northern belt south of the Middle Niger, lived the Igbomina subgroup, and west of the Igbomina, the Oyo subgroup – one of the largest, occupying the wide expanse of Yorubaland from the border with the Igbomina in the east to the border with the Ketu in the west. A small subgroup – the Ibolo – lived to the southwest of the Igbomina, sandwiched between the Igbomina and the Oyo. All the territory of these northern Yoruba subgroups was grassland.

Immediately to the south of the territory of the Okun Yoruba lived two subgroups, the Ekiti and the Akoko, both inhabiting the hilliest region of Yorubaland. Ekiti was one of the largest of the subgroups. West of the Ekiti were the Ijesa (another large subgroup), and west of them the Ife of central Yorubaland (one of the small subgroups). West of the Ife lived the Owu (another small subgroup), and west of them the Egba. North of the Egba lived the small subgroup named the Ibarapa. The middle belt of Yorubaland occupied by these subgroups was mostly tropical forest, with the grasslands intruding into the Ekiti and Akoko territories.

South of the Ekiti and Akoko were the Owo, and west of them the country of the Ondo, and then the Ijebu, and the Awori. The Ijebu were among the largest of the subgroups. The homelands of these subgroups lay in the belt of the thickest forests in Yorubaland. The Ijebu and Awori extended further south to the coast and occupied a considerable stretch of coastal lagoon territory.

South of this thick forest belt was the Atlantic coastland, a narrow stretch of mostly mangrove swamps broken up by innumerable creeks and lagoons. The easternmost Yoruba subgroup in this lagoon territory were the Itsekiri. The Yoruba subgroup next to them were the Ilaje. A thin territory of partly forests and partly swamps immediately to the north of Ilaje was occupied by the Ikale subgroup. West of the Ilaje and Ikale were the coastal Ijebu, and west of them the coastal Awori. These coastal subgroups – Itsekiri, Ilaje, Ikale and Awori – were all small. The coastal Ijebu were the southernmost tip of the large Ijebu subgroup.

The farthest western region of Yorubaland lay west of the Oyo, Egba, Egbado and Awori territories, stretching from grasslands in the north and touching the coast in some places. In today's terms, this area covers the middle and much of the south of the Republic of Benin and penetrates into the western provinces of the Republic of Togo. In this area lived a number of small Yoruba subgroups – the Ketu, Idasa, Sabe, Ahori, Mahi, Sha (or Itsha), and Western Ife. These far western Yoruba subgroups lived interspersed here and there with a people called the Adja or Aja (consisting of such subgroups as the Egun or Gun, Allada and Fon). There was considerable closeness between the Yoruba and the Aja. Like the Yoruba language, Aja belonged to the Kwa subfamily within the larger Niger-Congo family of languages. It seems obvious that when the Yoruba stream encountered the Aja people in this area, it continued and flowed past them westwards, so that over time Yoruba subgroups existed to the east, west and north of the Aja. With the Aja thus almost enveloped by the Yoruba, profound cultural affinities further developed between the two, with the smaller (the Aja) greatly influenced by the larger (the Yoruba) – in language, religion, and social and political institutions. Ultimately, the Yoruba and Aja became more or less one cultural area, and the Yoruba language became a sort of lingua franca for the two peoples, which means that while the Aja spoke their own language (which was strongly influenced by the Yoruba language) most of the Aja also spoke Yoruba.[8]

In this far western Yoruba country, the traditions also identify one more Yoruba subgroup named Popo, but this has created a problem, since no Popo subgroup is identifiable today. Most Yoruba traditions speak of an old, far western, subgroup of that name. At the same time some of the western Yoruba refer to the people of the much nearer area of Badagry and Ajase (who call themselves Gun or Igun) as Popo. The probability would seem to be that there existed an early Popo subgroup which settled in a thin line along the coast of what are now the Benin and Togo Republics, among the Aja, with the Ewe as their western neighbors. Being considerably isolated from other Yoruba subgroups, the Popo subgroup (and the kingdom which was founded among them at a later time) probably became absorbed over time into the cultures of non-Yoruba neighbors; and, therefore, the existence of the name Popo in places along the coast might be survivals from their name. Presumably from surviving traces of that name, the first European traders along the coast called the towns of Hula and Aneho (on today's western part of the Togo coast) Grand Popo and Little Popo respectively, but the people of the two towns did not, as far as is known, explicitly call themselves Popo and were not Yoruba-speaking (they were Gbe-speaking) by the time of the coming of the Europeans.

The experiences of the subgroups in this far western region appear to have been somewhat similar to the experiences of the Akoko subgroup in their rugged eastern homeland. It is obvious that the Akoko, too, encountered some non-Yoruba group or groups in these hills. Here, however, the Akoko seem to have completely absorbed such non-Yoruba elements. It is no longer possible to identify the descendants of such non-Yoruba group or groups, but their language or languages are not totally extinct, being more or less discernible in the dialects of the Akoko people (in fact, in some places still faintly discernible side by side with Akoko dialect). The complexity of dialects in Akoko was also increased, over time, by contacts with non-Yoruba groups to the east (the Akoko-Edo, Afenmai and Ishan) and to the north (the Kakanda, Ebira and Nupe).

In general, the subgroups differed from one another in dialect. But this must not be understood as meaning that each subgroup was completely homogenous in dialect. There were shades of local differentiations within the dialect of every subgroup. The most profound of such local differentiation existed in the Akoko subgroup, among whom dialect varied from village to village. In the larger subgroups, the differentiation in dialect resulted in what some historians have called "provinces" of the subgroups, each province speaking a variant of the subgroup dialect. For instance, the Ijebu had four large "provinces" – first, the province of western Ijebu which is known as Remo, second, the central Ijebu (around Ijebu-Ode), third, the coastal Ijebu, and fourth, the northeastern Ijebu (around Ijebu-Igbo). The Ekiti, occupying the rugged hills, had sixteen – hence the ancient Ekiti tradition of "sixteen heads of Ekiti." The large Oyo subgroup, occupying mostly open country, were considerably homogenous in dialect, and had roughly two provinces – first, the large body of population inhabiting northern and central Oyo territory, and second, the Epo to the south (in and close to the Osun Valley). The Ondo had four – the population around the Orosun Hill or Idanre Rock of eastern Ondo territory, the population of the northeastern (around Ile-Oluji), the population of the deep southern Ondo forests close to the Ikale and Ilaje, and then the populations of the rest of the Ondo forests (around Ode-Ondo). Finally, the Egba had three – the largest known as the Gbagura, in northern Egba territory, the Egba Oke-Ona on the River Ona close to the Remo province of Ijebu, and the Egba Agbeyin.

About the earliest settlements of Yoruba farming people in the forests, there are bodies of traditions in most parts of Yorubaland. Such traditions are found in nearly every town with a long history of existence in its present location. According to these traditions, some settlers inhabited, in great antiquity, the location where each of these towns now stands. The first researcher to write about these early settlements, using the oral traditions of Yoruba towns, was the anthropologist Ulli Beier. In an article entitled "Before Oduduwa," published in the 1950s, Beier identified many of these early settlements and the towns into which they later became absorbed.[9] Since then, interest in these early settlements of the Yoruba forests has grown, with the result that what we now know about the subject is quite considerable.[10]

The traditions concerning these early settlements are integral to the traditions of the founding of the Yoruba kingdoms. When, in a period from about the tenth or eleventh century AD (the period usually regarded as the Oduduwa period of Yoruba history), various groups went out (mostly from Ife) to establish kingdoms in the Yoruba forests, they came upon some pre-existing settlements everywhere, and it was among these settlers that they established kingdoms. The traditions are unambiguous that the early settlers and the groups that came among them to establish kingdoms belonged to the same ethnic stock, speaking dialects of the same language and sharing many other cultural attributes. In short, the early settlers were the scattered Yoruba settlers in the Yoruba forests, while the ones who came among them to establish kingdoms were bearers of a somewhat higher level of political organization that had evolved in the central region of the Yoruba country. About the founding of the Yoruba kingdoms, much more will be said in subsequent chapters.

The early settlers lived in small settlements; each settlement, by about the tenth century AD, was autonomous and had its own ruler and hierarchy of chiefs and its own shrines and rituals. Usually, however, these settlements lived in groups – that is, a few settlements were located at some proximity to one another in an area, and that group was separated from similar groups by expanses of forests. There is some uncertainty about what name we should call these groups. Some scholars call them "village groups," and others still other names. In most parts of ancient Yorubaland, especially in central and eastern Yorubaland, it would seem that each such group was known as an *elu*, and therefore, for simplicity, the name *elu* will be adopted in this book, and each settlement in the *elu* will be called simply a settlement or village.

Each *elu* evolved slowly over a very long time. First, one small settlement lived in an area; then, over a long time, other small settlements came one by one to take locations in the same area. Each settlement had evolved, according to the traditions, in the nearby forests and, under pressure of some difficulties there, had moved and relocated to what it saw as a better place. In this way, the *elu* came into being, surrounded by virtually unoccupied virgin forests on all sides.

We owe the clarity of these traditions to the manner in which Yoruba towns and cities arose in a later period of history. In that later era (the centuries beginning roughly from the tenth century AD) the distinct settlements or villages in each *elu* were amalgamated or compacted together to form a single new town or *ilu*, but each pre-existing settlement remained a recognizable quarter in the new town, and its former ruler became its quarter chief under the ruler or king of the new town. In that type of setting, each former settlement gave much attention to the preservation of its own remembered history – and the study of early Yoruba history is the richer today from that circumstance.

We must now attempt a synthesis of all the information available from probing these bodies of traditions. As the Yoruba group and its many subgroups expanded into the Yoruba forests, they settled in small villages – choosing for their locations the banks of rivers, streams and lakes (obviously to ensure reliable water supply), or the shelter of hills and rocks (for protection). In most locations, these small, primitive settlements were confronted by grave dangers, depicted in the traditions and legends as vicious, unforgiving, enemies. Chief among these enemies were wild beasts, hostile humans from other settlements, hunger and disease. The villagers, in some cases, lived in almost endless fear, which sometimes became so intense that adults ran away and abandoned children. Production of food was primitive, food was scarce, and whole families often had no more than a small, shriveled, yam tuber to share. Mysterious sicknesses wiped out settlements or forced survivors to pack and flee in panic.

These harrowing experiences were no doubt the results of the very primitive status of the technological, economic and social life of Yoruba people in those early days. Food production was primitive and food was scarce because these were the beginnings of the practice of agriculture. Farming tools (made of stone) were primitive, farmers cultivated only small patches of ground, and the types of cultivated crops were few. Wild beasts were hostile because the earliest settlements, intended to be permanent and supplied increasingly by agricultural production, were the first sustained intrusions of humans into the habitats of wild beasts. People feared strangers, and that bred sudden aggressions. The people of one settlement would surprise another settlement and abduct its people to increase their own settlement, because settlements feared remaining too small; smallness made them vulnerable to known and unknown human enemies. The mysterious sicknesses and deaths were probably the result, mostly, of the spread of malaria. When people cleared an opening in the forest and settled and made farms, they thereby created an area where the malaria mosquito could flourish.

However, it would seem that the people of the time gave purely supernatural explanations to their troubles. Thus, to appease the wild beasts, people began to worship the spirits that were believed to materialize through some of them, especially such large carnivores as the hyena and the leopard, and large reptiles like the crocodile and the boa constrictor, and set up shrines and rituals for the purpose. The mysterious sicknesses and deaths were attributed to the anger and malevolence of the spirits inhabiting the land over which people had come to establish their dwellings. The worship of primordial spirits of the earth (called *ore* or *ere* or *erele*) became the major cornerstone of their religious life. In time, each settlement that managed to survive "discovered" a protector spirit in a local physical entity like a body of water (a river, stream, lake or spring), a rock, a hill or a tree that was believed to have magical powers. In this way, according to traditions and myths preserved in rituals and festivals, arose the worship, for instance, of the Olota Rock in Ado (Ekiti), Olosunta Hill in Ikere (Ekiti), the Orosun Hill and Idanre Rock in Idanre, the spirits of virtually all the rivers and streams of Yorubaland by the settlements established along their banks, and the spirit of the sea by the settlements established along the sea coast.

Settlements also tended to relocate, repeatedly in many cases, in order to flee their terrifying experiences. To this, the end result was that settlements tended to relocate close together in places which came to be regarded as suitable (having reliable water supply, good for the crops, etc.) and, above all, safe. The process seems to be that when a settlement survived for long in a place and seemed to prosper there, other settler groups, seeking to share in the advantages of the place, would come and establish their own settlement nearby – and a group of small settlements (or an *elu*) would gradually emerge.

Most of these *elu* and the settlements or villages in them are still more or less easily identifiable in the traditions of most parts of Yorubaland, but only a few will be mentioned here. In the fertile valleys and low hills of the area that later became Owo town in the far southeastern forests, there grew Efene, Iyere, Igbe, Utelu, Upo, Okese, Idasen and some others. Around the foot of the

Olota Rock in the area that later became Ado (in Ekiti), there emerged Ilesun, Ijala, Idemo, Ilemo, Iremo, Isolo, Inisa and Ilaro. In the hill slopes and valleys which later became Ogotun (in Ekiti), there developed side by side more than eight settlements, of which Igbon, Isodu and Arun are the best remembered. In the thickly forested plains that later became Akure, many small settlements clustered together. Only a few of these are clearly remembered today, and they include Ipogun, Ikota, Ijomu, Oke-Aro, Obanla, Idopetu, Ilemo. Similarly in Ondo in the deep southern forests, only a few of the many early settlements are remembered – among them Oka, Ifore, Idoko, Akasa. In Ijebu-Ode, west of Ondo in the same deep forest zone, many settlements were founded, but only Idoko and Igbo now stand out clearly in the oral traditions. In the area now known as Ife (Olukotun) in Yagba in the far north-eastern region of Yorubaland, there emerged at least twenty small settlements. At Ife (Jumu) in the same region, there existed about thirteen.

In a 1969 report of a preliminary archaeological survey of Ife in central Yorubaland, Paul Ozanne pointed out that the Ife area features certain geographical advantages which must have been very suitable for early settlements.[11] The whole area lies in a high bowl surrounded by hills which form a watershed for many streams flowing out through gaps between the hills. Well protected from erosion, it also benefits from fog and clouds which, in the rainy season, form over the hills while the rain drains into the bowl. Into this bowl, the earliest settlers came in some unknown antiquity. Over time, other settler groups found their way into the area. According to Paul Ozanne, there were many settlements established there by the fourth century BC. By about the tenth century AD when great changes began to transform this area, there were, according to Omotoso Eluyemi, thirteen settlements, namely Omologun, Parakin, Iwinrin, Oke-Awo, Ijugbe, Iraye, Imojubi, Okeoja, Iloran, Odin; Ideta, Iloromu and Ido.[12]

In many communities in Yorubaland, it is still quite easy to identify the descendants of the earliest settlement in a place, because the rulers of earliest settlements usually held (and their descendants still hold) the priesthood of the local protector god or spirit. For instance, in the Ado kingdom in Ekiti, the Elesun, ruler of Ilesun (the oldest settlement in the place) is still much revered, even though the last holder of that title was defeated in battle and executed as far back as about the fourteenth century AD by the immigrant founders of the Ado kingdom. The influence of the Elesun sprang from the fact that he was the high priest of the spirit of the Olota Rock (in addition to being ruler of Ilesun). The other settlements that came later to the area feared the Elesun, who, according to some traditions, had his shrine in a cave or rock shelter in the Olota Rock and kept leopards as pets there, under the care of a senior priest who bore the title of Balota. Ado traditions claim that the people of the Ilesun settlement never came from anywhere but originated at the foot of the Olota Rock; and that the other settlements that came there in later times originated in the neighboring forests and later moved closer to Ilesun, especially in order to share in the protection given by the spirit of the Olota Rock.

In the Owo kingdom in the southeastern forests, the Alale, ruler of Idasin, the earliest settlement in the area, was high priest of the Ogho spirit, the protector spirit of the area. He exercised considerable influence over the rulers of the other independent settlements that later relocated to the area. The traditions have it that Idasin existed in Owo since the beginning of time. Of the other settlements in the place, some claim that their earliest ancestors came from a nearby forest known as Igboere, a forest early known as the grove of primordial earth spirits.

Early settlements in the forest area that later became the Akure kingdom recognized the Oba settlement, ruled by the Oloba, as the oldest settlement not only in the area but in the world. This settlement housed the shrine of the most feared of the ancient spirits inhabiting the depths of the earth, and was revered and feared on that account by the other settlements. In the deep southwestern forests where the Ijebu-Ode kingdom was later founded, one earlier settlement named Idoko exercised powerful ritual influence over the other settlements. Such ritual influence seems to have later developed some political character.

About what time, then, was the Yoruba country characterized by the existence of these settlement groups or *elu*? For a significant time marker we have Paul Ozanne's preliminary archaeological report, earlier referred to, which indicates that there were some settlements in the "Ife bowl" by about the fourth century BC. This would seem to indicate that by the fourth century BC, the *elu* pattern of settlements had begun, or already existed, in the Yoruba forests. During the roughly fifteen centuries that followed the fourth century BC, from what we know of Yorubaland in about 1000 AD (as will be seen in subsequent chapters), the *elu* pattern of settlement became the widespread mode of settlement for almost all the inhabitants of the Yoruba forests. The date, fourth century BC, is very important because by about that date the knowledge of iron smelting and iron working was spreading in West Africa, inaugurating centuries of great economic and social transformations in parts of the West African forests.

For about fifteen centuries or more, then, most Yoruba people lived in *elu* settings. The imprint of this is obvious in the culture of the Yoruba – in the composition of their towns and cities, in the structure of their communities and chieftaincy institutions, in their religious, economic and social institutions. The development of the character of Yoruba society in those fifteen centuries is the subject of the next chapter.

1. Head of Ooni of Ife. Work likely 12th–15th Century, Ife. Terracota. *Photo: C. Diame, 1961, IFAN.*

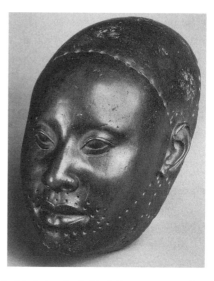

2. Mask head of Obalufon II, Ooni of Ife. Work dated 12th–15th Century, Ife. Copper. *[Photo: Phillips (1999).]*

3. Head of a man, Ife. Work dated 12th–15th Century, Ife. Zinc-brass. *Photo: Phillips (1999).*

4. Head of the queen of the Ooni of Ife. Work likely 12th–15th Century, Ife. Terracota. *Photo: C. Diame, 1961, IFAN.*

2

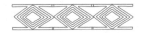

The Development of Early Yoruba Society

During the roughly fifteen centuries following the fourth century BC, the coming of the knowledge of the production and use of iron transformed the culture of the Yoruba and stimulated great cultural advances in their small settlements in the *elu* setting. According to archaeological evidence, the knowledge of iron came to the area now known as Nigeria as early as 700 BC. At Taruga in central Nigeria (about 55 miles, or 80 kilometers, southeast of Abuja), some remains of iron smelting activities have been dated to between 700 and 500 BC. How soon after this the knowledge of iron reached Yorubaland is not known; archaeological evidence has yielded dates in the second century AD, but it is almost certain that its beginning in Yorubaland belongs to considerably earlier dates.[1]

The history of the beginning of the Iron Age in Africa south of the Sahara is, in general, markedly different from its history north of the Sahara, in the Middle East and in the Mediterranean world. In these places, people first learnt to produce copper and its bronze alloy before they came to know how to produce iron. That is, there was a Copper/Bronze Age, which followed the Stone Age, and which lasted for centuries, before the Iron Age. In Africa south of the Sahara, on the other hand, the Stone Age was followed directly by the Iron Age, while the use of copper and bronze came later. For this reason, many archaeologists and other scholars insist that the knowledge of iron production must have come to sub-Saharan Africa from the Mediterranean world; either through Carthage (in modern Tunisia), or through Meroe (in modern Sudan), or from the Red Sea through Aksum in modern Ethiopia. Their principal argument is that knowledge of metals through copper and bronze is a precondition for the knowledge of iron, and that peoples who had not had any knowledge of production of copper and bronze could not possibly have discovered how to produce iron.

Other archaeologists and scholars, however, disagree with these views. They point out that the knowledge of iron could have been arrived at in West Africa through the processes of pottery production. The type of rock-clay from which iron is smelted (called *egun* or *eguru* in Yoruba) is the same type of clay for making pots. The firing of pots requires knowledge of production and management of high-heat fires. In the application of such intense heats to clay pottery, it is possible that raw iron (called iron bloom) could have formed from time to time and remained unrecognized for a long time – until, by and by, people recognized its nature and began to use it. It is significant that in some parts of West Africa the iron smelter was usually the husband of the woman potter. Moreover, the earliest date known for the evidence of iron production in West Africa (about 700 BC at Taruga) is considerably earlier than the beginning (about 500 BC) of iron at Meroe, the source from which West Africa is most generally supposed to have received the knowledge of iron production. In summary, the argument here is that knowledge of metallurgy through copper and bronze need not necessarily be a precondition for the discovery of iron, and that people in sub-Saharan Africa seem to have discovered iron as a by-product of pot production. The implication is that Yoruba women potters were probably the first producers and discoverers of raw iron in Yorubaland.

The available evidence suggests that in the centuries after 500 BC, then, the knowledge of iron was spreading gradually in West Africa. In Yorubaland, evidence of ancient iron works has been found in a few places. One at Ife-Jumu in northeastern Yorubaland has been dated to about 160 AD. Another site has been found near an abandoned town near Moniya in Ibadan in the Yoruba midlands. Other places famous among Yoruba people as places of iron production are Isundunrin, Ilorin, Ife (in central Yorubaland) and Idofin (in the northeast). The usual remains of ancient iron production are furnaces, kilns and heaps of iron slag.

Iron smelting was a very hazardous occupation, involving the use of dangerously high heats. Partly for this reason, no doubt, Yoruba people always located iron smelting centers at a considerable distance from human habitation, at a place in the forests where the iron-bearing type of rock-clay was available. The smelting equipment consisted of the furnaces (for producing the high heat) and the kilns (for holding the supply of clay over the heat). The smelting process involved heating the clay until the iron bloom formed and was separated from the rest of the slag. This was cooled and then sold, as iron ingots, to blacksmiths who would use it to fabricate tools – iron blades for machetes, hoes, knives, axes, arrows, spears, as well as for household utensils.

Early Yoruba people consigned iron smelting, and the fabrication and use of iron tools, to the patronage of one of their most senior deities, the god later known as Ogun, who was from earlier times worshipped as patron god of all working folks (probably, in these earlier times, with the name of Alaka-aiye – meaning, roughly, owner or wielder of the arms of all working people of the world). The iron-smelting center was a shrine of this deity, with all the adornment and paraphernalia of a shrine, and nobody who was not an initiate was allowed to come near it. The blacksmith's workshop was located closer to the village and sometimes inside the village, and the villagers could come there to buy or repair their tools. But it, too, was a shrine and, like the smelting center, was a place of frequent sacrifices to the patron god Ogun. Even people who only used iron tools in their daily occupations (farmers, hunters, wood workers, sculptors, and so on) were supposed to offer sacrifices to Ogun. So highly did the Yoruba people esteem iron as a factor in their lives.

After the discovery of crop and animal domestication (that is, agriculture), the discovery of iron was the greatest step taken by early humans in West Africa in the path of civilization. As material for tools, iron commands enormous superiority over stone. Iron-bearing clays are not as commonly available as stone, but they are sufficiently available in many places. Iron is much harder than stone; unlike stone, it can be molded or beaten into various shapes; and iron tools can, as desired, be made very sharp.

The knowledge of iron came in a particularly fortunate era in Yoruba history, coinciding, as it did, with the growth of the *elu* pattern of settlement. In practically all parts of Yorubaland, the traditions, folklore and legends seem all agreed that, for each settlement, greatly increased security and peace was a major benefit of living in an *elu*. By and large, an *elu* was a haven of security, peace and stability for its villages. Consequently, the *elu* setting was especially suited, and ready, to derive great advantages from iron when it was discovered.

In Yorubaland, then, the immediate impact of iron was the improvement of farming tools and methods. Iron tools gradually took the place of tools made of stone, bone and wood. The iron-bladed cutlass or machete (for cutting vegetation) and the iron-bladed hoe (for tilling and digging), fabricated, we may suppose, only crudely at first, improved over time, making it possible for each farmer to clear and cultivate larger farms than farmers of earlier times who had used stone tools. The areas opened up as farmlands pushed the primeval forests farther and farther back. Probably quite early, Yoruba farmers learnt from experience the wisdom of leaving every piece of farmland fallow periodically. That knowledge became an important asset for the management of soil fertility. As production increased, farmers evolved methods of storing and protecting harvested crops. Detailed information from traditions and yam festivals abounds all over Yorubaland about the handling of yam tubers, the most important food crop. The seasonal task of tying harvested yam tubers in rows on vertically standing stakes is celebrated with rituals and sacrifices in some parts of Yorubaland. That storage method ensured that the tubers were well aired and protected from pest and fungus infestation; it also ensured that they would not sprout suckers and deteriorate quickly.

All this, together with the gradual increase in the variety of food crops, made food progressively more available. Almost certainly, the increase in the availability of food led to the beginning of slow increases in human population in Yorubaland,[2] resulting in the emergence of more settlement groups (or *elu*) in more areas of the country, and an increase in the number of settlements in some *elu*. As the *elu* experienced population increases, the forests separating settlement from settlement in each *elu* gradually became open farmlands.

The coming of iron, and consequently the general improvement in tools and skills and in people's management of their natural environment, also resulted over time in improvements in the dwellings in which they lived. Gradually, we may suppose, people learnt to build stronger and better houses – ultimately with mud walls and thatched roofs made of selected durable wood, ropes and fronds. At some high point in this improvement in the building of houses, Yoruba people turned their skills to erecting buildings which kept each extended family group or lineage together under the same roof – a logical outcome of their way of life and their group psychology which had evolved over many centuries. The earliest *agbo-ile* (lineage compound) thus came into being, each consisting of many dwelling units in one single building. Each building developed as a number of courtyards, around which the dwelling units were arranged. Traditions, and group behavior that survived into the early twentieth century, would seem to indicate that the practice was to add a new courtyard when more living units were needed. It is not known how, in that type of approach, a group decided that an *agbo-ile* had reached optimum size and that another one needed to be started. But it did happen that, over many centuries, each *agbo-ile* came to contain about three courtyards as standard, while each settlement came to consist of a number of *agbo-ile*, or even some quarters – each quarter being a segment comprising a few contiguous *agbo-ile*.

Architectural and aesthetic improvements to the *agbo-ile* made it gradually stronger, safer, more comfortable, and more beautiful. The preparation of the earthen plaster for walls, and the setting up of walls, became more skillful, thus increasing the intricacy, safety and durability of wall structures. The weaving of the roof thatch became an art in itself, making it possible for roofs to last many generations with only minor repairs every few years. Minor roof repairs were done often, but roof replacements were done at intervals of generations, and each such replacement job was usually taken as an opportunity to improve, and restructure if necessary, the whole *agbo-ile*. Decorations became a standard part of the construction of an *agbo-ile*, and grew more and more detailed. It became standard practice to carve (using iron tools) and paint (or stain) the wooden pillars that supported eaves, typically in stylized anthropomorphic or animal idioms, and to carve wooden doors in bas-relief, especially the large main door to the *agbo-ile*. Decorations also came to include murals (called *iwope*) on wall surfaces – some of them frescoed or engraved. All these features improved gradually in quality and beauty from generation to generation. Ultimately, with the broad and sweeping verandahs, carved and painted posts holding up the eaves, and the murals on the walls (many in elaborate geometric compositions), the courtyards of some *agbo-ile* could look quite imposing. And all these decorations were extended to shrines also, so that shrines tended to be striking public buildings. In fact, the shrine became each settlement's prized possession over which skill and art were lavished. The pride over the beauty of shrines has continued to survive in the *oriki* (praise poetry) of many lineages. The *oriki* of many a proud lineage in many parts of Yorubaland includes lines such as these:

A ko 'le ebo fi iwope se gbehin re,

Bi 'le ebo ko sunwon, iwope re a wuni wuni

(We build our shrines and finish them with murals.

Even if a shrine building itself be not impressive,

Its murals would still captivate the passer-by.)

Rivalries and competition between settlements and between compounds in settlements resulted in other forms of artistic expression also. One such was the *oriki*, a form of poetry in which each group glorified itself and preserved in cryptic language the high points of its history. Over time, as the *oriki* tradition grew, every unit of society (the settlement, the lineage, the leadership titles, and even the individual) came to have *oriki*, and every *oriki* tended to be amplified and grow richer in the course of history. Group pride also produced facial markings given to children at birth, to proclaim their ancestry; as well as exclusive group festivals, seasonal and annual, filled with special group songs and exhibitions of masks; and loud, elaborate, funerals for departed parents.

All of these were features in the development of the identity and distinctiveness of the groups (settlements and lineages). That development had, perhaps, its most important product in the evolution of the Yoruba kinship system.[3] Every group conceived of itself as a "family"; and the culture demanded that marriage had to be exogamous – that is, people must, ideally, marry from "families" outside their own. As a result, each lineage contained many women who had been married from other lineages, and many members who were offspring of such women – facts loaded with potential to dilute lineage cohesiveness, identity and loyalty. The Yoruba responded to this by evolving a rigidly patrilineal kinship system. By this system, every child belonged only to its father's lineage, had to be raised in its lineage compound, and could only inherit title from it. As a corollary to this, when a woman married into another lineage, she became a member of her husband's group; she could never revert to membership of her father's group, and if she died her body had to be buried in the land of her husband's group. Hence, the Yoruba saying that after parents give their daughter in marriage, the appropriate thing to do is to remove her favorite childhood seat from their home and burn it (*B' a ba m' omo f' oko, a njo oota re ni*). This was most probably the root of the norm whereby Yoruba girls were given in marriage only when they were adjudged to be mature (usually about twenty years or older) and capable of being independent of their parents as well as of being able to fit quickly and maturely into their roles in their new homes. Yoruba folklore has many tales of very serious penalties for mothers who dared to cling to their newly married daughters.

The general improvement in tools and skills also accelerated the growth of division of labor, and the rise of distinct professions.[4] We do not know whether the making of stone tools ever developed into a special profession; but in any case, the making of stone tools ultimately ceased as a result of the coming of iron. Pottery remained the oldest craft profession. For many centuries before the knowledge of iron, women potters had made pots at locations where suitable clay deposits could be found in the forests near their homes. Almost certainly, the potter's possession of iron tools for her work (for instance for cutting the covering vegetation and digging up the clay) increased her production capacity, and may also have improved the quality of her pots. The association or guild of potters was probably the oldest professional guild or association in Yoruba history.

Hunting, too, developed into a distinct profession. Although all men continued to be involved in farming the land and doing some hunting, using the greatly improved tools (iron-bladed machetes, knives, arrows, spears, traps), over time some men came to be more employed in hunting than farming, and the group of professional hunters ultimately came into existence. From the folklore and rituals surrounding the profession of hunting, it would seem that hunters were highly regarded from the beginning. Not only did they contribute to the meat supply, they also served society in some other ways. People depended on them to help find in the forests good clay deposits for the potter and the iron smelter, as well as springs and brooks – sources of good water supply. But most importantly, according to the traditions, hunters provided security for their settlements. Closely allied to this, if a group or settlement needed to move and relocate, it usually depended on its hunters to find a good relocation site and the easiest path to it. The group of hunters in every settlement early

5. The entrance of an *agbo-ile* in Ibadan. *Photo: Toupet, 1964, IFAN.*

6. Decorated entrance of a compound in Oyo. *Photo: Toupet, 1964, IFAN.*

7a & b. Sculpted column in the palace of the Onire of Ire. Wood. *Photo: P.Verger, 1953, IFAN.*

8. *Agbo-ile* verandah post in the Oye Kingdom, Ekiti. Wood. *Photo: Drewal, et al., (1999).*

9. Murals in the palace of the Alaafin of Oyo. *Photo: Toupet, 1964, IFAN.*

became a highly regarded professional association or guild which developed its own unique folklore, its own chants, music and dance, and acquired a near-sacred public image – almost akin to that of the iron smelters or that of the blacksmiths.

What was true of hunting as a profession came also to be true of many other pursuits. Most women could plait women's hair, but some became professional hair plaiters in their community. Most farmers could climb palm trees and harvest palm wine, but it became a profession for some. Some older women and men in every *agbo-ile* could carry out circumcision for children, but some (usually women) came to be recognized as the professionals in the provision of this important service. Depending on the occupations common in their home area, many persons grew up knowing how to make raffia yarn, weave some raffia goods, spin cotton yarn on spindles, weave cotton cloth, weave mats etc. Each of these pursuits, however, came to have its professionals.

Yoruba people also began, after the coming of iron, to produce individuals who practiced art as a profession. The earliest sculptures would seem to have been done in terra cotta (that is clay) – almost certainly a development from the profession of pottery. The earliest carvings, made possible by iron tools, were presumably in wood – most of it, probably, for the decoration of houses and shrines. By the later parts of the first century AD, sculpture in stone appears to have become well developed also – as well as sculpture in metals, especially cast or wrought iron. Most of the growing sculptural art was devoted to the worship of gods and spirits and the celebration of rulers, leaders and heroes. A fuller attention will be given to this subject of the development of early Yoruba art in the next chapter dealing with the early history of Ife.

The production of palm oil remained always closely associated with farming, but it was nevertheless one of the most important industries in early Yoruba economy. The coming of iron tools (especially the machete and the axe) greatly improved the harvesting of palm fruits. The typical Yoruba oil mill, called *eku*, evolved to handle the increased fruit harvests. The *eku* was a large circular container built on an open rock surface, with the rock surface for its base (usually in some forest location). Inside it, the boiled palm nuts were pressed to extract the oil. The process, plus other ancillary processes, yielded not only the edible oil and fats, but also the palm kernel oil (used for medicaments and cosmetics) and various fuels for lighting, for cooking, and for use in high-heat furnaces (like the iron smelter's or the blacksmith's).

The improvement of tools and skills enabled the Yoruba farmer to incorporate more and more crops into his farming. At some point in this long process, cotton became one of the crops he cultivated. It would seem from some folklore connected with the cloth industry that cotton and the weaving of cotton cloth first appeared in the broad belt comprising the Yoruba savannah and derived savannah countries of the Oyo, Igbomina, northern Ekiti, northern Ijesa, Akoko, and the Okun Yoruba. This broad area was the vegetation belt most suitable in Yorubaland for cotton cultivation, and was also the natural home of most of the shrubs from which the Yoruba people obtained their dyestuff; over time, some of these shrubs came to be regularly cultivated (such as indigo). Cotton cultivation spread only slowly into the deep forests of southern Yorubaland, mostly into areas where agricultural activity resulted in more open vegetation. Even in such places, the cotton crop was prone to diseases because of the higher humidity of the southern Yoruba forest country. From the beginning, therefore, cotton cloth weaving in southern parts of Yorubaland depended heavily on cotton wool and dyestuff from the middle belt and the northern territories. Some Ekiti proverbs seem to indicate that the Igbomina were probably the earliest leaders in cotton cloth production in Yorubaland. Like the practitioners of other trades, weavers evolved early into local associations or guilds, with rules and obligations and a guardian deity.

Some sort of trading also evolved in the earliest Yoruba settlements.[5] As settlement groups or *elu* evolved, each settlement or village in an *elu* developed a market place of its own – so that there were many small market spots in each *elu*. All over Yorubaland, survivals of the separate early settlements have quite clear information in their traditions concerning their early marketplaces. Most probably, trading in each such marketplace evolved from simple exchanges of products among dwellers in the same village and, over time, became gradually more complex. The economic developments consequent upon the knowledge of iron would no doubt have speeded up the growth of trade as a factor in the lives of the early settlements. Increasing productivity in farming, in the production of palm oil and other palm products, in pottery, in the making of baskets, mats and cloths, and in the manufacture of iron tools and implements, coupled with the growing division of labor and the rise of distinct trades and professions – all these would have created the condition for increasing the growth of trade, first in each village and then between villages in each *elu*. A further development upon this, no doubt, was that particular village markets became known as the best places to procure or sell particular products – resulting in the gradual pooling of the *elu* into one market community.

It is not known what mode of exchange was employed in this earliest of Yoruba trade. Some traditions, reinforced by some surviving traces of practice, suggest some sort of barter of products for products. The use of cowry shells as currency almost certainly, as will be seen later, began in times before Oduduwa – that is, before the tenth century.

In the context of this age of varied growth and development, political organization of society also began and developed.[6] Each settlement had a rudimentary government from very early, under the leadership of a headman. The oldest living male member of the group, he was a sort of ruler and priest. His religious authority and ritual functions sprang naturally from his being the group's "father" and the nearest person to the departed ancestors of the group as well as to the primordial sprits inhabiting the earth upon which the settlement stood. He was keeper of the totem and other "secrets" of the group. The group's totem was an object treasured by the first father of the group (a charm, article of personal adornment, favorite tool or artifact, etc.) and believed to have been bequeathed by him to the group on his deathbed, to be kept as the symbol of the group's unity and identity. Sometimes, copies of the totem were made and given to members to keep or to wear on their persons, but the original was kept by the group leader and passed on to his successor. The group leader also kept and tended the group shrine, made the daily, periodic and seasonal rituals, and offered the sacrifices. His authority in trying and punishing offences was conceived of as flowing naturally from his religious authority and ritual powers. In modern political language, then, he was ruler, priest, judge and enforcement authority.

From this point, Yoruba traditions generally paint an implausible picture of sudden transformation of each village or settlement into one that had a government with an exalted ruler, subordinate chiefs, rituals and orderly laws. Such phenomenal transformation is made to seem as if it all happened in one generation, such as from father to son; but we are certainly right to assume a development that lasted many centuries and many generations. What most probably happened is that each group, which later became a settlement, started off as one small family whose surviving members kept in close association for generations until they became a lineage – that is, a group of families bound together by belief in common descent from a known ancestor. As the group grew larger, it kept regarding itself as one family, even if other persons joined it from time to time. The original family values of mutual loyalty and support, and individual acceptance of family rules and authority, continued as the group norm. The authority exercised by the father in the foundational family became institutionalized in the leader of the group. The original family demands on interpersonal behavior, and of group duty, became institutionalized into group rules and law. Continued expansion of group size and needs slowly generated devolution in the performance of group duties, which then gradually produced institutionalized offices and officers (that is, chiefs and priests) below the level of the group leader, complete ultimately with titles and insignia. The leader's own title had to proclaim that he was father, head, and embodiment of the spirit, of the settlement. Hence, in practically every settlement, the leader's title came to include the name of his settlement – as in Elefene (of Efene), Obajio (of Ijio), Olowagbon (of Igbon), Aro (of Ilaro) and so on.

Fittingly too, in addition to these specific titles, the evolving national culture began to identify and address the rulers with general, exalted, titles that set them apart from the rest of humankind. The Elefene, Obajio or Aro belonged to a special level of humans known as Olu or Osin or Oba – king. It seems probable that which common title people used for 'king' depended on which region they lived in. In some regions people used Olu, in others Osin, and in yet others Oba. An Ekiti tradition has it that in most parts of Yorubaland people first used Olu or Osin as leader titles.

At some very late point in the evolution of these settlements, their leaders began to wear a distinctive skull cap. Since the crowns of Yoruba kings have continued till our times to be regarded as sacred objects, it seems very probable that crowns started off as part of religious and ritual attire. For reasons unknown to us today, the ruler seems to have begun to wear some special cap as part of his religious garb as he performed the rituals and sacrifices at the shrine. Over time, wearing such a cap became a generalized part of his clothing while performing any of his other functions, even though the ruler's skull cap never ceased being regarded as a sacred, religious object. We have very clear descriptions of these earliest Yoruba "crowns" in the traditions. Moreover, some ancient recesses of some Yoruba palaces are believed to have samples of them. They were simple looking caps woven from pieces of certain types of raffia yarn at first, and much later from certain types of cotton cloth and yarn – not anything like the elevated dome-shaped or cone-shaped crowns of a later period of Yoruba history.

The important consequence of the emergence of many compounds in each settlement is that each compound slowly, over many centuries, took on some life of its own – a latter day lineage. Each settlement thus became a sort of super lineage comprising many small lineages. Particular leadership roles in the settlement became domiciled in particular compounds. When the bearer of any such title died, the inhabitants of the compound became responsible to the village for selecting his successor from within their compound. But since the title (and its duties) belonged to the whole settlement and not just the compound, the village must accept the appointee and install him. The system whereby the chiefs gathered in council around the ruler to manage the affairs of the settlement gradually evolved. In each compound, the oldest member was the compound head, vested by practice over time with judicial and other authority in the compound. As earlier indicated also, the farms pushed farther and farther away from the villages, even though the areas immediately outside each village remained the most intensively farmed. Moreover, from each village, paths radiated into the neighboring forests – to the sites of the palm oil mill or *eku*, the pottery, the iron smelter, the brooks and springs (sources of the village's supply of water). From the earliest times, these special forest locations and the farmlands were conceived of as common property of the village. In this way, the Yoruba laid the foundation of the system of land ownership that later became a very significant feature of their culture.

Although the oral traditions speak almost entirely of the roles of men in the ancient Yoruba villages, there are nevertheless glimpses of women's roles. The traditions are clear that, from the very beginning, women were the makers of pots – a very important service to their settlements. For reasons not entirely clear to us, women were also the traders from the beginning. It is probable that this was a consequence of an early division of labor whereby the men cleared and prepared the ground and raised the crops (with significant assistance and back-up services from the women), and the women harvested most of the crops and offered the surplus for exchange (or sale). When yarn making and cloth weaving came too, they became exclusive industries of the women. The typical Yoruba loom, from early times, was the vertical loom installed over a shallow pit in the house. The other type of loom which also became common in Yorubaland, the horizontal draw-loom, a specialty of the men, came much later – and it long remained exclusive to northwestern Yorubaland, that is to the Oyo country. The women were, in early times, the greater actors in the spinning, weaving and dyeing processes which, over time, gave Yorubaland its very important cloth industry.

But early Yoruba women may have been more active in the political process than the oral traditions would admit. For instance, it is possible that some very early influential position for women is what we have in very many folktales about a woman with the title of Anosin, represented always as first wife of the Osin (king). Within the palace of the Osin, the Anosin wielded authority second only to that of the Osin himself. This very influential female official always starts off in each folktale as a glowing embodiment of power and authority (and feminine beauty), and then she is shown as coming to a tragic end on account of her wicked use of her power over the other women of the palace. It is significant, however, that in none of these folktales is the legitimacy of her authority ever questioned; her tragic end is always caused by the manner of her use of her authority. This seems to imply either that having women in positions of authority was acceptable, and perhaps even common, in early Yoruba settlements, or that women did in fact occupy leadership positions but were, in a generally male-dominant culture, depicted as temperamentally incapable of using leadership positions well. The Anosin was probably commonly "mother" of the settlement while the Osin was "father" of it. Admittedly, the Anosin folktales do not rank as direct information about influential roles for women in early Yoruba settlements. About such roles for women in the kingdoms of later periods of Yoruba history, the oral traditions are replete with direct information. Women did become crowned rulers of Yoruba kingdoms in these later periods – and it does seem improbable that such eminence would have had no root whatsoever in earlier periods of Yoruba history.

Yoruba traditions hold up the development of herbal medicine as one of the triumphs of early Yoruba history.[7] Slowly, over many centuries, the Yoruba people in their villages accumulated solid knowledge of countless herbs and herbal preparations for various sicknesses, as well as considerable knowledge of the nature of many diseases. Professional herbalists called *onisegun* emerged, on whom the people of the village depended for the treatment of their sicknesses. Over time, indeed, specialization developed in this profession – so that there were those (called *onisegun aremo*) who specialized in the treatment of infertility in women, the management of pregnancy problems, the delivery of babies and the treatment of childhood diseases, those who specialized in the treatment of mental and nervous diseases, those who specialized in the fixing of bone fractures, and so on. From those early times, the profession gradually set up rules and procedures for the training of those to be admitted to it; fourteen years of apprenticeship becoming a sort of general standard. The profession also evolved meetings of members for the exchange of knowledge, and established strictly binding rules of professional assistance of member to member.

However, Yoruba herbal medicine, in spite of its ever growing knowledge of diseases and treatments, never freed itself from its origins – the belief that sicknesses were often caused by malevolent spirits. Therefore, even the soundest of herbalists continued to mix with his practice the appeasement of, or combat with, spirits, as well as divinations, sacrifices, rituals, incantations, protective amulets (around neck, waist and wrist), protective magical preparations (of powder or liquid) inserted into parts of the body through lacerations. All these started early and continued through later periods of Yoruba history as part of the herbalist's art.

In the context of high rates of infant mortality, the belief early developed that some children (especially of mothers who lost many babies in succession) were not ordinary children but spirits who came to the world as babies only for the purpose of tormenting certain women. Called *abiku* (born to die), these special children became the subject of a whole complex of lore, rituals and magical practices, all aimed at either warding them off from the women who were their victims, or forcing them to convert to real, ordinary, children if they were already born.

In earliest times also, having twin babies was regarded as a bad omen or a visitation by malevolent spirits. Yoruba people never ceased regarding twin babies as beyond the ordinary, but the attitude to twins gradually softened – until, in much later times, twin babies came to be regarded as friendly spirits or bearers of good luck, to be related to with special rituals and celebrations.

Belief in witches and witchcraft also became an important feature of Yoruba life – a witch being, according to Yoruba belief and folklore, a man or woman (most often a woman) who consented to hosting in her own person a malignant spirit sworn to causing harm to humans. Sicknesses which could not be explained or healed were usually attributed to witchcraft or the hostility of some spirit or deity. This usually provoked a heavy investment in sacrifices and rituals, and, if witchcraft was suspected, efforts to find and punish or appease the witch or to neutralize her powers. Herbalists developed potions which were believed, when ingested by suspects, to be efficacious in detecting the witch among them. And the penalty for being so publicly identified as a witch was death, sometimes by public stoning.

The religion of the people of the early Yoruba settlements, started in their earliest days, grew and amplified. To the original earth spirits and protector spirits of the neighborhood hill or rock or stream were, over centuries, added more and more gods and goddesses and spirits. Settlements and lineages deified prominent departed members and set up shrines to them – as special friends and protectors in the spirit world. As various occupations developed, patron gods and goddesses emerged for them – for farming and other working folks, for women traders in marketplaces, for weavers and dyers of cloth and yarns, for potters, for herbalists, etc. Certain natural phenomena (such as lightning and thunder, and the sea), certain diseases – all came to have gods or goddesses associated with them. Over time, some deities became generally accepted and worshipped throughout Yorubaland. The god later known as Ogun (originally patron god of all working people) seems to have been the first of such pan-Yoruba gods – hence his salutation as "*Osin-mole*" (first, or king, among the earliest spirits or gods).

By the tenth century, or perhaps even considerably earlier, the main outlines of Yoruba cosmology and religion had evolved. The Yoruba conceived of all existence as located in two realms – a lower realm known as *aye* (the earth or the world, the abode of humans), and a higher realm known as *orun* (heaven, the home of the spiritual beings). The realm of the spirits was conceived as consisting of two spheres – a higher and a lower. The higher was the place of the Supreme Olodumare who created all things and ruled over all of existence. This Supreme Being was first given the name Orisa – roughly meaning "the source from which all things emanated." Later, to his name was added Olorun (king of heaven) and Oluwa (king over all). Though some Yoruba groups (especially the southern and eastern peoples like the Ijesa, Ondo, Ikale, Owo and Ekiti) continued to apply the name Orisa to the Supreme Being, that name generally came to be used for the highest heavenly beings who were said to have been with the Supreme Being at the time when the Supreme Being created all things, and whom the Supreme Being later sent to the lower spiritual sphere where they became the most senior gods.

The Supreme Being's sphere was so far above the human's world that humans could not worship or relate directly with him. Therefore, only in a very few places in Yorubaland did shrines emerge for his worship. Generally, Yoruba people believed that no human could know what sacrifices would be acceptable to Olorun or Oluwa. At some late time, Olorun or Oluwa also acquired the name Olodumare, a difficult name that has been variously translated or deciphered. The central word in this name is *odu*, which means "fullness", or "totality." For this reason, Olodumare has been translated by some as "the absolute fullness that encompasses all." Olu Alana suggests that its best translation would be "the king – who holds the scepter, wields authority and has quality which is superlative in worth and … permanent, unchanging and reliable."[8]

The second heavenly sphere existed in very close proximity to the world of humans and was the home of all the other gods (collectively known as *imole*) and the spirits, all arranged in grades from the highest to the lowest. The highest category consisted of the *orisas* – namely, Orisanla (arch divinity), Ifa (god of wisdom and divination), Ogun (god of working people and of iron), Esu (messenger of the senior gods), and others. Of these, Orisanla came to be regarded as the most senior; he was believed to have assisted Olodumare in the act of creating man. A goddess named Odudu was regarded as wife of Orisanla and mother of the gods (*Eye umole* or *Iya imole*). In certain liturgies and localities, the name of this goddess later became confused with the name Oduduwa, the name of an important male personage in later Yoruba history. (Oduduwa was later deified, as a male god.) Odudu is still worshipped in some places in Yorubaland as Odudu, not Oduduwa; Odudu's shrine and rituals still exist in Ado (in Ekiti), where she is worshipped as mother of all mothers and their little children.[9]

The total number of the gods (*imole*) varied from region to region of Yorubaland – but 401 appears to have been the commonest count. By the tenth century, many of the gods were already pan-Yoruba in acceptance and worship. Such pan-Yoruba gods increased in number in later periods of Yoruba history. Each *imole* was concerned with a particular department or pursuit of human life and demanded a particular type of sacrifice and rituals. Below the level of the *imole* were countless spirits, each in its own way in frequent contact with human life.

Growing from the whole complex of Yoruba beliefs and religion, there emerged the powerful tradition of Yoruba divination – the telling of hidden circumstances and of the future through carefully learned processes.[10] Typically, the Yoruba assigned divination to the province of a god, Ifa, the god of divination. It is clear in the traditions that there were many kinds of divinatory practices and traditions in early Yoruba history, but over a long time they almost all became consigned to the province of Ifa. Some Yoruba traditions indicate a Nupe contribution to the earliest rudiments of the Ifa system in Yorubaland, but the extent of such contribution is uncertain. According to traditions recorded in the late nineteenth century by Samuel Johnson, there lived in Ife in pre-Oduduwa times a man of Nupe extraction named Setilu or Agboniregun (the latter being probably the name given him by his Ife hosts). Agboniregun, practicing Ifa divination, lived in some places in eastern Yorubaland (including Ado in Ekiti, and Owo) before he came to settle in Ife, where he acquired considerable influence on account of his Ifa divination, and where he initiated many people into Ifa mysteries and divination. Some apparently older traditions, however, have it that the practice of Ifa divination was introduced to the world by the benevolent act of the god of wisdom, Ifa, himself (through the instrumentality of his sixteen children), and that, in its early rudimentary form, it was common among the Yoruba, Nupe, Edo and Ibariba. The probable conclusion from these traditions and myths would seem to be that Ifa developed slowly from very early times in the context of the cultures of the Yoruba, Nupe, Edo and Ibariba region. Thereafter, Yoruba creativity elevated Ifa divination and mysteries and enriched them with a profound body of folklore, until the whole Ifa system became a sophisticated theme in Yoruba religion and culture, and Ifa became a very important Yoruba god – the god of divination and of hidden knowledge, the mouthpiece of the gods. In the long history of their development of Ifa and of Ifa mysteries, practices, divination and folklore, the Yoruba people gradually evolved a rarified body of lore, knowledge and wisdom known as Odu Ifa (roughly, the body or fullness of Ifa wisdom). In its final form, Odu Ifa became the longest corpus of poetry in Yoruba folklore, a massive and ever-growing cultic body of wisdom encompassing historical and mythological accounts, exalted precepts, snippets of divine wisdom, life-related instructions, and the profoundest in Yoruba philosophy. It developed, most certainly, from very many generations of the loftiest in Yoruba folk wisdom, and it was meant to be, and was, the special preserve of the select elite known as the *babalawo* (father of the secrets), the priests of Ifa. As the exalted profession of the *babalawo* developed, the initial "schooling" of a *babalawo*, consisting of intensive, unbroken, instruction in the practice of divination and in spiritual development, and unfaltering memorization of the entire Odu Ifa, was generally supposed to last for fourteen years, but in reality his education was a lifelong pursuit. The nature of the *babalawo's* life and profession demanded that he should be in regular contact, sharing and collaboration with other *babalawo*. In every settlement and in every *elu*, an association or guild of *babalawo* early came into being.

Another very important development in Yoruba religion and cosmology was the belief in the afterlife. The Yoruba believed that the dead went on to live in another place of existence (some part of the heavenly realm), from where they could see, interact with, and help humans in this world. For that reason, articles of clothing and of personal adornment, articles of food and of domestic value, were buried with the dead – in order to help them settle in their new otherworld homes. The newly dead was believed to be welcomed "home" by family members who had earlier died. The quality of life that one would have in the afterlife was believed to be determined by the good or evil life that one had lived in one's earthly life – and, for this reason, Yoruba society thought of its aged members as typically honest and trustworthy, in preparation for the afterlife. But there were also ways in which the living could assist their dead into a place of status and honor in the afterlife. One such way was a big, expensive, and prestigious funeral – the objective of which was to put on show (to both the living in this world and the people of the afterlife) the wealth and high status of the deceased, as well as his or her success in having many prosperous children. Another way, especially for the great and influential, was that the deceased's children would add a second burial ceremony far more expensive and more demonstrative than the first. For this second burial, the children of the deceased would commission a life-size naturalistic sculpture of their dead parent, which they would then dress in gorgeous clothes, put on show for a couple of days, and then bury. This is the second funeral ceremony known as Ako in Owo.[11] For the deceased who had been a great hunter in his earthly life, another kind of help was also commonly given. This was made necessary by the belief that the spirits of the animals that the deceased had killed as a hunter could ambush and harass him on his journey to the afterlife and make his journey unpleasant. To prevent such, the hunter's children would mount a standing, life-size, effigy of their deceased father, dressed in his clothes, on the way to his farm – and the belief was that the animals would fix their attention on the effigy as if it was the hunter himself, while the hunter made an undisturbed journey to the afterlife. This practice was known as *epade* or *ipade*.

The dead were also believed to reincarnate in their descendants, and to come occasionally to visit their communities. The belief in reincarnation led to the practice of giving personal names that identified some persons in every

Yoruba family as reincarnations of departed parents, and the belief in the occasional visits of loved ones from the other world produced the *egungun* cult. The annual calendar of religious rituals and festivals in every Yoruba community included one or two celebrations when *egungun* – represented by masked persons believed to be loved ones from the afterlife – walked the streets and visited homes. The *egungun* came in various types of masks (in combinations of cloth, fronds, varieties of raffia, beautifully carved wooden pieces, decorations with beads, cowry shells, etc.), and for various purposes. Some were very serious, very portentous manifestations specializing in performing rituals beneficial to society. Others went from home to home praying for and blessing people. Yet others entertained people with dancing or with sayings loaded with deep folk wisdom or with tales from Yoruba folklore. Some of the lighter ones just roused their community by fighting mock fights with people in the streets or by bearing whips and playfully chasing young people from compound to compound. In most communities, some prominent lineages came to have unique masks and *egungun* of their own. The *egungun* cult in every community had a highly revered priesthood, made up usually of men (since women were not supposed to be exposed to *egungun* mysteries), but always including one or two highly placed priestesses.

From a complex interplay of Yoruba religion and ritual practices and mysteries, of Yoruba knowledge of herbs, the power of herbs and of herbal preparations, of the mysteries of Ifa and divination, and of witchcraft and the occult, there ultimately evolved a more or less distinct profession whose practitioners came to be known as *adahunse*. The *adahunse* concerned himself very little (if at all) with herbal medications for health delivery purposes, or with treatment of the sick, or with divination as such. While he would usually know and employ any or all of these skills, his real focus was on the occult employment of herbs and other materials from nature, as well as the use of incantations, curses, charms, and amulets, to enable his clients to accomplish stated social purposes – good purposes such as success and wealth, evil purposes such as hostile occult interference in the lives and affairs of other persons, or power purposes such as protection from certain weapons, or ability to de-materialize, or the ability to engage in out-of-body actions. Usually feared by all the people of his community, the *adahunse*, in the full maturity of his art, had as his clients mostly rulers (kings, chiefs, warriors), the powerful, the influential and the ambitious, the practitioners of hazardous occupations such as hunting, and other persons seeking success or wealth, or seeking protection from physical or spiritual harm.

There were, altogether, many types of associations, guilds and cults in the early Yoruba settlements. But the most visible associations, to which everyone belonged, were the age-grade associations – called *egbe, otu or igbamo*. Age-grade associations very probably evolved in the earliest days of Yoruba settlements, no doubt in response to the needs of the settlements – to provide an appropriate pool of labor for each of the various functions for which the ruler needed to mobilize people. Depending on age, one team could be called upon to keep the open places in the settlement clean, another to keep paths clear of in-growing bush, another to effect repairs on public houses and shrines, another to give back-up services during large rituals and festivals, etc. Over time, the originally informal teams became formalized and institutionalized into age-grade associations. The youngest association in a settlement was constituted about every third year, and was made up of youths about nine to twelve years of age. The inauguration of the youngest age-grade association became a festival featuring consultations of the Ifa oracle, the ruler's giving of a name to the new association, and the association's election of its officers. Persons so elected held the offices for life, and there were two lines of offices – male and female. Over time, age-grade associations developed meetings, rules and regulations, seasonal and annual festivals, etc. Outside one's own family and lineage, the members of one's age-grade association came to be one's closest associates and support in all phases and happenings in one's life. The public duty of an association depended on its age – from the youngest who kept public places clean, to able-bodied youths whose males could be called to military service, all the way up to the most senior citizens who were revered as the very essential pool of wisdom and guidance for their village.

In the considerable security of life in the village and the *elu*, then, the Yoruba slowly molded the building blocks of their culture. In the ordering of economic functions, the organization of political life and governance, the molding of the relationship with the world and with the powers of the supernatural, the overall outlining of a world view, the centuries of Yoruba life in the village and the *elu* laid most of the essential foundations.

The primary building block of the village was the *agbo-ile*, the lineage compound.[11] Each constituting a home where many families lived together, all of them believing themselves to be one family, the *agbo-ile* was a wonderfully fertile ground for cultural development, growth and refinement. Almost all the adult male residents lived by farming, supported by their wives and children. A typical day in the *agbo-ile*, we may imagine, dawned with most residents, in their nuclear families, heading out to the farms, leaving behind the very old, the children, the nursing mothers, and those engaged in home-based occupations (like traders, weavers and dyers and, if there were any, herbalists, *babalawo*, blacksmiths, etc.). For much of the day, these home-bound folks kept the *agbo-ile* alive and busy with their various pursuits, while the children played various games in the dust in the open courtyards, under the eyes of the aged and the nursing mothers. The farming folks returned in the late afternoon, bringing head-loads of farm produce and firewood. In the rest of the evening, each family cooked for supper, the main meal of the day. The hours after supper were the great time for socializing in the compound – the men in groups around kegs of palm wine, and the women (still doing all sorts of light domestic chores, like spinning yarn on spindles) gathering the children, if there was no moonlight, to tell stories (usually folktales accompanied with songs and refrains). These night folktale sessions were beautiful experiences in education and artistic expression, and a major contributor to the famed Yoruba wealth in folklore. If the moon was up, the children, joined by those older children who had spent much of the day on the farms, played in the courtyards. Moonlit nights could be very lively, beautiful and noisy in the compound, as the children played running games, engaged in wrestling contests, or put up some drama from their perception of adult life – a wedding, a chieftaincy installation, a festival, a dance, an inter-group disagreement, or a group meeting. In this whole context, Yoruba people invented many types of one-to-one and team games. Lineage meetings were frequent in the compound – some for lineage business, others for the elders to settle quarrels or to try infringements of lineage rules of conduct.

The *agbo-ile* was a very major contributor to the economy of its village. Farm produce and other products flowed from each *agbo-ile* to the village market – food, articles of pottery, mats, baskets, cloth, cotton wool and yarn, etc. Some *agbo-ile* became famous as a source of certain products. Professions and trades tended to run in lineages.

Days of celebrations were many in the *agbo-ile* – village and lineage festivals and rituals, chieftaincy rites, domestic rituals, funerals of departed aged members, weddings. A wedding was a celebration of a new pact and relationship between two (usually unrelated) lineages (the bride's and the bridegroom's) and was always accompanied with colorful celebrations in both. In the full development of the Yoruba wedding over the centuries, the processes of the introduction of the contracting lineages to each other, the betrothal ceremony, and the ceremonial journey of the bride to her husband's lineage compound, all became greatly beautified by Yoruba creativity with dramatized banter, the giving of gifts, and the sharing of feasts. When all these were completed, the two lineages became linked together (ideally in perpetuity) by a bond of love and honor. The birth of a baby was a joyful event in the lineage compound – and for weeks, the oldest women members would serve the baby and its mother as nurses and house-help. Days of mourning were also quite frequent, and every death pulled the whole *agbo-ile* powerfully together in sorrow. Probably more children died in infancy than survived it. The death of a young adult kept an *agbo-ile* in mourning for days.

The *agbo-ile* buried its dead in the soil of its own compound and regarded them as continuing to be part of the lineage and as continuing to participate in its affairs. Children – both those who were living and those yet to be born – were regarded as important members of the lineage; in fact, the universal Yoruba belief was that the adults of a lineage held all its things in trust for its living and yet unborn children. In lineage caucuses, respectful references were commonly made to "the ones who went before" and "the ones who will come"; and some of the latter were regarded as direct reincarnations of some of the former – a belief often expressed in the names given to new babies. The *agbo-ile* took great care to involve its children in its affairs and rituals.

Quarrels, often featuring noisy verbal exchanges, were, on the whole, common – especially between women who happened to be married to the same husband. Over these and other kinds of interpersonal conflicts in the *agbo-ile*, the lineage leader (*olori-ebi*), spokesman for the departed ancestors, assisted by the lineage elders, exercised very powerful judicial and penal authority. In all matters pertaining to the lineage, the overriding principle was that every member (as descendant of the ancestors) had full rights to participate and express opinion, and ensuring healthy respect for the exercise of such rights was one of the most important duties of the lineage head, assisted by the elders.

10. Following the precepts of the oracle, Iya-Ibeji, a mother of twins, dancing in the market in Abeokuta. *Photo: P.Verger, 1948–49, IFAN.*

The *agbo-ile* was the place of education. The proper nurturing of an *agbo-ile's* children was the collective concern of all its adults. Every lineage raised its young in its own image, and equipped them with a strong knowledge of its history – especially its importance in the history of its village. This was the primary root of societal decency, and of the general historical consciousness, of Yoruba people. Children also learned the professions and trades common in their *agbo-ile*, and this is why trades and professions tended to run in lineages.

All in all, the early *agbo-ile* as part of the village was the most important factor in the beginnings of the evolution of Yoruba civilization. Throughout all the ebb and flow of Yoruba history even until the twentieth century, the *agbo-ile*, with its family group or lineage, was to remain the primary identifier, educator and maker of the Yoruba person.

There seem to have been considerable contacts between various regions and localities of Yorubaland in times often referred to as "before Oduduwa". Hunters are generally credited in the traditions as the pioneers who first opened up tracks in the primordial forests of Yorubaland, and as guides of early groups to good sites for the earliest settlements. From an analysis of these traditions, Saburi Biobaku writes: "A bold hunter usually led the way and when a suitable site was struck, he founded a town."[12] By the ninth or tenth century, however, Yorubaland had clearly long passed the era of initial path finders. Many centuries of ever-lengthening paths from settlement area to settlement area would seem to have by then linked up Yorubaland quite copiously, and fairly well defined corridors of traffic were known to wayfarers, almost all of whom were herbalists, diviners and traders. The professions of the herbalists (*onisegun*) and the diviners (*babalawo*) seem to have early developed some built-in dynamic that impelled their practitioners to go further and further afield in order to learn more and more and make wider and wider contacts. It became ultimately a character of the two professions that the *onisegun* or *babalawo* who was known to have traveled widely, to have resided in many parts of the country, to have established bonds with many members of his profession in distant places, was regarded as belonging to the peak of his profession. Such persons constituted a specially respected elite that traversed the country regularly and knew it quite well.

Then, trade also developed early beyond settlements and settlement groups (or *elu*). It seems clear from the traditions that the amount of long-distance trade traversing Yorubaland by the ninth century must have been quite considerable. Such trade no doubt accounted for the provision of iron to blacksmiths across the country. Some long distance trade in sea salt also seems to have existed – the earliest carriers of which would have been traders from among the coastal Ijebu. There was an ancient trade in herbal preparations, mostly a preserve of the herbalists. According to Robin Horton, by the ninth century AD, the Ife zone in central Yorubaland was becoming an area of some importance on the southernmost reaches of the trans-Sahara trade routes from the Mediterranean coast, through the Sahara Desert and the grasslands south of it and across the River Niger.[13] More will be said about this later. Suffice it to say now that this would mean that by the ninth century some goods from the Mediterranean and the Sahara Desert region were entering into the trade of Yorubaland. It would also mean that Yorubaland was by then on the verge of the development of rapidly increasing long-distance trade.

Until the very end of the period covered in this chapter (that is, roughly until about the tenth century), each individual settlement or village within an *elu* conceived of itself as a separate, autonomous, settlement, and resolutely clung to that perception. The forests which originally stood separating settlement from settlement in an *elu* turned from forest to farmland, thus making the whole *elu* area a more or less continuous opening in the forests. But that generally did not conduce much to a weakening of separateness. The farmland boundaries were well known and respected, and each settlement maintained its share of the paths dutifully to the end of its own land. Each settlement pushed additions to its dwellings only in directions away from neighbors' dwellings, and cleared more and more of the increasingly distant forests to provide for expansion to its farmland. The universal norm, sanctified over time by powerful religious and spiritual underpinnings, was separate, self-contained, settlements – each with its own ruler and chiefs, its own protector god and spirits and shrines, its own rituals and festivals, its own marketplace, its own blacksmith's workshop, its own, as much as possible, everything. For the rulers and citizens of each settlement in an *elu*, to honor this norm was to live in the will of the invisible powers that oversaw the affairs of humankind.[14]

However, strong forces gradually developed that slowly whittled down the norm. Most of these were economic. For instance, from time to time, a mat weaver or cloth weaver or blacksmith might become known as having some special artistic or other talent, and customers would come to him or her from all over. Some production facilities were not just replicable everywhere. For instance, iron-smelting facilities were, in the end, few in the whole country, and blacksmiths must depend for their raw iron on very distant smelters. This lengthened the arms of trade not only beyond the village but also far beyond the *elu*. As earlier pointed out, the construction of *agbo-ile* and shrines improved continually in complexity and decorations. Not every settlement could have the artisans and artists for these services; most settlements must employ people from other settlements or even from distant *elu*. Over time, a guild or association developed for each of these trades, and its members served clients far and wide.

Some village markets, as earlier pointed out, became known as the best places to sell or buy particular products, so that people from every village increasingly went there for those products. Over time, it became the way of life in the *elu* that some village markets were open on certain days and others on other days. In this way, the four-day market cycle peculiar to Yoruba commercial life evolved – each village market being open only every fourth day.

Professional associations and guilds grew to establish links with their counterparts in other villages. It was, no doubt, in the context of these wider linkages that the association of herbalists (*onisegun*) evolved their stringent, virtually sacred, rules of mutual help of herbalist to herbalist. This ensured that if one herbalist encountered a difficult case in his village, he could count on help from herbalists from other villages. The *babalawo* (priests of the god of divination, Ifa) developed identical links and rules, and so too did the guild of hunters. By and by, each of these guilds created festivals at the *elu* level.

Intensive and very powerful linkages arose from the exogamous nature of marriages. And, most importantly, even though each settlement had its own protector spirit, all the settlements in an *elu* acknowledged and made rituals to a common protector spirit for the whole *elu*, and held its high priest in great awe – and, from time to time, deferred to his ritual prescriptions or requests.

The great surprise is that in the face of all these unifying realities, the rulers and people of the villages in the *elu* setting persisted in regarding each of their villages as separate from its neighbors and as self-contained. The explanation, earlier stated, is that the religious or spiritual guarantees which sustained separateness as the norm were so powerful that no groups internal to an *elu* could challenge them. That, as far as everybody knew, was the way people lived, and nobody knew any person or group of persons who lived any other way. All of the linkages among the villages in the *elu* were looked upon, not as negating the separateness of each settlement, but as necessary support for it. The individual settlement was home; beyond that was the outside world. The rules of inheritance and succession fitted perfectly into, and reinforced, such a world view.

But the forces of change continued slowly to increase in impact. Ultimately, by about the tenth century AD, the Yoruba world was ready for major steps forward. As it happened, the first of those steps were taken at Ife in the heart of Yorubaland. The great importance of Ife in Yoruba history, therefore, is that it was the first Yoruba village group or *elu* to step out beyond the encrusted framework of many centuries into the bright lights of a higher political culture. The chapter that follows will tell that story of Ife.

11. Opa Oranmiyan, Ile-Ife. *Photo: P.Verger, 1953, IFAN.*

3

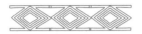

Before Oduduwa:
Ife in the Ninth to Tenth Century

All available evidence indicates that by about the beginning of the tenth century, each settlement in the Ife group had attained very high levels of economic, political, religious and social complexity, and that the group as a whole was poised for major transformational change. When that change came, it was so great that historians today are generally agreed that it amounted to a revolution – a revolution which not only transformed Ife but triggered a movement of profound change and transformation for the whole of Yorubaland.

Much is known today about the great developments in Ife in about the tenth century AD. It is also known that by about the eleventh century those developments had lifted Ife above every other Yoruba community in every sphere of human culture. The generality of Yoruba people then and after, awed by the image of Ife, transformed that city in their thoughts and folklore into a place of myth, mystery and legend. Ife became the first place that God created in the world, and the source of all earthly existence. For the Yoruba, Ife was *ondaiye* (the place of creation), *orirun* (the source of life), *ibi oju ti nmo wa* (the place from where the sun, or enlightenment, rises). It was generally believed that Ife was so close to heaven that one could meet one's departed forebears in its streets; and that in some hidden shrine in Ife could be found the gate to heaven. The gods that watched over the Yoruba race were believed to have their primary abodes in Ife. In later centuries, when communities in other parts of Yorubaland rose above Ife to greater heights of political and military power, the consensus and convention lived on that Ife's territory was inviolate to all Yoruba people, because to assault the Ife kingdom was to upset the supernatural guarantees that sustained order in the world. When, in the late nineteenth century, Ile-Ife was destroyed in war and lay in ruins, the oracles warned gravely from all corners of Yorubaland that the Yoruba country would never know peace until Ile-Ife had been resettled and accorded the respect and honor due to it.

Yet Ife's early greatness did not have its root in the mysterious and mythical, but in the concatenation of advantageous earthly circumstances. The present chapter will attempt to describe the economic and other developments in the *elu* at Ife in about the ninth or tenth century. The story of the revolution which followed upon those developments will be the subject of the next chapter.

As pointed out in previous chapters, then, we have the suggestion that there were thirteen settlements in the *elu* in the "Ife bowl" by the ninth or tenth century: Omologun, Parakin, Okeoja, Iloran, Odin, Ideta, Iloromu, Iwinrin, Oke-Awo, Ijugbe, Iraye, Imojubi, and Ido. However, it is important to note that there have also come down to us a few other important names not included in this list of thirteen. These include Ita Yemoo, Ilara, Orun Oba Ado and Idio. Also, some of the bigger settlements among the thirteen had quarters that were quite substantial in their own right, whose names keep showing up as separate settlements – a fact which tends to introduce some confusion into our attempts to ascertain the list of settlements. Finally, once the revolution commenced, the events occasioned by it were violent, tumultuous and long drawn out, and they caused the destruction of many settlements and the temporary emergence of others. The fact that the names of these settlements tossed about in the whirlwind of events also keep occurring in the traditions tends to add much to our difficulties. The consequence of all this is that, in the present state of our knowledge, our list of the tenth century Ife settlements is no more than tentative.

All that we can definitively say, therefore, is that by the tenth century, there were many settlements dotting the area of the "Ife bowl," an area with a diameter of about 20 kilometers (12.5 miles). Isola Olomola has made efforts to identify the locations of the better known of the settlements.[1] According to his findings, Iloromu lay along a stretch of today's Ife-Ilesa road; Ideta, remembered as the largest of the settlements, lay along today's road to Mokuro; Odin lay along the modern road to Ifewara; Ijugbe, Okeoja and Iraye were situated a few kilometers west of modern Modakeke, with Iraye being the farthest southwestwards; Ilare and Esije occupied the sites of today's Sabo and Eleyele, respectively; Iwinrin covered the area of today's Koiwo and Oronna quarters; Omologun covered part of what is now the campus of Obafemi Awolowo University; Imojubi lay along the modern Ife–Ondo road on the outskirts of today's city of Ile-Ife. The sites of Ido (which is said to have been a large settlement), Oke-Awo, Iloran and Parakin are difficult to ascertain.

Each settlement comprised at least a few quarters – each quarter being an intricate complex of compounds (or *agbo-ile*). If some physical difficulty (like a stream, a piece of marshy ground or a rock) had made it necessary to leave a sizeable gap between quarters, some quarters could look like self-contained settlements in their own right. Thus, for instance, Ijugbe consisted of four contiguous "villages" – Eranyiba, Ita-Asin, Ipa and Igbogbe; and Ideta consisted of three – Ilale, Ilesun and Ilia. Each *agbo-ile* was a large sprawling building consisting of a number of courtyards. A picture of these settlements in their last years of existence can be easily pieced together from traditions still vibrantly alive in many quarters of Ile-Ife today. Many of the *agbo-ile* were very old buildings. During dry seasons, there was a lot of roof repairing and roof replacement activity in every settlement, as well as of wholesale remodeling and improvement of some of the oldest *agbo-ile*. Many *agbo-ile* were proudly beautiful buildings – with carved wooden posts and doors, and murals on the walls of the courtyards. Usually in preparation for festivals, the women worked on these murals, cleaning them and renewing their paint, and there was much rivalry about this. Some of the traditions claim that potsherd paving of floors was already an old practice, and that some courtyards where kings lived were so paved. Some shrines experienced more decorating and more beautifying than even the richest *agbo-ile*. In every settlement, there was much activity in the building of new *agbo-ile*; food was plentiful; weddings were many.

Each settlement was ruled by its own king, who was also its high priest. Each quarter in every settlement was ruled by a high chief who was subject to the authority of the settlement's king. The quarter chief performed priestly duties for his quarter. In addition to his duties in his own quarter, he also served as an adviser and assistant to the king. In the process, some of the quarter chiefs had become so exalted that their titles rang out nearly as loudly as the titles of their kings. This is yet another reason why it is sometimes difficult today, when studying the traditions relating to this era of Ife's history, to be sure which titles belonged to kings and which belonged to quarter chiefs. Every *agbo-ile* had its own compound head (its oldest male member) who led the compound in ritual matters and dealt with small day-to-day matters peculiar to his compound. All relations in this whole system of government of a settlement were deeply rooted in religion – religious and spiritual bonds, proprieties, obligations, rituals. It is very clear in the traditions that a ruler in any of those Ife settlements of the tenth century was, much of the time, more a priest than anything else. The king, or chief, and the shrine belonged together, and the shrine was the heart of the settlement. The power of religion, the reality of supernatural sanctions, upheld and preserved the whole system.

Every settlement was surrounded by intensively cultivated farmlands. As a result, the whole "Ife bowl" was one expansive area, largely free of forests, criss-crossed by paths, a hub of human activities. Various kinds of crafts kept each settlement busy and generated a daily traffic of people between settlements. Each settlement had its own marketplace which opened every fourth day, and therefore women going to sell and buy were on the move between the settlements every day. The names of some of the settlements seem to indicate that they were generally recognized for certain special services. For instance,

Oke-Awo roughly means "village of the herbalist or diviner," and Okeoja "the settlement where the marketplace is located." While it is not known for sure whether these settlement names described their special functions in the area, it is known that some marketplaces had become, over time, bigger centers of trade than others, so that traders came to them not only from the Ife settlements but also from settlements in more distant parts of the country. Some Ekiti traditions strongly indicate that one Ife marketplace acquired the stature of a central marketplace in the Ife area. According to Olomola (relying on some versions of these Ekiti and Ijesha traditions), such a central marketplace did exist under the name of Oja Igbomoko, and traders came to it from as far away as parts of Ekiti. In early times, the people of the Ife settlements were known collectively as the Igbo – and Igbomoko therefore probably meant "a place for the gathering of the Igbo" (for buying and selling).

The settlements in the *elu* at Ife were therefore very close, not only physically but in many other respects – in their day-to-day pursuits, in their commercial life, in their sharing of special services, etc. The exogamous nature of their marriages interconnected all the settlements in a giant cobweb of human relationships. Consequently, significant events in any settlement (a festival, a wedding or a funeral) drew relatives from all the other settlements. By the tenth century, each settlement had grown so old and so diversified that some marriages could be contracted between persons of the same settlement, but most persons were the offspring of mothers married from other settlements. Some farmlands happened to be more desirable than others – because they were known to receive more rains usually, because they drained better, or because particular crops were known to do especially well on them. Therefore, farms belonging to farmers from different settlements tended to get interlocked in some areas, even though rigid respect for the traditional boundaries remained the norm. Some settlements became known as the leading producers of certain farm products. For instance, Ijugbe became generally recognized as the leader in the production of yams, which means that Ijugbe regularly produced large quantities of yam surpluses for sale. The other settlements generally believed that Ijugbe's success with yam cultivation was the result of a special favor from its protector god, but the cause, probably, was that Ijugbe's part of the farmlands was more suitable for certain types of yams. All the settlements also accepted the god of Ijugbe as the special giver of rains, the god to make sacrifices to for better rains for the farms – hence, the saying, "If the rains fail, make sacrifices to the god of Ijugbe. " In consequence, Ijugbe acquired some special prestige among the settlements.

Progressively too, long distance trade was becoming a major factor in the Ife group of settlements by the tenth century. Reference has been made to the traditions of parts of eastern Yorubaland concerning traders from those parts to Ife markets. The same traditions have it that the reason for the increase in this long-distance trade to the Ife area was that Ife was the only place to procure certain foreign, exotic, goods in the earliest times.

In an article first published in the *Journal of the Historical Society of Nigeria* in 1979,[2] Robin Horton looks at the agricultural, commercial, and industrial sectors of the economy of Ife by the ninth century, and concludes that by that date Ife's economy generally was experiencing great expansion. As indicated in Paul Ozanne's article earlier referred to, the Ife farmlands were mostly very fertile, received adequate rains in the rainy season, were mostly well drained, and were not prone to catastrophic erosion. These conditions provided the base for successful farming from the earliest history of the Ife settlements. That the settlements took good advantage of them and accorded agriculture the highest priority is shown in their traditions. Thus, we have the traditions relating to Orisateko, who is said to have been the hero (or god) who brought yam from heaven – a tradition which, most probably, suggests that some species of yams were domesticated in the Ife farmlands. Another version of the Orisateko traditions, however, has it that Orisateko was one of the most prominent people in the revolution that occurred in the tenth century, a strong man who resisted Oduduwa very successfully for some time. We can be sure that this means that big farmers were heroes in the settlements, and that farming was a very prestigious occupation there by the ninth century. This would seem to be confirmed by the traditions, earlier referred to, that Ijugbe enjoyed special prestige as a settlement because it produced rich surpluses of yams.

Also, the cultivation of the kolanut appears to belong to early times, and this crop seems to have become a very important one in the economy of the Ife area by the ninth century. The same appears to be true of the type of kola known as *orogbo* (*Cola garcinia*). By the ninth century, before Oduduwa, Ife was already a major producer of oil-palm products (palm oil, palm-kernel oil, palm wine, etc.) as well as of the raffia palm, *Raffia vinifera* – mostly palm wine. As will be related later in this chapter, Obatala (Oduduwa's most important opponent) was much given to these wines.

By the ninth century, then, Ife was a center of very prosperous agriculture. Such healthy agricultural production stimulated the growth of population. The traditions to the effect that new *agbo-ile* were always being built in all the Ife settlements by the beginning of the Oduduwa revolution testify to the growth of population, which, in turn, supplied more labor for agricultural production.

Also, and very importantly, the production of surpluses in agriculture created a strong base for the growth of trade – both local and long-distance trade.

For the early development of trade across the Niger with the West African savannah (and beyond, through the Sahara to the Mediterranean world), Ife occupied a particularly advantageous location. Directly south of the point at which the valley of the Niger describes a southward bend, the West African tropical forests also bulged northwards, so that a route from the Niger bend to this forest bulge provided the shortest connection from the Niger to the forests for the exchange of savannah and forest products. Ife lay in the middle of this forest bulge, making it a natural terminus of the earliest central north–south route in this region of West Africa. This made Ife the earliest center of the north–south trade in the Yoruba forests and established it as the earliest great commercial center south of the Niger. The trade stimulated the production of some goods and the gathering to Ife of others. The interaction of production surpluses and trade established the foundations of wealth. Ife thus began the journey into greatness – economic, cultural and political – much earlier than the rest of Yorubaland.

Other routes developed to connect this central route to other regions of West Africa. One such route pointed northwestwards to connect with the ancient city of Gao on the upper Niger, a city that by the ninth century was already a considerable center for the riverine trade as well as a terminus on trans-Saharan routes, and was later to become the capital city of the Songhai Empire. That a route such as this was already a factor in the Borgu and Yoruba region by the ninth century is, according to Robin Horton, indicated by a number of traditions and cultural evidence. Another route seems to have pointed southwestwards, connecting in the Ijebu forests with an ancient lagoon trade running east–west. The t-point junction of the two routes developed to become the commercial city of Ijebu-Ode. About the existence of an early east–west lagoon trade, there is much strong evidence. E. J. Alagoa has shown that a strong body of Ijo oral traditions points to the early existence of such a trade between the Ijo and the Ijebu waterside, oral traditions that seem to be confirmed by surviving traits of cultural connection between the Ijo and the people of the Ijebu waterside. Robin Horton does not mention yet another route – the one that almost certainly existed very early from Ife eastwards and southeastwards, along a general corridor consisting of the Ijesa, Ekiti and Owo countries, and that was later to provide the connection between Yorubaland and Benin. There seems to be no doubt that such a route already provided commercial and cultural links between central and eastern Yorubaland by the ninth century or earlier, as would seem to be indicated by Ijesa, Ekiti and Owo traditions, by the discovery of potsherd payments in Osi (Ekiti) and Ipole-Ijesa, and by considerable evidence of links between Ife, Owo and Benin sculptural art traditions.[3]

Before Oduduwa: Ife in the Ninth to Tenth Century

Perhaps the earliest export merchandise of Ife to the north was kolanut. The earliest scholars to study early kolanut trade in West Africa came to a conclusion that left out the Yoruba forests as a source of kolanut for the trade with the savannah. They postulated that the principal type of kolanut involved in the trade was the *Cola nitida* (*gooro*) which existed in the western parts of the West African forests (modern Ghana, etc.) but not in the Yoruba forests; and that the typical Yoruba type of kolanut – *obi abata* – was not a significant part of the trade. They also thought that the principal route of the kolanut trade started around Kumasi in modern Ghana and ran through the Niger bend to Hausaland, by-passing Yorubaland. In more recent times, however, these opinions have undergone some serious modifications. Babatunde Agiri has pointed out that *Cola acuminata* was also almost certainly a very significant item in the trade (as was perhaps also *orogbo*.[4] This would make Ife a major player in the kolanut trade.

Horses from the north were almost certainly also a part of this early trade. Some historians used to think that horses did not feature in the trade of the savannah with the forests until about the sixteenth century, but many scattered pieces of evidence now seem to contradict that view. The presence of a horse's head as a motif in ancient Igbo-ukwu brass art indicates quite strongly that horses were indeed known in the forests south of the Niger from quite early times. That conclusion is supported by some evidence from Yoruba traditions. Particularly strong evidence is found in the mention of horses in at least one verse of Odu Ifa. A strong body of Ife royal traditions is unambiguous that horses played a significant part in the import trade of Ife during the reign of Oduduwa, in the late tenth or early eleventh century. One *oriki* of Obokun, Oduduwa's grandson and founder of the Ilesa kingdom, describes him as *okunrin dudu ori esin* (black rider on a horse), and some very ancient shrines in parts of Yorubaland had sculptures representing deities riding on horses. It is also known that some centuries after Oduduwa's time, the rulers of the Benin kingdom in the deep southeast used horses, partly as prestige items, but partly also for very important communication. In spite of the difficulties created by the tsetse fly, horses appear to have been a regular part of the penetration of savannah animal species from beyond the Niger to Yorubaland from very early times. The most probable conclusion, then, is that the tsetse fly did not totally exclude horses, it only made them rare – and for that reason horses were prestige possessions of rulers and of the most important shrines. Ife most probably had a monopoly of the trade in horses in Yorubaland for a long time – which would account for the southern Ekiti proverb that he who desires to own a horse must buy one from heaven through Ife.

Ife also seems to have been a major center for the earliest distribution of salt in the Yoruba interior – salt produced by processing sea water in various parts of the coast (mostly by the Ijebu, Itsekiri, Ilaje and Ijo) and imported into Yorubaland through the Ijebu coastal towns. Salt from the Sahara later came to enhance the volume of salt in Yorubaland. Dried fish from the coast appears also to have been a major item of the ancient trade, and so was palm oil sold to the savannah lands in the north. Ekiti and Ijesa traditions also indicate that Ife was the earliest market in which to procure leather and leather goods, as well as exotic herbs and herbal preparations from the savannah and the sahel, and potash from the Sahara.

The use of cowry shells (*owo eyo*) as currency had very probably begun in the Ife market before the ninth century. Widespread Yoruba traditions point to the Ife as the first users of cowries in Yorubaland, a fact indicating that the earliest cowries came through the trans-Saharan routes. Imported from the Indian Ocean through the Middle East, cowries were used in Ife not only as money but also as ritual jewelry and ritual decoration. Cowries seem to have quickly spread over the Yoruba and Edo forests, to be imported also through the coast by the Portuguese after the coming of European trade centuries later.[5]

By the ninth century, then, Ife was a center of considerable agricultural and commercial prosperity. But Ife was also prospering as a center of industrial production and already experiencing increasing manufactures of iron, beads and various other products that were to make it by the twelfth century the greatest manufacturing and artistic center in the West African forests.

For the existence of a very strong iron industry in Ife by the ninth century, before Oduduwa, the evidence is unambiguous. Ife appears, indeed, to have already become the major center of iron production in much of West Africa by that date, as well as a supplier of raw iron and iron manufactures (tools, implements, artifacts) to much of Yorubaland. The shrine of Ogunladin (deified blacksmith of Oduduwa), in front of the Ooni's palace, has a pear-shaped hundredweight of wrought iron which was made in Oduduwa's time. This, clearly, is a work of very skilled blacksmiths – a level of skill which already existed before Oduduwa. Abundant evidence of a vibrant early iron industry has been found in other parts of Ife. For instance, excavations by P. Garlake at Obalara's land and at Woye Asiri have revealed, among other things, large quantities of iron nails, some of which seem to have been used in some large wooden construction. Even more importantly, the Garlake excavations unearthed iron slag and tuyeres (clay pipes through which air was passed into furnaces), clear evidence of an iron smelting industry. And, as it would seem, we do not have to look far to discover the source of the iron-bearing rock-clay for a smelting industry in Ife. Paul Ozanne points to ironstone quarries in both the southeast and northwest outskirts of the ancient city, from which raw materials were dug for smelting.[6]

Long before Oduduwa then, Ife had an iron-smelting industry and many blacksmiths' workshops producing a large variety of iron goods in quantity. Such a strong base for the production of farming tools in iron was one of the major factors which boosted agriculture, which then had serious impacts on population growth and the expansion of commerce. But the production of large varieties and quantities of iron products must have impacted almost all areas of life – the volume and quality of *agbo-ile* construction, plastic art in all mediums, long-distance travel and, eventually, the political ordering of the Ife group of settlements.

Ife also had a growing industry in bead production. In later years, under Oduduwa and his successors as kings of Ife, this bead industry was to grow into a very major source of wealth for Ife people, but its beginnings belonged to earlier times than Oduduwa's. The two types of beads produced in Ife were the blue, dichroic glass beads known as *segi*, and the red tubular type known as *iyun*. Concerning the source of the raw materials for Ife's bead industry, there has been some debate among scholars. Some believe that Ife bead makers did not get their raw glass by smelting original raw materials such as potash and silica (both found in ashes and sand), but by re-melting glass from glass products imported from mediaeval Europe through the trans-Saharan trade routes. In support of this view, some evidence exists of such re-melted imported glass in some of the Ife beads. However, other scholars have pointed to equally conclusive evidence of original smelting of glass in Ife, as indicated by the findings of some archaeological excavations in the city. It is important also that some Ife traditions have it that iron smelting and glass smelting generally went together as twin pursuits. What most probably happened, then, is that in the high-heat processes of iron smelting (or perhaps even pot firing), the exposure of potassium-rich wood ash, together with silica in ordinary sand, to very high heats, yielded Ife's earliest quantities of raw glass. Thereafter, facilities were established for regular smelting of glass for the production of beads. Then, a long time later, under Oduduwa and his successors, when the bead industry became very large, bead producers began to melt any glass to augment the raw glass from the smelters. Ife was an exporter of some beads before Oduduwa, through Ijebu traders to the coasts of West Africa, and through other traders to the Niger and beyond, especially to the Nupe country. With the coming of European trade in later centuries, European traders bought a type of bead called 'akori' in the Allada area and resold it on the Gold Coast. It has now been suggested that this akori bead was in fact *segi* bead from Ife.

Besides these manufactures, Ife was also an early and major center of production of cloth, pottery products, oil palm products, raffia products; certain types of mats, raffia-woven baskets commonly used as containers in long-distance trade, herbal preparations, etc. All in all, then, by the ninth and tenth centuries, Ife was a great and growing economy, certainly the richest and most dynamic place in the whole of the Yoruba forests.

Even in these very early times, Ife was already a place of considerable artistic activity. In a recent monumental work on Yoruba art history written by Henry Drewal, John Pemberton and Rowland Abiodun, the following stages and eras in the development of art in Ife have been proposed:

- Archaic Era, before AD 800
- Pre-Pavement Era, 800–1000
- Early Pavement Era, 1000–1200
- Late Pavement Era, 1200–1400
- Post-Pavement Era, 1400–1600?
- Stylized Humanism Era, 1600?–the Present[7]

Of these eras, only the first two concern us in this chapter. During the Archaic Era and the Pre-Pavement Era, that is the centuries from about 350 BC (when the first Ife settlements arose) to about 1000 AD, the people of the many small settlements in the *elu* in Ife decorated their lineage compounds and shrines with wall murals and paintings, as well as with carved and painted wooden posts and carved doors. They also produced beautiful clay figurines, as well as carvings in stone, and molded iron figurines – most of these, almost certainly, for decorating community shrines, *agbo-ile* shrines, and the abodes of rulers. Some of their stone sculptures were studded with iron nails – a sort of artistic expression whose purpose remains unknown to us. The Ife people of this period, especially the later centuries of the period, appear to have initiated the practice of beautifying some floors and courtyards by paving them with potsherd (pieces of broken pottery) and stones. Some of their most important shrines, and the abodes of some of their rulers, were, according to Ife traditions, decorated in this way.

Probably by, or before, the tenth century, some art in bronze or brass casting may have begun in the Ife settlements. Many archaeologists and historians believe that bronze/brass casting did not start in Ife until about the early eleventh century, but this is probably because much of the bronze/brass art of Ife has not been dated. At Igbo-ukwu, east of the Niger in the same forest zone as Ife, clear ninth century dates for bronze/brass casting have been obtained. Since it is fairly certain that the copper for bronze/brass casting at Ife and Igbo-ukwu were importations into West Africa, it seems very probable that both places obtained the raw materials and practiced bronze/brass casting at about the same time. By the tenth century, Ife had, as earlier pointed out, become a market of considerable importance as a terminus of the trans-Saharan trade – the early source of copper imports to West Africa. At any rate, the very high quality of Ife bronze/brass art by the eleventh century seems to be positive proof of some earlier beginning than the eleventh century.

The growth in population in Ife by the ninth century increased the sizes of the settlements, and growing prosperity enhanced the quality of life in many ways. Very importantly also, Ife's prosperity attracted increasing numbers of people into the area. Many of these were traders and others who ended up becoming members of the existing compounds and lineages; but increasing numbers were not getting so absorbed but tended to constitute a sort of floating population. Also, small coherent groups came, seeking to establish settlements and share in the prosperity of the Ife area.

In the face of all these developments, the traditional political arrangements in the "Ife bowl" could not possibly survive for much longer. From their various beginnings, each of these settlements had managed its own affairs as an autonomous kingdom religiously, so respected by, and respectful of, its neighbors. The traditional political leaderships clung tenaciously to this old order of things, but clearly the old order was due for radical change.

At first, and for some time, according to the traditions, the people in control of the old order compromised a little by allowing some change. The kings of the settlements worked out some system of cooperation among themselves, a sort of alliance (or confederacy, according to Abiodun Adediran) over which one of them presided as a sort of chairman. The details of this arrangement are not very clear, but, according to Adediran, the alliance was a very loose one. Membership was voluntary, and it was presumed that any of the kings could pull out at will. No central chieftaincy institution was ever considered, and every kingdom kept its autonomy and separate existence. Apparently, there developed some increased collaboration in ritual matters, allowing the chairman to call for, and preside over, joint sacrifices to the gods for the common welfare of all the settlements. But the chairmanship was not permanent but rotational, so that when the chairman died, the position passed to the king of another settlement. The oldest one among the kings, according to some traditions, was elevated to the vacant position, an arrangement which tended to make the chairmanship change hands frequently, thus guaranteeing that no chairman would develop undue ambitions. So far were the kings ready to go and no further.[8]

As it turned out, this arrangement proved very unstable. Even soon after its inception, conflicts surfaced. The first chairman of the alliance, according to most versions of the traditions, was Oranfe, ruler of the Ora settlement. He soon confronted some major challenge to his leadership. The nature of the challenge is not clear. Probably he found that some of the kings and their settlements would not accept his leadership in certain matters, or even that some of them conspired to replace him or abolish the alliance. According to the traditions, he survived the challenge and secured the support of the majority of the kings and settlements. A minor conflict seems to have occurred, since the traditions describe Oranfe's supporters as running through all the settlements proclaiming:

> *Gbogbo elu o o* Hear, all people in this elu,
>
> *E mo s'oni to Oranfe o* Oranfe has no rival;
>
> *Ora lo mo n' Ife o* Oranfe is undisputed leader in all Ife;
>
> *Elu gbogbo, Ora lo n' Ife!* Let all in the elu hear that!

Most of the kings who occupied the position of chairman after Oranfe do not appear to have fared well at all. The last of them was Obatala. In the very many traditional accounts of the events of these times in the history of Ife, the image of Obatala is generally a very unflattering one. Most versions of the traditions represent him as an alcoholic who was in the habit of getting drunk and falling into a stupor when he was needed to attend to important matters. Some versions represent him as a man crippled by some bodily deformity. It is difficult to miss in these traditions the tone of contempt for the leaders of this alliance arrangement. Almost certainly, what these traditions are trying to convey is that the system of alliance was grossly inadequate for the needs of the times, and that the men who led the alliance were incompetent. Ife was ripe for real change.

4

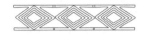

The Revolution in Ife: Tenth to Eleventh Century

In about the late tenth century, the storm that had slowly gathered over the political life of Ife burst. The result, according to all versions of the large wealth of Ife traditions, was a long period of conflict and turmoil, ending in a new political order.

Of the human actors in this revolution, the greatest, according to all the traditions, was Oduduwa. So monumental was the role of this man that, probably even from as early as his own life-time, popular traditions and legends elevated him to the awesome pedestal of father of the Yoruba race and founder of the monarchical system which thenceforth became their typical system of government. His successors deified him, and subsequent generations transposed him all the way back to the very beginning of creation and crowned him as the first human to walk the earth, the progenitor of the Yoruba race.

In much of the effort made during the twentieth century to study this revolutionary era in Yoruba history, the general direction was to look for Oduduwa's root in some distant foreign land outside of Africa, and to bring him as a conquering foreign prince to Ife. That direction was initiated by the Reverend Samuel Johnson in his famous *The History of the Yorubas* which was written in the final years of the nineteenth century and first published in 1921. According to Samuel Johnson, Oduduwa was leader of a group which left Arabia in the Middle East as a result of clashes between Islam and the traditional polytheistic religion of the place, and which finally found its way to Yorubaland and established itself over Ife. Until deep into the twentieth century, some of the best minds available to us in historical scholarship took up Johnson's lead and followed it, and therefore it is important that we briefly examine the roots of Johnson's ideas concerning early Yoruba history.[1]

A son of Yoruba emigrants (liberated slaves returning home) from Sierra Leone in the nineteenth century, Samuel Johnson was educated for the service of the church. After elementary education in the Church Missionary Society (CMS) mission school in Ibadan, he was sent, for secondary education, to the

CMS Training Institution in Abeokuta, where he studied from the age of 16 until he graduated at 20 (in 1866). He then returned to teach in Ibadan until 1882, after which he repeatedly featured in the peace-making missions seeking to end the wars among various Yoruba states in the last two decades of the nineteenth century. The book *The History of the Yorubas*, which he started to write in these years, was completed in 1897. At the Training Institution in Abeokuta, he had schooled under a German teacher named G. F. Bühler who, while training his students as church workers, gave them a very solid grounding in ancient history – the history of Egypt, Babylon, Greece and Rome. From such beginnings, Johnson developed a strong interest in the history and mythology of the Middle East. Moreover, Johnson's Yorubaland of the late nineteenth century was increasingly affected by the growth of Islam and Christianity, two world-shaping products of the Middle East. In particular, with Islam came the knowledge of Western Sudanese myths and legends through the writings of Muslims of the Western Sudan (including Hausaland) – especially some of the writings of Sultan Bello of Sokoto which contained some Sudanese myths about Yoruba origins. Above all, the nineteenth century was, in Europe, the golden age of the study of the history and civilization of ancient Egypt. The ancient Egyptian writings had just been deciphered, and the expanding knowledge of the wonders of ancient Egypt was creating great excitement in the world of scholarship. The writings of the emerging class of literate Yorubas were commonly laced with Egyptian and Middle Eastern references, analogies and mythology (a practice apparently regarded then as a mark of erudition) – as a reading of the Lagos newspapers of the time will abundantly show. All these influences combined to shape much of Johnson's *The History of the Yorubas*, and to account for his linking of all important details of early beginnings of Yoruba history to the Middle East. Thus, Oduduwa became a personage from the Middle East, and Oranmiyan's migration northwards to the Niger country became a journey with the Middle East as its intended destination. Indeed, the influence of Middle Eastern mythology pervades most of Johnson's early history chapters, all the way from his preface. In contrast, his accounts of the history of the Oyo Empire were assembled from oral evidence he collected in places like Oyo and Ibadan where memories of the disintegration of that empire were still quite fresh; while his accounts of late nineteenth century Yoruba history were products of his own eyewitness observations of many of the events.

Fortunately, while much effort was being expended in following Johnson's ideas about the beginnings of Yoruba history, there existed all around us, in Ife and other parts of Yorubaland, an enormous wealth of traditions, as well as evidence in the Yoruba political system and surviving practices and rituals, about Oduduwa and his era. Ultimately, a different direction in the study of

The Revolution in Ife: Tenth to Eleventh Century

Yoruba history developed (as part of a more scientific study of African history in general) which focused on the indigenous evidence, as well as other source material, for the reconstruction of early Yoruba history. Consequent upon these efforts, we now stand able to lay aside, with respect, the Johnsonian hypothesis about the origins of Oduduwa and of the Yoruba. All who study the history of Ife and of the Yoruba people are now generally agreed that the great political changes which began in Ife in about the tenth century were indigenous in their origin, in their unfolding and in their *dramatis personae*. It is on the soil of Yorubaland that Oduduwa was born and raised; it is only in that soil that his roots can be found.

The traditional accounts of the development and growth of the political troubles in Ife in Oduduwa's time are many and complicated. Countless versions exist, each with its own twist, orientation and emphasis. Even in spite of an intervening period of about one-thousand years, partisan differences and passions about these events are still quite real in Ife. Nevertheless, by carefully sifting through the infinite variety of traditions and versions, we can put together the basic traditional narrative that follows.[2]

Some small settlements had, for a long time, existed on hills beyond the immediate environs of the settlements in the Ife bowl. At some point in time, one of them moved down, staked claims to some land within the area and started to build a new settlement. Its leader was a man named Oduduwa. Before this group came, there was already an area that the old settlements generally regarded as land for strangers. It was into this area that the group now commonly represented in the traditions as the Oduduwa group moved. From the moment that this group arrived, it was unprepared to accept the claims of precedence by the older settlements; it was also not willing to have any dealings with the existing alliance of kings. All this led to the beginning of conflicts between the Oduduwa group and some of the older settlements, and these conflicts got worse over a long time.

At some point in the conflicts, an influential citizen of one of the old settlements, a man named Oreluere (or Ore), thought of a way to subdue Oduduwa and restore peace. He poisoned one of Oduduwa's daughters (another version says that he wounded one of Oduduwa's sons), confident that Oduduwa would come to him for herbal treatment for his sick daughter (or son). Oduduwa proudly refused to seek help and went about treating the sick by himself, but he did not have the necessary herbal knowledge and skill, and he did not make much progress. At last, he went to Oreluere for help. As Oreluere had hoped, this led to communication and then peace. But it turned out to be a short truce. Conflicts were resumed, and Oreluere became one of Oduduwa's leading adversaries. The confrontation was fierce. Oreluere and many of his men received terrible wounds in the fighting, but Oduduwa and his group were overpowered and forced to agree to pay tribute "of sheep and fowls." Yet, the Oduduwa group was not dislodged; it rebuilt its strength and was ready to fight again. As these new conflicts dragged on, some of the old settlements threw their weight in with Oduduwa. Some settlements were destroyed and scattered, new settlements sprang up here and there. The confusion, loss of lives, and destruction of property were beyond description. At last, all parties agreed to attempt to make peace, and Obatala, king of Ideta and chairman of the alliance of kings, was put in charge of the arrangements for general negotiations towards permanent peace ("permanent existence," according to the traditions). But Obatala was incompetent and unstable (often getting drunk), and his excessive claims to authority alienated many. By contrast, Oduduwa's excellent qualities of leadership won the admiration of even his most tenacious enemies. Many of these enemies chose to continue to fight Oduduwa, but more and more of them gave up the fight or decamped to the Oduduwa side. In fact, one of the decamping leaders, Obameri, became Oduduwa's general. Obatala became the leader of those still fighting Oduduwa, and his formidable home settlement of Ideta, of which he was king, became the backbone of the anti-Oduduwa war. However, he and his followers steadily declined in strength. A major attack led by Obameri dislodged Obatala from Ideta and forced him and his followers to withdraw to an area beyond the Esinminrin stream where they established their camp and named it Ideta-Oko ("Ideta in the woods"). At Ideta-Oko they increased their strength considerably and then embarked upon a series of determined campaigns to retake Ife, but a strong Oduduwa force under Obameri encamped at Odin to fight them off again and again.

In the end, all the parties, battered and decimated, desired peace. The toll in human suffering was heavy. Small groups of dislodged persons, hoping to find peace, established fragile little settlements on the farmlands. At Ideta-Oko, a smallpox epidemic broke out and caused terrible loss of lives, seriously weakening the Obatala forces. At last, a group led by a prince named Ojumu urged all for peace. The resulting peace agreement provided that Obatala and his followers be readmitted into Ife. Ideta-Oko was therefore broken up as its inhabitants returned to the ruins of Ideta. The peace agreement also provided for a new permanent existence (or constitution) under which the new people (the followers of Oduduwa) and elements of the old settlements would be fused together as the new government for Ife. By then, Oduduwa had become, far and away, the most dominant leader in Ife. Practically all were prepared to accept him as their ruler, and all looked up to him to lead Ife back to order and peace. Obatala had no choice other than to concede authority to him.

For the most part, then, peace returned. Only some of the most irreconcilable of Obatala's followers continued to hold out against peace. This faction, led by Obawinrin, king of the old settlement of Iwinrin, refused to return to Ife from Ideta-Oko, but rather moved further away from Ife to a place which became known as Igbo-Igbo (forest of the Igbo) from where they continued for a long time to harass the outskirts of the new Ife with lightning raids that usually left people dead and houses burning. Rather, however, than stultify the consolidation of the new Ife, as they were meant to do, these raids actually helped its growth as will be seen below.

Thus, the basic narrative of the events of the political turmoil as it has come down to us in the traditions. The first comment concerning this narrative is that the events described in it are preserved by the many traditional agencies concerned with the preservation of Ife's history — in the palace of the Ooni of Ife, in the compounds of the chiefs, in the many shrines at which Ife people traditionally worshipped, and in the Odu Ifa. Perhaps more significantly, many of the details of these events are preserved in some forms of Ife's art as well as in rituals of great importance in the life of the Ife kingdom. For instance, artists believed to be contemporary with the events left sculptures in stone representing Oreluere and showing the wounds that he and his followers suffered in the battles. Then there is a very important festival that the Ooni and the people of Ife celebrate annually to commemorate these events in Ife's history. Called Itapa (meaning, roughly, "the great conflict"), this festival does not merely re-enact some of the events of those times; it also stands for an annual reaffirmation of the legitimacy of the Ooni's kingship. During this festival, the priests of Obatala mark their bodies with white dots — in remembrance of the smallpox epidemic which had put deadly pustules on many people in Obatala's camp at Ideta-Oko. On the seventh day of Itapa, rituals are carried out to ward off smallpox from Ife. On the eve of the eleventh day, the whole populace of Ife is supposed to weep and wail in remembrance of the day on which Obatala and his followers were expelled from Ife in a terrible battle; and on the eleventh day, there is joyful celebration of two events — first, the peace agreement which ended the wars, and second, the readmission of Obatala and his followers into Ife. The Itapa festival is believed to have been instituted soon after the events it commemorates.

Not only were the events "carved in stone," as it were; some of the leading actors in them were too. Every culture has its own way of preserving the memory of its most important people. The Yoruba culture does so by deifying them and establishing shrines at which they can be periodically commemorated through rituals. Oduduwa was deified after his death and an Oduduwa shrine exists in Ile-Ife, with its own priests and regular rituals — a very important institution in the life of the Ife kingdom. Obatala too was later deified. In fact Obatala became identified with Orisanla, the most senior of the Yoruba gods. This strange elevation of Obatala to Orisanla seems like an attempt by his followers to make the statement that though Obatala had been defeated and relegated to insignificance by Oduduwa, he remained a most important personage in Ife's history. Even some of the lesser persons in this era of Ife history were later deified, such as Obameri and Oreluere.

What then were the causes of the collapse of order in the Ife bowl? Once the conflicts started, why did they become so vicious, and why was it impossible to make peace until all parties became virtually exhausted?

Most of the popular traditional accounts in Ife trace the beginning of the troubles to the arrival of the Oduduwa group and its unwillingness to recognize any rights of precedence or accept the order that had long existed. Obviously, this is no more than the orthodox version preserved by the people of the pre-Oduduwa settlements who have always been the majority of the population of the new city of Ile-Ife, created in Oduduwa's time. Even these same versions contain fairly detailed information pointing to the fact that the causes of the conflicts were deeper and wider. According to such details, settler groups had been finding their way into the Ife bowl since a very distant past. The rate of their coming had been generally slow – no more than a few groups in centuries. But the very considerable prosperity in the Ife area by the ninth century (in agriculture, trade, manufacturing, improvements in the quality of life, etc.) turned Ife into a very desirable place to go and settle. Consequently, a growing stream of immigrants arrived over a relatively short time. Those who came as individuals or families seeking inclusion in the old compounds and lineages were, by and large, so included and absorbed. But things were different for those that came as coherent groups seeking space to settle – fragments that had hived off from other settlements, or whole settlements that wanted to relocate. Claims of the older settlements, and rigid boundaries to the farmlands, created a situation in which such newly arriving groups could not easily settle in places immediately desirable to them. Even though virgin forests lay in all directions beyond the immediate area of the elu, the jostling and resentment of the newly arriving groups in the immediate elu area created a sort of artificial land hunger there. At first, under this pressure, the old settlements, according to the traditions, designated an area as strangers' area. And in that strangers' area small settler dwellings mushroomed. The group that was later to achieve prominence as the Oduduwa group was one of the larger groups in this medley. Ultimately, sporadic conflicts developed between the new arrivals and the older settlements, and that on a jaggedly widening front – each old settlement keeping aloof until the conflicts rolled to its door.

The Revolution in Ife: Tenth to Eleventh Century

As the resentment and hostilities grew, the political arrangement existing in Ife was incapable of dealing with them. A common authority did not exist. There was an alliance, for sure, but, as earlier pointed out, it was a very loose one as each of the old settlements jealously guarded its autonomy. More often than not, the chairman of the alliance was in some trouble with some rulers and settlements and could not get much accomplished at the collective level. In fact, the rulers in the alliance most often preferred to behave as if there was no alliance at all. In these circumstances, every chairman of the alliance seemed incompetent. As is clear from the traditions, sporadic acts of violence erupted between the so-called strangers and some of the older settlements in an irregularly widening front. Each old settlement kept aloof until the troubles rolled to its door.

At some point in this growing turmoil, Oduduwa became ruler of his little group and then leader of all the stranger elements. When that happened, the collective group of stranger elements acquired a leadership with unusual courage, vision and élan, and its strength and confidence exploded. With some of the old settlements already in ruins, the remaining old settlements at last acted together and appointed Obatala, until then an ineffectual chairman of the old alliance, as their leader. This pitched the two leading men in Ife – Oduduwa and Obatala – against each other, and the fighting entered its most terrible, most bloody, phase. As it happened, Oduduwa was a much better leader and statesman than Obatala, whose unstable behavior lost him the loyalty of some of his most capable followers – who then went over and offered their services to Oduduwa. The balance of strength shifted slowly in favor of the Oduduwa forces. By the time Obatala and his followers were expelled from Ife and pushed beyond the Esinminrin stream, most of the old settlements were in ruins. The pitched battles that followed after that only added to the destruction.

How long, then, did these conflicts and wars last? The traditional accounts all insist that the troubles in Ife, from the beginning to the end, went on for a "very long time." Some versions even have it that the troubles went on for 201 years. There is a strong probability that "201" is no more than typical Yoruba hyperbole; still, there seems to be no doubt that the era of troubles, starting with the early resentments and minor acts of hostility and ending with the Ojumu peace, went on for very many decades. Akin Ogundiran, after carefully researching the Ife traditions, has suggested that the conflicts started in the late ninth century and went on until the early eleventh century – and that would seem to be borne out by the generality of the traditions.

That raises the important question about the time span of Oduduwa's participation in the conflicts. The traditional accounts put Oduduwa and Obatala at the very beginnings of the conflicts to their very end, and then, after that, present us with very detailed information about Oduduwa as king ruling over the new unified city of Ife for many decades – altogether a very improbable construct. There is no doubt that Oduduwa and Obatala were the most prominent persons in the last stages of the wars. Neither, therefore, could have been actors, or even could have been born, at the beginning of the conflicts. An examination of most of the traditions fairly definitively establish that Oduduwa was born in the strangers' area of Ife to leaders of a small group that had relocated from one of the hills beyond the elu at Ife, that he grew up in the tradition of resentment in the strangers' area, and that his youth and Obatala's youth (both of them "sons of the soil") were spent in the tradition of growing conflicts in Ife. The traditional accounts put both men in the era of conflicts from its beginning to its end, obviously, because of their extremely dominant roles in its latter stages. In the light of this, it is reasonably certain that the group which became popularly known as the Oduduwa group in the traditions was led to the Ife area not by Oduduwa but by his parents or grandparents.

Not until practically everything lay in ruins and all parties were exhausted was meaningful compromise and peace possible. Obatala returned to the ruins of Ideta, and other surviving kings must also have returned to the ruins of their various settlements, determined, most certainly, to start to rebuild. But the world they had always known had vanished. In all directions, indefinable groups of displaced persons lay jumbled together, feebly casting around to start life anew. Very clearly, a new order was needed, but such a concept was far too strange and too high for most to grasp. Fortunately, in the midst of all the rubble, there was one man who understood the great need of the moment and, by understanding the need, came to an understanding too of the concept – even though (as far as we know) he does not seem to have had any precedent to go by. His name was Oduduwa. Probably because he was not a product of an old Ife settlement with some grand name or history, he was freed to see the realities and the need of the moment clearly. While the kings of the old settlements must have agonized about rebuilding them, Oduduwa dreamed of new possibilities and prospects. A completely new pattern of settlement was needed, a new settlement comprising all, under one leader who was king of all. Oduduwa began to gather together the pieces of that new settlement – Ile-Ife, the first city in the Yoruba forests, the first city of the Yoruba people.

To summarize then, by the ninth century, Ife had grown to a point where its old political system of many autonomous, small kingdoms could no longer hold it together. A large array of economic and social forces had created, more or less, a single Ife society. Trade was stretching the reach of that society to distant parts of the world. The growth of art in various forms and media shows that the human mind in this Ife society was expanding, exploring, and reaching out beyond itself. Even in religion, many of the gods worshipped in Ife were no longer merely gods of the small settlements, but gods of all the settlements and of a whole people, known and worshipped in distant parts of the Yoruba forests – some of them originating outside Ife. Powerful new professions and cults simply rejected the boundaries represented by the autonomous little settlements. Only the political arrangement (of many small, separate, autonomous, settlements), reinforced by powerful religious beliefs, was not changing at a rate commensurate with the multiple changes in other aspects of the life of the area. In the end, the irresistible forces of change simply ripped this political straitjacket to shreds, in the process creating a horrendous explosion that shattered lives and a lot of treasured possessions. From the smoldering ruins, the new pattern of life that had been straining to come into existence was about to be born.

Oduduwa was camped in the partly ruined compounds of Omologun when the fighting ended. Within days, he moved his base to Idio, a low hill gently sloping in all directions. From Idio, he embarked upon the huge task of allocating sites for all identifiable groups. When that was completed, he invited the kings of the old settlements to move with their people to the new locations that he had chosen for them. The massive movements of people began, each group to its predetermined location around the center of the new city. The old settlements, as well as the new ones that had sprung up during the wars, were abandoned. In all directions around Oduduwa's location, the new city of Ile-Ife slowly emerged.

As this proceeded, Oduduwa embarked on two important tasks – provision of security for the new city, and elaboration of the city's new system of government. Just as the city was forming, attacks on it began from Igbo-Igbo. Oduduwa therefore mobilized the citizens of the new city for the building of a protective wall round their city. And, as he and his people worked on building Ile-Ife's first city wall, he established the details of the new city government.

The "Oduduwa Constitution" as it emerged, took the following form. Ile-Ife had only one king – and that was Oduduwa himself, whose family became the royal family and (in the well known tradition of kingship in the Ife bowl) would provide the kings in succession forever. The city thus became one single kingdom under one king, and not an alliance, confederation, or federation of kingdoms. Each of the kings of the pre-Oduduwa settlements had used to hold the *are*, the sacred symbol of royalty. These were now surrendered to Oduduwa so that only Oduduwa as king of Ile-Ife could hold the *are*. With the *are* in his possession, the king of Ile-Ife became the legitimate leader of every single one of the old settlements and their lineages, and any claims to ultimate leadership by their former kings were thus terminated. Everybody thenceforth looked up to the king alone as their ruler, chosen and upheld by the gods, and it became the prerogative of the king to appoint any citizen to governmental roles and duties in the new society. The city was then delineated into quarters, each quarter under a quarter chief. The former kings, as found appropriate, were appointed quarter chiefs in their quarters, and other significant citizens were appointed quarter chiefs in other sections of the city. Below the level of the quarter chiefs, other chieftaincies were instituted in every quarter. Such chiefs, installed by the king and subject to his government, assisted in their neighborhoods the quarter chiefs. Like the kingship, every chieftaincy title (quarter chief or neighborhood chief) was hereditary in one lineage; when a chief died, members of his lineage nominated from among themselves a candidate acceptable to the king for him to appoint and install. The king also had the prerogative to establish chieftaincies for special duties – war chiefs, palace officials, etc. Some of such special-function chieftaincies were not hereditary, meaning that the king could select any notable citizens to them. In the palace, the king was served by officials known as *omode-owa*, employed mostly as royal messengers.

In the early years of the Ife kingdom, as its form of government gradually crystallized, there emerged a special extra-governmental body known as the Ogboni – a body comprising the highest political and religious leaders and other eminent citizens notable for their experience in public affairs and their supreme knowledge of the traditions. In its council, the Ogboni worshipped the primordial spirits of the Earth rather than the latter-day Yoruba gods. They held that the Earth was older than the gods, and that the Ogboni was older than the kingship. The membership of the Ogboni was bound together by extremely powerful oaths, and its meetings and other activities were conducted in uttermost secrecy. All this, and its uniquely prestigious membership, gave the Ogboni enormous respect and influence, and it used that influence to watch over the affairs of the kingdom – especially over the integrity of political institutions and of the performance of public officials (including even the king). In this watchdog role, it could (always in its secret councils) call to question, and penalize, any public officials, and employ powerful cultic sanctions against errant conduct that threatened the quality of public stewardship, the image of the government, or the welfare of society. By the mass of ordinary citizens, the Ogboni was viewed as a "cult" of powerful people, shrouded in secrecy, possessed of limitless spiritual capabilities, guarded by secret oaths, an institution about which even the highest chiefs spoke in muffled tones to even the members of their own families (if they spoke of it at all). Its council chamber called *iledi* (the house of secret bonds) was feared and avoided by members of the public. Its symbols, the brass staffs called *edan* (usually in pairs, male and female), had supernatural powers ascribed to them. As objects of protection, they were supposed to be able to foretell if danger or serious sickness was about to come to a member, to be able to ward off such sickness or danger, and to heal a sick member. As symbols of the judicial and penal authority of the group, and as objects of spiritual communication, they were believed to be able to travel long distances on their own (flying like birds), and to go through obstacles on their way. Therefore, any person declared guilty and targeted for punishment by Ogboni was believed to have no means of evading the punishment. As watchers over the realm, Ogboni held its members to the very highest standards of honesty and probity; and inflicted, through occult and ritual sanctions, terminal penalties on any member who infringed such standards. Their tenet of faith was that the Earth and the ancestors were the givers of the moral laws for the conduct of leaders of society, and that the Earth and the ancestors had charged the Ogboni in its council with vigilance over the moral laws, and had vested the Ogboni with limitlessly efficacious sanctions for their enforcement.[3]

Everything about the Ogboni points to the fact that it was modelled on some rudiment found in the culture of the small settlements of pre-Oduduwa times. What seems to have happened is that the leaders of the new kingdom under Oduduwa came to the determination that, in order to protect the offices and functions of their new kingdom from the corruption that could result from the frailties and wickednesses of humans, some type of higher institution was needed to watch over the institutions of state and to moderate the behavior of the state's officials and leading citizens. They then brought the Ogboni into being and upheld its influence and power. The Ogboni was to become a significant gift of Oduduwa's Ife kingdom to the political culture of the future kingdoms of the Yoruba people.

Oduduwa did not establish a new system of government. What he did was to take the old system of monarchy, which had developed and matured in Ife and other parts of Yorubaland before his time, and employ it in the service of a larger agglomeration of people, a wider polity. His greatness consists in his ability to conceive and create a more inclusive society with wider loyalties far above the small, encrusted, ancient kingdoms that he had known in his youth. Unknown to him (we must assume), he was showing to the Yoruba people in general a new line of development. The city of Ile-Ife and its type became the pattern of existence for most of Yorubaland, making the Yoruba the most urbanized people in the tropical African forests, an urbanism which impacted their cultural growth in countless ways and made them the proud possessors of what many regard as Africa's highest indigenous civilization. They are therefore right in their designation of Oduduwa as father of the Yoruba nation.

Soon, the first Ile-Ife wall was completed. It was about 7 km in circumference, with a maximum diameter of about 2.3 km. A second wall was embarked upon not long after that. Most probably, more people were coming to settle in the new city than first expected, and houses were springing up beyond the first wall, vulnerable to the attacks from Igbo-Igbo. This second wall had a circumference of about 15 km, with a maximum diameter of about 5.2 km.⁴

Concerning the attacks from Igbo-Igbo, a tale exists in Yoruba folklore about one of a later king's wives named Moremi. According to this tale, which various generations of Yoruba people have amplified and even set to song, this beautiful woman, determined that the Igbo-Igbo raids had to stop, deliberately let herself be captured and taken to Igbo-Igbo. While there, she became a wife to their ruler and was therefore able to learn all the secrets of the planning and execution of their raids on Ile-Ife. She then escaped and returned home, and the information that she brought enabled the government of her husband (said to be the Ooni Obalufon, probably Oduduwa's immediate successor) to defeat the Igbo and end their raids. Most of the people at Igbo-Igbo ultimately returned to live in Ile-Ife. The most touching part of this tale is that this woman, in preparation for her adventure, had asked protection from the spirit of a local stream, and pledged that, if she succeeded in her adventure, she would sacrifice her only son to that spirit. And when she returned alive and the Igbo raids were decisively brought to an end, she did take the painful step of sacrificing her only son. We do not know how much of all this is history and how much is fiction. However, there is no doubt that the story was meant to illustrate the fact that people were so much in love with their new city that they would make even the most painful personal sacrifices for its welfare.

Evidence is slim about the impact of Oduduwa's kingship on religion and rituals in his new kingdom. It would seem that the popularity of particular gods of the pre-Oduduwa settlements gradually waned, whereas the gods with the wider perspectives received increased emphasis. The cult of Ogun, in particular, became a special royal cult, and Ogun became, in addition to being the god of iron, also the god of war – the giver of victory in war.

Oduduwa devoted very special attention to the economy – first, the economy in general, and second, the establishment of economic support systems for the monarchy.⁵ There is unambiguous evidence that agriculture took some time to revive from the ravages of the recent wars. Oduduwa seems to have started the royal tradition of personal patronage of farming by the king, and to have raised some crops himself. The return of peace liberated the energies of the people, and according to the traditions, food slowly became plentiful in Ife again. The same happened in the production of cash crops, especially the major long-distance export, kolanuts. Though the Ife area was already a substantial center of trade before Oduduwa, most of the evidence in oral traditions indicates that the time of Oduduwa marked the beginning of a steep rise in trade.

Oduduwa himself appears to have made much personal contribution to this boosting of trade. He established a central market for the new city, providing for royal messengers to keep peace in it. By doing this, in fact, he established the tradition whereby every Yoruba king was supposed to establish a central marketplace (the king's market) in the vicinity of the palace, and serve as patron of the trading going on there. From Oduduwa, *oba* (king) and *oloja* (owner or father of the market) became synonymous in Yoruba political tradition; the palace and the central plaza of the market became inseparable.

About the great importance of long-distance trade under Oduduwa, a special note is called for. Some verses in Odu Ifa describe Oduduwa himself as having gained enormous wealth from exporting large quantities of kolanuts to the north and bringing many horses from there to Ife. The impression that one gets from other sources, however, is that it is doubtful that Oduduwa personally took that much part in trade. What the Ifa verses most probably mean is that, in Oduduwa's time, Ife traders made a lot of money from the kolanut and horse trades. The palace may have bought many horses, mostly for prestige, and horses seem to have been in common use among royal messengers and leading chiefs. The king's special attention to long-distance trade as a source of wealth is indicated in the provisions he made for orderly, peaceful traffic on the roads leading to and from Ife. Some traditions have it that Ipetumodu in the northern outskirts of Ile-Ife started as a customs post established by Oduduwa to guard Igbodo Nla (the Greater Gate) on the northern route, and to collect tolls there. Akalako, the first gate-keeper at this place, is said to have been one of Oduduwa's most trusted followers; in fact, before or during his tenure as gate-keeper there, he was given one of Oduduwa's daughters in marriage. So great importance did the king attach to the northern route. We do not have similarly precise information in the traditions about other routes leading into and out of Ile-Ife — southwest to the Ijebu country, and east to the Ijesa and Ekiti countries. It seems probable, however, that the town of Apomu, which later became a major trading center for the Ife kingdom, started its history under Oduduwa as a tollgate and market center on the Ijebu route. Somewhere also on the outskirts of Ile-Ife, a toll gate or guard post developed in Oduduwa's time that was later to acquire fame in Yoruba traditions. Known as Ita-Ijero, this place developed into a sort of rendezvous where groups from Ile-Ife usually gathered to start journeys to parts of Yorubaland. The overall impression from the traditions is that this famous spot was located on the eastern route. In the report of his archaeological survey already referred to, Paul Ozanne points out that on Ile-Ife's first city wall the entrance which pointed eastwards towards Ilesa and Benin had a "massive entrance enclosure." This was almost certainly a tollgate and guard post, and probably the spot known to the traditions as Ita-Ijero.

Oduduwa's time also marked a major upsurge in manufacturing, a development that was likewise directly stimulated by the king himself. His victories in the wars against the old pre-Ile-Ife settlements had owed much to his efficient attention to the production of weapons for his men. From the moment he became king in Ile-Ife, he attached very high priority to manufacturing. He even appointed a royal blacksmith named Ogunladin to head a large royal smithy close to the palace. Although the traditions are not explicit on this point, Ogunladin's smithy seems to have been a place for the manufacture of stockpiles of weapons (machetes, spear blades, arrow blades, swords, etc.) for Oduduwa's palace as well as other iron goods for the market. In general, the old iron industry (both smelting and fabrication) expanded rapidly under Oduduwa. It was probably in his time that the Ife area became decisively the central supplier of iron goods to different parts of the Yoruba forests.

Another industry whose expansion was closely related to Oduduwa's reign was the bead industry.[6] To elevate the glory of the monarchy before the people of the new city, Oduduwa is said to have turned to lavish use of beads in the royal regalia – in his crowns and clothes, as bracelets, wristlets, anklets, etc. (In early Yoruba society, beads, rather than gold, were the great treasure of personal adornment.) By and large, the chiefs, high and low, followed Oduduwa's example, though at comparatively more modest scales. As a modest imitation of the king's crown, the *oro* came into being, a chiefly cap adorned with beads. Some traditions even seem to suggest that some wall surfaces in Oduduwa's residence were studded with decorative beads. Beads became the favored package of gifts to the king and his chiefs on festivals and other special occasions. Such heavy demands for beads pushed the bead industry higher and higher, both in volume and quality. Increasing volumes of beads in head-loads left Ife along the trade routes. The king himself became the patron of all bead makers, and the traditions indicate that some sort of royal regulation of the industry was instituted. As bead production kept increasing, the traditional local smelting of raw bead glass failed to keep up with bead production, and bead manufacturers melted down other types of glass (glass products imported from Europe through the Sahara trade routes) to produce beads. All told, bead production and the bead trade became a very significant item in the economy of Ile-Ife, a source from which some citizens built substantial wealth. The richest of these was a woman trader named Olokun whom tradition has identified as one of Oduduwa's wives but who, more probably, was not related to Oduduwa at all. After her death, she was deified as goddess of the sea – the sea being regarded as the largest and richest body of water on the earth. Olokun also became the patron goddess of bead manufacturers and traders. In later times, the goddess Olokun became, fittingly, wife of the god Oduduwa.

The Revolution in Ife: Tenth to Eleventh Century

We will end this list of the high points of the Ile-Ife economy under Oduduwa by touching on the sculptural arts – that is art in wood, clay, stone and metals.[7] As pointed out in an earlier chapter, most of Ife's sculptures before Oduduwa were in wood, clay and stone – and, according to the traditions, a beginning in brass/bronze casting. Wood sculptures mostly served the decorative demands of home (*agbo-ile*), shrine and palace buildings. In Ile-Ife, the building of the *agbo-ile* rose to higher and higher levels of structural soundness and decorative beauty. The generally growing economic prosperity showed itself in the growing quality of compounds. A large class of wood sculptors arose, hired to work in new constructions throughout the city. The wooden carvings became generally more sophisticated. Wooden posts supporting eaves and decorating verandahs became more and more detailed images of men and women standing or kneeling to the task, the women with braided hair. Main doors to many *agbo-ile* became masterpieces of carvings in bas-relief. Similar sophistication, it might be added here, was true of the old arts of wall murals and engravings (known as *iwope*), and potsherd paving of courtyards and hallways.

Sculptures in stone and molded clay improved greatly in the urban culture of the new city, but very clearly, the medium specially preferred by the new monarchy was brass or bronze. The growing volume of trade from across the Sahara increasingly supplied the copper for this art. During the 400 years following Oduduwa's reign, it grew into a special symbol of Ife royalty.

As a final note to this chapter, it must not be imagined that the new monarchy under Oduduwa did not encounter any political difficulty. It did. Some members of the pre-Oduduwa ruling families continued to fret for some time about their loss of power. In fact, a few of them formed themselves into a secret cult with the name Imole, determined to resist, in particular, the loss of their traditional land. Some traditions even indicate that Oduduwa intended to build a grand palace but that distractions caused by political difficulties prevented him. On the whole, however, Oduduwa's reign was a long and peaceful one, and his methods and style of leadership were major contributors to that. In accordance with the agreement reached to end hostilities, Oduduwa made sincere efforts to create a leadership that welded all segments of the new society together. Besides appointing the former kings as quarter chiefs, he also included many members of their lineages in appointments to significant positions and generally made them feel accepted and honored in the new order of things. This policy of dignified inclusiveness weakened dissent and robbed it of support; it also tended to make persons in leadership positions proud to belong to the Oduduwa state system. After Oduduwa, such a policy became the proof of wisdom in an Ife king, and any king who was careless or negligent about it tended to invite trouble for himself and for his kingdom.

Moreover, life in the growing city was changing in many ways. The *ebi* (lineage) and its *agbo-ile* (lineage compound) remained the basic building block of society in the new urban setting (and would so remain till the twentieth century), but urban life rubbed off much of the pre-Oduduwa rigidities and exclusiveness of that structure. Tradesmen, artisans, artists, traders had a larger customer base to serve in one single community – an unprecedented opportunity to prosper; and urban competition stimulated professionalism and excellence. Every male was still, by general perception, a farmer, but city-based professionals of all types emerged. According to innumerable hints in the traditions, the city environment also bred entertainers, bands, bards, singers, story tellers, musical groups, as well as new instruments and styles of popular music. In various professions and pursuits, some men and women acquired city-wide prominence – for instance Ogunladin the master blacksmith, Elesije the great physician, Orunmila the master diviner, Olokun the richest woman trader, Obagede the large-scale plantain farmer, etc. The king's palace became the center of society, and its festivals became the magnet that pulled large cheering crowds of people together from time to time. To meet the people's expectations, the king and the palace tried harder and harder to glow and dazzle for society to gaze at and worship. There were people (and they were many) who could never forgive Oduduwa, but they would never even think of throwing out what he had given to all. After he had passed away, the leaders deified him and set up a shrine to his worship. Then, after some squabbling among them, they crowned their next king. The royal city of Ile-Ife, the heart of the kingdom of Ife – and source of light to the Yoruba people – had come to stay.

5

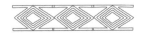

The Primacy of Ife: Eleventh to Fifteenth Century

The history of the Ife kingdom from Oduduwa (about 1000 AD) to about 1900 AD, falls roughly into three broad periods – the period from about 1000 to about 1500, the period from about 1500 to about 1800, and the period covered by the nineteenth century. The period from Oduduwa to the fifteenth century was a period of growing economic and political prosperity and power in the history of Ife. Not only did the kingdom grow and prosper at home, it also became the source of inspiration for major political changes in Yorubaland in general. In the course of the four centuries before the fifteenth century, kingdoms like that of Ife sprang up in most parts of the Yoruba forests, all of them acknowledging Ife's leadership, their rulers claiming Ife as the source of their origin and legitimacy. From the fifteenth century, a decline set in as powerful rivals (Benin and Oyo-Ile) emerged. By the end of this period in the eighteenth century, Ife was a small weak kingdom in the heart of Yorubaland, even though all other Yoruba kingdoms continued to regard it with awe. In the third period, from 1800 to 1900, Ife plunged into disaster. Its territory violated and subjugated, its city in ruins, the Ife kingdom shrank to a faint shadow of its former self, even though flickers of its old image were never totally extinguished in the cultural and spiritual sensitivities of most Yoruba people. Only the first period, the period of expansion and glory, belongs to this chapter.

After Oduduwa's departure from the scene, his aura continued to glow over everything and everybody. His subjects had, of course, seen kings before – indeed some of them had been kings themselves, many were descendants of kings, and most adults had lived in the small pre-Oduduwa kingdoms. But nobody had ever seen a king with the sort of stature and glory that Oduduwa had had as king of Ile-Ife. Not only did the chiefs and priests take steps to deify him, the collective imagination of the masses began to represent him as larger than life. Long before then there had existed, no doubt, the myth about Olodumare sending some heavenly beings to come and establish life on the earth. That basic story would no longer do. Oduduwa had to be part of it – indeed, he had to be the leader of the heavenly beings that came to the earth. Over the next centuries, the myth-making genius of the Yoruba nation amplified and embellished Oduduwa's part in the story of creation. The titanic fight between him and Obatala had to be woven into it. So, in the end, the full detail of the story came to be that Obatala had first led the heavenly beings coming towards the earth, but that he had got drunk on the way and Oduduwa had taken over and completed the mission, thus becoming the first man on the earth and the progenitor of the Yoruba nation.

Ife palace traditions have preserved an enormous body of information about the kings who reigned in Ile-Ife after Oduduwa, and therefore about the growth of the kingdom. Details of these traditions are sometimes difficult to understand and unravel, and sometimes seem to contradict one another. Nevertheless, historians have illuminated a path through it all that most can agree upon.[1]

Oduduwa's kingdom started as just the city of Ile-Ife – with, of course, the open farmlands around it, farmlands that the pre-Oduduwa settlements had gradually claimed from the forests over many centuries. One of the immediate consequences of the rise of a single substantial polity in the place of the many small ones was the emergence of a fairly strong state that was disposed, and able, to claim and use territory at considerable distances from its own immediate location. Oduduwa started the trend. As earlier pointed out, he established toll gates and guard posts to protect the trade routes into and out of Ile-Ife. Some such outposts were at greater distances out into the forests than any of the pre-Oduduwa settlements could have ventured – at Ipetumodu, Ita Ijero and Apomu, to mention the few definitively identified in the traditions. A kingdom was thus emerging which consisted not only of the city housing the king but also of other towns, villages and hamlets far beyond. Oduduwa thus initiated the structure of the typical Yoruba kingdom of the future.

For reasons not known to us, the Ife kingdom did not, eventually, go out for as much territory as it could easily have done, but remained comparatively small territorially until other kingdoms arose and limited the possibility of further expansion – especially Ilesa to the east, Owu to the west and, ultimately largest and strongest of them all, Oyo-Ile to the north. The forests southwards to the Oni River, part of the deepest forests in Yorubaland, were regarded as part of the Ife kingdom, and received some small Ife settlements at various times in Ife's history.

Territorially then, the Ife kingdom did not become as large as it could have. But that did not constitute any limit to the importance of this kingdom. For about five centuries, Ife was the most revered of all the kingdoms of the Yoruba

The Primacy of Ife: Eleventh to Fifteenth Century

people. Its territory was sacred and inviolate to all Yoruba people, by a universal consensus.

It is possible, from examining Yoruba traditions concerning the Ife kingdom after Oduduwa, to come to the conclusion that its ascendancy over Yorubaland for centuries was simply religious and spiritual. The typical Yoruba mode of speaking about ancient Ife tends to encourage such a conclusion, but such a conclusion would be only partly true. It is true that, though the general direction of Yoruba religion had evolved slowly over millennia in the Yoruba forests, it was at Ile-Ife after Oduduwa that most of the deities and leading spirits dominant in Yoruba religion were given final form and personality and then given to the rest of Yorubaland. The list is long, but suffice it to mention only a few here. A patron god of working people and of iron existed in all Yorubaland long before Oduduwa (probably, as earlier suggested, with the name Alaka-aiye), but it was the kingdom of Ife that finally gave him the name Ogun (the name of an Ife king) and made his cult a royal cult. Deities of wealth and of the sea certainly had existed, but it was in the Ife kingdom that they were combined as one and given the name Olokun, from the name of a rich woman contemporary of Oduduwa. Even the most senior Yoruba god, Orisanla, became Obatala (the name of Oduduwa's eminent contemporary) and was, thereafter, so known to all of Yorubaland. The ancient deity probably originally known as Elefon (and still so called in some eastern Yoruba kingdoms) had his name changed to Obalufon, the name of an Ife king. The ancient god of divination, Ifa, also came to bear the name Orunmila, the name of perhaps the greatest Ifa priest in about the time of Oduduwa. Of the other Yoruba kingdoms, only the kingdom of Oyo-Ile shared a little of such religious honor: the ancient god of lightning and thunder (very probably originally known as Jakuta) had his name changed to Sango, the name of an Oyo-Ile king. But even Sango was usually thought of as originating ultimately from Ife. For all Yoruba people after Oduduwa, therefore, Ife was the home of the progenitor of the Yoruba race and the home of virtually all pan-Yoruba gods – a place to honor and fear, a place to pay homage to in almost all religious observances.

The Ife kingdom was also the home of the most famous persons in Yorubaland for nearly five centuries, and the source of the greatest movements in the spiritual and cultural life of Yoruba people. After Oduduwa himself and his many famous contemporaries, the growing civilization of the city of Ile-Ife continued to produce great men and women – founders of kingdoms, great traders, farmers, priests, artists and artisans, *babalawo* (priests of the god of divination), *onisegun* (herbalists), *adahunse* (men of occult power), men and women lofty enough to be deified or to be counted among the gods and goddesses. The career of Orunmila was one of the most luminous of these great lives. Orunmila grew up in Ile-Ife as a great *babalawo*, a priest of Ifa. Then, according to many traditions, he embarked upon a career of life-long travel all over Yorubaland, practicing and teaching the very best in Ifa divination and mysteries, as well as spiritual development. In the process, he lived for a few years each in many places in Yorubaland, leaving his strong mark on religious and cultural life. According to some Odu Ifa verses, his longest stay was in Ado (in Ekiti) – and this has led to suggestions that he was probably of Ekiti extraction. At last, in great old age, Orunmila returned to live his last days in Ile-Ife. Some traditions claim that he was then crowned king of the Ife kingdom, but the preponderance of traditions negates that claim. But it is well known that he did wear a crown in his last days, a sort of sacred crown in honor of the god of divination. After his death, he was deified and his name became a second name for Ifa in all parts of Yorubaland. Stories about Orunmila constitute a significant body of stories in Yoruba folklore.

Orunmila's career was typical of men and women in a growing movement based in Ile-Ife, dedicated to the search for and dissemination of knowledge and enlightenment. The growth of such a movement was one of the great gifts of the city of Ile-Ife to Yoruba civilization – and it was one of the foundations of Ife's image as "the place from which the sun rises" (that is, the source of light or enlightenment). Many groups sprang up in the era of Ife's economic, political and cultural primacy, each seeking to advance its own brand of knowledge: knowledge of herbs, of the past (or history or mythology), of the invisible forces at work in the world, of divination, of the making of magically effectual articles (or charms), of the hidden "secret" meanings and power of words (called *ofo* or *ogede*), of hidden (occult) names for ordinary objects, of out-of-body projections, of access to the power of witchcraft for "wisdom" and other beneficial purposes – all of which Chief Isola Fabunmi (the Odole Atunobase of Ife) has described as the "esoteric sciences".[2] Some centers other than Ife became pan-Yoruba centers for some of these "esoteric sciences" – like Irun in Akoko and Otta in Awori for access to witchcraft, and Ire in Ekiti for acquisition of special bonds with, and power from, the god Ogun. However, Ife was the home of the greatest concentration of cultic knowledge and power. Traveling in order to know more and to teach was a common preoccupation of the cultic groups. As the Ile-Ife type of kingdom supplanted the old settlements in various parts of Yorubaland, members of these groups were able to travel more easily and to reside abroad in the new kingdoms. Ile-Ife became the place to which the "wise" came from all over Yorubaland and beyond to acquire some special knowledge – and to add to the stock of special knowledge – as members or initiates or adepts of the Ife groups and cults. It was no doubt in these centuries, and in this cultural atmosphere, that the Odu Ifa developed into the enormous complex of knowledge, myths and wisdom that has come down to us. What all this seems to add up to is that a cultural ferment (with a strong intellectual character) was in progress in Ile-Ife in the centuries following the creation of the city, a cultural ferment whose light gradually spread to the rest of Yorubaland. The spreading light also had revolutionary political ramifications, an account of which will form the subject of another chapter.

The foundation for all this cultural ferment, however, was the growing economic prosperity and power of the city of Ile-Ife and the kingdom of Ife. For nearly five hundred years (from Oduduwa's time, to the fourteenth century) the Ife kingdom was the richest and economically most powerful state in Yorubaland. Its preeminence in Yorubaland, in those centuries, was not merely spiritual and cultural, it was also economic. The economically expanding society of Ile-Ife multiplied opportunities for self-improvement as well as freedom to venture into cultural expressions and thought. That is why and how Ife became the heart of Yorubaland in nearly everything of cultural importance.

The economic foundations laid in the city of Ile-Ife in Oduduwa's time produced increasing wealth in the centuries that followed. Trade grew. The emergence of other centers of urban population in other parts of Yorubaland (of which an account will be given later) most definitely improved the channels of trade. This meant that more and more trade flowed into and out of Ile-Ife. After some time, some of the newly arisen kingdoms became important secondary centers of trade. Of these, perhaps the earliest were Oyo-Ile in the north, Ijebu-Ode in the southwest, Ilesa in the east, Owo in the southeast and some of the Ekiti kingdoms. Meanwhile, the coastal east–west lagoon trade was producing a significant center of trade in the far southeast, namely Benin. More will be said in a subsequent chapter about the growth of trade and trade routes in Yorubaland in this period of many kings and cities. Suffice it to say that until about 1400 Ife remained the hub of trade routes pointing in all directions in Yorubaland. Most goods from the savannah, the Sahara and the Mediterranean world found their way to Ile-Ife for onward distribution to the rest of Yorubaland and the Edo country, and goods from these territories to the north first went to Ile-Ife.

The result was that Ile-Ife grew for upwards of four centuries as a great trading center. Industrial production grew in response to the growing trade in Ile-Ife in those centuries. In general, too, agricultural production grew, though the traditions tell of some interruptions by drought and famine. And widespread Yoruba traditions tell of large growths in Ife's population in these centuries, and how the population growths engendered migrations from the Ife area to other parts of Yorubaland.

12. Sculpture from Ijebu-Ilesa. *Photo: P.Verger, 1948–49. IFAN.*

Continuing a trend initiated in Oduduwa's time, certain aspects of Ife's industrial production became special buttresses of the political system and, therefore, matters for close royal regulation. The most important of these was the bead industry. In the first place, increasingly from Oduduwa's time, beads became the distinctive material component of royal grandeur – beads in the making of crowns, insignia, scepters, ceremonial royal fans and horse-tail fly-whisks, beads on the royal person as necklaces, bracelets and anklets, beads woven into the royal regalia and into the braided hair of royal females. Secondly, and conceivably more importantly, as the new kingdoms emerged across the face of Yorubaland, beads became the most important material objects for establishing relationships between the Ife throne and the emerging royal dynasties. According to Akin Ogundiran, "These preciosities and symbols were crucial in the development of Ile-Ife as the primate center that many harbingers of dynastic institutions in the region visited and allied with to establish and validate their political power and ideology."[3] This one factor, almost certainly more than any other, guaranteed the status of Ile-Ife as the ever-beating heart of elite politics among Yoruba people for centuries. Would-be founders of new kingdoms, rulers of existing kingdoms, newly installed kings; all must procure, or obtain as ritualized gifts, the precious material symbols that only Ife could supply.

Not surprisingly, therefore, the Ile-Ife palace took the bead industry, as well as the making and distribution of its status products, increasingly under control. Apparently the average trader could always take or send beads to distant places in West Africa beyond Yorubaland. But inside Yorubaland, a significant part of bead distribution passed through channels dignified with palace rituals and royal glitter. The well-connected trader who was allowed into this sanctum could make for himself something more valuable than money; he could acquire status and influence. The artisan who lived by producing beaded crowns, insignia and other status products worked in dignified seclusion as a protégé of the Ife palace. Kings in palaces all over Yorubaland paid with fortunes for the objects essential to the exhibition of their legitimacy and grandeur before their subjects – beads, beaded crowns, beaded insignia and others. Below the level of kings, every chief of any rank bought some beads for status identity. Among ordinary citizens, the rich bought beads, usually as family treasure or for gifts to kings or chiefs, and most of the rest bought some beads for ritual and ceremonial family occasions.

The industrial processes involved in the production of beads were ultimately concentrated mostly in one area of Ile-Ife, about half a square mile in the northern outskirts, the area now known as Olokun grove. Many materials for bead production processes have been found there – including remains of furnaces and tuyeres, bead-polishing stones, ceramic crucibles for handling molten glass (with glass beads still fused with them). Various samples of glass beads and stone beads have also been found. Some other related manufacturing processes seem to have moved in with the bead processes. These included workshops for producing pottery and other ceramic ware, as well as others for the production of copper and brass sculptures.

Like the bead industry, sculptural art in brass or bronze became an important symbol of the Ife dynastic system. Several pieces of these naturalistic sculptures have been found in the ancient city, mostly in locations in and around the palace and in sacred shrines, and have been dated to the period from the eleventh century to the fifteenth. When these sculptures, especially the ones depicting naturalistic human heads and figures, were first unearthed in the early twentieth century, scholars wondered (among other things) what their purpose might have been, but it is now more or less generally agreed that they were produced for very important rituals in the funerals of the kings of Ife. Most probably, each was carried in procession as a crowned naturalistic head of the dead Ooni, mounted on an effigy, in a second funeral ceremony or *ako* (the practice of second burial earlier briefly described in Chapter 2). Available evidence indicates that the use of the brass/bronze sculptures in this way was an exclusive royal status symbol in Ife. After the effigy with its naturalistic brass/bronze head had been put on show, the head was buried at a shrine, to be unearthed (and reburied) whenever certain rituals connected with the late king needed to be performed.

Like all status ritualistic objects connected with the monarch, the brass sculptures were produced in secluded workshops and facilities. Each was produced during the lifetime of the Ooni whose head was being represented in brass or bronze, and it was most probably meant to be an exact portrait of him – accomplished through the lost-wax method of metal casting. (The lost wax technique involved first making a model of the king's head with a soft material like solid wax. A thick layer of soft clay was poured all over this wax carving and left to dry. When the clay had dried, heat was applied to melt the wax, which drained away through holes provided in the clay. The molten brass or bronze was then poured in to replace the wax, and when it had cooled and solidified, the clay covering was broken off). Since each brass/bronze sculpture was meant to be an exact representation of the king's head, these sculptures were almost certainly produced in much greater seclusion than were beaded crowns and insignia. Unlike beads and crowns and insignia, also, they were definitely not produced for export but exclusively for the Ife palace.

The production of these sculptures went on for about five centuries and then came to a more or less abrupt end in the fifteenth century. For five centuries, the sculptures had been a very important component of the symbolism of the Ooni's royal majesty. What seems to have happened is that, as the economic foundations of Ife's greatness eroded during the fifteenth century, much of the political greatness came to be lost, and economic and political realities brought some symbols of the Ooni's power and pageantry, such as the naturalistic brass representations of royalty, to an end.

The above naturalistic sculptures in brass or bronze for royal purposes were only part of a very rich and vibrant artistic culture in the kingdom of Ife, and in Yorubaland in general, in the centuries beginning with Oduduwa's time. The quality of wood scultures improved continually. Brass and bronze were also used in the making of accessories like bangles for ankles (*ide ese*), wrists (*ide owo*), and necks (*egba orun*), and for various ritual or decorative objects like stools, staffs, bells, vessels, and ceremonial or official rods. Silver also came into use – in accessories like bangles and rings, as well as in some decorative items for lineage compounds and palaces. The old art in iron grew, the blacksmiths generally becoming more skilled in fabricating ceremonial and ritual staffs (usually with stylized representations of birds) for the use of priests and devotees of various *orisa* and cults. The emergence of the many Yoruba kingdoms, cities and towns greatly facilitated the spread and growth of art in Yoruba society in these centuries – which, as would be remembered, Drewal, Pemberton and Abiodun divided into the following four eras: Early Pavement Era, Late Pavement Era, Post-Pavement Era, and Stylized Humanism Era.

In addition to many impressive sculptural products in wood, clay, brass/bronze, and iron, this period in Ife and Yoruba history also produced many important stone products – in stone carvings and stelae for shrines, and in human figures, many of which are naturalistic. Of all the stone works done in Ife, the most famous is the sculpture known as Opa Oranmiyan (Staff of Oranmiyan), which is located in a small shrine in the heart of Ile-Ife. Opa Oranmiyan is a shaft made of granite, standing over eighteen feet high (with an estimated one foot buried in the ground), and having iron nails studded in a curious pattern along its whole height. This stone sculpture was most probably produced to commemorate some important event in Ife's history, while its pattern of nail studs must also have had some symbolic meaning; unfortunately, both meanings are unknown to us today.

The brass and terracotta sculptures of Ife represent the best of naturalistic art in the history of tropical Africa. They would, suggests one scholar, "stand comparison with anything which ancient Egypt, classical Greece and Rome, or Renaissance Europe, had to offer."[4] The first European to see them (Leo Frobenius during a visit to Ile-Ife in 1910) wrote that they were "eloquent of a symmetry, a vitality, a delicacy of form directly reminiscent of ancient Greece".[5]

Because these sculptures, as naturalistic art, stand far above and beyond any other found in tropical Africa, there has been much debate concerning them. Frobenius expressed the opinion that, since no indigenous African civilization could have produced this level of naturalistic art, it must be that "a race far superior to the Negro had settled here." Such opinions persisted for decades, for quite understandable reasons. First, it seemed as if the tradition of brass or bronze casting was unknown in the modern city of Ile-Ife. Secondly, it seemed that similar art traditions did not exist in the region to which Ile-Ife belongs, including all the rest of Yorubaland. In short, then, the naturalistic sculptural art of ancient Ile-Ife seemed like an isolated occurrence in the history of the region, an isolation that thus raised legitimate doubts about its indigenous origins. However, in the course of the twentieth century, most of the supposed isolation disappeared. Some survivals of the brass/bronze sculptural tradition have been discovered in modern Ile-Ife; and evidence has come to light that the art tradition existed in many other places in Yorubaland (for instance in Owo, and in Obo-Aiyegunle in northern Ekiti, in Ijebu-Ode, etc). By the late twentieth century, therefore, there was no serious doubt left that the Yoruba people were in fact the creators of this naturalistic art tradition that ranks easily with the best in the history of the world.

Kings and Reigns[7]

It is against the general background described above, then, that the reigns of Ife kings from the eleventh century to the fifteenth century must be viewed. By and large, it was a long period of economic growth and political stability, punctuated by comparatively minor political troubles and short periods of drought and famine. Historical interpretations that see apparent intrusions into the royal line as proof of violent political disturbances most probably exaggerate.

One problem beset the successions to the Ife throne from the beginning: the system left fluid the choice of successor from among members of the royal family. The neighboring younger Edo kingdom of Benin, beyond the southeastern borders of Yorubaland, settled, when it emerged, for the principle of primogeniture (succession by only the first son of the king). Ife had earlier chosen to give the highest chiefs the power to choose the new Ooni from among princes of the royal family, including sons and grandsons of former kings. Such a system became the abiding Ife system and later the typical Yoruba system. It had the potential for political troubles, but it had the virtue of empowering the subjects to choose their king. Yoruba people, in fact, came to fall in love with, and become proud of, this system – because it emphasized the political rights of the people as against the possibility of excesses in the prescriptive claims of royalty. Indeed, as will be seen later, the Yoruba monarchical system as it developed from Ife was a system of limited monarchy. In its initial operations in Ife, the system of succession proved repeatedly problematic, but none of the problems seems to have ever developed into a full-blown catastrophic disruption.

Furthermore, one point that was made in the previous chapter needs to be reemphasized here. As much as possible, Oduduwa had included the preexisting leadership groups into the new leadership of Ile-Ife. After him, the chiefs and the people in general expected their kings to follow his example. As king followed upon king over a long time, this expectation became less and less troublesome; but in the reigns of the first few kings, it was a very serious factor in the way people assessed their kings. In the first few reigns, therefore, some kings who did not do well in this matter provoked reactions that led to political troubles.

Finally, from looking at the names of the kings as well as some versions of the traditions, some historians have come to the conclusion that the pre-Oduduwa ruling families must have somehow made their way to the throne of Ile-Ife at certain times in the years after Oduduwa. Such an occurrence is not necessarily improbable. However, since we do not have definitive information to this effect, we need to look also at other possibilities. For instance, intermarriages among the leading families must have been common. Intermarriages would produce situations in which the pre-Oduduwa ruling families would have members born into the royal family. In the contest for the selection of king, an influential family would normally support the princely candidate close to itself by blood – and the victory of such a candidate could be couched in the traditions as the victory of the influential family that pushed his candidature. Also, intermarriages could have resulted in the interposition of typical family names – so that some royal princes could bear names drawn from their maternal ancestry. We do not know for sure whether either of these things happened at any point, but the possibility of either needs to be borne in mind.

Oduduwa was succeeded by a man identified in the traditions as his son. However, the picture at this point is not too clear. Whoever succeeded him was, of course, officially his son; but the traditions are so complicated that this successor may have been his biological son or grandson, a close relative of his, one of his most loyal followers, or even one of his closest adherents from among the leading families of the pre-Oduduwa settlements. Some traditions name this successor as Ogun, but the name by which he has come down most clearly is Obalufon Ogbogbodinrin (probably Obalufon, follower, or maker, of the straight path) Obalufon Ogbogbodinrin is said to have been a very impressive personality. His subjects said of him that he shone like a large sun in the sky; hence, his other cognomen Osangangan-Obamokin (roughly, "the great sunlight that illuminates the earth at the height of day"). All traditions agree that his reign was long, and that it was peaceful most of the way. Towards the end of his life, he seems to have done something (or some things) that caused trouble with some sections of the kingdom's leadership. Whatever the problem was, it spilled into the reign of his son and successor, Obalufon Alayemore. By then, the dissidents had grown so strong that the king himself died fighting them. Alayemore's son or younger brother, Obalufon Ejigimogun, who was crowned after him, plunged straight into the same trouble.

At this point, there appeared on the scene one of the greatest, one of the most enigmatic, characters in the early history of the Ife kingdom, Oranmiyan. One of the youngest grandsons of Oduduwa, Oranmiyan was probably the foremost warrior prince and adventurer that the Ife kingdom ever produced. According to many traditions, after prolonged adventures that took him to Benin in the southeast and to the Niger Valley in the northwest, he returned to Ile-Ife, welcomed back by all as Akinlogun (hero in battle). Finding the king, Obalufon Ejigimogun, confronted by strong opponents led by a personage named Orisateko, he intervened, crushed Orisateko and his followers, drove Ejigimogun into exile, and accepted the throne. His intervention brought the troubles to a complete end. His reign was peaceful and long, lasting seventy years according to some traditions. He is remembered particularly for the attention he devoted to the development of the palace building. Under Oduduwa's immediate successor, Obalufon Ogbogbodinrin, the construction of a grand palace had gone a long way. Oranmiyan took the work in hand and, especially, remodeled what had already been built, changing the main entrance (the *geru*) to where it has remained till today.

After Oranmiyan, the Ife chiefs and people brought Obalufon Ejigimogun back to the throne – or installed his son of the same name. This king then settled into a peaceful and very long reign. The traditions say that he reigned for 240 years (*ojilugba odun*), but this is certainly hyperbole to emphasize the great peace which the Ife kingdom enjoyed during his long reign. In the palace traditions, there is preserved a saying that Ejigimogun reigned long and peacefully because he took great care to observe certain rules or laws or conventions (*esisun*).

What these *esisun* were is not explicitly spelled out in the traditions. However, it seems very probable that they comprised the agreements made to end the pre-Oduduwa wars, the principle of inclusiveness in the government, all of which Oduduwa had faithfully observed. This would therefore give us a clue as to the cause of all the troubles that had faced the kings before Oranmiyan. Towards the end of his long reign, Obalufon Ogbogbodinrin had probably flouted these rules and traditions and thus provoked organized resistance. His successors, Obalufon Alayemore and Ejigimogun, had foolishly tried to fight rather than compromise – until Oranmiyan had suppressed both sides in the strife. Oranmiyan as king had then gone back to a careful observance of the tradition of inclusion and, when Ejigimogun returned (or his son was enthroned) he promised to do the same and fulfilled his promise, and so had a long and peaceful reign. It is significant that when the opponents of Obalufon Alayemore had eliminated him decisively with military might, they did not install their leader, Orisateko, on the throne, but allowed the installation of Alayemore's son or brother. This could only mean that they were not fighting for the throne; they were fighting for certain principles of great importance, namely the *esisun*, the principles of conscientious, dignified, inclusion.

Obalufon Ejigimogun's observance of the rules was immortalized not only in sayings in the traditions. After his death, it was apparently laid down that he should be remembered in future installations of Ooni, and that every new Ooni should be reminded of what he had done to be such a good king. The ritual was therefore established whereby, when all other rituals of installation had been completed and the new king was to be crowned, the crown was first put on

The Primacy of Ife: Eleventh to Fifteenth Century

Ejigimogun's effigy and then taken off and placed on the new Ooni's head – a ritual which has continued till our times.

The peace that was thus established seems to have lasted for quite some time. Not until the time of Aworobiokin, some reigns later, do we hear of disturbances again. The palace traditions have it that Aworobiokin was assailed and assassinated during the processions of an Ogun festival. Various explanations have been given for this in the traditions. There are faint suggestions that Aworobiokin was only distantly related to the royal line and that he had employed some shady means to get the crown. But he also seems to have created trouble by seizing a well-connected man and sacrificing him at a ritual, thereby offending the victim's lineage. A general picture of political difficulties around this time is indicated by many traditions. Conditions are said to have got so bad during an interregnum that even a Yegbata (official leader of the king's messengers), a man named Lajua, had the audacity to have his friends declare him Ooni. And he probably held the throne for some time before he was assassinated. The tradition, made popular by Samuel Johnson in his *The History of the Yorubas*, of a radical change of the royal line from Oduduwa's descendants to some older Ife family, probably derives from the traditions relating to this period. Also, the Imole secret cult might have attained to its highest level of influence at this time, and to have had some impact on some selections of Ooni. Some traditions indicate that a woman Ooni reigned during this time. The political picture of this period is so cloudy, however, that a clear statement of its happenings and developments is extremely difficult. On the whole, what we seem to have here is a period characterized by frequent and tortuous succession disputes. The chosen system of selection of a king was still in its infancy, and it was prone to pitfalls, interferences and dissonance. Stories of seizures of power and change in the line of succession fit temptingly easily into the picture, but none of them are easy to authenticate. In the final analysis, the clearest feature in the picture is that the kingdom of Ife, in these its apparently stormy early years, continued to move forward as one kingdom, continued to grow in economic and cultural prosperity at home, and continued to rise in luminance, adoration and influence in the rest of Yorubaland.

The succession twists and turns came to an end in the reign of Lajamisan, the eighth or ninth Ooni in the list of Ife kings reconstructed by various scholars from the traditions. It would seem that this man's family was a distant branch of the royal line, and that it was his father, Aiyetise, who had brought the family into the main line by winning the throne and ruling briefly as Ooni, just before his son. According to the traditions, Lajamisan was a very rich prince, a large-scale yam farmer who became enormously rich because raw materials for making beads were discovered on his farm. He might also have had a bead-making business. He is said to have been so rich as a prince that he was regarded as second only to the Ooni in wealth in Ile-Ife. The traditions list another Ooni immediately after Lajamisan, an Ooni whose name is not given and who is remembered only by his cognomen, Oseganderuku (i. e. he who turns a virgin forest into open ground). This cognomen was, according to Adeagbo Akinjogbin, most probably Lajamisan's, coined in the light of his extensive farms and bead quarry operations. Lajamisan is important in the history of the Ife kingdom because, after him, the succession stabilized in his bloodline – so that all Ooni after him have come from it.

The next three or four centuries produced a long list of Ooni. Of these, some reigned for very long; many had only short reigns. Only the most significant happenings in these reigns will be mentioned here. Various Ooni added to the walls of the city, obviously to enclose new quarters springing up beyond existing walls. During most of this first long period of Ife's history from Oduduwa to the fifteenth century, the building of city walls does not seem to have been necessitated by any external dangers. After the Igbo-Igbo raids were silenced, Ife seems to have been free for centuries from external threats. The kings continued, in spite of that, to build the walls. City walls became part of the cultural definition of a city in Ife. The king owed it to his subjects to enclose, and include, all of them with walls. Kings also sought to immortalize their names by building walls, by adding to the grandeur of the palace, and by expanding the king's market place. The Ife palace grew bigger and bigger over the centuries, and grand new additions usually ended up replacing the older structures, resulting in a palace that kept spreading out. The main gate and front of the palace, in particular, became more and more imposing as the kings added tall structures and high gables. On and around the palace grounds, many of the city's main shrines were located – an arrangement which ensured that the palace was both the political and religious center of the city. Seasonal and annual rituals and festivals, as well as occasional royal audiences, brought the masses of the people to the palace courtyards from time to time to view and adulate their king. In the context of such celebrations, the *oriki* (or praise poetry) of royal glory grew apace, poetry to shout in adoration at the king whenever he graciously showed his person. The high-domed, or conical, beaded crown evolved, with dangling frills to veil the king's face. A code of behavior appropriate in or near the palace developed, the flouting of which could lead to serious penalties.

Meanwhile, the system of government of the Ife kingdom evolved slowly but surely. About the ultimate form of that government, more will be said in another chapter. In the kingdom of Ife, the final outlines of the monarchical government of the Yoruba people were developed in the first few centuries after Oduduwa.

The Primacy of Ife: Eleventh to Fifteenth Century

In the centuries of Ife's great wealth and influence, it does not seem to have had any significant military establishment. The traditions provide no account of external wars or military action; the impression one gets is that, after the suppression of the Igbo-Igbo raids, Ife did not have to defend its interests with any major force. Small royal establishments held the toll posts on the main trade routes to provide security and collect the king's toll. Beyond that, no military establishment seems to have been needed or created. The Ife kingdom gradually became the exalted leader of the world around, not by the use of arms, but by the influence of its commerce and the expansion of its enormous cultural heritage. As the other Yoruba kingdoms emerged, each of them acknowledged Ife as head, and looked up to Ife as source of life and light rather than as a rival. That was destined to change, of course, but that change did not come for many centuries. Until about the end of the fourteenth century at least, there was what we must call an Ife empire – an empire held together not by the force of arms but by the power of commerce, the belief in a common ancestry, and the manifest oneness of cultural heritage. Adeagbo Akinjogbin calls the linkages of Ife's ascendancy an "*ebi* system" – an acknowledgment by all rulers of Yorubaland that they belonged to one large family the ancestral source of which was Ife. In that kind of system, the important thing was not the actual source of the rulers of any particular kingdom, but the belief in the common ancestry. That system of belief held for centuries – and, even after the decline and fall of Ife, continued to hold.

13. Pottery, Ilesa. Terracota. *Photo: P. Verger, 1953, IFAN.*

Map 1. Yorubaland

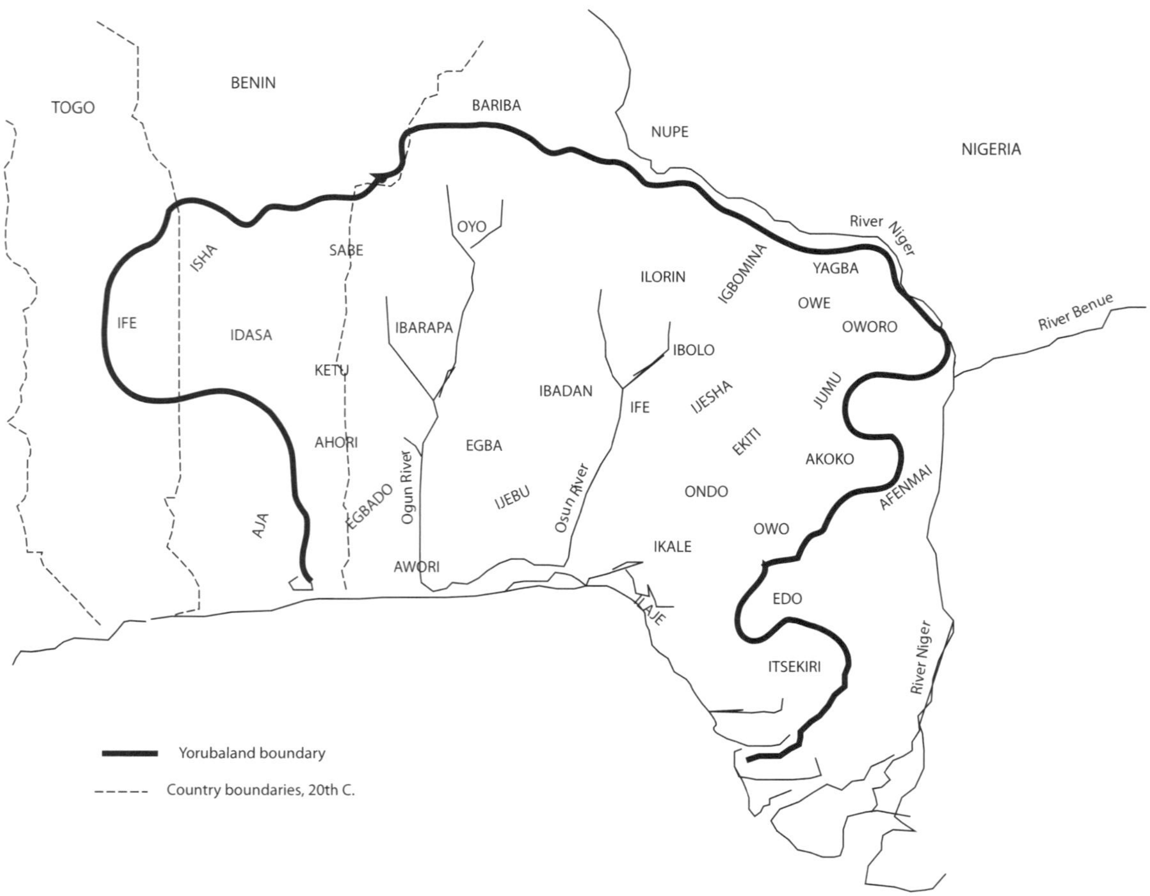

6

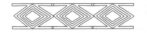

Traditions of Kingdom Founders

The welding of many pre-existing small settlements together to create the city of Ile-Ife and the kingdom of Ife marked a great leap forward in the political history of the Yoruba people. In the five or six centuries that followed the emergence of the Ife kingdom in the heart of Yorubaland, cities like Ile-Ife, each the capital of a kingdom like the Ife kingdom, rose up in nearly all parts of Yorubaland. As had happened in the case of Ile-Ife, every one of the emerging cities came into being by welding together a number of pre-existing small settlements, each of which had been a little kingdom in its own right. The basic scenario was the same in most cases. A group of Yoruba people (migrating from Ife, or later also from other places in Yorubaland) came to some Yoruba people living in an *elu*, or clump of small old settlements, in the Yoruba forests, and proceeded to weld itself and them together to form a town like Ile-Ife and a kingdom like Oduduwa's.

There exist in all parts of Yorubaland large bodies of detailed traditions about the creation of the Yoruba kingdoms, almost all of which have been collected in bits and pieces in writing in recent times.[1] Almost all these traditions link the creation of the kingdoms to Ile-Ife. Nearly every kingdom states in its traditions that its founder originated from Ife, that he was a descendant of Oduduwa, and that he migrated from Ife in the time of Oduduwa or close to it. Ife palace traditions have it that Oduduwa himself, on his deathbed, initiated the kingdom-founding movement by urging members of his family to go out and establish kingdoms like Ife in the rest of Yorubaland. One body of Ife palace traditions even puts a formal, ceremonial, face on the earliest migrations from Ife. According to this body of traditions, the princes gathered at the place called Ita Ijero (just outside the Ile-Ife city walls), held a farewell meeting, agreed and swore to certain conventions concerning their relationships with one another and with the Ife ancestral home, and dispersed to their separate destinations, each to found a kingdom of his own.

According to Samuel Johnson[2] in his *The History of the Yorubas*, the following were the first seven kingdoms founded from Ife by members of the Ife royal family: the Owu (that is Owu-Ipole) kingdom founded by the Olowu, the Ketu kingdom founded by the Alaketu, the Benin kingdom founded by Oranmiyan, the Ila kingdom founded by the Orangun, the Sabe kingdom founded by the Onisabe, the Popo kingdom founded by the Olupopo, and the Oyo-Ile kingdom founded by Oranmiyan. Johnson obviously relied only on traditions collected by him in the western parts of Yorubaland. It is known that in other parts of Yorubaland, the following are also mentioned among the earliest kingdoms founded by princes from Ife: the Ilesa kingdom founded by Ajibogun (also known as Obokun), the Ijebu-Ode kingdom founded by Obanta, the Owo kingdom founded by Ojugbelu (and his son Imade), the Ado kingdom in Ekiti founded by Awamaro, some other Ekiti kingdoms, the Ode-Ondo kingdom founded by the Osemowe, and others.

All these, however, are, according to the traditions, only a few of the kingdoms founded from Ife, since kingdoms continued, after the first wave of migrations, to be founded from Ife for centuries. In the same era also, kingdoms founded from Ife became centers from which migrant groups went out to found other kingdoms. Moreover, some kingdoms would no doubt have been founded without any origination from Ife or any other existing kingdom – by adventurous persons acting on their own strength, although benefiting from the general tradition evolving all around them. A complete count of the Yoruba kingdoms has never been done, but even a cursory count would seem to point to a number in excess of seventy. And even that would not include kingdoms that failed soon after they were founded and became absorbed by their neighbors.

Causes of the Migrations

All this raises the question: Why did people go out on these kingdom-founding adventures? What factors or incentives were at work in Yoruba society that made so many prominent persons leave their homes to go and found kingdoms and that made many ordinary folks go with them into largely unknown forests?

The Ife palace traditions quoted above present the earliest kingdom founders as only loyally responding to the expressed desire of their great progenitor. However, some verses of Odu Ifa offer a purely economic explanation. According to those verses, the Ife kingdom, very early in its history, suffered a severe famine caused by a long drought. The famine was made the more devastating by the fact that the city was overpopulated. The rulers of the kingdom therefore sought counsel from the Ifa oracle and, through a priest named Agirilogbon (a resident of Ita Asin in Ile-Ife), the oracle counseled that some of the people of Ile-Ife should migrate to other parts of the country. The rulers accepted the counsel and embarked on encouraging the Ile-Ife citizens, led by their princes, to go out and found new kingdoms like the Ife kingdom.²

Other Ife traditions give accounts of some migrations originating from Ife at the time of the wars between Oduduwa and Obatala – that is, migrations caused by the troubles in Ife before Oduduwa became king of all Ife. One such was the protest migration led by Obawinrin – the migration that founded the kingdom of Igbo-Igbo. Because Igbo-Igbo was bent on destroying the new city of Ile-Ife, it provoked against itself the patriotic and military energy of the new Ife kingdom, and perished in the outcome. Very probably, a similar protest migration at about the same time, in the same troubled circumstances, resulted in the founding of the Ketu kingdom in the far west. The hitherto popular tradition about the founding of Ketu has been that Sopasan, the founder of Ketu, was one of Oduduwa's grandsons. However, in recent times, Abiodun Adediran has recorded an Ife tradition which has it that Sopasan was in fact, like Obatala and Obawinrin, a ruler of one of the old, pre-Oduduwa, settlements in Ife. According to this tradition, Sopasan left during the wars and led his followers to the western parts of Yorubaland where they ultimately, after the Ife kingdom had been created, established the kingdom of Ketu. This tradition would, therefore, make Ketu the oldest existing kingdom established in other parts of Yorubaland by persons from Ife.³

Migrations caused by famines appear too to have occurred at various times in later periods of Ife's history, according to many Ife traditions. Periodic droughts and famines (usually separated by decades) are known to be generally characteristic of the region to which Yorubaland belongs. It would seem that whenever such occurred in Ife's history, Ife society tended to respond with migrations, a response conditioned by the history of earlier Ife emigrations. Consequently, we must conceive of emigrations as events that happened in Ife's history from time to time, bigger at some times than at others – some of them producing new kingdoms in various places in Yorubaland.

Furthermore, a typically Yoruba cultural phenomenon – chieftaincy contests and disputes – was also a common cause of kingdom-founding migrations. This occurred when a prince or descendant of a chiefly lineage, who believed that he was unfairly passed over in the selection of a king or chief, decided to go away, taking relatives and supporters with him. The first known emigration of this type occurred early in Ife's history, under the leadership of a very popular prince named Olojo Agbele who, after being passed over (unfairly in the opinion of most Ife citizens), left Ile-Ife with a large following and founded Ifewara kingdom in the forests south of Ile-Ife.⁴ Thereafter, hardly any significant Yoruba kingdom avoided this type of incident in its history. In most cases, such emigrant leaders ended up in other well-established cities and accepted some high titles there. The dynamic of this development was that Yoruba towns were usually seeking to get bigger, to extend beyond their walls (that is, *yadi* – break out beyond the city walls). For this purpose, Yoruba rulers frequently offered sacrifices to their gods, seeking supernatural help to increase their cities' populations. Therefore, an aggrieved prince who took himself and many followers away was punishing his town in a very hard way. And while the town he was leaving behind might be mourning, all towns on his way would offer him incentives to persuade him to stop and settle with them. Such events as this constitute a very common theme in Yoruba folklore. Most of such migrating princes would accept an offer and settle in some town; hence the very important fact that virtually every major town of the Yoruba has at least a few high chiefs (and quarters) whose ancestors had migrated in protest from other towns. However, there are traditions of many a protest migrant leader who persisted until he came to a suitable location where he and his followers founded a kingdom of their own. Not a few Yoruba kingdoms had this type of origin.

There were also a few kingdoms that seem to have originated from deliberate sponsorship by an existing kingdom, as an extension of the power and influence of the sponsor. The powerful kingdom of Oyo-Ile, at the peak of its greatness in the seventeenth and eighteenth centuries, sponsored the creation of a few kingdoms in the Oyo, Egbado and Igbomina countries. The old kingdom of Ketu also sponsored one or two kingdoms in the Ketu country. Most of the kingdoms over which Oyo nominees came to rule in Egbado in the eighteenth century were not founded from Oyo; they were old kingdoms over which Oyo came to establish influence. A kingdom that sponsored the creation of a new kingdom did so to protect its own interest in an area. For instance, Oyo sponsored the creation of Ede as an outpost against Ilesa's threats, and Offa in the Ibolo country, and Igbaja in the Igbomina country, as outposts against Nupe incursions. Ilesa founded Osogbo as an outpost against Oyo in the Osun valley.

Some traditions, both of Edo and local Yoruba provenance, claim Benin foundation of some kingdoms in eastern and southern Yorubaland. However, a close look at the traditions of those kingdoms indicates quite strongly that Benin foundation is very unlikely. A consideration of this matter belongs to another chapter; suffice it to say here that Benin's influence seems to have entered into the lives of these kingdoms at later stages of their history.[5]

Some kingdoms were founded, according to available traditions, by people fleeing from distress in established kingdoms – distress caused by military pressure from neighbors. Because Yorubaland was, on the whole, peaceful before the beginning of the nineteenth century, kingdoms with this type of origination appear to have been few. According to Ijesa traditions, the kingdom of Imesi Igbodo (now Okemesi) in Ekiti was founded by emigrants who went up the hills from Imesi-Ile as a result of Ilesa's military pressure on Imesi-Ile in about the seventeenth century.

Finally, there were obviously kingdoms that were founded by purely local persons – that is, talented and capable local men who, in the era of the foundation of the kingdoms, managed to carve out kingdoms in their localities. Presumably, too, in the era in which many of the new type of kingdom were emerging here and there in the Yoruba forests, there were instances in which the existing local structure, the *elu*, gradually evolved, on its own, to become a centralized kingdom. No Yoruba kingdom would acknowledge either of these kinds of origin, however, because it provides no link with a prestigious source. Yet, a close sifting of many traditions of origin would seem to indicate quite strongly that local origination was the source of at least some Yoruba kingdoms. Given the desire of every kingdom to be seen as having a great and prestigious origin such as Ife, a local personage who created a kingdom or became the ruler of a kingdom would almost certainly hurry to forge an actual or mythical link with Ife, making it possible for his descendants to claim that their ancestor originated from Ife

It is obvious from all the above, then, that the origins of Yoruba kingdoms were considerably more diverse than the Yoruba people and their traditions would like to acknowledge. Concerning this, some historians have, rightly, counseled caution in our acceptance of the traditions of the origins of Yoruba ruling dynasties, pointing out that, in particular, probably many of the traditions of origin from Ife are open to question or even doubt. Yet there is a sense in which all Yoruba kingdoms can be said to originate in Oduduwa and Ife. Oduduwa and Ife gave the Yoruba people their first kingdom, elaborated the structure of their type of kingdom, and pointed all of the Yoruba people in the direction to this higher level of political existence. This is more than enough to proclaim Oduduwa as the father of all Yoruba kings and people. Over many centuries before the nineteenth, the belief in Ife and Oduduwa as place of origin and progenitor of Yoruba kings ruled the lives of virtually all Yoruba people, and descent from Ife was the proof of legitimacy for Yoruba kings. No decline in the fortunes of the Ife kingdom itself seems to have been enough to shake this belief. For instance, at the time that Samuel Johnson made our first written collection of the traditions in the last decades of the nineteenth century, there was no incentive for any Yoruba kingdom to claim an Ife origin for its ruling dynasty. Ife was in ruins (for the second time in about three decades), its badly shrunken population was camped in a small farm village called Isoya, the site of the ancient city itself was covered by thick bush, and there was not even a king over Ife (the man selected as Ooni remained uncrowned in exile some forty miles to the south, in the village of Oke-Igbo in the Ondo country). In spite of this situation, the strongest and proudest states of the Yoruba people of the time unhesitatingly, and with all gravity, recounted to Johnson and other writers the traditions of the coming of Yoruba dynasties from Ife. Obviously, the most that we can say about this subject is that our knowledge of this important development in Yoruba history – the processes of the emergence of the Yoruba kingdoms and the growth of the powerful belief in Ife and Oduduwa as the source and springhead of Yoruba kings – is still limited.

Ways and Means of the Kingdom Founders

The kingdom-founding migrant groups and the dwellers in the old small settlements to whom they came, belonged to the same culture and spoke the same language, albeit different dialects of that language. Yoruba traditions about the founding of their kingdoms do not tell of some alien invaders, but of a movement generated from within the Yoruba culture and people. Robert Smith writes as follows:

> ... linguistic evidence seems to show that by the time they began to form the states ... the Yoruba had occupied more or less their present habitat for several hundreds or even thousands of years. ... the traditions relate that as the emigrants from Ife spread over the land, they almost everywhere encountered earlier settlers ... who were often hostile (not unreasonably, since they had prior claim to the land) but who apparently neither were unfamiliar nor spoke an unknown tongue. ... the Oduduwa cycle describes not a conquest from outside but a process of state-formation from within a people in which the leaders belonged to a dominant but probably not alien lineage.[6]

Fighting was quite common in the process of establishing the new kingdoms. Usually, the emigrant groups arrived, settled peacefully close to the old settlements in an *elu* and proceeded to establish interactions with them. In a few cases, such peaceful methods worked, and the immigrants slowly achieved the end of unifying themselves with all the settlements, with the migrant leader as king. But in most cases, their effort provoked reaction and resistance and war, sometimes war that went on over a long time.

The end result was always a new community, the beginning of an Ile-Ife type of city. At its beginning, the new community always comprised many clearly defined groups. First, there was each of the old settlements led by its own ruler. The immigrant group too consisted of segments. The overall immigrant leader had his own personal following (his family and relatives and other persons directly attached to him). Then there were prominent men who had agreed to come with him, each bringing a group comprising his own personal following (family, relatives and persons directly attached to them). Each such subordinate leader and his group constituted a clear segment of the total immigrant group – all together led by the creator and overall leader of the immigrant group. Each of the new cities was therefore a plurality in the fullest sense, a plurality that accepted the overall immigrant leader as king and then proceeded to build around him an expanding body of rituals, ceremonies, institutions and myths. As had happened in Ile-Ife under Oduduwa, the age-old outlines of monarchy as they had grown over hundreds of years in the old settlements were taken and applied to the larger community that came into existence.

If the new king was indeed a prince from Ife, building him up as a branch of the Oduduwa dynasty was easy. If he were someone other than an Ife prince, the task of building him up as a chip of the Oduduwa dynasty was less easy, but it would still be accomplished. For many centuries after the creation of the Ife kingdom, a king was, by definition, for all Yoruba people, a prince from Ife. From about the seventeenth century, after first Benin and then Oyo became dominant in the Yoruba-Edo region, some new (and even old) communities could feel comfortable with claims of Benin or Oyo royal origin for their kings – but even that with the very clear understanding that the Benin and Oyo dynasties themselves were branches of the Ife dynasty.

One other fact that emerges quite clearly from the traditions is that whenever the arriving immigrant groups and the old settlements fought, the immigrant groups almost invariably emerged victorious. Why was this so? Some historians have tended to assume the answer to be that the immigrants had iron weapons while the people of the old settlements did not. A close look at the traditions, however, would seem emphatically to contradict that assumption. There does not appear to have been any technological superiority of one group over the other. The immigrant groups and the old settlements belonged to a general Yoruba civilization in which the production and use of iron was long established. It is not impossible, of course, that some slightly more potent iron weapons were known to the immigrant groups, but there is no clear evidence (or even hint) about that in the traditions.

Numbers seem to have been a factor – the immigrant groups are usually represented as coming in large numbers. What this seems to mean is that they arrived with larger numbers of persons than each of the old settlements had. Such numbers were effective, it would seem, because the old settlements had no tradition of acting together and therefore could not collaborate against the immigrants. In one place where the old settlements managed to unite a little (that is, in Owo), they succeeded so much as to dislodge the immigrant group from its first chosen location and, thereafter, kept resisting and fighting for generations.

The most important reason for the victory of the immigrant groups, however, would seem to be the difference in worldviews between them and the people of the old settlements. Each of the old settlements was merely resisting threats to its old way of life – its small, exclusive, inward-looking existence. Each immigrant group, on the other hand, was animated by ambitions and dreams inspired by the city of Ile-Ife, the kingdom of Ife and the glory of the kings and chiefs of Ife – in short, by visions of the grand new world in which their own city would shine and they themselves and their descendants would reign as kings and chiefs like Oduduwa and his chiefs. They had left home on the quest for such goals (no matter where they came from), and even when they were faced with the toughest resistance, acceptance of failure was not an option for them. In many places, if the fighting went through twists and turns, they kept trying to find ways for the victory of their ideas and their mission. The traditions of many kingdoms show that the new polity emerged only after many compromises and truces. In short, a new idea of society was on the move in Yorubaland, and it would adopt any means to get to victory. As far as is known in the traditions, in no place was its goal ultimately and decisively thwarted.

The migrations for the founding of the kingdoms obviously occasioned considerable movements of people across the face of Yorubaland. Some of the migrant groups probably consisted of no more than a few hundred people. But some appear to have involved quite large numbers. The impression one gets from the accounts of the earliest emigrations led by princes from Ife is that they generated much excitement and attracted many people, and that people joined them from settlements along their paths. Oranmiyan's followership is spoken of as consisting of a very large army of mostly young people. Oranmiyan is also said to have never failed to attract some followers in any settlement that he passed through. And when the prince Olojo Agbele left Ife (on the migration that produced the Ifewara kingship), so many relatives, friends and sympathizers are said to have gone with him that he was spoken of for a long time afterwards as the prince who almost emptied some quarters of Ile-Ife. His following was so large because his was a protest migration against a broadly unpopular rejection of his candidature by the Ile-Ife kingmakers. In fact, when it was time again to select another king in Ile-Ife, the Ile-Ife chiefs invited Olojo Agbele to return from Ifewara and rule in Ile-Ife, so that he might bring some of the people back. Some of the Ifewara people did then return to Ile-Ife, but Olojo Agbele himself seems to have died before ascending the Ife throne.

The migrations continued for centuries, and transformed the political and demographic structure of Yorubaland. Their most visible physical heritage is the many cities of the Yoruba people, the cities of the kings. And their political heritage is the Yoruba kingdoms.

14. Orisanla priests, Ile-Ife. *Photo: R. Mauny, 1949, IFAN.*

15. Orisanla priests, Ile-Ife. *Photo: R. Mauny, 1949, IFAN.*

From all we know about these developments and their times, one important conclusion seems unavoidable — namely, that the era of the kingdom-founding migrations was a special era in Yoruba history. It was a long period in which the spirit of adventure was strong among the Yoruba people, a period in which they were ready to step out beyond the common run of their lives and venture into the largely unknown in order to accomplish the unique, the new and the glorious. The revolution that produced the city of Ile-Ife and the kingdom of Ife appears to have roused something noble, adventurous and big in the character of the Yoruba people.

16. Alaketu, Alayeluwa Agbolawoluowe Alade-Ife, Ketu. *Photo: E. Soumonni, 2009.*

7

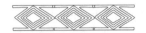

The Kingdoms of Yorubaland[1]

We will now in this chapter present a survey of the founding of the Yoruba kingdoms as made possible by the most prominent traditions. In doing so, however, we need to be mindful of the limitations in our present state of knowledge of this important theme in the history of the Yoruba people – some of which limitations have been pointed out in the previous chapter.

The Central Kingdoms

The territories of Ife, Ijesa and Owu are regarded in this chapter as the central territories of Yorubaland. The foundation of the main kingdom of the Ife country, the Ife kingdom, has been dealt with in an earlier chapter. The other considerable kingdom in the Ife forests was Ifewara, a short distance to the southeast. Ifewara was founded, as would be remembered, probably about one century after the foundation of Ife, by a prince, Olojo Agbele, who migrated from Ile-Ife after being rejected for the Ife throne. Olojo Agbele came with his large following to a group of old settlements, and these were glad to receive him as their king. His followers and the older settlers then joined hands to give him a proud kingdom, a replica of the one that had rejected him.

According to Owu and Ife traditions, the first member of Oduduwa's large family to leave Ile-Ife to found a kingdom was Olowu, son of Oduduwa's oldest daughter. His father was a commoner, a priest in Oduduwa's palace. On leaving Ile-Ife, he headed roughly westwards into the forests and, some distance from Ile-Ife, he established, in the country of the Owu subgroup, his kingdom of Owu-Ipole. The first location of this kingdom seems to have been somewhat further north of its final location where it later became famous from about the fifteenth century, about sixty miles west of Ile-Ife. In later centuries, other princes from Ife came and established kingdoms in other parts of the Owu territory, namely the kingdoms of Ogbere, Erunmu, Mowo, Okolo and others.

In the country of the Ijesa subgroup, immediately to the east of Ife, many kingdoms appear to have been founded from Ife. Of these, the best known are Ilesa, Imesi-Ile, Esa, Ipetu, Otan, and Igbajo. Ilesa was the greatest from the beginning. According to Ilesa and general Yoruba traditions, the founder of Ilesa was an Ife prince named Ajibogun (also known as Obokun).[2] One of Oduduwa's younger grandsons, Ajibogun is renowned in Yoruba traditions as the prince who offered to travel to the sea coast in order to fetch some quantity of sea water prescribed by the Ifa oracle for the treatment of Oduduwa's failing eyes – hence his other name Obokun (he who brought sea water). While he was away to the seacoast, many of his cousins had obtained blessings and emblems from Oduduwa and departed in various directions to found kingdoms for themselves. When Ajibogun returned from the coast, he asked for an emblem also. The grateful grandfather gave him his old war sword, the sword that he had used in many of his victorious battles (for which reason it was known as Ida Ajase – the sword of victory). Armed with Ida Ajase, Ajibogun headed eastwards and soon entered into Ijesa territory. Along his way, he found some of the followers of his cousins who had left Ile-Ife before him and he seized valuables from some of them.

In the Ijesa forests, he first settled with his followers at a place called Igbadaiye, where he lived for a number of years and died. His son and successor, Oke Okilo, continued the migration and brought the group first to Igbo Owaluse and then to Ilowa. Okilo's successor brought the group to a large group of very old settlements known as Ilamure, which he conquered and renamed Ibokun. From Ibokun they conquered another group of settlements of which the most prominent was Ilare, ruled by the Alare.

With the restlessness inherited from the founder of their group, Obokun, the group continued to move. Subsequent leaders, or Owas, of the group are said to have ruled at Oke-Osun, Ipole, Iwori, Ejioro, before they came to the location where they decided to make their final home – that is, Ilesa – in the time of the fifth or sixth Owa. When they arrived at Ilesa, there were some settlements there – Akogun (ruled by the Alakogun), Ibosirin (ruled by the Labosirin), Igbogi (under the Shindile), Lurere (under the Olurere), Asore (ruled by Alasore) and Okesa. At the settlement named Okesa, they met an important personage (probably the ruler of Okesa) who was a very successful farmer (his main crop being okro, *ila*, from which was derived his title, Obanla). All these settlements were made to accept the leadership of the Owa and to become parts of his new city of Ilesa. The Obanla was so important in the area that he was accorded the position of second in rank to the Owa, so that his title of Obanla became the highest chieftaincy title below the Owa. Before departing from Ibokun, the Owa had given the ruler of that town the title of Ogboni of Ibokun. Ibokun's main shrine became one of the most important in the Owa's kingdom, a shrine that had to be visited by every subsequent Owa as part of his installation rituals.

The Eastern Kingdoms

Eastwards, the Yoruba subgroups living in the hills and forests beyond the Ijesa country were the Ekiti and the Akoko. The Ekiti people insist in their traditions that a total of sixteen kingdoms were created in their country, but even they themselves usually identify more than sixteen names – Ado, Ikere, Ise, Emure, Akure, Ogotun, Efon, Ara, Ijero, Otun, Ido, Ikole, Ishan, Oye, Itaji, Aiyede, Obo, Omuo.[3] Osi and Ire, not usually listed today as kingdoms, seem to have been kingdoms of some stature in their early history. Some traditions have it that Osi was once a prosperous kingdom, but that it came upon disastrous times as a result of the hostility of its neighbors – the Ido and Ado kingdoms. Ire probably evolved locally from one of the groups of settlement (or *elu*) existing in the Ekiti forests before the time of Oduduwa. Its ruler, the Onire, traces his ancestry to the god Ogun, a claim confirmed by traditions of all Yoruba people, among whom it is generally believed that Ire was the original home of Ogun. The indication from all this seems to be that the god Ogun had his origin in Ire, that the Onire was the high priest of Ogun, and that when the kingdom-founding immigrants came from Ife and other sources to Ekiti, they kept off from this group of settlements and it evolved into a kingdom. Of the avowed Ekiti kingdoms, the last to be founded was Aiyede. The account of the founding of this kingdom in the mid-nineteenth century does not belong here with the accounts of the founding of the early Ekiti kingdoms, but will be treated as part of the developments of nineteenth century Yoruba history.

As analyses of their traditions and king lists seem to indicate, the early Ekiti kingdoms were probably founded in the course of the thirteenth and fourteenth centuries. Various versions of Ekiti traditions recorded in the early twentieth century suggest that Otun was probably one of the earliest to be founded. Almost all of these older kingdoms have it in their traditions that their founders were descendants of the Oduduwa royal line from Ife. Some traditions recorded in Odu Ifa indicate that the founders of the Ara, Oye and Ijero kingdoms were from Ife but from the bloodline of Orunmila, one of the greatest personages in the early history of the Ife kingdom. In every case, when the immigrant founders of these kingdoms came into the Ekiti hills, they had to contend with certain earlier settlements in order to establish their Ife-type kingdoms.

For instance, Ado palace traditions have it that the founder of the Ado kingdom was a prince of Ife, where he was known among the princes as Awamaro (the restless one) and Ewi (the speaker) on account of his restlessness and persuasiveness. He is said to have left Ife with his "older brother" Oranmiyan and to have gone to Benin with him, leading a small group of his own. After some years, he left Benin and headed northwards with his followers until he entered the Ekiti country. At Agbado he stopped for a few years, and when he wanted to continue on, the older men in his following chose to make their home at Agbado. Continuing eastwards with his younger followers, he came to Ado where he found some old settlements around the foot of the Olota Rock. The oldest of these small settlements was Ilesun, ruled by the Elesun. The other settlements regarded Ilesun as a sort of senior settlement, and feared the Elesun, who was believed to command enormous ritual powers as priest of the spirit of the Olota Rock, the protector spirit of the whole area. The Awamaro group settled peacefully at first, and then conflicts erupted between them and the old settlements. In the last of many clashes, Awamaro overpowered his opponents, cut off the Elesun's head, and proceeded to establish his kingdom, taking the title Ewi. But so influential did the Elesun's memory continue to be that each descendant of Awamaro, on being installed as the Ewi of Ado, must offer obeisance at the Elesun's grave. The former rulers of the old settlements and the leaders of the Awamaro group became the high chiefs in the new kingdom, and the new city of Ado comprised two broad divisions known as Odo-Ado (made up of the quarters of the old settlers) and Oke-Ewi (made up of the quarters of the Awamaro immigrants). Probably about a century later, a large immigrant group came from the kingdom of Ila in the Igbomina country. These were welcomed; their leader was accorded a high chieftaincy title, and a third main division to Ado city thus emerged, with the name Ila. Ila, under its sectional leader, the Alarierin, was also arranged into quarters of its own.

The traditions of the Ikere kingdom present a unique problem. An earlier line of Ikere kings, the Olukere, was at some point supplanted by another, the Ogoga. The Ikere traditions have it that the founder of the Ogoga line was a famous hunter of Edo origin who resided in Ikere and who used to be asked by the Olukere to attend to certain matters for him, including adjudication of disputes, because the Olukere, being also the chief priest of the spirit of the Olosunta Rock, was usually too busy with state rituals. From that, Ogoga, in ways that are not clearly explained in the traditions, became the king while the Olukere became entirely the high priest or ritual king. Beier suggests that the Olukere probably represents an early immigrant wave (from Ife), which founded the Ikere kingdom, while the Ogoga represents a late immigrant wave from another source. However, a close look at the available evidence indicates that while the Olukere very probably represents an early kingdom-founding immigrant group from Ife, the Ogoga dynasty seems to have been only the result of a purely internal change in leadership structures in the Ikere kingdom rather than the arrival of new immigrants, a change which took place at a late stage in the history of the Ikere kingdom (probably as late as the seventeenth century).

The founder of the Akure kingdom, according to Akure palace traditions, was a certain Asodeboyede, a prince of Ife, who is said to have left Ife at the same time as Oranmiyan. At Osu in the Ijesa country, he parted with Oranmiyan and headed eastwards into the Ekiti hills. For years, he wandered in the forests around Ara and Efon before he finally found his way to Akure. The main paths of the old route from Ife to the Edo country in the far southeast passed through this place, and Asodeboyede and his followers found in the area many small old settlements spread over a large area of forest. By pulling together the settlements in the most desirable part of the forest (notably Idopetu, Ilemo, Okearo, Ijomu, Obanla and others) he established the new city of Akure, the royal city of his new kingdom. Identical developments took place at about the same time at the place that later became Ogotun in western Ekiti. Some of the settlements in this place, of which Arun, Igbon and Isodu are the most remembered, were overpowered by an immigrant group from Ife and pulled together to form the city of Ogotun, the central city of the new kingdom of that name. At Ise in southern Ekiti, the immigrant group led by the Arinjale suppressed some earlier settlements and rulers, the most notable of whom was the Oluse. As at Ado, the rulers of the Ise kingdom that was thus created continued afterwards to give emphasis to rituals honoring the memory of the supplanted Oluse. When the founders of the Ijero kingdom came, they had to suppress some old settlements in the area in order to establish their new city and kingdom. The traditions of the Ijero area indicate that the ruler of one of the old settlements, the Oloku of Ouku, somehow successfully resisted being integrated into the chieftaincy structure of the new kingdom of Ijero. The traditions have it that the Oloku wielded such great ritual powers that the Ajero, king of Ijero, more or less decided to leave him by himself even though his settlement had been destroyed. The Oloku thereafter lived as a priest in a shrine just outside the city of Ijero, under a vow that he and the Ajero must never meet or see each other. The Oloku still lives at that location.

The hills of the Akoko country, immediately to the east of Ekiti, are a continuation of the Ekiti hills, but they are considerably more broken up and more rugged. This too is frontier country where the Akoko-Yoruba, the Edo and the Afenmai, and even faint strains of the Nupe from the north, meet and often intermix. Furthermore, unlike in Ekiti, there are clear signs that, in addition to early Yoruba settlers, there also lived in the Akoko hills, as earlier pointed out, certain small groups of people speaking languages that were not Yoruba. Finally, it is obvious from Akoko traditions that their country very frequently experienced military pressure from its neighbors – from the Edo, Owo and the Nupe.

Probably because of these conditions, kingdoms comparable in size to the neighboring Ekiti kingdoms never evolved in the Akoko hills. The traditions of the founding of the Akoko kingdoms are basically the same as of other Yoruba kingdoms. Migrants came from some distance, suppressed some older settlements and established a kingdom. Many trace their founders to Ife, but some (like Arigidi, Ishua, Afa, Ifira, Epeme and Ipesi) trace their founders to Benin, not surprisingly the Benin royal family. The kingdoms so established had typically Yoruba monarchical structures and insignia.

The Southern Kingdoms

The kingdoms of southern Yorubaland inhabited the thickest forests of Yorubaland and the lagoon territories of the Atlantic coasts. In these regions lived the following Yoruba subgroups: the Owo, Itsekiri, Ilaje, Ikale, Ondo, Ijebu and Awori.

The Owo[4] lived in the extreme eastern forests of this region, close to the country of the Edo, the southeastern neighbors of the Yoruba. According to Owo and other Yoruba traditions, the kingdom named Owo was the first kingdom established in the Owo forests by an immigrant group from central Yorubaland. According to the main body of Owo palace traditions, the founder of this kingdom was a man named Asunlola Ojugbelu, also known as Omolaghaye, a prince of Ife. Another body of traditions from Owo and from Odu Ifa traces Ojugbelu's ancestry not to the Oduduwa royal line but to Orunmila, one of the greatest priests in Ife in about Oduduwa's time. According to this version, Ojugbelu was one of Orunmila's sons, born to him in his old age, and some of Ojugbelu's brothers also founded the kingdoms of Ara, Ijero and Oye in Ekiti. A local Owo historian, M. B. Ashara, dates Ojugbelu's migration from Ife to the twelfth century, a date he arrived at by working backwards with the list of Owo's kings and by relating events in Owo's history to known nodal points in the history of the Benin kingdom.

After leaving Ife by the old eastern route, Ojugbelu and his followers are said to have taken a less known western branch of that route, and to have therefore gone through the area of the Idanre hills. They stopped in a number of locations on their way (at Uji and Upafa, both close to Idanre), hoping to settle and establish their kingdom. In each place, bad weather conditions or the intense hostility of earlier settlers compelled them to move on. South of the Idanre area, they came into extremely difficult forest country where they suffered lack of food and water. Finally, after another abortive attempt to settle at a place called Ugbo Ogwata, they came to a junction of paths on the old Ife–Benin route and started to build their kingdom. Ojugbelu had died during the long stop at Upafa, and it was his son, Imade, who brought the group to Owo.

When they arrived at this place, they found a number of small settlements, each a mini-state under its own ruler, that had long lived in the area – notably Efene, Idasen, Ilale, Omu, Utelu, Igbe, Upo, Okese, Oko. At first they were well received by some of these settlements. But when they tried to assert some sort of joint authority over all the settlements, resistance developed. In the hostilities that ensued, the Imade group found three of the old settlements particularly strong and difficult to overcome. The first was Idasen, headed by a ruler with the title of Alale. As priest and custodian of the much feared Ogho deity and shrine, the Alale commanded great influence with all the old settlements. The second was the Olomu who drove Imade and his people from their first site. And the third was the Elefene, who ruled Efene, perhaps the largest and strongest of the old settlements. The Alale, Olomu and Elefene managed to join hands again and again, and made attempts to unify all the settlements for the fight against the immigrants. While fighting against all these hostile forces, the Imade group went on determinedly establishing their new city. Some of the old settlements got tired of the fighting and gave up, but the fighting continued for many generations and through the reigns of many Olowos. Those settlements which made friends or were vanquished, were incorporated into the new Owo state and their leaders became important chiefs in it. The one or two who proved the most irreconcilable had their leaderships totally destroyed. The city of Owo grew, though slowly and with interruptions. Around the Olowo's residence on Oke Asegbo, the city took shape, each old settlement and each group among the immigrants establishing its own quarter, headed by its own chief, all acknowledging the supremacy of their king, the Olowo of Owo.

The kingdom of Ode-Itsekiri is the easternmost Yoruba kingdom on the coastal lagoons.[5] There has been much discussion among historians concerning how and when this Yoruba people got into this part of the western delta, and how and when their monarchial institutions originated. Their own traditions about their early history have tended to focus on the creation of their monarchy and its ruling dynasty. Those traditions follow more or less completely certain Edo traditions collected and preserved in writing by the Edo historian, Jacob Egharevba, in the early twentieth century.[6] According to these, in the reign of Oba Olua of Benin (dated by Jacob Egharevba to 1473–80) a Benin prince named Iginuwa, having become too unpopular to hope to be accepted as king of Benin after his father, migrated with some followers into the western delta. The Itsekiri versions have it that when this prince arrived in the delta, there were small groups of Yoruba-speaking people already settled in the area where he chose to settle. The Itsekiri traditions call these earlier settlers *umale*. Some of these *umale* moved away, but the rest stayed and accepted Iginuwa as their king, and so the kingdom of Ode-Itsekiri came into being.

Now, *umale* (rendered in other Yoruba dialects as *imole* or *umole*) is, as would be remembered, the generic name that the Yoruba people call the earliest earth spirits and deities worshipped by all Yoruba. The small groups called *umale* were almost certainly Yoruba elements worshipping, like other Yoruba people, a pantheon of earth spirits. Obaro Ikime[7] suggests that these people accepted Iginuwa as their king probably because they were impressed by the regalia of royalty that he brought with him. There might also have been additional reasons. According to Ikime, "The Benin court may have been bilingual for some time after the coming of the Ife prince (that is Oranmiyan) and … therefore the royal party from Benin may have spoken Yoruba as well as Edo." If this was so, then a group which spoke the Yoruba language (though also speaking Edo) would be quite easy for the pre-existing Yoruba settlers to accept. The Ode-Itsekiri kingdom that thus emerged later absorbed into itself various linguistic and cultural elements – Edo, Urhobo, Ijo. Nevertheless, its language has remained recognizably Yoruba – proof, no doubt, of the predominance of Yoruba elements in the kingdom throughout its history.

There remains the question when and how this Yoruba people arrived in this delta country. Their closest Yoruba neighbors to their west are the Ilaje, Ikale and Ondo. Their Yoruba dialect exhibits some similarities to these neighboring dialects. They named their royal city Ode-Itsekiri, a cultural trait that they share with other southern Yoruba subgroups among whom royal cities were called Ode (as in Ijebu-Ode among the Ijebu, Ode-Ondo among the Ondo, Ode-Aye and Ode-Irele among the Ikale). In parenthesis, among the northern and western Yoruba, royal cities were called Ile (as in Ile-Ife among the Ife, Oyo-Ile among the Oyo). The Itsekiri were, like the Ilaje, a Yoruba subgroup which formed from Yoruba elements penetrating this far to the coast as part of the general expansion of the Yoruba people beginning from Stone Age times. That expansion brought, at different times, the Awori, the coastal Ijebu, the Ikale, the Ilaje, and the Itsekiri, to the coastal lagoon country – with the Ilaje and the Itsekiri settling further east than the rest, and the Itsekiri settling further east than the Ilaje.

We have no definitive information concerning the chronology of Itsekiri history. The Iginuwa tradition indicates that by the time this prince came, small Itsekiri groups lived in small, heavily ritualized, settlements – similar to the small settlements common in Yorubaland before the creation of centralized kingdoms. What we seem to have in the Itsekiri case, therefore, is the Itsekiri version of the nearly universal Yoruba experience – a bunch of small local settlements upon which a centralizing group came, resulting in the creation of a centralized city and kingdom. Alagoa suggests that this Ode-Itsekiri kingdom was already in existence before the first Europeans came to the delta coast. His thesis is that when the first Europeans came looking to trade in the western delta in the last years of the fifteenth century, they naturally sought to trade in places where there were already authorities well established to see to the proper management of the trade. They focused, therefore, on Gwato in the Benin kingdom, and on the Ode-Itsekiri kingdom. We can safely say, then, that the Ode-Itsekiri kingdom had been created some considerable time before 1500.

The Ilaje subgroup, as earlier stated, were the closest Yoruba neighbors of the Itsekiri kingdom. A few Ijo settlements straggled between the two. The small Ilaje settlements spread out westwards from there all along the coast, in the lagoons and creeks and numberless islets until the boundary with the coastal Ijebu.

Not much is known about the pre-nineteenth century history of the Ilaje. The nature of their country made large centers of population impossible. But it does not seem to have made the concept of kingdom, of a group of settlements owing allegiance to a king, impossible. During the centuries marked by the creation of kingdoms in Yorubaland, the coastal spread of Ilaje settlements appears to have gradually come to recognize two kingdoms – an eastern kingdom with its royal center at the small old settlement of Ugbo ruled by the Olugbo, and a western kingdom with its royal center at another small settlement called Mahin ruled by the Omopetu. Roughly, the eastern Ilaje villages accepted the Olugbo as their king, and the western Ilaje villages acknowledged the Omopetu as their king.

The details of the process that resulted in the emergence of these two kingdoms are obscure. Like all the other peoples living in the lagoons, the Ilaje were principally a fishing people living in small, mostly remote, settlements. Their traditions, and even surviving practices, indicate that these settlements were shrouded in spiritual rituals based on the worship of various traditional Yoruba gods and water spirits. These deities and spirits mediated disputes on conflicting claims over fishing rights and enforced high standards of probity. Common shrines arose in a number of places, each exercising ritual influence over many settlements and stretches of water. Of such common shrines, the most influential seems to have been the shrine of the Aiyelala goddess, situated on a stretch of the Oluwa River which the Ilaje and their hinterland neighbors, the Ikale, regarded as boundary. Aiyelala was widely feared among the Ilaje, Ikale and Ijo because of her well-known devastating severity in the punishment of dishonesty.

The traditions have it that the Aiyelala shrine was instituted for the resolution of disputes, especially disputes over trade. Apart from fishing, then, trade seems to have very early developed as a major factor in the economic life of people in the Ilaje creeks and lagoons – trade eastwards to the Itsekiri and Ijo lagoons and the Benin coast, and westwards to the Ijebu coastal villages, to the Awori islands and to the Aja coast, and trade northwards with the hinterland through the Ikale country as well as through villages of the Ijo, the Ijo-Arogbo. More will be said about this trade later. Suffice it to suggest here that the need for order in contacts over fishing rights and over trade transactions, apart from instituting powerful shrines, most probably also resulted in wider political arrangements beyond the little settlements – ultimately leading to the emergence of two kingdoms. There are faint suggestions in the Ilaje traditions that, of the Ugbo and Mahin kingdoms, Ugbo was the older. Because of the nature of the Ilaje country, the kingdoms represented no more than loose relationships, which operated mostly in situations of inter-village disputes. For the most part, each settlement or village went its own way. The powers of the Olugbo and the Omopetu seem to have consisted mostly of potent ritual sanctions, although either king could occasionally cause boats of different villages to be pooled for intervention in serious disputes.

The immediate neighbors of the Ilaje towards the hinterland were the Ikale. The Ikale territory is a slice of territory stretching out roughly parallel to the Ilaje territory and the coastal line. Some Ikale settlements hugged the lagoons, but the majority occupied openings in the thick forests close to the coast.

The Ikale country was not only thick forest, it was also divided up by various bodies of water – the northernmost reaches of some lagoons and the southernmost reaches of rivers and streams flowing from the interior. These conditions would seem to have been responsible for the fact that no kingdom of any considerable size arose among the Ikale. Most Ikale towns seem to have started off as small camps in the forest. Typical Yoruba kingdoms ruled by crowned kings emerged, but each remained limited to just one town or not much more than that. Traditions of founders from other places in Yorubaland are common, but Benin input seems also to have been considerable in the early history of the kingdoms in these forests. It is difficult to determine how much of the Benin input went into the actual founding of any of these small kingdoms and how much went into subsequent developments in their history, but Benin influence is obvious in their political titles and in the structures of their monarchical systems. For almost all of these kingdoms, the most probable explanation seems to be that they were already in existence before a strong flow of Edo influence washed over them, especially in the centuries of Benin's commercial expansion.

The most notable of the Ikale kingdoms were Ikoya ruled by the Abodi, Ode-Irele under the Olofun, Osooro under the Rebuja, Idepe under the Jegun, Ode-Aye under the Lapoki, Ode-Erinje under the Orungberuwa, Ajagba under the Ahaba. Some Ikale traditions seem to suggest that the Abodi's kingdom of Ikoya was the first kingdom to emerge in the Ikale country.

The Ondo[8] subgroup lived in the expansive forest country north of the Ikale and south of the Ife. Some of the biggest rivers in Yorubaland flowed through this very thickly forested country. In addition, in the eastern part of the Ondo country, the Orosun Hill (including the Idanre Rock) rises abruptly, forming the highest peak in Yorubaland at 3098 feet above sea level. Probably because of these conditions, human settlements seem to have been few and widely dispersed in the Ondo forests, and the Ondo dialect showed marked differences from one population center to another. The dialect of the groups settled on the slopes of the Orosun evinced the most obvious differences from the rest, probably because of their considerable isolation.

Only three kingdoms seem to have been founded in the Ondo forests – Epe, Ondo (with its capital city at Ode-Ondo) and Idanre. Of these, the Ondo kingdom was the most successful from the beginning. An Edo tradition recorded by Jacob Egharevba has it that this kingdom was founded by immigrants from Benin during the reign of the Benin king, Ozolua. And Benin influence is evident in various aspects of the political culture of the Ondo kingdom – the insignia of office, the pattern of the hierarchy of chiefs and the functions of some principal chiefs. However, here again, the true picture seems to be that this kingdom was already in existence before it came under strong Benin influence. The core of Ondo's rather unique monarchical system – its special place for high-ranking women chiefs – bears much closer harmony with Ondo's own tradition of its origin.

According to the Ondo palace traditions, a royal wife in Oduduwa's palace in Ife had twins, one female and one male. Since having twins was regarded with horror or fear in those early days among the Yoruba, the woman was driven from the town with her twin babies. Accompanied by her relatives and sympathizers, she headed south into the forests until she came to Epe where there were some settlers in the Ondo forests. There the twins grew up, and the male twin established a kingdom. The female twin, Pupupu, later left Epe with her son, Airo, and found her way to the place where she too started a kingdom, naming it Ondo. When Pupupu and Airo and their followers came to this place, there were many old settlements there. By employing tact and the power of rituals, Pupupu and Airo won the acceptance of the rulers of these small old settlements, and so founded their royal city of Ode-Ondo. After Pupupu,

Airo ruled the new kingdom and established the line of kings with the title of Osemowe.

A slightly different version of this tradition was recorded by Samuel Johnson, most probably in Oyo, in the late nineteenth century. According to this version, the woman who had the twins and was driven south into the Ondo forests, was a wife of a king of Oyo, the Alaafin Ajaka. This would mean that the founders of the Ondo royal family were migrants from Oyo and not Ife; it would also put the founding of the Ondo kingdom in a later time than the other version of the tradition does. Yoruba traditions in general speak of the Ondo kingdom as one of the oldest Yoruba kingdoms – considerably older than Oyo-Ile – and the fact that the Ondo kingdom has one of the longest lists of kings (nearly fifty) seems to support this. What the Oyo tradition recorded by Samuel Johnson probably implies is that some close relationship developed between the Ondo and Oyo-Ile kingdoms at the early stages of the growth of Oyo's commercial and territorial expansion. As will be seen subsequently, the Ondo kingdom became an important center of trade on an early route which developed north–south through Oyo-Ile, Ife, Ondo, to the Ilaje coast. Some rivalry with Ife in the trade of the Ondo area might have given rise to Oyo traditions intended to claim a special closeness of Oyo rulers to the rulers of the Ondo kingdom.

According to the traditions of the kingdom of Idanre, its founders were immigrants from Ife. This kingdom was much isolated in early times, which is why the influences of the pre-Oduduwa settlers in the area seem to pervade the religion, rituals and political culture of the kingdom. At some point in its history, this kingdom had its political and main ritual centers established, not merely on the slope but right on top of a major peak, accessible only through a hard climb by rope ladders up bare rock surfaces.

The country of the Ijebu[9] subgroup lay west of the Ilaje, Ikale and Ondo territories, southwest of the Ife and south of the Owu and Egba territories. For reasons not well known to us today, the Ijebu country seems to have been very well populated in ancient times, with groups of settlements in many locations. Robert Smith suggests that the reason was the fertility of the soil in the Ijebu forests, and the variety of economic opportunities in farming and fishing along the coast. To these we probably should add the considerable opportunities in trade through these forests. As pointed out in an earlier chapter, trade through the Ijebu country probably accounted for most of the commercial traffic in southern Yorubaland in early times – traffic north–south connecting with Ife and beyond, and traffic east–west along and close to the coast. In spite of the general thickness of the Ijebu forests, therefore, the population volume and the amount of economic contacts seem to have resulted in the Ijebu dialect becoming quite homogenous.

Probably for the reasons stated above, the Ijebu forests attracted many migrant groups coming to establish kingdoms. And many kingdoms were therefore established there – namely Ijebu-Ode under the Awujale, Ofin under the Akarigbo, Makun under the Ewusi, Epe under the Elepe, Idowa under the Dagburewe, Ikija under the Akija, Ago-Iwoye under the Ebumawe, Ijebu-Igbo under the Orimolusi, Ijebu-Ife under the Ajalorun, etc.

Of all these kingdoms, that of Ijebu-Ode was the most successful and famous from the beginning. The traditions of this kingdom speak, as earlier pointed out, of many groups early settled in the location that was later to become Ijebu-Ode. In fact it would seem that before the immigrations which created the Ijebu-Ode kingdom, the early settlers there had evolved some fairly high level of political organization, resulting in the emergence of a sort of state, which we must call an Idoko kingdom. Details about this early Idoko kingdom are obscure, but it seems to have been a kingdom with some considerable strength, with some influence over some of the settlements in the locality. Some traditions have it that the Idoko kingdom was the builder of the first town wall in this place – a wall that was later to be the eastern sector of the great city wall of Ijebu-Ode. We do not know the circumstances or the processes of the emergence of the Idoko kingdom. But it is known that the area where Ijebu-Ode was later to rise up was a significant junction of trade routes from very early times. It is possible that such commercial opportunities and the wealth from them enabled one of the old settlements here to acquire political influence over some of the others.

Upon this scene, according to the traditions of the founding of the Ijebu-Ode kingdom, three different kingdom-founding migrations came. The first migration was led by Oluiwa who, with his followers, settled at Iwode, now an important part of the city of Ijebu-Ode. A second migration was led by Arisu, who settled in the Ijase area of the city. The third and most important migration was led by Ogborogan who is said to have come from Ife. After leaving Ife, the traditions say, Ogborogan went on a long, circuitous and adventurous journey through Imesi (in Ijesa) and through the Ondo forests before he entered the Ijebu country. All along this long route, he added more and more people to his following. By the time he arrived at Ijebu-Ode, he had become so famous that the people were excited to receive him. With shouts of *Oba wa n'ita* ("The king is in our streets"), the inhabitants welcomed him as their king. From this manner of his reception, he is said to have acquired the new name Obanta. The title Awujale, the title of Ijebu-Ode kings, was created in his time.

Some traditions attempt to explain this royal title, Awujale. One has it that on his long journey to Ijebu-Ode, Ogborogan defeated the ruler of Igbo in a wrestling contest, and that from this event the title of Awujale arose (meaning, one who knows how to fight on land). Samuel Johnson, on the other hand, has given us an Oyo tradition which claims that one king of Oyo-ile (the Alaafin Jayin) sent an *ilari* or palace messenger to southwest Yorubaland to adjudicate in a land dispute, and this messenger became the king of Ijebu – hence Awujale (one who resolved a land dispute). It is unlikely that we have in these traditions the true meaning of the title Awujale. Most Yoruba royal and chiefly titles derived from the Yoruba language (and its dialects) of an early age, and most sound-based decipherings of them in our times are, at best, suspect. As in the case of the Ondo kingdom, the tradition we have here probably represents an Oyo attempt to promote the picture of a special link between the rulers of Oyo-Ile and the rulers of Ijebu-Ode, the most important trading center in Yorubaland south of Ife.

The country of the Awori lay along and close to the coast, with an eastern boundary with the coastal Ijebu and a western boundary with the coastal non-Yoruba Aja people (of the modern Benin Republic). To the north of the Awori were the countries of the Egbado. Most of the Awori lived on the group of small islands in the area of Eko (now Lagos) Island and the low-lying forests in its immediate hinterland.[10]

Three kingdoms sprang up in the Awori country: Eko on a coastal island, Otta in the hinterland forests, and Badagry on the extreme western end of the Awori coast. Many small Awori settlements existed before the emergence of these kingdoms. According to Awori and other Yoruba traditions, Otta seems to have been the earliest kingdom created among the Awori. The traditions of Otta have it that the founder of this kingdom, an immigrant prince from Ife, came among Awori settlers in this place and consolidated them into his kingdom, the Otta kingdom ruled by the Olota. Some other Yoruba have it that Otta was one of the oldest Yoruba kingdoms.

According to the traditions of the Eko kingdom, its people first settled at a place called Iseri, a small settlement of mostly hunters and fishermen on the lower bank of the Ogun River, some distance southeast of Otta and a few miles inland from the coast. To this place, a prince named Ogunfunminire came from Ife and was accepted as king. Trade was beginning to grow in the coastal lagoons, trade eastwards with the coastal Ijebu and from there with the Ilaje, Ijo, Itsekiri and the Benin, and westwards with the villages of the Aja coast. In order to be able to catch more of this trade, most of the Iseri people, led by their king, undertook a series of relocations that brought them closer to the lagoons, leaving at Iseri a small remnant that has kept that little village alive till our times. The main body first relocated to Ebute-Metta, then to the edge of the lagoon at Iddo, and finally to the biggest island in the area, Eko Island. Here, incorporating into their community the scattering of other Awori settlers already living on the island, they established the permanent home of their kingdom, the Eko kingdom under their king who bore the title of Olofin.

The kingdom of Badagry came into existence on the Awori coast many centuries later than the kingdoms of Otta and Eko, in an area in which Awori and western Aja settlers (known as Gun or Igun) lived close together. In the 1730s, some Dutch traders established a trading post on the lagoon at this place, and it quickly attracted settlers from among the Awori, Igun and other Aja elements. The Aja became the predominant group in Badagry at the outset, and therefore its earliest leadership was almost entirely of Aja origin. The form of a kingdom quickly evolved, somewhat different from the typical Yoruba kingdom in the sense that its king, the Akran, had very little control over the various sections of the town beyond his own section. The origin of the Akran title-holders is traced to the Aja kingdom of Mewe. Because of the strong Aja presence and influence in the origins of this kingdom, some students of Yoruba history wonder whether we are right in identifying it as a Yoruba kingdom. The area, however, was Awori territory with many small Awori settlements inhabiting the sandy swamps around it, and many of such Awori ultimately became part of the new town and kingdom of Badagry. Also, Badagry almost immediately came under the influence of the Oyo Empire and, as a result, the number and influence of Yoruba elements grew in it.

The Western Kingdoms

The Egba kingdoms are concentrated today in the city of Abeokuta and control the forests around it, especially on both sides of the River Ogun, but until the early nineteenth century their country extended much further to the west and included the site of the modern city of Ibadan.[11] This original Egba territory shared a boundary with the Owu to the east, with the Ijebu and Awori to the south, with the Ibarapa and Oyo to the north and with the Egbado to the west. The Egba, as earlier pointed out, comprised three branches or provinces. Of these, the largest were the Egba Agura (or Gbagura), occupying the northern parts of the Egba forests. The second were the Egba Oke-Ona, so called because their territory was on the banks of the Ona River, close to the Remo province of Ijebu. And the third branch was the Egba Agbeyin who occupied the western parts of the Egba forests. According to Egba traditions, many immigrant groups, each out to create a kingdom, came into the Egba forests during the fourteenth and fifteenth centuries. Some came from Ife, and some from other parts of Yorubaland, especially from northwestern Yorubaland (that is, the Oyo country). Many of the towns that thus emerged in the Egba forests traced the ancestry of their rulers to Ife or Oyo. Only five towns, however, became known as kingdoms, ruled by kings wearing the beaded crowns of Yoruba monarchs. Of these five, there were two among the Gbagura (Iddo, under the Agura, and Ilugun, under the Onigun); one among the Egba Oke-Ona (Oko, ruled by the Oloko or Osile); and two among the Egba Agbeyin (Kesi, ruled by the Ojoko, and Ake, ruled by the Alake).

The country of the Ibarapa lay roughly north of the Egba country, southwest of the Oyo country, and east of Egbado. Between the Ibarapa and their Egba neighbors, very close relationships developed. Similar to the Egba country, a number of kingdoms were founded in the Ibarapa country, some of them by immigrant rulers whose origins are traced to Ife and other places in central Yorubaland. From the late sixteenth century, the Ibarapa country came under very intense Oyo influence – as a result of the expansion of Oyo influence in the era of the Oyo Empire. As a result, the population of some of the Ibarapa towns came to have a strong Oyo component. Today, the leading kingdom of the Ibarapa country is Eruwa.

Immediately north of the Awori country, and west of the Egba, Ibarapa, and Oyo, was the country of the Egbado, west of the Ogun River. The Egbado had the Aja to their west and southwest. One important peculiarity of the Egbado country was that the Egbado people lived in considerable intermixture with communities of other Yoruba subgroups like the Awori from the south and other Yoruba groups from the west, as well as communities of non-Yoruba elements like the Aja from the west. From about the third decade of the seventeenth century, large numbers of Aja and Yoruba elements fleeing eastwards from pressure by the rising power of Dahomey, and then of Oyo elements attracted southwest towards the trade through the Egbado country, came to add to the demographic diversity of the Egbado country.

The kingdoms that emerged in the Egbado country, therefore, were of widely diverse origins. According to Egbado traditions, the earliest kingdoms were founded in the fourteenth and fifteenth centuries by immigrant princes of Ife origin. Erinja and Ilobi are the two most important in this group. Probably not much later than Erinja and Ilobi, the two kingdoms of Ilaro, under the Olu, and Ijana came into existence. During the two centuries after these, Awori migrants from the south created the kingdoms of Ado and Itakete, and Aja migrants from the southwest created the kingdom of Ipokia. Then during the seventeenth century, as the power of the Fon kingdom of Dahomey grew and its pressure on the peoples to its south and east increased, mixed crowds of Yoruba and Aja peoples came east into the Egbado country and founded such kingdoms as Aiyetoro, Igan and Egue.

The subgroups and kingdoms of the far western Yorubaland now live beyond the borders of Nigeria in the modern Republic of Benin and the Republic of

Togo. Samuel Johnson counts three kingdoms of this area among, according to him, the oldest seven kingdoms of the Yoruba people, founded by Oduduwa's grandchildren in Oduduwa's lifetime. The three are the Ketu kingdom ruled by the Alaketu, the Sabe kingdom ruled by the Onisabe, and the Popo kingdom ruled by the Olupopo.

Both Ife and Ketu traditions agree that the founder of the Ketu kingdom was a certain Sopasan, who left Ife in Oduduwa's time and founded Ketu.[12] There is however, as would be remembered, some question about Sopasan's ancestry – one tradition claiming that he was a grandson of Oduduwa, and another tracing his ancestry to one of the pre-Oduduwa settlements in Ife. Further details of Sopasan's migration have it that the group led by him split into three after crossing the Ogun River. One group under Sopasan himself and his nephew, Owe, continued roughly westwards and ultimately founded Ketu. A second group first headed northwest, but was forced to turn back south and continued until it founded the kingdom of Sabe. The third group headed north up the Ogun River and eventually founded a kingdom identified in this tradition as Oyo (probably an early arrival in the Oyo country before Oranmiyan).

Before finally settling and founding Ketu, the first group led by Sopasan and Owe stopped and settled in a number of places – first at a place called Oke-Oyan (probably near the future location of Saki), and then another location called Aro. Sopasan died at Aro and Owe took his place. In the reign of Ede, the seventh ruler of the group, the group moved again. It then again split into three. One party led by a hunter named Idofa founded a town and named it Idofa, after its leader. A second party founded Igbo-Ora in the country of the Ibarapa. And the third party led by Ede himself was guided by a hunter named Alalumo until it eventually settled at Ketu and established the final home of its kingdom.

Other migrant groups, some of them from Oyo, later established a number of small kingdoms in the Ketu country. Of these, the most important was Ifonyin. The Ifonyin kingdom later became a center from which other kingdoms were founded – first Ihumbo and Ikolaje, and later Ilase.

The above body of traditions, then, gives accounts of the founding of the kingdoms of Ketu and Sabe in the far west. The same traditions, as well as other related traditions, supply more details about the process of the founding of Sabe. According to them, after the Sabe migration separated from the main group led by Sopasan, it moved under its leader, Salubi, north into the Bariba (Borgu) country and founded the town of Paraku. Salubi died at Paraku. His second successor, Ajogun, later moved the group to Kilibo where they remained for a long time under as many as nine reigns. This place would have become their final home, but serious pressure from the Bariba forced them to give it up and to head back southwards until they came into the country of the Sabe subgroup. Here, they found a number of small old settlements that they had to suppress before they could establish their kingdom.

About the Popo kingdom, we do not have today traditions as detailed as the above – other than that its founder was a prince of Ife and that it was one of the earliest kingdoms founded from Ife. As pointed out in an earlier chapter, although Yoruba traditions are emphatic about a Popo Yoruba subgroup and kingdom, neither has been identified anywhere. One possible answer to the puzzle was earlier suggested: namely that both the Popo subgroup and kingdom were probably absorbed into the cultures of their Aja and Ewe neighbors, leaving faint survivals of their name in various places in these western counties. But another answer is also possible (and seems to be favored by some historians). According to this, Popo was probably not the name of any definite group but the name by which the Yoruba referred loosely and generally to the countries of the distant west, a name which acquired strong currency in the era of the expansion of the Oyo Empire in the seventeenth and eighteenth centuries. In the light of the widespread presence of Popo in Yoruba traditions and folklore, however, the former possibility would seem to be considerably stronger than the latter.

At various times, some other kingdoms were founded in these far western frontiers of Yorubaland, also by persons from Ife or other places in the Yoruba heartlands. Among these were the kingdoms of Ifita, Igede, Iloji, and some kingdoms among the subgroups called the Sha and the Ife, some of whom are now in the Republic of Togo. Some traditions trace the origins of the Sha kingdoms to the Ijesa country in east-central Yorubaland and of the Ife to the Ife kingdom in central Yorubaland.

Probably centuries after the founding of the old kingdoms of Ketu and Sabe, two other kingdoms were founded in the general area not far from Ketu. One was the kingdom of Idassa, and the other the kingdom of Ohori Ije. The latter was founded in the land of the Ahori subgroup to the south of Ketu. The traditions of Idassa have it that the Idassa kingdom was founded by a man named Jagun Olofin who came from the Egba country.

The Extreme Northeastern Subgroups

In the extreme northeastern region of Yorubaland, close to the Niger–Benue confluence, the area believed to have been the earliest home of the Yoruba as a people, there live today many small subgroups of the Yoruba: the Owe, Ikiri, Abunu, Oworo, Yagba, Gbede and Jumu.[13] These Okun Yoruba had the Ekiti and Akoko as their neighbors to the south, and Igbomina as their neighbors to the west, and non-Yoruba peoples, the Nupe and the Kakanda, as their neighbors to the north and east. Their territory is the area where Yoruba people closely touch and interact with other peoples of the Niger–Benue confluence, namely the Nupe, Ebira, Kakanda and Igala.

For reasons not known to us today, this region of Yorubaland did not experience the centuries-long revolution that resulted in the creation of the Yoruba kingdoms. As a result, the subgroups in the region have no traditions of kingdom-founding migrant personages and groups from Ife or elsewhere in Yorubaland, no centralized Yoruba kingdoms, and no typical Yoruba monarchical institutions and paraphernalia. Instead of typical, centralized, Yoruba kingdoms, what have evolved among them are decentralized state formations – examples of which are found in Ife Olukotun among the Iyagba and Ufe Jumu among the Jumu. In Ife Olukotun, for instance, a sort of supreme ruler with the title of Ajalorun (later Olukotun) emerged, but this did not involve the abolition of the original leadership titles or the creation of central institutions. The original rulers, with the titles of Olu or Oba, continued to preside over their own hierarchies of chiefs and over their own little states, each of which was a combination of some lineages, with its own cycle of rituals, its own set of prohibitions and taboos, its own area of land. All these, plus the differences between their pantheon of deities and the typical Yoruba gods, strongly indicate that the Yoruba subgroups in this region are directly descended from groups largely unaffected by the major kingdom-founding developments that transformed the rest of Yorubaland.

The Northern Kingdoms

To the west of this land of the Okun Yoruba lay the country of the Yoruba subgroup known as the Igbomina (or Igboona). The Igbomina country has the Oyo country to its west, the Ibolo country to its southwest, the Nupe to its north, and the Ekiti and Ijesa to its south.

The Igbomina[14] seem to have had especially close relationships with their Ekiti neighbors in history, and the two are very similar in many respects. As in the Ekiti country, many kingdoms were founded among the Igbomina, notable among which were Ila, Ajase, Isanlu, Omu, Aran, Oro, Igbaja, Iwo, Esie, Eku Apa, Ora, Oba, Idofian and Oro-Ago. Of these, the kingdom of Ila enjoys an elevated status in Yoruba traditions on account of the fact that the ancestry of its ruler, the Orangun, is traced to a line very close to Oduduwa. The founder of the Orangun dynasty is said to be one of Oduduwa's daughters named Adetinrin. Guided by the Ifa oracle, Adetinrin set out from Ife, intent on founding a kingdom. Moving with her followers in a northeastern direction, Adetinrin entered into the Igbomina country and settled at a place called Igbo Ajagunla, named after her son Ajagunla. Adetinrin died at this place and was succeeded as the ruler by Ajagunla with the title of Orangun. Here, the group came under some hostile attacks, and therefore in the reign of Amota, one of Ajagunla's successors, they decided to relocate to a new place which they called Ila Yara. At Ila Yara, the group prospered considerably for a long time, the best remembered kings of the period being the Orangun Ogboye and the Orangun Oboyun. But Ila Yara later came under attacks also. One Orangun named Arutu died fighting and was deified by his subjects. The group again decided to move, but then it split into two when a prince named Apakimo led a splinter group to found another town. The splinter group first called its new town Ila Okiri, but later changed its name to Oke-Ila. Each of the two sister towns called its ruler the Orangun, but there was never any question in Oke-Ila about the paramountcy of the Orangun of Ila in the Ila family.

The other Igbomina kingdoms were founded in the Igbomina country after Ila, mostly by persons tracing their origins to Ife. A few, however, trace the origin of their founders to Oyo; of these the most notable were Ajase Ipo (believed to have been founded by a daughter of an Alaafin), Iwo, ruled by the Oniwo, Irese, ruled by the Elese of Igbaja, and Ora, ruled by the Olora. The exalted ancestry of the Orangun made the Ila kingdom the most senior Igbomina kingdom from these beginnings.

The country of the Ibolo, sandwiched between the Igbomina and Oyo countries, is small. The Ibolo and their much larger Igbomina neighbors were so closely related in their history that some Igbomina traditions regard the Ibolo as a branch of Igbomina. A number of kingdoms were founded in the Ibolo country – Offa, Ikirun, Okuku and others. Of these, the most prominent in history was Offa. Offa traditions trace the origin of the founder of the kingdom to the Oyo country. The Offa kingdom takes great pride in its peacock (or *okin*) symbol (for which reason Offa people are known as "*omo-olokin*"), and the Offa people are reputed among all Yoruba people for their passion for wrestling – hence the saying, "*Ijakadi l'oro Offa*" ("wrestling is Offa's favorite festival"). According to Okuku traditions, the founder of the Okuku kingdom was a prince of the Ara kingdom in Ekiti who emigrated in protest after he was passed over in a selection to the Ara throne.

All of the vast territory of the rest of northern Yorubaland, extending all the way to the country of the Ketu to the west, was the home of the Oyo sub-group.[15] Their northwestern neighbors were the non-Yoruba Bariba of Borgu, and their northeastern neighbors the Nupe, both peoples of the Niger Valley. To the south, the Oyo country straddled the countries of the Ijesa, Ife, Owu and Egba.

Many kingdoms were founded in this broad, mostly grassland, country, only a few of which are clearly remembered in the traditions – Oyo-Ile, Ogboro, Adikun, Iresa, Igbon, Ijeru, Iganna, Iwere, Asia, Okeho, Igijan, Saki, Igboho, Ibode, Ipapo, Kisi, Iseyin, Ilobu, Ifeodan, Iwo, Idese, Ede, Ogbomoso. A few of these kingdoms were founded in the Oyo country before Oyo-Ile. Most were younger than Oyo-Ile. Most have it in their traditions that their founders originated from Ife. A few (like Ede) were founded somewhat later in history by persons from Oyo-Ile. Of all the kingdoms of the Oyo country, Oyo-Ile became the richest, most powerful and greatest.

According to Oyo, Ife and general Yoruba traditions, Oyo-Ile was founded by Oranmiyan, one of Oduduwa's youngest grandsons. A man of great bravery, Oranmiyan set out from Ile-Ife as a youth, leading a large group of brave youths like himself. The traditions of the Edo, the southeastern neighbors of the Yoruba, give an account of his first exploits after leaving home. According to these Edo traditions, the Edo people in Oranmiyan's time were ruled by some ancient rulers known as the Ogiso, under whom the Edo country plunged into profound disorder. Some of the Edo leaders therefore sent a message to the ruler, the Olofin, of Ife (identified in their traditions as Oduduwa himself, although more likely to be one of Oduduwa's successors), urging him to send help for the reorganization of their country. The king of Ife responded by sending Oranmiyan. On arrival, Oranmiyan was welcomed by some of the Edo leaders but resisted by others. He suppressed the resistance and then settled down and established order and a strong monarchy. After some years, he decided to leave, saying that the kingdom, known as Benin, really ought to be ruled by an indigenous Edo prince. He then installed as king his son, Ewuare, born to him by one of his Edo wives. The young king Ewuare became the progenitor of the dynasty that led and developed the Benin kingdom and made it the most powerful kingdom on the shores of West Africa.

Yoruba traditions confirm these Edo traditions and add that not long after returning to Ife as a great hero, Oranmiyan set out again, this time northwards into the Oyo country, desirous to found a kingdom of his own (as many of his cousins had done). He traversed the whole breadth of the Oyo country before he found a suitable place to settle – in the northwestern borderlands of the Oyo country, just south of the Niger Valley, an area where small Oyo settlements existed interspersed with a scatter of small Bariba and Nupe settlements. Unifying together some of the settlements in the area, he established his kingdom, the kingdom of Oyo-Ile. The title, Alaafin, probably arose early as the title of the rulers of this kingdom. Some years later, Oranmiyan returned to Ile-Ife, leaving his sons in charge of Oyo-Ile.

17. Alaafin of Oyo, Oba Adeniran Adeyemi II in ceremonial regalia surrounded by members of his family. *Photo: R. Mauny, 1948–49, IFAN.*

8

The Politics of Kingdom Rule

The Yoruba kingdoms came into existence during the long period of about six or seven centuries starting in about the eleventh century. The present chapter will attempt to describe general trends and themes in their history, with the exception of the Oyo-Ile kingdom, in the period ending with 1800. From the sixteenth century, Oyo-Ile achieved such successes that set it above the general family of Yoruba kingdoms and made its history a significant chapter in the history of the Yoruba people. Consequently, a subsequent chapter will be devoted to the outstanding history of the Oyo-Ile kingdom.

Citizens of the Royal Cities

The immediate, most visible, result of the creation of each kingdom was the emergence of the new king's city, *Ilu-alade*, which we shall here call the royal city or royal town. In every kingdom, the royal city amalgamated the populations of the pre-existing settlements and the immigrant founders of the kingdom. The most important consequence of the amalgamation was the almost sudden rise of a town of considerable population. From about the eleventh century to about the eighteenth century, then, Yoruba people saw such significant centers of population springing up all over their homeland.

As soon as one of these cities arose, inhabitants of settlements in the neighboring forests tended to migrate into it and thereby quickly increase its population. Usually, most of these people came as single families or lineages; but sometimes whole settlements moved. The total effect of all this was that the Yoruba became increasingly an urban-dwelling people. Ultimately, they became the most urbanized people in the tropical African forests.

How large in population the cities were by 1800 is indicated here and there in the traditions. As earlier pointed out, some scholars have estimated that at the peak of the growth of Ile-Ife by the thirteenth or fourteenth century, its population was probably about 70,000. Oyo-Ile would seem to have been more than twice that number by 1800. By 1800 also, some other Oyo towns (such as

Ikoyi, Igbon, Iresa, Igboho) ranked among the largest in Yorubaland. The cities that are reputed to have been the largest in Yorubaland outside the Oyo area – namely Ilesa, Ijebu-Ode, Owu-Ipole, Owo, Ode-Ondo, Ado (Ekiti), Akure and Ikere – reached the peak of their growth considerably later than Ile-Ife. The fairly definite impression conveyed by the traditions is that, by about 1800 (by which time Ile-Ife's population had declined), some of these cities were larger than Ile-Ife in population and physical size. Below the level of these largest cities, there were many royal towns of fairly large size all over the country – Ila in the Igbomina country; the Ekiti towns of Otun, Ikole, Ara, Ijero and Efon; Idoani in the Owo country; Ifewara, Ketu, Sabe; the Egba towns of Iddo, Ilugun, Kesi and Ake. Royal towns of the Akoko country were generally small. Generally small too were those of western Yorubaland from the Egbado country westwards – with the exception of Ketu, Sabe and Ifonyin. However, the extension of the political dominance of Oyo-Ile to these western regions in the seventeenth century and the coming of many Oyo settlers, boosted the population of some of the towns there – especially Ketu, Ifonyin, and the Egbado towns of Ilaro and Ijana.

In most cases, it would seem, the creation of the royal city was effected by destroying the pre-existing settlements and massing all their population and that of the immigrants together in one area, just as had happened in the case of Ile-Ife. The founders of Ilesa destroyed many pre-existing settlements, and so did the founders of Owo through a long-drawn-out war. In Ijebu-Ode, however, Obanta and his followers simply took control of the place as they found it, and then began to build the structures of one common city – a palace, the king's marketplace, and city walls. The founders of the Ado kingdom under Awamaro in Ekiti did much the same as Obanta. The old settlements here were stretched out around the foot of the Olota Rock. Awamaro left them where they were, and settled his immigrant followers as a continuation of the chain around the foot of the rock. Then he established a palace and the king's market place, and began to build the city walls.

Thus, as would be remembered from an earlier chapter, the population of each royal city or town was made up of many distinct segments – many distinct old settlements each under its own ruler, and many distinct segments of the immigrant group, each under a sub-leader who accepted the leadership of the overall immigrant leader. In the new royal city or town, each of these segments settled as a quarter under its own leader as quarter chief, and they and their quarter chiefs acknowledged the over-all leader of the immigrant group as king.

Creating the Royal Government[1]

From the above steps, there followed the formulation of the system of royal government in the royal cities – a process that was apparently made easy for most cities by the fact that the basic outlines of a Yoruba monarchical system had become generally familiar. The initial order of seniority among the quarter chiefs was based on various factors. In general, the leading chiefs of the largest quarters became, in principle, the most senior chiefs in the new kingdom. But in practice, almost in every kingdom, other factors influenced the order of seniority – such as how high the ancestry of the new quarter chief had been in the place from which the immigrant group came; whether the new quarter chief had been, in his own right, a famous person before joining the migration; and how personally close to the new king the new quarter chief was. If, subsequently, a migrant group arrived to join the king's city, the King's Council met to decide the appropriate slot in the whole system for the newly arriving immigrant leader. Over time, the King's Council established lower chieftaincies for the streets of each quarter, to assist the quarter chief. A quarter chief could recommend to the king's government the creation of such a lower chieftaincy, and also recommend the lineage to be vested with it.

Before we go any further with this description of the typical system of government of the Yoruba kingdoms, it is important to make the following notes. First, as earlier pointed out, the foundational model replicated from kingdom to kingdom was basically the same – namely, the system that had evolved in the villages or settlements of the widespread *elu* in pre-Oduduwa times. However, circumstances and historical experiences varied from kingdom to kingdom and, consequently, the ultimate details of government came to vary in subtle ways from kingdom to kingdom. Secondly, it is also not possible to give accounts here of the many centuries of the gradual evolution of the system of government in all the kingdoms. For such in-depth accounts and descriptions, we must look to specific studies of each kingdom – the type that, gratefully, we have in (among others) such works as Pemberton and Afolayan's joint book on the Ila kingdom, Karin Barber's book on the Okuku kingdom, and Olugbadehan's work on the Owo kingdom – in addition, of course, to works by local historians and chroniclers.[2] Only the briefest outline of the system in its ultimate maturity is presented here.

The initial highest group of the quarter chiefs became the King's Council (or Inner Council), and its membership usually numbered five (occasionally more, but hardly ever more than seven). In addition to providing leadership in their quarters, the members of the King's Council met with the king daily in the palace (as the King-in-Council) to take all decisions affecting the kingdom.

The King-in-Council also served as the kingdom's highest Court of Appeal. The king was prohibited from taking decisions of state outside this King-in-Council, but all its decisions were presented to the people as the king's decisions.

The highest council of state bore different names in different kingdoms (Olori-Marun, Oyo Mesi, Ihare, etc.) but its composition and functions were roughly the same in all kingdoms. The composition of this council was deemed as perpetual; the chieftaincies included in it could not, usually, be removed, and the number of its members could not be increased or decreased without an exceptionally important decision of the council itself.

Below this highest level of government, there were other important councils on which the other quarter chiefs served. Each of these met in the palace also, not every day but each on its traditionally appointed day of the week. The "king's decisions" on any matter were reported first to these meetings as appropriate and, at this level, they would be discussed and the message could be sent up to the king to modify them.

When the "king's decisions and orders" had been thus formulated and finally settled, they were communicated to the populace through well established channels. Usually, the simpler decisions and orders were announced to the people of the royal city through an official town crier who would go through the streets in the cool of the late evening, at short intervals strike a gong to attract attention, and then proclaim, "The king, the owner of the world, greets you all, and says so and so". At the sound of the gong, the citizens would stop everything and listen, and when the announcement was completed, they would answer back from their homes, "May the king's will be done." Besides this occasional process, royal decisions and orders in general reached the citizenry through the detailed and powerful channels laid out in the system. Each quarter chief informed meetings of the lower chiefs and lineage heads of his quarter; each lower chief informed meetings of the people of his street; each lineage head informed the meeting of his lineage compound. The high chief who served as the official liaison between the royal government and the Baale (ruler or minor king) of a subordinate town or village informed the Baale, and the processes carried out in the royal city were then replicated in the subordinate town or village. All the chiefs and officials involved in these processes also bore the very important responsibility of seeing to the implementation of the king's decisions and orders in their respective areas of authority.

In addition to serving on the various councils of state and as the executive in their various spheres of authority, most highly placed chiefs also bore some executive responsibility in the kingdom at large. The most senior member of the King's Council served as Prime Minister and was regarded as second-in-command in the kingdom. Holders of other titles served in lower, but important positions – special friend of the king, liaison officer between the king and other organs of state, bearers of particular duties in the king's installation ceremonies, overseer of the palace, overseer of the marketplace, officer in charge of particular city gates, keeper of the king's regalia and crowns, officer in charge of the purse, etc.

Of these various special functions, perhaps the most important was the selection of a new king. The monarchy was hereditary in the royal family, but, as earlier pointed out, all male members of that family (sons and grandsons of former kings) qualified to be selected as king. In general, the Yoruba people rejected the principle of primogeniture (automatic succession of a king by his oldest child) and even any succession of a king directly by his own biological son. In some kingdoms, this was carried so far that certain categories of a king's offspring were totally excluded from selection as king. For instance, at different points in the history of the kingdoms, it came to be laid down in the Ado (Ekiti) kingdom that the Ewi's first son (titled Abilagba) could never be selected as Ewi, and in the Oyo-Ile kingdom that the Alaafin's first son (titled Aremo) could never be selected as Alaafin.

A small standing committee of the highest quarter chiefs served as the Council of Kingmakers. Selection by this body was always final, and any agitation after the selection was deemed an extremely high crime. While the Council of Kingmakers was still busy considering the candidates, however, its members could be lobbied by agents and supporters of the candidates and by other members of the public. But while the council was obliged to keep itself open to the currents of opinion in the public, it owed the very critical responsibility of not letting any citizen have any idea how its mind was working. Its members were forbidden, on oath, to divulge its information even to members of their own families. For this reason, its members would reject no candidate's gifts – or, if the decision were to accept no gifts, would reject gifts from all candidates and their agents. The level of accountability and discipline expected of the Council of Kingmakers was very high. And once the selection was made, the chosen prince was handed immediately to the officials and priests responsible for the first steps in the process of installation. Usually, most members of the public might not even be aware a king had been chosen until the heavily ritualized installation process had gone some way.

Another small standing committee of high chiefs bore a responsibility that could occasionally be far from pleasant. The Yoruba system provided that a king could be removed if he habitually acted beyond the established controls on royal power, or if he made himself repulsive through greed, tyrannical tendencies or immorality. In such situations, a committee of the high chiefs existed to counsel, admonish or even rebuke the king in strict privacy. If the king would not mend his ways, the situation could develop to the point that this committee would bring the matter before the other councils of state as well as before the Ogboni (described in Chapter 4) – and the decision could be taken to remove the king. Once, however, a Yoruba man had been installed king, he could never revert to ordinary citizenship in his kingdom or in any other kingdom. Deposition or exile was therefore not an option. The small committee of chiefs would approach him respectfully and urge him to "go to sleep" because the duties of kingship had become too burdensome for him. In some kingdoms they would present him with a covered empty calabash, in others a parrot's egg. All these symbols had only one meaning – the king was being asked to remove himself with dignity by committing suicide, and he would do so. Briefing the incoming king about all this (and instructing and equipping him for it) was part of the process of installation. Usually, the new king lived in a special compound outside the palace for a few months for such briefing as well as for important rituals, while the palace was being prepared to receive him.

All the chieftaincies touched upon above, from the very highest quarter chieftaincies to the lowest street chieftaincies, were, like the monarchy, hereditary in particular lineages. When the holder of any hereditary chieftaincy died, his lineage selected from among its members a suitable candidate for the king's government to accept and install. Being suitable meant that the candidate enjoyed strong support of his lineage and was adjudged by the king and his council as deserving of the position and as an asset to the interests of the kingdom.

The use of selection in the appointment of public officials (kings and chiefs) usually meant that each Yoruba kingdom or community was served by very capable persons. To earn selection as a chief, for instance, one had to be strongly acceptable to one's lineage, be broadly respectable in the community, be a manifestly good manager of one's own nuclear family, be a hard-working and achieving person. The selectors of kings looked for these same qualities in the princes, as well as for a modest yet princely bearing. In short, to be selected and inducted into the formal titled elite, the Yoruba person had to belong to an elite of character and personality.

The extensive use of the hereditary principle, and its linkage with important public functions, tended generally to underpin stability in a Yoruba kingdom. It meant that, virtually in perpetuity, the same lineage gave the kingdom its Prime Minister, or its special friend of the king, or its liaison officer between the king and other agencies of government, or the performer of a given function in the installation of the king, or one of the members of the Council of Kingmakers, or one of the members of the special committee of chiefs that could advise the king to "go to sleep". Each lineage whose titled member held any such special functional position from generation to generation ended up acquiring an expertise for that function, a high sense of commitment to its demands, integrity and accountability in its performance, a sense of mission, and an aura of dignity. Cumulatively, this tended to impart a dignity and gravity to the functioning of the government and to the offices of state. It also safeguarded against errant and erratic functioning of the agencies of government. It preserved the internal, predictable, relationships essential to the orderly existence of the government and of society.

Besides the hereditary titles, there were some titles that were not hereditary – like those of the war chiefs, commanders of the citizen armies in time of war. Usually, the king's government appointed from the citizenry for these titles, men who had distinguished themselves in some way; an arrangement which usually produced very capable military commanders. Holders of military chieftaincies held their titles for life.

Over this whole system, the Yoruba king or Oba reigned in every kingdom of the Yoruba people, surrounded unceasingly by grandeur, pomp and ceremony. To his subjects, he was so high above all humans that it was prohibited to call him by his personal name; instead, he and the high chiefs chose an appropriate cognomen for him – some grand composition from the history or circumstance of their kingdom, or from their hopes for the new reign. In the various kingdoms and dialects, the Oba's inexhaustible *oriki* included countless names – such as *Ekeji Orisa* (companion or lieutenant or likeness of the gods), *Alaye* (owner of the world), *Alase* (owner of all power or authority), *Agbogbomoja-ekun* (the all-powerful leopard that stalks the wicked and the lawless, and therefore the strength of the weak against the injustice of the strong), *Iku* (death – that kills, so that society, and order in society, may live), and *Baba-yeye* (father and mother – for every one of his subjects). He was too much like a god to visit any private home or to be seen ordinarily in the streets, and if his natural parents were alive, he must never set eyes on them. He must never step on any floor that had not been broom-swept that day, and he must drink or otherwise use only water that was freshly fetched from the springs that day. Those who fetched his water had to be unmarried young females, and they had to do so naked – and protected from meeting anybody on their way. Those who prepared his food did so under the strictest supervision. He must not be seen by anybody while he ate or drank. If he needed to drink when people were present, he must be screened off in the act. For his subjects, it was a great blessing to see their king on the few festivals when he ceremonially showed his person – adorned, on his throne, in gorgeous clothes, and wearing the beaded crown with the dangling beaded frills veiling his face. If he graciously spoke to the assembled crowd, no citizen would hear his voice; one of the high chiefs would echo his words. On a daily basis, even the highest chiefs greeted the Oba on their knees before the throne (even if he was not there), and any citizen passing by the gate of the palace paid respect on bended knees.

Universally, Yoruba people thought of the title of king as a title exclusively for men. In reality, however, many Yoruba kingdoms had women rulers in their history. An immigrant princess from Ife, Adetinrin, was the founder of the Ila kingdom in the Igbomina country, and another woman founded the Ode-Ondo kingdom. The warlike kingdom of Ilesa had at least two women rulers – Yeye Waye in about the late fifteenth century; and Owa Ori (or Yeye Wari) probably in the second half of the seventeenth century. It is significant that each of these women rulers led the Ilesa kingdom successfully during times of intense military challenges. A woman Ewi, Yeye Loreowu (so named because she lived at Orere-Owu just outside the palace) also led the Ado kingdom through serious internal strife, probably in the seventeenth century. Every kingdom also had a high female chieftaincy, the holder of which was the most senior woman in the realm and a member of the high councils of chiefs. And usually, there were special chieftaincies and priesthoods for women who performed certain functions, such as in the marketplace and in certain palace rituals. Finally, in every kingdom, one of the wives of the king was a titled wife, a position that entitled her in some kingdoms to sit by the king in some public appearances and to speak in some councils of chiefs. It is most probably this titled wife that we see in some bronze figures of early Oonis, figures made in Ife between the twelfth century and the fifteenth. Typically, these bronze figures show the Ooni and a female companion standing side by side, each wearing a crown, arms locked, with the king's left leg locked over his companion's right leg. These figures seem to symbolize the statement that the king's titled wife was very important in the affairs of state.

The Ogboni as an institution went out from Ife with the founders of the earliest kingdoms, and became a very important factor in the typical Yoruba monarchical system in all kingdoms, exercising very powerful influence on the affairs of state, even until the twentieth century. One recent study has suggested that the Ogboni's influence was muted for some time – before the nineteenth century – in the Oyo-Ile kingdom of the Alaafin, a suggestion contradicted by some other studies. The available evidence is, on the whole, fuzzy concerning the place of the Ogboni in old Oyo in the imperial era. But the evidence is unambiguous that after the Alaafin's kingdom relocated its royal base southwards in the fourth quarter of the nineteenth century, the Ogboni was very influential in its affairs.[3]

Most of what has been written in the above paragraphs concerns the commanding heights of the governmental system of the Yoruba kingdoms. However, it is important to note that, on the whole, governance involved the broad spectrum of the community – that is, that the system was considerably open and participatory. Thus, for instance, the political system featured, from the lowest to the highest levels, important, established, meetings. The primary level, or base, of the system, was the lineage in its compound. The lineage had many important corporate assets, interests and functions, for which general and special lineage meetings were held. There were all-member meetings to take decisions on the care, maintenance, improvement, or expansion of the lineage's sprawling compound, the management of issues arising from members' use of parts of the lineage farmland and the conditional admission of non-members thereto, the sharing of certain common goods (like the tolls paid by non-members for permission to use the lineage's farmland), arrangements for weddings and funerals of members (and for participation in such events in other closely related lineages), arrangements for festivals and rituals, selection of the chief (if a chieftaincy title was domiciled in the lineage), reception and consideration of decisions and directives from higher levels of government. And then there were special leaders' meetings for the settlement of disputes and quarrels, for trying cases of indiscipline and assigning punishment, for consultation of the oracles and carrying out of sacrifices for the welfare of the lineage, and for the disposal of a deceased member's belongings. Beyond the lineage compound, the age-grade associations, of which all citizens were members, had appointed days for their all-member meetings – for the purpose of carrying out their duties to the community, and for mobilizing support for members during important events in their lives (and also for holding association feasts and festivals). Each chief of a street had appointed days for meetings with lineage heads in his street (and also held occasional meetings of all the people of his street) – mostly for the purpose of disseminating the decisions and directives of the king's government, and for other matters affecting the street. For these types of purposes too, each quarter chief had appointed days of meetings with the street chiefs, and with the lineage heads, in his quarter. Over most important matters, it was established practice that the palace government consulted directly with leaders of lineages and age-grade associations, as well as with leaders of professional and trade associations – like the hunters' association, market commodity associations, the diviners' association, the herbalists' association, the priestly leaders of all cults, etc. Very important also was the fact that, as would be remembered, every citizen was in a position to influence the selection of a prince as king, through contact with the Council of Kingmakers or its members. In every kingdom, there were days traditionally designated as days of town meetings, when citizens who cared to come would solemnly gather at the palace (always early in the morning) with the high chiefs (with the king in usually concealed attendance), hear their chiefs over important current issues, ask questions and express opinions. In every kingdom also, there were one or two special festival days in the year on which people paraded peacefully in crowds through the streets and openly voiced criticisms of their chiefs and king (and satirized them), usually in impromptu and crudely composed songs – without any intervention from the authorities and without any repercussions whatsoever. Also, in every Yoruba community, certain classes of persons (like musicians, singers, humorists, *egungun* masquerades, and certain categories of priests) enjoyed a near sacred freedom to voice their feelings or thoughts (whether serious or humorous) about kings, chiefs, prominent citizens, and everyone else.

On the whole, therefore, the typical system of government of a Yoruba kingdom had a considerably democratic character, and the Yoruba people in general were strongly established in the tradition of participation in the making of decisions that affected their lives in the community. At every level, (even on the occasions when ordinary citizens gathered for meetings with the chiefs in the palace), the system enshrined freedom of speech; in fact, at certain levels (such as in the lineage), it was regarded as a sacred duty of the leader to ensure that every component section of the lineage and every individual had a say before a decision was concluded – because every member was regarded as a chip of the ancestors. As for the women of the lineage (called *obirin-ile* – women married into the compound), no compound would take an important decision without involving and hearing its women. In fact, in certain matters (like weddings and some aspects of some festivals), leadership in the compound sometimes belonged more to the women than to the men. Lineages took meticulous care to involve their children in everything, and children's celebrations were common in lineages. For their part, the age-grades operated in a tradition of very conscious respect for the opinions of members. In the affairs of age-grade associations, it was not uncommon for a well-attended meeting to decide to suspend decision on an issue if it was felt that absent members needed to be given a chance to voice their opinion. And if things were shared in a meeting, the association would go to great lengths to see that absent members received their shares, no matter how small the shares were. Participation in an age-grade's community tasks was compulsory for all members, and members who were absent for reasons other than sickness had to make some payment to their association. The effect of all this on the individual was that he or she was usually confident to speak (and could be quite eloquent) as a member of the community, and was used to being respected by those who held positions of authority over him or her in the community.

This, then, is the basic outline of the system of government under which Yoruba people lived in their many kingdoms until Europeans came and imposed foreign rule on Yorubaland. To complete the description, a number of facts need to be briefly noted. Although each kingdom gave its own unique institutional and functional interpretations to various details of the system, the governments of the kingdoms were, in essence, remarkably similar. Chieftaincy titles, and the functions assigned to titles, might vary somewhat from kingdom to kingdom, but a Yoruba person traveling through, or relocating to, another part of the country knew broadly what to expect in terms of governance, the laws, and the functionaries of state. This served to a great extent to facilitate contacts, internal migrations and relocations, and broad intermixture and integration of Yoruba people throughout the Yoruba homeland.

The system was not without significant weaknesses, however. One of the most important weaknesses inhered in the system of selection of kings from members of the royal family. In spite of the Olympian solidity and responsibility presumed of the Council of Kingmakers, selection occasionally generated an open contest and dispute, with all that this implied. The laws made it a high crime to protest after the selection had been made, and that sometimes meant criminal trials and stiff punishments – including executions. But even though an aggrieved prince might not be able to protest (with his supporters) in the streets, he could cause other painful troubles for the state: he was free to emigrate, taking family, friends and sympathizers with him – usually a very sad event in the life of a royal town. The fear of provoking this painful outcome always weighed heavily with the Council of Kingmakers and made its members usually meticulously cautious and responsible; but sometimes, its very best performance proved insufficient to prevent this trouble. One cumulative consequence of all this was that interregnums or short-term disruptions were not unknown in the system. Similar problems also attended the selection of chiefs at lower levels of the system. Given the large number of chiefly positions in each kingdom, chieftaincy contests and disputes tended to be a rather frequent feature of the life of every city.

Another source of weakness was the provision for the removal of kings. Ordinarily, this provision was very infrequently invoked and, whenever invoked, usually passed quite quietly. But it was not unknown for kings who were urged to "go to sleep" (or who saw it coming) to slip out of the palace and flee into exile, and whenever that happened, it usually shut down the high functions of the monarchy – because then the royal funeral rites could not be performed, a new king could not be enthroned, and vacant chieftaincy titles could not be filled. In such a tight predicament, the high chiefs commonly fabricated legends (such as that the king turned into a great animal and went into the wild, or that he simply entered into the earth) – in order to calm the populace, and in order to manipulate the priests into agreeing to undertake alternative rituals. But the problem would usually not end with the installation of another king; the authorities of the kingdom would for long be engaged in efforts to ensure that the news of their self-exiled king would not seep back home. It could be a very destabilizing circumstance. And, therefore, it was quite common for self-exiled kings to be quietly invited back to their thrones.

Finally, the limited monarchy of the Yoruba presupposed a king who was well adjusted to, and respected, the systemic limitations placed on royal power, and the whole system was managed in ways that were designed to ensure this. For instance, it was for this reason that the Council of Kingmakers took care, ideally, not to select as king a prince who was powerful, rich or influential in his own right – for fear that their king might claim later that he had obtained the throne on his own strength. Consequently, the history of every kingdom is replete with stories of rich or influential princes who were passed over for their humbler brothers or cousins. Many details in the installation rituals, and the intensive briefing of the new king in a special compound for some months before being taken to the palace, were designed to communicate and inculcate the true nature of the kingship. So too were many seasonal and annual rituals, including the ritualized recounting of the kingdom's history during certain festivals. In spite of all this sophisticated structuring, however, and in spite of all the grandeur attending to kings, it sometimes happened that a kingdom would find itself with a king who exhibited inappropriate ambition or troublesome independence – a king who thereby brought stress upon the whole system by threatening the balances crucial to its stability. Also, though much more rarely, Yoruba traditions tell of chiefs below the level of king who became ambitious and aggressive, and sought to readjust the systemic balances in favor of their particular chieftaincies – thus setting off unhealthy rivalry or conflicts among chiefly lineages. Whenever any of these situations developed, the monarchical system experienced troubles and even instability.

It says much for the strength and resilience of the system, however, that, in spite of these weaknesses, it survived in considerably good health for many centuries. Of course, modifications had to be adopted in each kingdom from time to time along the way, but the intrinsic character of the system was never seriously altered.

Religion and the State

As had been the case in the small ancient settlements before Oduduwa's time, the governance of every Yoruba kingdom was deeply rooted in religion. The king was, as earlier pointed out, a "companion of the gods." Every act, function or affair of state was anchored on the gods of the nation. The annual calendar of every kingdom was marked with many days of public festivals, holidays and feasts for the gods, some such festivals occasioning mammoth public celebrations usually centered on the palace. Shrines, large or small, stood at significant locations in every town or village – at town gates, at many locations in the palace, at the market place, and in every quarter. Besides such public shrines, every lineage compound had a small shrine of its own, at which the leader and elders of the lineage performed rituals and offered sacrifices to the gods and the ancestors for the welfare of the lineage.

The Yoruba king was a sacred king. His selection, installation and daily life as king were all shrouded in religious mystery, rituals, observances and sacrifices. The installation of a newly selected king involved a round of rituals at many shrines (located not only in the royal city but also in some towns and villages in his kingdom), as well as initiation into various mysteries. When the process was completed, the king emerged from it a sacred being. Therefore, for any citizen to touch the person of a king (not to talk of striking him) was ultimate sacrilege. Typically, there were, in the year, only a very few days in which some sacrifices were not offered in the palace to one or more of the hundreds of gods worshipped by the Yoruba people. The king was the highest priest of the kingdom, and all the high priests of all the cults were, in principle, his assistants. Unlike all other persons, he was supposed to be a priest in the worship and rituals of all gods in his realm. The cult of Ogun (the god of all working men, of iron, and of war) was the special royal cult to which the king paid more attention than he did to other cults. In the Oyo-Ile kingdom, however, the cult of Sango (the god of thunder and lightning) early developed as another, and somewhat higher, royal cult. For the welfare of his kingdom, the king bore the important duty of regularly seeking counsel from Ifa, the god of divination, and of offering prescribed sacrifices to the other gods. The king's highly ritualized burial and the location of his grave were perhaps the most closely guarded secrets of every kingdom.

The Yoruba were very sophisticated in the use of symbols and icons to express deep and powerful statements, and everything around the king conveyed profound messages. Thus, every significant detail of the palace building – the carvings of the wooden pillars and doors, the murals on the walls, etc. – all were iconographic statements relating to aspects of the origins of the kingdom, the Oduduwa source of its royal dynasty, the all-pervading oversight and care of the gods, the perpetual presence of the kings who had ruled in the palace, and the visible and invisible powers or authority of the king. The conical beaded crown, said to originate in Oduduwa's time (and therefore known as the great crown or the crown of Oduduwa), was loaded with great iconographic meanings. The dominant (front-placed) one among the faces depicted on the beaded patterns on the crown is usually said to represent Oduduwa's face. The other faces (commonly sixteen in number) represented the sacred assembly of the kings who had reigned on the particular throne. The crown therefore was no ordinary ceremonial head covering, but the object holding in itself the unification of the life forces (*ase* or power) of the progenitor of the Yoruba nation, and the royal ancestors of the reigning king. When, therefore, the crown was put on the king's head, his life force was added to the powerful combination of life forces inherent in the crown – thus making it a sacred object with unimaginable visible and invisible powers, the visible totemic image of the invisible essence, power and authority of the kingdom. For this reason, the Yoruba regarded the king's crown as an *orisa* or deity. The conical crown usually had a beaded figure of a bird on its top, and sometimes other smaller birds (usually numbering from four to sixteen) attached to the sides near the top. Pemberton and Afolayan (writing specifically about the crown of the Orangun of Ila) wrote as follows:

> Henry and Margaret Drewal have shown in their studies of bird imagery in Yoruba iconography that birds are associated with the power … of women or "our mothers" … It is their hidden, procreative power, a power that can give birth but can also be used to deny others their creative power. It is woman's power upon which the continuity of a husband's patrilineage depends. And … "without the mothers" (a king) "could not rule". Furthermore, the large bird at the peak of the crown is attached to a peg the other end of which is bound to a packet of powerful ingredients … placed in the top of the crown … The packet touches the top of the Oba's head … which is thought to contain (his) life force … It makes the Oba powerful over all kinds of spirits …[4]

With the crown on his head, the Oba embodied the supernatural entities and forces that sustained the existence of his kingdom and all life and order in it. The king's enhanced *ase* (power and authority) was seen as ensuring human increase in his kingdom, the health of his people, good rains and healthy crops, peace and order, etc. Pemberton and Afolayan add:

> Such a power must not be looked upon or approached without fear and trepidation … Chiefs and townspeople must remove their shoes, men prostrate and women kneel before him, addressing the Oba without looking directly upon his face. Servants must roll on the ground … as gestures of absolute subjection.[4]

If the Oba left the palace (only on festival or ritual processions), he was surrounded by his entourage (made up of his chiefs and priests and servants) and was barely visible to his other subjects. Nobody must walk to meet him and his entourage; all must stand by the roadside, and those who wished to join his entourage could only do so after he had passed them by. The king must not witness the birth of a child, and he must not see a baby who had not yet had its birth hair shaved – the hair on the head of a newborn baby came from the spirit realm, and this property of the spirit realm must not encounter the spirit of the king. Also, the Oba must not see or touch a dead body or see a grave dug for burial; a corpse was a threat to the king's life-giving power.

The King's Palace

Usually the first public facility constructed in every royal city was the palace. For this, an effort was usually made to find a distinctive location, normally a low hill around which the new city could evolve. Imade built the first Owo palace on the low hill known as Oke Asegbo (Asegbo Hill), where the Owo City Hall now stands. His successors moved it to a better location on Oke Ekusi (Ekusi Hill) where it now stands. Awamaro built the Ado (Ekiti) palace on the gently rising hill known as Oke-Adodo, where it served as the hub linking the group of quarters of the old settlers (at Odo-Ado) and those of the immigrants (at Oke-Ewi), and where it stands today. The Ijebu kingdom of Ofin built the Akarigbo's palace on Oko hill, a beautiful location overlooking most of the royal town. In the hilltop city of Efon in Ekiti, the Alaaye's palace was built on a distinct little peak.

In every kingdom, the main palace buildings were surrounded by many acres of ground, most of which was left under virgin forest. A wall (known as *gbagede*) was then built to surround the palace and its grounds, with access through one large gate. It was a measure of a king's success that he added to, or improved upon, the palace buildings, especially its gate structures. As a result, the growth of the palace constitutes an important theme in the traditionally preserved history of every Yoruba kingdom. The biggest and most powerful kingdoms had the most impressive palaces. In the forest country of Yorubaland by the eighteenth century, the palaces of Ijebu-Ode, Owo, Ilesa, Ode-Ondo, Akure and Ado (in Ekiti) seem to have been the most impressive – the Owo palace being, according to most Yoruba traditions, the largest, followed by the Ilesa palace, and then the Ijebu-Ode, Ode-Ondo, Ado (Ekiti) and Akure palaces. Like its city walls, Ila-Yara's palace was famous for its grandeur, before the city was abandoned. Owu-Ipole most certainly had one of the most impressive palaces also, but it was destroyed in the early nineteenth century. Owo palace traditions identify the two Owo kings who contributed most to the greatness of the Owo palace. The first was Ogeja, who probably reigned in the fifteenth century, and the second was Osogboye, whose reign has been dated to the early seventeenth century. Ogeja moved the palace from its first Oke-Asegbo location to Ekusi Hill where he laid out large palace buildings. And Osogboye, reputed in Owo traditions as the greatest of the Owo kings, added grand extensions and beautifications and enclosed so much land within the palace wall that the Owo palace came to earn the reputation of the largest palace in all of Yorubaland. Palace walls (*gbagede*) were different from city walls; they were, like house walls, built of molded mud plaster, but made much thicker and higher than any house wall. A visitor to Ilesa in the mid-nineteenth century wrote: "Surrounding the ruler's palace was a great wall, some 18 to 20 feet high and five to six feet thick."[5]

In every kingdom, therefore, the palace buildings tended to grow into a sprawling establishment with many, and ever increasing, halls and courtyards. In most palaces, the oldest buildings became, in a few centuries, no more than a museum or curiosity, visited only on certain festivals and rituals by persons in the innermost circles of government. Somewhere in some deep recesses of the palace grounds, the bodies of deceased kings were buried. However, the popular myth, propagated by the highest chiefs and priests, was that kings never died but turned to rocks or other objects or simply entered into the earth. Partly for this reason, partly to preserve the awe attaching to the king, cultivation of any part of the palace grounds was strictly forbidden in every kingdom – forbidden even to the king himself. In many kingdoms, the palace forest was known as *igbo-orunkoja* ("the forest through which even ants may not crawl") or some other such fearsome name.

The Yoruba palace started in every kingdom, no doubt, as the compound where the king and his family lived and where central government business was done. However, centuries of myth making around the king turned it into a place of mystery where only the sacred person of the king resided, where his chiefs went to transact government business with him. In most kingdoms, the mundane features of human life were ultimately exiled from the palace – like women giving birth, babies crying, persons dying or being buried, voices raised in anger or quarrel or excitement, people leaving for or arriving from farms, market places or other pursuits. The practice developed, therefore, that the compounds of the highest chiefs housed some members of the king's family and the chiefs acted as foster parents to young children of the kings. Meanwhile, the palace grew apace in the popular mind as a place of mystery, a place of strange happenings and strange encounters, a special type of sacred shrine.

City Walls

While working on building their palace, the founders of each kingdom usually also embarked on building their city wall. The experience too was more or less the same everywhere. No sooner was the first wall completed than another one longer in circumference, or a loop to enclose more land space, was commenced – made necessary, presumably, by unexpected influx of people from the neighboring forests.

The typical Yoruba city wall, called *yara* or *odi*, was a combination of trench and earthworks. The deeper and wider the trench, the higher were the earthworks. Against the weapons employed in warfare in their times, the Yoruba city walls provided a reasonably formidable defense. The invader must first climb to the top of the outside earthworks, then drop to the bottom of the trench, and then attempt to climb up the perpendicular wall of the trench, with the inner earthworks still waiting for him to scale on the inner top of the trench. The trenches were usually some fifteen feet deep, the better ones being considerably deeper, and, in most cities, much more than twenty feet wide at the top, with the earthworks heaped on both sides, higher on the inside than on the outside. Nature usually helped to increase the efficacy of these walls. Good rainy seasons left considerable depths of water at the bottom of most trenches, making a descent into them very dangerous. A stretch of thick vegetation was usually planted, or allowed to grow, on the outside of the wall, to make an approach to the outside earthworks difficult. Gates, called *bode*, punctuated the wall system, each gate secured with a guard post under the command of a palace official with the title of Onibode, some of whose staff also collected the customs and tolls on merchandise. Some of the highest chiefs acted as superintendents over particular gates. Most walls enclosed considerable acreages of farmland with their cities, as a sort of reserve for times of prolonged emergencies.

The first written reference to any Yoruba city wall is found in an early sixteenth century note by a Portuguese trader on the West African coast, Duarte Pacheco Perreira,[6] who wrote, "Twelve or thirteen leagues upstream from Lagos there is a large town called Geebuu, surrounded by a very large ditch." The Ijebu-Ode wall, called the Eredo Sungbo, parts of which still survive, has, according to Robert Smith, "a circuit of some eighty miles and appears to enclose an area of some 400 square miles around the town of Ijebu Ode. It is still in places twenty feet high, with an outer ditch of twenty to twenty-five feet in depth."[7] Smith's description is of the Eredo as it existed in the late twentieth century, over five or six hundred years after its construction, of which the last one hundred years have seen much house building and other construction works that have reduced much of the wall's earthworks and trench. In its pristine condition, say by the end of the eighteenth century, it must have been a truly gigantic structure, with trenches reaching depths of thirty feet in parts and earthworks as high as twenty feet or more. In 1855, the CMS missionary in Ibadan, David Hinderer, visited Ijebu-Ode and described the trench of the Eredo as a "wonderfully deep trench".[8]

Besides the Oyo-Ile walls (which will be described in another chapter), the greatest city walls in the country seem to have belonged to Ijebu-Ode, Owo, Ilesa and Owu-Ipole. The total destruction of Owu-Ipole in 1822 makes a description of that city and its walls impossible; but Yoruba traditions speak of that city and its defenses as truly magnificent. According to Owo traditions, Owo embarked, under Osogboye in the early seventeenth century, on the construction of very mighty city walls. The end product was widely regarded as one of the greatest in Yorubaland. Of the Ilesa city walls, we have some mid-nineteenth century descriptions by a literate visitor – William H. Clarke, who traveled extensively in Yorubaland in 1857–8 and spent three days in Ilesa. His assessment was that Ilesa surpassed Ilorin in size, population, and in the strength of its defenses. Of Ilesa's defenses he wrote: "Four or five miles from the town, my attention was drawn to three separate ditches ten feet wide, cut through the woods and running, how far I could not tell."[8] The missionary David Hinderer visited Ilesa about the same time and described it as

> one of the larger towns of the country, in extent perhaps next to Ibadan. … The walls are at least fifteen feet high and no less than six feet thick, with a trench around it of about twenty feet in depth, whereas inside there are high trees close to it all at a distance of about ten yards one from the other, so that a scaffolding can be erected between their branches to defend the walls from it. Hundreds of human skulls are tempered into these walls; at the north gate I counted upwards of a hundred, all of which are of war captives.[10]

Ado (Ekiti) had a fortunate location in a high bowl formed by a nearly semi-circular range of hills comprising the Olota Rock and two or three smaller hills. Streams from these hills flowed through the town in a general southern direction; at the southernmost end of the town, their confluence formed a wide marshy area before a single stream (called the Ajilosun) drained away into the southern forests. The hills and the marshy area (where there were some small lakes) provided protection around much of Ado. It was only in the gaps that Ado people needed to construct city walls, but these wall segments had some of the deepest trenches and highest earthworks in the country. Relentlessly quarried for laterite for modern buildings since the early twentieth century, some of the earthworks and their ditches still survive here and there.

Most other royal towns of Ekiti had similarly fortunate locations owing to the hilly nature of the Ekiti country. Ijero, Ikere, Ara and Ido perched partly on the slopes of hills, and Effon and Imesi-Igboodo (now Okemesi) on top of steep-sided hills. The Olosunta Hill and rock provided a near perfect defense for much of the city of Ikere. "The hills," says an Ekiti proverb, "make the Alaaye (king of Effon) defy all invasions." Even these, as well as most other Ekiti towns, had some wall systems. In the Ekiti, Akoko, Igbomina and other hilly areas of Yorubaland, some towns arranged large rocks to form balustrades and ramparts serving as walls.

The King's Marketplace

The creation of a king's marketplace or *oja-oba* was one of the most important developments in every new royal city. Trade was very important to the Yoruba people, and the kings took seriously the provision of facilities for its proper running. As soon as the building of the palace commenced, therefore, an area in its foreground, a short distance beyond the palace gate, was cleared and measured out for the king's marketplace. A marketplace close to the palace, usually located just outside its front walls, became an unalterable attribute of the Yoruba royal city or town.

The king himself was the grand patron of the marketplace, although one of the chiefs would traditionally stand in for him as master in charge. Palace messengers laid out the marketplace to the satisfaction of the traders themselves, ensuring that vendors of each particular article of merchandise had one area (called *iso*) allocated to them. While the traders constructed their sheds and the facilities for spreading out their wares, palace messengers planted shade trees, needed to prevent excessive heat in the marketplace and also to provide some decoration. When the marketplace became functional, senior palace

18. Market scene, Ibadan. *Photo: R. Mauny, 1949, IFAN.*

messengers did patrol duties in it as peace officers and also collected tolls authorized by the king's government. The sellers of each article usually formed a market commodity association – of which the king was usually patron, even though each association would also appoint other citizens as additional patrons. In short, then, the influence of the king pervaded the marketplace. In fact, the creation of the king's market place was a major item in his establishment of sovereignty over his new kingdom. The king's marketplace was a special and symbolic banner of royal sovereignty; therefore, whenever it was time for the authorities to announce the death of a king, they would order the symbolic act of having the tops of the shade trees of the king's marketplace trimmed.

In many of the royal cities, the king's marketplaces grew into sprawling establishments occupying tens or even hundreds of acres. Besides Oyo-Ile, the largest king's market in the country by about the seventeenth century was at Ijebu-Ode, followed probably by Owo and Ilesa, Owu-Ipole, Akure, Ado (Ekiti) and Ila, the greatest centers of trade in southern and eastern Yorubaland by the seventeenth century. Every one of the kings' marketplaces became a link in the great chain of long distance trade that inter-connected all of Yorubaland.

Subordinate Towns and Villages

Many kingdoms never expanded their sovereignty beyond the royal city and its farmland. All of the Akoko and Ikale kingdoms, some of the Ekiti, Ijesa and Egbado kingdoms, and most of the far western Yoruba kingdoms stagnated in their royal cities.

Of the rest, some acquired only a few towns and villages, while others acquired quite considerable territory with many towns and villages in it. The Ekiti kingdoms were generally small territorially, the three largest ones being Ado, Akure, and Moba (with Otun as capital). During the first two or three centuries of the history of the Ado kingdom, it gradually expanded the territory under its control until it came to rule over twenty subordinate towns in a kingdom stretching from northwest to southeast for some sixty miles, the largest kingdom in Ekiti. The Owo kingdom was somewhat larger than that, consisting of forest territory more than seventy miles in length from north to south with more than twenty towns. The Ilesa kingdom quickly became the largest Ijesa kingdom, while the Olowu's kingdom dwarfed the other kingdoms of the Owu. The Osemowe of Ondo ruled over a large forest kingdom extending all the way from the Oni River in the north to boundaries with the Ikale and Ilaje in the coastal lagoon country, and from the Owena River in the east to indefinite forest boundaries with the Ijebu in the west, certainly one of the largest kingdoms in Yorubaland.

Among the Egba, the Gbagura are said to have had some 144 small towns located at short distances from one another, of which seventy-two came to owe allegiance to the Agura of Iddo and seventy-two to the Onigun of Ilugun. Each of the other Egba kingdoms – Kesi ruled by the Ojoko, Ake under the Alake, and Oko under the Oshile or Oloko – also came to rule over tens of small towns. By about the eighteenth century, the Ijebu-Ode kingdom was perhaps the largest forest kingdom of the Yoruba people. To the south, this kingdom shared a boundary with the Awori of the Lagos kingdom on the coast; to the east it shared a boundary with the Ondo, to the northeast with the Owu and Ife, and to the west with the Egba and the small kingdoms of the Ijebu-Remo province.

These territorial expansions were accomplished in diverse ways during the long period starting from the founding of the first kingdoms in about the eleventh century to the eighteenth century. As earlier pointed out, in most kingdoms, when the royal city was being established people came out to it from the neighboring forests. The traditions of many kingdoms show that these immigrants to the city usually continued to preserve their farming and land-use interests in their former villages, ultimately producing the situation whereby the city regarded those villages as subject to itself. Often, farming, fishing or trading activities by city people resulted in the emergence of subordinate villages and towns in the neighboring forests. Quite often also, villages, unassimilated old settlements or mini-states, and independently emerging settlements, sought protection of the nearby city. Most such protected settlements became fully absorbed as subjects of the city government. In some cases, however, such towns or villages acquired a status of semi-independence, or even maintained their independence, within the kingdom, each thus existing as a state within the state. In Ode-Ondo, for instance, the Oloja of Idoko, in return for special religious services done for the Osemawe, was allowed to keep his own hierarchy of chiefs very much like the Osemawe's, even after Idoko had become absorbed into the kingdom of Ode-Ondo. The relationships of Igbara-Oke to the Akure kingdom, and Ilawe and Igbara-Odo to the Ado kingdom, seem to have belonged to this type. Finally, every ultimately large kingdom contained towns and villages that were conquered by the armed forces of the royal city.

It would seem, as Ade Obayemi has suggested,[11] that by about 1600, absorption, destruction and conquest of independent mini-states and settlements by centralized kingdoms had been completed in most parts of Yorubaland. By then, in effect, centralized kingdoms shared boundaries with one another all over Yorubaland. In many cases, kingdoms responded to the situation by setting up border posts as a means of protecting and stabilizing their boundaries. For instance, when the Oyo-Ile kingdom and the Ilesa kingdom came to share a border, Oyo-Ile established Ede, and Ilesa established Osogbo, as border posts.

Subordinate towns and villages were known as *ereko* – that is, settlements of the farmlands. Usually, a subordinate town or village retained the line of rulers it had had before coming under the authority of the city. In some cases, however the city authorities placed their own nominee over an *ereko* town or village, usually in instances where some vital interest (like an important road junction) required special control.

Every substantial *ereko* settlement was organized like its city, under the headship of a local ruler called the Baale, and cadres of chiefs. The Baale, followed by his chiefs, owed allegiance to the king in the city. Usually, a high chief in the city government was appointed to act as liaison between the city government and the government of a particular *ereko* town or village. This usually meant that the high chief transmitted messages between the king's government and the *ereko* government, received in his compound the Baale and his chiefs on their official visits to the city, and led them to the palace if they had business to do in the palace.

The king's government owed the *ereko* towns and villages the duty of defending them, of coming to their aid in emergencies, and of intervening to sort out their most difficult disputes. The king's palace also served as the final court of appeal in any cases arising in an *ereko* town or village. On their part, *ereko* towns and villages owed the king the duty of contributing men and materials to his army in time of war, as well as to repairs, expansions or improvements of the palace or the city wall. Routine levies and impositions on subordinate communities were not usually part of the Yoruba system; instead there was a general culture of support and gifts to the king on important festivals and jubilees.

One Band of Brothers

Most Yoruba traditions concerning their kingdoms deal with the relationships of these kingdoms, first with their "source," the Ile-Ife kingdom, and then with one another. The most widespread of the traditions have it that the character of those relationships was clearly established at Ile-Ife before the first emigrant princes went out from there to found kingdoms. According to these traditions, earlier referred to, the Ita Ijero meeting laid down, on oath, two important undertakings – the first, that all kingdoms established outside Ife would forever honor Ife (the *orirun* or springhead); the second, that all Yoruba kings would forever relate to one another as brothers.

Traditions of many Yoruba kingdoms contain popular accounts of periodic rituals involving the sending of official envoys to the palace, or some shrine, in

Ile-Ife. When kings consulted the Ifa oracle about the welfare of their kingdoms also, prescriptions in rituals and sacrifices issued by the oracle often included that certain objects be sent to or obtained from Ile-Ife, or that certain rituals or sacrifices be done at some Ile-Ife shrine. All this must be seen against the backdrop of a national culture in which reference to Ife's name was a constant, unavoidable, factor in all worship, all rituals and all divination. Moreover, Yoruba and Benin traditions have it that whenever a Yoruba kingdom or the Benin kingdom enthroned a new king, envoys were sent to the palace of Ife to inform the Ooni that "a new sun had arisen" over their kingdom, and that the Ooni would then send gifts back to the new king as a token of his pleasure. These traditions have some strong corroboration in a Portuguese document of the middle of the sixteenth century, which states as follows:[12]

> Among the many things which the King Dom João learnt from the ambassador of the King of Beni, and also Afonso de Aveiro, of what they had been told by the inhabitants of those regions, was that to the east of the King of Beni at twenty moons' journey – which according to their account and the slow pace at which they travel, would be about two hundred and fifty of our leagues – there lived the most powerful monarch of those parts whom they called Ogane. Among the pagan princes of the territories of Beni he was held in a great veneration, as are the Supreme Pontiffs with us. In accordance with a very ancient custom, the Kings of Beni, on ascending the throne, sent ambassadors to him with rich gifts to inform him that by the decease of their predecessor they had succeeded to the Kingdom of Beni, and to request him to confirm them in the same. As a sign of confirmation this Prince Ogane sent them a staff and headpiece, fashioned like a Spanish helmet, made all of shining brass, in place of a scepter and crown. He also sent a cross, of the same brass, and shaped like something religious and holy. Without these emblems the people would consider that they did not reign lawfully, nor could they call themselves true kings. All the time this ambassador was at the court of the Ogane, he never saw him, but only some silk curtains behind which he was placed, like some sacred object. When the ambassador was taking his leave, he was shown a foot from within the curtains as a sign that the Ogane was behind them and granted the request he had made; this they reverenced as though it were something holy.

While the above text seems to confirm quite clearly, and in detail, the traditions that are common in the Yoruba–Edo region, it is important to note that some questions have been raised about it. Writing in the 1960s, A. F. C. Ryder[13] expressed the opinion that the "Ogane" of this text could not have referred to the Ooni of Ife, since the Ooni lived northwest of Benin while the text said that the Ogane lived east of Benin. Ryder then suggested that the Ogane should be sought not in Ife but in the region close to the Niger–Benue confluence or somewhere else east of Benin. However, other scholars have cast serous doubts on Ryder's conclusions. The art historian, Frank Willet, has shown how very close were the art traditions (especially the brass/bronze sculptural traditions) of Ife and Benin, a fact which proves considerable closeness in the history of the two societies.[14] And then there is the existence of very many other traditions linking Ife and Benin – including the Oranmiyan traditions, and the existence of a quarter (and shrine) in Ile-Ife with the name of Orun Oba Ado (roughly, "tomb of the kings of Benin") where, according to Ife traditions, the heads (or perhaps effigies or totems) of deceased Benin kings used to be interred. It has also been suggested that "east" in the text was some sort of mistake; or that it came from foreigners' misunderstanding of the well-known, common, reference to Ife as "the place from where the sun rises,"[15] or that it may have arisen from the fact that the most popular routes from Benin to Ife probably initially pointed northeast (to avoid the thick forest and big rivers west of Benin) before bending around in the Akoko Edo hills to descend to Idoani and Owo.[16] Whatever may be the correct explanation, there seems now to be no doubt that the "Ogane" of the Portuguese text was the Ooni of Ife. Robert Smith concludes that the manner in which the Ooni and Ife are generally regarded in the Yoruba–Edo region leaves hardly any doubt that the Ogane of the Portuguese text was the Ooni of Ife.[17] Finally, it ought to be added that attempts to find the Ogane in the area of the Niger–Benue confluence or anywhere east of Benin, as suggested by Ryder, have been totally futile.

Newly installed Yoruba kings (as well as the kings of Benin), then, sent to inform the Ooni of their ascension to the throne, and received totemic gifts from him to convey his confirmation or pleasure. It seems quite certain also that Yoruba kingdoms occasionally sought help from Ife towards the resolution of some of their political disputes, especially disputes requiring clarification of some point of history. Moreover, as would be remembered, important symbols of royalty and legitimacy – beads, beaded crown, beaded scepter (*opa akun*), beaded ceremonial fan and walking stick (*opa ileke*) and beaded horse-tail flywhisks – were obtained only from Ife for some centuries, often through channels that originated from, or passed through, the Ile-Ife palace. Some connection with the Ife dynasty was the universal proof of legitimacy.

In the course of the fifteenth century, however, Ife's primacy over Yorubaland waned – rapidly over a short time, it would seem. The beginning of the decline appears to have been marked by a long war or a series of wars to which Ife traditions give much prominence. According to the traditions, Ife had to go to war in the reign of the female Ooni, Luwo Gbagada, probably in the first half of the fifteenth century. Luwo is listed as the twentieth Ooni in some Ife kings' lists. Soon after she came to the throne, Ife had to embark on a long war known to Ife history as the Ara War.[17] The war continued into the reign of Giesi, probably her immediate successor. The Ara in the war is not clearly identified but there seems to be no doubt that it was the Ara kingdom in Ekiti. So important was this war that Luwo ordered all able-bodied young men to enlist in the army, arresting and even executing some who would not – as a result of which she became known in history as the Ooni who nearly depopulated Ile-Ife. The emergency also called for improvements by Giesi to the wall defenses of Ile-Ife, including the planting of a thick belt of trees between the city and the walls.

Concerning the cause of the war that occasioned all this tough mobilization, the traditions offer little clear information. From the way in which the account of the war is usually rendered, it seems quite clear that this was a war fought at Ara rather than a war against Ara – a war in which a large Ife army was camped at Ara to confront a serious enemy. The enemy is not clearly identified, but other traditions relating to the Ekiti and Ijesa countries in about the fifteenth century point to clear probabilities. Changes in the configuration of trade routes had turned the Ekiti and Ijesa region into a very important area of trade by the fifteenth century. Trade routes from the Nupe country on the Niger, southwards to Benin on the coast, increased the commercial importance of the Ekiti kingdoms in between, and threatened to reduce the commercial importance of Ife to the people of the Ekiti area. The first Benin invasion of the Ekiti country occurred in the early fifteenth century, as also did Nupe invasions of the Ekiti and Ijesa areas through the Igbomina country. It would seem that, in defense of its commercial and security interests, the Ife kingdom sent a large army to Ara in order to curtail the military activities especially of the Nupe in the Ekiti country, and that the Ife army needed to encamp at Ara for a long time for the purpose. Back home in Ife, steps were taken to strengthen Ile-Ife's defenses in case the Nupe, whose western wings were active in the Ijesa area (about which more will be said later), should decide to veer further west and attack Ile-Ife.

In short then, by the fifteenth century, Ife's control of almost all the trade of Yorubaland was beginning to unravel, while Nupe incursions into Ijesa threatened the kingdom. All this compelled Ife to invest in large, prolonged, military ventures, a step which it had never had to take in all the centuries since the fight against Igbo-Igbo in the eleventh century. The military ventures appear to have been successful in the short run. Benin avoided a direct clash with Ife by shifting its operations largely eastwards where, to some extent in Akoko and on a large scale in Afenmai (called Kukuruku by the Nupe), Benin forces came into heavy clashes with the Nupe. The armies of Ilesa also repulsed the Nupe in Ijesa.

But these successes were not sufficient in the long run to avert a downturn in Ife's fortunes. The essence of the situation worked irresistibly against Ife. The rise of the many royal cities all over Yorubaland over the centuries had opened up the country, strengthened communication and commerce, and greatly boosted Ife's central commercial position and prosperity. But by the fifteenth century, the royal cities had become so many largely independent commercial centers, served by routes that pointed in all directions. Ife was ceasing to occupy a central position commercially. The Benin kingdom from the southeast and the Nupe from the northeast tried to channel the whole eastern arm of Yoruba trade to their own advantage, compelling Ife to plunge in in order to stop them. But the Benin initiative, at least, appears to have continued to prosper in spite of Ife's efforts. With the coming of European traders to the Benin ports from the closing years of the fifteenth century, its monopoly of the importation and distribution of European goods established Benin decisively as the controller of most of the trade of eastern Yorubaland. Not long after that, Oyo-Ile, finally freed from the limitations imposed by its neighbors (the Bariba and the Nupe), began to seize major shares in the trade of Yorubaland. To the northeast, Oyo-Ile defeated the Nupe and seized most of their share of the trade of northeastern Yorubaland, and established a link with Benin in northern Ekiti (with Otun as a sort of commercial boundary). To the west, Oyo-Ile took control of the trade through Owu with the Ijebu country, as well as the trade through the Egba and Egbado countries. Ife therefore declined, commercially and militarily. The traditions also indicate that Ife suffered in the fifteenth century from some long droughts and famines, which thus added to the general economic decline of the kingdom. It seems very probable in fact that the population of Ile-Ife began to decline in the fifteenth or sixteenth century, and continued slowly to decline until the nineteenth century.

The economic and political influence of Ife in Yorubaland thus declined from the fifteenth century on. By the late eighteenth century, the Ife kingdom seems to have become one of the smaller and weaker of the kingdoms of Yorubaland, and the city of Ile-Ife had become considerably smaller than many other Yoruba cities. Nevertheless, the traditions are unambiguous that Ife in decline continued to be regarded by the generality of Yoruba people as the place of origins, the abode of the gods of the race, and the home source of all Yoruba kings. For the most part, kings continued to send envoys to Ile-Ife to announce their ascension to the throne, and the envoys continued to return with totemic gifts. Kingdoms confronted by serious internal disputes or problems continued to send to Ile-Ife for the clarification of knotty issues of history, or for the performance of rituals and sacrifices prescribed by Ifa. To such envoys, Ile-Ife was still a city of awesome mysteries, even though it had not the size, the population and the bubbling economic life of the cities from which they had come, and even though its king did not command the manifest power of the kings that they served. In the reign of the Ewi Amonaola ("he who knows the road to wealth") in the early eighteenth century, Ado people proudly added to the *oriki* of their king the lines that proclaimed him as:

Ate'pa ileke b'Ooni s'ore

Ajewo oro f'Ooni.

(He who walks with the beaded stick and counts the Ooni as friend,

He who flaunts wealth that the Ooni does not have.)

But though economically, politically and militarily weak, the Ife kingdom was nevertheless master of its own territory, which no Yoruba king would dare to violate.

Concerning the undertaking that all Yoruba kings should relate to one another as brothers, the subsequent record is mixed. Traditions describing periodic exchanges of messages and gifts between kings are found all over Yorubaland. In fact, in some cases, such practices have survived into modern times. For instance, it seems to have been a common practice that newly installed Ekiti kings used to send messengers to inform other Ekiti kings, and that gifts were usually exchanged on such occasions. On important state festivals also, Ekiti kings used to receive messages and gifts from other Ekiti kings. In the Ado kingdom, the great annual royal festival was the Idiroko, during which the Ewi sat in state in Igbamote, the people's courtyard of the palace, with large cheering crowds of his subjects in attendance, and his chiefs (followed by dancing members of their lineages) came to pay homage to him. For this festival, the Ewi received royal messages, visitors and gifts from all over Ekiti. So too did the Olukere of Ikere during the annual grand festival of the Olosunta. Most Ekiti kingdoms, in fact, had such festivals; some of the rich kingdoms like Ikole, Ara, Iddo, Effon, Oye, Ado, Ikere and Ijero had more than one. Perhaps the most popular and best-attended festival in Ekiti belonged to the Arinjale's kingdom of Ise in southern Ekiti. This festival, called Alile, was a gorgeous celebration of beginnings during which, among other things, families with marriageable girls displayed them in the best of clothes and the girls sang to admiring crowds from all over Ekiti. Large numbers of visitors, royal messengers, and friends annually streamed to Ise for this festival, some for the king and some for the families involved in the celebrations.

Interactions of these types seem to have developed into special relationships between some Ekiti kingdoms. The Ewi of Ado, the Elekole of Ikole, and the Ajero of Ijero, for instance, seem to have become a special group of brothers – a group whose tie Ekiti folklore explained in a story.[19] The story had it that a woman named Eyemode married and had sons in succession for the Elekole, the Ewi and the Ajero, and that her three sons reigned as contemporaries on the thrones of the three kingdoms, thereby establishing a special bond among them. It is not known whether this is history or myth, but it seems fairly certain that for some time at least the Elekole, Ewi and Ajero regarded themselves, and were regarded by other Ekiti kings, as having a special relationship that set them apart.

Patterns of relationships similar to those among Ekiti kings existed in every subgroup region of the Yoruba country. In fact, the general Yoruba belief was that the kings in a Yoruba subgroup constituted a sub-family of the Yoruba family of kings.

Some traditions also indicate that Yoruba kings in general believed that it was their duty individually and collectively to adjudicate in difficult disputes within or between kingdoms in the Yoruba family. Scattered accounts of such interventions exist in many traditions. According to one Oyo tradition recorded in Johnson's *The History of the Yorubas*, the Alaafin Jayin of Oyo (probably in the sixteenth century) sent a senior *ilari* (palace envoy) to settle a dispute between Owu and Iseyin. A dispute over the succession to the throne of the Ara kingdom was, according to some traditions, settled by officials from some (unidentified) kingdoms. As a result, civil war was averted, and the aggrieved candidate left peacefully and ultimately founded, with his many followers, the kingdom of Okuku in the Osun Valley.[20]

Akure traditions preserve a detailed account of a series of interactions of this type among some kingdoms. According to this account, about the middle of the seventeenth century, one Owa of Ilesa, Atakunmosa, fell out with his chiefs and people. Atakunmosa slipped out of his palace and fled (before his chiefs could urge him "to go to sleep"). Fleeing south on the popular trade route, he stopped at Akure and then continued to Benin, where he stayed as an exile for a few years in the palace of the Oba of Benin (regarded as a member of the Oduduwa family of kings). He left Benin and retraced his steps to Akure, and stayed for a few more years in the palace of the king of Akure, whose title originally was Ajapada. At Akure, he at last received his subjects' invitation to return to Ilesa and to the throne. The traditions imply that the Oba of Benin and the Ajapada of Akure had been interceding for him with the Ilesa chiefs. Atakunmosa thereafter reigned very successfully, remembered by Ilesa as perhaps the greatest king in its history. His stay in Akure resulted in a blood link between the Akure and Ilesa dynasties. One of Atakunmosa's daughters married the Ajapada, and the son born of the marriage later became king of Akure. When he was a baby, this son was given the name Olufadeji by Atakunmosa. With him the title of Akure kings changed from Ajapada to Deji.

Likewise, evidence of very ancient territorial settlements between kingdoms abounds all over Yorubaland, settlements arrived at as resolutions of disputes. Ondo and Ikale traditions indicate the existence, in the forests between them, of such markers of agreed boundaries. The Ikole and Ado kingdoms in Ekiti have it in their traditions that they once established an agreed boundary marker between their two kingdoms at a place that they gave the name of Okiti Eyemode. Perhaps the best known of such ancient territorial markers was the one established at Apomu, probably in the seventeenth century, by the kingdoms of Ife, Oyo-Ile and Ijebu-Ode. Because of perennial conflicts involving traders from these kingdoms in the Apomu area, the three kings set up at Apomu a marker which they named Apimo, on oath that their kingdoms would never fight one another. Some traditions have it that the name Apimo (modified to Apomu over time) replaced the original name of this old Ife market town. The usual materials for such markers were cairns (heaps of stones) and the ritual tree called *peregun* that is believed to be able to survive all conditions (including forest fires).

Brothers against Brothers

Another face of the relationships among Yoruba kingdoms, however, featured conflicts and wars. In spite of the undoubted acceptance by all Yoruba kings of the brotherhood of all of them, differences in success, prosperity and power led, in the end, to territorial and other ambitions that produced conflicts. Ultimately, the general picture came to be that a successful and ambitious kingdom tended to aspire to dominance over kingdoms in its own subgroup – that is, to unify the subgroup into just one kingdom. In a number of cases, indeed, very successful kingdoms aspired to even greater expansion than that, into Yoruba territories beyond their own subgroup territory.

Owo and widespread eastern Yoruba traditions have it that the Owo kingdom experienced great success from quite early in its history. Its location on some of the busiest trade routes in Yorubaland resulted in quick wealth and power. Growing threat of military conquest by its close southeastern neighbor, the powerful Edo kingdom of Benin, challenged this kingdom into becoming a considerable military power in its own right. By the fifteenth century, Owo had, according to Oladipo Olugbadehan in his thesis, established an impressive forest kingdom with boundaries with Ekiti to the north and northeast, Akoko to the north, and with Benin in the southeast.[21] It soon absorbed the nearby kingdom of Idoani, an important town on the route to Benin. In the forests of the south of the Owo country, close to the boundary with Benin, a number of small kingdoms emerged – Ifon, Sobe, Imoru, Ajagba, Ute, etc.

Owo claimed sovereignty over these, in spite of resistance that was destined to go on for centuries. Having thus established its dominance over the whole of the Owo subgroup territory, the Owo kingdom then began strong bids to conquer the Akoko country and absorb its kingdoms. Repeatedly throughout the seventeenth century, Owo armies swept through the Akoko hills. These efforts reached a climax in the reign of the Olowo Ajaka, the most warlike ruler in Owo's history, about 1760–80. According to Owo palace traditions, Ajaka, whose mother was from Akoko, invaded the Akoko country more than once and subdued many of its kingdoms. From Ajaka's time, Owo generally regarded the Akoko kingdoms as subordinate to itself.

In Ekiti, the two kingdoms of Ado and Ikere, both founded in about the fourteenth century, began to clash early in their history. According to traditions recorded by the Ado historian, Rev. Anthony Oguntuyi, Ado claimed that the Elesun, whom the Ewi had subdued to establish the Ado kingdom, had used to have some authority over the early settlements in Ikere before the founding of the Ikere kingdom. On the basis of that claim, the Ado kingdom, as it expanded, sought to establish a claim over parts of the territory of the Ikere kingdom. The clashes that thus ensued went on intermittently for centuries, Ado fighting under the Ewi and Ikere fighting first under the Olukere and later under the Ogoga. Whenever either felt stronger, it launched an invasion – off and on, all the way till the last years of the nineteenth century. Ado seems also to have had a feud with the Ido kingdom in the territory around Osi, as well as around Ifaki. The Ado–Ido feud resulted in sapping the strength of Osi, which had started off as a kingdom with some prosperity.

A somewhat similar feud existed for centuries between the two southern Ekiti kingdoms of Ise and Emure. Only a few miles apart, these two kingdoms seem to have been perpetually involved in trying to swallow each other up. Their hostilities continued too into the nineteenth century.

The Ijesa kingdom of Ilesa, as would be remembered, embarked on a career of conquests even before it had fully established itself in the eleventh or twelfth century. It became, early in its history, a meeting point of very important trade routes, and grew to become one of the most powerful kingdoms in Yorubaland. Local wars feature strongly in the traditions of this kingdom, wars against the other kingdoms of the Ijesa country. These wars appear to have resulted in the splitting up of some Ijesa royal towns like Imesi and Otan. A section of Imesi migrated up the hills into the Ekiti country and founded the Ekiti kingdom of Imesi-Igboodo (now Okemesi), and a section of Otan moved northeastwards and founded Otan-Koto (now Otan Aiyegbaju). Igbajo was the most fortunate of these other Ijesa kingdoms. Secure on top of a hill, it was able to resist Ilesa. The power of the Ilesa kingdom reached its peak in the late seventeenth century in the reign of Atakunmosa, reputed to be the greatest warrior king of the later eras of Ilesa history. On the whole, although the Ilesa kingdom did not achieve its ambition of making its Owa the ruler of all the Ijesa, it did make the Owa the highly exalted senior brother among the Ijesa kings. The Ilesa kingdom also brought pressure to bear on kingdoms of western Ekiti, notably Ogotun and Effon, in the seventeenth century. Effon's location on the hills made repeated aggressions against it futile; but Ogotun appears to have become tributary to Ilesa for some brief period.

Like the Ilesa kingdom, the Olowu's kingdom of Owu-Ipole early developed into a commercially rich and militarily strong state. It was particularly well located to benefit from the trade that flowed from the Ijebu country in its south to the Ife country in the east and the Oyo country in the north. Unlike Ilesa, it dominated its small Owu subgroup from the beginning, so much so that no other kingdom in the Owu country could become anything higher than a subsidiary of the Olowu. What such kingdoms lost in independence, however, they gained in wealth and in the pride of being led by the Olowu, who was for some time widely regarded as the most powerful king in central Yorubaland. In general, the Owu people gloried in the militarism of the Owu-Ipole kingdom and earned, among other Yoruba people, a reputation for aggression, toughness and arrogance. On the younger kingdom of Oyo-Ile in the north, the Olowu exerted pressure, forcing Oyo-Ile at some point in its early history to pay tributes. Then when in the seventeenth century Oyo-Ile became the greatest Yoruba kingdom and the center of a large and expanding empire, the Olowu's kingdom became a subsidiary of Oyo-Ile, and the Owu people became very proud as the Alaafin's foot soldiers in the central forests of Yorubaland. By the eighteenth century, therefore, the Owu were feared and spitefully spoken of by most of their neighbors – the Ife to the east, some of the Egba to the west, and some of the Ijebu to the south.

In the Ondo forests, the kingdom of Epe, for reasons that remain unclear, remained small, poor and stagnant. The Idanre kingdom was largely isolated because of its hill location, but derived considerable wealth from the trade that flowed through the ancient paths in the valley below its hills. It is not known whether this kingdom ever developed territorial ambitions or some military power. The Osemowe's kingdom of Ode-Ondo, therefore, controlled almost all the Ondo forests. It became a fairly rich trading and military power, taking advantage especially of trade with the Ikale and Ilaje on the coastal lagoons, and with the Ijebu to the west and southwest, the Owo to the east, and the Ife to the north. Conflicting ambitions over control of the trade routes, exacerbated by uncertainties over territorial boundaries in the deep southern forests, caused this kingdom to get into conflicts from time to time with some of its

Ikale neighbors – especially, according to Ondo traditions, with such kingdoms as Ode-Aye, Irele and the Abodi's kingdom of Ikoya. Attempts to settle these disputes resulted in a number of negotiated boundary markers in a number of locations in the southern forests.

In the Ikale country, the Abodi's kingdom of Ikoya seems to have emerged early as the most powerful kingdom. However, the nature of the Ikale country – thick forests broken up by lagoons, rivers and swamps – compelled each Ikale kingdom to remain fixed in its own forest patch. Much as among the Ekiti, the Ikale kings remained a family of equal brothers throughout their history, with hardly any traditions of conflicts among them.

In the Egba country, a certain ebb and flow seems to have characterized the configuration of power among the kings. Over the Gbagura, influence was originally shared about equally by the Agura of Iddo and the Onigun of Ilugun. In the rivalry between the two, the Agura became gradually more powerful – until he finally established influence over the whole of the Gbagura province. Rather than accept the leadership of the Agura, the Onigun ended up attaching his own kingdom to the province of Oke-Ona. Among the Egba Agbeyin, a similar rivalry went on between the Ojoko of Kesi and the Alake of Ake. The Ojoko was originally the principal king in this province. Conflicts between him and the Alake gradually increased the Alake's influence, until the Alake became the principal king in the province.

In Ijebu, the Awujale early became the richest and most powerful king – acquiring a specially exalted status and influence among the Ijebu kings, as well as certain privileges which no other Ijebu king could claim.[22] Among such privileges may be mentioned the exclusive ownership of *odi* (a special kind of court official) and *apebi* (a special priest who performs the crowning of the Awujale), and the right to have brought to him from all over Ijebuland the skins and some other parts of certain animals regarded by the Yoruba as royal property – such as elephants, bushcows (African buffalo), and leopards. The Awujale also occupied the very influential position of patron of the powerful Osugbo (the Ijebu version of Ogboni) council of Ijebu-Ode, to which all other Osugbo councils in the Ijebu country were subordinate. And he enjoyed the important ritual supremacy of holding certain great and colorful festivals annually, one of which culminated in the gathering in Ijebu-Ode once every year of the sixteen *Agemo* priests (earth fertility high priests), each accompanied by large numbers of followers, and each bringing a sacred load to bless and to honor the Awujale. In short, then, the Awujale was supreme among the Ijebu kings, and, by and large, he could, whenever there was need to, influence the affairs of all kingdoms in the Ijebu forests. Considering the large expanse and the wealth of the country over which he was thus the most influential ruler, the Awujale would seem to have regularly been the most powerful king in the southern Yoruba forests, and, in the centuries of the greatness of the Alaafin, second only to the Alaafin in Yorubaland. This political picture in the Ijebu forests would seem to have been generated mostly by the magnitude of trade in the Ijebu country and the nodal position of Ijebu-Ode on the overall complex of trade routes in that part of Yorubaland.

In Igbomina, the Orangun of Ila was generally regarded as the most senior king from the earliest, because of his descent from a line clearly traced to Oduduwa. However, research by Funso Afolayan, to whom we are indebted for an impressive study of Igbomina history, shows that while the cultural antecedents and political seniority of the Orangun were generally acknowledged all over the Igbomina country, he does not appear to have exercised any form of serious political hegemony over the Igbomina kingdoms before the nineteenth century. A few of the Igbomina kings, most notably the Olomu of Omu Aran and the Olupo of Ajase Ipo, increasingly came to challenge and threaten whatever paramountcy might have originally been attributed to the Orangun. One important cause of this state of affairs was the constant Nupe aggression on the Igbomina country, a military pressure which became intensified in the eighteenth century and resulted in the destruction of Ila. The failure or inability of the Orangun to resist and contain the Nupe threat weakened his prestige and influence among the Igbomina kings. In this situation, when, during the seventeenth and eighteenth centuries, the Oyo-Ile kingdom of the Alaafin became a great power in northern Yorubaland, some of the Igbomina kings (especially the Olomu of Omu Aran and the Olupo of Ajase Ipo) happily established military alliances and political association with the Alaafin, and thus considerably enhanced their power, prestige and influence vis-à-vis that of the Orangun.[23]

Migrations and Other Folk Movements

Migrations of people in large or small groups, families and individuals, within Yorubaland, were a very important phenomenon in the history of the Yoruba kingdoms and of the Yoruba national society. The primary, kingdom-creating, migrations had resulted in the emergence of kingdoms and cities in Yorubaland, and the populations of the cities had been generally enhanced by migrations from their neighboring forests. After these, a second generation of migrations moved significant groups and elements from kingdom to kingdom and imparted what one might call a "national flavor" to every significant city and kingdom of the Yoruba people.

A substantial part of the second-generation migrations were protest migrations – of persons going away from a city where they felt that they had been unfairly denied a royal title or chieftaincy or other position. As earlier pointed out, most leaders of such migrations ended up as chiefs in other cities and kingdoms. Every Yoruba royal city had at least a few such chiefs, always heading quarters constituted by the followers who had come with them. Besides this, Yoruba people seem to have very commonly reacted to disasters (communal troubles, famines, epidemics, etc.) by migrating to other parts of their country – as individuals, lineages, or even whole settlements. And, moreover, the Yoruba elite in general appear to have been very prone to migrating. It was common that if a famous king ruled over a kingdom, persons of substance and fame came from far and near to live in his city, share in his glory, and contribute to his fame. Kingdoms or kings or other accomplished persons who prospered or became famous usually attracted distinguished persons. This represents a major theme in Yoruba folklore.

Such migrants included not only politically ambitious persons but also famous diviners, herbalists, *adahunse* (providers of occult services), magicians, wise men, and famous women traders, from other royal cities or from provincial towns within the same kingdom or other kingdoms. Typically, such immigrants struck root in their new homes, quite often were offered chieftaincy titles, and entered into high offices of state. All over Yorubaland, there are stories of rich women who married king after king across the country and had children for some, and thus became famous. It was common for the most distinguished professionals to spend their professional lives migrating all over the Yoruba homeland, living a few years in each place and then moving on. Such persons were the icons of the Yoruba national society. If they were *babalawo* or medicine men or "wise men", they usually left groups of their disciples in many cities. One of such men, according to Ade Obayemi, was Atakunmosa, the seventeenth century Ilesa prince who in later life became king of Ilesa.[24] A renowned medicine man, Atakunmosa lived in many towns – Ikole, Ara, Ado, Ikere, Akure – before he was crowned king of Ilesa. When he left Ilesa as a result of disagreement with his subjects, he spent some more years abroad, during which time he lived briefly in Benin, Owo and Akure, before he was invited back to his throne. According to certain traditions, a sort of national summit meeting was held periodically (at fixed intervals of perhaps seven or eight years) by the highest and best of "wise men" from all over Yorubaland. According to Chief Isola Fabunmi of Ife, the general populace, only faintly aware of these summit meetings, commonly fearfully spoke of them as gatherings of witches and wizards. The typical agenda of such meetings appear to have been exchanges and demonstrations of esoteric knowledge and power.

Finally, most really good musicians, dancers and other entertainers (male and female) usually traveled the country extensively to ply their trade. The best often spent most of their lives traveling and living away from home, sometimes as guests and clients of kings. Widespread traditions indicate quite strongly that *alarinjo* (traveling entertainment) groups were constant features of social life in all Yoruba cities. To the itinerant entertainers must be added masked entertainers (*egungun*), the best of whom usually traveled far from home. Some kingdoms were famous all over Yorubaland for their *egungun*. *Egungun* from parts of Ekiti are said to have been eagerly awaited annually (during the dry season) in even distant towns like Otta and others in the Awori and Egbado countries. *Egungun* from various towns in the Oyo country were usually the most numerous, most diversified in the types of their masks, offered the most varied entertainments, and were leaders in traversing the country from end to end. *Igunu*, the Nupe type of *egungun*, were also often drawn into Yoruba culture as regular entertainers in Yoruba towns, far from their own country on the banks of the Niger. Visual artists (especially sculptors) are treated as special national assets in Yoruba traditions. The best of them usually became widely famous, and usually lived their lives sojourning in town after town (as guests or under the patronage of kings, chiefs and priests), carving decorative posts, doors, and other pieces for palaces, shrines and famous lineage compounds. Some families of great sculptors remained nationally famous for generations. All of the above was also generally true of some other types of artists and artisans – like the makers of beaded products (crowns and insignia), and the makers of bodily decorations (facial marks and body tattoos). In short, the Yoruba national community in the era of the kingdoms, cities and towns, commonly circulated its brightest and best.

All these trends in the cultural, political and economic behavior of Yoruba people in the long era of the Yoruba kingdoms (eleventh to eighteenth century) were profoundly influential in molding the Yoruba nation into a strongly intermixed, and continually intermixing, people. They account for the fact that countless Yoruba towns and villages, as well as quarters, chieftaincies and significant lineages in practically every Yoruba town, are traceable to distant places of origin within the Yoruba homeland. And they played a great part in the molding of the remarkable homogeneity of Yoruba civilization, in the enrichment of Yoruba culture, and in the reinforcing and strengthening of Yoruba national consciousness.[25]

19. Orangun of Ila, Oba Adetona Ayeni. *Photo: J. Pemberton III, 1971.*

20. Ooni of Ife, Oba Adesoji Aderemi. *Photo: Atanda (1980).*

21. Alake of Egbaland, Oba Ladipo Ademola II, Abeokuta. *Photo: P. Verger, 1948–49, IFAN.*

22. Ewi of Ado Ekiti, Oba Daniel Aladesanmi II. *Photo: Atanda (1980).*

9

The Kingdoms and the Economy: Part I

Broadly, in terms of economic development, there are two periods in the long era of the kingdoms in the history of the Yoruba people: from the eleventh century to the beginning of the sixteenth century, and from the beginning of the sixteenth century to the end of the eighteenth, with the coming of coastal trade with Europe in the early sixteenth century as the dividing line. The creation of many kingdoms, cities and towns in Yorubaland from about the eleventh century acted as a powerful stimulus to transform economic life. It produced a growing urban culture, which reordered the general economy – farming, manufactures, trade, arts and artisanship, entertainments – in many ways. Then in the early sixteenth century, European coastal trade entered upon the scene, generating very significant transformations. In this chapter, we shall look at the whole economic picture and its two periods, again excluding, as much as possible, details that pertain specifically to the Oyo kingdom and empire, since Oyo constitutes the subject of a subsequent chapter.

The Main Pillar: Peasant Farming

The civilization that ultimately produced the Yoruba kingdoms was developed over many hundreds of years by a farming people whose agricultural economy became progressively more efficient and more productive as a result of the growing sophistication of iron tools as well as increasing numbers of cultivated crops. Agriculture was the pillar of the economy before and after the creation of the Yoruba kingdoms. The emergence of the royal cities, as well as other major towns, as the kingdoms were springing up, widened opportunities in other occupations – like house building, government and military service, the arts, artisanship, entertainment, priestly occupations, health care and herbal occupations and, very importantly, commerce. But agriculture remained the employer of the vast majority of people in the Yoruba kingdoms.

A fortunate combination of suitable soils and adequate rains made most of the Yoruba homeland good for agriculture. The only decisively poor agricultural belt consisted of the coastal lagoons, creeks and swamps, the home of the Itsekiri, Ilaje and Ikale kingdoms, the coastal Ijebu towns and some of the Awori. The inhabitants of these places lived mostly by fishing, and, from ancient times they supplied dried fish to the rest of the Yoruba homeland. Some of them also manufactured salt from seawater and provided the rest of Yorubaland with its earliest supplies of salt. The coming of imported salt from Europe from the sixteenth century on gradually destroyed the ancient salt industry, but European trade in general opened up new commercial opportunities for these coastal Yoruba people – commercial opportunities about which more will be said later.

Immediately north of this belt came the belt of Yorubaland's thickest forests – the home of the Owo, Ondo, Ijebu and Egba kingdoms. Next came a belt of slightly lighter forests, and finally the broad belt of grasslands characterized by tall grass, scattered shrubs and trees and, along the rivers and streams, patches of thick forests. The thick forest belt, as earlier mentioned, bulged northwards in the area of the Ife kingdom (roughly central Yorubaland), and then from the Egbado country westwards, the open grass belt bulged southwards near to the coastline, putting much of the Egbado and the far western Yoruba kingdoms (and their Aja neighbors) in light forest and grass territory. The Akoko and Ekiti kingdoms lay partly in the lighter forests and partly in the grasslands, the Ijesa and Ife kingdoms mostly in the light forest belt, and the Oyo and Igbomina kingdoms in the grassland belt.

The lighter forest and grassland belts were the best areas for agriculture in general, the land in the grasslands being considerably more fertile than in the thickest forests. Certain types of yams did particularly well in the valleys and hill slopes of the Ekiti, Ijesa, Igbomina and Ife countries, and therefore these kingdoms were the most prolific producers of yams in Yorubaland. The grasslands were the best for cereals (mostly millet and maize) and most types of beans. Therefore, foods made from cereals and beans featured more prominently in the diets of the Igbomina, the Oyo and the Okun Yoruba. The oil palm grew abundantly in all parts of Yorubaland, somewhat more in the lighter forests and grassland belt than in the thickest forests. Palm oil and palm wine production were very important items of agricultural activity in all parts of Yorubaland. Another type of palm tree called *oguro* (*Raffia vinifera*) did well only in swampy areas – in many places along the lagoons and in swamps along riverbanks. Its most important product was palm wine, but it also supplied fronds for a highly valued roof mat. As pointed out in an earlier chapter, cotton and the shrubs from which dyes were derived grew best in the more open country, making the Igbomina and Oyo areas the leading producers of cotton and dyestuff. On a journey through these parts of Yorubaland early in the nineteenth century, the Englishman Richard Lander[1] recorded seeing extensive plantations of cotton and indigo in the farmlands around every town. "In the vicinity of Katunga (i.e. Oyo-Ile) and most other large towns," he wrote, "indigo is cultivated to an extent of from five to six hundred acres." The beans from a bean tree (locust beans, known in Yoruba as *irugba*) that grew scattered in the grasslands yielded a highly valued aromatic called *iru*, of which the Igbomina, Oyo, northern Ekiti and northern Ijesa were the leading producers. The Yoruba type of kolanut, *obi abata* grew well in all parts of the forests, but the large-scale production of it for export to the trans-Niger countries appears to have been a monopoly of the Ife kingdom for some centuries. From there it expanded westwards to the Owu, Ijebu and Egba countries and, later, to the Ijesa and Ondo countries. Large-scale production of *orogbo* developed in much the same way.

The raising of livestock was not a significant feature of Yoruba farming. Unlike their northern neighbors (the Hausa and Fulani and others beyond the Niger), the typical Yoruba farmer did not rear herds of cattle or flocks of goats or sheep. In the extreme northwestern part of the Yoruba country, in the Oyo grassland, it was common for rich families to own some heads of cattle (and also goats and sheep), for the care of which they procured labor (as employees or slaves) from beyond the Niger. For the rest, the typical Yoruba livestock were goats and sheep – and birds like chickens, ducks, pigeons, and sometimes turkeys – all of which were raised free range around the home, and almost all of which were owned by the women. Most women owned one or two goats or sheep and a few birds, which they raised in their compound homes; some of the wealthier women had many, and frequently derived considerable income from sending a few to the marketplace for sale from time to time.

Urbanism

A active peasant-based urbanism evolved all over Yorubaland. Surrounding each city or town were farmlands spreading out for miles. Members of the predominantly peasant population of each urban center left home in the morning to work on their farms, and returned to their city or town in the late afternoon. On their farms they built the barns for preserving the harvest, and usually makeshift huts (called *aba*) where they cooked and sheltered from sun and rain while away on their farms. These were the daily farms called *oko etile* (near-town, or precinct, farms), which were normally not farther than five miles from the city. Of the farmers who owned precinct farms, a few would also have farms in the more distant forests near the ultimate boundaries of the land that belonged to their city. In such distant farm locations called *oko egan* (farms of the forests), there developed small outposts called *abule* consisting of small, fragile, family homes. Farmers could stay in the *abule* for many days; a few turned the *abule* into semi-permanent homes. Small towns or villages called *ileto* existed in every kingdom, but the pattern of life in them was the same as in the city – with family compounds, near-home farms and distant farms. Even in such villages, most residents would claim that their ultimate homes belonged in a lineage compound in the large local town or city. By and large, the ideal home for the Yoruba person came to be an apartment in a lineage compound in a city or town. Emotionally, and almost completely in fact, the Yoruba people, after the creation of their kingdoms and cities, became a nation of urban dwellers.

Krapf-Askari describes Yoruba towns and their farms as follows:

> The classical plan of a Yoruba town resembles a wheel: the Oba's palace being the hub, the town walls the rim, and the spokes a series of roads radiating out from the palace and linking the town to other centers. Beyond the walls lie the farmlands; first the oko etile or "farms of the outskirts", then the oko egan or "bush farms", merging imperceptibly with the oko egan of the next town.[2]

Manufactures

The emergence and growth of many cities and towns in all parts of Yorubaland, and the consequent growing demands of an urbanizing people, stimulated manufacturing in general. In the process, regional specialization was also generated. Over time, the country looked to the towns of the Osun Valley for its best quality dyes,[3] certain types of dyed cloth, and iron goods; to Ife, Ijebu, Ilesa and Ondo for iron products; to western Ekiti (especially Ogotun) and eastern Ijesa (especially Ipetu) for the best mats and raffia products; to the towns of the northern Oyo country for leather and the best quality leather goods; to certain Ekiti towns for different types of pots as well as certain types of cloth; to the Akure and Owo areas for the best cosmetic camwood and some types of cloth, to Ife for beads and beaded products.

The manufacturing enterprise of dyeing (of yarn and fabrics) deserves some note, because of its importance in the economy. Every community had at least a few dyeing establishments known as *idi-aro*, where giant pots were sunk in the ground for compounding and holding dye solutions. These facilities were major pillars of the cloth industry – the largest industrial enterprise of the Yoruba people. Usually, *idi-aro* were owned by the richest women in the community. They were very expensive to establish, since each of the giant pots normally cost a fortune. They usually passed from mother to daughter over many generations, and, therefore to own one was, in most cases, to be a descendant of a long line of rich people. And the *idi-aro* was invariably a good and lucrative investment. The owner usually owned a large yarn and cloth production business of her own based on her *idi-aro*. In addition, she made a good income from the fact that her *idi-aro* regularly served very many small yarn and cloth producers – persons who would rent pots (for compounding dye solutions and then dyeing whatever they chose) for a length of time, and others who would only come to dye some piece of yarn or fabric in dye solutions already prepared by the facility owner. Most Yoruba dyeing had the objective of producing various shades of two basic colors – blue and black, from the lightest blue all the way to the darkest black. This was because indigo was the most easily produced and commonly used dye. Production of other colors (especially shades of red and brown) was usually a specialized process, carried out with different types of dye solutions by persons with special training for it. Most brown or brownish-grey fabrics were not woven from dyed cotton yarn, but from naturally brown or brownish-grey yarn derived from a species of silkworm that grew on the bark of a tree found in the Yoruba forests. A French slave trader on the West African coast in the early eighteenth century, as will be seen below, described this brown or brownish-grey cloth (the highly prized fabric which the Yoruba called *sanyan*) as "cloth made of the bark of trees".

Commerce

All the developments of the period added up to create enormous benefits for trade. The emergence of kingdoms, cities and towns opened up the country by developing and strengthening the channels of transportation and communication. Regional diversity in agricultural products, and the growth of regional specialization in manufactures, pushed up the volumes of internal trade. Generally increasing agricultural and industrial productivity generated increasing exports to places within and beyond Yorubaland. Increasing sophistication of economic demands consequent upon growing urbanization boosted the volume of imports from distant lands. The Yoruba became a great trading people, their women, especially, ranking among the best traders in Africa. Long-distance traders called *alajapa* began to rank among the elite. Every one of the Yoruba cities, with its king's marketplace, became an emporium, generating, receiving, distributing and sending out merchandise on a large scale. In very distant parts of the West African region, Yoruba trading colonies emerged – as far north as the Hausa country beyond the River Niger and the Kanuri country on Lake Chad, and also far eastwards and westwards. Some Yoruba traditions even seem to suggest that Yoruba trading colonies might have existed as far west as the valley of the Senegal River and as far east as the lands of the Congo. Inside Yorubaland itself, Hausa and Nupe trading communities arose in most cities, and traders from even further north (especially Tuaregs from the Sahara) became frequent features of the trading population. So much regard was had for the Hausa and Nupe trading communities that Yoruba kings generally became their patrons, and many a king set aside space for them to live in or near his palace, close to the king's marketplace. When increasing numbers of the Hausa traders came to be Muslims, Yoruba cities usually gave them land to build their mosques close to the marketplace – so they could observe their prayer breaks near their merchandise.[4] In eastern and southern Yorubaland, Edo resident trading communities emerged in many towns.

The Coming of European Trade

The above, then, is our picture of the economic life of Yorubaland before the coming of European trade in the sixteenth century. From the founding of the first Yoruba kingdom (Ife) until the early sixteenth century, the trans-Saharan trade networks provided the major links between Yorubaland and the economies of the wider world outside of Africa. These trans-Saharan links had been in existence even before the founding of the Ife kingdom, and had contributed to the factors that had produced it. Thereafter, they had continued to be important in the economy of Yorubaland, as channels of imports from, and exports to, distant parts of the world – the Mediterranean basin, the Middle East, Asia and Europe. From the early sixteenth century, however, a major, totally different, new channel of contacts with the wider world emerged – namely overseas routes between the coasts of West Africa and Europe. The trans-Saharan channels continued in existence, of course; but they quickly became much less important than the channels over the Atlantic Ocean.

The first Europeans to come to the coasts of West Africa were the Portuguese, who were seeking a sea route around Africa to Asia. They came to the coast of Benin in the 1470s. By then, the Benin kingdom and most of the Yoruba kingdoms were already mature states; and some of them (like Ife, Benin, Ilesa, Ijebu-Ode, Owu, Ode-Ondo, Owo, Oyo-Ile, Ila, and some of the Ekiti kingdoms) were already substantial trading and expansionist states. According to Ila palace traditions,[5] the king of Benin sent envoys to inform the Orangun as well as other kings (like the Ooni of Ife, the Owa of Ilesa and the Ewi of Ado) that some strange white people had visited his kingdom, and some of these kings sent envoys down to Benin to go and see the white people. The envoys returned home with gifts of European articles for their kings from the Oba of Benin – especially pieces of European velvet cloth. The Ewi who first wore such velvet clothing was given the cognomen Owamuaran (the king who wears the velvet cloth).

The Portuguese established a trading station (called a factory) at the Benin port town of Ughoton (Gwarto) and other stations at other places like Ode-Itsekiri. At these places, they bought peppers, ivory (elephant tusks), cloth woven in Benin and Yorubaland, dyestuff, etc. The cloth was sold further west on the coast, especially in exchange for gold, which was derived from Mina (in present day Ghana). The imports included various European manufactures – cloth, metal implements like knives, swords and domestic utensils, ceramic ware, beads, alcoholic beverages, royal luxury articles such as ceremonial umbrellas, expensive cloth, carpets and bugles. Benin traders took these imports to distribute in the interior (mostly in Yorubaland) and brought back from there articles for export, and the wealth and power of Benin were tremendously enhanced. Many towns in eastern and southern Yorubaland became important centers of Benin trade and housed large numbers of Benin traders.

From the opening years of the sixteenth century, European coastal traders established more and more trading locations on the coasts of the Bights of Benin and Biafra. In general, the coasts of Yorubaland did not have natural harbors capable of taking large ships. European traders were attracted by the island of Eko (which the Portuguese began to call Lagos) but the approaches to it were made very difficult by sand bars. On the Ijebu and Ilaje coasts, there was no access even comparable to Lagos. As a result, the major centers of European trade with the Yoruba interior developed away from the Yoruba coasts – in Benin on the western delta of the Niger to the east, and on the Aja coast to the west (where the Aja town of Offra became the leading port, to be superseded in the late seventeenth century by the port of Whydah).

Still, some trade with Europeans started on the Yoruba coast, especially at Lagos and on the Ijebu coast, and grew slowly during the sixteenth century. As would be remembered, these coasts had long been part of an ancient lagoon route connected to the Yoruba interior especially through the Ijebu country and the Ogun River. Later, in the early eighteenth century, Badagry emerged as a new port near Lagos. Although on a smaller scale than through Benin, European goods entered through the Yoruba coastal towns into Yorubaland, a considerable part of such goods penetrating through the coastal Ijebu towns.

Increasingly during the following three centuries, European industrial products became part of the life of Yoruba people. Possession of exotic European goods (like clothing, jewelry, cookware, enamelware, liquor, mugs, even fancy bottles for presenting liquor or palm wine) became part of the symbols of status in Yoruba society. European traders also brought cowries from the Indian Ocean. Strangely, even though the Benin kingdom started in about the sixteenth century to employ some European guns in its wars in parts of Yorubaland, no

Yoruba kingdom armed its soldiers with European guns until the close of the eighteenth century.

Patterns in Internal Trade

The cobweb of trade routes linking all parts of Yorubaland from the beginning of the era of the kingdoms in about the tenth century, to the time of the coming of European trade in the sixteenth century, was essentially a development on route patterns that had long existed, about which much has earlier been said. The growth of trade with Europeans along the coast from the sixteenth century gradually transformed trade and modified the pattern of trade routes. One important change was the rise in the commercial importance of the Yoruba coastal towns like Ode-Itsekiri and Lagos. In spite of the natural obstacle to port activities in Lagos, the volume of its trade as a port slowly grew, and with that, the volume of the old lagoon trade around Lagos multiplied, and the short lagoon routes connecting the Ijebu coastal towns with Lagos assumed heightened importance, generally strengthening such towns as Ikorodu, Igbogun, Epe, Ejinrin, Lekki and Makun. East of the Ijebu coast the Ilaje towns of Mahin, Ugbo and Atijere saw more trade also, but their lack of direct entry to the sea caused them to remain small and insignificant. For much of the sixteenth century, in fact, the ports of the Benin kingdom held the primacy of place among ports important to Yorubaland, and that boosted the importance of the routes through eastern Yorubaland – Owo, the Ekiti towns, Ilesa, Igbomina, to Oyo-Ile and the Nupe country on the Niger. Towards the end of that century, with the development of the Aja coastal towns as important ports, routes southwestwards through Egbado, the far western Yoruba kingdoms (Ketu and others), and through the Aja country, gradually became Yorubaland's busiest routes, to which the trade of Oyo-Ile came to be mostly channeled.

With the rise of Oyo-Ile as the greatest market town in Yorubaland from the late sixteenth century, Oyo shifted the preponderance of the trade generally westwards from Ife, so that Owu more or less came to replace Ife as the preferred central channel of trade with Ijebu, a shift which benefited the Egba towns considerably. The greatest beneficiaries of the general westward shift in trade, however, continued to be the Egbado towns. In the east, with the growth of trade directly northwards with Oyo-Ile through Ijesa and with Nupeland through Igbomina, and directly southwards with Benin, the traditional commercial connection of the eastern Yoruba (Ekiti, Owo and Akoko) with Ife gradually shriveled. Owo continued to be a great center of trade, while Akoko and Ekiti towns northeast of Owo, on the corridor to the Nupe country, grew very rapidly as trade centers. Ikare, Akure, Ikere, Ado, Ara, Otun,

Ikole and some other Ekiti towns became major market towns. Commercial transactions became so large and complex in Ado that one Ewi of the late seventeenth century, Ewi Owakunrugbon (the bearded king), set up at the gate of the Ado palace (overlooking the market place) a powerful shrine named Esu Owakunrugbon, at which difficult commercial disputes could be resolved on oath. The Oye town of Egosi became a major center where Ekiti, Akoko, Yagba, Owo, Benin and Ijesa traders met for trade. Owo, with its subordinate towns of Idoani and Okeluse, remained always a significant junction of many routes and the entrepot at which much of Benin's trade with Yorubaland was done. A special market seems to have developed in Ikole for the sale of undyed Ekiti, Akoko, Igbomina and Yagba cloth (called *ala*). In the Akoko country, a famous periodic market place named Osele developed, attracting Nupe, Benin, Owo, Ekiti, Okun Yoruba and other traders.[6]

As would be obvious from the above, the shifts in the paths of trade tended to leave the south-central parts of Yorubaland – Ife southwards to Ondo, Ikale and Ilaje – considerably lagging behind the regions to the west and east. In addition to those stated above, other reasons were the lack of any ports on the Ilaje coast to attract European trade, and the fact that the Oni River constituted a major obstacle on the road southwards to Ode-Ondo from Ife. Directly north from Ode-Ondo, two towns arose on the banks of the Oni River to handle the trade and traffic across the river – an Ondo town named Oke-Igbo on the southern bank, and an Ife town called Ifetedo on the northern bank. According to Ondo and Ife traditions, however, the river was too prone to flood in the area. Another Ondo town, Ekun (later known as Ile-Oluji), further east in the same forest south of the Oni River, did not fare much better, in spite of its slightly better contact with Ilesa through the Ijesa villages of Odo and Iperindo in the forest north of the river. In the forest south of Ode-Ondo, the Ondo authorities established a trading outpost named Odigbo (literally, "forest gate"), as a junction of the north–south routes and the old east–west forest route from Owo through the Ondo country to the Ijebu country.

These route pattern modifications fitted easily into the age-old complex of market centers linking all of Yorubaland together. As the country had developed, every town or village had one central marketplace and, depending on the size of the town or village, a number of smaller ones. Of such markets, some opened for trade mostly in the morning, others mostly in the late afternoon (from about 3 pm). In 1826, in Oyo-Ile (then the largest of all Yoruba cities), Clapperton saw "seven different markets which are held about three or four o'clock."[7] The central markets of the main cities and towns, as well as some of the lesser ones, were held every four days.

The whole of Yorubaland had, over many centuries, evolved into "market districts," of which there were hundreds.[8] Each market district encompassed many towns and villages and therefore many marketplaces. Each market district was divided into a few sub-districts. The largest of the markets in each sub-district were held every eight days and were therefore known as *oja isan* ("nine-day" markets). One or two markets close to the center and outer boundaries of the whole market district were held every sixteen days (and were therefore known as *oja itadogun* ("seventeen-day markets"). The overall picture, then, was that the leaders of each market district were the *oja itadogun* (seventeen-day markets); the leaders of the market sub-district were the *oja isan* (nine-day markets), and the leaders of the community markets were the *oja orun* (five-day markets).

Every market place had some small, residual, trading going on every day – usually in perishables like vegetables, peppers, and fruits. Then on every fourth day the whole of a community converged on the *oja orun* markets; on every eighth day the sub-district converged on the *oja isan* markets; and on every sixteenth day the whole district converged on the *oja itadogun* markets. The leader markets in each unit were staggered, so that the owner of a large trading business could take her outfit to as many as possible. The big traders usually knew the schedule for virtually all sub-district and district markets across the country. Usually, *oja isan* markets were much larger than *oja orun* markets, and *oja itadogun* markets were the largest – in some cases spreading over many tens of acres of land.

The best known of these large periodic market places was (besides Oyo-Ile), Apomu, situated in Ife territory close to the junction of the territories of the Ife, Owu, Ijebu and Egba kingdoms. But a few others are also known: the Osele market in Ikare in the Akoko country; Egosi in the Oye kingdom in northern Ekiti; Osogbo, a northern Ijesa town in the Osun Valley, close to the Oyo, Ife and Igbomina countries; Saki in the Oyo country, connected to the Egba, Egbado, Ife and Owu countries, and serving as a starting point of the road to the Bariba country and to Gonja; Akure in the southern tip of Ekiti serving the Ekiti, Owo, Ondo, Benin and Ijesa countries, Okeluse and Idoani in the Owo kingdom, serving Ekiti; Akoko, Owo Nupe, Benin, Afenmai and Okun Yoruba traders. Of the great market centers, the ones near the boundaries of Yorubaland with non-Yoruba peoples served as the links between the Yoruba homeland and these non-Yoruba territories. The market system in the Aja country was, however, essentially a western part of the Yoruba market system, and the Aja marketplaces were in every way Yoruba, filled invariably by Yoruba traders and conducting business in the Yoruba language.

The Kingdoms and the Economy: Part I 165

One description by a French slave trader on the coast of the Yoruba-Aja region during the first years of the eighteenth century provides some idea of Yoruba-Aja markets. Between 1702 and 1712, this trader visited the port towns of Whydah and Allada three times, and has left us the following description of a market place in that area:[9]

> One beautiful morning, walking by the market where without exaggeration, there were more than six thousand black men and women, I noticed several things which surprised me. The first was the order and the arrangement of the tents, the different quarters for each kind of merchandise, the peace and order which existed ... This market, surrounded and decorated with trees, could probably be four times bigger than the New Market in Amsterdam, where you have two or three thousand square feet; it was packed full like an egg... it was full of round tents covered with mats.... At least there must have been about two hundred of them and in the center there was a small square place, about forty or fifty feet square, into which led all the roads... These roads were divided into sections; each section was reserved for only one type of merchandise or for those that are related to one another. In one section were the traders of tobacco and pipes. In another traders of dyed cloths, in another those of white cloths; here were mat traders and of baskets, there the sellers of boiled fish, sellers of palm oil occupy one area, while the sellers of cooking pots and earthen pots occupy another; fruit sellers were in their own places, those who sell legumes also were in theirs; sellers of cotton cloth and of cloth made out of bark of trees also had their particular places... In general, everything in this market is arranged in a manner to give pleasure, without confusion... In each section there are five or six tents where one buys food and also places where one buys drinks... I took notice that everything went on without noise, without quarrel, without shouting and in a most tranquil manner. When night approached, each one took his tent, folded his wares, and went away...

About one hundred years later, another traveler, the Englishman Hugh Clapperton, wrote the following description of another market place during a visit to the Yoruba interior:[10]

> We came through the market, which, though nearly sunset, was well supplied with raw cotton, country cloths, provision, and fruit, such as oranges, limes, plantains, bananas, vegetables such as small onions, chalots, pepper and gum for soups, also boiled yams and accasons. Here the crowd rolled on like a sea, the men jumping over the provision baskets, the boys dancing under the stalls, the women bawling and saluting those who were looking after their scattered goods. Yet no word or look of disrespect to us.

The Yoruba marketplace, then, was typically a pleasant place, laid out in order so that merchandise of the same type was displayed side by side. Shade trees, planted in some order, provided both shelter and decoration. Traders built their own tents in accordance with specifications acceptable to the authorities (especially to the leaderships of the market associations), or used portable tents. Sellers and buyers alike paid careful attention to the preservation of law and order, even though their haggling usually generated a lot of noise. Commotion or disruption in a market place was, among all Yoruba, regarded as a terrible omen, and saying that a town's marketplace broke down was equivalent to saying that the town itself broke down. Therefore, any breach of the peace in the marketplace was visited with very severe penalties and called for ritual sacrifices. The Yoruba marketplace was much more than a place of buying and selling; it was the heart of its community – a place which exercised powerful influence on the government, the place of some of society's most powerful shrines and rituals, the place where young people found and courted their future spouses. Sellers of the same or similar merchandise formed a commodity association, with its own officers, rules, rituals and festivals. These market commodity associations were the richest, and among the most influential, associations in every Yoruba community. Between them, they established the site rules for the market place and bore most of the responsibility for maintaining law and order there. The president of each association, with the title of Iyalaje, was one of the most influential persons in society.

The American Baptist missionary, T. J. Bowen, wrote in the 1850s an eyewitness account of one day in the life of a Yoruba marketplace which specialized in evening trade. In an evening market, some trading usually commenced early in the morning, for the sale of produce. Then in the late afternoon, as stated earlier, the real crowd of traders and buyers arrived. Bowen wrote:[11]

> The most attractive next to the curious old town itself… is the market. This is not a building but a large area shaded with trees, and surrounded and sometimes sprinkled over with low thatched roofs surmounted on rude posts. Here the women sit and chat all day, from early morning till nine o'clock at night to sell their different merchandise. The principal marketing hour and the proper time to see all the wonders is in the evening. At half an hour before sunset, all sorts of people, men, women, girls, travelers, lately arrived in the caravans, farmers from the field and artisans from their houses, are pouring in from all directions to buy and sell and talk. At the distance of half a mile their united voices roar like the waves of the sea. The women, especially, always noisy, are then in their glory bawling out salutation, cheapening, giggling, conversing, laughing and sometimes quarreling, with a shrilling and compass of voice which indicates both their determination and their ability to make themselves heard. As the shade of the evening deepens, if the weather allows the market to continue and there is no moon, every woman lights her little lamp, and presently

the market presents to the distant observer, the beautiful appearance of innumerable bright stars.

Rooted in a local market, but operating far and wide in order to serve it and other markets, there were two classes of big traders. The first, known as the *alarobo*, did business as gatherers of local produce from the producers, for wholesale distribution to retailers in local markets. The other, known as the *alajapa*, did business as long-distance traders all over the Yoruba homeland and beyond, taking the products of one part of the country to local retailers in other parts. Persons engaged in these levels of commerce were usually the richest in society, and commanded large trading establishments employing large numbers of porters. The *alajapa* usually became very knowledgeable about trading conditions in various parts of Yorubaland. Those of them who took trade beyond Yorubaland often became fluent in foreign languages.

These owners of large trading businesses, and the numberless small traders, kept the roads throughout Yorubaland constantly busy. Human porters carried their goods. Usually, the big trader sent out large teams of porters in different directions, with herself leading the most important team, while members of her family or trusted servants led the others. After traveling over much of Yorubaland in the 1850s and meeting these teams everywhere, T. J. Bowen described Yorubaland as "a land of caravans." Some caravans could number many hundreds of people. In some parts of the country, especially in the more open grassland areas of northern and western Yorubaland, horses played a small part in the carrying of people and of goods.

The trade routes were paths trodden by humans (and, in some areas, horses) over many centuries. In accordance with ancient practices, each town cleared the sections of the paths that traversed its territory, the clearing being done on the days of certain festivals by the male population. According to Samuel Johnson, the paths in the Oyo area of northwestern Yorubaland were cleared twice a year – during the *egungun* and *ayan* (drum music) festivals. In the thick forests of the south (in the Ijebu, Egba, Ondo and Owo areas) clearing was done more often. Each kingdom was responsible for maintaining peace on the paths that went through its territory. Usually the paths were well maintained and protected. The authorities of kingdoms, towns and villages, had vested interests in ensuring good paths, since the best and safest paths attracted the most traders and trade. If there was some threat of danger on a road, the local authorities would usually send armed escorts to accompany the caravans. The English explorer, Clapperton, traveled on the road from Badagry on the coast to Oyo-Ile in 1825–6 and his general assessment was that the road was good and peaceful, and quite pleasant in some sections.[12] Unfortunately, the transcriber of his notes had difficulty with the Yoruba place names, as a result of which some of the towns visited by him are now impossible to identify. Between a town named "Dagmoo" in his diary and the town of Ihumbo, Clapperton noted that the road surface was "rather uneven" and that the forest on either side of it was thick and impenetrable. Soon after, however, between "Atalaboloo" and Ilaro, the road lay "through fine plantations of yams" and was "nearly as level as a bowling green." Between Ilaro and Ijanna, the road lay "through large plantations of corn and yams and fine avenues of trees" in some sections, and through "plantations of millet, yams, avalanches (sic), and Indian corn" in other sections. Between "Ega" and "Emado," the road was "a long broad and beautiful avenue of the tallest trees." Between "Washoo" and Saki, the road lay through a mountain pass that was "grand and imposing, sometimes rising almost perpendicularly, and then descending in the midst of rocks into dells, then winding beautifully round the side of a steep hill." Of the towns that lay on Clapperton's route, he noted of Eruwa that it was "large and very populous," and of "Kooso" (Koso) that it was "a large walled town." These western parts of Yorubaland had started to experience minor political troubles by the time of Clapperton's 1825 visit. For instance, he wrote of one small town that it had suffered destruction and that its "gate and the ditch are now all that remain." In spite of such political conditions, Clapperton met streams of traders on the road, all going about their business without molestation. He himself commented at a point that he had done sixty miles in eight days and changed carriers many times, and yet he had not had even the smallest thing stolen from him.

Some three decades after 1825, by which time Yorubaland's political troubles had widened and deepened, many literate foreign travelers traversed the country, passing through many towns ruined or troubled by war. Even in such circumstances, they met streams of traders on the roads. From late 1855 to early 1856, the pioneer Anglican missionary, David Hinderer, accompanied by Dr. Irving, traveled from Ibadan to Ijebu-Ode at the invitation of the Awujale Ademiyewo Fidipote.[13] After leaving Ibadan, Hinderer and his companions passed through the ruins of many Egba towns. At Idomapa, the road divided, one arm going direct to Ijebu-Ode and the other to the Remo area. They chose the Remo branch and, after passing through the ruins of a few more Egba towns, came to the Remo town of Ipara, their first Ijebu town. In spite of the melancholy sight of ruined towns, Hinderer noted that "a beautiful country opened before us on all sides." At Omi, they joined the company of a large caravan of Ijebu traders and, soon after, Hinderer noted that their path led through "a most beautiful palm field, abundance of kola trees ..." Most of the road from there to Ofin, and from Ofin to Ijebu-Ode, was quite good, in spite of some political trouble on the approach to Ofin. It was during this visit that Hinderer described the ancient wall around Ijebu-Ode (the Eredo Sungbo) as "a wonderfully deep trench." From Ijebu-Ode they headed down to Ikorodu on the Ijebu creeks.

In 1855, A. C. Mann, a missionary based in Ijaye, traveled from Ijaye to Ilorin, passing through Ogbomoso and the ruins of the formerly great city of Ikoyi. In 1858, Hinderer traveled the road from Ibadan to Iwo, Ede, Osogbo, Ilesa, Ile-Ife and Apomu. And in the same year, the American Baptist missionary, T. J. Bowen, and the English commercial traveler, Daniel May, traveled various roads that led to the Ijesa, Igbomina and Ekiti countries.[14] It was during his travels in northern Ekiti that May met Esugbayibi building the town of Aiyede close to Isan. All of these travelers found that, in spite of wars in many places, the roads through Yorubaland were reasonably well maintained and safe, and carried a heavy traffic of traders.

Fundamental Commercial Advantages

For the establishment of this strong commercial civilization, the Yoruba people benefited from a number of initial fundamental advantages.[15] The most important was that theirs was a large country linked closely together by one language and one culture – the largest of such units of territory in all of the tropical forests of Africa. From the territories of the Okun Yoruba and the Akoko close to the western banks of the lower Niger, all the way westwards to the homelands of the Itsha and Ife of modern Benin and Togo, and from the seacoast northwards to latitude 9° north (on the southern banks of the River Niger), Yorubaland occupied about half of the West African tropical forests. Though this vast country was not one but many states, all its states had the same basic system of government, and all its people lived the same pattern of community and economic life, married and raised their children in more or less the same way, worshipped the same pantheon of gods and spirits, and spoke mutually intelligible dialects of the same language.

In fact, by the time that the trade with Europe started, the Yoruba language had become the lingua franca for peoples beyond the Yoruba ethnic homeland. Writing about the Aja kingdom of Allada in 1668, Dapper said: "Their own mother tongue is by them little regarded; therefore they seldom speak it; but they are obliged to speak mostly Alkomijs which in their country is regarded as a noble language."[16] One Father Columbin of Nantes visited the coast of West Africa as head of the French mission in 1634 and 1640. In a letter to the higher authorities of the mission, he wrote as follows about the Benin kingdom:

> In this kingdom the people may very easily be led to embrace the faith, and priests can live here with greater ease than in other parts of Guinea because of

the healthy climate … Their language is simple; it is called Licomin language and is universally used in these parts, just like Latin in Europe.[17]

Europeans along the West African coast called the Yoruba Lukumi, Lucumi or Alkomin (and endless variations of it) and the Yoruba language Alkomijs, Licomin (and other variations). Thus, Dapper's Alkomijs and Father Columbin's Licomin meant the same – the Yoruba language. The use of the Yoruba language, therefore, linked together not only all parts of the Yoruba homeland but also areas extending beyond. As earlier pointed out, the Aja country, commercially, was essentially part of western Yorubaland. Such an expansive cultural and linguistic continuum provided great opportunities for commercial development.

The creation of the Yoruba cities and towns, some housing the thrones of kings, all ruled by well-organized governments, was another important factor. It opened up and civilized the Yoruba forest and grass homeland and turned it into a land wherein people could roam at will.

Finally, the whole of the Yoruba homeland, together with its cultural and economic extensions to the east and west, had one single common monetary system, one currency – namely cowries. In the whole area, cowries were an ancient currency. From their earliest contacts with the Benin and Yoruba coastland in the early sixteenth century, European traders found cowries as its common currency. One French trader wrote in the eighteenth century: "Cowries are the currency of the country and consequently they are accepted for all goods, even gold, which they regard as no more than an article of trade. Among the Blacks you can buy with cowries anything that gold or silver will buy in Europe."[18] A small amount of trade by barter seems to have survived in some parts of the country until the nineteenth century (for example, the exchange of beads for other goods), but in general, cowries were the currency, and its value was roughly the same in most parts (though there were minor differences in some places). To make trade easier, even European traders had to harmonize their own currencies with the cowry currency, determining how many cowries were equivalent to their own pound or franc. The existence of the common currency in cowries facilitated trade in the broad region comprising the Yoruba, Edo and Aja countries – and even beyond.

The Impact of the Atlantic Slave Trade

In the opening years of the sixteenth century, some slaves became part of the export cargo on European ships leaving the port of Benin. Some of the first slaves were taken to supply labor to the islands off the coast of West Africa (São Tome, Principe and Fernando Po) where the Europeans began to develop plantations of sugar cane. Some were also taken to Europe as domestic servants. Then, as various European nationalities (Portuguese, Spanish, Dutch, French and English) acquired islands in the West Indies and embarked on large-scale plantations there and in Brazil, the demand for slaves increased, and these nations entered into the trans-Atlantic slave trade on a big scale. By the beginning of the seventeenth century, slaves were already dominating the export trade from the coasts of West Africa and Central Africa (that is, Angola and the Congo region).

The ports on the Aja coast (Whydah, Jakin, Offra, Apa and, later Ajase or Porto Novo) and the ports of the Niger Delta east of Benin (Calabar, Bonny and New Calabar) handled the overwhelming part of slave exports from the Bights of Benin and Biafra for about 250 years, from the early sixteenth century to about the middle of the eighteenth century. Compared to these, the number of slaves exported from the coasts of Yorubaland during the sixteenth and seventeenth centuries was small. The Portuguese trader, Duarte Pacheco Perreira, wrote in the sixteenth century about the Ijebu coast that "the trade which one can conduct here is the trade in slaves, who are sold for brass bracelets, at the rate of twelve to fifteen bracelets for a slave, and in elephants' tusks."[19] Some slaves were exported from some parts of the Yoruba coasts, then, but these were, according to available data, few. Small too was the number of Yoruba exported from the port of Benin and from the ports of the Aja coast.

In short then, during the sixteenth and seventeenth centuries and the first half of the eighteenth (1500–1750), the number of persons exported from Yorubaland as slaves was small – according to some estimates about 240,000, that is less than an average of one thousand slaves per year. And probably most of these were not persons of Yoruba descent, since Yoruba people bought many slaves from the Nupe, Borgu and the Hausa on and beyond the Niger whom they then sold on the coast, and since the Oyo people, beginning from the seventeenth century, sold many of their Nupe, Bariba and Aja captives – products of the Oyo wars of expansion.

Why then were Yoruba people so comparatively little involved as part of enslaved human exports from West Africa from the sixteenth to the middle of the eighteenth century? Historians have suggested various answers to this question. Most believe that the answer is to be found in the fact that Yorubaland in general was comparatively peaceful through most of this long period. Conflicts occurred between Yoruba kingdoms in a number of regions of the country, but these were mostly local affairs of usually short duration and small impact. Much more important than such conflicts was the general belief among Yoruba kings that they belonged to one family. Of that family, the most powerful from the seventeenth century was the Alaafin of Oyo, and the available evidence indicates that most other Yoruba kings recognized him as their powerful brother, while many of the kingdoms (like most of the Igbomina kingdoms, and many other kingdoms in the far west, the Egba and Owu kingdoms) were absorbed, with varying statuses, under the Alaafin's overlordship. But military conquest does not seem to have been Oyo's usual way of dealing with other Yoruba states. Oyo's great wars of expansion were fought not against Yoruba kingdoms but against non-Yoruba peoples like the Bariba of Borgu, the Nupe, and the Aja. To the Igbomina country for instance, Oyo armies came, not to conquer the Igbomina, but to expel the Nupe who were making a strong bid over that part of northern Yorubaland. And, according to Biobaku, the establishment of Oyo's suzerainty over the Egba was accomplished without violence, and the Egba were pleased to have the Alaafin's protection. Widespread traditions indicate quite clearly also that the Alaafin frequently employed his enormous influence to settle disputes between Yoruba kingdoms and even within some kingdoms. From the southeast, the Benin kingdom was a great power like Oyo, but, on the whole, the Benin kingdom was much more a great trading power in southern Yorubaland than anything else. Benin did not employ its power in endless or even frequent aggression and raids but in sharp, focused, actions that were meant to deal with particular (mostly commercial) problems; and for long periods in the seventeenth and eighteenth centuries Benin did not, or could not, launch such actions. Among Benin's neighbors in southern and eastern Yorubaland, its image in general was not that of a raider but that of a strong, well-ordered, kingdom that insisted on being respected – in particular, on having its traders treated well. On the whole, the power and influence of Oyo in the northwest and the power and influence of Benin in the southeast were together strong guarantees of order and peace in the Yoruba–Edo world. Old sayings and proverbs among the Ekiti portray the two as pillars of order.

The very nature of Yoruba society itself seems to have been fundamental to this fabric of order and peace. The lineage in its *agbo-ile* was a formidable guarantor of respect for its members. It was also a formidable defense for strangers lodged under its shelter – whether permanent or long-time residents or transient travelers. Abusing or violating a member of a lineage, or a stranger resident with it, was usually sure to lead to civil commotion. It was a grave matter when a lineage complained that the king or chief had ill-treated its members, and, historically, many kings' troubles with the political system started from such complaints. One of the early kings of Ife was assassinated in the streets during a festival procession, and one of the reasons given in the traditions is that he had laid hold on a man and sacrificed him during a ritual – as a result of which he had angered the man's lineage and other lineages related to it. The honor of the lineage was very important to its members, and every lineage had close connections with some others. In the plural society that was every Yoruba community, people in general, and the rulers in particular, were customarily cognizant and respectful of these facts.

Beyond each community too, governments behaved towards one another in much the same way. Respect for persons from other communities was strict law in every Yoruba community. A community that, for whatever reason, sought trouble with its neighbor would usually attack the neighbor's citizens who had come to trade or to do other business, knowing quite well that the authorities of that other community were almost sure to respond with some aggressive action.

All these patterns of sensitivity, then, tended to protect the individual and his freedom and dignity. It was crucial to the freedom with which Yoruba traders (mostly women), herbalists, diviners, entertainers and others endlessly traversed their country to ply their trades. Even in spite of disruptions caused by long wars in Yorubaland in the second half of the nineteenth century, the culture of widespread, long-distance, trade and travel proved irrepressible.

Concerning the sources of the few Yoruba persons who ended up as enslaved exports from the sixteenth century to the end of the seventeenth century, the available evidence is not very strong. It seems fairly certain that most Yoruba governments came to adopt the practice of authorizing the sale of convicts – especially hardened criminals who were embarrassments to their lineages and had been renounced by them. Richard Lander noted, during his visit to Oyo-Ile in 1826, the age-old Yoruba practice of dealing with such a convict. The "ministers of justice" would, he said, inflict incisions over his facial marks, thus irreversibly disfiguring him.[20] This was a notice to society that the man had been rejected, renounced and expunged by his lineage. Usually, he would run away to some distant place, but even there he would suffer life-long rejection and scorn and die miserably. With the coming of the Atlantic slave trade, such criminals were authorized to be taken to the coast and sold to European traders – but their numbers were, on the whole, small.

Some other slave exports – almost certainly the overwhelming majority of Yoruba in slave exports in the sixteenth and seventeenth centuries – resulted from occasional invasions of Yoruba frontier territories by non-Yoruba neighbors. Although the Oyo armies had expelled the Nupe from the northern and northeastern parts of Yorubaland in the early seventeenth century, the Nupe never ceased sporadic incursions into the countries of the Igbomina, the Okun Yoruba, the northern Ekiti and the Akoko. Captives from these raids were usually sold into slavery and formed part of the slaves from the Nupe country that found their way into slave ships along the coast through the labyrinth of mostly concealed slave routes to the coast. Also, although the Benin kingdom was essentially not a slave-raiding state, some war captives from Benin wars in eastern Yorubaland were sold as slave exports. And, in the far western region of Yorubaland, the rising kingdom of Dahomey from the late seventeenth century embarked on much military activity among other Aja and neighboring Yoruba peoples, as a result of which some Yoruba were among the increasing numbers of slaves sold at the ports of the Aja coast.

Some historians have suggested that a good part of Yorubas who ended up on slave ships were domestic slaves. The supposition is that, before the coming of Europeans the institution of domestic slavery was common and widespread in Yorubaland, that domestic slaves were a substantial part of labor in the Yoruba economy, and that when Europeans came asking for slaves, Yoruba owners of slaves had them to sell. It has been assumed that there was, among every African people, a large class of domestic slaves waiting to be sold to Europeans. In recent studies, however, this view has been shown to be untrue about many African peoples; for example, Walter Rodney has shown that among the peoples of the Upper Guinea coast there was no slave class waiting to be sold to European slave traders.[21]

Similar conclusions appear to be true of Yorubaland. In his thesis on the Owo kingdom, Oladipo Olugbadehan finds that Benin traders, increasingly active in Owo from as early as the fourteenth century, never bought slaves in Owo – because, according to him, there were no slaves to buy. Benin invasions occasionally produced Owo war captives, some of whom were sold into the coastal trade.[22] Similarly, no Ekiti traditions speak of Benin traders buying slaves in any Ekiti town, but traditions of Ekiti communities and lineages losing some members to Benin invasions abound.

What would seem to have been the case is that there were indeed domestic slaves in Yoruba society long before the coming of Europeans, but that selling and buying of slaves was rare. A person captured in any of the few internal wars of the Yoruba kingdoms became an *eru* – meaning, roughly, a "slave." Usually, many (often most) of the *eru* would end up as palace servants, and the king would reward the most worthy of his chiefs (especially the war chiefs) with the rest. This made the owning of *eru* virtually an exclusive preserve of the powerful and influential, before domestic slavery became common and widespread in the nineteenth century. Also, before the *eru* status became grossly degraded in the nineteenth century, an *eru* was only technically a slave. If he served the palace, there was no status difference between him and other palace servants; his rank, and how high he could rise in the king's service, depended on his character and capabilities. In palaces all over Yorubaland, persons who came as *eru* commonly rose to the highest and most influential of positions and even married kings' daughters. If an *eru* belonged to someone lower than the king he could, besides serving his master, raise crops of his own (on the farmland of his master's lineage) or establish some other enterprise. Unless he had some serious character blemish, he could (and often would) marry his master's relative or even daughter, and that would usually transform him into a member of the lineage, with nearly all the rights and privileges of membership. (If there was a chieftaincy title in the lineage, he could not, usually, aspire to it, but his sons later could.) He could also inherit from his master's belongings. He could serve in the king's armed forces if war came, and distinguished performance there would usually raise him to honor and influence. Character was, for an *eru*, the all-decisive factor. If an *eru* exhibited extremely poor character and committed criminal or shameful acts, his master could punish him. However, it was a serious crime to kill an *eru* or subject an *eru* to life-threatening treatment. Universal fear of hurting an *eru* (and thereby committing a serious crime) is, according to Chief Isola Fabunmi of Ife,[23] illustrated by the dire warning expressed in the words of this old Ife folk song:

Mo nre 'le o	I must leave you
Oku ole	You fool of a coward;
O b' eru ja!	You want to fight an *eru*!
B' eru ba ku sio lorun	If the *eru* dies by your hand,
K' o a ti se?	What are you going to do?

In fact, the master's penal authority over his *eru* covered small domestic offences only; if the *eru* committed a serious crime, the master could not usurp the judicial and penal authority of the state. Legally, a master could sell his *eru*, but selling was not a common part of the system. Selling was punishment – an extreme act of rejection and renunciation, and it was not commonly resorted to. And there is some evidence that selling was not even a decision that the master could take entirely on his own – without the input of the people of his lineage compound. Hence the saying "*Bi a o ba ta eru p' owo, ajoro omo ni.*" (If an *eru* is to be sold, the decision would have to be taken by a caucus of the free people – of the lineage.)

Some corroboration for this is provided by Richard Lander, visiting Yorubaland in 1825–6 and in 1830.[24] Lander wrote that the conditions of slaves in Yoruba society were much better than those of slaves of European planters in the Americas or even of slaves employed as domestic servants in European homes. Of the domestic slave in Yoruba society he wrote:

> If his character be good and his honesty unquestioned, the slave ... is admitted into the house of his master, placed on an equality with himself and male

children, thrusts his hand into the same bowl of tuah (food) as they, shares their confidence, and participates in all their pleasures and amusements.

Concerning the selling of domestic slaves, Lander wrote:

> An instance is never known of a dependent (domestic slave), having an unblemished character, and active industrious habits, being sent to the coast to be sold; in fact everyone considers this to be the greatest punishment that can be inflicted upon him …Those (domestic slaves) sent to the sea-side from the interior are invariably the scum and refuse of the country – freebooters, lawless refractory fellows, adulterers, and even murderers.[25]

And the available evidence strongly indicates that, as would be remembered, even such persons were few on the slave ships before the late eighteenth century.

In summary, in the present state of our knowledge, the available evidence would seem to suggest the following picture concerning the part played by domestic slavery in the sale of Yoruba people into the Atlantic slave trade. Before the advent of European coastal trade, there existed in Yorubaland certain types of subordinate statuses of which servitude was a component – notably the *iwofa* and *eru* systems. The *iwofa* system never involved sale of persons; the *eru* system could, but did so very infrequently. Neither, legally, permitted inhuman handling of the subordinate persons. The slave trade with Europeans on the coast from the sixteenth century started to generate slaves from various other sources – essentially from among captives in on-going wars, rather than from any pre-existing domestic pool. Of such wars some were local wars between Yoruba states, others were invasions of Yorubaland by non-Yoruba neighbors (like Benin, the Nupe and the Bariba), and yet others were Yoruba invasions of the countries of non-Yoruba neighbors (Oyo invasions of Nupe, Bariba and Aja territories). Among the Yoruba, the Oyo, being rulers and citizens of the most powerful (and expansionist) Yoruba kingdom, and being almost perpetually at hostility with non-Yoruba neighbors, became the most drawn into the slave trade, selling their war captives, and buying other slaves from the Nupe, Bariba, Hausa and Aja for sale. The Oyo-Ile kingdom started to expand over one century after the coming of European coastal trade, and independently of it. Oyo's widening expansion and the growth of the coastal trade coincided as major developments of the seventeenth and eighteenth centuries. In the process, the two developments converged and, by the late eighteenth century, Oyo had become a considerable slave-trading power, deriving some growing wealth from the sale of slaves. Tapping into the slave trade became more and more attractive to ambitious Oyo people, and by the last decades of the eighteenth century, many prominent Oyo men and women were involved in the trade. Oyo's trade

The Kingdoms and the Economy: Part I 177

in slaves brought coast-bound slaves through many of Yorubaland's trade routes – especially the trade routes passing through the Owu and Ijebu territories, and the Egba, Egbado and far western Yoruba territories. In these places, the people living near the coast became the middlemen on the trade, buying from the Oyo traders and selling to the Europeans on the coast. Of such middlemen, the Ijebu became the most numerous and richest.

One of the results of the growing trade in slaves was the expansion of personal ownership of domestic slaves, especially in the Oyo country, but also in other parts of Yorubaland (particularly places close to the ports – Ijebu, Awori, Egbado and the farther western Yoruba subgroups). Another, according to widespread Yoruba traditions, was the beginning and growth of kidnapping of people for sale, mostly to coast-bound traders. Kidnappings were probably few, but they were made to seem numerous by rumors and popular fears; therefore, it is not surprising that the authorities in many kingdoms took action against kidnapping. It was most probably in order to keep out strangers who might be kidnappers that the Ijebu-Ode authorities turned their great city into a land where strangers who could not give clear accounts of themselves faced the danger of being arrested and sacrificed at the shrines. Ilesa traditions are unambiguous that some of the skulls displayed on the Ilesa city walls were of suspicious strangers. And Ado (Ekiti) traditions speak of suspicious strangers dragged to the palace and made to swear at the Esu-Owakunrugbon shrine, or sacrificed at the shrine if their accounts of themselves proved unsatisfactory. Both the slave trade and slavery gradually grew (in the western parts of Yorubaland more than in the eastern) during the late eighteenth century – ultimately, as will be seen in subsequent chapters, reaching a climax by the second quarter of the nineteenth century as a result of the Yoruba wars of that century.

In the 250 years between 1500 and 1750, in summary, the effects of the slave trade on Yorubaland would seem to have been almost unnoticeable. The number of Yoruba people involved in slave exports was generally small. In terms of regions of Yorubaland, the most affected in these years (especially from the seventeenth century) would seem to have been eastern Yorubaland – as a result of Benin invasions in Owo, Ekiti and Akoko, and Nupe aggression in the countries of the Igbomina, Okun Yoruba, Akoko, and parts of northern Ekiti and northern Ijesa. Of the comparatively few Yoruba persons exported as slaves during these 250 years, the majority most probably came from these places. Of the rest, a slowly increasing number would have come from the regions of Yorubaland more directly exposed to the influence of the coastal trade – Ijebu, Awori, Egbado, Egba, Oyo, and the various Yoruba subgroups in the southern parts of the modern Benin Republic (Ahori and others). These western subgroups would also have increased in the slave exports from about the late seventeenth century as a result of the rise of the Dahomey kingdom and its tendency to aggression against its neighbors. The expansion of Oyo towards the southwest from the end of the seventeenth century, while greatly increasing the number of Aja slave exports, would also have increased the number of Oyo elements ending up on slave ships.

In the last fifty years of the eighteenth century (1750–1800), most of the above trends gradually intensified and produced marked increases in the number of Yoruba people being exported as slaves (resulting in an estimated total of about 300,000 for the fifty years). For instance, Nupe aggression intensified in the lands of the Igbomina, Okun Yoruba, Akoko and northern Ekiti. Increased participation in the slave trade by Oyo people (as well as the gradual deterioration of security in the Oyo homeland owing to growing political instability) markedly increased the number of Oyo elements in the slave exports. All these and other factors continued to intensify into the nineteenth century, resulting in sharp increases in the number of enslaved Yoruba people being exported in the course of its first half.

10

The Kingdoms and the Economy: Part II

This chapter continues our consideration of the economy of the Yoruba kingdoms from about the eleventh century to the end of the eighteenth century. Here, we will focus on specific features and institutions of the economy. In-depth studies of some of these subjects (such as royal finances, savings, credit and loans systems) have intensified in recent times, we are indebted to such studies. We will then conclude this chapter with a general eighteenth century economic and social overview – the eighteenth century being the concluding century of the period covered here and in the previous chapter.

Royal Finances

Much, even most, of the financial resources available to the king's government in every Yoruba kingdom came from tolls and taxes on commerce.[1] With the exception of produce from local farms, all merchandise was subject to some tolls at the gates. The *onibode* (gate keeper) was therefore, in every kingdom, a very important public official – usually a trusted palace servant honored with a chieftaincy title. In many kingdoms, these positions became hereditary in certain lineages, with the result that such lineages became trusted pillars of the monarchical system. The amount of revenue accruing to the government of a kingdom from tolls depended on the volume of trade, especially long-distance trade, passing through its gates – and for this reason governments paid very particular attention to the quality of their roads and to the protection of peace on their roads.

Tolls and taxes from the king's marketplace constituted another source of income. Practice in the collection of such market tolls and taxes varied from kingdom to kingdom. In general, it was accepted by all traders that the king's servants could demand customary payments to the king on the *iso* (stall or location in the market) or on particular articles of merchandise. It was also generally accepted that the king could, through his servants, demand from traders payments or gifts on important state occasions like festivals, rituals and sacrifices, repairs and other work on palace buildings, and towards the support of war efforts. Palace servants usually received liberal gifts from traders for themselves on a more or less regular basis, and so did wives of the king whenever they came to the market to buy. Again, the amount of royal revenue from the various tolls, levies, and taxes from marketplaces depended on the volume of trade. The kingdoms that were great centers of trade and had many large marketplaces commanded rich treasuries.

Another source of royal revenue derived from a kingdom's subordinate towns and villages (*ereko*). Again, although gifts to the king on important state occasions, and contributions in men and materials to work on the palace and on city walls and to the king's war efforts, were standard practice, details of practice varied from kingdom to kingdom. Unlike most kingdoms, the Oyo-Ile palace seems to have developed early the practice of regular annual and seasonal levies on its subordinate towns and villages, levies graduated according to their sizes and means. At the peak of the power and greatness of the Oyo Empire, every kingdom in the Oyo country sent regular annual tributes and gifts to the Alaafin. It was common practice in some kingdoms that the king occasionally sent high chiefs to visit the subordinate (or *ereko*) towns and villages, with the understanding that such envoys would return with rich gifts for the king.

There were, moreover, in every kingdom a large number of traditional rules, observances and practices, as well as many provisions and customs of the judicial system that generated revenue (in money, materials and services) for the king. If the palace intervened and settled disputes within or between lineages or individuals, all sides were customarily required to send gifts to the king in order to thank him. When prominent members of a lineage contested a vacant chieftaincy title in their lineage, the candidate who was believed to be closest or most acceptable to the king usually had the best chance of winning among members of his own lineage. This always meant gifts to the king, and to his wives and servants, by contestants for chieftaincy titles. The traditional rules laid it down that a candidate for installation to any chieftaincy title must make some payment to the king, and the type and amount of such payment were graduated according to the importance of the title in the political system. All Yoruba regarded certain animals in the wild (such as leopards and elephants) as royal property. Therefore, any hunter or farmer who killed any of them must surrender it to the king. Surrendering the skin, or in the case of the elephant, the tusks, was usually sufficient for compliance. During ceremonies (festivals, funerals, weddings, etc.) any lineage that slaughtered certain types of animals (especially a cow) was customarily expected to send a part of it to the palace. Funeral rites for notable citizens included gifts to the king, and many families would make such gifts very rich – as a means of bragging about the prosperity of their departed parents. In many kingdoms, gifts of this type evolved into well regulated taxes. In general, gifts to the king and the chiefs during important festivals were regarded as part of civilized life and, in all parts of Yorubaland, the rich were constantly engaged in a lively rivalry over this. Together, all of these customary payments and gifts amounted to a substantial flow of resources to the palace, especially if a kingdom had many rich, proud, lineages, and rich citizens (big farmers, traders, artisans). Hence the old saying that it is foolish to count the king when counting the rich people in a town: though the king might have no visible business, the cumulative flow to him from the wealth of all citizens made him much richer than even the richest citizen.

Finally, Yoruba kings derived some income from their own primary production – in agriculture. Many a royal town had a large plot of land immediately outside the town walls, known as *oko oba* or *oko owa* (king's farmland), where the king's servants and slaves raised crops for him on a regular basis – usually out of bounds to the general populace. Apart from supplying the king's large family and palace establishment, yields from such farms also supplied the open market. Typically, when the king's servants brought his produce to the market, other traders deferred to them to let them sell it before spreading out their own goods of the same type for sale. The king usually had more servants and slaves than any of his subjects; even though many of such servants and slaves were employed in state and palace duties, the rest probably cultivated farms for the king that rivaled those of some of his richest subjects. As will be seen later, Yoruba rulers in the nineteenth century generally maintained extensive farms – and in doing so, they were certainly continuing a well-established Yoruba tradition.

Labor in the Economy[2]

On the lineage farmland (in the near-town farms and the distant forest farms) the individual male member of a lineage was free to farm as much land as he had the capacity for – with the strict provision, of course, that he should not encroach on land already being used by other members or on land deliberately left fallow. He could clear and farm any number of plots. In general, he had the right of first return to any piece of land he had first cleared of virgin forest and farmed and then left fallow. Effectively, his limitations were the labor available to him and the efficacy of his tools (hoes, cutlasses or machetes, and other iron-bladed tools like axes and knives).

The primary source of the farmer's labor supply was his nuclear family – himself and his teenage sons and unmarried young adult sons, assisted by his wife (or wives) and unmarried daughters. To increase this primary labor base, ambitious men married many wives and raised many children. Beyond this, there were some supplementary labor sources. Youthful married (and therefore independent) sons, as well as sons-in-law, usually came in once or twice in the year to give free assistance on particular tasks – like land clearing or tilling. Then there were two systems of mutual labor pooling – one called *owe* and the other called *aaro*. To create (or call) an *owe*, a farmer set a date and invited his relations (young male members of his lineage and related lineages), his sons-in-law, his married sons, his sons' friends and others, to come and work with him and his family on his farm, usually on heavier tasks like cutting the bush or tilling the soil. Labor given on *owe* was pure grant: it did not have to be repaid or reciprocated. *Owe* usually lasted one day or, at the longest, two, and was commonly called by ambitious farmers – as well as by older farmers past their prime. Depending on the number of men present, it could get a lot of work done – especially because it was usually characterized by a lively rivalry among the young men. *Aaro* was a system of labor pooling by a group of friends to work in rotation on one another's farms. The *owe* or *aaro* day was usually a day of work and fun, with food and palm wine provided by the host for the lunch-break and the end of the day.

Hired farm labor also existed. Usually a married young man would, in addition to work on his own farm, set some time aside to hire out his labor for some income in cash or kind (especially seed yam). Sometimes, such young men would form a work team and go around to offer their services to one big farmer after another, even far beyond their own towns or villages. Also, a young man faced with a projected large expenditure (for a parent's funeral, a parent's installation as chief, or his own plan to take one more wife) might partly shut down his own farming for a season in order to go and accumulate cash, either through a series of quick farm jobs or through one long employment with a substantial farmer. Available for employment in the same way on farms were young men who had completed their training as apprentices in a trade or craft and needed money to perform the prescribed ritual and celebration of their graduation.

Exploiting combinations of these sources of labor, an ambitious farmer could cultivate as large a farm as the technology (the iron-bladed machetes and hoes) made possible. Within this context, quite sizeable farms became generally common all over Yorubaland. No doubt, most farmers produced for subsistence or just a little above it, but the most ambitious went far beyond the level of subsistence farming and established extensive farms for the market, becoming thereby men of considerable wealth. At some point or other in their history, most lineages had one or two such great farmers, and their accomplishments passed into the lineage praise poetry (or *oriki*).

For the manufacturers and the craftsmen, the most important source of labor was the apprenticeship system. To become a blacksmith, coppersmith or artist, cloth weaver, mat weaver, raffia products weaver, cane and rattan craftsman, wood sculptor, carpenter, mud-wall builder, tailor, herbalist, diviner, etc., a young person had to learn under a master. Each industry or craft had its own number of years for apprenticeship, and the apprentices, as they matured in training, served as the master's labor force. After training, some would remain behind and become part of the master's permanent staff; others would go to work for other masters or start out on their own.

For production, master manufacturers and artisans also employed a system of subcontracting jobs to smaller people. In the cotton-weaving industry, for instance, large-scale producers, as a supplement to the labor directly available to them, often had to farm out weaving jobs to people in the community. Women and men who had good weaving skills but who were engaged mostly in other pursuits (nursing mothers, small traders, farmers, for example) would register their names with the large-scale producer, and the latter would contract weaving jobs to them whenever needed. Such contract workers were paid in cash – and therefore, contract jobs were a good source of income for many small people in the community. In the case of the contract weaver (known as *alagbawun*), it was the duty of the large-scale producer to give clear specifications of the cloth to be woven and to supply the appropriate lengths and colors of yarn. A woman *alagbawun* worked on her own pit-loom in her own home compound. The men's weaving facility was more elaborate and more expensive to create; therefore a male *alagbawun* usually rented or begged working space in a facility near his home.

Apart from its use in various types of production, this system was also used in the raising of the typical Yoruba livestock – goats, sheep, hens, etc. Under this arrangement, the richer woman gave to the poorer a female animal (known as *eran-osin*), for her to take care of in her own home compound. According to an ancient rule, the owner took the animal's first offspring, and then shared subsequent offspring equally with the caretaker. In this way, a rich woman could have very many heads of livestock scattered throughout her community. On the other hand, the system enabled poorer women to own some livestock.

Commerce leaned heavily on large numbers of porters to convey merchandise. Small traders (like women taking some goods from their homes or from their husbands' farms to the local marketplace) carried their own goods, usually assisted by young members of their family. The small long-distance trader taking goods to markets in neighboring towns or villages usually employed a few porters. The major long-distance trader employed tens or even hundreds of porters, usually traveling together with groups of other traders' porters in caravans.³ Porters were usually young people – mostly young women, although young men were not excluded from earning some quick income in this trade. Probably most Yoruba women had some experience of portering in their youth. The average young woman would usually offer her service in conveying merchandise from her town to another town a few miles away; on her way back home she would convey goods for another employer. For a trader well known to her and her family, she might carry goods to very distant places across the country or even beyond. Many a long-distance trader started as long-distance porter.

On waterways, on main rivers like the Ogun and on the coastal lagoons, goods were conveyed on canoes, mostly small dugouts. Ilaje boatmen were the most famous Yoruba in the canoe trade. The average Ilaje young man owned his own canoe with which he fished and, from time to time, conveyed goods for traders for pay. Some of the more substantial citizens in the Ilaje and coastal Ijebu and Awori country owned many canoes, operated by hired hands (usually youths working part-time), and employed in carrying goods for traders. Canoe men from among the neighboring Ijaw were usually intermingled with Yorubas (Itsekiri, Ilaje, Ijebu and Awori) as carriers on the Yoruba coast.⁴

Women were the backbone of commerce in Yorubaland. As earlier pointed out, some who later became big traders started as porters. Others started small trading as girls, buying goods from a village in their region and selling in another village or town. For instance, buying pots from the royal town of Isan in northern Ekiti (as well as from Ara in the Ikole kingdom or Obo in the Ado kingdom) for sale in other Ekiti towns was a favorite beginner's trade for Ekiti girls. On the market days in these pot-manufacturing towns, crowds of young women usually arrived from all over Ekiti, each departing at the end of the day carrying a stack of new pots. The small capital needed to start this trade was usually begged or borrowed from parents, or gradually built up through the mutual savings system known as *esusu*. Carrying stacks of pots was a hard task, but with luck and persistence, the small trade in pots could grow and diversify into other merchandise. Similar opportunities existed in all regions of Yorubaland for young women to start some trading – salt and dried fish on the coastal lagoons, different types of cloth in various parts of the country, dried fish from the Niger, dyestuff in the towns of the Osun valley, locust-bean aromatics (or *iru*) processing and sale by young women in the grasslands of northern Yorubaland, carved specialty calabashes from many parts of Ekiti, Ijesa, Igbomina and Oyo, raw leather as well as finished leather goods from the Oyo country (where the town of Shaki was perhaps the most famous leather market), small-sized earthen pots and vessels (for cooking soups, and for use as dishes, ceremonial vessels, decorations, and medicinal crucibles) from various towns scattered all over the country, cosmetic camwood (or *osun*) from the towns and villages of Owo and southern Ekiti (especially Akure), shea butter from the Igbomina country and from the Nupe country on the Niger, grinding stones from Ekiti and Akoko. With the advent of trade with Europe from the sixteenth century, a whole new range of merchandise entered into the trade. Traders from Benin, the Aja coast and the Yoruba coast (Itsekiri, Ilaje, Ikale, Ijebu and Awori) first brought the European goods for distribution in the Yoruba interior, where experienced, knowledgeable and well-connected local traders established trading relationships that enabled them to obtain more and more of the European goods for sale.

Another common means whereby the rich acquired labor (for their farming, manufacturing and trading) was through the system known as *iwofa* (the pawning of persons). Very early in their history, the Yoruba seem to have created this system, whereby a borrower agreed to pawn himself or herself (or, more commonly, a young relative) to the creditor as security for a debt. This was an agreement freely contracted between the creditor and the borrower and witnessed by important persons like chiefs or palace officials. The creditor and the borrower agreed that the pawned person would serve the creditor until the debt was fully paid. As soon as the debt was fully paid, the pawned person was set free. A pawned person could not be ill-treated or humiliated; if ill-treatment or humiliation was satisfactorily proved before the authorities, the agreement lapsed instantly and the creditor had no further claims on the debtor. If the pawned person was a grown up girl, the creditor (or any member of his or her lineage) could not marry her; any such marriage instantly discharged the debt. The death of the pawned person terminated the agreement and fully discharged the debt (that is why creditors usually insisted on healthy young persons as pawns). If the pawned person ran away and could not be found, the debtor must provide a substitute or pay the debt. Pawning, therefore, was not slavery; it was freely negotiated, limited, servitude. There was no odium or stigma attached to it; it was generally regarded as an honorable way whereby a person in desperate need of money could borrow it from a rich person. It was a favorite method of raising capital for business and the rich usually preferred to enter into it with persons who intended to use the money for business (especially trade, or quick production of goods like cloth to meet pressing market demands). The *iwofa* system was commonly used in all parts of Yorubaland, and the typical wealthy farmer or trader or large manufacturer or artisan usually had some pawned persons in his or her labor force.

Finally, Yoruba people also had an old institution of domestic slavery, but, as the available evidence overwhelmingly suggests (and as has been shown above), domestic slavery does not seem to have accounted for a significant proportion of labor in Yorubaland until the last decades of the eighteenth century. Before the late eighteenth century, owning of domestic slaves was almost entirely a monopoly of the ruling classes of society.

Women in the Economy[5]

The importance of Yoruba women in the economy of their country deserves a special treatment in this chapter. Unlike most other West African peoples whose women did some of even the heaviest and roughest farm tasks, the Yoruba regarded farming as an exclusively male occupation. In practice, this translated to the exclusion of women from the heavier farm tasks – cutting the bush, tilling the soil, weeding the growing crops, some of the heavier planting (especially seed-yam planting) and the most demanding categories of harvesting (like digging up yams or harvesting nuts or palm wine from palm trees). In all these tasks, the job assigned to women was to provide back-up services to their men – to cook while the men worked, fetch water, carry supplies (like seed-yam from storage to the farm) or harvested crops (like yams to storage, or palm nuts to the processing facility). Women were also responsible for carrying farm produce to the points of sale and for selling it. Women did all the light harvesting of maize, beans and cotton, as well as the gathering of kolanuts, shea-nuts and locust-bean fruits, to mention only a few. While the Yoruba woman did not, unlike women in many other West African cultures, do the heaviest farming tasks, her contributions to the agricultural economy were absolutely indispensable to its prosperity.

Yoruba women also were responsible for much of manufacturing and for most crafts and arts. Heavier industrial processes like metal smelting and its ancillaries (like metal fabrication or sculpturing) belonged only to men; as did the rougher aspects of home construction like the building of walls and roofs. But almost all others belonged to the province of women – the weaving of cotton cloth and raffia products, production of yarn from raw cotton, almost all dyeing processes, the making of pots and other ceramic goods, glass and bead production, production of mats and the finer baskets. Both men and women sewed garments, though men predominated in the making of beaded goods like crowns and other royal articles. When men had finished constructing a building, the women took over and did the entire plastering and decorating. The very important industry of oil processing from palm nuts engaged more men than women, but the contributions by women were significant. Women gathered, shelled, cleaned and dried the kolanuts for market, an important export-oriented industry of the Yoruba forests.

Much more so than women in any other African cultural group, Yoruba women dominated the commercial life of their country. From the smallest local trading to the largest long-distance trading, women were the operators. Women created the trade networks that molded Yorubaland's market districts and sub-districts, and the longer trading relationships that connected it with the rest of West Africa. Yoruba people were used to trading with men traders from, and in, other lands, yet Yoruba culture always regarded trade as a woman's enterprise and never put any considerable number of men in commercial pursuits before the late eighteenth century. After Olokun, the rich Ife bead trader of Oduduwa's generation, we do not have names of the great women traders until the nineteenth century. But Yoruba traditions in general are unambiguous that women controlled commercial wealth in Yorubaland and that every city or town had a long succession of rich women traders.

Savings and Capital Formation in the Economy[6]

The emergence of widespread urban centers in Yorubaland consequent upon the creation of the kingdoms produced major transformations in agriculture, manufactures and commerce. In the context of such developments, major changes also arose in such important economic activities as the saving of money for significant economic and social needs. Though there may have been rudimentary practices in such matters in times before the kingdoms and the urban centers, it was almost certainly in the urban setting that the influential Yoruba systems known to us today evolved – namely, *ajo* and *esusu*, as well as Yoruba money-lending institutions. The growth of comparatively large farms for regular production of surpluses for urban populations, the establishment of, and supply to, large urban workshops, the growth of long-distance large-scale trading (as seen, for instance in the activities of the *alajapa* and *alarobo*), and higher levels of expenditure on family occasions (like funerals, chieftaincy installations, or weddings) in the urban setting – all these almost certainly generated the savings systems, the beginnings of capital formation and the money borrowing and lending systems that the Yoruba people evolved.

Ajo is a shortened form of the word *akojo*, meaning "that which is gathered or pooled together" or "the act of gathering together".[7] The traditions concerning *ajo* strongly suggest that it started in early urban practices whereby individuals saved money with notable persons in their social and family circles – for instance, residents of *agbo-ile* with *agbo-ile* elders, members of age-grade associations with the officers of their associations, members of market commodity associations with the more substantial traders in their associations. From such beginnings, there developed the institution of the *alajo* – that is, a person (usually a significant citizen, like a chief or successful trader, trusted for his or her integrity) who made a profession of receiving and saving money for other citizens. To avoid confusion, it developed that each individual depositor had to deposit the same amount of money at regular intervals of time – say every *orun* (five-day) or *isan* (nine-day) market day. To receive back the accumulated savings, the depositor must give the *alajo* an advance notice, the length of which was agreed to at the beginning of the relationship. A depositor's last installment constituted a payment to the alajo for his or her services. The accumulated deposits did not earn any interest. It was common for the *alajo* to offer this service until grand old age.

As should be easily obvious, the *ajo* system suffered an important weakness: its level of security was low. The *alajo* was often also a money lender, which meant that he sometimes loaned out some of the money received from depositors. If any of the loans went bad, the *alajo*'s obligations to some depositors were likely to be disrupted, and such depositors would suffer loss or, at least, painful delays in receiving their money back. Sometimes, on the other hand, the disruption emanated from depositors – if any depositor failed to bring in the deposits as arranged, he could slow down the *alajo*'s fulfillment of his obligations to other depositors. Still, the *ajo* system had its attraction, especially as a result of its simplicity: the depositor had a direct one-to-one relationship with the *alajo*, and could give notice and call in his or her money whenever he or she chose. Consequently, the *ajo* system lived on quite strongly, and it was considerably modified and strengthened by the coming of literacy from about the late nineteenth century.

Side by side with the *ajo* system, however, there evolved another system that was much more secure, that was participated in by many more people in every town, and that had a much bigger impact on the economy. This system was known as *esusu*. *Esusu* is from the Yoruba word 'su', meaning 'pour'. As used in this financial system, 'pour' has two meanings – 'pour' as in pour together (or pool together) and 'pour' as in pour out (or disburse). In its operation, *esusu* ran as a "pooling-and-disbursing" of funds at predetermined intervals of time, in a chain stretching over a predetermined length of time. Samuel Johnson describes the operation of an *esusu* as follows: "A fixed sum agreed upon is given by each (member) at a fixed time (usually every week) and place, under a president; the total amount is paid to each member in rotation."[8] And a twentieth century scholar, using the English pound-and-shilling currency of his time, has illustrated the operation of an *esusu* thus:

> … imagine a simple case where twenty members contribute one shilling each, monthly. At the end of twenty months, which completes the cycle in this case,

each member will have contributed twenty shillings or one pound and will, on one occasion, have received the amount of one pound in return.[9]

Esusu pervaded all of Yorubaland and, usually, many *esusu* groups existed at any given time in every Yoruba town. The smallest and simplest *esusu* consisted of a few members (say twenty) who, under the leadership of one member as president, agreed to contribute a fixed amount of money at agreed intervals (say weekly). Each member would bring his or her contribution to the president at the agreed place on the agreed day of every week (usually the local market day). After receiving all the contributions for the day, the president would give all of it together to one member, which member was said to "gather" (or *ko*) the *esusu* for that day. The order in which members would gather the *esusu* was agreed to in a meeting of all members before the first contribution was made – usually with the assistance of the Ifa oracle. This example, then, would be described as a twenty-member twenty-week *esusu*. In most cases, such a simple twenty-week *esusu* would operate for twenty-one weeks (so that each member would make twenty-one contributions and receive the total sum of twenty contributions) – the contributions of the first week being kept by the president to cushion the operation (so that unavoidable lateness by members to bring in their contributions would not harm any member whose turn it was to gather the *esusu*). Usually, depending on the community, the first contribution being thus withheld would end up, at the end of the cycle, as a "thank you" gift to the president for her services – although the president was also usually expected to end the cycle with light refreshments for the group. Lateness by any member in bringing in a contribution was treated as a very serious offence, and default was out of the question. Penalties were always stated in advance – usually including fines or expulsion (and the terrible possibility of refusal of admission to future *esusu* groups). A member who was expelled lost her place on the list of members and must wait till the end of the cycle to receive back whatever she had contributed.

Esusu varied very widely in size, number of members, duration, and complexity of operation. An *esusu* in the largest categories could comprise over 200 members and have a duration of over two years. The membership of a complex *esusu* might have internal subgroups, each under a leader who was responsible for collecting the contributions from members of his or her subgroup. In such cases, it was the subgroup leaders only that dealt directly with the group president. Often, subgroup leaders were persons who were using the position to understudy the group president in preparation for starting *esusu* groups of their own.

Every *esusu* accommodated within itself persons of little income and the economically more comfortable. This was done by institutionalizing the agreed amount of each individual installment and calling it *"owo"* (hand). While a weaker member might hold only one "hand" (*owo kan*) in an *esusu*, a richer member might hold two or three. This meant that the former would make one contribution, while the latter made two or three; and that the former would occupy one spot on the list of members (for gathering the *esusu*) while the latter would occupy two or three dispersed spots.

The *esusu* system was one of the most sophisticated inventions of Yoruba economic life. Although we have no documentary mention of it before the nineteenth century, Yoruba traditions in general are unambiguous that *esusu* had its earliest roots in the ancient Yoruba tradition of pooling assets for the mutual benefit of persons in groups. Of such practices, mention has been made of *owe* and *aaro* – systems of labor pooling in farm work. One other was the *owu-oya* system, in which women spinners of cotton yarn pooled an agreed length of yarn weekly or thereabouts, the collective contribution of each week being gathered by one member – exactly as in *esusu*. Created in the cities and towns most probably in the early history of the kingdoms, the *esusu* system of monetary asset pooling was the peak invention of this whole cultural trend.

At the height of its development, *esusu* was three things in one: a societal bonding organization, a vehicle for savings and capital accumulation, and a mutual credit institution. Typically, membership of any one *esusu* spanned various lineages and lineage compounds, various age-grade associations, various occupations, various strata of society, sometimes even various neighboring towns. As such, an *esusu* bonded together many traditional segments of society, as well as the rich with the poor. Also, membership of an *esusu* constituted a very reliable way to save money and create some significant capital. It enabled its members to put money together gradually with a level of discipline beyond what they could have mustered as individuals. The total amount of savings generated through *esusu* week by week, month by month, in an average Yoruba city or town must have been very large indeed. For all cities and towns of Yorubaland for, say, one whole year, the savings generated by all *esusu* must have constituted an enormous capital. It is believed that probably most of the capital that came into individuals' hands through *esusu* was consumed in family and social events like funerals, chieftaincy contests, chieftaincy installations, weddings, individual and family rituals and festivals. But, from the hands of traders, artisans, cotton cloth producers, owners of dyeing stations (*idi-aro*), and others like them, some of the capital from *esusu* went into the expansion of trade, and into production facilities and supplies. For instance, the giant earthen pots that were sunk into the ground and used for dyeing were so expensive that to buy one (not to talk of buying a few to establish a dyeing station), one needed the kind of capital derivable from an *esusu*. The long-distance trader (the *alajapa*), the local wholesaler, the large-scale retailer in the local marketplace, the sellers of expensive (and therefore capital intensive) merchandise like livestock, metal goods, export kolanuts, the owners of metalworking establishments – all usually had deep roots in the *esusu* system for the capital needs of their businesses. Although precise data and numbers on the impact of the *esusu* system on the economy are unavailable to modern historians, there seems to be no doubt that substantial parts of the high peaks of the Yoruba economy before the twentieth century relied very much on the *esusu* system.

Finally, in effect, when a member of an *esusu* (with the exception of the last member on the members' list) gathered the contributions, he or she took a loan from the *esusu* group, a loan secured by his or her continued contributions. Such loans were interest-free and were available only to members.

Altogether, then, the *esusu* system served many of the purposes that banks serve today. It provided for savings, for loans and credit, as well as for capital formation for all sorts of capital needs. Because of its great impact on economic life for many centuries, it has continued to exercise much influence in Yoruba society today, in spite of the proliferation of banks and similar financial institutions.

Open Loans and Credit Systems

The loans available in the *esusu* system were closed loans – that is, they were not available to the general public but only to members. However, there were other types of loans that developed in the Yoruba cities and towns, systems making loans and credit available to the general public.[10] Rich traders were probably the earliest providers of open loans in most new urban centers, but over time, there arose persons known uniquely as money lenders – usually traders or *alajo* who increased money lending in their businesses or who converted completely to money lending. Since these loans carried interest, money lenders were known as *olowo-ele* – providers of interest-bearing loans.

Interest on loans was not always in cash; quite often it was in the form of human labor or in goods and products. For instance, the *iwofa* system (earlier described) did not only provide security for a loan, it also provided interest on the loan. The borrower gave a pawned person to serve the lender, but still had to pay the loan in full. As long as the loan was not fully paid, the pawned person continued to serve the lender. The pawned person's service to the lender was therefore a very exorbitant interest on the loan. Hence the common experience was that loans covered with *iwofa* arrangements tended to be paid back more quickly than other types of loans.

Very similar to loans covered by *iwofa* arrangements was another type of loan designed especially for borrowers who were farmers. These were usufruct loans for which the borrowers pledged farms. The farm pledged could be either of annual crops like yams, cereals, legumes, cotton, etc., or of perennial crops like kolanuts or indigo. If the farm was of an annual crop, the borrower surrendered the farm as security and pledged the harvest thereof as the loan repayment – and the lender was therefore entitled to come whenever the crop was ripe and harvest it. Almost invariably, the cash value of the harvest far exceeded the amount of the loan, thus returning to the lender a heavy interest on the loan. The lender's security and profit were even better in the case of perennial crops, since the lender, while holding the farm as security, would keep harvesting it until the loan was otherwise repaid – the harvests thus constituting a usurious interest on his loan. In short, the city or town money lenders often did very well for themselves in their dealings with farming folks. Usually, most farmers worked two or more farms; if the need arose to borrow money, the practice was to set one of the farms aside for the loan transaction.

Some money lenders dealt only in cash – that is, cash loans and cash repayments and interest. Each such money lender usually had a standard length of time for his or her loans, at the end of which the loan and interest had to be paid together. Again, the interest rate was usually very high (commonly 100 percent for one year, which made calculation easy). For people of small means, taking this type of loan was very risky. Consequently, only the most desperate availed themselves of such loans – persons faced with sudden funeral expenses or under pressure to pay older and troublesome debts or strangers who had no other source of funds to turn to. Occasionally, owners of businesses resorted to this type of loan to raise quick funds for urgent business needs.

In the recovery of capital and interest in cash, default was more often experienced than in the recovery of other types of loans. The excessively high interest rates tended to load borrowers with burdens that could prove too heavy, a situation that greatly increased money lenders' risks. However, since rich money lenders were members of the politically influential elite, the rulers of society allowed them to employ draconian methods of debt recovery and such methods came to be emulated generally by others who had debts to collect. The creditor would usually start by reporting a difficult debtor to the debtor's lineage head or to his street chief – and that would usually prove sufficient. Failure at those levels might ultimately lead to reporting to the quarter chief of the debtor's quarter of the town. Commonly, a chief would set a mandatory date for payment (or dates for installment payments) and then put in place a follow-up arrangement to ensure that his orders were carried out. (Reporting debtors to the palace was uncommon.) If the debtor kept evading payment at all these levels, he risked punishment; he also risked the probability that the creditor might obtain official permission to employ a legalized rare pressure as a last resort — namely, the use of a paid, licensed, distrainer. Samuel Johnson describes the procedure as follows:

> The Yorubas have a peculiar method of forcing payment out of an incorrigible debtor. When a creditor who has obtained judgment for debt finds it impossible to recover any thing out of the debtor, he applies to the town authorities for a licensed distrainer. This individual is called *Ogo*; he is said to *d'ogo*, i.e. to sit on the debtor (as it were). For that purpose, he enters the premises, seeks out the debtor, or ensconces himself in his apartment until his appearance, and then he makes himself an intolerable nuisance to him and to the members of the house generally until the money is paid.
>
> The distrainer is a man of imperturbable temper, but of a foul tongue, a veritable Thersites. He adopts any measure he likes, sometimes by inflicting his presence and attention on the debtor everywhere and anywhere he may go, denying him privacy of any kind, and in the meantime using his tongue most foully upon him, his own person being inviolable, for touching him implies doing violence to the person of the authorities who appoint him to the task. He demands and obtains whatever diet he may require, however sumptuous, and may help himself if not quickly served. If he thinks fit, he may hold on any poultry or cattle he finds in the premises, and prepare himself food, and all at the expense of the debtor. He must not take anything away but he may enjoy the use of anything he finds in the house.[11]

This obnoxious process was usually very effective in the recovery of debts, because it targeted not only the debtor but also the lineage compound where he lived. The distrainer could easily bring a stigma upon a compound and its residents; and, in any case, his antics were a distasteful disruption of life in the compound. Therefore, the common experience was that the residents would intervene, either by contributing money to pay the debt or by collectively offering to the creditor a satisfactory payment arrangement. The use of a distrainer could, however, prove ineffective if the debtor was disreputable in his compound on account of his being a habitual difficult debtor who had brought in distrainers or other debt-related troubles in the past. In such a case the creditor was out of luck — except that he might obtain permission from the authorities to seize and hold valuables (especially livestock) belonging to the creditor or his closest of kin until the debt was paid.

Besides the various types of loans, Yoruba urban communities also had a strong tradition of purchasing goods on credit. At the highest levels of commerce, credit was a very important factor in the business relationship between local traders and the long-distance merchants who brought European and other goods for distribution in the interior. Such long-distance wholesalers, and the interior-based long-distance trader (the *alajapa*) who took merchandise to distant markets, commonly depended, for their trade, on relationships of trust with significant local retailers. At the level of retailers, too, selling on credit was a regular feature of business.

Upon this tradition of commercial credit, a notable practice was developed by itinerant Ijesa traders in about the eighteenth century.[12] Going from town to town, these Ijesa traders (always men) went to people in their homes and retailed to them short lengths of imported European cloth throughout the length and breadth of Yorubaland, probably most of it in the Oyo cities and towns where the levels of affluence and fashion were quite high in the seventeenth and eighteenth centuries. The trader would come, make a sale on credit and move on, to return on other rounds later to collect payment, usually in small installments. The Ijesa traders engaged in this style of trade came to be known as *osomaalo* – from the methods they sometimes had to use for collecting the more difficult debts. The *osomaalo* would station himself on the homestead of the difficult debtor, and announce repeatedly that he absolutely would not leave until he had been paid – which, in his Ijesa dialect, was rendered as *oso ni maa lo gb' owo mi* (I am going to keep crouching here until I receive my money). The *osomaalo* was usually himself under great pressure. Quite often, he had received his consignment of cloth on credit from a bigger merchant, or he was no more than a small subsidiary to a bigger merchant; he must pay his principal and make some profit for himself, and he could not afford to abandon even the smallest debts. So he would crouch rather than sit, because that way he had a better chance to attract everybody's attention to his difficult plight and to the debtor's lack of consideration.

The *osomaalo* was, in his own way, an important agent of cultural change and progress. He brought inexpensive cloth of European manufacture to all cities and towns of Yorubaland, and made it available to all (including even the poor) on deferred payments which he was willing to receive in easy installments. Usually, most of his transactions went smoothly, and only in few cases did he need to "crouch" to compel payment. Some of the more successful *osomaalo* had subordinates to assist and represent them while they made wide sweeps of the country. Of the smallest ones, each usually confined his rounds to a given district. The *osomaalo* continued to be important in the commercial life of Yorubaland until deep into the twentieth century.

An Eighteenth Century Overview

In spite of a perceptible decline in human rights and security in parts of Yorubaland by the end of the eighteenth century, on the whole it marked a climax to the centuries of growing socio-economic prosperity. By the end of that century, Yorubaland was a country of many rich towns and villages (many of including very large walled cities), prosperous farms growing a large variety of crops, well kept and peaceful roads bearing endless streams of travelers and traders conveying various types of merchandise, a proud land of culture in the arts, crafts and entertainment. By the eighteenth century, the lineage compound (*agbo-ile*) had reached its peak in beauty and decoration and comfort – much of which could be seen until well into the twentieth century. The average compound featured large verandahs around the courtyards and low eaves (which together protected the living and sleeping rooms from sun, heat and glare), wooden posts (supporting the eaves) and wooden door panels – all carved in great detail, very detailed wall colorings and decorations (often with furrowed patterns and inscriptions that had symbolic meanings to the lineage), and, commonly, a small garden in which herbs were grown, and a compound frontage planted with decorative shade trees. In every town, these compound beautifications had their most glorious expressions in the king's palace and, to a lesser extent, in the compounds of the high chiefs. The Yoruba culture of color, music and gaiety in festivals, ceremonies, funerals and weddings, so often marveled at in the twentieth century by neighboring peoples, had attained its maturity by the eighteenth century.

In royal cities across the land, kings ruled in varying grades of splendor, adorned in beaded regalia and the proud, beaded crown of Oduduwa, with a long white feather (known as *iyere okin*) swaying on top of it. Every palace, expanded and refined down the centuries, proclaimed the glory of its king by its grand gate, its gabled roof, its sculptured pillars and its many courtyards each of which had a function, a name and a history. Masses of the residents of every royal city gathered in the palace on those festivals when the king, adorned in his best, his face veiled behind the shimmering beaded frills of his crown, with the beaded scepter in his hand, graciously showed his person to his adoring subjects. When he spoke to the crowd, one of his chiefs echoed his voice and his every word was greeted with a torrent of *oriki* praise poetry from thousands of voices. The huge drums of royalty known as *gbedu* drums, their wooden trunks gorgeous specimens of sculptural art, boomed to play some royal beat and, depending on the kind of festival, the king danced – a brief series of steps to an ancient royal song laced with history – as his people roared their adoration. If this was the royal festival of Ogun (god of iron and war), the king would step beyond the palace gate on a procession through certain parts of the city, with his chiefs and thousands of his subjects in his train, in loud jubilation.

A brief survey of some of the kingdoms will illustrate this general picture of peace, stability and prosperity.[13] The Ilesa kingdom was at the peak of its power and prosperity, reached during the glorious reign of the warrior king, Owa Atakunmosa, in the last years of the seventeenth century (see Chapter 8). Ilesa's trade with Oyo in the north and Benin in the south prospered; Ijesa traders ranked among the best in Yorubaland both in commercial expertise and versatility, and in the range of their operations, as colonies of Ijesa traders mushroomed as far west as places that are today in Togo and Ghana.

Many of the Ekiti kingdoms joined the ranks of the richest Yoruba kingdoms. The cognomens of two of the Ewi who ruled the Ado kingdom for most of the century speak loudly of prosperity, comfort and peace. The Ewi Amonoola (meaning "he who knows the road to wealth") reigned, according to Anthony Oguntuyi, from 1722 to 1762 – a long reign celebrated in Ado traditions for its prosperity and glory. Amonoola's successor, Afunbiowo (meaning white as money – that is cowries), reigned from 1762 to 1781, also in great wealth and splendor, although his subjects complained of him that he was greedy and crafty.

Various traditions, sayings and proverbs project a picture of wealth and beauty in most Ekiti kingdoms prior to the nineteenth century. The Ikole kingdom was pictured as being so rich in cloth production and sales that Ikole people used to clothe the trees in their streets, while the Elekole's regalia used to spread out in folds after folds. Ekiti people sang of the kings of some of their richest kingdoms (like the Ewi of Ado, the Elekole of Ikole, the Deji of Akure and the Alara of Ara) as being so rich that parts of their stores of money (in cowries) needed to be spread in the open to air every day. And one piece of poetry had it that when the Ewi went on the annual ritual visit to a shrine called Otu, the priests there became rich from the beads that dropped from his clothes and that all the bush along the way twinkled with lost beads.

According to Ijebu traditions, the eighteenth century was a period of surpassing prosperity, stability and greatness for the Ijebu-Ode kingdom, as well as for most of the other Ijebu kingdoms. The Ijebu-Ode kings of the period bore such grand cognomens as Tewogbuwa (he who had power and glory placed gently in his hands), Gbelegbuwa (he to whom power and glory came in the peace of his home), Fusengbuwa (he who celebrated to receive power and glory). These kings were perhaps the richest in southern Yorubaland in their time. Ijebu-Ode did enormous amounts of trade with the interior and the coast. The names of the most influential age-grade associations in Ijebu-Ode during the century proclaimed the peace and stability of the time – such names as

Legbeta, Lewuru, and Ilesegun. By the end of the century, this kingdom seems to have started buying some guns for its armies – the first Yoruba kingdom to do so. Ijebu traders, tutored by the experience of many centuries, were reputed to be the best among the Yoruba and were a major source of imported European goods. They traversed Yorubaland intensively, set up agreements with local traders everywhere, and settled as wholesalers in almost all prominent towns. Recent studies show that Ijebu-Ode and the other Ijebu towns were centers of great art in brass, bronze, terracotta and wood. Ijebu's direct access to the European coastal trade made brass abundantly available, greatly enhancing sculptural art in this medium; and strong contacts and trade with Owo and Benin added to the richness of the art of the Ijebu country.

Under the umbrella of the Alaafin of Oyo, the Owu and Egba kingdoms enjoyed much prosperity for most of the eighteenth century. The same was true of the kingdom of Ila in the north. Shielded by Oyo-Ile from frequent incursions by Nupe raiders, this kingdom at last began to derive full benefits from its location on the trade routes connecting Yorubaland with the Nupe country on the Niger. It was during the eighteenth century that the glory of the Orangun of Ila, widely respected as one of the oldest Yoruba dynasties, had a chance to glow.

Osogboye's long reign in the seventeenth century had raised the power of the Owo kingdom to great heights, more or less permanently securing Owo against Benin invasions. But it had also introduced elements of the Benin style of monarchy characterized by a strong dose of royal autocracy. The conflicts between this style of monarchy and the Yoruba tradition of limited monarchy caused instability in Owo's political system for a long time after Osogboye. But the Owo kingdom proved adroit at expanding economic prosperity even in spite of its constitutional troubles. The eighteenth century was therefore the most glorious era in Owo's history. Free from disruptions caused by Benin's military threats, Owo's trade with Benin reached great heights. Owo and Benin traders mingled freely on the Owo–Benin routes as well as in all parts of eastern and southern Yorubaland. Owo's traditions speak of a new class of very rich citizens, mostly traders, of prosperous farming and plentiful supplies of food, of a new era of bountiful industrial and artistic production. Owo's cloth industry boomed, and in particular, Owo became the new center, clearly at last replacing Ife, for manufacturing the beaded products of Yoruba royal grandeur – crowns, scepters, etc. Working at home in Owo or scattered abroad as protégés of various Yoruba kings, Owo bead-setters made the new generation of Oduduwa crowns for Yorubaland. Second only to Oyo-Ile, Owo experienced a ferment in the entertainment arts. Various types of new drums and musical instruments, various styles of popular music, many colorful troupes of musicians, went out from Owo and gave most of Yorubaland many bright new additions to its popular entertainment. The eighteenth century is also believed to have witnessed the height of Owo's art in brass/bronze sculptures, terracotta sculptures, ivory carving, etc. Indeed, the available evidence suggests that by this time Owo had come to surpass Ife in the arts. Owo developed the art of carving ivory to perfection, and became the major supplier of ivory figurines to both Yorubaland and Benin. Artfully mixing Yoruba and Benin royal regalia (with its super-abundance of beads), the Olowos shone, as their subjects said, like the sun in the sky, and attracted streams of spectators from all over Yorubaland to some of the annual royal festivals of Owo. The eighteenth century also saw the peak of Owo's expansion, as a result of which the Olowo could claim that most of Akoko belonged to his kingdom.

In the far western region of Yorubaland, Ketu was the most successful and most powerful Yoruba kingdom. As the pressure of Dahomey on its neighbors increased during the century, Ketu was better able than the rest to resist, defeating a Dahomey attack in 1760. Ketu fared less well against another Dahomey attack in 1789, but was still able to claim victory when it was over. At home, this kingdom enjoyed much stability under its own version of the Yoruba constitution of limited monarchy. Its council called Kobalede (meaning, "teach the king to speak"), made up of between sixty and seventy chiefs, acted as a sort of parliament that met with the king regularly to take all decisions of state. The traditions of Ketu speak of considerable prosperity under its late eighteenth century kings – Oje (1748–60), Ande (1760–80) and Akebioru (1780–95). Many of the trade routes connecting Oyo-Ile with the Aja and western Yoruba countries benefited Ketu and brought much wealth to its citizens. One of the Ketu towns, Meko, grew particularly rich during the century.

No written eyewitness descriptions of Yorubaland beyond the coast in the centuries covered in this chapter (eleventh to eighteenth century) are available. From the first years of the nineteenth century, however, travel accounts of European visitors to the Yoruba interior began to furnish such descriptions. By the time that the first of these visitors (Hugh Clapperton) came in the 1820s, the western and northwestern parts of Yorubaland were, as earlier pointed out, already experiencing some political troubles. Even then, the records of Clapperton and his companions paint a picture that gives a lot of information about what Yorubaland must have been like in the eighteenth century.[14]

Clapperton and his team, including notably his servant Richard Lander, started from Badagry on the Yoruba west coast at the end of December 1825 intent on collecting information about the course of River Niger. Traveling slowly northwards through western Yorubaland, they made it to Oyo-Ile in late January 1826. What they had to say about the generally good and peaceful condition of the roads and of traveling traders and marketplaces has been earlier touched

The Kingdoms and the Economy: Part II 199

upon. Here we will note some of their minor observations about the general civilization and conditions of Yorubaland.

From the moment they left Badagry, the group never had to go any long distance before coming to a town. They were traveling through a well-populated country, with towns and villages not far apart. Outside every town or village, according to Lander, were "fields of Indian corn," numerous "plantations of cotton," "extensive plantations of corn and plantains," "rich plantations of yams." After they had emerged from the thicker forest territory near the coast, they saw palm trees growing abundantly everywhere, sometimes appearing to belong to plantations. In the farmlands after Ijanna, Lander recorded that they saw groves of "cocoa and female cocoa trees, scattered on all sides" – by which he presumably meant coconut trees. After a town whose name he recorded as Choko, Lander wrote that they came through some "low mountains, on the summit and in the hollows of which were several hamlets, inhabited by an industrious race, who had extensive plantations in the valleys below, where the palm tree flourishes in great abundance." They were probably, at this point, passing through an area of forest farms (*oko egan*).

Lander observed that as his group penetrated further and further into the Yoruba interior, the population generally grew denser, the towns grew bigger, the land got more intensively cultivated, "and civilization became at every step more strikingly apparent." "Large towns" he wrote, "at the distance of only a few miles from each other… lay on all sides…" He tried to guess the population sizes of some of the towns. The town which he called Koofo (around which, according to him, "several extensive cotton plantations lay"), he thought, had a population of about twenty thousand (though an Englishman, used to the small family homes of his own country, would naturally underestimate the population of a town filled with packed, sprawling, lineage compounds). He did not attempt to guess the population of Shaki, but recorded that it was a "populous town," and that its king had "a considerable number of towns, and many thousands of people, under his protection." About many other towns, he simply wrote that they were "densely inhabited."

Lander found the location of many of the towns to be well chosen, attractive and very impressive. So likewise were their layout and decorations. "Bidgie," he said, was a "pleasant town," "Laboo" was "delightfully situated on rising ground, commanding an extensive and noble prospect; the approach to it is through a beautiful walk of trees…" The city of Shaki was "perched" attractively "on the top of the highest hill" in its region. The entrance to the town he called Aja was "through a spacious avenue of noble trees," and "Chiadoo" was "seated on a gentle declivity." Usually too, the towns were clean. Lander spoke of hill slopes and valleys "studded with cleanly [sic] habitations."

Most of the bigger towns, according to Lander, were walled. Some of the towns of the thick forests near the coast were "defended by a strong stockade or a mud wall, and sometimes by both together." But most town walls consisted of "a thick mud wall and deep trench." In many towns the wall was shielded by "trees of large dimensions… planted so as to form a belt… which in case of necessity might easily be converted into an excellent means of defense…" At another place, he wrote,

> Ateepa, like most towns of any magnitude in the country, is furnished with a strong wall, made of earth, and a belt of trees within it, by reason of a thorny creeping shrub climbing round the trunks, like the ivy to the oak, and throwing out vigorous shoots, had become so thickly entangled as to form a secure barrier which, except by the narrow gateway at the entrance, was impervious to man and beast.

Lander noted the public shrines in some of the towns. Of the town which he called Bookhar he wrote,

> Near the entrance of the town, on the left side of the road, stands a solitary fetish hut, of large dimensions, with a number of wooden figures, carved in bass relief, some in a kneeling and some in a recumbent posture, placed outside the walls; these idols the inhabitants worship, and ascribe miraculous powers to their agency.

In the "beautiful walk of trees" which formed the approach to the town of "Laboo," there were between the trees "fetish houses" – "which are held in greatest veneration by the inhabitants." Outside Badagry, the Clapperton group saw "a solitary fetish-hut, ornamented in front with a species of small shining stones which abounds in this country."

Finally, Clapperton and his companions caught some glimpses of Yoruba art in a few places. The wooden images which they saw outside the wall of the big shrine at "Bookhar" were no doubt part of the artistic decorations of that shrine. In a town which Lander called Engwai, they saw "several busts of men, as well as figures of tigers, crocodiles, serpents… carved of blocks of wood, and extremely well executed…" Then Lander added, "The natives of that part of Africa appear to have a genius for the art of sculpture, which is in great repute with them; and some of their productions rival, in point of delicacy, any of a similar kind that I have seen in Europe."

Concerning the inhabitants of these towns and villages, Lander had varied remarks. Sometimes, he could not understand the ways of his hosts and, therefore, occasionally allowed himself to lapse into rude, ethnocentric comments. He was, in particular, sometimes irritated by the crowds which gathered to gaze at members of his group (even when they were trying to sleep) and by the fact that he and the other members of his group were called "red men." He was frustrated too because, for most of the way, they could not find men to bear hammocks for pay. "We were," he wrote on one occasion, "...unfortunate in our inquiries for hammock men, not a single individual in the town being willing to engage himself in what all ranks conceive to be an occupation fit only for horses." In one town, some young men did agree to carry Clapperton in a hammock. Clapperton got into the hammock and they lifted it onto their shoulders; "but," wrote Lander, "the bearers had proceeded only a few paces when it was, for some unaccountable reason, suddenly let [it] down, and the fellows scampered away as fast as their leg could carry them." However, Lander's team had no difficulty whatsoever about recruiting carriers to carry their loads.

More generally, however, Lander was appreciative of the people whose towns and villages he passed through. His assessment was that "the inhabitants ... pay the greatest respect to the laws, and live under a regular government." A few incidents illustrated the orderly government. All the way from Badagry to Oyo-Ile, Clapperton and his companions regularly found agencies and evidence of orderly control by the government of Oyo-Ile and by the local governments. When they came to a district where Fulani rebels from Ilorin had attacked and burnt villages, they found that the royal government of Oyo-Ile had provided armed guards to protect traders and travelers on the roads. Lander wrote, "We passed several hundred of men, women and children, with heavy loads on their heads, who had been traveling the whole of the previous night... They were carefully watched by overseers (one of whom was appointed to each fifty) who were all armed, either with short swords or bows and arrows ..."

Lander also found the people generally very hospitable, cheerful and good-natured. He wrote "we experienced as much civility from them as our countrymen would have bestowed upon us in our native land. They were, generally speaking, neatly dressed in cap, shirt (tobe) and trousers, and very cleanly in their personal appearance." The large town of Ihumbo had just suffered some aggression (the political troubles of the nineteenth century had already started in that locality) and much of it was in ruins. Nevertheless, the people showed as much friendliness and hospitality as if there was no problem – "Singing and dancing and music playing were kept up during the whole night, with as much spirit and good humor, as if the people had been the happiest in the world." At "Assoudo" he remarked that the people were "pleasing in their manner." The people of the towns they passed through in one district "all bore an air of novelty, cheerfulness, beauty, and grandeur, that I have never seen surpassed." In general, "we were everywhere received on the road with acclamations and songs of welcome."

He found that the Yoruba were a very musical and happy people. In town after town, his group was surrounded by crowds of men, women and children, "the ladies enlivening us with song … and the men blowing on horns and beating on gongs and drums." In one town, their hosts liberally offered "an intoxicating beverage called Otee (a kind of ale made from millet) which made everybody light-headed and cheerful." When Clapperton fell sick in one town, the local herbalist gave him a potion to drink which worked like magic.

King after king welcomed them with touching kindness and some of Yoruba royal grandeur. While they waited to be ushered into the presence of the king of Ijanna, the women of the palace "struck up a native tune, which they sang loudly and with much feeling." Lander added, "there was a solemnity and pathos about it that reminded me of the most impressive church music in my own country." When the women stopped singing, "the band played a lively air, in which the singers occasionally joined, and at the conclusion of the concert a message was sent from the king … for the red men to make their appearance." When they were ushered before the king of Shaki, "the king was seated under his verandah, surrounded by a hundred of his wives and musicians and drums and fifes … the latter struck up a native air, the ladies keeping time with their feet, and accompanying the instruments with their voices." In many places on the journey, kings and chiefs kindly lent horses to the Clapperton team.

Generally, Lander had much to admire in the kings. He said of the king of "Bidgie" that he was "a fine young man named Lollakelli." At "Bookhar" not far from Badagry, Lander wrote that when the visitors were invited before the king, "we found (him) in earnest conversation with his elders … altogether forming the most venerable looking group of human beings I ever saw." For more details he added that the king was

> a tall thin man, well stricken in years, and respectably dressed in a silk tobe and trousers of country cloth. On his head he wore a cap thickly studded with various colored glass beads… and small gold colored tassels of beads hung from it to the shoulders. The cap was neatly and fancifully made.[15]

After one of his visits to the Alaafin Majotu in 1826, Lander wrote as follows:[16]

> The monarch was richly dressed in a scarlet damask tobe, ornamented with coral beads, and short trousers of the same color with a light blue stripe, made of country cloth; his legs as far as the knees were stained red with hennah, and on his feet he wore sandals of red leather. A cap of blue damask, thickly studded with handsome coral beads, was on his head; and his neck, arms and legs were decorated with large silver rings.

We will conclude this picture of Yorubaland from Lander's account with his description of a scene of some Yoruba girls in carefree recreation at a beautiful spot just outside the walls of their town, not far from Oyo-Ile, in January 1826. Lander wrote (on Sunday, January 22, 1826):

> At noon we descended into a delightful valley, situated in the bottom of a ridge of rocks, which effectually hid it from observation till one approached almost close to it. It was intersected with shimmering streams and purling rills, the elegant palm, and the broad leaved banana, covered with foliage, embellishing the sheltered and beautifully romantic spot. In the center was a sheet of water, resembling an artificial pond, in which were numbers of young maidens from the neighboring town of Tschow, some of them reposing at full length on its verdant banks, and some frisking and basking in the sunbeams, whilst others of their companions were sporting with the Naiads [sic] of the sacred stream; but all of them visibly delighted with the pleasant recreations which they were enjoying so prettily and innocently. We stood for a season gazing on them with pleasure; but no sooner were our white faces observed by the young ladies, than their amusements instantly ceased, and the sable beauties simultaneously rushing from the water, snatched up their apparel, and with their uncovered associates, concealing their faces with their hands, ran away and hid themselves behind the trunk of trees, looking as coy and bashful as did their mother Eve in the Garden of Eden.[17]

All these accounts by Richard Lander, then, represent what most of Yorubaland would have been like by the end of the eighteenth century – except that the few ruins of towns and villages which Lander saw along his way would not have featured. Much further to the east, in the Igbomina country, a traveler would have seen some ruins and encountered some wars in the last decades of the eighteenth century – the effects, as will be seen in a later chapter, of Nupe incursions. Earlier in the eighteenth century (say by 1750), however, a traveler through Igbomina would not have seen any towns or villages devastated by Nupe raids. All indications are that, through most of the eighteenth century (at the peak of many centuries of prosperous growth), most of Yorubaland was a country of happy, productive and hospitable people, a land of farmers, artisans, craftsmen, and caravans of traders, of crowded marketplaces, of musicians, artists and story tellers, of what Lander called "regular government," and of law, peace, and order.

The growth and development of the wealth in the visual arts and in folklore, for which the Yoruba have become famous worldwide, belonged mostly to these centuries up to the eighteenth. The order and prosperity resulting from the rise of many towns and cities all over Yorubaland, and the culture of beauty and grandeur which became the character of the monarchical establishments, enhanced the flowering of artistic expression. Of Yoruba sculptural art in metals (especially in brass, bronze and iron), many of the pieces on display in our times have been found in the city of Ile-Ife. But that high quality of art in metals was a nationwide phenomenon. Most towns that were major centers of trade were also major centers of art – for example Owo, Ijebu-Ode, Owu-Ipole, many of the Egba towns, many of the Ekiti towns, Ode-Ondo, Ila and many towns in Igbomina. Lander's statement about "a genius for the art of sculpture" was true of the people of all Yoruba communities.

Countless pieces of impressive carving in wood have been found in all parts of Yorubaland, especially from shrines, palaces and lineage compounds. The Staff of Oranmiyan in Ile-Ife represents the highest in extant Yoruba monumental sculpture in stone. But sculpture in stone was common to all parts of the country. Across the country, countless shrines had stone images of *orisa* (sometimes riding on a horse) and human guards (called *adena*). In the Igbomina town of Esie in northeastern Yorubaland, there exists in one location a large collection of impressive stone carvings (about 1000 in all), all of them figures of humans variously dressed and adorned, most with prominent headgear and beaded accessories and many representing various social roles – chiefs, priests, warriors, etc. Many questions remain difficult to answer concerning these sculptures. They appear to have been gathered together from different places, but it is not known from where, when, or for what purpose. There is no doubt that they were produced by artists of the Igbomina and Ibolo areas – scattered pieces of similar stone sculpture have been found in some places in that general part of the country. Virtually all pieces in the collection are damaged – a fact which seems to indicate that they were probably gathered in distressed circumstances (like flight from war), or that the collection was set upon for destruction after it was gathered together. While these and other questions remain unanswered, however, there is no doubt that these stone images of Esie represent very significant examples of the best in Yoruba sculptural art in stone.

As Drewal, Pemberton and Abiodun note in their monumental book on Yoruba art, "The Yoruba-speaking peoples of Nigeria and the Popular Republic of Benin, together with their countless descendants in other parts of Africa and the Americas, have made remarkable contributions to world civilization ... In the arts, the Yoruba are heirs to one of the oldest and finest artistic traditions in Africa ..."[17] Most of that great artistic tradition of the Yoruba people was accomplished in the urban civilization of the Yoruba kingdoms.

11

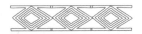

The Frontier Effect

The southern border of the Yoruba homeland is the Atlantic coastline. To the west, north and east, are land frontiers with non-Yoruba neighbors. The types of relationships that developed along these land frontiers played very significant parts in the history of what we may call the Yoruba frontier kingdoms.

While the frontiers in general constituted grounds for cultural and economic inter-fertilization, the Yoruba frontier kingdoms, along most stretches of the frontiers, and for most of their history, also lived under military and political pressures from formidable, hostile, neighbors. By and large, faced with these pressures, the affected kingdoms developed strengths that enabled them to survive and, in one important case, to overcome and subdue the hostile neighbors for some centuries.

Along the Western Frontier

The western frontier had a character entirely its own. Much has earlier been said in this book about the relationship of the western Yoruba and their Aja neighbors. In summary, settlements of the Yoruba and Aja early became interspersed and this had resulted in much cultural affinity between the two peoples long before the Yoruba began to create kingdoms, starting with Ife in the tenth or eleventh century. From the late sixteenth century, the Aja people also began to create kingdoms, closely patterned after the Yoruba kingdoms. Of these, the most important were Savi (of which Whydah was a dependent port town) and Weme, both on or near the coast, Allada (or Ardra) about twenty miles inland from the coast, and Dahomey, whose capital town, Abomey, lay still further inland on the Abomey plateau. As Savi's port town of Whydah became a major center of the slave trade in the course of the seventeenth century, the whole Savi kingdom came to be referred to as Whydah. Allada was the earliest to be founded, in about 1575, and was generally regarded by the Aja people as "father" of all their kingdoms. In general, these kingdoms were strongly influenced by Yoruba culture and had substantial Yoruba populations. In fact, the Fon leadership groups of the Dahomey kingdom, founded in 1625, emerged from a mixture of Aja and Yoruba elements.

Not long after it came into existence, the Dahomey kingdom began to exhibit great ambition. By the late seventeenth century, it was already causing anxiety for its neighbors, Yoruba and Aja alike. Dahomey pushed towards the coast and brought pressure to bear on all its neighbors. Its aggression forced many people, both Yoruba and Aja, to migrate eastwards into the Egbado country, resulting, as would be remembered, in the emergence of new towns there as well as in increases in the populations of some old towns.

At this point, the Oyo-Ile kingdom from the northeast, by then a very strong power, entered the scene. Oyo armies swept through the area and the Yoruba and Aja kingdoms there, including Dahomey, became tributary to Oyo-Ile. The details of all this belong to a subsequent chapter. Oyo-Ile continued in control until the last years of the eighteenth century when, because of internal and other problems, its hold began to weaken. This gave Dahomey the chance to reemerge with considerable strength, and thus to become a great threat to all of the kingdoms of western Yorubaland in the nineteenth century – as will be seen in our chapter on that century.[1]

Along the Northern Frontier

Along the Yoruba northern frontier, their neighbors were the Bariba and the Nupe, two peoples of the banks of the River Niger. Between these peoples and the Yoruba, much cultural inter-fertilization occurred throughout their history. Not only were the Nupe and Yoruba closely related during their evolution into distinct groups, they thereafter remained very special neighbors to each other. Along the southern banks of the Niger, early settlements of Bariba, Nupe and Yoruba people lived side by side; in some cases, in fact, Yoruba (Oyo) and Bariba elements occupied the same villages in the western parts of the Middle Niger valley, while Yoruba (Oyo and Igbomina) and Nupe elements inhabited the same villages in some areas in the eastern parts of the valley. The Nupe were the closest trading partners of the Yoruba from the north. The fact that the Nupe lived on both the northern and southern banks of the Niger (their main population concentration being in the northern banks) gave them great influence over the river crossings and made them the major connection between Yorubaland and the countries beyond the Niger. In language, in religion, in their styles of clothing, and in a large spread of other cultural practices and customs, centuries of very close relationships resulted in profound similarities between the Yoruba and Nupe. Yoruba traditions acknowledge Nupe inputs into significant features of important Yoruba institutions such as Ifa divination and *egungun*, while Nupe traditions acknowledge Yoruba origins of such institutions as the Ogboni cult and facial markings among the Nupe. Countless family ties straddled the ethnic boundary between the Nupe and the Yoruba, a factor of considerable importance in the evolution of political institutions and titles among the two peoples. Of foreign traders on Yoruba soil, only Nupe women traders were usually admitted to membership and leading positions in market commodity associations.[2]

Yet, political frictions characterized the relationship of these peoples in the frontier areas. Aribidesi Usman[3] has identified two broad periods in the development of these frictions. First, in the early history of Igbomina and Nupe settlements, only small, local frictions commonly occurred — minor frictions over land, water and other resources between neighboring villages or village groups. Probably a similar situation existed between early Bariba and Oyo settlements to the west. Usman then identifies a period, starting from about the thirteenth century and continuing until about the seventeenth century, when a reverse migration of Yoruba people from the southern forests to the northern grasslands took place. This migration increased Yoruba populations in northern Yorubaland in general and in particular in the Oyo and Igbomina countries. As the numbers of the Yoruba increased, their non-Yoruba neighbors felt threatened. Settlements that had been originally wholly or partly Nupe became predominantly Yoruba and the Nupe, in order to hold or regain position, fought back. Again, almost certainly, similar developments were taking place between the Oyo Yoruba and the Bariba further to the west.

It is significant that this period of increased frictions was the period of the founding of kingdoms in Yorubaland. As Yoruba kingdoms arose in the Niger area, they faced stiff opposition by the Nupe or Bariba. The history of Owu, Ketu, and Ila illustrates the experiences of the earliest Yoruba kingdoms close to the Niger. Owu finally flourished in the country roughly west of Ife; but there is evidence that its first location was further to the north, in the Ogboro area, and that it was pushed south from there by the Bariba. The Ketu kingdom first took a position in the territory to the west of the hills where Oyo-Ile was later founded. Bariba opposition forced it to give up that location and migrate to the south, where it finally settled down. And the Orangun's kingdom of Ila was forced to move from location to location for a long time. At last, in about the fourteenth century, Ila chose a good location and embarked upon building for its defense a very formidable wall system. Ila's city walls became famous in Yorubaland and Ila itself became proudly known as Ila-Yara (Ila of the great walls). Protected behind its famous walls, Ila settled down and prospered; the glory of the Orangun finally shone forth.

Map 2. Yorubaland and frontier kingdoms in the western Sudan

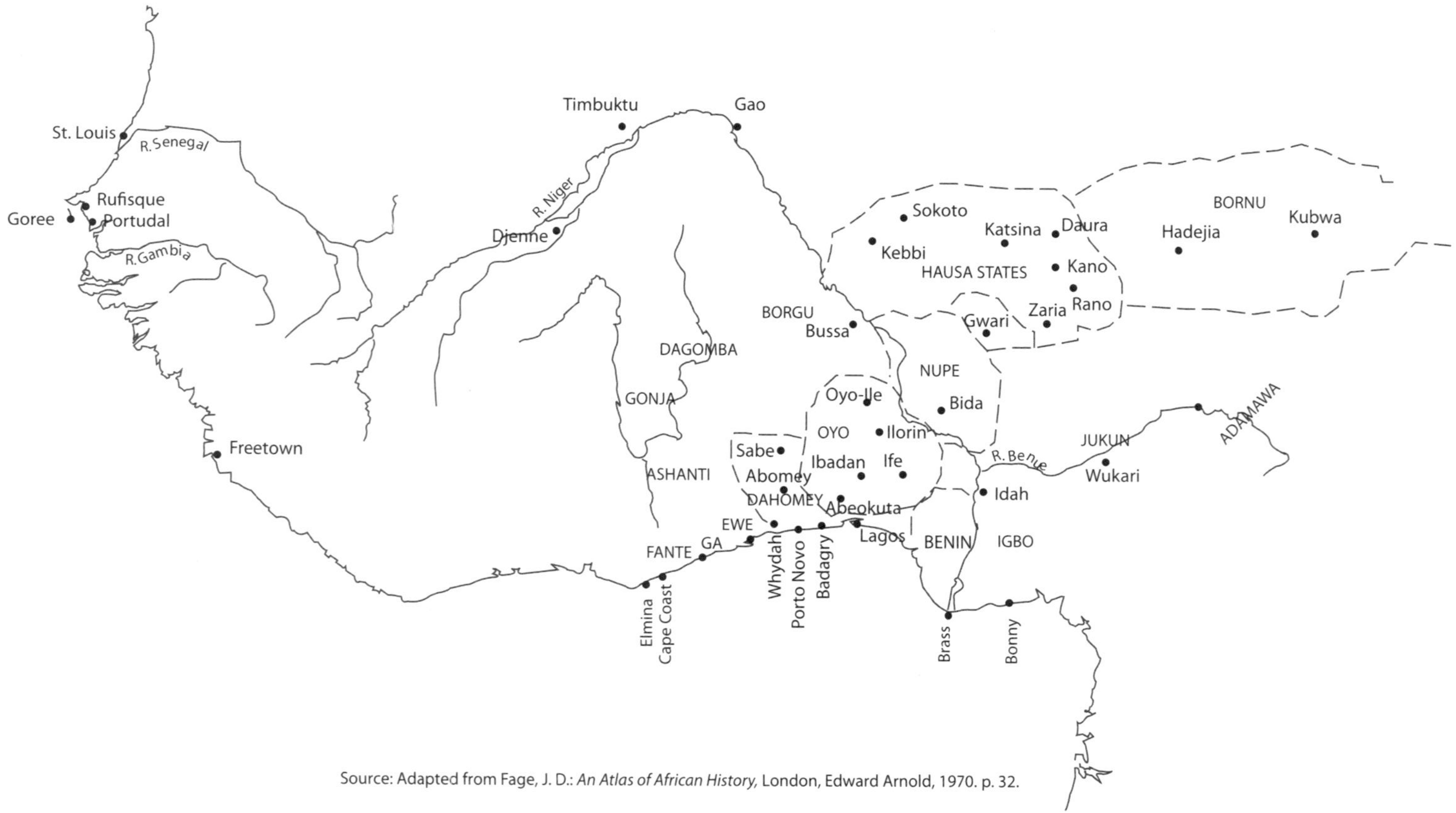

Source: Adapted from Fage, J. D.: *An Atlas of African History*, London, Edward Arnold, 1970. p. 32.

Even then the Nupe never ceased harassing Ila and other Igbomina towns. In about the fifteenth century, the various Nupe groups became united into one centralized kingdom under Edegi (or Tsoede). With that, their aggression became better led and better directed, mainly towards the seizure of channels of trade. From Igbomina, the Nupe broke south in the fifteenth century into Ijesa, northern Ekiti and Akoko and even threatened Ilesa. Ilesa traditions count at least two Nupe invasions of Ijesa, against both of which the Ilesa forces were victorious. At the same time, Ife sent armies, as earlier related, to Ara in Ekiti to join with the Ekiti in repelling the Nupe. This situation continued until the sixteenth century.

One very important consequence of the Nupe and Bariba hostility was that the Yoruba lost some of their foothold on the southern banks of the Middle Niger. In the area to the west of the country where Oyo-Ile was later to be founded, the Bariba pushed Oyo and Ketu settlers down southwards. Further east, the Yoruba who had lived in the Jebba-Mokwa area were absorbed by the Nupe. The Gbedegi of that area are now mostly Nupe in culture, but they were probably originally Yoruba. Bishop Ajayi Crowther reported witnessing some rituals of the Gbedegi on the Niger in the late nineteenth century, rituals being conducted in the Yoruba language – and noted that the persons conducting the rituals did not understand the language that they were using.

From the seventeenth century, a new development gave a fresh impetus and purpose to Nupe aggression. The Atlantic slave trade was growing on the coast of West Africa. From then on, Nupe incursions into the territories of their neighbors (the Gbagyi in the country north of the Niger Valley, and the Yoruba south of it) increasingly took on the character of slave raids – what some historians have described as "smash and grab operations, with little consideration for long-term exploitation"[4] – commercial or political.

During the late sixteenth century, however, Oyo-Ile emerged as a very powerful kingdom in the Oyo country. Its military power soon penetrated into the Igbomina country, a demise that began the process which was later to establish Oyo-Ile's overlordship over much of the Nupe territory south of the Niger. For the Ila and other Igbomina kingdoms, there followed two centuries of comparative peace, shielded by Oyo-Ile's power. Nupe incursions did not completely stop, but they became fewer and less effective. But then, two centuries later, by the second half of the eighteenth century, Oyo-Ile's power began to wane. This opened the door to a new intensity of Nupe aggression. Three of the Nupe kings of the mid to late eighteenth century – the Etsu Jibrilu (1744–59), Majiya I (1769–80), and Mu'azu (1780–95) – are particularly notable for their violent raids. Many Igbomina towns – Isanlu, Oba, Oke-Aba, Oke-Ode, Oro-Ago, and even Ila – were either forced to evacuate or were reduced to tributaries by the

Jibrilu raids. Weakened by internal dissension, Ila people lost the will to fight, and their great city fell to the enemy, their king, the Orangun Arutu, dying in the process. After evacuating Ila-Yara, Ila people split into two, one continuing to bear the name Ila, the other taking the name Oke-Ila, both kings retaining the Orangun title. Not surprisingly, the two only became more vulnerable to Nupe aggression. The raids under Majiya I were even more devastating. Majiya's cavalry forces galloped on whirlwind raids throughout the Igbomina country, sacking and burning towns and villages and capturing men, women and children for sale. The flourishing town of Igbole in the Olusin's kingdom, Odo-Eku, Oro, as well as many villages in the Ibolo area (near Offa) fell to Majiya's attacks. So also did Gbagede, the royal town of the Olupo's kingdom. The Olupo Dalla II died fighting at the head of his people, a fate shared by some other Igbomina kings. To the east of Igbomina, the territories of the Iyagba, Abunu, Ikiri, Owe, Gbede and Oworo, lacking centralized kingdoms, became easy raiding ground for the Nupe. In fits and bursts, the Nupe activities extended into Akoko and northern Ekiti. The Nupe made a habit of stationing resident officials in ravaged towns, but, according to traditions in the affected places, the presence of such an official did not shield any town from being raided again and again. As the eighteenth century drew to a close, then, the kingdoms, towns and villages of much of the Igbomina and the Okun Yoruba reeled under the Nupe scourge.

It says much for the strength and resilience of the Yoruba kingdoms and towns in these places that nearly all survived. Kingdoms smashed in their original homes took their kings, political systems and religious properties, and struck root in other locations. Even the smallest of towns did the same. Usually, such groups sought sites that held out particular advantages (especially hilly places) where they would be better able to defend themselves. Also, trade survived. Yoruba traders and their Nupe counterparts (both mostly women) kept trade flowing, albeit with interruptions and in the midst of grave hazards. Even as late as the 1850s, by which time wars were even more widespread, foreigners who traveled through part of Igbomina and northern Ekiti found trade flowing quite vigorously on the trade routes.

Along the Eastern Frontier

Along the eastern frontier, almost all the important developments impacting Yoruba people were concentrated on the southeast.[5] Further northwards on the eastern frontier, their neighbors were all small national groups stretched out along the western banks of the Lower Niger – namely, the Kakanda, Ebira and Afenmai. Between each of these peoples and their Yoruba neighbors, much cultural interaction and exchange occurred throughout history, resulting in significant similarities in language and ways of life. The dialects of the Yoruba subgroups in these areas (notably the Okun Yoruba and the Akoko) bear strong marks of the languages of their non-Yoruba neighbors, who all spoke Yoruba as a second language. Movement of farm labor appears to have been regular across the borders, resulting in many small Ebira settlements on farmlands in parts of Ekiti and Akoko.

In the mostly thickly forested country of the southeast, Yoruba kingdoms shared boundaries with the Edo and Edo-related peoples like the Akoko-Edo, Afenmai and Ishan. This was an area of intensive cultural interactions resulting in mixed populations, common occurrences of bilingualism, free borrowings among languages, pockets of immigrants outside their own ethnic areas, widespread inter-ethnic marriages, a free flow of trade and of human movements. Politically and in geographical features, the immediate Yoruba frontier was divided into two areas: a southern half consisting of mostly low-lying thick forest country, the home of the kingdoms of the Owo forests; and a northern, generally hilly territory, covered by lighter vegetation, the home of the Akoko kingdoms. Most of the intermixing of cultures and peoples took place in the northern half, where the Akoko lived in very close contact with their Akoko-Edo and other neighbors. To the south, the Owo country was separated from the main centers of Edo population (and from Benin) by some fifty miles of the thickest forests in the Yoruba–Edo region. Even then, the Olowo's kingdom of Owo and the Edo influenced each other's culture in many ways, to the extent, for instance, that Owo's Yoruba dialect came to bear a strong imprint of the Edo language. In the extreme southeastern Owo forests, the small kingdoms – Ifon, Sobe, Ikaro, Ute, Imoru, Ajagba – all ended up having varying degrees of Edo influence in their culture and dialect; some had considerable populations of Edo immigrants.

Some of the oldest and busiest trade routes in southern Yorubaland passed through this whole area, carrying trade between all parts of Yorubaland, Benin and the countries of the Edo and neighboring peoples. The city of Owo became the shining light of this frontier area, a city of culture and art, the transition center of the flow of artistic traditions between ancient Ife and Benin. Available archaeological evidence reveals that Owo, an early center of the art of bronze casting, benefited from, and enriched, the ancient Ife and Benin traditions of bronze casting. Within Yorubaland it was, almost certainly, second only to Ile-Ife as a place of art for centuries, before eventually superseding it. In general, Yoruba and Edo monarchical culture and royal regalia had a common base, characterized by a preference for beads as the precious adornment of rulers. In the course of history, the Edo took the beaded component of this royal grandeur and embellished it gorgeously, until the Oba of Benin, when adorned for public appearances, dazzled the eye in his super-abundance of beads. The Owo, Akoko, and most Ekiti kingdoms borrowed liberally from this Edo tradition, as well as from Benin royal festivals, chieftaincy titles, and styles of palace buildings. For much of their history after the rise of the Benin kingdom, in fact, the Owo, Akoko and southern Ekiti peoples of this area looked as much eastwards towards Benin as they did westwards towards the main centers of Yoruba civilization.

In the traditions of these Yoruba kingdoms, however, the greatest emphasis belongs to the political relationships that developed with Benin.[6] Founded in about the twelfth century, Benin had by the fourteenth century unified all the Edo, and the Edo-related Akoko-Edo, Afenmai and Ishan peoples, under its own leadership, thus becoming a kingdom of considerable power. Owo was the earliest Yoruba kingdom founded in the area, probably in the late twelfth century also. Though Benin and Owo were separated from each other by a wide country of very thick forests and some fairly large rivers, the two soon established close commercial and cultural contacts – relationships that were made the richer by the fact that both looked, spiritually, commercially and culturally, northwestwards towards Ife and were connected to that ancient kingdom through the same old routes. In spite of such relationships, however, rivalries over the trade routes led to hostilities. The growing power of Owo seemed to threaten Benin's free access to the rich trade of the further Yoruba country, thus provoking Benin into taking military action.

A first invasion in the early fifteenth century, led by a famous chief named Iken, ended in disaster. The Benin army entered Owo after some resistance and took some booty, but when it started to leave for home, Owo people sprang a massive surprise. A rout followed and Iken himself was killed. Many of the Benin men chose to make new homes in Owo and the surrounding villages rather than return to Benin. The rest quietly returned home. A number of less famous invasions followed, about whose outcome there is much confusion in Benin and Owo traditions. By the late fifteenth century, an arrangement had been made guaranteeing special protection for Benin traders in Owo and for Owo traders in Benin. Benin and Owo traditions agree that this arrangement included a provision that Owo would, from time to time, send a prince to live in the Benin palace, but do not clearly explain the significance of this. Some Benin traditions claim that its implication was that Owo was subject to Benin; but others claim that the purpose was to signify Owo's continued faithfulness to the agreement to let Benin traders go peacefully through Owo to the further interior. Some Owo traditions claim that it was a means of emphasizing the new era of close friendship between Benin and Owo.

As it turned out, this arrangement greatly served the interests of both kingdoms. According to Owo traditions, a large colony of Benin traders sprang up in Owo and a large colony of Owo traders sprang up in Benin. From Owo, Benin trade spread rapidly into Ekiti and Akoko. Akure, to the north of Owo, became a major center of Benin trade, with a large colony of Benin traders. Another sizeable Benin trading community emerged in the junction town of Igbara-Oke on the route to Ilesa. Smaller colonies of Benin traders developed in Ikere, Ado, Ara, and as far north as Otun, the Ekiti town which Benin traders came to regard as a sort of outer limit to their trade. Owo traders also came to feature prominently, through Benin, in the coastal lagoon trade with the Itsekiri, Ilaje, Ijebu, Awori and Aja – and, soon, with European coastal traders, when these appeared from about the 1480s.

Wherever there was a sizeable colony of Benin traders, they had the habit of organizing themselves into a community with its own "chiefs," topped by a head chief with the title of Olotu-Ado or Olotu Ekiran. They also developed the practice of sending their tributes to the Oba of Benin through their Olotu-Ado. Usually, these head chiefs wanted to be seen and treated as representatives of the Oba of Benin. Their unmet expectations in this regard came to play some part in causing conflicts with Benin. According to Akure traditions, the first coming of Benin troops to Akure, during the reign of Oba Ewuare of Benin in about the middle of the fifteenth century, was caused by a major confrontation between the Akure government and the leadership of the Benin trading community over a dispute between some Akure and Benin traders in the Akure marketplace. After Akure, the Benin troops penetrated into southern Ekiti – to Ikere, Ado, Ara, Ogotun, Ise, Emure, in which towns sizeable Benin trading communities already existed. According to accounts in the traditions, the Benin army engaged in no actual fighting in any of these kingdoms – with the exception of Ado. While passing through Ikere, the army got drawn into some on-going hostilities between Ado and Ikere. The details are unclear, but Ikere did succeed in winning the support of the Benin army for its forces preparing to fight against Ado.[7] Apparently, Ado people themselves made this possible; misunderstanding the original intentions of the Benin troops, Ado rulers seem to have been hostile to them and to have made some attempt to prohibit their entry into Ado territory. Some minor fighting occurred between Ado men and the Benin forces, but it quickly came to an end in some mutual understanding and the Ado rulers then decided to welcome the Benin men and to allow them to come into and through Ado. However, the news of the fighting had spread to some of Ado's subordinate villages; therefore, when the Benin men passed through these villages, they were met with hostility. This provoked a number of minor engagements, as well as the strange action whereby the Benin commanders took away some villagers found on farms and highways (from Are, Afao, Iluomoba and Agbado) and resettled them in Ikere where they were made to settle in new quarters under their old village names. Some of the Benin men, returning home through Akoko, entered into some of the mostly small Akoko kingdoms. Wherever the Benin men went, some chose to settle as traders, artisans, etc., thus adding to the number of Benin settlers. In fact, the overall impression from Owo, Ekiti and Akoko traditions about Benin's men in arms is that hardly any of them should be regarded as exclusively a soldier. Every one was a trader, a herbalist or an artisan (blacksmith, coppersmith, bead setter, etc.) and the lure of opportunities for their trades far from home was a cardinal motivation for their enlisting in their king's service. Consequently, Benin men in arms tended to go beyond their objectives and roam far beyond, more or less like commercial exploration groups. Many also tended to end up settling in the places that they visited.

Some decades after these events in the early fifteenth century, the news spread all over Yorubaland that some strange white people had come to Benin from over the seas. Then, the Benin traders began to come with exotic European goods. Benin wholesalers became sought after among retailers in all marketplaces, especially in Owo, Akoko and Ekiti. Trade along the old lagoon waterways multiplied in volume as Edo, Owo, Itsekiri, Ijaw, Ilaje, coastal Ijebu and Awori traders took increased parts in trading there, as far west as the Aja coast or even beyond. Since Benin was for a long time the main source of entry of European goods into Yorubaland, its increasingly large trading influence penetrated into the southern kingdoms of Yorubaland – to Ikale and, from there, to Ondo; from the coastal Ijebu and Awori to the Ijebu interior and even to Egbado.

Benin's closest interaction with Yorubaland remained, however, with its immediate neighbors – the Owo, Akoko and Ekiti. After the first Owo–Benin clashes in the fifteenth century, Benin did not come into confrontation with Owo again (and did not send armed men beyond Owo) until the early seventeenth century. The cause of the new conflicts with Owo was the challenge posed to Benin by the Olowo Osogboye who, according to the Owo historian, Ashara, reigned between 1602 and 1648. Osogboye had lived as a young prince in the Benin palace and, according to Benin traditions, was a very personable teenager and very much beloved in Benin. Strangely, without the courtesy of informing the Oba of Benin, he secretly returned to Owo – which action was seen in Benin as a breach of the cordial relationship between Owo and Benin. The Oba of Benin sent envoys to ask the Olowo to make him return but he eluded the envoys. About one year later, the reigning Olowo, Omaro, died, and Osogboye, young, knowledgeable and ambitious, ascended the Owo throne.

Osogboye came to the throne with grand schemes in his head: he would remodel the Owo monarchical system after Benin's and he would make Owo, militarily and otherwise, the equal or even the superior of Benin. His charisma energized his subjects; at his bidding, they embarked on the construction of a gigantic wall system for their city. Owo youths were trained and drilled for war, until their young king was satisfied that his army was an equal to Benin's. His schemes worked. When the expected Benin invasion came, Owo was ready for it. The large Benin army marched into a well-laid ambush outside the village of Ute and was routed. Two other invasions did not do any better, although some residents of Owo villages and farmsteads were taken away as war captives.

Benin's war against Osogboye's Owo in the early seventeenth century appears to have led to a second wave of entry of Benin's men in arms into the Ekiti and Akoko countries. The exact reasons for this are not known. Two small groups entered the Akoko country from the Akoko-Edo area. Another small group entered Akure. After Akure, this group broke into a few units and fanned out into Ekiti. Unlike the fifteenth century invasions, these seventeenth century forces included units that carried guns. The Ekiti and Akoko in their traditions give the impression that most of the effect of the gun was produced by its terrifying noise. One of their sayings has it that when the king of Benin waged war on the earth, the god of noise (Ogbomudu) waged war in the sky. Another feature of these invasions was that some of the Benin units took away some captives from farms and roadways, not as hostages or *eru* (slaves) but as people to be sold in Benin to traders who would sell them to traders on the coast. The fear generated by the rumors from Owo that Benin people would sell captives to traders from beyond the seas, according to Ekiti traditions, provoked hostility to Benin residents in some towns and villages.

As had happened in the early fifteenth century, the Benin men again found themselves in conflict with the Ado kingdom. Apparently, because Ado was, as would be remembered, often fighting wars of expansion against its neighbors, the Benin had come to think of Ado as an overambitious and unfriendly kingdom. As the noise of the Benin guns reverberated outside the Ado city walls, Ado people took the decision that if the enemy entered their city, nobody should flee from the guns but everybody should die fighting in front of his compound. Consequently, when the Benin troops entered Ado, they found themselves opposed on every street. Almost all of the fighting was with traditional weapons such as bows and arrows, spears and swords. Ado people remember this as the bloodiest fighting ever in the history of their town. By evening, there were dead bodies in front of many compounds, bodies of both invaders and defenders of the city. The engagement became known in Ado traditions as *Ogun*

Oluponakusupona — "the war in which all resolved to die fighting in front of their homes."

Other Benin units went to other parts of Ekiti. In spite of their guns, they were met with resistance in most places. One unit went all the way north to Otun and then attempted to go further north into the Igbomina country (by then mostly under Oyo-Ile's protection). Just beyond Otun, some local Igbomina forces, reinforced by some Oyo cavalry, stood in their way and they withdrew.

Following these events, some of the Ekiti kings, according to some Ekiti traditions, seem to have bought a few guns. However, there is no evidence that any Ekiti kingdom ever used such guns in warfare. The kings who bought guns seem to have kept them as prestige possessions only. The occasional noise of guns from the Ado palace (during some festivals) earned one Ewi of the time the additional cognomen of Akulojuorun ("he who booms in the sky").

Owo, Ekiti and Akoko people did not experience another coming of Benin troops for about two centuries – that is, until the early nineteenth century. For all the rest of the seventeenth century and the whole of the eighteenth, Benin suffered serious internal weaknesses of its own. Then in the second decade of the nineteenth century (Oguntuyi, the Ado historian, puts it as 1818),[8] Benin sent some men into Ekiti. The king of Owo was officially informed by Benin that their destination was Akure and not Owo. Even then, Owo refused them passage through any part of its territories and raised a large army to enforce its refusal. Going by the ancient route through the forests south of Owo, around by the foot of the Orosun Hill (near Alade and Idanre), the Benin men, again some carrying guns, entered Akure. Even better than in the seventeenth century, Akure prepared to defend itself and killed many of the leading Edo residents. Days of fierce fighting followed, with the Akure forces led by the Deji Osupa himself. In one of the engagements, the Deji was killed and one of his sons was taken captive. From Akure, small groups of Benin men went to parts of southern Ekiti and through Ikere and Ado to Otun. Ado traditions mention their passage without giving any account of fighting. The traditions speak of a minor clash between a small Benin contingent and the forces of the Otun kingdom, resulting in the death of some Benin chiefs. Other Benin chiefs then acted to revive the friendship with Otun, even offered their services to the Oore of Otun in a small war between Otun and one town, Aaye, that was in rebellion against him.

On the whole then, there was not much of actual fighting in the Benin expeditions into Owo, Ekiti and Akoko. An interesting perspective on the subject was given by the Oore of Otun to this author during visits to the Otun palace in the 1970s.[9] According to the Oore, the true picture was that Ekiti kingdoms did not really see Benin as an enemy. The comings of Benin's armed men were few and very far between; no generation of Ekiti people witnessed two of such, most generations saw none. The Oba of Benin was regarded as a "brother" to some Ekiti kings. Paying tribute to the Oba of Benin was out of the question. Forming a coalition to fight him was also out of the question – and so, for the most part, was making even solo preparations to fight him. In Ado and Akure where bloody battles occurred, there were special factors at work. In Akure, the large Benin resident trading community was irresponsibly ambitious and frequently came into conflict with the Deji's government. Ado people fought because they believed the Benin men were supporting Ikere against Ado. Most people taken away by the Benin men as captives were seized on the roads or on their farms. Some communities that put up some resistance did so for fear of the alleged slave trading practices of the people of Benin.

On the whole, the movements of Benin's men in arms appear to have been intrinsically actions in support of trade and traders. Benin was a great trading state whose rulers paid very close attention to its citizens' trading activities. The Oba of Benin himself was the patron of some of the most important trading associations that organized trade to various territories outside of Benin. It is in the context of the activities and traditions of these trading associations that we must understand most statements in Benin claiming many distant lands as places in which the Oba of Benin had influence. Olfert Dapper, using such sources derived from Benin in the seventeenth century, wrote as follows:

> The kingdom of Benin... is borded on the north-west by the kingdoms of Ulkami, Yabu, Isago and Udobo, to the north by that of Gabu, situated at an eight days journey above the great town of Benin; to the east by the kingdoms of Itsana and Forkado or Ouweri... How far the kingdom of Benin extends from south to north is yet unknown, as some places lie at a great distance of eight or nine days traveling beyond the town of Benin, near Ulkumi...[10]

J. Barbot, using Dapper without acknowledgement and adding some details of his own, wrote in the eighteenth century that the Benin kingdom "borders to the north-west on Alkomy, Jaboe, Isago and Oedobo... Its extent from south to north must be near two hundred leagues." He also added the information that "Towards Alkomy, the Benin kingdom is very well peopled."[11] Captain H. L. Galway, who visited Benin in 1892, wrote that the Benin kingdom had used to extend "up to within fifty miles of Lokoja, at the confluence of the Niger and Benue Rivers."[12]

Deciphering these statements is not easy. Of the place names, Ulkami or Alkomy (as would be remembered) meant the country of the Yoruba. In that case, "the kingdoms of Ulkami" meant the Yoruba kingdoms. Dapper's statement that the Benin kingdom was "bordered on the northwest by the kingdoms of Ulkami" would therefore mean that, to the northwest, Benin shared a border with the neighboring Yoruba kingdoms (that is, the Owo and Akoko kingdoms). Dapper's further statement that the Benin kingdom shared a border on the northwest also with "Yabu, Isago and Udobo" presents a much bigger difficulty. It is not known for sure what Isago and Udobo would have referred to – probably Isoko and Urhobo. It has been suggested that Yabu probably referred to Ijebu. If so, then Dapper's statement in this regard would contain an exaggeration. The Benin traded with the coasts of Yorubaland all the way to (and beyond) the powerful Yoruba kingdom of Ijebu-Ode, but the Benin kingdom is not known to have encompassed these territories. Ijebu was a name certainly well known in Benin as a result of the activities of Benin traders. Dapper learned that, to the north, the Benin kingdom was bordered by the kingdom of Gabu. It has been suggested that Gabu probably referred to Abaw on the Lower Niger. Barbot's statement that, "towards Alkomy, the Benin kingdom was very well peopled" would seem to refer to the populous Ishan and Akoko-Edo countries, the homes of many villages in close proximity. Captain Galway's 1892 statement that the Benin kingdom extended to about fifty miles south of Lokoja on the Niger–Benue confluence is consistent with what is known of the extent of the Benin kingdom in the country of the Edo-related Afenmai, the eastern neighbors of the Yoruba Akoko and Okun Yoruba. In this Afenmai country beyond the eastern borders of Yorubaland, the Benin kingdom had for centuries clashed with the Nupe. The sum total of all this would seem to be that the Benin kingdom with its vassal territories shared borders with Yoruba kingdoms to the west and northwest and a little to the north, that it covered the Edo, Ishan, Akoko-Edo and Afenmai countries, and that, along the western bank of the Lower Niger, in the Afenmai country, it extended to quite close to the Niger–Benue confluence in an area where it was frequently at war with the Nupe.

It will be helpful, however, to supplement the above conclusion with local information on the Yoruba areas concerned. In an earlier article on this subject, this writer had suggested a considerably wider and deeper political influence for Benin in eastern Yorubaland.[13] On a closer look at the evidence, however, and in the light of subsequently clearer understanding of Benin and eastern Yoruba history, that earlier position can no longer be sustained. Before Osogboye (1602–48), the Owo kingdom had a sort of bilateral treaty relationship with Benin. From Osogboye's time, Owo affirmed its independence more aggressively and became less friendly.

In the bigger Akoko towns, Benin (Edo) trading communities were many, and some of them were quite large. Apart from the leaders of the resident Edo trading communities (known as Olotu-Ado), there were, at some times in the history of some of the bigger towns, Benin officials known as *balekale*. The duties of the *balekale* were to watch over the interests of the Benin traders and to transmit tributes to the Oba of Benin. The traditions of these places have it that such tributes were collected from members of the Edo resident communities — and some corroboration for this would seem to be provided by the fact that, after the British had conquered the Benin kingdom in 1897, some Edo resident communities in Ekiti and Akoko still sought to send their representatives to take their tributes to the Oba of Benin. The situation would seem to be that distant Edo trading communities regularly kept contact with their homeland's rulers by sending their tributes to their Oba, especially on certain royal festivals in Benin, and that the Benin government reciprocated by sometimes sending men (or troops) to visit these trading communities and *balekale* to live, and represent the Benin Oba's interests, among them. About the relationship between the *balekale* and the local Akoko rulers, the traditions offer no clear information; the overall impression would seem to be that the *balekale* had no significant status *vis à vis* the rulers of the native Akoko communities. On the whole, Akoko traditions are very proudly emphatic about the Akoko people's love of freedom. Basic to their lack of large political units was a tenacious love of individual and community freedom, aided by the fragmentation of their country by rocky hills.

Among the Ekiti, Benin's influence was felt most strongly in the Akure and Ikere kingdoms. Akure was the Ekiti city on the busiest spot on the highway connecting central and northern Yorubaland with the south and with Benin through Owo. Because the Ado-Akure community that came to accumulate in Akure was very large, its leaders were often very ambitious for recognition in Akure. Their demands and comportment frequently generated conflicts between them and the Akure people, many of which escalated into serious communal violence, sometimes lasting for months. Such eruptions did not only usually cause serious loss of lives and property in the Ado-Akure community, they also disrupted the flow of trade — and therefore attracted the attention of the Benin government. It was to deal with this situation (to protect the Edo resident traders and free the flow of the trade), that Benin troops were sent to Akure. The available evidence indicates that Akure never acknowledged Benin's overlordship. However, according to a statement by Akure chiefs in 1897,[14] Akure used to send, for an unknown length of time, "yearly presents" to the Oba of Benin — probably briefly following the seventeenth century Benin invasion of Akure, the invasion in which Benin troops first used guns. According to the same 1897 statement, during the same brief period, Akure used to send messengers with gifts to inform the Oba of Benin of the installation of a new Deji of Akure. But even during that brief period, the Akure chiefs seem to have usually neglected or refused to send messengers to Benin while installing their king and the insistence by the leaders of the Ado-Akure that it be done usually provoked conflicts. For most of the late seventeenth century and all of the eighteenth, while Benin was too weak at home to influence events in distant places, the Ado-Akure seem to have mellowed and given little or no trouble, and the rulers of Akure had no trouble from Benin. However, in about 1815, when the Deji Osupa was crowned, the then leadership of the Ado-Akure community chose to remember a thing that had been long forgotten and began to make trouble over it: they protested the fact that the Akure chiefs had sent no messenger to the Oba of Benin, and they even sent a messenger of their own. This, together with an on-going trouble over the killing of an Edo trader named Ogonto in the Akure marketplace, led to very bloody conflicts between the Akure people and the Ado-Akure community. A certain Chief Osagwe who came from Benin and presented himself as an official envoy of the Oba of Benin was killed by the Akure people and the conflicts greatly escalated. About three years later, as the violence was still continuing sporadically (causing serious material and human losses to the Ado-Akure trading community, and which seriously disrupted trade), Benin sent an army. This 1818 war was a brief and sharp affair, with no known lasting political outcome. After it, Akure was never again to see Benin arms, as Benin's power sank lower and lower thereafter. As for the Ado-Akure, increasingly unsure of Benin's protection and patronage, almost all had become simply Akure people by the end of the nineteenth century, although some of them continued dutifully to send their tributes to the Oba of Benin.

 Benin's pressure was never as strong in Ikere as in Akure. The Benin resident community in Ikere was much smaller and tended generally to harmonize with the native Ikere society. All in all, Benin seems to have treated Ikere as a commercial ally in southern Ekiti. During the seventeenth century, as would be remembered, a prominent member of the Benin resident community, a famous hunter who was a close friend and confidant of the then Olukere and lived close to his compound, became ruler of Ikere. It is not clear how the transfer of governance to this man took place. Ikere traditions say that the Olukere often used the assistance of this friend of his in settling some disputes in the city whenever he himself was too busy with the rituals of the Olosunta. Most probably, the Olukere then died and during the interregnum, common in Yoruba kingdoms, Ikere people continued to resort to the late Olukere's friend as judge in their disputes; the interregnum continued longer and longer, until the *de facto* leader became, more or less, a *de jure* leader; and when he died (probably while the interregnum still lasted), his son succeeded him and gradually assumed royal attributes – and a new dynasty thus came into being. Ikere traditions are emphatic that neither the Benin government nor any Benin arms had any input into this important change in Ikere's political history. After it had happened, how did it affect Ikere's relationship with Benin? Again, Ikere's traditions give no clear information about this. A certain measure of increased closeness between Ikere and Benin may be assumed, as well as increased Benin–Ikere trade, but there is no indication of any loss of independence by Ikere.[15]

In most of the rest of Ekiti, Benin's political influence appears to have been about nil. About June 1897, a certain Joseph Williams, clerk and interpreter for the Niger Coast Protectorate, visited many Ekiti towns for the express purpose of proving that Ekiti ought to belong to the Niger Coast Protectorate because, according to him, Ekiti towns had used to be ruled by Benin. He reported that at Ilawe, Igbara-Odo, Ogotun and Ara (all in southwestern Ekiti) there was acknowledgement that some gifts and some tributes had been sent to the Oba of Benin in the past. The set preconception with which Joseph Williams had come to these places makes his account unreliable. Moreover, the well known fact that members of Benin trading colonies in Ekiti towns had used to send tributes to the Oba of Benin in the past creates confusion around Williams' reference to tributes. When asked about this later (in 1975), Ara chiefs remembered that the first white man to visit their town had succeeded only in talking to the leaders of the then small Edo resident community and not to the then Alara and his chiefs, because the Alara's palace and most of the town was still in ruins as a result of the Ibadan destruction of Ara some years earlier. Ogotun, Igbara-Odo and Ilawe chiefs had no remembrance of Williams' visit. Williams also reported that the rulers of Ado, Otun, Ijero, Effon and other towns, though admitting that Benin troops had sometimes come through their towns and villages in the distant past, denied having been subjects of the Oba of Benin or ever paying tributes to him.[16]

The Southern Frontier

Benin also came to have some influence in another part of Yorubaland – in the small Awori island kingdom of Eko or Lagos, beyond the Ijebu coast.[17] By the late sixteenth century, owing to the growth of the coastal lagoon trade, Lagos and the other small Awori settlements had come to have sizeable resident populations of Ijebu, Benin, Ilaje, Ikale, Owo, Egba, Egbado, Aja and Ijaw traders. In about 1600, conflicts between some of the non-Awori communities on the one hand and the indigenous Awori people ruled by the Olofin on the other, was affecting the trade so much as to attract the attention of the government of Benin. Some expeditions were sent to the aid of the Benin community. The claim by Egharevba, the Benin historian, that one such expedition was led by the Oba Orhogbua himself is improbable, and probably amounts to no more than a statement of the great importance of the westward lagoon trade to the Benin people at this time. For some time, the Benin and some of the other non-native communities, under the leadership of a Benin chief named Asheru, exercised some prominent influence and this much would seem to be corroborated by the statement of a German named Andreas Joshua Ulsheimer, who (according to Robert Smith in his *Kingdoms of the Yoruba*) wrote in 1603 that Lagos Island was a military camp under the command of Benin officers.

The Benin and Lagos accounts differ in a number of respects, however. While the Benin account asserts outright conquest by Benin people, the Lagos account describes many indecisive conflicts between the Awori population and the Benin and some other non-native resident communities, and an ultimate settlement as a result of which the latter came to have a part in the governance of the island. But the conflict remained unresolved; Asheru died soon afterwards in one of the clashes and a certain Awori man named Asipa, described in Lagos traditions as an Iseri chief of Ife royal descent (but in Benin traditions as grandson of an Oba of Benin) graciously led the party that conveyed Asheru's body to Benin. The Benin traditions say that, in Benin, the Oba Orhogbua was so appreciative of Asipa's gracious action that he accorded him recognition as ruler of Lagos. In any case, Asipa did become king of Lagos – the progenitor of a line of Lagos kings.

It is not improbable that, hidden in this picture as presented by the traditions, was a conflict or succession dispute among factions of the indigenous Awori ruling family of the Olofin. In that case, Asipa might have been the princely leader of a faction that sought and won the support of some of the non-native resident communities, especially the Benin. These non-native communities and the Asipa faction became victorious for a brief while; but skirmishes continued, and in one of them, the Benin leader, Asheru, was killed. After Asheru's death, Asipa further courted the support of the Benin by making the personal sacrifice of leading the men who took Asheru's corpse to Benin. With the support of his indigenous faction and the Benin and some other non-native resident communities, Asipa ultimately became king.

In the present state of our knowledge of Lagos history in general, the above would seem the explanation most harmonious with known trends of the history of the island kingdom. In the development of the coastal lagoon trade following the advent of European trade, Lagos Island had become, by the end of the sixteenth century, a focal point of considerable importance, so important, in fact, that a very sizeable number of Benin, Ilaje, Ijebu, Itsekiri, Aja and Ijaw traders had come to reside there. The politics of succession to the throne of the kingdom could no longer remain simply an indigenous affair. It is, therefore, in the light of such a situation that the early seventeenth century political history of Lagos would seem to be best understandable.

We must now complete this section with a statement on the impact of the Benin kingdom on the kingdoms of eastern and southern Yorubaland. Politically, as is obvious from preceding paragraphs, even in the regions of Yorubaland closest to Benin (Owo, Akoko and Ekiti), its influence was, on the whole, very small or non-existent. That does not mean, however, that the impact of Benin was small. On the contrary, its overall impact was considerable, but this had very little to do with arms, armies, conquest, overlordship, vassalage, tributes and such other factors and indices of military and political power and control. Benin was certainly a great kingdom for much of its long history, but the common assumption that all, or even most, of its impact was accomplished or sustained through the force of arms or through political control is certainly untrue. Ade Obayemi says that even in the case of the mini-states of the Edo-speaking and Edo-related peoples now believed to have been "clients of Benin" (the Ishan, Akoko-Edo and Afenmai), "the greatness of the city (of Benin), the impressiveness of its culture, the attractiveness of its rituals and the prestige and power of the Oba were in many respects more important than military intervention in shaping, cementing or defining" the relationship between them and the Oba of Benin.[18]

In the case of the Yoruba kingdoms of eastern and southern Yorubaland (Owo, Akoko, Ekiti, Ilaje, Ikale, Ondo, Ijebu, Awori), Benin's influence was owed rather to the same factors, as well as to commerce, than to conquest and control. All the evidence from the traditions of most of these Yoruba kingdoms emphasizes the attractiveness of Benin. Benin was, to them, a Yoruba kingdom whose common citizens happened to speak a non-Yoruba language. According to Ikime, as would be remembered, the Benin palace almost certainly spoke both Yoruba and Edo; and Yoruba was the language of trade for most of Benin's long-distance traders. The traditions of origin, the fundamental idioms, and the spiritual, historical and mythical underpinnings of Benin's monarchy were exactly the same as those of the Yorubas; but some of the presentations and expressions of Benin's royal ceremonials were different and exotic and, therefore, attractive. As the bronze statues of the earliest Oonis (made from the twelfth to the fifteenth century) strongly indicate, the forms of Yoruba and Edo royal regalia (with their abundant use of beads) derived from a common Ife base, but in time, as earlier pointed out, Benin amplified the beaded elements enormously and very attractively. Popular stories about the fame of the Oba of Benin, the pomp and pageantry of his royal appearances and festivals, the elevated, dramatic use of the common properties of Yoruba royal regalia in the regalia of its kings, its stylized, glimmering, sword of state and the king's ceremonial sword bearers – these were parts of the themes and subjects of Yoruba poetry and folklore and songs. Particularly, the fact that for eastern and much of south-central Yorubaland, Benin was the source of exotic imported European goods for about a century, added much to its fame and mystique in these places. Culturally, the Yoruba and Edo peoples were so close in many respects that they do not seem to have seen themselves as different peoples – until the twentieth century. To see traces of Benin's culture in any of these Yoruba kingdoms and interpret them as evidence of Benin's conquest and overlordship is to miss the point completely.

The history of the Owo kingdom illustrates all this most clearly.[19] Geographically, Owo is the closest Yoruba kingdom to Benin. Of all Yoruba kingdoms, Owo bears the strongest traces of distinctly Benin culture. But Owo was never conquered or ruled by Benin; in fact, Owo saw itself as Benin's rival. From the reign of the Olowo Osogboye, Owo did become a credible rival – with an impressive city, imposing city walls, proud multi-courtyard palace, large marketplaces, a rich artistic culture, a powerful military establishment, and empire-building ambitions and agenda of its own. For all these developments, the fear of Benin was a major motivator. Benin was the great threat that the rulers and people of Owo must watch and be prepared for.

Yet, for Owo, Benin was a source of great trade and wealth. Even more importantly, throughout the history of the Owo kingdom, many kings of Owo wanted and tried to be like the Oba of Benin. According to Olugbadehan, some Owo kings, on their ascension to the throne, took cognomens that were culled from the Edo language, because they believed that high-sounding exotic Benin names added to their stature before their subjects. Renrengenjen, the ninth Olowo on some of the Owo king lists, created a Benin-type royal festival (the Igogo festival) featuring a high-voltage royal procession very similar to the festive processions of Benin kings. Successive Olowos borrowed features from Benin's royal regalia to add to their own, until the point was reached that when the Olowo fully dressed up for some festivals, he looked almost completely like an Oba of Benin.

Attempts by Owo's rulers to remold their kingdom in the image of Benin extended into even more fundamental things. The Olowos in general admired the sort of power exercised by the kings of Benin over their kingdom. Under the system of succession by primogeniture, Benin kings were born and not (like Yoruba kings) selected from a pool of princes and did not have to compete within a royal lineage group. For a brief while in the late seventeenth century, Owo rulers instituted a system whereby each Olowo would be succeeded directly by one of his sons. It was so unpopular with the masses as well as with many of the chiefs that a return had to be made quickly to the traditional system of selection.

But the greatest point of attraction for Owo kings was the power of the Oba of Benin to create new chieftaincy titles at will at all levels of the Benin political system. This enabled him to tilt the balance of power within any group of title holders at any time, with the effect that he could build support for his personal power in the political system and thus wield powers that a Yoruba king could not. The Yoruba system did not allow a king such personal latitude over the creation of chieftaincy titles, but successive Olowos bent the system, starting from the time of Renrengenjen. By creating new chieftaincy titles and vesting such titles with authority and influence determined by the king, the Olowos slowly increased their personal power. They also gradually pushed aside the foundational cadre of chiefs of the Inner Council, the Ighare chiefs, and confined them increasingly to ritual functions. The Ighare chiefs watched in dismay as this or that Olowo created a new title, conferred it on a friend or a total stranger, included the new title on the list of members of the Inner Council, or even made its holder a high official like a Prime Minister, thus increasing his own personal power by putting in the highest levels and offices of government persons who owed their elevation and loyalty personally to him. These developments reached their most successful climax under Osogboye. In fact, with the probability of more Benin invasions always hanging over his kingdom, Osogboye ruled more or less like an Oba of Benin.

Olugbadehan describes the growing development as follows:

> Successive Olowos, starting with Renrengenjen, had slowly reduced the influence of the Ighare chiefs by creating chieftaincies loaded with influence and authority, many of them held by persons who owed their elevation to individual kings and operated in ways that promoted and upheld royal prerogatives and absolutism. ... The Olowos had fallen into the habit of creating and elevating chieftaincies to suit their purposes; in fact, the tendency was that each Olowo tried to outdo his predecessors in the creation of highly bloated, highly glamorized, chieftaincy titles for his relatives, friends and cronies, as well as in the pushing down of formerly exalted chieftaincies. The Oshorun (or Sashere) title tumbled from its lofty position (of Prime Minister). The Ojumu and Oshowe titles were created at the same time by the Olowo Omasan and belonged to the same level as first class titles, but the Oshowe ended up as a second class title, while the Ojumu title managed to stay aloft, close to the top ... The newly created chieftaincies became, without the Ighare chieftaincies, the new Inner Council around the king – an Inner Council that did not have a name because it had no traditional basis for its existence.[20]

Olugbadehan adds that by the end of Osogboye's reign:

> ... The Ighare chiefs had become virtual outsiders to the governance of the Owo kingdom, a kingdom of their creation. The other chieftaincies were endlessly rivaling one another for royal elevation and endlessly being reshuffled down or up, and a configuration of power (as well as a disorder in chiefly ranks) unknown to Yoruba political culture, existed.[21]

Not surprisingly, these developments nurtured a tradition of endemic conflicts in the highest levels of Owo's political system. During a royal procession in an Igogo festival, the chiefs assassinated the Olowo Renrengenjen. Two reigns later, the Olowo Ogeja started a new palace on Ekusi Hill, partly for the purpose of making the king safer. Before his death, he had finished a high thick wall around the new palace grounds, as well as many of the palace buildings. The Ighare chiefs complained that the new palace isolated the king from the town. After Ogeja's successor, Imagele, had completed his installation rituals, the Ighare chiefs put up an armed resistance to prevent him from occupying the new palace. Imagele had to fight his way into the palace.

Given the plural nature of the composition of a Yoruba polity, the political changes alienated many groups (especially lineages), which felt displaced or threatened. During Osogboye's reign, his charisma and popularity silenced most voices of dissent, but after he left the scene, it became rapidly obvious that the Benin type of almost total royal power was impossible in Owo. Lacking his charisma, Osogboye's successors generally tried to rule like him, and thereby created a situation in which "a collapse of the whole (political) system seemed a possibility" from time to time.[22] Political violence became common, and chaos repeatedly threatened. It developed that the newly created chiefs would start by uncritically supporting a king and then, after they had become well established, they would join the other chiefs in opposing the king's exercise of powers that had no basis in the traditional constitution. Usually, a king would respond by creating new chieftaincies and reshuffling the chiefly ranks, but that would usually buy him victory for only a short time.

The kings' habit of creating high chieftaincies yielded its worst result in about 1750 when the Olowo Adedipe, in order to set up strong support for his throne, created for his younger brother, Oludipe, the title of Ojomo and vested that title with such powers and assets as made the Ojomo an uncrowned second king. Even while the two brothers were still alive, the conflict between the Olowo and the Ojomo inherent in such a situation blew wide open – and it was destined to keep generating profound disruption in the political life of the Owo kingdom even deep into the twentieth century.[23]

23. Gbedu drums, Ilesa. *Photo: P. Verger, 1948–49, IFAN.*

The Olowos had considerable success, then, in their attempts to appear like the Oba of Benin; but their efforts to make the constitution of the Owo kingdom mirror Benin's only led them and their kingdom into serious political troubles. No other Yoruba monarch in the frontier area with Benin tried or succeeded as much as the Olowo to appear like the Oba of Benin, but there was hardly any that did not try at all. Even in regions of southern Yorubaland considerably removed from Benin, its royal culture had some influence over the packaging of monarchs and royal ceremonials.

Map 3. Oyo Empire at its greatest extent (c. 1780)

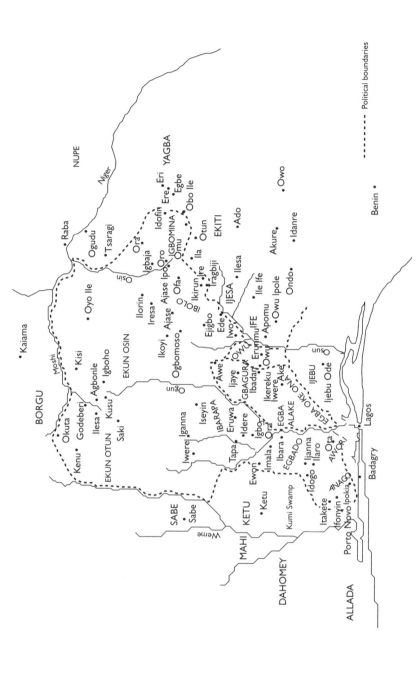

Source: Law, R. C. C.: *The Oyo Empire, 1600–1836: A West African Imperialism in the Era of the Atlantic Slave Trade*, Oxford, Clarendon Press, 1977.

12

The Great Oyo Empire

The kingdom of Oyo-Ile is regarded in Yoruba traditions as one of the younger of the early Yoruba kingdoms. It is believed to have been founded considerably later than such kingdoms as Ketu, Owu and Ila. However, by the seventeenth century, Oyo-Ile had become the greatest of all Yoruba kingdoms – richer, stronger, and territorially very much larger than any other. By the eighteenth century, its capital city of Oyo-Ile, known to its northern Hausa neighbors as Katunga, was the center of an empire comprising most of northern and western Yorubaland as well as substantial territories of non-Yoruba peoples like the Nupe, the Bariba and the Aja. During the eighteenth century, armies of the Alaafin of Oyo were pushing far westwards beyond the Aja country, defeating at least one army of the Ashanti kingdom in parts of what is now the Republic of Togo, most probably in the country of the Yoruba Itsha and Ife of modern Togo Republic. Now known to history as the Old Oyo Empire, the Alaafin's empire was the largest ever in the history of the tropical forests and grasslands of West Africa south of the Niger.

What circumstances or factors were responsible for advancing Oyo-Ile, initially a small kingdom located in the extreme northwestern corner of Yorubaland, to such military power, such territorial expansion and such greatness? One factor, without doubt, was adversity. The location that the founders of Oyo-Ile chose for their kingdom turned out to be a very difficult one. Before it had had time to establish roots, the small kingdom was attacked relentlessly from many directions. The principal enemies were the Bariba of the Borgu country to the northwest, and the Nupe to the northeast, both of them formidable peoples of the banks of the Niger. This was, in short, frontier territory between the Yoruba and these peoples; for some time both of them had been attacking Yoruba settlers in the region and forcing them to move southwards. Older Yoruba kingdoms in the region – Ketu, Owu and Ila – had encountered the Bariba and Nupe hostility. Both Ketu and Owu had been forced to abandon their original locations and relocate at some distance to the south. Ila would not relocate southwards, but it was compelled to move its capital town from location to location in search of safety.

The location chosen for Oyo-Ile had yet another problem. It was, as its later history would show, a very desirable spot on the oldest routes connecting the trans-Niger grasslands and the forests of central West Africa across the Middle Niger. That meant that many groups of people had some interest in the area and would fight to uphold their interests. That included various Bariba and Nupe groups as well as the older kingdom of Owu from the south.

In short, the location of Oyo-Ile was like the eye of a whirlwind that would not subside. Buffeted relentlessly by Bariba and Nupe groups, the infant kingdom agreed to pay tribute to some of them at certain times. Threatened also by Owu from the south, Oyo-Ile paid tribute to the Olowu for some time. To survive at all, Oyo-Ile needed to be not just strong, but so overwhelmingly strong as to be able to overcome and suppress its enemies. Mostly learning from those enemies, Oyo-Ile built a military establishment that became the terror of all its neighbors and conquered many kingdoms and peoples. Like some other significant Yoruba frontier kingdoms (notably Ketu, Ila and Owo), Oyo-Ile survived its initial frontier afflictions and prospered; unlike them, it went on to build the largest empire south of the Niger.

A second factor was the good natural defenses of Oyo-Ile's ultimate site. After the kingdom's early relocations, it finally returned to settle on the site that was destined to be its home until the 1830s. The site lay under the protection of a range of rocky hills, which afforded it considerable security. Richard Lander described as follows his first sight of Oyo-Ile, by then a great city, in January 1826:

> …on attaining the summit of a lofty ridge, we came in sight of the city of Katunga, lying to the south of us, at the base of a granite mountain, and apparently embosomed in beautiful trees. Between the ridge and the city was a fertile valley, highly cultivated, and extending to the westward as far as the eye could reach; while the view to the eastward was bounded by a granite rock, shivered into fragments, and at no great distance from the place on which we stood.[1]

After the kingdom had built great city walls, taking advantage of these natural defenses, the city that emerged was widely regarded by neighbors as impregnable. For over two centuries, no enemy came even close to directly threatening the city.

Thirdly, the region in which Oyo-Ile was established was one of the most favorable for agriculture in West Africa. This was the Yoruba savannah grassland or savannah low woodland [see Chapter 9], gently undulating, with occasional low hills and rock outcrops. Its high points formed a watershed territory from which streams flowed either south to the Osun and other south-flowing rivers, or north to the River Niger, making the whole area a well-watered region. Its soils were among the most fertile in Yorubaland. Very prosperous farming in these circumstances made for rapid population increases in the Oyo-Ile kingdom and the Oyo country around it. By probably as early as the late fifteenth century, the Oyo country was the most thickly populated part of Yorubaland and had a disproportionate share of its heavily populated cities and towns. Once the Alaafin had established varying types of overlordship over all the kingdoms, cities and towns of the Oyo country, he ruled over a large and prosperous area from which he could almost endlessly draw men and material resources into his armies. These armies grew bigger and stronger, until they became all conquering.

Fourthly, the largely open grassland nature of the Oyo country and all the Yoruba and Aja countries to the west of it greatly assisted the growth of an empire. Employing horses in the open grasslands, Oyo-Ile came to control far-flung communications, establish far-flung administrative and commercial networks, and send armies to subdue and control very distant lands. At the peak of the power of the Old Oyo Empire, its officials spread out from the Nupe country on the Middle Niger all the way southwestwards to the coast of what are now the Lagos State of Nigeria and Benin Republic, and westwards all the way into the modern Togo Republic.

Fifthly, Oyo-Ile lay on, and in the end controlled, the most important trade routes across the Middle Niger. It was therefore in a position to dominate most of the trade between Yorubaland, the Aja country and much of West Africa south of the Niger on one side, and the trans-Niger countries, the Sahara and the Mediterranean world on the other. This was an enormous source of wealth to the kingdom and to its citizens. Very importantly also, Oyo-Ile came to control the importation of horses from beyond the Niger, from Hausaland and from Bornu, a factor that contributed most to its military superiority.

Finally, Oyo-Ile enjoyed all the benefits of being a kingdom of the Yoruba people, the largest single people in the West African forests, occupying more territory than any other people of the region. Oyo-Ile never extended its control over large areas of Yorubaland – especially the southern and easternmost parts. But its people were Yoruba and, therefore, all of the homeland was theirs to trade, travel, do business, and reside in at will. Its king, the Alaafin, was a member of the Yoruba family of kings and, as his power grew, his influence was enhanced by the fact that all other Yoruba kings regarded him as their fortunate and powerful brother. Yoruba people commonly said that nobody could ever get more fortunate than the Alaafin (*A kii l'ori ire ju Alaafin Oyo*); and a Yoruba person bragging about his fame or popularity would commonly use the hyperbole,

"*Alaafin Oyo mo mi*" – "the Alaafin of Oyo knows me." There is strong evidence in Yoruba traditions that, at the peak of the power of the Alaafin's empire, Yoruba kings, in general, deferred to him in various ways, including in the resolution of their internal and inter-kingdom difficulties. In far western Yoruba kingdoms (such as Ketu) which were independent of the Alaafin's authority, his armies, while campaigning in those parts against the Aja people, were regularly sure of hospitality, supplies and other types of support. The same would seem to have been true in the Orangun's kingdom of Ila for the Alaafin's armies campaigning against the Nupe in the northeast. Every one of the other independent Yoruba kingdoms of the southern and eastern forests (Ijebu-Ode, Owo, Ilesa, Ondo, the Ekiti kingdoms, etc.), ultimately developed some sort of strong ties with the Alaafin. Where his military and political power did not reach, that is, his membership of the large family of Yoruba kings extended his influence quite potently.

Early Beginnings

According to Yoruba traditions, the founder of the Oyo-Ile kingdom was Oranmiyan, said to be one of the youngest grandsons of Oduduwa. The time of its foundation, in the light of calculations done from lists of kings in various Yoruba local histories, was probably in the late twelfth or early thirteenth century. Oyo traditions have very popular accounts of the founding of this kingdom, and so too do many traditions widespread in Yorubaland. Samuel Johnson recorded some of them in Oyo, Ibadan and other places in western and central Yorubaland in the nineteenth century. The core of these traditions is that Oranmiyan set off from Ile-Ife and headed northwards. Samuel Johnson, in his attempt to fit this northward migration into his own general theory that Yoruba people originated from the Middle East, wrote that Oranmiyan's purpose was to go to the Middle East to avenge the expulsion of his ancestors from Arabia.[2] Oyo and other Yoruba traditions, however, simply have the Oranmiyan migration as an episode in the general story of the founding of Yoruba kingdoms. After Oranmiyan entered the country of the Oyo subgroup, where old Oyo settlements dotted grassland territory, he continued to the far northwest, to the frontier country near the Niger, where small Oyo, Bariba and Nupe settlements existed, closely interlocked. There, one Bariba chief helped him to locate a good place to settle. (The story is that the Bariba chief gave him a charmed python that guided him to the location.) Unifying a few old settlements at that location, he began to establish his kingdom. He also married the daughter of a Nupe chief, usually identified in the traditions with the name Elempe.

The traditions indicate that the first years of the Oyo-Ile kingdom were peaceful. But such a peaceful period did not last long. Oranmiyan's friendship with one Bariba chief and his connection with a Nupe chief by marriage did not prove sufficient to secure peace with all the Bariba and Nupe groups. Oyo-Ile was attacked repeatedly by various Bariba and Nupe groups. The difficulties became so intense that Oranmiyan, himself a famous warrior prince, decided to move the base of the kingdom to a less troublesome site, at a place called Oko. At Oko, the kingdom had peace for some time. But then the need arose for Oranmiyan to return to Ile-Ife. After installing his oldest son, Ajaka, on the throne, he left for Ile-Ife.

The traditions paint the time after Oranmiyan's departure as an extremely difficult period for the kingdom. Threats from the Owu kingdom in the south compelled it to start paying tribute to the Olowu. Some of the stronger Bariba and Nupe groups overran it and forced it to pay tribute. In fact, Ajaka appears to have been displaced for some time by these unforgiving enemies. At last, he stepped aside and gave the throne to his brother, Sango, son of Oranmiyan's Nupe wife, who was believed by the chiefs to be the more warlike prince.

With Sango as king, the situation began to improve. The secret of the military power of the Nupe and Bariba was their use of cavalry. Sango embarked on buying horses from some of the Nupe, his mother's people. When the Olowu sent his officers to demand the tribute, Sango refused to pay. The Olowu sent an army to compel him to pay, but Sango's men so decisively defeated the invaders as to silence the Owu threat once and for all. After that, Sango moved the base of the kingdom from Oko back to its original location. When the Bariba and Nupe attacked, he fought them fiercely and beat back attack after attack, capturing many horses in the process. Sango's life was so filled with terrible battles and surprising victories that his subjects and enemies alike credited him with supernatural powers.

Sango died in the prime of his life. One of the supernatural powers which he claimed himself was the power to make lightning. According to Oyo traditions, while demonstrating this power to his chiefs and courtiers one day, he accidentally burnt down the palace. Either out of embarrassment or out of fear of his subjects, he took his own life. But his people, out of gratitude for all he had done for their kingdom, deified him, giving his name to the god of thunder and lightning and set up shrines and rituals for his worship. The cult of Sango became the special cult of Oyo-Ile kings, unlike in most Yoruba kingdoms where the cult of Ogun (god of iron and war) was the royal cult.

The above is the best known and most widely accepted traditional account of the beginnings of Oyo-Ile. However, there are some other less well known accounts. One tradition recorded by E. M. Lijadu says that Oyo-Ile was founded by a Nupe hunter from the Nupe town of Ogodo on the southern banks of the Niger. Another, recorded by Leo Frobenius during visits to Yorubaland, has it that there were two successive dynasties in early Oyo-Ile, one originating from the Nupe and the other from the Bariba. Then too, there are suggestions by some historians that some details in the well-known Oranmiyan tradition itself are open to interpretations pointing to Nupe or Bariba founding of Oyo-Ile. Thus it has been suggested that the story that a Bariba chieftain helped Oranmiyan to find the location at which to settle could mean that Bariba folks were in fact the founders of Oyo-Ile; while the story of Oranmiyan's marriage to the daughter of a Nupe chieftain could also support the claim of a Nupe foundation. From all this, a conclusion has been proposed by Robin Law in his book on Oyo history, that Oyo-Ile was not founded by a prince from Ife at all, but that the Oranmiyan tradition was a creation aimed at conferring Yoruba legitimacy on the rulers of Oyo-Ile. Law writes that of the traditions of Bariba, Nupe and Oranmiyan foundation of Oyo-Ile,

> Skepticism seems most justified with regard to the one that connects the Oyo royal dynasty with Ile-Ife. Given the strong prejudice among the Yoruba that only descendants of Oduduwa could validly claim royal status, a tradition of origin from Ile-Ife might readily have been fabricated in order to create a spurious legitimacy for the rulers of Oyo.[3]

Against these suggestions, however, the following picture needs to be considered. The demographic nature of the area where Oyo-Ile was founded was, as earlier pointed out, frontier country where, according to Aribidesi Usman, supported by Yoruba, Nupe and Bariba traditions, Bariba, Nupe and Yoruba settlers and settlements were already closely interspersed by at least the eleventh century. Further and further southwards from the frontier area, Oyo-Yoruba settlements increasingly predominated. Now, Oyo traditions are unambiguous that Oranmiyan went all the way north to the frontier area where Oyo, Bariba and Nupe settlements lived closely side by side. The obvious probability then is that the town which he created combined some early Oyo, Bariba and Nupe settlements. Indeed, that this is more than mere probability is attested to by the well-known fact that Oyo-Ile, as it grew, contained many Bariba and Nupe families (ancient, pre-Oranmiyan families in the area), subjects of the Alaafin, who played significant roles in Oyo-Ile's history – its society, religious and political life, its military, and its cultural and artistic growth. From this strong probability, other probabilities flow as follows: At first, the inhabitants of the old settlements received Oranmiyan peacefully – and therefore the Bariba chief who is said to have helped him to find a location to settle and the Nupe chief whose daughter he married would be chiefs of the early settlements who welcomed him peacefully when he came. But, over time, the existence of his Oyo-Ile kingdom in this frontier area attracted more and more of Oyo settlers, until the point was reached that the Oyo population seemed to be on the way to taking over the whole frontier area and swallowing up the Bariba and Nupe population. To this growing threat, the Bariba and Nupe elements ultimately reacted with violence, confronting the young town of Oyo-Ile with some troubles internally and then Bariba and Nupe attacks from the surrounding country. Memories of the pre-Oranmiyan settlements and chiefs would survive, resulting in lingering traditions of Bariba and Nupe foundation and dynasties. Such a historical development as this harmonizes more or less perfectly with the scenario described by Aribidesi Usman for all the frontier area south of the River Niger in about the eleventh to the thirteenth century.[4] It makes many details in the Oranmiyan tradition more obviously meaningful – the initial brief period of peace in the new kingdom, the subsequent violence and need to evacuate to Oko, Sango's return of the kingdom from Oko to the original location, and the persistence of Bariba and Nupe hostility. It accounts for all the surviving traces of traditions of Bariba and Nupe dynasties in the foundation of Oyo-Ile, while upholding the Oranmiyan tradition. With regard to Sango, the picture would be that though his mother was Nupe, he was raised as a prince of the Yoruba by a Yoruba father and king, and that his loyalties were firmly Yoruba.

After Sango's death, Ajaka was again made king. During his second reign, Ajaka sat on a much safer throne and ruled over a militarily stronger kingdom – all the fruits of Sango's achievements. Not much is said in the traditions about this reign other than that Ajaka fought a number of successful engagements against the Nupe.

Not much detailed information, likewise, is available about the next few reigns, covering probably near 200 years. Ajaka was succeeded by his son, Aganju. According to traditions recorded by Samuel Johnson, when Aganju died, his son Kori was too young to be made king, so one of his wives named Iyayun served as regent for a few years. Kori was a youth when he was crowned Alaafin, and he ruled for many years. Kori was succeeded by Oluaso. One other Alaafin of this early period, Oluodo, is usually excluded from the list of Alaafins because, according to some traditions, he drowned in the Niger in the course of a war against the Nupe. Apparently, he drowned soon after he was crowned Alaafin and the chiefs did not have his body for the royal funeral rituals, as a result of which the palace traditions treated him as if he never reigned.

During this early period when these kings ruled in Oyo-Ile, it was only a small kingdom – no more than one of the small towns in the northern parts of the Oyo country. The fact that Oranmiyan had to go all the way to the northwestern extremities of Oyo territory before he could stop to establish his kingdom points to the strong probability that other towns had prior claims to the territory. One such town would be Ogboro. Another would be Owu. Owu might still be in the area near Ogboro, or, if it had relocated further south, might still be known to have interests in the area. Yet another would be Adikun. In this regard, local traditions concerning the early relationship of Oyo-Ile with some of these towns are very important. Some of these traditions have it that the king of Oyo-Ile did not originally have a crown and that he later seized the one belonging to the Aladikun of Adikun. Such stories of seized crowns are common all over Yorubaland. Usually they mean that a town that was originally regarded as a leading town in an area was later superseded by another. Adikun was some 45 miles to the southwest of Oyo-Ile; it may have been bigger and more important than Oyo-Ile in early times. Some Ogboro traditions also claim that the first Onisambo of Ogboro, some 50 miles west of Oyo-Ile, was a senior brother of Oranmiyan. Again, in the codes of Yoruba political language, to say that a ruler was a "senior brother" of another was to say that he was superior to him in some way. The kind of superiority that the early rulers of Ogboro had over the early rulers of Oyo-Ile is now not clear. Ogboro was probably a considerably bigger town than Oyo-Ile in early times.

In these early times, Oyo-Ile began its journey to political and territorial greatness by establishing, first, some superiority and dominance over the Oyo towns nearby. Compelled to learn the art of war in order to survive the Bariba and Nupe attacks of its early years, Oyo-Ile had managed to free itself from paying tributes to Owu, and then had kept the Bariba and Nupe at bay. While continuing the clashes with the Bariba in the northwest and the Nupe in the northeast, Oyo-Ile began also to use its growing military muscle to acquire dominance over other Oyo towns to its west, south and east. According to the traditions of Ogboro to the west, Oyo-Ile made war on Ogboro during the reign of the Alaafin Aganju. In these wars, some of the towns in the area (Igbonna, Imeri, Tede and others) came to the aid of Ogboro. Ogboro lost or was worn down over time, so that it accepted the leadership of the Alaafin over the area. Oyo-Ile also most probably fought Adikun to the southwest. In short, Oyo-Ile was doing in the country of the Oyo subgroup what the Ilesa kingdom was doing in the country of the Ijesa. However, Oyo-Ile came off more successful than Ilesa. While the Owa of Ilesa never became anything more than the senior brother among the kings of Ijesa, the Alaafin gradually became the great king of all the Oyo (much like the Olowu among the Owu subgroup). This position was achieved, most certainly, only slowly over a long time, but was probably completed by the sixteenth century.

While making this progress in the Oyo country, Oyo-Ile continued to fight the Bariba and Nupe. The traditions indicate clearly that, after some time, it ceased being merely a defender and took the war into the country of the Nupe. In fact, Oyo-Ile forces seem to have crossed the Niger and taken the war into the heartlands of the Nupe, as the tradition of the drowning of one Alaafin in the Niger during one war against the Nupe would seem to suggest.

Fall and Revival of Oyo-Ile

In the early sixteenth century, however, disaster befell the Oyo-Ile kingdom. The Nupe, who had been divided into many small chiefdoms throughout all their early history, became unified about this time into one kingdom under Edegi, also known as Tsoede in Nupe traditions. Nupe armies entered into Igbomina and northern Ijesa and Ekiti. A strong Nupe army invaded the Oyo country, overcame the defenses of Oyo-Ile and overran Oyo-Ile city itself. The reigning Alaafin was Onigbogi, successor to Oluaso. Oyo-Ile was sacked, and its inhabitants fled in all directions. Onigbogi fled northwestwards into the Bariba country where, fortunately, one Bariba chief offered him hospitality. The Oyo-Ile kingdom ceased to exist; only the Alaafin Onigbogi and the few chiefs and attendants around him remained as testimony to its existence.

But this terrible disaster was to prove only a brief interlude in the history of Oyo-Ile. The kingdom rallied and then marched forward more decisively than ever before. Its greatest days were about to dawn.

According to Oyo traditions recorded by Samuel Johnson, Onigbogi had a Bariba wife, the daughter of the leading chief of one of the Bariba groups. It was this woman's father who gave him hospitality. He was allowed to settle with his followers in a small town which Yoruba people called Gbere – probably Gberegburu, some 60 miles northwest of the deserted city of Oyo-Ile. Onigbogi died at Gbere and was succeeded as Alaafin by Ofinran, his son by the Bariba wife. Joining, or joined by, some Bariba, Ofinran participated in raids into the Oyo country. One such raid resulted in the destruction of the Oyo town of Irawo. Thereafter, a clash of interests developed between the Alaafin and his Bariba hosts and resulted in disagreement between them. Ofinran therefore left the Bariba country and returned southeast into Yorubaland, where he took up residence in the Oyo town of Kusu, about 50 miles west of Oyo-Ile. Ofinran died at Kusu and was succeeded by Egunoju who moved his throne first briefly to Shaki and then to Igboho about 40 miles from Oyo-Ile. Igboho was founded by the Alaafin Egunoju as a new capital for the kingdom. Egunoju and three successors (Orompoto, Ajiboyede and Abipa) ruled at the new capital before, at last, Abipa moved the throne back to Oyo-Ile.

It was at Igboho that the Alaafin's government established solid measures for returning home to the city of Oyo-Ile. Apparently, learning the lesson of their disastrous military failure against the Nupe, the Oyo government took steps to set up a powerful cavalry force. Cavalry had been a feature of Oyo-Ile's armies since the time of Sango, but at Igboho it became the core of its military strength. Another major military development at Igboho was the upgrading of the Eso, described by some historians as the Alaafin's "praetorian guard," and by others as the Alaafin's imperial guard or noble guard. The town of Ikoyi was founded by the Alaafins at this time, and it became the center where the bulk of this elite force was trained and stationed. Ikoyi thereafter grew to become the greatest military center of the kingdom, outside the city of Oyo-Ile. From this account about Ikoyi as well as Kusu and Igboho, it is certain that the Oyo-Ile authorities in exile began a major incorporation of the human and material resources of the rest of the Oyo country into the efforts to rebuild their kingdom. The unrelenting threats by the Nupe and Bariba facilitated the willing cooperation of other Oyo kingdoms. The ultimate outcome of this development was the emergence of a consolidated Oyo kingdom under the leadership of the Alaafin. It is important that the nature of this "consolidated Oyo kingdom" be understood. The various kings of the Oyo country did not become subordinate Baales in a kingdom of Oyo-Ile; they continued to be kings over their kingdoms. But they were kings who willingly pooled all the assets and resources of their kingdoms and allowed the Alaafin's government to direct the use of it all, for the common good.

Some measures of a cultural nature, believed to have potential for strengthening the kingdom, were also adopted in exile. One was the elevation of the Ifa cult to a state cult. Oyo traditions have it that the Alaafin Onigbogi's mother, Arugba, a native of Otta in Awori, had suggested just such a step in the good days of Oyo-Ile, but that the authorities had ignored her suggestion. After the kingdom collapsed under Onigbogi, the belief spread that it was because the gods were angry with Oyo-Ile on account of its disregard for Ifa, the god of divination. At Kusu, therefore, Ofinran officially had rituals and observances set up giving a new prominence to the Ifa cult in the affairs of the kingdom. The cult of *egungun* was elevated in the same way. *Egungun* was common to all Nupe and Yoruba, but Oyo-Ile had never recognized its power as a state cult. On the other hand, the Nupe had much regard for *egungun*, and harnessed its spiritual support for war by sending *egungun* mask-bearers with their armies. At Igboho, the Alaafin's government made the *egungun* cult a state cult and, from then on, *egungun* mask-bearers became constant companions of Oyo-Ile armies.

Not surprisingly, as soon as the exiled Oyo-Ile government appeared in the Oyo country again, its old enemies, the Bariba and Nupe, rose to the attack. In the reign of Orompoto at Igboho, a strong Bariba raiding group came to attack Igboho. Orompoto's army met them at Ilayi and crushed them. Not long after, in the reign of Ajiboyede, Orompoto's successor, the Nupe came with a large army – and penetrated to Igboho itself. In a fierce and close-fought battle outside Igboho, the Nupe army was put to flight and its commander, a chief named Lajomo, was taken captive. These two decisive victories, then, served notice on Oyo-Ile's enemies that it had come back to life, and that the balance of military strength had shifted. Without any serious enemy left to oppose him, the Alaafin Abipa decided to take the government of his kingdom back home to its own city of Oyo-Ile.

In the last days at Igboho, some of the high chiefs, reluctant to abandon their compounds or to leave their unharvested farms behind, tried a trick to frustrate or delay the departure. Knowing that the Alaafin was sending a party of men to reconnoiter the site of the old city, they sent in advance some persons whom Yoruba people call *eni orisa* (people of the gods) – the Basorun sent a hunchback, the Asipa a leper, the Alapini an albino, the Shamu a man with a deformed jaw, and the Akiniku a cripple. When the royal survey party came to the site of the old palace, these strange persons, carrying torches in the nearby woods, roamed around all night screaming "Ko s'aye," "Ko s'aye" ("No room!" "No room!"). Frightened, the royal messengers went back to report to the Alaafin. But the Alaafin quickly found out what was happening and sent some hunters to go and round up the fake phantoms. From this episode, the Alaafin Abipa was given the cognomen Obamoro – "the king who caught ghosts," a cognomen still applied to the Alaafins. The story of the Alaafin's catching of the fake ghosts is still reenacted at Oyo on certain festivals and at the time of the installation of Alaafins.

After departing from Igboho, the Alaafin stopped for a short time at a place called Kogbaye, to allow certain repairs on the palace to be completed. From Kogbaye, Abipa and his chiefs made the final triumphal journey to Oyo-Ile [see Chapter 8].

The return of the Alaafin to Oyo-Ile was a great event. Many days of ceremonies followed, during which sacrifices were offered in the palace and in many places in the city. From all over Yorubaland, kings sent fraternal messages to the Alaafin. According to the traditions, only the Owa of Ilesa did not send any and, for a long time, the leaders of Oyo-Ile held it against the Ilesa kingdom.

Igboho was to remain from then on an imperial city – a sort of second capital city, ruled by a representative chosen by the Alaafin. It has survived till the present, and its ruler continues to be appointed in the same old way. Also, the graves of the Alaafins who were buried there can still be seen, all marked by large earthen ramparts tended by an important official.

Growth and Power

The reign of the Alaafin Abipa who brought the government back to Oyo-Ile has been dated to about the last quarter of the sixteenth century – about 1570–90. Back in Oyo-Ile, the government settled down remarkably quickly – the monarchy, the palace organization, the chieftaincy system, and all other institutions. The explanation for such an accomplishment must be that all arms of the government had remained functional during the years of exile, especially in the years spent at Igboho. Moreover, while the Alaafins had moved gradually towards home, many important families seem to have also taken steps to return from the places to which they had been scattered.

The years following the return of the Alaafin to Oyo-Ile proved to be years of phenomenal achievements by the kingdom. From being a small kingdom, it expanded rapidly to become an empire, so that the Alaafin became an emperor whose territories included Yoruba kingdoms and non-Yoruba peoples. At the peak of the greatness of the Oyo Empire in about the middle of the eighteenth century, its main components were as follows: First, the country of the Oyo subgroup became what may be described as the metropolitan province of the empire. The Alaafin ceased being merely the king of Oyo-Ile and became the king of a consolidated kingdom of all the Oyo people, with Oyo-Ile as his capital city. Of the other Yoruba included in the empire, the Egbado were in many respects close to the Oyo; the Alaafin became effectively the king of all the Egbado. In the other Yoruba provinces of the empire – Owu, Egba, Igbomina, some far western kingdoms in Idassa and others – the kingdoms accepted the Alaafin as their overlord and protector, and paid regular tribute to him. Then, there were the non-Yoruba provinces, made up of some part of the country of the Nupe on the southern banks of the Middle Niger, much of the Bariba country all the way west to the River Moshi, and the country of the Aja all the way southwest to include their coastal towns and west to their boundaries with the Ewe and Akan.

The expansion of the Alaafin's authority over all these territories was accomplished at a fast pace. The chronological growth of the expansion is difficult to trace, but it is well known that its ways and means differed from province to province. In the country of the Oyo subgroup, apart from the early conflicts between Oyo-Ile and other Oyo towns (like Adikun and Ogboro), the establishment of the Alaafin as king of all Oyo people was not accomplished with the force of arms. From quite early in the history of the Oyo-Ile kingdom, its commercial weight, derived from its advantageous location on the north–south routes across the Niger and east–west routes in the country south of the Niger, had gradually made it the economic heart of the Oyo homeland. This had, no doubt, gradually boosted Oyo-Ile's political stature. At the same time, the growth of its military muscle, consequent on its responses to Bariba and Nupe pressures, had gradually made Oyo-Ile the strong kingdom in the Oyo country, and its foremost defender against the Nupe from the northeast and the Bariba from the northwest. From the south also, the ambitious Ijesa kingdom of Ilesa seems to have early constituted a threat to Oyo settlers on and near the banks of the Osun River. In the reign of the Alaafin Kori, Oyo-Ile authorities established the town of Ede on the Osun to defend this area, a clear indication that Oyo-Ile early began to see itself as a defender of the Oyo country. By the time of the Nupe sack of Oyo-Ile, the security needs and the political destiny of the Oyo-Ile kingdom and of the rest of the Oyo homeland had become closely knit together. With the Oyo-Ile government away in exile at Gbere, the Oyo country was wide open to Nupe and Bariba raids. The Alaafin Ofinran, as would be remembered, collaborated with his immediate Bariba hosts in raids into the Oyo country, but his interests were different from theirs. While they were merely carrying on their tradition of raids into Oyo territory, his purpose was to confront and frustrate the Nupe there. This, no doubt, was why, after the Bariba had destroyed the Oyo town of Irawo, he broke with them and returned into Oyo territory. From then on, the Alaafins, in their struggle to resuscitate their kingdom, had at their ready disposal the human and material resources of the whole of the Oyo country. The founding of Ikoyi by the Alaafins, their development of Ikoyi into a great military center, and the incorporation of the rulers and populations of all significant Oyo towns into one military system, followed. All these developments made possible the creation of the powerful army that crushed the Bariba and Nupe invaders. The great armies that went out from then on to conquer an empire for the Alaafins were all mass armies of the consolidated kingdom of the Oyo people. As the empire grew to cover many lands, the supply of men for the Alaafin's armies was augmented from time to time from populations of Yoruba kingdoms outside the Oyo country (the Igbomina, Ibolo, Owu, Egba, Ibarapa and Egbado kingdoms), but the masses of Oyo men remained the large heart of the Alaafin's armies.

Abipa's successor, Obalokun, who began to reign probably in 1590, is credited with initiating a deliberate policy of territorial expansion. After him, for nearly 200 years (until about 1780), there followed a long list of kings under whom, in general, more and more territories were added to the empire – Ajagbo, Odarawu, Kanran, Jayin, Ayibi, Osinyago, Ojigi, Gberu, Amuniwaiye, Onisile. Samuel Johnson, to whom we are indebted for the fullest and earliest recording of Oyo traditions relating to these kings, has tended to give considerable emphasis to the remembered moral lapses and weaknesses in their personal characters. In spite of the personal weaknesses of many of the Alaafins of this long period, however, the Oyo Empire continually grew both territorially and in economic prosperity. The tradition of military excellence was sustained and the army remained strong. Oyo armies became much better than their rivals (the Bariba and Nupe) in the use of the cavalry. Horsemanship and marksmanship (with bow and arrow) became the passion and favorite sport of Oyo youths, skills at which they trained and competed tirelessly. On a second visit to Oyo-Ile in 1826, after a journey through Bariba, Hausa and Nupe countries, Richard Lander commented that Oyo people

> … have the reputation of being the best bowmen in Africa; and the young men soon become excellent marksmen by frequent practice and steady perseverance… They amuse themselves daily by attempting to discharge arrows through a small hole made for the purpose in a wall, at a great distance from the standing ground, and I have frequently seen individuals accomplish this difficult task three successive times … from a distance of up to one hundred yards. … it requires great and unceasing practice to attain to so much perfection.[5]

Yoruba people usually fought their wars during dry seasons – when heavy downpours were rare, the roads were unlikely to get muddy, the rivers and streams were low or dry, and farm work was light. In imperial Oyo-Ile, the military campaigns of each dry season were opened with a grand ceremony in the palace, the highlight of which was that the war chiefs would kneel before the throne and ask the Alaafin, "Who are your enemies?" The Alaafin's answer (derived, no doubt, from decisions earlier arrived at in high councils of government) constituted the armies' marching orders for the season.

Most of the greatest warriors of Yoruba history were produced by, and served, the Oyo Empire in its era of growth. Iba Magaji served both Obalokun and Ajagbo as Basorun, and commanded the earliest campaigns that conquered most of the Nupe and Bariba countries. Kokorogangan, the first person to bear the title of Are Ona Kakanfo (see below), established the tradition of valor and ferocity in battle for all future holders of that title. He and his contemporary, the Basorun Akindein, were the heroes of the earliest campaigns in the Egbado country. The Basorun under the Alaafin Ojigi, the personage known to history by the nickname Yau Yamba, is reputed to have been one of the greatest generals in the history of the Oyo Empire. After a long string of victories in wars, he succumbed to a freak accident on a campaign to Offa in the Ibolo country.

Below the level of these topmost warriors, the empire was regularly blessed with a large number of brilliant commanders and soldiers who made the name of the Alaafin feared over a large part of West Africa. The most distinguished of these were appointed as the Eso, the seventy titled military officers who commanded the armies in battle and reported directly to the Alaafin through the

Oyo Mesi, the highest council of state. An awesome reputation and ethos of bravery and honor attached to the title of Eso. According to Samuel Johnson, each Eso "wears an Akoro (or coronet) and carries in his hand no weapon, but a baton or staff of war known as The Invincible". Many popular sayings pertained to the Eso. One has it that:

> One of two things befits an Eso:
>
> An Eso must fight and conquer (or)
>
> An Eso must fight and perish.

Another says:

> An Eso must never be shot in the back,
>
> His wounds must always be right in front.[6]

In the early seventeenth century, the Alaafin Ajagbo created the title of Are Ona Kakanfo, the highest Eso of all the Esos. The creation of such a title was a very important sign of the time – a time of boundless territorial ambitions and tremendous military pride in the center of the Oyo Empire. The Kakanfo commanded specially selected elite forces and operated as a sort of field marshal. The Kakanfo was supposed to be the fiercest warrior in the land. At his investiture, the holder of this title shaved his head completely "and 201 incisions are made on his occupit with 201 different lancets, and specially prepared ingredients from 201 vials are rubbed into the cuts, one for each. This is supposed to render him fearless …."[7] Thereafter, the Kakanfo, while shaving his head, must leave the lacerated part unshaved, as a result of which the hair there would grow and be plaited into a tuft or pigtail, giving him a fearsome appearance. The Kakanfo was supposed to be continually engaged in battles; the longest he could stay without fighting was two years. Because he was supposed to yield place to nobody, the Kakanfo was not allowed to live in the capital city. As a result, Kakanfos always lived in provincial towns and villages. All told, the Kakanfo was a strange creation – the creature of a kingdom that envisioned itself as perpetually at war. The negative potentialities of it ought to have been obvious to the leaders of the Oyo Empire, but in the euphoria of almost invariably successful wars of conquest, they were not. While the wars and the conquests lasted, the Kakanfo was an intoxicating, invaluable, instrument of state policy.

Another creation of the time was the practice of sending multiple armies out at the same time, with the purpose of impelling them to outperform one another. This practice was begun under the Alaafin Ajagbo who made it a habit to send out four armies to different directions each time, one commanded by the Basorun, another by the Agbaakin, a third by the Kakanfo, and a fourth by the Asipa. Continued after him, it was a major contributor to the near-invincibility of Oyo armies in battle.

Territorial Expansion

The homelands of the small neighbors of the Oyo, namely the Ibarapa to the west and the Ibolo to the east, were the earliest non-Oyo territories to be incorporated into the Alaafin's expanding kingdom, almost certainly during the reign of Obalokun, Ajagbo's successor, in the last years of the sixteenth century and the first years of the seventeenth. During the same reign also, the Alaafin's armies followed the Nupe into the Igbomina country, pushed them out of there, and then overran most of the western parts of the Nupe territory on the southern banks of the Niger. The northern and western Igbomina kingdoms (with the exception of the Orangun's kingdom of Ila) became subjects of the Alaafin, paying tribute to him, and contributing men and materials to his armies whenever so requested. Some Igbomina chiefs even commanded some of the Alaafin's armies. The Igbomina kingdoms which thus came into the Oyo Empire enjoyed regular protection by the Alaafin's armies against Nupe incursions. The town of Igbaja was established as a fortified post for such defense purposes. As for the Nupe people in the areas conquered by the Oyo armies, they too began to pay tribute to the Alaafin. As far as is known, however, they were not required to supply men for his armies. The eastern parts of the Nupe country south of the Niger, where the Oyo armies did not conquer, remained a source of incursions into Igbomina, but, on the whole, the power of the Oyo Empire kept them at bay for nearly two centuries. The kingdom of Ila never became part of the territories controlled by the Alaafin in the Igbomina country; but it too was considerably shielded from Nupe incursions by the presence of the Alaafin's armies in most of Igbomina.

The Alaafin also attempted to expand his authority towards the south. Giving the excuse that the Ilesa authorities had sent no goodwill message at the time of the Alaafin Abipa's return to Oyo-Ile, the Alaafin's government ordered an invasion of the Ijesa country. A cavalry force entered into the Ijesa forests, but it was repulsed by the Owa's army and lost many men in the process.

In the direction of the northwest, a series of invasions of the Bariba country suppressed Bariba groups all the way to the banks of the Moshi River. Like the Nupe, the conquered Bariba became subjects of the Alaafin, paying regular tribute to him.

In the southwest, as Oyo armies came sweeping through the Egbado country, its kingdoms and towns embraced the Alaafin's overlordship. The Alaafin's control over Egbado came ultimately to be second only to his rule over the

Oyo country itself in its detailed administration. As would be remembered from earlier chapters, Oyo created new towns in Egbado or gave new responsibilities to old towns. Some of these, as imperial towns, had their governments closely controlled by the Alaafin; the rulers of some were even appointed by the Alaafin; and some of the latter had for rulers servants of the Alaafin appointed and sent directly from Oyo-Ile. In the wake of the Oyo armies came large numbers of Oyo traders and migrants from the Oyo country, increasing the population of many Egbado towns and considerably modifying the demographic composition of the Egbado country. By the eighteenth century, Egbado had become profoundly transformed by the influence of Oyo, and its people were among the most loyal subjects of the Alaafin.

The Egba and Owu kingdoms, neighbors of the Egbado to the east, also became tributaries of the Alaafin, with the obligation to support his armies with men and materials. According to Egba traditions recorded by Biobaku, among the Egba, as among the Egbado, no military resistance was offered to the Alaafin's armies. By and large, the Egba were glad to be protected by his great power, and the Owu rulers were proud to be seen as his friends in south-central Yorubaland.

As it developed then, most of the territorial expansion of the Oyo Empire was towards the southwest. This has led to suggestions that the rulers of Oyo were simply pursuing a policy aimed at establishing trade with Europeans along the coast. While the territorial expansion did boost Oyo's trade enormously, trade *per se* does not seem to have been the objective. The central objective was to expand the Alaafin's imperial control in all directions. The southwest, where open grasslands penetrated all the way to quite close to the coast, proved easier for the Oyo cavalry than other directions. Thoughts of expanding in other directions were never given up; however, the experiences of the Oyo cavalry in places like the Ijesa country made invasions of thickly forested territories highly unattractive. With regard to seeking trade relations with Europeans on the coast, indeed, the Oyo-Ile authorities would seem to have had some reluctance, arising from their experience in the reign of Obalokun. According to Oyo-Ile traditions, Obalokun received friendly messages from a European monarch and, to reciprocate, sent a large party of men (numbering 800) to take his goodwill message to the coast, but none of the men was ever heard of again.[8] This made the Oyo-Ile palace very suspicious of all Europeans for a long time. It is in this regard significant that the Oyo-Ile authorities never attempted to equip their armies with guns from the coast, even though they could very easily have done so.

Oyo's expansion into the country of the Aja people followed naturally upon the expansion into Egbado.[9] Even when Oyo-Ile had been only a small kingdom, it had done considerable trade with the Aja country through Egbado and the Ketu kingdom. By the time of the warrior king Alaafin Ajagbo, that is, about the middle of the seventeenth century, the Egbado country and most probably the territories of the far western Yoruba kingdoms (with the notable exception of Ketu), even as far as the small Aja kingdom of Weme on the Popo Coast, had come under the control of the Oyo Empire. That made Oyo-controlled territories neighbors of the Allada kingdom, the oldest and most important of the Aja kingdoms. Moreover, the founding of the Dahomey kingdom (another Aja kingdom) some distance to the north of Allada in about 1625, and Dahomey's general aggressiveness, as it grew stronger, against all its neighbors, was destined to threaten the oldest routes carrying Oyo's trade through the area as well as parts of territories that Oyo considered to be Oyo-controlled land. As a result, Dahomey was to become an important military objective in Oyo-Ile.

Statements by some European coastal traders that an Oyo invasion of the Aja country took place between 1680 and 1682 are now regarded as doubtful. But a major Oyo invasion did occur in the 1690s. Some political trouble developed in the kingdom of Allada, and an aggrieved group of Allada citizens sent a delegation to Oyo-Ile in 1698 to urge the Alaafin to intervene. In response, the Alaafin sent an envoy to advise the king of Allada to put his house in order. In blatant contravention of well-known Yoruba and Aja laws, which protected envoys from even the faintest molestation, the Aja king seized and killed the Oyo envoy. Oyo armies therefore marched out. According to Oyo traditions, the offending king fled and vanished (and the Oyo commander, on return to Oyo-Ile, was disgraced for not bringing him captive). The Allada kingdom was viciously ravaged and large numbers of its people were taken captive.

The available evidence shows that the Allada kingdom never truly survived this disaster. In the years that followed, its power and influence sank lower and lower. Since Allada had been regarded by all the Aja as their foremost kingdom, its decline altered the pattern of relationships among Aja kingdoms. Whydah, a port town of the kingdom of Savi, developed to become a major slave port on the West African coast (and the Savi kingdom itself became better known by the name Whydah). Thanks also to perpetual meddling by European slave traders in the internal affairs of both Whydah and Allada, as well as in their relationships with each other, both suffered endless internal dissensions and ultimately went to war with each other, a development that weakened Allada the more and weakened Whydah also. The younger kingdom of Dahomey, located farther in the interior, saw the situation closer to the coast as an opportunity for its own commercial and territorial expansion. In 1724, Dahomey invaded, conquered and occupied Allada, and three years later prepared to do the same to Whydah. Agaja, the king of Dahomey, was about to become ruler over a kingdom stretching from the Abomey Plateau to the coast.

The Oyo authorities were not prepared to accept the developments in the Aja country. Following Oyo's conquest of Allada in 1698, the Alaafin had regarded it as part of his empire. In late 1726, therefore, a large Oyo army headed for war with Dahomey. The Dahomey army was armed with guns, and Agaja was confident that it would overcome the Oyo cavalry. He was mistaken. The ensuing battle was sharp and short. A huge number of Dahomey soldiers fell, and the rest scattered. Agaja himself first fled into a swampy thicket to hide, and then came out and surrendered, agreeing to pay heavy tribute to the Alaafin. Believing, like all observers, that Dahomey was finished militarily, the Oyo army returned home. But Agaja soon proved that he was far from finished. In 1727, he overran Whydah. Then, when he heard that a very large Oyo army, commanded by the great warrior Yau Yamba, was coming towards Dahomey, he evacuated and burnt his capital city of Abomey, made his subjects abandon their villages and flee into forest areas where the Oyo cavalry could not reach them, and he himself took refuge in a forest. The Oyo army came and found the country empty – no towns, villages, houses, farms, food. Consequently, they quickly returned to their own country, and as soon as they left, the Dahomians returned and rebuilt their homes. Yau Yamba and his officers became resolved to crush this troublesome little kingdom. Early in 1729, they were back again on the road to Dahomey. Once again, Agaja played the only card available to him. After burying his palace treasures, he burnt Abomey again and instructed his subjects to burn everything and flee into the forests. This time around, the Oyo army would not go away quickly or easily. Special units were sent to pursue the Dahomians into many of their hideouts, capturing many and killing more. While these operations went on, the main Oyo army dug its feet deep into the country and refused to go away. The dry season passed and the rainy season began, but the Oyo army did not leave. In the Dahomian hideouts, the hidden supplies of food began to run out, with consequent starvation and deaths. By the time the Oyo army finally left, Agaja and his people had suffered tremendously. But, as they were settling down and putting the shattered pieces of their lives together again, news came that yet another Oyo army was coming. The Oyo authorities had apparently decided that the way to beat Agaja and his people was to wear them down. Agaja sued for peace, requesting the Director of the Portuguese fort at Whydah to arrange things between him and the representatives of the Alaafin's government. In the peace treaty that resulted in 1730, Dahomey accepted the overlordship of the Alaafin and agreed to pay him annual tribute. Oyo accepted the reconstitution of the Dahomey kingdom to include former Dahomey, Whydah and a part of Allada (that is, virtually all of the Aja country), with its capital moved from Abomey in the interior to Allada near the coast. The remaining part of Allada, with a strong Yoruba component, was constituted into a separate small kingdom with the name of Ajase (called Porto Novo by the Europeans). Dahomey sent a young prince named Togbesu to live in the Alaafin's palace as a pledge that it would faithfully carry out the terms of the treaty. Also, the Alaafin gave a daughter in marriage to the king of Dahomey, and received a Dahomey princess in marriage.

The expanded kingdom of Dahomey (made up of almost all the Aja country) thus became a province of the Oyo Empire. From about the early 1740s, however, strains again appeared in Oyo's relationship with Dahomey, largely because Dahomey could not pay the tribute regularly. Some minor Oyo invasions occurred in 1742 and 1743, and thereafter it looked again and again as if a major Oyo invasion would follow. In 1748, therefore, Togbesu, by then king of Dahomey, entered into another treaty with Oyo, reaffirming the 1730 treaty. He also obtained Oyo's permission to return the capital of Dahomey to the town of Abomey in the interior. Thereafter, until the end of the eighteenth century, Dahomey remained a peaceful province of the Oyo Empire.

The Alaafins also had thoughts and plans of expanding their empire to the south and east. In the reign of the Alaafin Ojigi, an army was sent to the Ibolo country. The details of this campaign are obscured in the Oyo traditions by the account of the accident that caused the death of its illustrious commander, the Basorun Yau Yamba. Oyo traditions say that the army was going "towards Offa" when Yau Yamba sustained the fatal accident. That does not help us to answer the question whether the campaign was against Offa, or whether its objective was the territories beyond Offa and the Ibolo country – the territories of the Okun Yoruba and the Ekiti. As would be remembered, by as early as the reign of Ajagbo in the late sixteenth century, the Ibolo country, of which Offa was the leading town, had become part of the Oyo Empire. As early as the early seventeenth century, Oyo-controlled territory had extended to the Igbomina country immediately north of Otun in northern Ekiti, where a Benin army had, in that century, encountered Oyo's frontier troops. It seems fairly certain, then, that Yau Yamba's army was sent to use Offa as base for a campaign for new territorial acquisitions in the territories of the Okun Yoruba and probably also northern Ekiti. The timing of the campaign would be some years after Yau Yamba's monumental campaigns against Dahomey, probably in the 1730s. The sending of an officer of Yau Yamba's stature is a strong indication that the Alaafin's government had major objectives for this campaign. Unfortunately, the campaign ended in a disaster. According to Oyo traditions, just before Offa, Yau Yamba fell with his horse into a deep ditch, broke his neck, and died – and, as a result, the campaign was called off.

The reign of Ojigi represented the high water mark of the territorial expansion of the Oyo Empire. The whole expanse of the Oyo-Yoruba country constituted its metropolitan province. To the northeast, in the Nupe country, it controlled a large slice of Nupe territory, up to the southern banks of the River Niger. Northwestwards, it included Bariba territory up to the banks of the Moshi River. Eastwards, it included most of Igbomina and all of the Ibolo country to a boundary with the northern Ekiti. Southwards, it shared a long boundary with the Ijesa and Ife, with Ede on the Osun River as a frontier post, and then it dipped down to include the Owu, Egba and Egbado territories, as well as a slice of Awori territory on the Atlantic coast and, from the 1770s, the kingdoms of Badagry and Ajase (Porto Novo). Westwards, it included the far western Yoruba countries of Sabe, Ahori and Idasa, and all the territory of the Aja people to beyond the River Mono east of the kingdom of Atakpame.

Late in his reign (probably in the early 1740s), the Alaafin Ojigi sent an expedition to trace the outer boundaries of his empire. Johnson's rendering of the tradition concerning this expedition relates that Ojigi:

> ... in order to show his undisputed sovereignty over the whole of the Yoruba country, including Benin, sent out a large expedition which struck the Niger in the north, near the Ibaribas, and coasted along the right bank until they arrived at the coast and returned to Oyo by the Popo country.[10]

The claim that the Oyo Empire included Benin is certainly an exaggeration, but it did have its northern boundary on the River Niger and its southern boundary on the Atlantic Ocean. By the time of Ojigi, Oyo people seem to have been referring to the southwestern (or Aja and western Yoruba) territories in general as Popo country. The kingdom of Atakpame lay in Aja territory northeast of the area that Oyo armies and traders referred to as Popo country, in the territory west of the River Mono. Atakpame itself was probably never subject to Oyo. However, in 1764, an Oyo army stationed in the area of Atakpame clashed with, and defeated, an Ashanti army in the territory west of Atakpame – probably in an area that is now Yoruba territory in the Republic of Togo.

The Alaafins had a great festival, a sort of jubilee called Bebe, with which they celebrated long or successful reigns. When the Alaafin Agboluaje celebrated the Bebe in the 1760s, 1060 vassal rulers (according to Oyo traditions) came to Oyo-Ile to honor their suzerain.

Administration of the Empire

In essence, the Oyo Empire was a large Yoruba kingdom, ruled according to the typical Yoruba system of government applied over a vast territory. At the head of it all was the Alaafin, a typical Yoruba divine king. Like the kings of all Yoruba kingdoms, the Alaafin was selected from the pool of princes of one royal lineage. For the selection, all princes (sons and grandsons of former kings) were eligible – with the singular exception of the oldest son of the recently deceased king. From the early seventeenth century, this one prince, with the title of Aremo, was allowed to be freely associated with his reigning father in matters of government, and then he had to die (by committing suicide) when his father died. Succession by primogeniture was, as would be remembered, generally rejected by Yoruba kingdoms; Oyo-Ile's requirement that the Aremo must die represents a particularly drastic rejection of it. The purpose, as in all Yoruba kingdoms, was to ensure that the right of the people to select their king would not be interfered with by one privileged prince.

As in all Yoruba kingdoms, in theory, by popular sayings, and as demonstrated in civic ceremonies and rituals, the government was the Alaafin's government, and he was supposed to have the power of life and death over his subjects. But, in reality, in the Yoruba system of limited monarchy over which he reigned, he was subject to well established, powerful, institutions, as well as to elaborate rules and prohibitions. The high Inner Council of chiefs, named the Oyo Mesi, consisting of seven of the most powerful quarter chiefs of the capital city of Oyo-Ile (the Basorun, Agbakin, Samu, Alapini, Laguna, Akiniku and Asipa), met with the Alaafin daily in the palace to make all laws and take the highest decisions of government. Such laws and decisions were then announced to the kingdom as the Alaafin's word. Outside that system, the Alaafin might not try to operate. In the generally militarized mode of existence to which this kingdom was forced by circumstances, the high chiefs of the Oyo Mesi were also the highest military chiefs. They also bore the responsibility of selecting new kings, and of removing an unpopular king by asking him, if matters came to such an end, to "go to sleep" [See Chapter 8].

The highest officer in the Oyo Mesi was the Basorun who bore responsibilities akin to those of a Prime Minister or Chancellor and presided over the Oyo Mesi in council. Of the other members of the Oyo Mesi, the Agbakin had charge of the worship of Oranmiyan in addition to other duties; the Laguna was the kingdom's highest ambassador (a sort of foreign minister) in the most critical situations; the Asipa was, in the council of the Oyo Mesi, the Ojuwa (he who distributed presents given to the Oyo Mesi); the Alapini was the officer in charge of the *egungun* mysteries and, over time, he became the head of all religious affairs. The lineage to which the Alapini title belonged was an old Nupe lineage.

Below the level of the Oyo Mesi existed many councils and committees of chiefs, each for a particular function of state, the individual members of which bore specific state responsibilities. In and around the palace, a large number of officers, high and low, ministered to the needs of the king, the king's personal family, the palace, and the palace shrines and rituals. This palace establishment grew to include hundreds of people. The highest rank of palace servants was that of the eunuchs who had charge of the personal affairs, and the wives and children, of the king. Usually, a eunuch was a very substantial royal official who had his own large compound where he served as guardian to the king's children and nursing wives. Absent in other Yoruba palaces, the institution of eunuch would seem to have been a borrowing from the cultures of the western Sudan beyond the Niger. Below the eunuch was a large number of Ilaris, male and female, who served as the king's messengers and personal servants. The most experienced of the Ilaris were sometimes sent as envoys to foreign governments or to special jobs in the provinces of the empire. Among the eunuchs and Ilaris, some performed purely religious functions in the palace.

Far more than any other Yoruba kingdom, the political system of the Oyo Empire emphasized military strength and preparedness. Apart from the high military chiefs of the Oyo Mesi, almost every other chief, no matter what functions he performed in the state, was also supposed to be a military officer, able and ready to command troops. High military positions enjoyed enormous respect and honor in the society, and the upbringing of the youths of the Oyo homeland devoted much emphasis to military skills. Some cities close to Oyo-Ile particularly focused on military training and preparedness. Among these were Koso, the town founded to the memory of Sango, Igbogun, Igboho, Iresa, Ogbomoso and Ede, but the most important was Ikoyi. The Onikoyi, ruler of Ikoyi, was the greatest provincial military chieftain. Young men who emerged into adulthood with the best military distinctions anywhere in the Oyo country stood a chance of being appointed by the Alaafin's government as military officers. Of such officers, the most honored were the Eso, seventy in number, about whom something has earlier been said. The Are Ona Kakanfo was usually referred to as the Eso of the Esos, and so he was in essence; but, usually he was not appointed from among the Esos – the position was usually given to a provincial ruler who had strong military credentials.

The earliest Alaafins personally led their armies to war. As would be remembered, one of the earliest Alaafins (Oluodo) drowned in the River Niger while leading his army in a war with the Nupe. A later Alaafin (Ajiboyede) nearly lost his life in the battle with the Nupe outside the walls of Igboho, during the exile. From the time of Abipa, Ajiboyede's successor, the Alaafins no longer led their armies in person. That task fell to the great war chiefs.

The above, then, is a brief summary of the central government of the Oyo Empire. Outside Oyo-Ile, the rest of the Oyo country constituted the metropolitan homeland of the empire, its base and main support. This Oyo country was made up of many kingdoms, each with its capital city (where its king lived) and smaller towns and villages (where Baales lived). All these kings accepted the Alaafin as the supreme king of all Oyo people, paid tribute to him, and held all the human and material resources of their kingdoms available and expendable in his service. It is important to repeat the fact that these kings were not Baales under the Alaafin; they were kings (Obas) over their own kingdoms – kings in a "consolidated kingdom" of all Oyo people, over which the Alaafin was unanimously accepted as supreme king and commander in chief.

The whole Oyo homeland was conceived as comprising three provinces called Ekun Otun and Ekun Osi (both belonging to the center), and the Epo province (in the far south). These three, plus the Ibolo country in the east, constituted what may be described as the metropolitan heart of the empire. The Ekun Otun province comprised some Oyo towns and all the small Ibarapa country.

In the Ekun Osi (to the east of Oyo-Ile), the main kingdoms were Ikoyi under the Onikoyi, Igbon under the Olugbon, Iresa under the Aresa, Ijeru under the Ompetu, Ogbomoso under the Soun. In the Ekun Otun (to the west of Oyo-Ile) the main kingdoms were the kingdoms of Iganna under the Sabigana, Iwere under the Oniwere, Asia under the Alasia, Okeho under the Onjo, Igijan under the Bagijan, Saki under the Okere, Ibode under the Alapata, Igboho under the Ona Onibode, Ipapo under the Elerinpo, Kisi under the Ikisi, Iseyin under the Aseyin, Ado under the Alado, the Ibarapa kingdom of Eruwa under the Eleruwa, Oje under the Oloje. In the Ibolo province, the main kingdoms were Ikirun under the Akirun, Ilobu under the Olobu, Ife-Odan under the Adimula, Offa under the Olofa. In the Epo province, the kingdoms were few: Iwo under the Oluwo, Idese under the Ondese and Ede under the Timi. By the late eighteenth century, Osogbo, originally a frontier Ijesa town, had become an important cosmopolitan center of trade, and had received so many Oyo settlers as to become predominantly Oyo. As a result, it was regarded generally as a kingdom in the Epo province of the Oyo Empire.

Outside of these provinces of the metropolitan center, the common characteristic of Oyo's imperial administration of each subordinate kingdom was the stationing of an official representative of the Alaafin's government, with the title of Ajele, in every important town. The main duty of the Ajele was to collect the tributes and send them to Oyo-Ile. However, Oyo traders and others away from home regarded the Ajele as the Oyo official at whose residence they could receive hospitality and protection. The Ajele also ensured that the local authorities maintained and protected the trade routes. As would be remembered, in a number of Egbado towns regarded by Oyo authorities as especially important for commercial or strategic reasons, the Alaafin's government established various kinds of nearly direct control.

At the peak of the greatness of the Oyo Empire by about 1750, the Alaafin's government controlled an enormous treasury – from the regular tributes, from the tolls on trade, and from, according to the Oyo traditions, a seemingly endless stream of gifts from all over the empire. The positioning of an Ajele in important towns of every vassal state to collect the tributes made their collection generally very efficient. For most vassal rulers, the annual delivery of the tributes was usually a festive occasion. No vassal ruler or Ajele wished for a situation in which the tributes were not rendered in full when due. In this regard, more information is available about Dahomey's experience than about any other vassal state of the Oyo Empire, because of Dahomey's close contact with literate European traders on the coast. From such information, it is known that the Dahomey economy, which came to depend heavily on the slave trade, declined considerably from about the 1740s. As a result, until the end of the century, there were some years when Dahomey could not come up with all its tributes when due. Whenever that happened, the Dahomey rulers incurred the intense displeasure of the Alaafin. In fact, on some occasions, Dahomey found itself on the verge of being punished like a vassal state in full rebellion against the Alaafin – to the Dahomey rulers a very frightening predicament. It would seem, therefore, that the Alaafin's government did not tolerate any laxity in the payment of the tributes by the vassal states; after all, payment of the tributes was the most measurable proof of a vassal state's loyalty.

Imperial revenues from tolls and dues on commerce, most certainly, also grew as the empire expanded. Trade was always a major factor in Oyo-Ile's strength; and the empire, as it grew, became one sprawling trading state. To traders from all parts of the Oyo homeland, the empire was a vast land of opportunity. By the late eighteenth century, many prominent men in Oyo-Ile were building wealth from trading; even most of the Alaafins of the period were rich traders before they came to the throne, and some of them continued to own large trading establishments, using their wives as organizers of their business to distant parts of the empire (especially to the Egbado province, all the way to the coast at the ports of Badagry and Porto Novo). Oyo-Ile, and the rest of the Oyo homeland, had some of the largest and busiest markets in the empire, of which Akesan (Oyo-Ile's central marketplace) was the greatest. Apart from Akesan, Clapperton visited six other marketplaces in Oyo-Ile, just as he had seen vibrant markets in every town along his route from Badagry to Oyo-Ile. From all this great commercial activity, the Alaafin derived much revenue on a regular basis – from city gate tolls, marketplace dues, levies on particular articles of merchandise, and so forth.

Moreover, gifts to the Alaafin were a major source of imperial revenue – gifts on special occasions and festivals from vassal rulers and chiefs, gifts from newly appointed kings and chiefs, gifts from funeral celebrations of prominent citizens, etc. In fact, in some vassal provinces, a given proportion of the moveable wealth of prominent deceased chiefs was required as gifts to the Alaafin. Again, the clearest information about this comes from Dahomey. Some time in the 1780s, the then Mehu of Dahomey died and the Dahomey king, Agonglo, had a major part of his moveable belongings and some of his wives sent to the Alaafin Abiodun. The Alaafin was dissatisfied with the amount that was sent, and he expressed his displeasure so vehemently that Agonglo had to buy more items and some women slaves to send to the Alaafin.[11] Such acrimony over the sending of inheritance gifts to the Alaafin would seem to have been uncommon, however. The families of most great men were proud to show off their late father's wealth by sending rich gifts to the Alaafin.

From about the second quarter of the eighteenth century, the slave trade became increasingly important in the economy of the Oyo Empire as well as in the revenue base of the Alaafin's government.[12] Oyo gradually became the chief supplier of the slaves sold on the Yoruba coast, resulting in increased volumes of slave exports from the ports of Ajase (Porto Novo), Badagry and Lagos. The usual pattern of the trade was that the Oyo traders sold to coastal middlemen (like the Ijebu and Awori for the Lagos market and the Egbado and Awori for the Porto Novo market). The main sources of Oyo's slave supplies to the coast are known; however, the relative numerical importance of each source in the whole volume remains unclear. As would be remembered, Richard Lander recorded, during visits to Oyo-Ile in 1826, that convicted criminals were a source of slaves sold to the coast by Oyo. Since convicts belonged to the state, this must have been a source of royal revenue exclusively. Very probably, from the time of the serious political troubles in Oyo-Ile in the third quarter of the eighteenth century (in the time of the Basorun Gaha), the number of ordinary persons convicted of offences and sold into slavery increased significantly. Captives in war constituted a probably much larger source – from the Oyo wars in the Nupe, Bariba and Aja countries. Oyo also bought large numbers of slaves from the Nupe and Bariba, and from Hausaland, mostly for resale on the coast, and partly also for sale to native buyers in the Oyo homeland who owned slaves for domestic and other types of labor. European slave traders on the coast were aware in the late eighteenth century that large numbers of the slaves being supplied to the coast were bought by the Oyo from the Nupe country and from Hausaland. Sultan Bello of Sokoto wrote that the Hausa country sold many slaves to the Yoruba. The slaves bought from the Nupe comprised probably mostly Nupe, and the rest comprised partly Yoruba (of Igbomina, Okun Yoruba,

Akoko and Ekiti origin), partly Kakanda, and partly Gbagyi (northern neighbors of the Nupe). Most of the Oyo trade in slaves belonged to private Oyo traders, but some part belonged to the royal establishment, bringing revenue to the palace. Tolls on the slave traffic also brought increasing royal revenue but never seems to have amounted to more than a small part of all tolls. Moreover, tributes from the vassal states regularly included some slaves, most of whom were usually absorbed into the royal service; the few who were sold yielded some revenue for the king's government. Finally, criminal kidnapping contributed to the number of slaves reaching the coast through the Oyo traders. The number of the kidnapped was probably small at any time, but, understandably, popular fears and sentiment exaggerated it – and have passed the exaggerations into the traditions.

As for the provincial administration, it seems to have been completely self-supporting. The typical Ajele lived off the province where he was stationed; in fact, most Ajeles did well for themselves and became quite well-to-do dignitaries. Royal messengers traveling through the provinces also usually received rich gifts for their master and for themselves. As earlier pointed out, the provinces also supplied men to the Alaafin's armies – often forming contingents commanded by their own rulers. According to Igbomina traditions, one seventeenth century king of Omupo in Igbomina, the Olomu Aperan, reputed to be a very gifted warrior, repeatedly commanded armies side by side with chiefs of the Oyo country (the Onikoyi, the Olugbon and the Aresa) in the Alaafin's wars. Archibald Dalzel, in his *History of Dahomey* published in 1793, talks of a 1784 campaign in which a strong Dahomey army, joined by troops from some western Yoruba kingdoms, and supported by Lagos, fought for the Alaafin. Dalzel wrote: "The operations of the Dahoman army were directed by the Eyeo messengers... and nothing of importance was undertaken without their [the Oyo messengers'] concurrence."[13] Two years later, the Dahomey army was again on the move for the Alaafin – against Weme. When they finished with Weme, they proposed to go on and attack Ardra and Porto Novo, but the Alaafin did not approve, telling them that Ardra was Oyo's "calabash out of which nobody should be permitted to eat but himself."[14] In short, then, the Alaafin's government was able to raise substantial armies at home and from the provinces for imperial objectives.

We must not conclude from incidents in the revenue collection practices of the Alaafin's government, however, that his overlordship in the provinces was habitually rough or brutal. It was not so for the most part. In fact, both at home and in the provinces, the government of the Alaafin seems to have been, until the mid-eighteenth century, mild and benevolent, and, towards the non-Yoruba subjects of the Alaafin, the Oyo imperial government seems to have been remarkably open, generous and trusting. For instance, it was established imperial policy that the representative of the Alaafin as ruler of Ijanna (the Onisare of Ijanna) in Egbado had to be an Oyo-Ile palace servant who was of Nupe origin, and many Nupe and Bariba notables were regularly employed in important positions in the Oyo government and army. From about the middle of the eighteenth century (as will be seen in the next chapter), Oyo-Ile experienced at home an increasing deterioration of the quality of leadership, and this manifested partly in increasing oppression of the common people even at home, as well as in some harshness in dealings with the provinces. Before then, the government of the Oyo Empire attached much importance to order and respectability. The overall impression from the Oyo traditions is that, by and large, the functionaries of government maintained dignity and gravity in the performance of public duties, that this ethos rubbed off on the Alaafin's officials and representatives in the provinces, that the average citizen of the empire was imbued with much pride, and that the citizens of even the most distant provinces felt comfortable about being protected by the power and authority of the imperial government of the Alaafin.

By the time that Clapperton and his team traversed part of the western provinces of the empire from Badagry to Oyo-Ile in 1825–6, standards of governance had fallen very seriously in the empire. The Alaafin's government had become too preoccupied with its own troubles in and around Oyo-Ile to exercise much control in the provinces. Yet, the foreigners still saw much orderly government, many respectable public officers, a country that respected the law and citizens who went about their daily affairs in peace and order. At Oyo-Ile, at the end of his second visit to the city in 1826, Richard Lander commented that, but for the "solitary exception" of the compulsory suicide of the Aremo and a few other persons at the death of the Alaafin, the people and rulers of the empire were "mild in their manners and charitable in their dealings." The Oyo Empire, he said, "is a fine kingdom, peopled with a mild, affectionate and unassuming race."[15] We know today that all that so impressed him in 1826 were no more than residues of the high qualities of an earlier time when, before the mid-eighteenth century, the government and the empire had been at their strongest and best.

A Country of Great Culture

The general peace, prosperity and pride enjoyed during the middle period of the empire produced a very significant flowering of Yoruba civilization in the Oyo homeland. The ancient Yoruba arts of sculpture in various media (terracotta, wood and metals – iron, copper, brass, bronze, silver) flourished in

Oyo-Ile and other Oyo cities and towns. Of course, the Alaafin's palace represented the epitome of artistic decoration, with the palaces of the lower kings of the Oyo homeland coming close behind. The Alaafin's palace had the tallest and proudest gables (called *gobi*) in the land as well as the most gorgeous array of decorative sculptures – together constituting a spectacle that attracted admirers from distant places in the empire.

Some of the public shrines in Oyo-Ile and other Oyo cities were also heavily decorated with sculptures, as well as with murals and other types of paintings. Richard Lander has given us a description of the principal shrine of Oyo-Ile in 1826. This shrine, according to him,

> is the largest and most fancifully ornamented of any of a similar kind in the interior of Africa. It is a perfect square building, each side of which is at least 20 yards in length. Directly opposite the entrance is an immense figure of a giant bearing a lion on its head, carved in wood, and beautifully executed. About twenty-six or twenty-seven figures, in bass-relief are placed on each of the sides of the hut, but all in a kneeling posture, with their faces turned towards the larger figure, to which they are apparently paying their devotions. On the heads of the small figures are wooden images of tigers, hyenas, snakes, crocodiles, etc., exquisitely carved and painted, or rather stained, with a variety of colors.[16]

Only the king and his high chiefs could enter onto the "highly polished" floors of this shrine for their daily devotions and rituals. Lower members of the society must do theirs outside the shrine. There were, according to Lander, fifty other shrines in Oyo-Ile, all of them "on a smaller and less magnificent scale" than the main shrine described above – but each beautifully decorated with sculptures and other works of art.

Yoruba music attained some of its richest products in imperial Oyo. Bata music, with its tight drums, almost metallic sounds, choppy, explosive rhythm, responded to with equally choppy and explosive dance movements, started in Oyo as sacred music to Sango, the god of thunder and lightning. But it became part of popular music and dance, even though its popular exponents usually dressed in ways reminiscent of the ritual clothing of Sango worship. Oyo was also the home of Gangan and Dundun – the talking drums – with their almost endless variations of music and rhythm for popular occasions (royal appearances, large family occasions, small band presentations with singing and dance, etc.). From Oyo cities and towns, small and large troupes and solo drummers went with all these types of music to other parts of Yorubaland. It was quite common for some of these troupes to be away from home for years, weaving themselves into the local popular music culture of one town and then moving on to the next town.

Also, from Oyo of the imperial era we have decisive evidence of Yoruba entertainment that was theatre or drama – with stage, trained professional actors, plot, acts and scenes, costumes, properties, etc. Strong rudiments of theatre and drama were a feature of many Yoruba rituals, especially re-enactment features in sacred rituals (such as in the installation of kings). From such roots, there probably generally developed a tradition of distinctly popular (secular) theatre and drama, but the only written description of it comes to us from imperial Oyo. Clapperton and Lander were invited to one such theatre production during their visit to Oyo-Ile in January 1826.[17]

The theatre stage was a large enclosure (near the palace), covered with lovely green grass, "as level as a bowling green" and "rendered particularly pleasant by the refreshing shade afforded by clumps of tall trees." "A lofty fan-palm tree grew in the center of the place, under the branches of which the actors were accommodated … and a temporary fence erected around its trunk screened them from observation whenever they chose to be concealed." The main productions for that afternoon were "pantomimes," the type of show usually held for kings visiting Oyo-Ile. (One vassal king was visiting that day and was in the audience.)

After a prelude of loud drums, horns and whistles, the first act began and consisted of "dancing, capering, and tumbling by about 20 men enveloped in sacks, which novel and elegant divertissement was continued with admirable spirit for a full half hour." Lander remarked that in the art of tumbling, these dancers

> cannot be excelled by any people in the world; their evolutions in the air are perfectly astonishing, and by the suppleness and pliability of their limbs, by their bending and turning, and twisting themselves into all manner of shapes, one would be almost inclined to believe that they have not a single bone in their bodies…

The second act, accomplished with very intricate costumes and masks, consisted of a fight on stage between a large snake (a boa constrictor) and a huge, whimsical, ugly monster armed with a sword. By using sacks sewn in particular ways, and by very deft acting, two actors joined end to end to form the big snake on the stage. When they were done and the snake revealed itself, it looked very much like a natural boa constrictor, skin and all, about 14 feet long. The sword-bearing monster had a headpiece so intricately made that he could change his expression and mood as often as he wished. With the sword, he tried to kill the snake, while the snake went after him, coiling and wriggling every way like a real snake, opening and shutting its jaws and darting out its forked tongue. All these evoked thunderous roars from the audience. Finally, after nearly half an hour of the fight, the monster managed to attack the snake from its tail, hacking at it furiously with the sword, causing the snake to twist and writhe in agony – at which point many masked actors sprang to the stage and carried the wounded snake away backstage.

The third and last act consisted of the "representation of the caricature of a white man" – by an actor with chalky white skin, mimicking the supposed walking and movements of a white man. This figure provoked the most uproarious laughter and applause of the afternoon, with the audience pointing in the direction of the two white men in their midst, and directing the white men to see their copy on the stage. Clapperton and Lander "entered most cordially into the good humor of the moment."

Each one of the first two acts was followed by an intermission of many minutes. And each intermission was filled with a concert of drums and whistles, accompanied by songs from a choir of female voices, generally joined in by the audience. A long concert of drums, whistles, horns, singing and dancing brought the whole presentation to an end.

Such theatres were part of the regular repertoire of entertainment in Oyo cities and towns. Theatre groups, known as *alarinjo* (traveling entertainers), accompanied by drummers, dancers, singers, acrobats and mascots, all from the Oyo country, were regularly to be found on tour in all parts of Yorubaland and the Oyo Empire.

The Oyo homeland in the era of the Oyo Empire, then, was a land of great and dynamic culture. Its huge cultural outflow played a very important part in promoting the image and influence of the Alaafin in the rest of Yorubaland and much of West Africa. The royal festival named Bebe served as occasion to put on show the beauty of Oyo-Ile and the glory of the Alaafin and Oyo-Ile chiefs. Celebrated by the Alaafins who reigned long or whose reigns were adjudged by them and their chiefs to be successful and prosperous, Bebe was the biggest and loudest royal festival ever designed by any Yoruba kingdom. At its best, it was an ambitious royal jubilee supposed to last a full 10 years, during which rulers and chiefs of the Oyo homeland, vassal rulers and chiefs from all the tributary states of the empire, very senior messengers of kings of other Yoruba kingdoms, ordinary citizens, rich and poor, from all over Yorubaland and the Oyo Empire, were invited to converge on Oyo-Ile, to honor the Alaafin and give gifts to him, to bask in the greatness and beauty of Oyo-Ile and gaze with awe at the palace and its great king, to join in mammoth dancing celebrations and parades, and to partake of the surpassingly rich hospitality of the Alaafin's government and royal city. The Alaafin and his kingdom, sitting atop a sprawling and prosperous empire, took the beauty of Yoruba civilization to very great heights.

24. Festival celebration in Yorubaland. *Photo: P. Verger, 1956, IFAN.*

25. Entertainer in Oyo. *Photo: Toupet, 1964, IFAN.*

13

The Fall of the Oyo Empire

By the middle of the eighteenth century, the Oyo Empire stood at the peak of its territorial greatness, its prosperity and wealth, its pride and glory. Oyo armies stood on the banks of the Niger in the land of the Nupe, on the shores of the Atlantic Ocean, on the River Moshi in the land of the Bariba, beyond the River Mono in the land of the Aja and Ewe. Oyo's provincial officials (the Ajeles) in their thousands held small courts throughout the expanse of these lands to represent the affairs and the majesty of their king and master, the Alaafin. The capital and heart of the empire, the city of Oyo-Ile, boomed with a population larger than that of any other in the African tropical forests, with a volume of commerce far beyond that of any other city in the forest interior of West Africa, with the sound of songs and music, and of dance and theatre; and scintillated with famous artists, artisans and entertainers, with great priests and medicine men, with wealthy traders and proud warrior chiefs. Many great cities, some only a little smaller than Oyo-Ile itself, dotted the Oyo kingdom, each a center of great wealth and power. The ruler of it all, the Alaafin, glowed and shimmered in glory, while at festivals women dancing in the adoring streets sang songs proclaiming him as *ori aiye* – the head, or apex, of the world.

Yet, by the end of the same century, this empire had gone a long way in disintegrating, and in the fourth decade of the nineteenth century it collapsed completely. The collapse was so total that by 1835 the great city of Oyo-Ile was abandoned and left desolate. Today, only some stretches of its once mighty walls can still be seen; the city itself is covered by thick grass and shrub inhabited by wild beasts.

Historians will long debate and search for the cause or causes of this strange, almost sudden, disaster. This chapter will attempt to tell what we know today of this sad story in the history of the Yoruba people.

The beginning of the troubles, which ultimately led to this collapse, is traditionally traced to the late eighteenth century, the time of the Basorun Gaha, c. 1754–74.[1] Gaha belonged to the lineage of the famous Basorun Yau Yamba (some traditions say that he was Yau Yamba's son). Before coming to the position of Basorun, Gaha had won brilliant honors as a warrior, and was extremely popular with the people of the capital city. He also had the reputation of commanding great ritual powers and potent charms. Only seventeen days after he was sworn in as the Basorun in 1754, he embarked on a series of policies and actions aimed at suppressing the Alaafin and making himself (as Basorun) the absolute ruler of the Oyo Empire. To isolate the reigning Alaafin Labisi, Gaha arrested and summarily executed prominent persons who were known to be Labisi's friends and supporters. He then set up a reign of terror which intimidated and silenced all who would have opposed him. Replacing the Ajeles in the provinces with his sons, relations and servants, he diverted tributes from the provinces to himself. The Alaafin Labisi became so intimidated that he could not even sit on the throne to perform the functions of a king. Rather than continue in such disgrace, Labisi did what Yoruba kings were supposed to do in dire extremities – he removed himself with dignity by committing suicide.

Gaha then put on the throne a prince named Awonbioju, who is said to have been a young friend of his. To Gaha's surprise, however, Awonbioju as king refused to treat Gaha as a superior. Only 130 days after Awonbioju came to the throne, therefore, Gaha forced him to take his own life. The next Alaafin, Agboluaje, lasted longer on the throne. Humbly managing his relationship with Gaha, he even celebrated a Bebe festival for three years and had vassal kings and chiefs come from all over the empire to honor him in Oyo-Ile. But in the end, Agboluaje too came into a conflict with Gaha and had to commit suicide.

To succeed Agboluaje, Gaha raised to the throne a prince named Majeogbe. While appearing openly to submit to Gaha, Majeogbe recruited famous occult practitioners (*adahunse*) to make powerful charms and formularies that would hurt or destroy the over-mighty Basorun. When Gaha became paralyzed in both legs, the Alaafin believed that his charms were working and he and his team of *adahunse* intensified their efforts. The paralysis, however, did not seem to have much effect on Gaha's hold on power. Finding ways to hide his paralyzed legs from the public, he continued to exercise despotic authority. According to the traditions, Gaha would have made himself king if such a thing were not impossible.

In the end, however, Gaha's excessively crowded life began to take effect. The paralysis in his legs (which was almost certainly brought on by a stroke) proved to be the first major sign of a general deterioration of his health. He is said to have begun to look prematurely aged, and to have also started to lose his usual mental sharpness. More and more, his affairs fell into the hands of lesser men – his sons, relations, cronies and servants, who generally used their influence for greed and for vicious oppression of vulnerable persons belonging to lineages and groups known to be opposed to Gaha. Many mindless acts of oppression committed by these people, including murders and seizures of defenseless citizens for sale into slavery, are preserved in the traditions. The result was that Gaha began to lose popularity – and as he did, his men's acts of oppression increased. Picking some petty quarrel with the Alaafin Majeogbe, Gaha finally got rid of him. Then he installed on the throne a prince named Abiodun.

Abiodun was a rich trader with trading connections and friends in the provinces of the empire. He was an intelligent and astute person. Though determined to get rid of Gaha's illegal authority, he knew that he could not win in an immediate confrontation with the old man, and that he had to employ all his astuteness and guile. He knew too that he could not depend on the mostly intimidated opponents of Gaha in the capital city. He turned to the provinces for support, and gradually knit together a formidable plot led by all the greatest provincial war chieftains – the Kakanfo Oyabi at Ajase, Opele the ruler of Igbogun, the Onikoyi, and others. While these schemes prospered, he bided his time and waited on (and flattered) Gaha so much that even Gaha himself became tired of it.

While all these were happening, Gaha grew visibly weaker in many respects. His popularity in the city continued to decline; his health continued to deteriorate; and the financial resources available to him shrank. His servants' oppressive conduct grew more and more sordid. As a result of their ineptitude and corruption, the amount of tributes reaching Gaha fell off sharply, and most prominent people in the provinces became Gaha's enemies.

More importantly, however, all the developments in the capital city began to have ominous effects in some of the tributary states. The first signs of trouble appeared in the northeast, where the Nupe became more and more audacious to raid in the Igbomina country. Under the Etsu Jibrilu in the 1760s, the Nupe cavalry forces destroyed many Igbomina towns and villages. The rulers of the Oyo Empire were too preoccupied with their own power struggle in Oyo-Ile to be able to do anything about the Nupe raids. Jibrilu's successor, the Etsu Majiya I who started to rule in 1769, intensified the raids.

At last, in 1774, Abiodun and his supporters were ready to strike. On the appointed date, the provincial war chiefs led their forces towards Oyo-Ile. In the supreme command was the Kakanfo Oyabi, with the Alaafin Abiodun by his side. When this huge army reached the gates of the capital city, the Oyo-Ile chiefs who were opposed to Gaha opened the city gates, and the Basorun's quarter came under a mighty siege. Gaha himself, descendant of great warriors and hero of many battles, led the defense. In spite of his weakened health, he was still a very formidable commander. Gaha's forces therefore put up a ferocious defence. They were, however, greatly outnumbered by the invaders who were also commanded by some of the empire's most talented warriors. Slowly, the invaders pushed their way forward until they rolled over Gaha's quarter and came face to face with his compound. Around that compound, the fiercest fighting ensued – the invaders losing countless men to sharp-shooters hidden in the roofs. At last, the invaders burst into the compound, set it on fire, and took Gaha captive.

Gaha was brought to the palace and made to grovel in the dust before the victorious king, Abiodun, now seated in glory on the throne. For the rest of the day, Gaha lay in the dust, while the crowds that had used to adulate him were allowed to come and taunt and humiliate him. The traditions have conflicting accounts of his end. One account has it that his body was burnt to ashes, another that his body was cut to pieces and the pieces were scattered all over the empire.

But that was not the end of the fighting. After destroying Gaha's quarter and all its leading men, the victors went on to do the same to the compounds of the great warrior chiefs who were seen as rivals of the Alaafin. When this awful rampage was over, the Alaafin Abiodun ruled supreme over a city that was pockmarked with the smoldering ruins of great compounds from which the most valiant of men had gone out for two centuries to conquer and hold an empire for the Alaafin. Effectively, though not yet manifestly, the military glory of the kingdom of Oyo-Ile was gone. The terminal manifestation of this truth would not come until about sixty years later; but when it came, there would be no strength to hold or save anything.

Thus, Gaha's career as Basorun brought incalculable disaster upon the kingdom. Before we continue, then, we need to ask the question: Why did Gaha bend all his power and influence into such unrelenting hostility against the Alaafins? What were the roots of this disastrous disruption of the Oyo-Ile monarchical system?

A close look would seem to indicate quite strongly that the answer is to be found in the native character of the Yoruba monarchical system as it played out in its Oyo-Ile version. Because the Oyo-Ile kingdom became immensely successful as an empire builder, one tends to be led away from seeing its essential internal weaknesses. In fact, as the type of government established by the Yoruba people went, its Oyo-Ile version was very unsuccessful in matters of inner cohesion and stability. Oyo traditions, recorded by Samuel Johnson for the two centuries of territorial expansion and imperial greatness, never failed to lay out, reign after reign, the symptoms of internal discordance and instability in the Oyo-Ile monarchical government. Of the seventeen kings who reigned from the end of the sixteenth century (when Abipa brought the government back to Oyo-Ile after the exile) until the end of the eighteenth century, only four (Abipa, Obalokun, Ajagbo and Amuniwaiye) died natural deaths. Of the rest, not less than nine were forced to "go to sleep" (that is, commit suicide), one was poisoned, and one died in a palace fire caused by violent conflicts with his chiefs.

For each of these contrived deaths, the traditions give two reasons – first that the king ruled like a despot and second, that he exhibited some unacceptable moral weakness. Samuel Johnson lists the offences as follows: "unchecked despotism, unrestrained license, insatiable greed, and wanton voluptuousness."[2] A look through the reigns as listed reveals, however, that the charge of moral turpitude was true only in a few cases. In cases where no moral problem existed, kings were still forced to commit suicide. Of the eighteenth century Alaafin Ojigi, for instance, the traditional record has it that he was "personally a very good man,"[3] a warrior king who added much to the empire and ruled with dignity at home – without question, one of the greatest men who ever ruled in Oyo-Ile. Yet, his high chiefs, only because of some excesses committed by his Aremo, called on him to commit suicide. The third successor after Ojigi, the Alaafin Onishile, was a man of great talents. He was the great warrior prince of whom it was popularly said that "his horse can leap over a town wall."[4] Under him there was so much prosperity in the kingdom that, according to the Oyo traditions, the common musical instrument known as *sekere*, which is usually strung with hard nuts and seeds, was widely strung with cowry shells and expensive beads – with dyed silk threads replacing the usual cheap cotton threads. This king was also reputed to have considerable artistic gifts. He brought those gifts into the decoration of the palace, and commissioned silver doors for its innermost chambers. In spite of all his admirable qualities and contributions, for which he was very popular with the generality of his subjects, his high chiefs still contrived a pretext for asking him to "go to sleep."

In short, then, it seems obvious that the Yoruba monarchical system as it played out in Oyo-Ile suffered an endemic disease. The system was, in its origins, built upon a plurality of lineages, and its inner strength and health inhered in checks and balances, and a healthy observance of such checks and balances by all groups. Oyo-Ile does not seem to have ever succeeded in managing and upholding the checks and balances. And the root causes of that failure were the pressures exerted by Oyo-Ile's frontier location. An emphasis (or perhaps over-emphasis) on military strength, imposed by the Nupe–Bariba frontier, while conferring enormous power on the Alaafin's kingdom, did violence to the checks and balances in its government by putting too much influence in the hands of the military-leader lineages. The earliest Alaafins, from the time of Sango, were warrior kings who led their armies to war and who therefore arrogated to themselves powers normally considered by Yoruba people to be beyond royal prerogatives. The conflicts that could result from such a development would seem to have been part of Oyo-Ile's experience from quite early in its history. In fact, it does seem very probable that the tradition about Sango's failed experiment with lightning, resulting in a palace fire and his suicide, was a cover for a conflict at the palace, resulting in the burning down of parts of it – leading the king, so rejected by his leading chiefs, to take his own life. (It is instructive that, centuries later, a similar fire and suicide ended the reign of another Alaafin – the Alaafin Karan in the seventeenth century.)

After the return of the government to Oyo-Ile under the Alaafin Abipa, the Alaafins no longer personally led their armies; that task fell to the great chiefs of the Oyo Mesi, assisted by a large and varied cadre of military officers. This greatly elevated the top chiefs and sharpened the rivalry between them and the kings. In response, the kings built up an enormous palace establishment employing many hundreds of people (much larger than that of any other Yoruba palace), which sometimes behaved like an alternative government. Luxuriating at the very top of an empire which spread out from the Niger to the sea, the Alaafins set up a glistening palace that resounded always with pomp and glory – all to emphasize that they were the kings. In this palace setting, petty acts of excess occasionally occurred – like the Alaafin Ayibi's order for the execution of the parents of one of his wives, in order to demonstrate the extent of his powers as Alaafin to that wife; or the Alaafin Amuniwaiye's adultery with his *babalawo*'s wife. But these acts of moral weakness were not the reason why the high chiefs rose up to demand their kings' deaths; they were only the excuses and pretexts. An intense rivalry was going on between the monarch and the high chiefs (backed by their influential lineages). As the chiefs saw it, the kings were attempting to establish a royal autocracy; to stop it, they had again and again to exercise their power of forcing the king to "go to sleep." Systematically resisting the Alaafins, disputing and arguing with them or their servants, was out of the question. It was messy, and could damage the standing of the whole government before the citizens. And its potential for civil commotion was too high, especially if a popular Alaafin was on the throne. Nobody would dare to strike (or even touch) the person of a king – that was an unimaginable violation of powerful spiritual prohibitions and taboos. However, the way to stop an Alaafin by summarily eliminating him was clearly set out in the traditional constitution, and it could be accomplished quietly in the deep recesses of the palace, out of the knowledge of the general citizenry. Oyo-Ile chiefs resorted to this constitutional device more frequently than the chiefs of any other Yoruba kingdom – because the Alaafins (being in possession of almost unlimited resources) attempted much more successfully than any other Yoruba monarch to tilt the balance of power in favor of the king, in violation of the checks and balances underpinning the unity of the plurality that constituted a Yoruba kingdom.

At least two of the peculiar features which came into being along the way in Oyo-Ile's political system, are explicable in the context of the rivalry between the Alaafins and the high chiefs. One was the creation of the position of Are Ona Kakanfo. The other was the provision that the Aremo must die when his father died. The Alaafin Ajagbo's intention in the seventeenth century in creating the title of Are Ona Kakanfo (to which the Alaafin alone could appoint any citizen of his choice), was to establish a counterbalance to the growing influence of the great war chiefs of the Oyo Mesi. (It is significant that Ajagbo's first choice for the post of Are Ona Kakanfo was his personal friend, Kokorogangan, from outside Oyo-Ile.) In that case, the provision, made later by the government, that the Kakanfo must never live inside the capital city, was an act of damage control by the Oyo Mesi. As for the mandatory death of the Aremo, it is clear from the traditions that the Alaafins had generally grown into the habit of associating their oldest sons with themselves in the functions of the throne, as well as in the enjoyment of the pomp and circumstance of power. The Aremo's home became a sort of second palace, and some of the tributes from the provinces of the empire were designated as the Aremo's. The chiefs could not make the Alaafins change the trend; but they could establish a constitutional provision that effectively cut off the Aremo with his father. It is significant that the harsh constitutional provisions relating to the Aremo did not come into existence until the seventeenth century, by which time the political and economic greatness of the Oyo Empire was beginning to have the effect, among other things, of placing at the Aremo's disposal enormous resources and influence. In a few other Yoruba kingdoms (such as in Ado in Ekiti) kings' oldest sons were barred from being selected as kings; but there was no insistence on their dying with their fathers. Again, the difference arose from the fact that the Alaafins made their Aremos live like second kings.

Some historians have suggested that the late eighteenth century troubles of the Oyo kingdom were caused by the effects of the Atlantic slave trade. According to this line of reasoning, Oyo's increasing participation in the slave trade brought increasingly large amounts of wealth to the coffers of the Alaafins, and thus produced, in the late eighteenth century, the situation whereby the high chiefs became envious of the Alaafins and the palace officials – a development which ultimately resulted in conflict and the disintegration of the kingdom. Other historians have, however, advanced strong objections to this suggestion. The most important of these is that, on the basis of available evidence, income from the slave trade was never so important a factor in the Alaafin's revenue. According to Ade Ajayi and other historians, the revenue of the rulers of Oyo was not much related to the slave trade, but came mostly from taxes on trade in the marketplaces and the toll gates, from tributes and gifts rendered by the provincial rulers and the vassal rulers, from large-scale primary production on the kings' farms, and from trading ventures (in regular merchandise) in which the Alaafins employed many of their wives and servants. Though the revenue and assets accruing to the Alaafins from the operation of the slave trade were considerable and growing, they were quite a small part of the whole revenue and assets of the Oyo government. Besides, the slave trade never became so intense in Oyo and other Yoruba kingdoms in the eighteenth century as to command the capacity to disrupt the political system. While the participation of Oyo people in the slave trade did increase from the middle of the eighteenth century, the slave trade did not occasion, in the kingdom and its provinces, slave raids or similar disruptions (the types that were common in many other parts of tropical Africa), and the kingdom enjoyed orderly government and the protection of the roads – conditions that were still largely intact even as late as the time of Clapperton's visit in the late 1820s.

Adeagbo Akinjogbin has offered the suggestion that the conflicts between the Alaafins and the high chiefs were a product of their divergent views, in the late eighteenth century, about the future of the Oyo Empire.[5] According to him, while the Alaafins favored a cessation of expansionist wars and advocated a stable exploitation of the empire that had already been created, the great warrior chiefs favored further and further expansion. Almost all the Alaafins of the eighteenth century were traders before coming to the throne, princes who had traded to various parts of the empire; others leaned heavily on influential supporters who were rich traders. The high chiefs, on the other hand, were sons and descendants of warrior chiefs, men who were raised for military leadership. Because the two sides did not find some way to reconcile their opposing views, so goes this line of reasoning, the prolonged crises of the Basorun Gaha's time (in the last half of the eighteenth century) resulted.

The basic details of this line of reasoning seem to be borne out by some of the available information. The Alaafins and the great war chiefs, conditioned by their divergent backgrounds and world views, appear to have wanted for the empire different types of future. However, this was only a late eighteenth century development – at the time when the empire had already been built to its farthest reaches. The constitutional conflicts in the government, on the other hand, had been ongoing almost from the inception of the kingdom. The sharp differences generated by the realities of the late eighteenth century only served to provide a new battleground for the age-old conflicts between the Alaafins and their topmost chiefs. The inability to reach a compromise in the late eighteenth century was conditioned by the endemic hostilities in the government.

The Basorun Gaha did not merely try to impose his view on the running of the empire; the more important thrust of his doings was to readjust the balance of power decisively against the Alaafins. In the process, he went into unimaginable excesses and thus enabled a very intelligent Alaafin to strike back – and strike back devastatingly not only against Gaha but against all the powerful warrior chiefly lineages. The Alaafin Abiodun's success readjusted the balance of power sharply in favor of the kings, but it did so at a price that the kingdom could not afford to pay without critically losing military strength. By destroying the top levels of the warrior lineages, Abiodun destroyed the foundations of Oyo's military power.

Meanwhile, Abiodun went on to rule in great pomp and glory, until about 1789. His reign is popular in Oyo traditions as a very prosperous one. Trade in particular prospered greatly. Oyo traders went far in all directions, not only in the Oyo Empire or the rest of Yorubaland, but into countries far beyond those territories. Many created considerable fortunes for themselves. The Alaafin Abiodun's personal popularity in the provinces kept the empire more or less intact. By nature a very pleasant and diplomatic person, he kept the friendship of the provincial kings and chiefs and the loyalty of the vassal kings and chiefs.

There were, however, obvious negatives in the Abiodun regime, but they were either not seen as serious or not even seen as problems at all. The Nupe continued to raid the Igbomina country – while the Alaafin's government lauded itself on the peace and prosperity in the empire. The participation of Oyo people and traders and, therefore, of Yorubaland in the slave trade increased greatly – and was to continue to do so until the end of the century and into the nineteenth century. The pattern, as far as can be ascertained from Yoruba traditions, is that Oyo people were the suppliers of most captives, while Oyo, Ijebu, Owu, Egba, Awori and Egbado traders received the captives and took them for sale to European slave traders at the ports. Probably as many slaves as were exported were kept in Yorubaland as domestic slaves, employed in domestic services, trade and farming. As pointed out in the previous chapter, Oyo traders bought large numbers of Nupe, Hausa, and Bariba and Aja slaves for export as well as for sale into domestic service. Judging from the large crowds of Hausa, Aja and Fulani slaves who were freed or who fled to Ilorin from all over the Oyo country from about 1817, the total number of non-Yoruba persons in the Oyo slave trade appears to have been very considerable. Still, the available evidence suggests that the number of Yoruba (especially Oyo) persons who ended up as slaves increased steadily from the last decades of the eighteenth century. Also, more and more ambitious and capable Oyo men and women ventured into the slave trading enterprise. Kidnapping and other nefarious activities, and the fear of them, grew – and so did insecurity for the poorer, weaker and more vulnerable members of society. For instance, an Oyo-Ile prince named Awole (who was then a trader), employed a close friend of his to help attend to his porters on a trade trip to Apomu in the Ife kingdom. At Apomu, he secretly went to slave traders and offered to sell his friend as a slave to them. The price was agreed, Awole received payment, and the traders went and grabbed the unsuspecting friend, and bound him for the journey through Ijebu to Lagos. Fortunately, Apomu's law enforcement officers came on the scene and released the poor man and arrested his perfidious friend and prince. Such a story describes symptoms of a societal disease that was growing. But under the Alaafin Abiodun, the overwhelming sentiment among the rich and influential was gratitude to the Alaafin for peace and prosperity in the empire.

The glory of Abiodun's reign was a façade, but the façade dazzled so brilliantly that Abiodun's subjects could not see what was happening to their kingdom and empire. The titles of Basorun and others continued to exist, and men continued to be appointed to them from the shells of the same old lineages, but none of these chiefs now commanded the support of a great proud lineage or the power and confidence of his predecessors. For the first time in Oyo-Ile's history, the Alaafin could act at will and rule without needing to wait for, or lean upon, a powerful Oyo Mesi that commanded the devotion of the masses. The old constitution was dead. A new one unknown to Oyo history had taken its place – one featuring almost unrestrained royal despotism. A royal administration free of "troubles" constituted by the great chiefs might be attractive to the Alaafin's friends and supporters, but it stood on feet of clay. A loveable and skillful Alaafin like Abiodun at the top of it might appear to keep the structure of government, kingdom and empire intact and strong; but as soon as lesser men occupied the throne, the façade would come crashing down. In times before Gaha's and Abiodun's, if an Alaafin were insufferable or incompetent, the kings and chieftains of the Oyo country would still have great Basoruns, Agbaakins and others like them in the heart of the imperial government to embrace. After the suppression of the power, prestige and influence of the great central chiefs, an insufferable or incompetent Alaafin commanded enormous capacity to take the whole system to its grave.

The most potent cause of the failure of a state is the disloyalty of its politically influential citizens and functionaries to its constitution and traditions. The era of Gaha and Abiodun produced such influential disloyalties to the fundamental principles and traditions of the Oyo-Ile kingdom. When Gaha dedicated his talents, power and influence to the toppling of the Alaafin from his exalted place at the top of the system, he initiated a process of demolition and destruction. When the Abiodun reaction suppressed the power, prestige and influence of the great lineages and great chiefs, it completed the process. The core pillars of the strength of the Alaafinate were devastated by Gaha and Abiodun. After that, the great state of the Alaafins only limped painfully, inexorably, towards its demise. The superficially glorious reign of Abiodun was, therefore, no more than a transition. The "consolidated kingdom of the Oyo people" that was the great pillar upon which the empire stood must have very respectable leadership from the Oyo-Ile center to sustain its integrity and strength; and it fed on the glory and euphoria of successes and victories. When the Oyo-Ile center fell manifestly sick after Abiodun and the succession of victories and parades stalled, the consolidated kingdom became quickly unglued – and the empire that it upheld disintegrated.

No Oyo army won any significant victory after the Gaha–Abiodun era till the very bitter end in the 1830s. Under Gaha, an Oyo army defeated an Ashanti army in the far west in 1864 and that may have been an attempt to keep expanding the empire's boundaries; but nothing was ever heard again of action in this border area, and Gaha's great enemies and preoccupation were the Alaafins and their known supporters at home. Under Abiodun, the Oyo army invaded the Bariba country in 1783 in order to suppress a rebellion against Oyo rule. The Oyo army was heavily defeated and lost many of its leading commanders. Except for that unsuccessful war, and a victory over the Mahi in 1788, Abiodun put the Oyo military almost completely to sleep. When, for instance, there were signs of disobedience and unrest in some coastal dependencies of the Oyo Empire in 1782–86, Abiodun asked his loyal vassal, Kpengla, the king of Dahomey, to go and suppress the revolt for him because those places were too far for his own army to go to![6] It was in this period that Oyo's superiority in cavalry was allowed to slip away – a development with terrible consequences later on. When later Alaafins tried to wake up the army, the edge was already too far lost. As will be seen later, some of the last Alaafins of Oyo-Ile, especially the very last three (Majotu, Amodo and Oluewu), though no great warrior princes, were certainly men of some competence and considerable dedication to the kingdom's greatness; their great weakness was that they did not have the sharp military tools that their warrior predecessors had had. It might be suggested that by the time of Gaha and Abiodun, the empire had reached optimum expansion and that a powerful military, therefore, was no longer needed for expansionist wars. But it cannot be suggested that, at any time, a strong military was not needed for holding the empire. It certainly was needed. That was the nature of the empire that the Alaafins and their people had created. When the Oyo kingdom slipped into losing its military superiority, it risked losing everything.

Abiodun died in about 1789 and was succeeded by his cousin Awole – the same prince and trader whom we have earlier met at Apomu. Tall and handsome,

Awole did not, unfortunately, possess the qualities of character that had enabled Abiodun to keep the kingdom and most of the empire in apparent unity, happiness and prosperity. He was a distrustful, vindictive and scheming ruler. As a result, Oyo traditions have mostly saddled him with the responsibility for the collapse of the kingdom and empire. According to the traditions, his meanness and vindictiveness pushed him into contravening a very important ancient prohibition: he ordered an attack on a town in the Ife kingdom. The account is that when Awole had been arrested for illegally selling his friend at Apomu, he had been brought before the Baale of Apomu, and the Baale and his chiefs had tried him, found him guilty and ordered him punished. When Awole became Alaafin, therefore, one of the first things he wanted to do was to punish the Baale of Apomu in retaliation; so he ordered the Oyo army to attack and sack Apomu. Shocked by the Alaafin's orders, the commanders of the army hesitated and agonized at a place called Gbeji. While they did so, the Baale of Apomu fled for refuge to the palace of the Ooni of Ife. His flight to the Ooni's palace suddenly threatened to provoke a culturally unacceptable situation – a war by the Ooni against a Yoruba kingdom. While the Ooni and the Ife chiefs mulled over this, the Baale of Apomu himself came to the decision that, rather than cause such a culturally unthinkable conflict, he would give his own life to save his town. Returning to Apomu, he directed his chiefs to take his head to Oyo-Ile to appease the Alaafin and he committed suicide.

Though an actual attack on Apomu was thus averted, Awole has nevertheless passed into Yoruba traditions as the first Yoruba king ever to raise hands against the Ife kingdom. How much importance the historian should attach to that is debatable. In some Yoruba traditional elite circles, there exists some residual belief that Awole's invasion of the Ife kingdom initiated his own destruction as Alaafin and the destruction of the traditional and spiritual foundations of peace in Oyo and all of Yorubaland.

However, at a less spiritual, more earthly level, Awole also went on to do many things to destroy his own authority as Alaafin. Even while the Apomu affair was still in progress, the traditional account noted that the Alaafin Awole's character was generating problems between him and many chiefs. The first was Afonja, the new Are Ona Kakanfo who lived in Ilorin, some forty miles southeast of Oyo-Ile. Awole himself had just appointed Afonja as Kakanfo, but deeply distrusted him because Afonja, who was related to the royal family through his mother, had aspired to be Alaafin at the time that the chiefs had selected Awole. His hostility towards Afonja was commonly known among the other chiefs. At the same time, his inept handling of a number of small issues, and his penchant for cursing and for invoking the anger of the gods and ancestors in little matters, created enmity between him and many other chiefs – including the Basorun and the Owota (one of the Esos). News of palace intrigues against Afonja reached him easily, and the Onikoyi, who was close to Afonja, also became offended. Thus, both at home in Oyo-Ile and in the rest of the Oyo homeland, Awole raised up enemies against himself.

In this atmosphere, Awole ordered a military campaign against the Nupe – in 1790 or 1791. For about thirty years, the Nupe had raided the Igbomina country, without the Oyo-Ile government doing anything about it. A Dahomey tradition (echoed by a contemporary report by a European on the coast) claims that, in fact, the Nupe had, by 1791, reached the point of actually demanding or extracting tributes from Oyo-Ile as payment for not invading the Oyo country itself. This is not corroborated by either Oyo or Nupe traditions and is, almost certainly, an exaggeration – a swipe by Dahomey against its Oyo overlord. Whatever might have been his reason, Awole did order the army out against the Nupe. The army marched out, and returned defeated. Suzerainty over the Bariba had been lost in 1783; now in 1791 Oyo also lost its suzerainty over the Nupe. Province by province, the empire was melting down. The return of the defeated army could only have added more to the gathering gloom around the Alaafin.

The storm finally burst when Awole ordered the army, led by the Kakanfo, the Onikoyi and the Baale of Igbogun, to attack the town of Iwere, against which he apparently had some complaint. The royal servants who accompanied the army had been instructed not to disclose its real destination to the Kakanfo until it had reached the vicinity of Iwere. When the army stood outside Iwere and the royal servants told the Kakanfo that his orders were to sack Iwere, the Kakanfo and the other commanders immediately refused to carry out the king's orders. They suspected, correctly, that the king's objective was to destroy the Kakanfo and not Iwere. Iwere was reputed to be one of the best naturally fortified towns in the country, protected by steep rocky hills and approachable only by steep narrow paths. An inadequately prepared attack on Iwere had a good chance of failing – and failure would mean that the Kakanfo must take his own life. Moreover, the Kakanfo and the other war chiefs could not see what the Alaafin had against this town – probably nothing more than his characteristic animosities from the past; and they were not eager to give their services to such. Even more importantly, Iwere did deserve to be respected; it was the hometown of the mother of the late and beloved Alaafin Abiodun, and the lineage compound where she had grown up as a girl was a place of attraction to travelers and traders on their way through the town. The army went into a full mutiny, led by its commanders. The royal servants were gathered together and slaughtered. Then the army headed back towards Oyo-Ile. Outside the capital city, they stopped and camped, unsure what to do next. When the Alaafin invited the commanders to come and see him, they refused to go to him. At last, they came to a decision: the king must go. An empty calabash was respectfully sent to the king. He knew what it meant – and he complied, after, according to the traditions, invoking the anger of the gods and ancestors and pronouncing his last terrible curses on his chiefs and kingdom. He had reigned for seven years, 1789–96. When the news of the king's death was received, the army entered the city in triumph, and some of the men did some looting (thus symbolically conquering the city), before their commanders ordered them to disperse to their homes.

The spirit of rebellion against the Alaafin, and of disrespect for the city of Oyo-Ile, that had been thus engendered did not, however, disperse. Both in the capital city and in the provinces, discontent (even disgust) with the Alaafin's government grew. During the few months of interregnum after Awole, the Basorun Ashamu, Chief Bada of Saki, acted as regent – the first person from the provinces to be thus appointed as the Basorun. During this regency, the Egba provinces rose in a massive revolt against Oyo's overlordship. The Egba people had always been unhappy about the less responsible ones among the Oyo Ajeles, some of whom were greedy and rapacious and behaved as superiors of the Egba kings. In the course of the late eighteenth century (almost certainly during Gaha's time), the greed and exactions of such Ajeles appear to have become excessive. Taking advantage of the interregnum in Oyo-Ile, with a provincial chief acting as regent, one Egba chief named Lisabi began to organize the Egba people for an overthrow of Oyo rule. Lisabi belonged to the Egba Alake province; he was born at Itoku and lived at Igbein. Reputed to be very tall and broad, Lisabi was a wonderful organizer and leader of men.

Lisabi started his organizing by taking advantage of the traditional system of *aaro* – combination of local farmers for helping one another on their farms. Working secretly, he linked the small local groupings together throughout the Egba country to form one secret organization. Then he changed the objective of the organization and turned it into a sprawling underground army, with the new name of Egba Olorogun. When all was ready, Lisabi gave the signal for a general uprising by killing the Ajele at Igbein (sometime around 1797). Within days, about 600 Ajeles were killed in all ports of Egbaland. The Alaafin's government set up a large army made up of contingents from Oyo, Egbado and Ibarapa. Since Oyo-Ile could no longer command the services of leading war chiefs like the Kakanfo Afonja or the Baale of Igbogun, the army that proceeded to Egbaland was officered by men with smaller names. This army crossed the Ogun River and headed for Igbein, Lisabi's hometown. Lisabi formed the men of Igbein and surrounding towns into an army and, as its commander, showed how good a general he was. He ordered the people of Igbein to desert their town, and he then hid his army in ravines where the Oyo army could not see them. The Oyo army easily entered the town, but as they searched round in it, Lisabi's hidden men descended upon them. The Oyo army was completely routed. Lisabi had won independence for the Egba people – and the Oyo Empire had lost its Egba provinces.

As for Lisabi, he continued for a long time, according to Biobaku's account of his life, to bring varied benefits into the life of his Egba people.[7] He gave his people laws. He taught them to aspire to trade far and wide (including taking their kolanuts to the countries beyond the Niger) so that they might become rich and, as he put it, wear the best types of clothes. He taught them to defend themselves. Lisabi seems to have lost much of his popularity in his last years, and the reason for that is not clear. According to Biobaku, his insistence on recruiting men into military service probably conflicted with the labor needs of families on the farms. Some traditions have it that he died in a forest, probably during a Dahomey invasion; others suggest that he was killed by some other Egba chiefs who were jealous of his influence.

In the dust and despondency caused by the military disaster at Igbein and the loss of the Egba country, a prince named Adebo succeeded Awole as Alaafin. Adebo found himself to be a king in name only, unable to command the loyalty of his chiefs and subjects. Loss of respect and affection for the Alaafin and the capital city of Oyo-Ile, already growing during Awole's reign, increased dramatically. The Alaafin, the palace, and the capital city had used to be objects of pride and adoration in all parts of the Oyo country; by Adebo's time they had become objects of some embarrassment, generally derided in crude sayings and songs. Many songs contrasted the reigns of Abiodun's successors with what was regarded as Abiodun's glorious reign. One song, for instance, claimed:

> In Abiodun's time we scooped money (cowries) with the calabash,
>
> In Awole's time we packed our belongings (ready to flee).

It became quite common for kings in the Oyo homeland to distance themselves from the Alaafin and from the affairs of Oyo-Ile in order to retain the loyalty and admiration of their own subjects. To be a citizen of the capital city of Oyo-Ile had used to be a matter of great pride in all parts of the Oyo homeland; by Adebo's time it had become something to be almost ashamed of. The Alaafin's Ilaris previously walked the earth with great authority in all Oyo towns and villages; by Adebo's time, they dared not even show their faces in some Oyo towns and villages. A falling away of prominent Oyo rulers and chieftains seemed more imminent by the day.

At last, towards the end of Adebo's short reign, it came. Opele, Baale of Igbogun, was the first prominent chieftain to announce his independence.

Some lesser chiefs soon followed suit. In short, even the central homeland of the Oyo Empire had begun to break into fragments.

The Alaafin Adebo reigned for only months and was succeeded by Maku, who also reigned for only a few months. When Maku died in about 1799, his reign was followed by a long interregnum, which lasted until about 1802. He was then succeeded by Majotu, whose reign lasted until 1831. All these kings reigned over an empire that had shrunk to only a small rump of its former self, and a kingdom that was breaking up. During Majotu's reign, in 1823, Dahomey asserted its independence.

During these reigns and interregnums, each of those Oyo chieftains who had declared themselves independent of Oyo-Ile struck out to carve a separate kingdom for himself in the Oyo homeland. The first to take action was Opele, the Baale of Igbogun. Opele set up his own army, and with it he took Igbo-Owu and Idofian, but he died fighting while attempting to take Igboho.

Probably during the long interregnum between Maku and Majotu, the Kakanfo Afonja at Ilorin declared his independence. Because Afonja, from this point on, became the most important person in the final disintegration of the Oyo Empire, it is necessary to give some details about him. Afonja's father was Alagbin, Baale of Ilorin. Alagbin's grandfather, Laderin, was the founder and first Baale of Ilorin, succeeded by his son Fasin; Fasin too was succeeded by his son Alagbin, and Alagbin by his son Afonja. The Laderin royal family of Ilorin enjoyed considerable fame in the Oyo country for its valor and leadership qualities. Afonja's mother was a member of the Alaafin royal family of Oyo-Ile. After the death of the Alaafin Abiodun, Afonja, Baale of Ilorin (but related to the Oyo-Ile throne through his mother), surfaced as one of the princes being considered by the Oyo Mesi for selection as Alaafin. He is said to have had many friends and admirers in influential circles in Oyo-Ile. However, it was Awole that was selected. Soon after Awole became the Alaafin, he invited Afonja to Oyo-Ile and conferred on him the title of Are Ona Kakanfo. Awole was very suspicious of Afonja, because of Afonja's popularity in Oyo-Ile. His appointment of Afonja as Kakanfo, therefore, was not out of love, but a stratagem for keeping Afonja out of Oyo-Ife. But since Afonja's popularity only continued to rise, Awole finally tried to destroy him. The result was the Iwere campaign, the revolt of the army, and the death of Awole.

After Awole's death, Afonja's name surfaced again very prominently among the princes being considered by the Oyo Mesi. But by then, Afonja had become the type of powerful, rich or influential prince that Yoruba kingmakers usually would not select as king. So, Afonja was passed over and Adebo was selected. After Adebo's short reign, Afonja was again rejected and Maku, said to be a close friend of Afonja, was chosen. Very probably, the Oyo Mesi reckoned that the selection of Afonja's friend would pacify Afonja. If so, they were wrong. When Afonja received the traditional message that "a new moon has risen at Oyo-Ile," he snapped back, "And let that moon set quickly." Like Adebo's, Maku's reign too was very short. After a poorly planned campaign led by him to suppress Igbogun's independence failed, his dispirited chiefs asked him to save face by going "to sleep."

While the long interregnum following Maku's death dragged on, Afonja finally came to the conclusion that he would never get selected as Alaafin, and he began to think of other ways to achieve his ambition. A close look at his activities indicates quite clearly that what he desired was a realignment of power in the Oyo country that would replace the Alaafin's dynasty with his own dynasty, which would then revamp and reestablish the greatness and glory of the Oyo Empire. This would require, most of all, a great military establishment with which to unify all of the Oyo homeland under his own leadership. As for the Alaafins, they would be allowed to hold the city of Oyo-Ile as a one-city kingdom inset in the new consolidated Oyo kingdom ruled by Afonja. With the united energy of all Oyo people, the authority of the empire would be reestablished on all its former provinces and more territories would be conquered. The capital city of the new empire would be Ilorin.

The condition of things in the Oyo homeland seemed to favor all these plans. The prestige of the Alaafin and of Oyo-Ile had fallen terribly in most places, and so had the Alaafin's authority almost everywhere. But there was also universal nostalgia about, and yearning for, the former greatness of the empire. People sang songs praying that the Alaafin Abiodun's times would come back. In spite of the loss of almost all non-Oyo provinces, what remained of the empire was still quite large and potentially mighty. The rich Egbado province was still strongly loyal to the empire. In spite of the weakening of imperial authority and the ravages of the slave trade, the fabric of law and order still held – so that even as late as the late 1820s a foreign visitor could still describe the Alaafin's domains as a "fine kingdom."[8] Even as things stood, a vigorous and talented ruler could still re-solidify the Oyo base of the empire, bring back the enthusiasm and glory of military victories, and turn the tide. Looking all around him, Afonja must have felt that he was specially created for such times and such accomplishments. After the death of Opele, Baale of Igbogun, no leading person in the Oyo homeland stood nearly as high as the Baale of Ilorin and Kakanfo of the Oyo Empire.

First, then, Afonja renounced his loyalty to the Alaafin and asserted his independence. Secondly, he began to work on raising Ilorin from a small town to a town big enough to be capital of the kingdom and empire of his thoughts. There were many small villages in the vicinity of Ilorin – Kanla, Ganmo, Idofian,

Elehinjare, Oke-Oyi, Igbon, Iresa, Ibare and others. One by one, Afonja persuaded the inhabitants of these villages to relocate to Ilorin. He had a friend named Solagberu who lived in the large town of Kuwo and who had become a very rich and influential person there. Afonja persuaded him to relocate to Ilorin, bringing his large family, relatives, friends and followers with him. Solagberu came and settled a large quarter which he named Oke Suna – quarter of "the faithful ones" – because he was a Muslim convert. Using Solagberu's Islamic connections, Afonja also persuaded a well-known Fulani Muslim preacher named Salih (called Alimi by the Yoruba) to come and reside at Ilorin. Alimi had come on visits to Ilorin and many other Oyo towns before, preaching Islam and selling charms. Alimi came and invited his sons down from Sokoto. The coming of Alimi was especially important to Afonja's plans; Afonja needed Alimi to make charms for him for the wars he was about to embark upon. Within a few years, Ilorin had become quite a large city and continued to grow.

Thirdly, Afonja embarked on building up his war machine. As foundation, the chieftains who had constituted the pillars of his command as Kakanfo stayed by him. Of these, the most important were Toyeje, the Baale of Ogbomoso, who commanded Afonja's right wing, and Fagbohun, Baale of Jabata, who commanded his left wing. The system, as it had traditionally operated, was that each of these commanders raised and trained in his own home area the troops that he would bring into battle under the Kakanfo's supreme command. Over and above them, moreover, the Kakanfo himself could issue calls to men in all parts of the country.

Probably in about 1801, Afonja was suddenly confronted by a major crisis. Ojo Agunbambaru, one of Gaha's sons who had escaped as a youth to the Bariba country at the time of the massacre of Gaha's people, returned to the country at the head of a large army which he had recruited in the Bariba country. Claiming to be fighting for the Alaafin and the kingdom, Ojo Agunbambaru went after Afonja and, as his army moved through the country, some sympathizers joined it. Afonja marched his own army out to meet Agunbambaru, but he was defeated in three successive battles and had to fall back on Ilorin. Agunbambaru then besieged Ilorin. Again and again it looked as if Ilorin would fall, but Afonja managed to hold on until Agunbambaru's army was worn down. Then in a main engagement, Afonja won a victory outside the walls, thereby forcing Agunbambaru, though his army was still mainly intact, to withdraw from Ilorin and return to the Bariba country.

With this victory over Agunbambaru, Afonja's fame increased enormously. Before the coming of Agunbambaru, he had had no rival in the country. After the victory, he became the undisputed military lord of the whole of the Oyo homeland. From all over the Oyo homeland, young men went to offer their services to him – either directly under him or under the chiefs belonging to his command.

Then, in about 1817, Afonja took an action that must rank as one of the most momentous in Yoruba history. He offered freedom and protection to Muslims and slaves who would flee to him in Ilorin.

To understand this action, a brief background is necessary. Islam had long established some presence among the Yoruba people, but until the beginning of the nineteenth century it had never caused any tension or encountered any intolerance – except briefly under the Alaafin Awole. But thanks to the influence of a radical Islamic movement which emerged in Hausaland in about 1804, Islam in Yorubaland became radical and aggressive, therefore provoking violent reaction in many towns in the Oyo country. A full account of this situation belongs to a later chapter; suffice it to say here that many Muslims were killed or forced to flee from their homes, some of them coming to live around Solagberu and Alimi in Ilorin, the city whose ruler, Afonja, had declared himself independent of the Alaafin's kingdom. As these Muslim refugees came, the men among them, sizzling with anger against the Alaafin and the Oyo rulers who had persecuted them, were very zealous to join Afonja's army and fight for him against the Alaafin's establishment and against the communities from which they had fled, even though Afonja's political plans and wars had nothing to do with their Islamic faith, and even though Afonja himself showed no desire to convert to Islam. From this circumstance, Afonja came to the idea that he could easily and quickly build up a large army by tapping into the fears and anger of Muslims in the Oyo homeland. Moreover, there were very many slaves of foreign origin (mostly Hausa, but also Nupe, Bariba, Aja and Fulani) in Oyo homes all over the kingdom, kept as cowherds, farm hands, stable tenders, rope makers, barbers, etc. Most of the Hausa among these were known to be Muslims. Afonja decided that offering these slaves their freedom and protection in Ilorin could yield a big addition to the army that he could amass from the Yoruba Islamic community. Afonja obviously had no understanding of the religious implications and possibilities of his idea. His was just a talented military mind seizing upon a ready opportunity to create a massive war machine.

Afonja made his proclamation in 1817, and provoked an immediate surge of Muslim migration to Ilorin from all over the Oyo homeland. Most of the refugees were Oyo people, but a large number consisted of slaves of foreign origin (Hausa, Nupe, Bariba, Aja and others) fleeing from their owners. Since the Hausa were the majority among these, Oyo traditions tended to refer to them all as Hausa. Training and arming these men as they came, Afonja achieved his ambition of amassing a very large army.

As the refugees flocked to Ilorin, they swelled Afonja's army. Beyond that, however, a bond of unity developed among them, especially among the mass of former slaves – partly because of the latter's ethnic affinities, partly because most were Muslims, partly because they were one mass of poor, common people. They became known, and called themselves, Jamaa (an Arabic word meaning 'community of Muslim folks'). They created symbols of identity for members of their group – large metal rings which they wore on thumbs and fingers and with which they greeted one another (by touching ring to ring). Needless to say, the Jamaa brotherhood did not involve Afonja at all, and it is obvious from all available evidence that he never sought to be involved. In effect, two parallel structures emerged in Ilorin – Afonja's army and the Jamaa brotherhood. Judging from the subsequent behavior of the Jamaa, the mood in the brotherhood was partly one of gratitude to Afonja, partly of intense anger of the Oyo refugees towards the traditional political establishment of the Oyo country, and partly of vengefulness among the ex-slaves towards the masters from whom they had fled. Moreover, the highly placed among the Yoruba Muslim refugees tended to stick to Solagberu for their religious observances, while the larger group of common people of the Jamaa of all cultures coalesced around Alimi. Thus, signs of trouble were not slow to appear.

But these were only the beginnings. In its ultimate outcome, Afonja's proclamation of freedom and protection for Muslim refugees was to turn out to be a great disaster. In the mass of the ex-slave foreign-born Jamaa, he had set up an army of men who had no stake or interest in his political doings, and who had good reason to use their new-found powers in his military establishment to hit back at their former slave owners and at the country of their former enslavement. As he would soon discover, he had created a monster that would devour him and devastate his country.

For the time being, the immediate effect of the refugees and the Jamaa was to enhance Afonja's striking capability. Having no reason to fear any serious opposition, he embarked on bringing the whole of the Oyo country under his own authority. His strategy seems to have been to start by subduing the farthest provinces, and then move from there to the more central ones. That way, by the time he came close to Oyo-Ile, any force that the Alaafin could raise to oppose him would be small. He overran parts of Igbomina, and from there descended on the Ibolo province, taking such heavily populated towns as Iresa, Ejigbo, Ilobu and others. In the Epo (Osun) province, some young chiefs formed a military band (in imitation of Afonja), aimed at carving out an area of authority for themselves. Their band, named Ogo Were, began to attract considerable attention. Afonja hurried south to the Epo province, took most of the towns there and stamped out the Ogo Were.

Afonja's military campaigns were all easy successes. There was no town, warrior or group strong enough to resist him in the country. Even the Alaafin Majotu watched helplessly as Afonja and his large army took town after town. But in the end, it all turned out to be futile – or even worse than futile. Afonja never completed the territorial conquests of his desire. He was stopped in his tracks by forces of his own creation. The Hausa and other foreign-born members of the Jamaa, whose numbers kept increasing as more and more slaves fled from their masters, became a curse, first on the country and then on Afonja himself. In every town against which Afonja commanded them, they made a point of going into horrid excesses of ravaging, looting and destroying. Even worse, they developed the practice of going off on their own, usually in small bands, to attack towns and villages, their objective being to loot, and extort valuables from defenseless householders – and thus carry away loads of brazenly stolen goods. One such band would enter a town or village, billet themselves on the compound of a well-to-do citizen, eat and drink to excess, snatch and extort things from the residents of the compound, and then use the compound as a base for attacks on other compounds. They particularly enjoyed returning to the homes where they had been slaves before, in order to humiliate their former masters and take away valuables. Since these brigands were generally regarded as Afonja's servants, nobody usually dared to raise a finger against them, for fear of offending and provoking Afonja. In towns and villages across the Oyo country, people therefore began to pack their belongings and leave – all of them heading southwards, beyond the Osun River, into the territories of the Ijesha, Ife, Owu and Egba. These migrations marked the beginning of a new era in Yoruba history.

As for Afonja himself, it took him long before he saw that the Jamaa, especially the foreign-born group in the Jamaa, were a danger to the country and to himself. Blinded by the euphoria from his military victories, he became conceited and arrogant, absolutely sure that nothing could hurt him. Many people in his immediate circle warned him about the Jamaa's behavior and its probable repercussions on himself, but he was too self-assured to listen. Those who persisted in warning him became his enemies. In fact, one of such men, Fagbohun, chief of Jabata, a close relation of Afonja and commander of the left wing of his forces, in the end had to keep a distance from Afonja for fear that he would kill him. By the time Afonja became wise to what was happening, the Jamaa had grown beyond control. He threatened again and again that he would disband them or wipe them out, but they only grew more unruly. Finally, resolved to take action against them, he at last looked around to make alliances with his own people, like the Onikoyi and other important chiefs of the Oyo country. But he never got far with that. The Jamaa learnt about his plans and revolted.

For the mass of lowly Oyo persons in the Jamaa, Afonja's plan represented a serious threat that they would be surrendered again to the religious persecutions from which they had fled to Ilorin. For the foreign-born, most of whom had been slaves before, Afonja's plans threatened a return to slavery. A huge number of the Jamaa, particularly of the foreign-born, armed with bows, arrows, spears and swords, besieged Afonja's compound. He and the few men who were with him when the mob arrived were totally surprised and massively outnumbered by their assailants. In his extremity, Afonja called on Solagberu for help. By his arrogance during the time of his military victories, however, he had alienated Solagberu. But Solagberu's attitude was mostly influenced by his religious faith. For him, a Muslim chief, choosing to fight for an unbeliever (even though a friend) against a mass of co-religionists was a hard decision. Solagberu hesitated and hesitated, and never took a decision.

Still, Afonja fought like the Kakanfo that he was. After his compound was set on fire, he took the fight to the streets, and kept hacking down surge after surge of his adversaries – until his noble body was shot through by countless arrows and spears. That was about early 1824.

With the death of Afonja, Alimi, surrounded by the mass of the Jamaa, became the leader and commander of the faithful and therefore the strongest man in Ilorin. According to Ilorin traditions, Alimi was often heard to say that the clash between Afonja and the Jamaa had been caused by an unfortunate misunderstanding. Being a Yoruba man and a Muslim, Solagberu thought that he would have the support of Alimi to become the ruler of the town. Only slowly did it become clear to him that the alien family of Alimi and his sons had taken over Ilorin, with the support of all the Hausa and Fulani Jamaa and the overwhelming majority of the Oyo Muslim refugees. Effectively, Solagberu's support did not extend much beyond his Oke Suna quarter.

Most people in the Oyo homeland had shown no interest in the growing problems between Afonja and his Jamaa forces. Many saw it as a trouble that he had brought upon himself, and most believed that he was more than strong enough to resolve it in some manner that would be to his benefit. When therefore he had tried, in his last days, to make alliances with some of the prominent people of his country, they had been mostly slow or hesitant to respond. But when the news of his death at the hands of the Jamaa came, it shocked the country profoundly. A resolve widely developed to drive the foreigners out of Ilorin, disband the Jamaa and punish its ringleaders. A national army hurriedly formed for the purpose. Toyeje, the Baale of Ogbomoso, who had commanded the right wing of the late Kakanfo's forces, was promoted as Kakanfo and put in command. An Ilorin army, made up of Alimi's Jamaa of all ethnicities, and Solagberu's followers, marched out. The two armies met at a place called

Ogele. Toyeje's cavalry was much smaller than the combined Ilorin cavalry. A sanguinary battle ensued. The cavalry decided the day. As Toycje's army broke and fled, the Ilorin cavalry pressed hard after them. In town after town they rallied and put up a stand, but they never managed to mobilize enough strength to check the Ilorin cavalry. Therefore, many towns in the Ibolo province were destroyed and deserted. The human suffering in such places was horrendous. An endless stream of persons, who had snatched some belongings and fled, jammed the roads leading to the south. The old and infirm, and in many cases, children, were abandoned and left to perish. In the few Ibolo towns that survived (like Offa, Erin, Igbona, Ilemona) as well as in towns to their immediate south, large refugee populations appeared. Quickly taken off the streets by the lineage compounds of these towns, they became heavy material burdens on the residents. Outside the immediate area affected by the Ogele battle, in the central and western provinces of the Oyo country, the news of the battle and its aftermath frightened many people into packing and heading south. Some towns and villages in the Oyo country were becoming empty.

In spite of all these disasters, the Oyo people were far from ready to leave Ilorin in the hands of foreigners. Alimi died, and his older son Abdulsalami assumed the title of Emir of Ilorin – and that, to most Oyo people outside Ilorin, was an outrage. Preparations were therefore set in motion for another attack on the foreign rulers of Ilorin. This time, a large army marched forward and besieged Ilorin. An alliance was also made with the Nupe ruler, Majiya II, who came at the head of a Nupe army to support the Oyo army. But this campaign turned out to be a very difficult one. Most of the towns around Ilorin for miles had been destroyed in the previous campaign, and therefore there were no farms to supply food to the army. Starvation became a common experience of both the invaders and defenders of Ilorin. It was the season of the ripening of the pods of the *irugba* (locust-bean) tree, and the army sent men to go fetching them from the country around – from which the campaign became known as the Mugbamugba War (the war in which soldiers lived on locust beans). The Nupe army gave up and left. And, once again, it was the Ilorin cavalry that ultimately decided the outcome of this war. The old Oyo superiority in cavalry had completely disappeared – or, more correctly, the Oyo people of Ilorin and their foreign compatriots had completely inherited the former Oyo supremacy in cavalry.

After this, it became increasingly difficult for Oyo leaders to make concerted attempts to free Ilorin. In fact, the failures in the wars against Ilorin slowly bred despondency, part of the result of which was that some of the leading chiefs began to quarrel, or even fight, amongst themselves. There had, for years, been no generally accepted overlord over the Oyo people, and each

Oba managed his own affairs as an independent ruler. This, in fact, was the fundamental reason for the failure of the attempts to drive the foreigners out of Ilorin. The campaigns were poorly coordinated. The Alaafin still reigned in Oyo-Ile, but he was no longer relevant to the affairs of most parts of the Oyo country. In the midst of this fragmentation and confusion, in fact, a strange short war occurred – a war in which the Onikoyi was opposed by most of the other chiefs and Ikoyi was besieged by a combined army, including, most surprisingly, an Ilorin army commanded by Solagbaru.

In Ilorin, the result of this state of affairs in the Oyo country was that the hold of Alimi's family on Ilorin became tighter and more confident under the Emir Abdulsalami, the older of Alimi's two sons. About one year after Afonja's death, Solagberu and the Emir Abdulsalami fell out, and a civil war ensued in Ilorin. Though generally respected in the town, Solagberu had no real contact with the mass of the Jamaa, and his solid support was limited to his Oke Suna quarter. In the conflict that ensued, therefore, his Oke Suna, supported by only a small part of the Jamaa, was quickly overwhelmed – and he died fighting at the head of his men. With the death of Solagberu vanished any immediate hope that an Oyo citizen of Ilorin would rule the city.

Ilorin became an Islamic Emirate, ruled by Alimi's descendants as a royal family – a royal family which then sought links with the Islamic Jihad movement going on beyond the Niger. And all that was due, ultimately, to Afonja. Alimi and his sons had Afonja to thank for bringing them to Ilorin and for creating an army for them. Though Afonja never converted to Islam, the creation of an Islamic emirate in Ilorin was essentially the work of his hands.

All the evidence indicates quite strongly that the Oyo people of Ilorin, constituting much more than 90 percent of the town's population, did not understand, or even give any thought to, the political implication of an emirate over their town – or to the links which the Emirs then forged beyond Yorubaland. To them, this would seem to have represented no more than the victory of their Islamic religion – and the Emir was seen almost entirely as a commander of the faithful. All the evidence would seem to show that, politically, their attention was focused entirely on the threats of the rest of the Oyo country against Ilorin and, as will be seen in subsequent chapters, on the place of Ilorin in the evolving political picture of Yorubaland. As long as Ilorin was in danger from the rest of the Oyo country, and as long as the Oyo people of Ilorin were consumed by their anxieties and desires about the place of Ilorin in the rivalries among the new states of Yorubaland (of which Ilorin became one of the strongest), questions about the legitimacy of an emirate, of Alimi and his sons as rulers over that emirate, and of the Emirs' extra-Yoruba connections, could only seem like distractions – and that was to be so throughout the nineteenth century. In short, to the Yoruba people of Ilorin, Ilorin was, politically, simply one of the Yoruba states absorbed in the epochal struggle among states of Yorubaland; no other goings-on of a political nature concerning their town were significant enough to attract their serious attention at all. The Alimi family's links with Sokoto beyond the Niger appear to have been seen by the Yoruba of Ilorin as, essentially, no more than a private family matter; and it never seems to have affected the life of their town in any significant measure. Compared with the emirates created by the Fulani jihadists in Hausaland beyond the Niger, Ilorin was far from being a typical Fulani emirate. It is nearer the truth to call it a Yoruba Islamic emirate.

In 1826, about two years after Afonja's death, the English explorer Clapperton and his team traveled through parts of the Oyo Empire and visited Oyo-Ile. The Alaafin Majotu granted them audience, especially because he thought that they had means of helping his country reestablish unity and peace. In spite of all the disasters that it had gone through, the country and its capital city still impressed the Clapperton team as a considerably well ordered state. In the Egbado province, they saw some destruction of one or two towns caused by local conflicts. And then, not far from Oyo-Ile, they saw some villages destroyed by Jamaa rampages. For the rest, the country was still, in their view, in good shape. Clapperton's assistant, Richard Lander, was of the opinion that the Alaafin's kingdom was a beautiful one in many respects, and that all the Alaafin needed were a few big guns (cannons) with which to drive out the troublers of his country and restore order. Lander, accompanied by his brother John, revisited Oyo-Ile in 1830 and again had some interviews with the Alaafin Majotu. The country was in worse condition than it had been in 1826, and the Alaafin appeared weaker and more helpless. Still, in Lander's opinion, Majotu's kingdom was not beyond being restored to order and strength.[9]

According to Oyo traditions, after the first visit of the white men, Majotu made a strong attempt to knit the Oyo homeland, the heart of the empire, together again. He is said to have personally made a plea to the leading chieftains of the country, urging a revival of the unity and power of the empire, under the leadership of the Alaafin. So successful was he that all the leading chieftains assembled at Ikoyi for a conference, with the Onikoyi as host. The conference started on a strong note of hope, as everybody present seemed agreed on a return to a general allegiance to the Alaafin and a revival of the kingdom. But, as the meeting progressed, the influence of suspicion became unconquerable. In particular, the assembled provincial notables saw how abjectly depressed the status of the chiefs of the Oyo Mesi had become in the affairs of the city of Oyo-Ile, and feared that that was the type of fate the Alaafin desired for them too in the affairs of the empire. With that, no decision could be taken to rally round the Alaafin. The fate of the kingdom and its empire was sealed.

In summary, then, the last years of Majotu's reign were terrible years for the empire and for the Oyo homeland. It was Majotu's misfortune to sit on the throne of an empire whose vassal provinces were breaking away while its core kingdom was also breaking up. After years of increasing restiveness, Dahomey (under Gezo) revolted and was lost to the empire in 1823. The year after that, the Jamaa revolt and Afonja's death turned Ilorin into a potent center of rebellion, and of aggression against the rest of the country. After a series of shakily united actions to free Ilorin, the various local rulers in the Oyo homeland did not only go their separate ways, they actually fell into squabbling and fighting with one another – and as the 1820s drew to a close, the internal conflicts intensified. One such conflict resulted in the destruction of Ikoyi.

The general disintegration of the Alaafin's power had gradually led to the loosening of Oyo's control in Egbado. When Clapperton and his exploration team traveled through Egbado in December 1825, there were already signs of local weakening of Oyo's control there, evidenced by the fresh ruins of at least one town recently attacked by another town. By about 1830, Egbado was at last lost to the empire, as various Egbado communities went on and found their own way. The disintegration of Oyo rule became so complete, for instance, that even one Ilari (named Dekun) who had represented the Alaafin at Ijanna, renounced his allegiance to Oyo and set himself up as an independent ruler at a town called Refurefu. Then came a two-year drought and famine, followed by an epidemic of a respiratory disease. Most families lost members to that epidemic. The aged Alaafin Majotu himself succumbed to it in 1831.

Majotu was succeeded by Amodo, who reigned for only about two years. In the last years of Majotu's reign, Ilorin had sent armies to attack towns in the area of Oyo-Ile, but they had not had the courage to attack Oyo-Ile directly. Probably in the brief interregnum before the Alaafin Amodo was crowned, a small Ilorin army came and entered the capital city and sacked some streets of it, taking away some booty from the city and parts of the palace. Following upon this, the rulers and people of Ilorin more or less regarded their town as the central city of the Oyo country (just as Afonja had desired), and Oyo-Ile as a tributary of Ilorin. The new Alaafin Amodo was absolutely unprepared to reconcile himself to being regarded as a vassal of Ilorin, and was perpetually consumed by the search for a way to reverse the situation, even though his position as the Alaafin continued to weaken markedly almost by the day. Tributes had ceased to come from any part of the Oyo country. Even worse, many of the Oyo chieftains had become allies, secretly or openly, of Ilorin, through the influence of their relations and friends who had become prominent citizens of

Ilorin. Operating from such a position of strength, the leadership of Ilorin had considerable success in encouraging disunity among the chieftains of the Oyo country, and in inducing them to fight petty wars against one another, wars in which Ilorin's army supported this or that chieftain, resulting in the destruction of some of their strong cities. Even then, the Alaafin Amodo never gave up the struggle to put together a coalition of Oyo chieftains to rid the country of the Ilorin emirate. Unlike his predecessor Majotu, Amodo was totally unprepared to live with the thorn of Ilorin's rebellious population and foreign ruling family in his country's foot.

In 1832, his striving bore some fruit. At his urging, a coalition of Oyo chieftains raised a fairly large army, and the Alaafin sent it against Ilorin. But this army had very little chance of succeeding. Its commanders were too badly divided by suspicion and intrigues. Outside Ilorin, at the small village of Kanla, the Alaafin's army and the Ilorin army met. A hard battle followed, but the Ilorin forces again won the day. Broken hearted, Amodo returned to Oyo-Ile, resolved to continue the fight. As he saw it, that was his destiny: as descendant of the great Alaafins, he could not accept the loss of Ilorin to what he regarded as a rebellious mob and a threat to all order. Unfortunately, a short time after the Kanla war, a huge fire razed parts of the palace and destroyed much of its treasures. Amodo did not survive that for long. In 1833, he died quietly in his palace.

Amodo's successor, Oluewu, a tall, handsome prince, ascended the throne with a clear mission — to take Ilorin back and then revive his empire. By his time, the rulers of Ilorin had become more confident of their power and more demanding of tributes and other signs of their power in the country. Soon after Oluewu ascended the throne, therefore, the Emir (then Shitta, brother of Abdulsalami) invited him to Ilorin. Though the Alaafin was, on the whole, respectfully treated by the people and rulers of Ilorin, he could only feel the humiliation of being made to go there by the Emir. Moreover, as the Alaafin was leaving Ilorin, Shitta ordered the seizure of one of the royal Gbedu drums from the Alaafin's attendants — apparently hoping that its possession would increase his legitimacy before the Oyo citizens of Ilorin. Oluewu felt deeply insulted, and decided that it was time for him to fight. Consequently, when Shitta invited him again to Ilorin (so that he might ceremonially accept conversion to Islam), he refused to go. The Emir responded by sending an army to ravage the suburbs of Oyo-Ile and to threaten Oyo-Ile itself. At the invitation of friends among the Ilorin chiefs, some Oyo chieftains went to the assistance of the Ilorin forces. Oluewu got ready to fight and invited the Bariba to help him. A Bariba army came to Oyo-Ile. The Ilorin army, assisted by some of the Oyo chieftains, was driven back from the gate of the capital city as well as from nearby villages. The

Bariba archers dislodged the Ilorin army besieging the small town of Gbodo, and many in the Ilorin cavalry, while fleeing from the town, drowned in the flooded streams of the rainy season.

Thus assured of Bariba help, the Alaafin issued a general proclamation urging his country to rally round him for a final attack on Ilorin. Most Oyo towns were by then friends or allies of Ilorin. The Alaafin therefore decided to make a detour, with his Bariba allies, through some of these towns in order to give them courage to rise up and fight with him. The large army that resulted then marched towards Ilorin. Frightened by these developments, the Emir gathered a much larger army than ever before, even recruiting troops from the Nupe country on the Niger. When the two armies met, the Ilorin army was very much larger and immediately tried to overwhelm the Alaafin's army with its superior numbers. The Alaafin's army fought back bravely and routed the Ilorin army, inflicting heavy casualties on them. That victory did not prove decisive, however, as the Ilorin cavalry managed to counter-attack and salvage the situation. Still the Alaafin had good reason to claim victory for the day and to have high hopes of ultimate victory.

As the Alaafin and his Bariba allies, thus elated, got ready for the final onslaught on Ilorin, some more leaders and towns of the Oyo country also arrived to join the Alaafin's forces. At sunrise, a confident Alaafin advanced on Ilorin. Ilorin had never been attacked by an army of such magnitude, and fear and consternation gripped the city.

On this second day, however, the hidden weaknesses in the Alaafin's army surfaced. Many of the Oyo chiefs in the Alaafin's army were not completely loyal to his cause. Among the chiefs, suspicions and fears about the Alaafin's intentions were rife – largely because the Alaafins would not give up attempts to suppress the Oyo-Ile chiefs. For instance, it was known by all that when Oluewu's Bariba allies had arrived in Oyo-Ile for the current war, Oluewu had first employed them against a Basorun whom he had regarded as too outspoken. Sent by the Alaafin, some of the Bariba troops had besieged that Basorun's compound, forcing him to commit suicide. The Oyo chiefs could not but wonder what the Alaafin would use his Bariba allies to do after Ilorin had been subdued. Would he unleash them on the leading rulers of the Oyo country? Rather than being grateful to the Alaafin's Bariba allies, therefore, the Oyo chieftains treated them spitefully, and privately ridiculed them as crude barbarians. Not only were some of the chiefs secret friends of the rulers of Ilorin, many who had relatives that had fled as Muslims to Ilorin and had become notable persons there were not sure that they wanted Ilorin and its inhabitants devastated. Wars between Ilorin and any Oyo forces were wars of Oyo people against Oyo people, and the Oyo of Ilorin (reinforced by large numbers of foreign-born co-religionists) were more united in purpose and derived much fervor from their Islamic faith and their memory of religious persecution. In the circumstance, the Alaafin could only be victorious by decisively winning a straight short encounter. When the final fighting spilled over to a second day, the hidden fissures in his forces had time to manifest and exert destructive impact.

Quite early in the second day, therefore, elements of the Ilorin cavalry broke through a shaky wing of the Alaafin's army and attacked from the rear. In the vicious fighting that followed, large numbers fell on both sides. The Bariba king commanding the Bariba troops fell, fighting furiously till the end. At the height of the fighting, Oluewu's oldest son galloped up to his royal father, saluted him goodbye, and plunged back into the thick of the battle. Both father and son, fighting as true princes, perished that day. Some traditions have it that the Alaafin Oluewu, wounded almost to the point of death, was picked up on the battle-field and taken alive into Ilorin where, still proudly refusing to acknowledge the Emir as ruler, he was executed. The once great empire of the once mighty Alaafins, still fighting on the offensive till the very end, went, at last, to its grave.

The city of Oyo-Ile did not survive the terrible news. For more than two hundred years, it had been the abode of surpassing power and glory. It would not wait to endure abject subjugation. For years, some citizens had been leaving and heading towards the south. As soon as the news of the battle and the fate of the Alaafin came, the remaining residents began to pack their things. This was no panic flight, or flight under pressure. Families calmly packed their belongings and set out, many coming back repeatedly for more of their things. Most went south, some found their way to towns still standing in the Oyo country, some went to the Bariba country to the west, and some even went to relations living in Ilorin. Slowly, over many days, the lineage compounds, the palace, the marketplaces, the streets, all emptied – as the light went out on the once proud, but now dead, city of the Alaafins.

26. Aremo, Prince of Oyo. *Photo: P.Verger, 1948–49, IFAN.*

14

Yorubaland in the Nineteenth Century: The Wars of Change

In the history of the Yoruba people, the nineteenth century was a century of tumultuous happenings, of the coming and growth of powerful new influences, and of profound, transformational, changes. Starting from the Oyo part of Yorubaland and the other Yoruba kingdoms that had been parts of the Oyo Empire, wars swept through the whole of Yorubaland and, as they did, they set afoot a whole array of demographic, economic, social and political developments and changes. From about the second decade of the century, Islam, which had existed in traces in Yorubaland, spread faster and wider than before. From about the middle of the century, Christian missions penetrated Yorubaland and quickly spread all over. Christianity brought with it Western education, and thus inaugurated the emergence of a literate, Western-educated, elite. At the same time, the legal abolition, and gradual demise, of the Atlantic slave trade, opened up a new era in which the productive economy of Yorubaland was gradually drawn into the economy of Europe and the wider world. Also at the same time, European political influence grew, culminating, at the end of the century, with the imposition of European imperial rule over all Yoruba people.

The present chapter will deal only with the wars and their consequences. The next chapter will focus on the other influences, developments and changes. This approach is adopted only for the sake of simplicity, since the wars and all the other developments were intricately interwoven in their courses and effects.

Causes of the Wars[1]

In the last chapter, we gave an account of the disintegration and collapse of the Oyo Empire – and of the Oyo kingdom that had constituted the core of the empire. The wars generated by that process of disintegration were not merely the first wars in nineteenth century Yoruba history; they proved to be the precursors of wider storms of war that came to rage all over Yorubaland for the rest of the century. The disintegration of the Oyo Empire and kingdom destroyed the pre-existing system of order and security in Yorubaland and created a situation whereby all centers of power, old and new, had to scramble to establish new systems and patterns that would guarantee order and security. Those efforts created conflicts and wars which the Yoruba people were not able to put an end to – until European powers intervened and imposed their own system of order, security and peace.

For two full centuries prior to the nineteenth century, the Oyo Empire had exercised powerful influences for peace in Yorubaland – both indirectly and directly. Indirectly, the Oyo kingdom, plus the Yoruba provinces in the Alaafin's empire, amounted to a very substantial part of Yorubaland – about half of its land area and probably more than half of its total population. For two centuries, this large area under the Alaafin's rule enjoyed orderly government, peace, prosperity and pride. The Alaafin's Yoruba domains were like a wide umbrella of peace and order, shielding and transmitting peace to the rest of Yorubaland. In short, in an indirect, intangible, but very real way, the Alaafin's domains laid down the standard of order and peace, and thus encouraged and guaranteed order and peace in the rest of Yorubaland. Directly, widespread Yoruba traditions attest to the Alaafin's interventions in disputes within and between Yoruba kingdoms beyond his own domains – interventions that usually succeeded in maintaining or restoring peace. The Alaafin's name and aura were great, and he employed them directly to uphold order and peace in the Yoruba homeland.

When, therefore, in the course of the first decades of the nineteenth century, the Oyo Empire disintegrated, as also its base (the Oyo homeland), and the once proud state of the Alaafins fell into dissolution, a major pillar of peace in Yorubaland crumbled. It is not difficult to imagine the sort of effects that the disruptions and violence in the Oyo homeland would have produced in the rest of Yorubaland – reports of terrible conflicts among princes of the Oyo country; of blasted towns and villages; of massive flights of people from their homes and their towns; of Alaafin after Alaafin isolated and helpless in his palace while Oyo princes destroyed their country; of an obscure resident foreigner at Ilorin taking advantage of the mess created by Oyo leaders to become a terror to the whole land; of countless towns shattered before the Ilorin cavalry and of endless crowds of destitute refugees in desperate flight for dear life.

But much worse was soon to follow, as the reports ceased to be merely reports. By the middle of the second decade of the century, the refugees from the Oyo country began to arrive in the rest of Yorubaland, especially in the Yoruba middle belt – frightened, many of them detached from family and loved ones, destitute, having lost all the substance of their earthly labor, often made violent by desperation, in their thousands and tens of thousands. The well-to-do or highly placed Oyo citizen might be able to flee in some order, but that was beyond the overwhelming majority of poor and vulnerable folks. Their numbers increased exponentially in the two decades that followed, and probably did not begin to decrease until the last years of the 1830s. For the people of the towns and villages to which they came, these must have been very traumatic times. At least in one area of the Yoruba midlands, in the Egba and Owu countries, their coming turned out to be much worse than traumatic; it became unbelievably destructive. Many towns and villages in those parts suddenly found themselves under vicious attacks by crowds of people too desperate to talk accommodation or hospitality.

The story of a man named Dado, though by no means typical of most, is illustrative of what these terrible times could do to a person.[2] Dado was a man of some reputation and of strong military credentials from the Oyo homeland. He did his last military service as a member of a company of valiant men who, determined never to stop resisting Ilorin, kept fighting in engagement after engagement until their number dwindled close to zero. Kurunmi, later ruler of Ijaye, belonged to this company. The survivors retreated to the small town of Ika-Odan near Ijaye. Having lost wives, children and all earthly belongings, they had become so brutalized and calloused by their experiences that most of them were in no mood to wait on the good will and hospitality of the Ika-Odan people, but turned their military power on their hosts. So they violently seized homes, belongings, farms and wives and turned their hosts who would not run away into menial servants. When they had eaten up everything available in Ika-Odan and its farms, they extended their forays into Ijaye farms. Ijaye farmers rose up and attacked these marauders, and a skirmish ensued. Kurunmi urged a gentler, conciliatory, approach, but Dado denounced him and the rest and led a small group to attack Ijaye. The people of Ijaye were driven from their farms into their town, and then the whole population, unready for war, fled the town – apparently believing that they would be able to return after their desperate guests had gone away. The company then moved from Ika-Odan and took possession of Ijaye, and decided to make Ijaye their permanent home, with Dado as their leader and ruler.

As ruler, Dado turned out to be a disaster. He had no interest in farming or other civil pursuits. All his thoughts and utterances were about fighting wars. Those of his colleagues who settled down and raised farms he accused routinely of cowardice. At last, his colleagues could no longer stand him, and they drove him and his few adherents from the town, and chose Kurunmi as their ruler. Dado wandered from there with his group until he came to a little town called Tobalogbo. Frightened by his military reputation, the ruler and chiefs of Tobalogbo came out to meet him and offer their hospitality. But, as they stood before him, he ordered his men to fall on them and kill all of them. He then entered the town and thoroughly looted it. With the booty from there, he went on to Aborerin near Iberekodo, and built a large compound where he resided for some time with his new wives, his children and his followers. But he was not able to settle down. The Egba had meanwhile founded Abeokuta and some Oyo refugees and others had established a new large town at the destroyed Egba village of Ibadan, and Ibadan and Abeokuta were engaged in some conflicts. Dado left Aborerin with his family and joined Ibadan in a campaign in which Ibadan was fighting at Oniyefun against Abeokuta. When the Ibadan forces were defeated there, Dado narrowly escaped with his life, but he lost his whole family and all his belongings. From then on, lonely and destitute, he wandered from place to place, including even a visit to some relatives in the city of Ilorin, and a short residence at Ibadan as a guest of an Ibadan chief. Finally he wandered back to Ijaye, where Kurunmi had him arrested and executed.

No other prominent refugee from the Oyo country is known to have become as dissolute as Dado, but the experiences of Ika-Odan, Ijaye and Tobalogbo were not very dissimilar from the experiences of many other towns and villages in the Egba country at the hands of some of the most desperate refugee groups. Things were extremely hard for the refugees and, for many of them, the temptation to lapse into brigandage was strong. Many small towns and villages in this part of the country were not just violently seized but totally destroyed.

In short, then, the coming of large streams of refugees from the Oyo homeland southwards to other parts of the Yoruba national homeland was, for an initial, fairly long period, productive of much violence and destruction, and very serious deterioration of security, especially in the west-central area of the Yoruba middle belt. In the years that followed, new significant centers of population crystallized in this middle belt area and went through a process of consolidation, a process that occasioned much stress as well as conflicts and wars. Thereafter, the maturing new states went through a period of rivalry amongst themselves, featuring, again, conflicts and wars. From these, one new state emerged the most successful and strongest of all. Back in the shattered homeland of Oyo in the north, one old city under a new, and foreign, leadership and carrying the banner of a new religion, had emerged as the sole powerful successor of the destroyed kingdom of the Alaafins. From its base in the north, this new kingdom, Ilorin, intent on imposing its own version of order on all of Yorubaland, continued to pursue the refugees southwards, bringing relentless pressure to bear on the new states emerging in the middle belt. From among the latter, the most successful, Ibadan, stood up to resist the pressure from the north. It succeeded wonderfully; and, because of that success, it developed bigger ambitions, namely, to prevent the northern kingdom from establishing a foothold anywhere in the vulnerable areas of northeastern and eastern Yorubaland. That ambition, because it met with success after success, became transformed into yet a bigger ambition – to establish control over all (or almost all) of Yorubaland, to build a new empire of the Yoruba people. The empire-building venture too, though it encountered varying degrees of local resistance almost everywhere, proved successful, so much so that it looked as if Yorubaland was at last about to find a viable new order. But a major surge of resistance, widespread and considerably unified, then rose to confront the nascent order in a long, final, series of stubborn wars. While these major wars were in progress throughout the century, many types of local disputes and hostile relationships were being played out in local wars. Also, while Yorubaland in general was thus preoccupied in wars, foreign neighbors (first the Nupe and then the Dahomey) took advantage and repeatedly invaded Yorubaland.

The Owu War

The first war outside the Oyo homeland, then, was the Owu War, c. 1812–22.[3] The Owu War was, indirectly and directly, caused by the troubles of the Oyo country. The remotest root of it was planted when the Alaafin Awole ordered the Oyo army in c. 1793 to attack and sack the Ife market town of Apomu. As would be remembered, the Baale of Apomu, finding that the Ooni of Ife was not able to save Apomu, gave his own life in order to save his town. Hatred for Oyo authorities, resulting from this, never died at Apomu and other Ife villages near Apomu. Years later, as the power of the Alaafin's government disintegrated, Oyo traders trading at Apomu or passing through to the Ijebu country came under occasional attacks by the people of Apomu and the other Ife villages. By then, the Alaafin was no longer able to help his subjects. However, two of the leading chieftains of the Oyo country, Adegun (the Onikoyi of Ikoyi) and Toyeje (the Baale of Ogbomoso) sent messages to the Olowu of Owu (Akinjobi) urging him to help stop the attacks on Oyo traders. Thereupon, an Owu army went into action and suppressed Apomu and some other Ife villages. This led to a brief war between Ife and Owu (c. 1812) in which the Ife army was defeated. Ife then embarked on bigger preparations for war and asked the Awujale of Ijebu-Ode for help. The rulers of Ijebu-Ode under the Awujale had long resented what they regarded as Owu's over-ambition over the trade routes that connected the Ijebu country with most of the Yoruba interior. Now, they bristled at Owu's sacrilegious disrespect of Ife. An Ife–Ijebu alliance was formed, and it declared war on Owu in 1817.

At the bottom of all these developments around Apomu were the centuries-old rivalries for the control of the large trade in the market town of Apomu and the routes through the Apomu area. At the height of the power of the Oyo Empire, the Oyo traders had come to dominate this trade – with the strong support of the Owu people, who benefited enormously from being supporters of the Alaafin's government and friends of Oyo traders. As would be remembered, this had considerably marginalized Ife (even though Apomu was an Ife town), and generated hostility between Ife and Owu. The growing disorder in the area threatened Ijebu's trade, and Ijebu was poised to intervene there – especially to stop what was widely perceived as Owu's excessive aggressiveness and its disrespect of Ife's interests.

The usually formidable Owu army marched out to meet the Ife–Ijebu allies, but the allies proved to be stronger – especially because the Ijebu army was armed with guns bought from European traders on the coast. The Owu army fell back on their city, which was then besieged by the allies. The Oyo chiefs who had got Owu into this situation could not help the Olowu; they were too preoccupied with the troubles in their own country. As the siege dragged on, large numbers of Oyo men – refugees fleeing from their own country – joined with the allies outside the walls of Owu-Ipole. The invaders thus became too strong for the defenders, and Owu-Ipole's defenses collapsed in c. 1822. The Olowu (by then a warlike king named Amororo) managed to escape. The invading armies, greatly swollen by the Oyo refugees, then broke into the city and completely wiped it out. According to widespread traditions, the Ooni ordered that a curse be placed on the site of Owu-Ipole, with an interdict that it would never again be resettled.

Owu-Ipole survivors fled, and so did the inhabitants of all the smaller Owu towns – some southwards into northern Ijebu, but most into neighboring Egba villages. The victorious allies, greatly swollen in numbers by the continually arriving Oyo refugees, followed them into the Egba country because some of the Egba villages had helped the Owu during the siege of Owu-Ipole. One by one, all towns and villages in the eastern and central parts of the Egba country were destroyed. The Egba people, plus most of the Owu, then fled westwards. When they came under the Olumo Rock in the far western part of the Egba country, they settled down and began to build a new town which they named Abeokuta.[4]

Thus ended the Owu War. It needs to be added that the siege of Owu (c. 1817–22) was contemporary with Afonja's creation of his Jamaa army in Ilorin in 1817, and his conquest of parts of the Oyo country. Owu was destroyed in 1822 and Afonja died in 1824. As will be remembered, Afonja's death was followed by unsuccessful attempts by Oyo armies to dislodge the Fulani from Ilorin, and by the firm establishment of an Islamic emirate in Ilorin.

The Wars of Newly Consolidated States

While the disintegration of the old order proceeded in the Oyo homeland in the north, important consolidation of new centers of population began in the late 1820s in the Yoruba midlands to the south. In the west of the region, Abeokuta, founded in 1830, quickly became one of the largest aggregations of population in Yorubaland. Its political evolution was guided by the fact that it had received substantial populations of the three arms of the Egba people as well as survivors of the Owu kingdoms. Abeokuta therefore became a state comprising many kingdoms – namely the Owu under the paramountcy of the Olowu, and the kingdoms of the Egba Alake, the Egba Agura and the Egba Oke-Ona.

A steady stream of Oyo refugees had continued to swell the populations of northern Ijesa towns, Ife towns and villages, and the mostly depopulated Owu and Egba countries. Three major settlements sprang up in the latter area. In the small village of Ago-Oja, a group settled under the leadership of an Oyo-Ile prince named Atiba, a son of the Alaafin Abiodun. Ago-Oja was the birthplace of Atiba's mother. Ago-Oja's name became changed simply to Oyo. In the deserted Egba town of Ijaye, another group settled, as would be remembered, ultimately under the leadership of a warrior named Kurunmi. After most of the commanders of the allied Ife, Ijebu and Oyo troops that had destroyed the Owu and Egba towns and villages had returned home, a large group of the troops camped at a deserted Egba village named Ibadan, which quickly developed into a regular town. From this point on, most of the accounts of the nineteenth century wars center around the history of these refugee settlements – Abeokuta, Ibadan, Ijaye and Oyo – and the Islamic kingdom of Ilorin in the north, which became one of the most powerful states of the Yoruba people.

At Ibadan, the first person acknowledged as ruler was an Ife warrior chief, Okunade, the Maye of Ife. Highly respected and feared for his military reputation, Okunade set out to impose strong discipline on the crowd of refugees who constituted most of Ibadan's new population. He was particularly hard on the poor and destitute among the refugees, because he regarded them as unruly. His efforts led to a revolt, and the revolt quickly developed into a civil conflict in which the Maye, supported by his Ife soldiers, many Oyo refugees, and many Egba and Owu who had returned to live in Ibadan, was confronted by the majority of the refugees. The Maye's supporters outnumbered his opponents, who trembled at the very mention of his name, but it was the fear and desperation of his opponents that won the conflict. When he finally fell into their hands, they could not believe what had happened, and they did not know what to do with him – until one of them took courage and struck him dead. After that, the town was gripped for many days with the fear that he would somehow return.

Ibadan gradually settled down after this confusion, and established the rudiments of government. As it took shape, Ibadan's system of government was strange to Yoruba culture and traditions. For all Yoruba people, government had always meant monarchy. Ibadan evolved a republican system of government featuring two parallel lines of chiefs – a civil line and a military line. The civil line was topped by the Baale, and the military line by a chief bearing a military title like Basorun or Aare. As the Ibadan system was ultimately established, rising up the ladder in each line of chiefs was by promotion. Any person, no matter his ancestry, could be appointed a junior chief, and then rise up the ladder in his line. The qualification was merit – a combination of good character and contribution to the progress of the city. Therefore, with good character and continued good civic record (and luck) the junior chief could rise to the top. As the Ibadan system thus de-emphasized traditional Yoruba lineages and lineage claims, a new type of "family" group and new type of *agbo-ile* developed in Ibadan. Each such group coalesced around a prominent person and built a compound for itself. The binding force in this new type of *agbo-ile* or compound was not belief in a common ancestry but attachment to one leader. If the leader happened to become significantly successful in the Ibadan political system, more of the people arriving in Ibadan would gravitate towards him and join his compound. As a result, the *agbo-ile* of some of the highest chiefs tended to be large, sprawling, compounds. A very successful trader could build up a large compound also. Later in the century, one of the largest compounds in Ibadan was owned by a rich woman trader named Efunseyitan Aniwura, by then the Iyalode (highest woman chief) of Ibadan.

Over time, Ibadan became a very attractive place to ambitious people from all over Yorubaland. Yoruba people who were strongly attached to their tradition and culture (like kings and traditional chiefs) tended to deride Ibadan as "a people without a king." But the ambitious young person who wanted to succeed in commerce, in some trade, or politically, could not resist the lure of this wonderful new city where one could become a big person regardless of one's lowly parentage or one's place of origin. As a result, people poured into Ibadan from all corners of Yorubaland. And as Ibadan grew bigger, so did the opportunities it offered. Ibadan was well located to trade in all directions: southwards to Lagos through Ijebu or Abeokuta routes, southwestwards through Egbado to Porto Novo; eastwards through Ife, Ijesa, Ekiti, Akoko, Owo, to Benin; northwards to the Niger through an endless number of routes. The large and growing population provided a growing customer base for local traders and for artisans of all types. And when Ibadan began to succeed in war and empire building, it became the ideal home for young men who wanted to distinguish themselves in valor and in politics. And so they came from the homelands of all Yoruba subgroups – even from as far as the land of the Okun Yoruba close to the Niger–Benue confluence. As they came also, they brought their various versions of the Yoruba cultural heritage. Migration into successful towns had always been a trait in Yoruba history; with Ibadan, that trait produced its greatest pre-twentieth century fruit.

At Ijaye, not far to the east of Ibadan, another large population of refugees accumulated. The settlement had a rough beginning, as would be remembered, under the leadership of Dado. After Dado was removed from the scene, his place was taken by Kurunmi. With Kurunmi as leader, Ijaye grew very rapidly as large groups of refugees came to it, attracted by Kurunmi's reputation. A man of considerable personal charisma and military brilliance, Kurunmi quickly built Ijaye into a well ordered city with a formidable military machine. Like Ibadan, Ijaye evolved into a state without a king. It grew into a military dictatorship ruled by Kurunmi who was much loved, even adored, by his people. Much has survived in the traditions about the person of this man. He was one of the most resourceful generals of nineteenth century Yoruba history. He was fond of illuminating his speeches with colorful proverbs. He loved to sing and dance and, when excited, would couch his proverbs in songs and dance to them. He was also impulsive by nature, and as he grew old that trait seemed to worsen, but he never ceased being a great military commander and leader of men.

The new town of Oyo under Atiba's leadership also grew into a big city. Until 1835, Atiba continued, as a prince of the dying old Oyo kingdom, to take part in the affairs of the old kingdom while slowly building his new town. He was in the Alaafin Oluewu's campaign against Ilorin in 1835, the campaign in which Oluewu perished, resulting in the abandonment of Oyo-Ile. After that terminal disaster of the old empire, Atiba was crowned Alaafin in his new town. Many urged him to return to the abandoned Oyo-Ile and rebuild it, but he chose to establish a new center for the Oyo kingdom. A man of enormous capabilities and great dreams, Atiba embarked on a very intelligent and expertly orchestrated effort to substitute his new Oyo for the dead Oyo-Ile, and to make himself the direct inheritor of the power, greatness and glory of the Alaafins of the imperial era. He was so successful at this that the leaders of Ibadan and Ijaye agreed to subscribe to his dreams and plans. According to such dreams, the Old Oyo Empire would be revived – or would be regarded as still in existence. Atiba would rule over it all as the Alaafin. The new town of Oyo would be the new imperial capital. The rulers of Ibadan and Ijaye would be the Alaafin's Basorun and Kakanfo, respectively. Ibadan would defend the Ekun Osi of the empire (that is, the Osun and Ibolo areas) and Ijaye would defend its Ekun Otun (that is, the Upper Ogun region and the regions to the west). Ultimately, the revamped empire would drive the Fulani out of Ilorin. The very important step was taken of conferring the titles of Basorun on Oluyole of Ibadan and Kakanfo on Kurunmi of Ijaye. At Oyo, the Alaafin began to build a large, prestigious, palace befitting the dignity of the new imperial capital – a beautiful, though smaller, replica of the great palace of Oyo-Ile.

Beyond those steps, however, the Alaafin Atiba was not able to go. It soon became clear that Ibadan and Ijaye, not Atiba's Oyo, were the real centers of power, and that each had expansionist or imperial ambitions of its own.

By 1840, then, many centers of large population had emerged across the breadth of the central region of Yorubaland. Many towns of the Osun Valley (Iwo, Ede, Ejigbo, Ikirun), northern Ijesa towns (Osogbo, Igbajo, Otan, Ada), as well as some Ife towns (Ikire, Gbongan and the cluster of villages in the Origbo suburb of Ile-Ife), had swollen up rapidly, many of them expanding far beyond their old town limits. A large refugee town named Modakeke sprang up as a twin to the ancient city of Ile-Ife. But the most important creations of this time of consolidation were the five new cities – Ibadan, Ijaye, new Oyo, Abeokuta, and Ilorin.

As Ibadan and Abeokuta settled down, a jostling for territorial advantage immediately arose between them. Ibadan leaders were concerned that Abeokuta occupied a strategic location that could block their access to the trade routes through Egbado to the port of Ajase (Porto Novo). Ibadan therefore embarked on a series of campaigns to drive Abeokuta from its location, campaigns which resulted in Ibadan–Abeokuta battles in villages between the two major towns. In these mini-wars, the Ijebu-Ode kingdom usually supported Ibadan, because the Ijebu were also concerned about Abeokuta's competition with Ijebu traders in the coastal trade with Lagos and the rest of the Awori country. Whenever Ibadan went into conflict with Abeokuta, Ijebu sent help to Ibadan, and Ibadan reciprocated whenever Ijebu declared war on Abeokuta. On a few occasions too, Ibadan managed to secure the assistance of Ijaye under Kurunmi. Against all these, Abeokuta proved remarkably able to stand its ground, recording a number of victories over the allies – over Ijebu in a battle that was fought on the Owiwi Stream, and over Ibadan at the village of Oniyefun. An Ibadan attempt to attack Abeokuta itself failed in a battle outside Abeokuta (which became known as the Jabara War). A major Egba campaign against Ijebu led to a long siege of the Ijebu town of Iperu, but it too failed when a strong Ibadan force came to the aid of Ijebu. For most of the late 1820s and early 1830s, therefore, the relationship of the Ibadan–Ijebu allies with Abeokuta featured a series of conflicts and inconsequential victories and defeats. Against the opposition of Ibadan and Ijebu then, Abeokuta settled down and began to prosper. In fact, during the same years, Abeokuta exerted military pressure on the neighboring Egbado towns and took control of Ilaro and Ijanna. To the south, Abeokuta attacked the old Awori kingdom of Otta. With the help of troops from the Lagos kingdom and from Ibadan, Otta held on for months against the Abeokuta invaders, but eventually fell.

While Ibadan (supported by Ijebu and, sometimes, Ijaye) and Abeokuta thus preoccupied themselves with their local wars, the consolidation of all the new states, and the peace or even the existence of the old states of midland and southern Yorubaland, was threatened by determined enemies from the west and north. From the west, the kingdom of Dahomey, freed from Oyo rule by about 1823, began immediately to put pressure on neighboring provinces of Yorubaland. Dahomey did not only desire control of the trade routes in the Egbado country, it also wanted to seize territory for agricultural purposes. Dahomey armies intensively harassed the Egbado towns, particularly Ijanna, Ilaro and Refurefu, and ultimately destroyed Refurefu. Abeokuta moved in force into Egbado, however, and stopped Dahomey by, as earlier pointed out, taking control of Ilaro and Ijanna. The situation was to remain this way until the 1850s when Dahomey finally made a frontal attack on Abeokuta, only to be firmly repulsed.

From the north, the Oyo emirate of Ilorin was much stronger, more persistent, and more successful. Ilorin had developed into a predominantly Islamic Yoruba kingdom, and most of its troops and commanders were of Yoruba (mostly Oyo) stock, with a strong complement of Hausa and Fulani commanders and troops – essentially the army which Afonja had created for Ilorin, though with additions and modifications over time. Ilorin forces pushed southwards until they came to the Osun Valley and even harassed towns and villages as far as the Ife kingdom. About 1835, the populations of the Ife towns of Ikire, Gbongan and the Origbo villages were forced to flee into Ile-Ife. In the last years of the 1830s, it looked as if nothing could stop the Ilorin from pushing all the way to the coast to "dip the Koran in the sea." The fate of the new towns – Ibadan, Ijaye, Oyo and Abeokuta – as well as of the old kingdoms south of them in the Awori and Ijebu countries seemed to hang in the balance.

In 1840, however, the tide suddenly turned. Ibadan had started to confront the Ilorin forces by 1838. At Osogbo in 1840, the Ibadan army met formidable Ilorin forces and routed them very decisively, destroying their dreaded cavalry, killing or capturing most of their horses, and capturing many of the Ilorin commanders. Thereupon, Ibadan forces pushed northwards, dislodging Ilorin forces and pushing them all the way beyond Offa, to only a short distance from Ilorin itself. Ibadan decided not to make any attempt on the narrow territory between Offa and Ilorin because it was too firmly controlled by the Ilorin cavalry. The boundary of Ilorin's domain came to stabilize at this line.

Ibadan thus saved the consolidation of the new towns and cities in the middle belt of Yorubaland. People who had been forced by the Ilorin threat to flee their towns in these places returned. The inhabitants of the Ife towns of Ikire, Gbongan and the Origbo villages returned home from Ile-Ife.

Ibadan's Territorial Expansion

One of the most important consequences of the Ibadan victories over Ilorin at Osogbo and beyond Osogbo was the emergence of an Ibadan Empire. For the towns of the Osun Valley and those north of there to Offa, acceptance of Ibadan's protection occurred as a matter of course. They had joined hands with the Ibadan forces in dislodging those of Ilorin, and they needed Ibadan's protection against their return. As a result of the influence of a native son of Ikire, Ajobo, who had become a prominent chief in Ibadan, Ikire willingly accepted Ibadan's protection. Employing the well-tried system of provincial administration of the dissolved Oyo Empire, Ibadan placed Ajeles in all these towns and villages to watch over their security, to receive tributes for Ibadan, and to prod the local rulers to send troops and other types of help to Ibadan whenever such was needed.

Ibadan's attention was soon attracted to other areas beyond the Osun Valley. After some lull in Ilorin's military activities, its forces returned to the fight in about 1846. It was impossible for them to drive directly south as they had done before. Ibadan solidly barred the way in that direction. Therefore, they veered southeastwards into the Ekiti, Igbomina and Ijesa countries. In the thickly forested parts of these generally hilly countries, Ilorin forces, depending heavily on cavalry, fared badly. Making very good use of their hills and forests, the Ekiti and Ijesa people drew the Ilorin cavalry into an endless series of ambushes. As remnants of defeated cavalry troops tried to find their ways out of the forests, their pursuers, assisted by local farmers, chased them with shouts of "Pole! Pole!" (that is, "fall" or "drop", the cry with which farmers chased farm thieves). From this, Ilorin's abortive invasions of Ekiti and Ijesa became known as the Pole War. In the northernmost parts of Ekiti, as well as much of Igbomina, however, where the forests gave way to mostly tall grass, the Ilorin invaders fared somewhat better. The Ekiti kingdoms of Otun Moba and Obo came under intense pressure. The Ilorin forces occupied the town of Aye in the Moba kingdom (a town which had been in revolt against the Oore of Otun) and from there tried to subdue Moba's capital town of Otun. In about 1847 the Oore, king of Moba, sent to Ibadan for help. Ibadan armies therefore headed for northern Ekiti and the Igbomina country, against the Ilorin forces. After dislodging them from northern Ekiti and neighboring parts of Igbomina, the

Ibadan armies fanned out into the rest of Ekiti, Ijesa – and, later, Akoko where Nupe raids were going on.

In most of Ekiti and Ijesa, the Ibadan forces met with varying degrees of resistance. The city of Ilesa had one of the best defenses in Yorubaland and had to be besieged again and again. The Ajero of Ijero put up a strong defence for the town of Ikoro in his kingdom and asked for help from other Ekiti kingdoms. Some of them sent help, and the Ibadan army found itself confronted by a fairly large and dogged coalition which was subdued only after many long and fierce encounters.

In northern Ekiti, a fairly formidable power emerged in the person of Esugbayibi, founder of a new kingdom named Aiyede. Esugbayibi was born in the small town of Iye in far northern Ekiti. As a young man, he won renown as an intrepid fighter against the Nupe and then the Ilorin invaders of his homeland. In about 1855, he migrated a little southwards to the woods between the kingdoms of Isan and Itaji in northern Ekiti, bringing with him some followers, mostly warlike young men. His plans were to establish this new settlement as a strong base for his war against Ilorin. More and more people came to join his new town, and this encouraged him to declare it a kingdom with himself as king, with the royal title of Ata. He soon proved to be as astute a politician as he was a tough warrior. Seeing Ibadan expelling Ilorin forces from Ekiti and taking control of most of Ekiti, he decided to strengthen Aiyede with an alliance with Ibadan. In 1857, he went to Ibadan and offered to defend its interests against Ilorin and the Nupe in northeastern Ekiti, and the rulers of Ibadan entered into an agreement with him appointing him as a sort of special vassal of Ibadan in northern Ekiti. (The English commercial traveler, Daniel May, visited Aiyede a day or two after Esugbayibi returned from Ibadan.) Esugbayibi's real intention, however, was to protect his young kingdom and ensure its independence, and he had no desire to defend Ibadan's interests or to be subject to Ibadan. In the next two decades, Aiyede as an independent kingdom, generally believed to be a close friend of Ibadan, attracted many more settlers and grew tremendously. From the information reaching Ibadan, Aiyede looked more and more like a rival, rather than a vassal or agent, but Esugbayibi's diplomacy continued to prevent an Ibadan attack.

In the Igbomina and Akoko countries, also, Ibadan encountered resistance, although the mostly small towns of Akoko did not have the strength to cause too much trouble for the Ibadan forces. The people of the Igbomina town of Oro-Ago, located on a rocky hill, hid behind rocks on their hill and attacked the Ibadan troops with all sorts of missiles from there, until the latter gave up and left – and went on to subdue Oro, Esie, Iludun and other Igbomina towns in that area.

In spite of all these difficulties, Ibadan had, by about 1859, subdued most of the Ekiti, Ijesa, Akoko and Igbomina kingdoms and stationed Ajeles in them. Only a few kingdoms still remained independent, notably (besides Aiyede) Ado in Ekiti, and Owo. Owo was reputed to be the most powerful kingdom in eastern Yorubaland. But its real strength against Ibadan resided in the fact that Owo controlled the road to the Benin market, which was vital for Ibadan's procurement of guns and gunpowder. Not only did Ibadan leave Owo free, Ibadan leaders actually made friends with Owo rulers. One Ibadan chief named Ayorinde, who had fled from Ibadan to escape some punishment there, came to live in exile at Owo and, in order to appease his superiors at home, he organized large purchases of guns and gunpowder for Ibadan from Benin through Owo. As for Ado, the largest Ekiti kingdom, its warlike reputation seems to have discouraged attack by the Ibadan war chiefs operating in Ekiti.

By 1850, the Ife kingdom too had become part of the Ibadan Empire. As the new cities of Ibadan, Oyo, Abeokuta, Ijaye and Ilorin had grown to become the strongest states in Yorubaland from the 1820s to the 1840s, the Ife kingdom too had stirred itself. Under the influence of a radical youth movement advocating that Ife too should launch into an expansionist program (a movement of which the best known leader was a prince named Aderinsoye – or Aderin or Derin for short), Ife had developed a fairly strong military which, apart from defending its borders against some little encroachments by Ilesa, had turned its attention southwards to the Ondo kingdom in the deep southern forests. Earlier in the century, the people of Ondo had installed a very rich prince named Arilekolasi as their king, who, leaning heavily on his personal friends and large army of personally owned slaves, had proceeded to defy the traditional limitations on royal power, and institute a very unpopular despotism. This had provoked a revolt by the Ondo chiefs and prominent citizens, as a result of which Arilekolasi had been made to commit suicide in about 1845. In reaction to this, Arilekolasi's slaves, stationed at Oke-Igbo, had started a rebellion. In late 1845, taking advantage of this disruption in Ondo, the Ife forces had occupied the Ondo border town of Oke-Igbo and forced Ode-Ondo itself to be evacuated. But, from the southern forests of their kingdom, the Ondo people had kept up a stiff counter-attack that had gone on year after year. While this was happening in the southern forests, the Ife kingdom itself ran into serious trouble at home. In 1849, a violent conflict erupted between Ile-Ife and its twin town of Modakeke, caused partly by attempts by some prominent Ife lineages to limit Modakeke's access to farming land, and partly by unresolved questions about the status of Modakeke in the Ooni's kingdom. Angry crowds of Modakeke people burst into Ile-Ife, burning and destroying Ife houses. Ibadan intervened, calmed tempers, and made it possible for the people of Ile-Ife to rebuild their houses. Consequent upon this, both Modakeke and Ile-Ife (and by implication, all of the Ife kingdom) became dependencies of Ibadan, and Ibadan Ajeles were stationed in them and in the other towns of the kingdom.[5]

By 1859, then, Ibadan's first wave of campaigns had expelled Ilorin completely from the Ekiti and Igbomina countries and created an empire comprising most of the kingdoms of Ibarapa, Osun, Ife, Ijesa, Igbomina, Ibolo, Ekiti and Akoko. To the southwest, the city of Abeokuta blocked any possible Ibadan expansion. The kingdoms of the deep south – in Owo, Ondo, Ijebu, Awori – remained beyond Ibadan's control, and so too, did the towns and villages of the Yagba, Owe, Jumu, Bunu, Oworo and others near the Niger–Benue confluence. The Upper Ogun region and the country to the west of it were regarded as territory under Ijaye's influence. The city of Ilorin, with a narrow stretch of territory to the west and south of it (some of which territory was only reluctantly conceded by Ibadan), was consolidated as the new Ilorin kingdom. From this time on, Ilorin generally avoided direct confrontations with Ibadan's armies.

The primary secret of Ibadan's victories in all its campaigns was that it was always able to put much larger numbers of men in the field than any opponent. And that ability stemmed ultimately from what we must call the Ibadan dream. When Ibadan decided to launch a campaign to a given destination, the practice was to appoint a senior chief to lead it. For the inner core of his army, the chief had the men of his compound – his following. The chief would then seek other chiefs (of lower ranks) to join him with their followings. If the leading chief's reputation as a commander and leader was good, many lower-ranked chiefs would apply to him for a chance to serve under him. After leaving Ibadan, the army would have, in towns already under Ibadan's control, men waiting to join up. The latter would have been recruited and prepared by the Ajele in each town, with the help of the local ruler. There was usually no difficulty in raising these provincial additions to the army. The Ajele would put his energy into raising the men, because his reputation in Ibadan, and his future prospects, depended on it. The local ruler would cooperate with the Ajele – except if the ruler wanted to start a revolt (and that was too risky). As for the men sought for recruitment, more usually came forward than were needed. Almost everywhere, young men wanted to be part of the Ibadan adventure – an excitement that first infected the towns and villages of the Osun country and, slowly at first and then increasingly, grew in the Ife, Ekiti, Ijesa, Akoko and Igbomina towns and villages. Serving Ibadan held out a huge promise. If one attracted attention in the battles, one could end up in some position in Ibadan. Usually one would start as a junior chiefling in a chief's compound. Having thus become a notable man in a large compound, one had started the rise upwards in the Ibadan system – with one's compound and chief rooting for one. A chief had vested interests in the growth of his young men; as they progressed in the system, so too did his own influence. Growth for the young man could lead to any of many types of elevation – an appointment as Ajele in the provinces, an official envoy, a chief in Ibadan itself, etc. There was some preference for men from the provinces in the appointment of Ajeles. How high one rose from there depended, as earlier pointed out, on one's character and performance – plus, of course, the fortunes of one's compound. Once this picture of Ibadan became generally known, many men recruited into its armies in the provinces would not return home, but would go with some chiefs to Ibadan, there to start a career that could lead to unknown heights. And when an Ibadan army engaged in battle, its men fought with a fury that was fuelled by this Ibadan dream.

In other respects too, Ibadan's base for expansionist wars was very solid. Ibadan traders ensured an endless flow of arms and ammunition from the ports of Porto Novo, Lagos and Benin. Many of them built substantial fortunes from this trade. To purchase arms and ammunition, Ibadan chiefs sold some of their war captives to traders who took them for sale to the dwindling number of ships still engaged in the Atlantic slave trade. Increasingly, products of the land were also sold to buy the arms and ammunition. Of these, the leading product was palm oil, of which Ibadan became a major source, since it could procure supplies from all over the provinces of the Empire. Some Ibadan chiefs themselves owned or sponsored large caravans carrying pots of oil, in addition to the almost endless flow of caravans owned by Ibadan traders.

Food supply was also well provided for. At home in Ibadan, the people of the chiefs' compounds worked extensive farms. Most of the labor on such farms was supplied by enslaved war captives; but other members of the compounds also worked on the farms on a more or less regular basis. More will be said in the next chapter about trends in the development of farming in Ibadan and the rest of Yorubaland in the nineteenth century; suffice it to say here that the large population of Ibadan was very productive of farm crops, and that its large armies never had problems about food supply. Moreover, food supply for Ibadan armies was also heavily supplemented by food from the provinces. The Osun country served as the bread basket for most of Ibadan's earliest campaigns in Ekiti, Ijesa and Igbomina. Later, these provinces added substantial contributions of food themselves.[6]

The Ijaye War[7]

By the late 1850s then, Ibadan had become the greatest single power in Yorubaland. However, that eminence was not undisputed. Kurunmi of Ijaye, for one, disputed it vehemently. As would be remembered, Kurunmi as ruler of Ijaye had started off being friendly with the rulers of Ibadan and giving them help on many occasions. On their part, they had also shown much deference to Kurunmi on account of his being older and more famous than they. That was in the early years, the 1820s and 1830s. As Ibadan flourished from about 1840 and went on to conquer an empire, the relationship between Ijaye and Ibadan deteriorated from just cool to very hostile. Various factors contributed to that. Not only did the Ibadan chiefs cease respecting Kurunmi, they increasingly put it to him that their own leader was his superior. They demanded that, since the Basorun was senior to the Kakanfo in the traditional order, Kurunmi as Kakanfo should come to Ibadan to pay homage to the Basorun Oluyole. In 1854 a high-powered meeting of leaders of Ibadan, Ijaye, Abeokuta and Ijebu was held at Ibadan to decide to put an end to all wars and cease selling Yoruba people as slaves. Those decisions were taken, but no positive result followed. For Kurunmi, the fact that the meeting was held at Ibadan and not at Ijaye, and that the Ibadan rulers were generally treated as more important than he, became causes of resentment and outrage.

Behind all this growing hostility was the issue of territory. The Alaafin, Kurunmi and the Ibadan rulers had originally agreed to consign the Ekun Osi to Ibadan and the Ekun Otun to Ijaye, with the very clear understanding that the Alaafin would be king over both. Ibadan had gone on to expel Ilorin from the Ekun Osi and then gone far beyond to establish an empire for itself. Both Kurunmi and the Alaafin were alienated by this. But between Kurunmi and the Alaafin, territorial problems also developed, as Kurunmi set out to establish Ijaye's control over all of the Ekun Otun (mostly the Upper Ogun region) which, being close to Oyo, ought now, in the Alaafin's expectation, to be at least partly controlled by Oyo. As Kurunmi increasingly took control of the area and showed no readiness to concede much to the Alaafin, intense hostility brewed between the two. The situation became really explosive when Ibadan, having become the overlord of the Ekun Osi as well as of Ife, Ijesa, Ekiti, Igbomina and Akoko, began to show interest in the Upper Ogun area. Some towns in the area (notably the large town of Iseyin), attracted by Ibadan's greatness, began to gravitate towards it.

From this cauldron of bad blood, hostile actions began to issue – Ibadan against the Alaafin and Kurunmi, and Kurunmi against Ibadan and the Alaafin. When in one of such little acts of hostility on the farmlands a small Ibadan contingent was completely crushed by its Ijaye opponents, hostile feelings towards Ijaye became a raging fever in Ibadan. The Balogun Ibikunle who spoke up for conciliation with Kurunmi in the Ibadan council of chiefs was accused by his colleagues of (of all things!) cowardice, and was reprimanded and fined.

The stage was being set for a show-down between Ibadan and Ijaye. By and by, the Alaafin came to reckon that Kurunmi was a greater threat to his interests than Ibadan was, and tried some cooling of tempers towards Ibadan. As a result Ibadan tended to be intermittently well disposed towards the Alaafin. On one such occasion of good feeling towards the Alaafin, for instance, Ibadan chiefs, in 1855, invited the leaders of some Oyo towns and urged voluntary acceptance of allegiance to the Alaafin as well as peaceful relations with Abeokuta and the Ijebu kingdom.

The explosion finally came in 1860 when the Alaafin Atiba died and he was succeeded by his Aremo, Adelu. In his last days, Atiba had persuaded the Oyo chiefs to set aside the well-known traditional rule and to crown the Aremo after him. Atiba had also broached the matter to the Ibadan rulers and obtained their concurrence, but he had left Kurunmi, the Kakanfo, in the dark. Therefore, when Adelu was crowned Alaafin, Kurunmi flatly demanded that Adelu should die (as tradition demanded) and that another prince be crowned the Alaafin. He then greatly escalated hostile actions against the new Alaafin in the Upper Ogun area. War flared between Ibadan and Ijaye. Known to history as the Ijaye War, this war quickly developed into a siege of Ijaye by Ibadan. Abeokuta declared support for Ijaye and sent an army to its defence. For five years the fighting raged. Ijaye was reduced to starvation but its defenders, commanded by Kurunmi, known to be the greatest general in the land, held their city. When it looked as if Ijaye might crumble, Kurunmi's valiant sons threw themselves into a series of vicious attempts to break the siege – and all died in the bloody clashes. Then, in 1865, Kurunmi himself, advanced in age and broken-hearted, died – and the defenses of Ijaye collapsed. Ogunmola, then the Balogun of Ibadan, led the final charge into the doomed city, and personally saw to the total destruction of every bit of it, compound by compound. Ijaye's people scattered in all directions, a large portion fleeing to Abeokuta while others fled to Oyo and the towns of the Upper Ogun and even to Ibadan. In later years, as wild vegetation established itself over the once proud city of Ijaye, people coined the sad saying, "*Owo ope Ijaye I'a o ti beere ogun Ogunmola*" ("Only from palm trees growing in Ijaye at the time will the world ever be able to ask questions about Ogunmola's assault on Ijaye."). With the elimination of Ijaye, Ibadan at last became the undisputed dominant power in Yorubaland.

A Decade of Minor Wars: 1866–76

The decade following the Ijaye War (that is 1866–76) was a period of minor wars in various parts of Yorubaland. Most of these wars were campaigns whereby Ibadan consolidated its control over most of Yorubaland. These campaigns produced the man regarded by many as the greatest warrior chief and political leader of Ibadan in the nineteenth century – Momoh Obadoke Latoosa (alias Asubiaro). Latoosa had come to Ibadan as a young man from his village of Ilora, where he had been a farmer. Entering into service in Ogunmola's following, he gradually distinguished himself. By the time of the Ijaye War, he had become one of the foremost men in Ogunmola's command. He rose rapidly thereafter, and in 1871 was appointed the highest war chief of Ibadan, the Are Ona Kakanfo. A man of dazzling talents, considerable charisma, great political ambition and military brilliance, Latoosa came to rule over the Ibadan system with a completeness unknown before his time.

Conceding only a few towns to the Alaafin, Ibadan established control over the Upper Ogun region. This was done almost without any fighting, since Ibadan's dominance was so total that most towns in the area happily accepted its protection.

In the eastern provinces of the Ibadan Empire, in Ijesa, Ekiti and Igbomina, some towns had revolted against its overlordship while it had been preoccupied with the Ijaye War. As soon as the Ijaye War ended, Ibadan returned to clear up such pockets of revolt. The most important of such campaigns was the attack on Ilesa in 1868, resulting in a siege in which Ilesa was very stubbornly defended for months. This confrontation brought into the limelight an Ijesa warrior named Ogedemgbe who was the foremost hero in its defence. As a youth, Ogedemgbe had lived in Ibadan and served under one of the Ibadan chiefs, and had then returned home to organize for himself a similar following. At last, when it became obvious that the defence of Ilesa could no longer hold, the Ibadan army allowed Ogedemgbe to leave the city with his followers (known as the Ipaiye). Ilesa was then re-subdued. Ogedemgbe went to live at Itaogbolu in the Akure kingdom and, two years later, he had the satisfaction of joining with a southern Ekiti coalition, based in Igbo Alawun near Itaogbolu, to frustrate an Ibadan campaign against part of the Akure kingdom. In the heart of western Ekiti, Ibadan moved against the kingdom of Ara. The Ara people, warlike and proud, stoutly defended their city, and many months of siege followed. When Ibadan finally broke through Ara's defences, many of the prominent citizens of the town, rather than surrender, killed themselves and their families.

In these years also, Ibadan took steps to subdue a few kingdoms that had not been subdued before, the most notable of which were the Ado and Aiyede kingdoms in Ekiti. An army commanded by Latoosa, by then the Are Ona Kakanfo of Ibadan, suddenly veered off its course in the dry season of early 1873 (probably in the month of March) and entered into the Ado kingdom. After overrunning the villages of Igede and Uyin, the Ibadan army drew up against the city of Ado itself. Ado had had no reason to expect an Ibadan invasion, and its hurriedly mobilized defenses collapsed quickly. Large numbers of Ado people fled eastwards into the towns of the Gbonyin district or southwards to Ise. When Latoosa's commanders entered the Ewi's palace on the second morning, the tall regal person of Atewogboye, fully dressed in royal splendor, came out to them, and asked them to take him directly to Latoosa himself. When they answered that Latoosa had gone on to Ifaki some thirteen miles away, he insisted that they should take him to Latoosa there. Surprised to see the king, Latoosa received him with all the honors due to a king, rebuked the officers who had dared to bring him so far out of his palace, and sent him back with messengers carrying loads of gifts for him. Meanwhile, the news that the Ewi had left his palace with Ibadan officers had caused a wild stampede in the general population of Ado, with almost all the people fleeing to Gbonyin and to Ise. When the Ewi returned home, therefore, it was to a virtually empty town.

As for the Ibadan officers on the spot, apparently confused by Latoosa's treatment of the Ewi, they took no step to set up even a rudiment of Ibadan overlordship – no Ajele and no standing unit of troops. About two or three months later, in the spirit of the old hostility between Ado and Ikere, a small army came from Ikere and attempted to destroy what was left of Ado. It was the rainy season, and the flooded Ajilosun stream gave the invaders much trouble. Still, as the main body struggled with fording the stream, an advance guard reached the southern wall of Ado at the Ijigbo gate, where they assembled their large arsenal of guns and gunpowder – under the command of a man named Olaleetan, an Ibadan trader and adventurer and Ikere resident. Ado traditions represent Olaleetan as the leader of the invasion, but he was probably no more than the commander of the guards protecting its arms and ammunition. While this advance group waited for the main body coming up through the flooded stream, the remnants of people who had returned to Ado surprised and scattered them there, and captured their cache of arms and ammunition, as well as their commander, Olaleetan. The main body of invaders disintegrated and scattered, many perishing in the flood and the nearby swamps.

After that, running hostilities persisted in the farmlands between Ado and Ikere for over two decades, during which time a small force under a young man named Faparusi established itself on a hill between Ado and Ikere and defended Ado's farms. A further sequel to the Ibadan conquest of Ado was that the city of Ise was accused of seizing some of the Ado people who had fled there and selling some of them into slavery. Partly because of that, a coalition comprising two Ado war chiefs, Aduloju and Falowo, the Ijesa chief, Ogedemgbe, and some other Ekiti chiefs, laid siege to Ise in 1874 – until Ise fell in 1875.

In 1875, too, Ibadan finally moved to put an end to the independence of Esugbayibi's kingdom of Aiyede in northern Ekiti. The Ibadan army, led by

Latoosa himself, expected Esugbayibi to be difficult to crack, but what awaited them in northern Ekiti still surprised them. Under Esugbayibi's talented leadership, a fairly large coalition of some northern and central Ekiti forces waited for Latoosa at Ijesa-Iye near Isan. Latoosa had to take the field himself, and his Ibadan hordes scattered Esugbayibi and his allies from Ijesa-Iye. Esugbayibi retreated to Aiyede, and ordered his subjects to evacuate Aiyede and flee into hiding. He himself then fled with his soldiers to the thickly wooded hills of Omu and Ijelu. Latoosa followed him there and sent huge numbers of Ibadan soldiers to storm up the thorny wooded fastnesses of the Omu and Ijelu hills. Esugbayibi surrendered, and accepted for Aiyede the status of a tributary to Ibadan.

A division of the victorious Ibadan army, engaged in some small actions on its way back home through western Ekiti, was afflicted by a mysterious sickness which killed very many of the men. The Ibadan authorities believed that it was caused by poisons put in food and water by farmers in those parts. The event became known in Ibadan as *Ogun Wokuti* (the war in which dead bodies were piled up on road sides).

All these events in Ekiti amounted, however, to no more than scattered spots of war. By and large, the Ekiti, Ijesa and Igbomina provinces of the Ibadan Empire remained peaceful in these years, while Ibadan's control grew firmer and more detailed. In Akoko, Ibadan's provincial administration had always been rudimentary and patchy, Akoko being seen at Ibadan as a sort of distant frontier province. Not much improvement seems to have been effected in Ibadan's administration in this province in the years after the Ijaye War.

During these years, one phenomenon which had started to show up as early as the the first years of the 1860s in the Ijesa, Ekiti, Akoko and Igbomina provinces of the Ibadan Empire became very marked. Some of the most ambitious and capable of the provincial men who had gone to Ibadan and participated in the Ibadan system, returned, after some years, to their homes, and established personal followings – in imitation of the Ibadan chiefs. A few ambitious men who had never left home, also followed suit. There were very many of these new leaders, but the best remembered are Ogedemgbe, Arimoro and Ogunmodede in Ilesa, Aduloju and Falowo in Ado (Ekiti), Fajembola in Egosi (in the Oye kingdom), Odu in Ogbagi (Akoko), Bakare in Afa (Akoko), Fabunmi in Okemesi, Adeyale in Ila (Igbomina), Apampalaso in Omuo, Faboro in Ido, Akata in Ijero, Agada in Efon, Oluborode in Ikogosi, Apoti in Ipetu-Ijesha, Are in Otun, Samo in Akure, Ayikiti and Prince Aderin in Ife.[8]

Almost all of these people built up large followings by attracting to themselves their young relatives and other youths. Some, like Fabunmi, transformed their age-grade associations into militant groups. Most augmented their followings by marrying many wives and raising large families and by buying healthy young war captives. Almost invariably, men who entered these groups as captives or slaves grew to become well-established persons and raised families of their own – within the group. Many of the leaders turned their large groups to farming and became rich thereby. Some (like Fajembola who lived in Egosi, a major trading center in the Oye kingdom in Ekiti) used their groups to venture strongly into trade and became very rich. Almost all gave some military training to men in their followings and built up an arsenal of guns and gunpowder, and some actually used them all in some military activity. In particular, those of Ekiti and Akoko were usually drawn into fighting the Nupe in the Akoko country as well as in the countries of the Yagba and others in the far northeast. For instance, Aduloju established his base at Imesi-Lasigidi in the district of the Ado kingdom closest to Akoko, and from there went to fight the Nupe in Akoko and the country to the north. Some who were descendants of chiefly lineages were honored with their forebears' chieftaincy titles in the traditional political system of their home kingdoms. Of the latter, the most notable was the prince who, after returning to Otun and acquiring much influence, was later crowned the Oore of Otun, choosing the cognomen Okinbaloye.

Wherever these men lived; they stood out in society and were highly respected and influential. In general they were known as Ologun (war chief). Soon, many young men who had not been to Ibadan at all began to adopt these people's ways – each establishing a following, building a new compound (separate from the compound in which they had grown up), and becoming rich, powerful and influential. Of such men, one was Esugbayibi (later the founder of Aiyede), another was Aso Ogundana in Ikole; in the last decades of the nineteenth century, a number of young men emerged in the Ado kingdom as Ologun – the most notable among them being Oso Akerele, Agbemu, and Faparusi (who became a hero for his prolonged defense of Ado farms in the direction of Ikere). In short, then, the political and social system which had evolved in Ibadan became the base from which a new type of elite class arose in the eastern regions of Yorubaland.

In the other regions of the country, the war between Ife and Ondo continued in the Ondo kingdom, resulting in the destruction of some Ondo villages. This war was to be the cause of the first British intervention in the politics of the Yoruba interior. From 1869, the British administration of Lagos (which had become a British colony in 1861) sent a number of missions to the Ondo country, to explore ways of restoring peace there. The British objective was to open a new trade route from Lagos to the Yoruba interior through the Ilaje, Ikale and Ondo countries, a route that would be free from the political troubles that plagued the routes through the Ijebu and Egba countries. In 1872, a senior official of the British administration of Lagos, Roger Goldsworthy, persuaded Ondo and Ife to put an end to hostilities. The Ondo people resettled Ode-Ondo, although Ife would not yet agree to give up Oke-Igbo. With the restoration of peace, Lagos traders streamed to take advantage of the new route through Ondo.[9]

From about 1870, Ibadan at last began, from northern Ekiti, to enter into the countries of the Okun Yoruba – the Yagba, Owe, Jumu, Bunu, Ikiri and Oworo in the farthest northeastern corner of Yorubaland, an area which the Ibadan people referred to as Ile Iyagba – that is, the land of the Yagba. The foreign enemies here were the Nupe, but the Ibadan authorities never clearly figured out what to do about them. In principle, Ibadan wanted the Nupe out of the whole area and desired control over all its towns and villages. But Masaba, ruler of the Nupe emirate of Bida, was engaged in very adroit diplomacy in many directions and appeared sincerely desirous of friendship with Ibadan. Among Ibadan leaders, therefore, the mood was that this ruler could become an Ibadan ally against the Ilorin – or that, at least, he should not be provoked into becoming an Ilorin ally against Ibadan. All this tended to create confusion for Ibadan's men in the field, so that while some Ibadan forces fought the Nupe in some places, others ignored Nupe activities in other places, and still others collaborated with Nupe forces in yet other places.[10] Back home in Ibadan, meanwhile, the whole area was usually counted as part of the Ibadan empire, even though the type of massive effort that could have cleared the Nupe out was never given consideration. One Ibadan chief did propose such an effort. Chief Ayorinde, as would be remembered, had lived in exile in Owo and had helped Ibadan's war efforts from there. In the late 1860s, he moved to Irun in Akoko and began operations against the Nupe in Ile Iyagba, seizing some villages from them. He then, in the 1870s, asked Ibadan for reinforcements to enable him push the Nupe out. However, not only did his plan run foul of the prevailing mood among the Ibadan leaders, he himself was not trusted in Ibadan – as rumors were circulating that he intended to create an independent state for himself in the northeast.

In the event, many of the war chiefs of Ekiti and Akoko developed ambitions, and became active, in Ile Iyagba – as well as even in Akoko. Between Aduloju and the younger warrior, Ogedemgbe, who had been acquaintances in Ibadan, a close friendship developed in these years. Still unable or unwilling to return home to Ilesa, Ogedemgbe lived in the Ekiti and Akoko area and was a frequent visitor to Aduloju's camp at Imesi-Lasigidi. The two of them, and Falowo, ultimately formed an alliance, with the very ambitious objective of driving the Nupe out of all northeastern Yorubaland (that is Akoko and Ile Iyagba, or Okun Yoruba, territories), and replacing Ibadan's control with their own.

Taking advantage of gaps and soft spots in Ibadan's establishment, Aduloju and Falowo subdued a few Akoko villages before striking boldly northwards into Ile Iyagba. Their most celebrated success against the Nupe occurred at Egga far to the north. On their return to Akoko, they joined with Ogedemgbe to start a siege against the important market town of Idoani in the Owo kingdom. Apparently, their purpose was to establish this town as the center from which they would carve out a new state comprising parts of Akoko, parts of Akoko-Edo, most of the Okun Yoruba territories, and possibly parts of the Owo kingdom. Unassisted by Owo, Idoani held on stoutly for more than a year, and finally fell in late 1876. Not long after that, some allied troops set out from Idoani for an attack on the city of Owo itself. Their venture turned out to be ill-fated. Outside Owo, they fell into a well laid ambush and perished almost to a man, and Ogedemgbe and the other leaders of the alliance hurried to deny knowledge of the venture.[11]

From Idoani, the allies then entered into Akoko-Edo and the neighboring provinces of the Benin kingdom. Subduing village after village and encountering no real resistance, they moved closer and closer to the city of Benin. According to Akoko, Akoko-Edo, Idoani and Ekiti traditions, they ultimately began to think of continuing all the way to Benin and subduing that famous city itself. However, talk of attacking Benin increasingly generated nervousness among their men. Finally at a village called Iruekpen, Ogedemgbe's singer, a man named Oniku (a citizen of Ise in Ekiti), voiced the men's misgivings in a song, and urged the leaders to let the men forage for booty and turn back. At first angry with Oniku, the leaders later thought the matter over and decided to return to Idoani.[12]

Back in Akoko, Aduloju took some more villages and then retired to Imesi-Lasigidi to commence large-scale preparations for a siege of Afa, one of the strongest towns in Akoko. Soon after, messages began to circulate in Ekiti, urging all Ekiti people to rise and unite to drive out the men of Ibadan. A very major phase in the nineteenth century wars was about to start.

Anti-Ibadan Wars of Resistance[13]

That major phase of the wars opened with a big bang in Ibadan on Monday, July 30, 1877. On that day, after massive and careful preparations, Ibadan declared war on Abeokuta. Next morning, an army larger than Ibadan had ever sent out on any campaign, bristling with confidence and wildly cheered by large crowds of Ibadan people, marched out towards Abeokuta. It was led by Momoh Latoosa, the Are Ona Kakanfo, by then the most dreaded war commander in all of Yorubaland.

According to Ibadan's plans, this was to be a short sharp war to destroy or subdue Abeokuta and thus eliminate Abeokuta's control of the trade routes to Egbado and the ports of Porto Novo and Lagos. Following the Ijaye War, all states still independent in Yorubaland had increasingly stood in fear of Ibadan. It seemed only a matter of time before Ibadan would conquer Abeokuta and even Ijebu-Ode and Ilorin, and the small kingdoms of the Egbado country. The Alaafin's pretensions about being the king over Ibadan had become completely meaningless; indeed, the Ibadan chiefs increasingly treated the Alaafin as a vassal, demanding of him gifts and services that only a vassal would give to an overlord. The Alaafin dared not oppose Ibadan openly, and so he became a secret enemy, surreptitiously giving encouragement to Ibadan's enemies. Abeokuta tightened control on the trade routes through its territory, and Ijebu-Ode, after some hesitation, followed suit – all in order to curtail Ibadan's access to guns and gunpowder from the coast. Ibadan's efforts to persuade Abeokuta, especially, achieved nothing. Therefore, the Ibadan chiefs, after satisfying themselves that the Ijesa, Ife, Ekiti, Akoko and Igbomina provinces were peaceful and under good control, decided to change the Egba situation by force. Hence the declaration of war in July 1877. Latoosa was confident that success would come very quickly. This, he thought, was the war that would end all wars.

Immediately, things began to go against Ibadan's expectations. Rather than end quickly, the campaign against Abeokuta met strong resistance and dragged on – until days became weeks and weeks became months. Ibadan took steps to make friends with Ijebu-Ode in order to isolate Abeokuta and ensure that the routes through Ijebu would be kept open. Again, after a short vacillation (caused by the opposition of the Ijebu traders to any closing of the routes), the Ijebu-Ode government took its decision. The Awujale Ademiyewo Fidipote accused Ibadan of aspiring to become master of the whole world (that is, the Yoruba world), and ordered more stringent closure of Ijebu routes against Ibadan traders. Ibadan sent an army to force the Ijebu routes open; the Ijebu army met it at the Ijebu border town of Oru, and a second front to the war emerged.

Meanwhile, the people of the Ekiti, Ijesa, Igbomina and Akoko provinces of the Ibadan Empire had watched all these developments with interest. In 1878 the Ekiti revolted. The trouble started in the small kingdom of Okemesi (then known as Imesi-Igboodo). Reacting to the Ibadan Ajele's assault of a woman who was prince Fabunmi's wife or the wife of his close relative, prince Fabunmi attacked the Ajele's residence, killed the Ajele and some of his officials and hangers-on, and burnt down the house. Knowing that Ibadan would respond with a punitive mission, Fabunmi dispatched urgent messages to all parts of Ekiti, urging the kings and war chiefs to rise and destroy the agents of Ibadan's rule in their towns and villages. The response was immediate almost everywhere.

Ibadan Ajeles were set upon and killed or forced to flee. In a few terrible days, the network of Ibadan's provincial administration in Ekiti vanished.

Leaders all over Ekiti knew, however, that Ibadan commanded the means of returning with devastating vengeance. Consequently, they moved the revolt to a higher level. The war chiefs mobilized their men and headed for Fabunmi's Okemesi, in the border hills of northwestern Ekiti, and many of the kings sent high-powered envoys. Days of serious meetings followed. Before the meetings ended, the decision was taken to form a confederacy known as Ekitiparapo. Fabunmi was appointed commander-in-chief of the Ekitiparapo armed forces, and teams of men were sent to all parts of Ekiti to appeal for more men, and for contributions of food, guns and gunpowder. Other teams were sent beyond Ekiti to war chiefs, rulers and prominent persons in Ijesa, Igbomina and Akoko. From all these places, troops, food and war materials flowed to Okemesi. When the two most famous war chiefs in these provinces – Aduloju and Ogedemgbe – did not show up, strong messages were sent to them (to Aduloju at Imesi-Lasigidi, and to Ogedemgbe at Idoani). Meanwhile, the decision was taken not to wait for Ibadan to attack, but to take to the offensive, with the objective of marching through Osun to Ibadan and taking the city. Envoys were sent to Ilorin to seek its support and the Emir, after hesitating for some time out of fear of Ibadan, promised to send an army to join up with the Ekitiparapo forces.

When they were finally satisfied that their forces were reasonably ready, the Ekitiparapo leadership ordered their men to march down the road through the old kingdom of Imesi-Ile, to Igbajo. At Igbajo, an Ijesa border town strongly defended by an Ibadan garrison, they met their first resistance. They overcame the opposition and took Igbajo. Then they rolled down the hills to the plains of the Osun Valley and headed for Ikirun, the largest town in this part of the valley. Here, they faced their first big trial. Even with the help of the Ilorin contingents, they did not have enough forces to surround the big town fully; so they held the eastern and northern parts of the Ikirun walls, apparently hoping that they would have enough time to move up the troops being formed behind them and completely surround Ikirun.

In Ibadan meanwhile, the authorities decided to take firm steps to meet the Ekitiparapo challenge, and a large army was sent out under the command of the Balogun Ajayi Jegede (better known by his nickname Ogboriefon). Ogboriefon easily entered Ikirun from the southwest and early the next morning, he took the field against the Ekitiparapo confederacy and their Ilorin allies. The Ekitiparapo and Ilorin forces seem to have had some difficulty with coordinating, which gave Ogboriefon a good chance to scatter and decimate them in one single day. Of the many prominent men lost in the day, the most painful to the confederacy was prince Adeyale of Ila. The Ilorin troops and many others fled directly north. When they came to the small Otin river a short distance to the north of Ikirun, it was unexpectedly flooded. Hotly pressed from behind, many plunged into the flood and drowned – so much so that the bodies of men and horses formed a bridge for later arrivals to run or gallop over. From this, the battle earned the name Ogun Jalumi (the war in which men plunged into a flooded river and perished).

Most of the Ekiti, Ijesa and Igbomina forces fled northeastwards in the direction of Ekan and Otun. Ogboriefon followed them in hot pursuit. In town after town they rallied and tried to fight back, but Ogboriefon's forces were just too strong and too fast for them. It looked as if nothing could save the rebellious provinces from the might of Ibadan. However, as the victorious Ibadan forces stood outside Ekan, ready for the assault, urgent messages arrived from Latoosa in Ibadan, ordering Ogboriefon to return home. Ogboriefon and his men gave up the pursuit and started off for Ibadan.

Latoosa's orders saved the Ekitiparapo. Apparently, he did not think much of their capabilities, and attached much more importance to the war against Abeokuta and Ijebu. He was soon to be proved wrong. In the days and months that followed, the Ekitiparapo, operating mostly out of Otun in northern Ekiti, picked together the shattered pieces of their organization and military machine, mobilized more support, and got ready to move again. They tried everything, but failed, to persuade Aduloju to come and lead them; they even sent some troops to the aid of Afa (which Aduloju had besieged) in order to frustrate him there, in the hope that the old warrior would then come to fight for them. But even after Afa fell, Aduloju did not leave Imesi-Lasigidi. He considered himself too old for the big venture that the Ekitiparapo had taken on; even the Ekitiparapo messengers reported that he was so old that he could no longer see well. Falowo wanted to go, and sent messengers to tell the Ewi so; unfortunately, while preparing to leave, he died as a result of an accident, and his followers, led by two young men named Agbemu and Oso Akerele, were too dispirited by the loss of their leader to venture out. As for Ogedemgbe, he finally decided to go – after much hesitation, and after seemingly endless questions about the true level of resolve among the Ekitiparapo leaders. When Ogedemgbe finally arrived, the much younger and much less experienced warrior, Fabunmi, gladly surrendered to him the position of commander-in-chief. Early in 1879, the Ekitiparapo forces finally marched again, down the same road as they had done in the previous year.

After easily overrunning Igbajo, they again advanced on Ikirun. Outside the walls of Ikirun, a large Ibadan army, led by the Seriki from Ibadan, confronted them. A number of minor engagements followed. Then, rather than wait for a major engagement, the Ekitiparapo forces retreated in perfect order back up the hills and past the ruins of Igbajo. In the farmland between Igbajo and Imesi-Ile, they stopped, chose a defensible position, and dug in to await the Ibadan army. When the Ibadan army came, it was much larger than the Ekitiparapo army, and it was by then led by no less a commander than Latoosa himself. After the Ibadan army threw itself against the Ekitiparapo position a few times without much effect, it became obvious that the two armies would be there for some time, facing each other. It turned out to be a long time, punctuated almost daily by fierce battles. By 1880, the two camps had developed features of regular towns – each with a large marketplace, workshops (mostly blacksmiths' workshops), and extensive farms in the surrounding farmlands.

Soon after the war started, important help was offered the Ekitiparapo from an outside source. Since early in the nineteenth century, a community of persons returning from slavery in the Americas and recaptives (people freed from captured slave ships) whom the British had resettled in Sierra Leone (all known as emigrants), had been settling in Lagos. After the Ekitiparapo was formed in the interior, the Ekiti and Ijesa among the emigrants in Lagos formed themselves into an Ekitiparapo Association, Lagos. The traders among them used their commercial connections to procure for the Ekitiparapo army some new types of fire-arms which were then unknown to West Africa – breech-loading guns like Snider rifles, Martini Henry rifles, and Winchester repeaters, all new developments in fire-arms technology in Europe. The possession of these new guns gave the Ekitiparapo some superiority in the daily battles for some months, and created considerable distress in the Ibadan camp. But neither side was able to dislodge the other, and the stand-off continued. After some time, too, the Ibadan army got some supply of the new guns.

The Ekitiparapo won the diplomatic battles almost overwhelmingly, since all other significant centers of power in Yorubaland were afraid of Ibadan and desired that Ibadan should be humbled. Diplomatic agents of Ibadan and the Ekitiparapo traversed the country tirelessly, and came across each other in many places. Ilorin reaffirmed its alliance with the Ekitiparapo, and it was strengthened with an exchange of some troops between the allies. Ilorin also stationed a large army just north of Offa, to wait for an opportunity to intervene actively. Throughout the war, the Ekitiparapo leaders occasionally had reason to doubt the sincerity and intentions of their Ilorin allies, but the alliance did hold together till the end. In Ijebu, the Awujale Ademiyewo Fidipote unswervingly rejected all overtures from Ibadan (against the insistent opinions of the leading Ijebu traders) and made it clear that he supported the struggle of the Ekitiparapo. In 1882, Ife revolted against Ibadan and declared support for the Ekitiparapo. In response, Ibadan sent a small army to join with Modakeke to sack Ile-Ife, forcing the people of Ile-Ife to withdraw to a village called Isoya.

The Ekitiparapo sent an army under Fabunmi assisted by Arimoro (an Ijesa chief), and the Awujale sent an army under the Seriki Ogunsigun, to the aid of Ife, and a new war front emerged on Ife soil. The Alaafin established secret contacts with the Ekitiparapo and frequently sent them messages of encouragement. Openly, however, he had to appear to support Ibadan – but the Ibadan leaders had good reason to believe that he secretly supported the Ekitiparapo, and frequently threatened him on that account. Abeokuta remained at war with Ibadan. Ekitiparapo agents made strenuous efforts to persuade the Osemowe of Ondo to bar Ibadan traders and supporters from the newly opened routes through the Ondo country. But Ibadan's agents were very busy in the palace of the Osemowe too. The outcome was that the Osemowe, while making it clear that he endorsed the aspirations of the Ekitiparapo, chose not to take sides but to allow all parties free use of the routes through his kingdom. However, Ife territory lay north of Ondo, and the Ondo routes therefore passed through Ife territory; and with the revolt of Ife against Ibadan in 1882, Ibadan experienced increasing difficulties on these routes. In the far southeast, Ekitiparapo agents also worked hard to persuade the Olowo of Owo to deny Ibadan traders the use of the routes through Owo to Benin. Just as in Ondo, Ibadan agents worked hard in Owo too. In the end, the Olowo adopted the same posture as the Osemowe; but Ibadan had serious troubles on the routes through Owo since the northern reaches of those routes all passed through territories of the Ekitiparapo.

In late 1882, a slight break occurred in the nearly solid front against Ibadan. The strong class of Ijebu traders, who had always complained that the blockade of the Ijebu routes hurt their trade, at last won the support of Chief Onafowokan, the Balogun of Ijebu forces. Faced by a revolt of influential citizens championed by the Balogun, the Awujale Fidipote fled into exile. The Balogun then opened the routes, thus allowing Ibadan traders to pass through. However, even he was so distrustful of Ibadan that he kept the army intact and ready at Oru. The ultimate benefits to Ibadan of the Ijebu situation turned out to be very little. Abeokuta immediately started raids into Ijebu in order to disrupt the routes there, while the Seriki Ogunsigun and his army near Ife continued to uphold the policies of the exiled Awujale.

The sum total of the results of the diplomatic contests, then, was that while the Ekitiparapo won allies, supporters and sympathizers, Ibadan won virtually none. In effect, indeed, the Ekitiparapo became the front-line prosecutors of a broadly based national war against the awesome dominance of Ibadan. That national war saddled Ibadan with the stand-off with the Ekitiparapo, with other engagements with Abeokuta on the Abeokuta farms, with Ijebu at Oru, with Ilorin at Offa, with Ekitiparapo, Ife and Ijebu in Ife. From the 1880s, the Fon kingdom of Dahomey added to Ibadan's burdens. Dahomey had launched major attacks on Abeokuta in 1851 and again in 1864, and had been repulsed on both occasions. Dahomey had also been fighting with Abeokuta over the Egbado towns. Now taking advantage of Ibadan's preoccupation with wars on many fronts, Dahomey began harassing the Upper Ogun region of the Ibadan empire (the towns of Iganna, Okeho and others), and continued to do so until the 1890s. As far as the war between Ibadan and the Ekitiparapo was concerned, Ibadan's multiple commitments and problems made it possible for the Ekitiparapo to stand in the field, head to head with the mighty Ibadan, indefinitely.

As would already be obvious from all the above, the stand-off between Ibadan and the Ekitiparapo in the farmlands between Imesi-Ile and Igbajo occupied center stage in the political life of Yorubaland throughout the last two decades of the nineteenth century. Generally known as the Kiriji War (a name derived from the noise of guns in the daily battles, especially the noise of the ricochet from the new high-velocity rifles), it caught and held the attention of all Yoruba people.

By 1885, both sides in the Kiriji War had started to show signs of war-weariness. Then in that year, Latoosa died in the Ibadan camp, and the affairs of the Ibadan war effort fell into the hands of much lesser men than he. The situation was ripe for a cessation of war. Consequently, persons representing the British government of Lagos, assisted by CMS emigrant pastors, came to the Kiriji War front in 1886 and succeeded in persuading the Ibadan and Ekitiparapo leaders to agree to terms of peace, resulting in the 1886 Treaty of Peace signed by the Ibadan chiefs and the war chiefs and some of the kings of the Ekitiparapo. The same commissioners went to Ife and worked out a treaty of peace there.

Neither of these treaties, however, brought the war situation to an end. Though Ibadan and the Ekitiparapo adhered to the terms of the treaty and abstained from further fighting, neither side trusted the other well enough to be willing to be the first to start breaking up camp. As a result, the two sides sat there facing each other for seven more years. As for the treaty in Ife, its most important provision – namely, that the people of Modakeke should disband their town and relocate westwards near to Ibadan – proved unacceptable to the majority of Modakeke people. Therefore, the situation around Ife remained unchanged: Modakeke kept its place, Ile-Ife people continued staying at Isoya, and the Ibadan, Ekitiparapo and Ijebu armies stayed put, though no further fighting occurred.

In the far north, in the area immediately south of Ilorin, some change in the line-up took place in 1887. Apparently wrongly believing that the era of wars had ended, the people of Offa let a dispute over the succession to the throne of the Olofa get out of hand. The commotion between the contending parties became so bad that the Ibadan defenders of Offa, rather than let themselves be drawn into it, left the town in disgust and withdrew south to Ikirun. One of the Offa parties then jubilantly invited the Ilorin army (that had long camped a short distance to the north) into Offa. The Ilorin army entered, and its leading commander, Karara, the Balogun Gambari, ordered that all the chiefs and prominent citizens of both Offa parties be assembled and slaughtered. Karara's army then viciously looted and took possession of Offa. Thereafter, Ilorin resumed hostile thrusts towards the south – into the country between Offa and Ikirun. However, the Ibadan army at Ikirun continued to be a terror to Ilorin. In these circumstances, the Ilorin activities consisted merely of flash raids, which were quickly abandoned as soon as Ibadan troops appeared. These activities continued until 1893. In the years following the collapse of Offa also, the Ilorin chiefs sent some representatives of theirs to some Igbomina towns, and behaved as if such towns were subject to Ilorin – and this caused much disappointment and anger in the Ekitiparapo camp.

For the Ekitiparapo leaders, the years 1886–93 were years of careful watching of Ibadan's actions, and of considering how to handle Ilorin's pretensions. They were therefore years of deliberations about the future of the Ekitiparapo Confederacy. Concerning this, many ideas emerged in their deliberations, but ultimately the most popular was that the populations of Ekiti, Ijesa, Igbomina and Akoko be relocated into a few large cities comparable to Ibadan. This envisaged the abandonment of all old towns and villages and the moving of their residents to the few large cities, strategically located. The objective was to ensure that the people of the Ekitiparapo territories would ever in the future be able to preserve their freedom against Ibadan or Ilorin or the Nupe or any other aggressors. Before this massive program could be embarked upon, however, the Ekitiparapo camp had to be broken up in 1893, and all its chiefs and people had to return to their homes.

The years 1892–3 saw the termination of all major wars – as European powers along the West African coast embarked on seizing territories in the hinterland. The scramble by European countries for African territorial possessions had begun. In 1892, the British sent a military expedition to conquer the Ijebu country and make its routes open to Lagos, and the French conquered the Fon kingdom of Dahomey and the Aja country. Early in 1893, some senior officials of the British colony of Lagos came into the interior, made a treaty with Ibadan, got Ibadan to return its armies home, and saw to the disbanding of the Kiriji War camps. All thoughts that wars might be resumed in the future, and all thoughts of the Ekitiparapo leaders for the future of their confederacy, quickly dissipated as the British and other Europeans established their rule over all of Yorubaland.

The Last Wars

Only in the far northeastern Yorubaland, in the homeland of the small subgroups (Yagba, Jumu, Bunu, Oworo, etc.) which Ibadan called Ile Iyagba, was the fire of war still burning after 1893. In this corner of Yorubaland, the years of the Kiriji War had witnessed a great expansion and intensification of Nupe raids, together with some elaboration of Nupe control in some places. Nupe raids and capture of people for slaves had caused the emergence of many refugee settlements. It had also generated very intense anti-Nupe hostility, not only in these Yoruba towns, villages and settlements, but over a much larger area including neighboring Afenmai and Ebira countries. As Nupe traders, troops, and persons representing Nupe control were routinely attacked and killed everywhere, the position of the Nupe gradually weakened. The climax to these generalized acts of resistance had occurred in 1885 when, outside the Iyagba town of Ife, local farmers had ambushed and brutally killed an important Nupe prince – Audu Bida – from Bida, and the group of people in his company. In response, Bida had prepared a major invasion – and the leading persons all over the Okun Yoruba towns and villages had called for a unified front to resist.

In 1894, in a refugee settlement named Ogidi, representatives of the various oppressed subgroups and communities met and formed a grand alliance for the purpose of liberating their country from the Nupe. This Ogidi Alliance borrowed its organization, strategies and tactics from ideas of the Ekitiparapo, and, at its peak, it commanded forces drawn from the Ijumu, Iyagba, Oworo, Owe, Ikiri, Bunu, and even Akoko and some Ekiti – with some support from even the neighboring Ebira. The various northeastern Yoruba communities wiped out all traces of Nupe control and claims by killing Nupe agents or by forcing them to flee, as young men flooded to join the armed forces of the Alliance. The Nupe forces, led by their cavalry, confidently expected that they would quickly disperse the forces of the Alliance. But, in fact, in the fighting that ensued, the Alliance forces, continually enlarged by the arrival of more fighting men, grew steadily stronger than the Nupe forces. Fighting in fervently hostile territory, the Nupe troops increasingly found their movements restricted and their food supply in jeopardy. Their increasing use of force to seize food from farmers only heightened the hostility and the consequent difficulties. In contrast, the morale of the Alliance was boosted by its improving strength in manpower, food supply, and widespread local support, and by encouraging showings against the Nupe forces in the frequent engagements. After some months of fighting, the leaders of the Alliance became so confident of victory that they even began to consider plans for advancing into the Nupe country itself in order to destroy Bida and free their people who were being held as slaves there.

While the conflict thus raged, a small constabulary of the British agency that was taking over the lands of the Niger, the Royal Niger Company, appeared in that part of the country. In June 1896, it clashed with elements of the Nupe forces and lost many of its men. Thereupon, the Royal Niger Company prepared for major operations against the Nupe. Assisted with men, food and intelligence by the Ogidi Alliance and by the general population of the anti-Nupe communities, Royal Niger Company forces advanced on Bida in January 1897. Surprised, the Nupe forces disengaged from their fight against the Ogidi Alliance and retreated to their own country, but they failed to save Bida. Bida capitulated on January 31, 1897. Nupe pressure on northeastern Yorubaland thus came to an end. The Ogidi Alliance was disbanded, and so were most of the refugee settlements of the area. Crowds of enslaved men and women freed themselves and returned home from the Nupe country. With that, the last of the wars in Yorubaland in the nineteenth century came to an end.[14]

Effects of the Wars

The first visible effect of the Yoruba Wars of the nineteenth century was the widespread destruction of cities, towns and villages. For some 700 years the Yoruba people had built cities and towns all over their country; in the course of one century they smashed many of the biggest and best of them. The areas most profoundly affected were the territories of the Oyo, Egba and Owu subgroups. The great city of Oyo-Ile, for two centuries the greatest and most prestigious city of the Yoruba people, perished completely. So did many other cities in the Oyo homeland – for instance Ikoyi, Kuwo, Igbogun. Owu-Ipole, the proud city of the Olowus, and the Egba royal towns of Ake, Oko, Kesi, Iddo, Ilugun, all suffered the same fate, not to count the many small Owu and Egba towns that were obliterated. Ijaye, the old trading town of the Egba people, revived and flourished for some five decades, and then was wiped out. Even the ancient sacred city of Ile-Ife ("the place from which the sun rises") did not avoid the nineteenth century depredations. Torn down twice over, however, it managed to rise again each time. For a people who pride themselves as builders of, and dwellers in, large cities and towns, it is surprising how easily the Yoruba people allowed themselves in the nineteenth century to plunge into the destruction of the proud icons of their history. One resident of Lagos (who had probably visited the interior, especially towns in eastern Yorubaland), lamented, in a letter to a Lagos newspaper, the shattered towns and palaces, with the following lines quoted from a poem:

> The spider holds the veil in the palace of Caesar,
>
> The owl stands sentinel on the watchtower of Afrasiab.[15]

On June 4, 1851, some weeks after the CMS missionary, David Hinderer, started his Christian mission in Ibadan, he toured the ruins of Owu-Ipole. And he noted in his diary:

> This afternoon, I rode out to the place of old Owu which is only two miles from my lodging. Owu was an old very large town … It was destroyed about thirty years ago and is now converted into farms by the Ibadan people but main ruins still remain … To think of the awful and bloody scenes such a large place must have witnessed at the time of its destruction makes one shudder and feel indignant.[16]

And William H. Clarke, who visited Ila in 1858, wrote the following sad comment on the condition of the Orangun of Ila, whom he described as "the monarch of Igbomina":

> If there is a being that deserves our pity and sympathy, it is the unfortunate one whom the ravages of time have reduced from opulence and power to a state of poverty and penury. Such seemed to be the condition of the monarch of Igbomina. Whatever the country and capital may have been in its palmy days, there are marks sufficiently evident to prove that those days are no more, that the power of royalty is lost and the kingdom exists only in name.[17]

The human suffering consequent upon all the devastation and acts of war was grave. The seemingly endless battles and raids resulted in the scattering of countless lineages and families, and in the loss and destitution of many of their members. Persons torn from their roots and homes, and wandering without clear destinations, constituted a large pool of vulnerable targets for adventurers and criminal kidnappers in most parts of the country. Even among groups managing to flee in some order, loss, deprivation and destitution were common experiences. Intense distress bred brigandage, disloyalty and perfidy, manifesting in kidnappings, the sale of friends by friends, and callous reward of hospitality and kindness with vileness and terror. In many parts of the country, refugee settlements sprang up, each the scene of hard struggles by individuals and groups to survive. The traditional norm of respect for peaceful traders on highways survived quite well in most parts, but greatly increased hazards from acts of war and crime increased the frequency and sizes of traders' caravans as a mode of travel. On the whole, for probably most of the century, the incidence of human distress would seem to have been greater in the Oyo and Igbomina provinces in the north, and the broad middle belt stretching from Ife westwards into the Egbado country. From about the 1880s, the extreme northeastern region of Yorubaland, under Nupe pressure, witnessed greatly increased distress also.

The wars and the accompanying raids, brigandage and kidnappings, resulted in the enslavement of countless Yoruba men, women and children. Most, in the early parts of the century, came from the Oyo and Igbomina areas – consequent upon the disruptive conflicts in the Oyo country, the Nupe raids in Igbomina, Afonja's campaigns in Igbomina and Oyo (1817–24), and the campaigns of post-Afonja Ilorin in the Oyo homeland and in the Ibolo country (1824–36). With the Owu War (1817–22), the spate of enslavement entered into the Yoruba midlands – the countries of Ife, Owu, Egba and northern Ijebu. The years of the sharpest increase in enslavements, as well as exportation of Yoruba slaves, then, were the years from about 1817 to about 1830, reaching a peak in 1826. Thereafter, the conflicts between Ibadan and Abeokuta (with frequent Ijebu and Ijaye interventions), the campaigns of Kurunmi's Ijaye, the war between Ibadan and Ijaye, the Dahomey and Abeokuta campaigns in Egbado, widened the area of enslavements in central and western Yorubaland. From the 1850s, Ilorin's campaigns in Igbomina, Ekiti and Ijesa, and Ibadan's campaigns of expansion eastwards, resulted in the enslavement of large numbers of Ijesa, Ekiti, Akoko and Igbomina people. Ibadan armies regularly arrived back in Ibadan with thousands of enslaved captives, and a number of slave markets sprang up in Ibadan city. From about 1850, the number of Yoruba slave exports began to decline markedly; by 1867, it stopped completely. But that did not mean the end of enslavements; it only meant that enslaved war captives were absorbed into productive enterprises in Yorubaland itself. From the 1870s, Ibadan, Nupe, Ilorin campaigns and raids in the countries of the Yagba, Oworo, Owe, Ijumu, Gbede, Ikiri, Abunu of northeastern Yorubaland, as well as military activities by Ekiti and Ijesa warriors in the area, resulted in very intensive enslavement of the people of the area. Very many of the war captives from these areas accumulated in the Nupe country, as well as in Ibadan, Ilorin and parts of Ekiti. From about 1880, the kingdom of Dahomey embarked on annual campaigns in parts of the Upper Ogun area (the towns of Iganna, Okeho, etc.), campaigns that continued until Dahomey was conquered by the French in 1892. These campaigns resulted in the taking of many people from these Upper Ogun towns as captives to Dahomey. As late as 1897, Ilorin was still sending intermittent raiding expeditions into parts of the Okun Yoruba and Akoko.

All of these material devastations and human distress were, however, no more than accompaniments of a revolution that was changing the face of Yorubaland and Yoruba society and culture in many significant ways in the course of the nineteenth century. One important direction of the revolution was the transplantation of human populations. As some cities and towns vanished, others sprang up elsewhere. New centers of population (like Ibadan, Abeokuta, new Oyo, Ilorin, Sagamu, Aiyede, Modakeke) gave Yorubaland new centers of culture, commerce, art, and political experimentation. Some of these new cities – because of their population size, unique evolution, and location – were destined for special roles in the subsequent development of Yoruba society. For instance, Ibadan has come, in the twentieth century, to serve as a sort of "national" political capital of Yorubaland; Abeokuta, the early headquarters of Christianity; Ilorin, the Yoruba headquarters of Islam. The emergence of Modakeke as twin town to Ile-Ife, and the swelling of Ife towns and villages by refugees, boosted the population of this "ancestral heart" of Yorubaland and thereby has enhanced its share in the twentieth century economy and politics of Yorubaland. The port town of Lagos had a peculiar experience of its own, from direct and indirect consequences of the wars. Refugees, traders and slaves from the Yoruba interior added considerably to the population of the island kingdom. At the same time, liberated slaves returning from the Americas and from Sierra Leone, came to constitute a substantial part of its population. Most of the latter were Yoruba, but a few were of non-Yoruba origin (especially Nupe and Hausa). The coming of all these people, with their various shades of the Yoruba culture, varying degrees of Western education, and varying levels of experience and skill in commerce and the professions and trades, transformed Lagos into a cosmopolitan society and made the people of Lagos the advance guard of Yorubaland in the development of a world-oriented economy.

Also, in broad terms, the wars changed the pattern of population spread in Yorubaland. Yorubaland had entered the nineteenth century more heavily populated in its northwestern region – especially in the Oyo country. By the middle of the century, the heavier population had shifted to the Yoruba middle belt – by then the home of such heavily populated centers as Osogbo, Ede, Ejigbo, Ikirun, Iwo, Ife-Modakeke, Ikire-Apomu, Gbongan, new Oyo, Ijaye, Ibadan, Abeokuta. Further eastwards in this middle belt, northern Ijesa towns like Igbajo, Iree, Ada and Otan as well as northern Ekiti towns like Otun, received some influx of Oyo and Igbomina from the north. Even as far south as Ido, Ado and Ikere in Ekiti, fairly large populations of Oyo resident immigrants emerged. In the distant west also, the region of Egbado and Ketu, for two centuries an area under Oyo political and commercial influence, witnessed a considerable influx of Oyo immigrants. Even some areas south of the middle belt received some of the shifting population, with some of the Owu and Egba flowing into northern Ijebu. In contrast, much of the northernmost reaches of Yorubaland became thinly populated, the northwest (the area of Oyo-Ile) being the hardest hit.

The ultimate, and very important, consequence of all these population movements was a mixing and intermingling of Yoruba subgroups far more profound than probably ever before in Yoruba history. This process of mixing started with a layer of Oyo migrants spreading out over all the other subgroups – thicker in the middle belt, but reaching even to the coast. In the important port towns of Lagos, Badagry and Ajase (Porto Novo), the migrations resulted in substantial Oyo populations. The peculiar development of Ibadan, as well as its empire-building successes, greatly reinforced the process of subgroup mixing. Ibadan grew as a city of all Yoruba subgroups in a way that no other city in Yoruba history can claim. Oyo, Ife, and Ijebu refugees and soldiers, and Egba and Owu stragglers, started the new Ibadan off. Then the peculiar and open meritocracy of Ibadan's political and social system attracted many from all subgroups of the Yoruba people. Later, Ibadan's conquests and style of provincial administration produced a powerful backwash of the mixed population of Ibadan to most of Yorubaland. Adversity threw the Egba and Owu together in Abeokuta and, later, brought to them crowds of persons of mostly Oyo descent from the smoldering ruins of Ijaye. Adversity also drove a seemingly endless stream of Oyo and Igbomina people to Ilorin, until Ilorin became one of the largest cities of the Yoruba people. Dahomey aggression provoked migrations of Egbado, Ketu and Idasa people eastwards, some to Abeokuta and some to the Awori kingdoms of Otta, Badagry and Lagos. Nupe aggression threw many Yagba, Jumu, Oworo, Abunu and others together in many refugee settlements which later developed into regular towns, and drove others southwards into Ekiti, Akoko and Owo. Esugbayibi, the founder of Aiyede, was a refugee from far northern Ekiti, and most of the earliest citizens of his Aiyede were Yagba, Oworo, Jumu; later, his kingdom attracted mostly Ekiti. Because Owo remained a peaceful haven throughout, it attracted many immigrants from Ekiti and Akoko. Following the opening of the Ondo road in the 1870s, many immigrants came from other parts of Yorubaland to live in Ondo, Ikale and Ilaje. Some Ekiti and Ijesa people from Lagos even established a new town, Aiyesan, in the southern tip of the Ondo forests, close to the Ilaje coastal towns.

Throughout the century, the enslavement of captives in the wars, raids and kidnappings kept a steady stream of human transplantations going. Until 1867 when the Atlantic slave trade finally ended, many of the enslaved captives were sold into the export trade, and the rest were held in the country, either sold locally or kept by their captors. After 1867, the internal trading in slaves accounted for all slave sales – a development whose economic consequences will be discussed in the next chapter. Now, as would be remembered, the Yoruba culture, as it typically processed slavery, usually transformed a slave into a member of his owner's family and group. This made domestic slavery a potent vehicle of subgroup mixing in war-torn Yorubaland. For instance, the areas of the greatest trade in about the second half of the century (Ijebu, Abeokuta and Egbado, the city of Ibadan, Ilorin, Lagos, towns on the newly opened Ondo road, and towns on the Owo road) received large numbers of domestic slaves from other parts of the country – from Oyo, Ife, Ijesa, Akoko, Igbomina, Ekiti, and the Yagba and neighboring territories of the far northeast. Most of these forcibly transplanted persons became parts of the fabric of the society of the places to which they were taken in Yorubaland. Many enslaved Yoruba also accumulated in Dahomey and the Nupe country. In the last three or four years of the nineteenth century, British and French overlordship offered all these persons a chance to return to the places from which they had been forcibly moved. Huge crowds of freed slaves returned home from the harsh slavery in Dahomey and the Nupe country. Inside Yorubaland itself, however, comparatively few took advantage of the chance to return home, and those were from among the persons less established where they lived. For perhaps the majority, made up of persons who had developed deep roots where they lived – women who were mothers and grandmothers (sometimes of well-established citizens), men who had become significant citizens, successful traders, or even chiefs, – there was no possibility of giving up everything and returning anywhere. In the course of the early twentieth century, as many such persons established contacts with their places of birth or their ancestral roots, the whole of Yorubaland became interconnected by a new web of far-flung family relationships.

Another direction of the revolution was widespread experimentation with new political systems in the quest for order and security. For many centuries until the beginning of the nineteenth, almost all Yoruba people had lived in kingdoms, and the monarchical system had been the more or less sanctified way to govern society. In the first decades of the nineteenth century, however, the greatest and most glorious of the kingdoms collapsed, and its collapse spread disorder and insecurity all over the country. In the troubles and distress that followed, while some new centers of population still clung to the traditional type of monarchical government (as in new Oyo, Modakeke, Aiyede etc.), many others sought alternative ways of reestablishing order and security. There were many such centers of political experimentation, but only a few will be mentioned here.

The large group that crystallized in Ibadan pointedly rejected a kingdom and the lineage system that produced a kingdom's hereditary type of leadership. Instead, they set up a new system of open participatory meritocracy, and of compounds each of which housed not a lineage bound together by common ancestry but people bound together by allegiance to one leader. To ensure that the rivalries among the leaders would not wreck the system, the laws laid down prohibitive penalties for the use of force to achieve elevation or promotion. In spite of that, big noisy rallies and even occasional brawling became endemic in Ibadan's political life. But Ibadan proved so mightily successful that its people could always laugh off the common reproach by the people of other Yoruba communities that street commotions were the disease of Ibadan.

Abeokuta sought security in one large city of many kingdoms. In effect, for most of the century, the leading chiefs (that is, the Olorogun chiefs from the three sectors of the Egba, and the chiefs of the Owu kingdom) provided the functional government of the city. And, judged by the prosperity of Abeokuta and its ability to defend itself, the system worked – although not without difficulties. Since each of the component Egba kingdoms had its own Olorogun chiefs, a federal Olorogun command needed to be set up. Choosing the leader of the federal Olorogun proved to be a sticky point at the beginning. A contest ensued between Sodeke from Iporo in the Ake kingdom and Deliyi from Ijemo, with the Ijemo people claiming that since they owned the land on which Abeokuta was founded their own chief should lead the federal Olorogun. A civil war nearly ensued at this point, and was averted only by the Ifa oracle's warnings that a civil war in Abeokuta would gravely displease the gods. Sodeke became leader of the federal Olorogun and thus led Abeokuta until his death in 1847. Later in the century, the Alake was promoted as the most senior of the Abeokuta kings – not, however, without resistance by the other kings, until British rule took over.

Many emerging communities chose, on their own, Abeokuta's type of a composite community in an easily defensible location – Sagamu in western Ijebu, Oke-Agbe in Akoko, Isanlu and others in Igbomina, Oke-Odan in Egbado, and the refugee settlements (comprising Yagba, Jumu and others) in the far northeast. Sagamu resulted from the flocking of a number of Ijebu Remo towns together in the town of Ofin. In the new composite town, the host king, the Akarigbo of Ofin, ultimately became accepted as the leading king. The refugees from many Egbado towns forced together at Oke-Odan settled down as quarters in Oke-Odan. Each quarter then established its own governing council consisting of war chiefs and elders; and a federal council was created, consisting of representatives from the quarter councils. The presidency of the federal council was rotated among the Balogun of the quarters. In Igbomina, the royal town of Isanlu became greatly swollen by refugees from many Igbomina kingdoms, attracted there by the reputation of the Olusin, who had stoutly and successfully held his town against successive attacks by Ilorin and Ibadan. Here, the Olusin became paramount ruler over many refugee communities and rulers. Ultimately, a novel integrative arrangement was evolved whereby two of the guest royal families (both being traditionally older than the Olusin royal family), were included as princes in the selection of kings to the Olusin's throne. Not much is known about the hilltop town of Oke-Agbe where the people of a number of Akoko towns (Oge, Afa, Ido and others) flocked together. It is known, however, that some integrated chieftaincy system was ultimately evolved there. Because of perpetual Nupe harassments, the refugee settlements of the Okun Yoruba areas never managed to evolve stable collective systems. They remained segmented settlements, each segment ruled by its own leaders. In the confusion, one Owe chief, the Obaro, sought security and influence by giving some help to the Nupe. As reward for his help, the Nupe accorded him recognition as controller over all the Owe as well as the Jumu, and quite a substantial centralized state seemed to be coming into existence under the Obaro. However, the rise of the Ogidi Alliance, and its challenge to the Nupe, pushed the Obaro's influence back to his own Owe village of Kabba.

Ilorin's Yoruba culture quickly absorbed and assimilated the groups of resident foreigners (mostly Hausa, Fulani and Nupe) – in a city bound together by fervent submission to one proselytizing faith (Islam) and ruled as a theocracy under a king (Emir) of Fulani descent. Making the system work proved quite difficult. The struggle against giant Ibadan bedeviled Ilorin's internal politics by giving too much influence to its group of war chiefs known as Baloguns, Yoruba and non-Yoruba. The internal power struggle between the Emirs and the Baloguns became manifested in divergent policies towards Ibadan. The Emirs generally wanted some accommodation with Ibadan. Ilorin had only narrowly avoided destruction by the Alaafin Oluewu in 1835 and, five years later, had again avoided destruction only because the victorious Ibadan forces had chosen not to go on and attack Ilorin itself. In the opinion of the Emirs, Ilorin needed to be cautious in its dealings with the mighty Ibadan. The Baloguns, in contrast, wanted a continuation of aggressive drives in various directions, even in spite of Ibadan's near invincibility – a risky ambition, since (as the Emirs feared) it could provoke an Ibadan attack on Ilorin city. The Hausa Baloguns would not stop thinking in terms of the victories of the past, and the Yoruba Baloguns and leading Oyo people who had flocked to Ilorin hated the thought of conceding leadership in Yorubaland to Ibadan. Intrinsically, the contest over the policy towards Ibadan became a contest for the control of Ilorin's life and direction. By the mid-1890s, the Baloguns were winning the contest so decisively that in 1895 a frustrated Emir Momoh took his own life. The triumphant Baloguns then installed Suleiman as Emir. The typical Yoruba system (of kings selected by high chiefs and exercising constitutionally limited authority) had thus ultimately established itself here; but the Royal Niger Company's conquest of Ilorin in 1897 obliterated it – and British rule was to replace it over time with the type of emirate system (of near-autocratic Emirs) found in Hausaland in the north.

Nevertheless, Ilorin had been a considerable success. At home it had enjoyed much security and prosperity; and it had believed itself (with some justification) to be second only to Ibadan in military strength in Yorubaland.

Over the refugees gathered at Ijaye, Kurunmi succeeded, by sheer force of personality, in establishing a scintillating personal dictatorship. However, how he purposed or expected to have this system of leadership continue after him never became clear. As things turned out, the city and the system perished with him.

The emergence of the large refugee town of Modakeke as twin to, rather than an integral part of, ancient Ile-Ife created the need for bold experimentation in political, economic and social engineering. For one thing, old Ile-Ife lineage claims to the farmlands conflicted with the desires and needs of the people of Modakeke for free access to farming land. For another, between the heavily traditional ancient town and the open and impatient new town, a whole range of social and political uncertainties and incompatibilities emerged. Unfortunately, the leaderships of the two towns failed to rise together adequately to the challenges facing them, and the stress generated proved uncontainable, resulting in immediate violent conflicts and a tradition of same.

Finally, the enormous success of the Ibadan system spawned in many parts of the country (especially in the eastern Yoruba territories most affected by the Ibadan conquests), a large crop of leaders fashioned after the Ibadan type. As the century wore on, these men became noticeably more powerful, more independent and more influential. At least a few of them (for instance, Aduloju, Ogedemgbe, Esugbayibi and Ayorinde) gave thoughts to creating states of their own in eastern Yorubaland. The Kiriji War interrupted almost all of such ambitions, but it also did much to increase the influence and confidence of this crop of leaders in general. It was they who led the Ekitiparapo war effort, and it was they who, on behalf of all the kingdoms in the Ekitiparapo, negotiated the 1886 Peace Treaty. And, through it all, their power over the kings in the Ekitiparapo had steadily increased. Not surprisingly, therefore, when the fighting was over, they had no doubt that they could obliterate the old political structure of most of eastern Yorubaland and create a new structure according to ideas of their own. It is not known how far these people would have gone – because the coming of British rule terminated their revolution.

Map 4. Early Christian missions in Nigeria

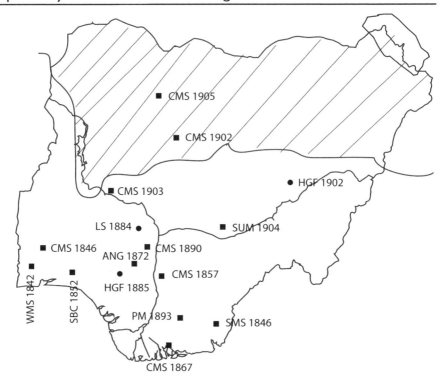

- ■ Protestant Missions
  CMS Church Missionary Society
  PM Primitive Methodists
  SBC Southern Babtist Convention
  SUM Sudan United Mission
  WMS Wesleyan Methodist Missionary Society
  ANG Anglican Mission

- ● Roman Catholic Missions
  HGF Holy Ghost Fathers
  LS Lyons Society (Society of African Missions)

  ▨ Islam dominated regions, 19th C

Source: Adapted from Fage, J. D.: *An Atlas of African History*, London, Edward Arnold, 1970. p. 50.

15

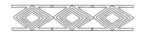

Yorubaland in the Nineteenth Century: Other Agencies of Change

While Yorubaland was being shaken and transformed by the wars of the nineteenth century, other powerful forces of change were also at work in the country. Of these the most important were a great surge in the spread of Islam, a major change in the pattern of relationship with the outside world, and the coming of Christianity and Western education.

The Spread of Islam[1]

Some account, as would be remembered, was earlier given of the intersection of Islam and the political developments in the Oyo country in the early nineteenth century. Here, we will give an account of the massive progress of Islam itself, resulting in the fact that by the end of the century, a very substantial part of the population of Yorubaland had become Muslim.

It is not known when Islam first made contact with Yorubaland. According to an Ilorin tradition, the word *Imale* (the Yoruba name for Muslims) originally meant a person or people from Mali (the great, strongly Islamic, empire which ruled much of the Western Sudan in the fourteenth century). This would seem to suggest that some Muslims (traders or preachers) from Mali first brought Islam to Yorubaland in about the fourteenth century. In the course of the centuries up to the eighteenth, Islam became well established in the Hausa kingdoms, the trans-Niger neighbors of the Yoruba people. Throughout those centuries, commercial and social contacts between Yorubaland and Hausaland were very strong. Hausa traders, more and more of whom were Muslims as time passed, traded and lived in probably all parts of Yorubaland while Yoruba traders traded and lived even in the farthest Hausa kingdoms as well as in Bornu on the Lake Chad, another Islamic country. By the eighteenth century, there were Hausa resident communities in many Yoruba towns, especially in the more important trading towns, and Islam was the predominant religion in those communities. The tradition that made every Yoruba king the patron of aliens in his kingdom resulted in the circumstance that Hausa traders lived as guests in many Yoruba palaces, and built the earliest rudiments of their prayer houses at the edge of marketplaces on palace foregrounds. During Clapperton's travel through Yorubaland from Badagry to Oyo-Ile in 1825–6, there were small Hausa communities in a few large towns along his route.

In spite of all these contacts with Islam, however, Yorubaland did not experience the kind of widespread and deep islamization that Hausaland did. The indigenous religion of the Yoruba people held its ground against the incoming faith. That does not mean that there was any intolerance of Islam. There was, by and large, none. Yoruba cultural perception of religious faith made it easy for members of the same lineage, in the same *agbo-ile*, to belong to different religious cults and worship different gods. When Islam came, it found its place in this cultural setting, so that the Yoruba convert to Islam practiced his Islamic worship in complete social harmony with the people of his lineage in the same compound. The Yoruba king who housed and fed alien Muslim traders and priests did so as "father" of all people in his kingdom and patron of aliens, and, for him, there existed no conflict whatsoever between his doing that and his worshipping the gods of his ancestors.

Though, therefore, Yoruba converts to Islam were many as the nineteenth century opened, they amounted to no more than a very small minority of all Yoruba people. Most of such converts would seem to have lived in the cities and towns in the Oyo country – Oyo-Ile itself, Igboho, Iseyin, Ikoyi, Kuwo and Ogbomoso, as well as the northern Ijesa town of Osogbo. In almost every one of these towns, the king's palace housed some foreign Muslims, and there were some native converts. In Igboho, the roots of Islam seem to have gone all the way back to at least the sixteenth century; Igboho traditions tell of Muslim preachers in the times when the Alaafins lived in Igboho. In the southern provinces of the Oyo Empire, some native Muslims also lived in the port towns of Badagry and Ajase, in both of which places there were some Oyo and foreign, mostly Hausa, Muslims. Further eastwards in Yorubaland (that is in Ekiti, Igbomina and Akoko), evidence of Islamic presence by the opening of the nineteenth century is difficult to find. In such places, through the influence of Nupe Muslim traders, there were probably scattered Muslim converts. Ado palace traditions trace the origins of the Muslim Hausa and Nupe trading community resident in a wing of the Ewi's palace to the reign of the Ewi Amonoola in the eighteenth century. The important point here, however, is that by the beginning of the nineteenth century, all these added up to no more than a thin trace of Islamic influence in Yoruba society.

The nineteenth century changed that – and changed it quite dramatically. Two separate, different, factors made for such a big change: first, a sharp increase

Yorubaland in the Nineteenth Century: Other Agencies

in Islamic evangelism, and second, developments in the political life of Yorubaland. In the first decade of the nineteenth century a radical Islamic movement led by a Fulani cleric, Usman dan Fodio, launched a jihad against the Hausa kingdoms from Sokoto. The jihad eliminated the old Hausa dynasties (which had also been Muslim), and replaced them with new rulers (Emirs) espousing dan Fodio's radical, puritanical, brand of Islam. The movement also generated a huge wave of evangelism – in preaching, teaching and writing. This wave spilled over into Yorubaland immediately, bringing many preachers of the new radical doctrines, some of them Fulani, some Hausa and some Arabs, who spread out into various parts of Yorubaland. The city of Oyo-Ile alone had as many as five of them early in Alaafin Majotu's reign (in the first decade of the nineteenth century). Available evidence indicates that most of the new preaching and most of its preachers in Yorubaland were concentrated in the Oyo country. Of these preachers in the Oyo cities and towns, two became particularly notable – an Arab named Muhammad Dan Haja Gumso, and Alimi (about whom much was said in the previous chapter). Some preachers also went far southwest into Egbado as well as coastal towns like Badagry, Lagos and Ajase and, presumably, into Ijebu and eastwards into Igbomina, Ekiti, Ijesa and Akoko. Most of the clearest information about their activities, however, is from the Oyo country.

The new evangelism featured preaching to street-side audiences, fervent criticisms of traditional Yoruba religious and social practices that did not meet the truest standards of Islam, and the teaching of Arabic, the language of the Koran. Considerable emphasis was given to children, and classes were formed for the teaching of the Arabic alphabet to them.

Wherever these activities reached, their immediate effect was to infuse new energy and new fervor into existing Muslim converts and Muslim communities, resulting in bold communication of the faith by believers, and the gathering in of converts. In some cities in the Oyo country, it looked as if an all-sweeping Islamic era was about to dawn in the first two decades of the nineteenth century.

Then the reaction started. Though religious tolerance was a strong character of Yoruba culture, the new wave of Islamic activities was seen by many as disruptive in their communities. Yoruba people had very deep respect for individual religious preferences and, therefore, had no objection to Islam; but the wholesale and disrespectful denunciations of all traditional religious and social ways jolted and shocked most hearers. In Oyo-Ile, the leading priests of the different traditional cults went into action. Insisting that the new wave of Islamic evangelism and activities were inimical to the welfare of the kingdom, they wanted the Alaafin Majotu to do something to put an end to the growing danger. Lander, who collected most of his information about this Oyo-

Ile situation from leading Muslims like Gumso, presents the Oyo high priests as acting merely in defense of their own positions, power and influence. He wrote:

> The priests became sensibly alarmed at the rapid progress of another and strange belief, so inimical to their best interests, and tending to the injury, if not the complete overthrow, of the power and influence which they themselves and their ancestors had exercised for a series of ages over the minds and actions of the votaries of paganism.

But in fact, the priests were not alone in their reaction. The Alaafin himself did not have much difficulty in agreeing with them, nor did other functionaries of the Oyo-Ile government. The kingdom and empire were going through difficult times in Majotu's reign, and significant leaders of society seem to have been nervous about the growing Islamic fervor and noise as yet another source of trouble. Moreover, the available evidence is even more unambiguous that the fervent aggressiveness of the preachers and Muslim converts simply offended the cultural sensitivities of most people, accustomed as they were to a calm acceptance of, and respect for, individuals' religious choices. Lander wrote that the preachers were fond of "disseminating, with too great eagerness, their opinions amongst the worshippers of idols."[2]

The high priests at last went in a body to the palace and demanded that the Alaafin Majotu should act without delay, warning gravely that if he failed to do so, he might lose his empire. In response, Majotu convened a secret meeting with the priests (and presumably also his chiefs) in the palace, and the meeting decided that the solution was to eliminate the Muslim preachers physically. Some days later, public officials carried out the decision. Gumso was lucky. One of the Alaafin's wives came to alert him only seconds before his appointed executioners came to his residence in the palace, and he fled with no clothes on his back, and escaped. Alimi was also probably in Oyo-Ile that day – which would account for the popular tradition that he was once driven out of Oyo-Ile by the Alaafin. Some preachers were killed at their residences; some others were gathered to the palace and executed. Undoubtedly, the victims included some prominent Oyo-Ile converts who had been active in the Muslim community.

From Oyo-Ile, the reaction spread to other Oyo cities and towns, with more or less the same consequences. For the first time in the history of Yorubaland, public policy in a kingdom declared a religious group as enemies of the state. In many cities, even in cities where the Alaafin's influence had become very small or non-existent, members of the public, with the connivance or even assistance of important chiefs, insulted, abused and physically molested or killed Muslim converts.

The basic details of events at this point are well known – the flight of a few Muslims to Solagberu and Alimi in Ilorin, Afonja's offer of refuge to all Muslims, the rise of the Jamaa as a force, its devastations in the country and its ultimate revolt against Afonja, ending in Afonja's death.

In terms of the progress of Islam in the Oyo country, the period covered by these events and subsequent developments up to the end of the century divides into two – the period from 1817 to 1840, and the period from 1840 to the end of the century. The unruly behavior of the Jamaa while fighting under Afonja (1817–24), and their penchant for destruction and rampage in Oyo towns and villages, produced a terrible effect on the spread of Islam. It provoked a heightening of reaction against Islam, resulting in intensified molestations of Muslim converts almost everywhere in the Oyo country. Consequently, more and more Muslim converts fled to Ilorin. While increasing the concentration of Muslims in Ilorin, this development depleted the ranks of Muslim activists, preachers and teachers in most Oyo cities. In many cities, many Muslims who chose to stay among their relations rather than flee to Ilorin lost the will to hold on to their Islamic faith.

In terms of the growth of Islam, the revolt of the Jamaa against Afonja and his death in the fighting that resulted (around 1824) led to one set of consequences in Ilorin and a totally different set in the rest of the Oyo country. Ilorin became decisively an Islamic fortress as more and more Muslim converts fled there from the rest of the country. Inside this Islamic fortress, a fight for dominance quickly developed between the group around Solagberu and the group (mostly the more radical, more puritanical, Oyo Muslims and the equally radical foreign-born Jamaa) around Alimi. Islamic purists around Alimi increasingly accused Solagberu and the people around him of allowing too much of traditional Yoruba practices (called *bada* in Arabic) in their lives, and therefore of not practicing a sufficiently true Islam. On the other hand, some of the most influential Oyo citizens in Solagberu's group increasingly resented the growing influence of the foreigners in Ilorin and their rampages and destruction in Oyo towns and villages. In the fight that ultimately ensued, Solagberu's Oke Suna was vanquished and he himself was killed. Alimi and his sons thus became the undisputed leaders of the Islamic community in Ilorin and the commanders of an Ilorin jihad to conquer Yorubaland for Islam. An Islamic emirate was born in Ilorin.

In the rest of the Oyo country, the news of Afonja's death at the hands of the Jamaa and the establishment of foreign rule over Ilorin, only greatly intensified popular hostility to Islam. The victories of the Ilorin Jamaa forces over Oyo armies sent to avenge Afonja's death and free Ilorin, and the terrible devastations caused by the Ilorin cavalry among civilian populations, pushed the hostility to Islam to great heights. In many Oyo towns, only the Hausa trading communities remained as Islamic outposts in a land seared by anti-Islamic anger, and the authorities of many towns prohibited even them from openly professing their faith or teaching the reading of the Koran to the children, "on pain of death."[3] As for Oyo-Ile, from the time of the killing of the preachers, no Islamic preacher dared to enter the city. By the time of Clapperton's visit to that city in 1826, Islam had long been virtually forgotten there – although the Lander brothers were later to see some Hausa Muslims there in 1830. Some preachers moved south into Egbado, hoping for more freedom there, but with mixed results. In Ilaro they apparently did not encounter much hostility; but in Ijanna they lived under intense official suspicion and restrictions.

Faced with this dismal picture with regard to the spread of Islam, the Emir of Ilorin at the beginning of the 1830s (by then Shitta, Alimi's second son) attempted to convert the Alaafin Oluewu to Islam, hoping, no doubt, that a Muslim Alaafin would open up opportunities for Islam in the Oyo country. After first inviting Oluewu to Ilorin for a friendly visit, the Emir then invited him a second time – for the express purpose of asking him to undergo the Islamic conversion ceremony known in Ilorin as "tapping the Koran." Oluewu, as would be remembered, refused to go – because the Emir had been posturing as politically superior to the Alaafin. Instead of accepting the invitation, the Alaafin embarked on military preparations aimed at wiping out Fulani rule in Ilorin. The outcome was a major invasion of Ilorin led by Oluewu himself, assisted by some Bariba allies. Oluewu lost the war and perished in it, and the news of that led to the abandonment of Oyo-Ile by all its people. The desertion of Oyo-Ile, and continued Ilorin military pressure southwards, resulted in the desertion of many cities, towns and villages.

In their outcome then, neither the military successes of the Ilorin emirate nor the attempt to convert the Alaafin did any good for the spread of Islam. The root of this failure was the mixing of political and religious ambitions by the Muslim leaders of Ilorin. It was not necessarily impossible for the Emirs and chiefs of Ilorin to convert the Alaafin to their faith, but as long as the Emirs claimed primacy over the Alaafin, no Alaafin was likely to accept anything from them. As long as they were perceived as foreign conquerors and rebels by most Yoruba people, Ilorin people stood little chance of converting many outside Ilorin to their faith. Moreover, because of the well known tendency of the non-Yoruba Jamaa to destroy, vandalize and loot, the reputation of vandals and destroyers preceded Ilorin armies everywhere. Consequently, inhabitants of towns or villages assailed by Ilorin armies, rather than surrender (and thus accept the religion of Ilorin), fled and deserted their homes. Almost everywhere in the Oyo country, being a Muslim became synonymous with being an agent of the Ilorin invaders and destroyers, and therefore a traitor and subversive. In their attempts to spread their faith, the Islamic rulers of Ilorin made no careful attempt to understand Yoruba society and its sensitivities. They purposed to conquer a Yoruba empire for themselves and then give it their religion, but, by and large, such an approach proved counter-productive in Yorubaland. "By 1840 then," writes Gbadamosi in his study of Islam in Yorubaland, "the picture of Islam among the Yoruba was largely a dismal one, depicting considerable depletion and disarray."[4]

From the first years of the 1840s, however, very significant changes began to appear in this picture, and Yorubaland rapidly evolved into a very different field for the propagation of Islam. The crucial factor was the defeat of Ilorin by Ibadan at Osogbo in 1840, the speedy roll-back of Ilorin's forces to the gate of their own city, and their permanent containment at more or less that boundary. As it became obvious to all that Ibadan's power was a dependable guarantee against Ilorin's campaigns of conquest and destruction, towns and villages largely settled down – towns and villages that had survived in the Oyo country, and towns and villages in the fringe areas like northern Ife, Ijesa and Ekiti.

Another important factor was the lesson which Islamic preachers and activists had learnt. First, Ilorin was not going to be able to come to the aid of any Muslim who, by any insensitive Islamic activities, got himself into trouble where he lived. Secondly, the type of frenetic, aggressive explosions of Islamic fervor common in the first two decades of the century did not work with Yoruba people; it only provoked resistance and hostility. Yoruba people, that is, were not opposed to Islam as such; they were only strongly opposed to the insensitive trampling down of their religion and traditions, and the norms of their interpersonal culture. Even in the worst of times in the 1830s Muslims (foreigners and indigenes alike) who had gone their ways in a calm and civil manner had converted friends and relatives to Islam.

Finally, by 1840, there existed for the first time on Yoruba soil an Islamic city. With most of the front-line activists for Islam in Oyo towns pushed into Ilorin by persecution, Ilorin had become a very strongly Islamic center of worship, preaching and learning – a budding Mecca for Yoruba Muslims, an Islamic resource center of growing importance and influence in Yorubaland. As fears of military pressure from Ilorin receded, contacts between inhabitants of Ilorin and the rest of Yorubaland slowly expanded. Traders from Ilorin slowly established confidence to ply the trade routes all over Yorubaland, even to the coast through Ijebu, Egba and Ondo. People from all over the country went to Ilorin to see their relatives who had fled to Ilorin and had become citizens there; and people from Ilorin went to search for relatives who had been dispersed to various towns. Slowly but surely, Ilorin was reintegrated into the family of Yoruba cities and towns (in spite of its non-Yoruba Emir) and, as that happened, its religious influence in Yorubaland grew. The concatenation of these three factors – Ibadan's containment of Ilorin's military aggression, the growth of a more carefully considered and more culturally appropriate approach by Islamic preachers and activists to Islamic evangelism, and the emergence of Ilorin as a Yoruba Islamic resource center – improved the prospects for Islam in Yorubaland continually for the rest of the century.

One common consequence was that Muslims among Oyo people who had migrated to the middle belt and southern parts of Yorubaland were able at last to start openly practicing their faith and quietly propagating it.[5] For instance, in Ilaro, an Oyo-Ile prince named Adeyemi and his Muslim family became the nucleus of an Islamic community. They had started cautiously before 1840 to gather the few Muslims in the town. In the years after 1840, the new community grew considerably, with Adeyemi, who had a fair knowledge of the Koran, as its leader. Thereafter, generations of the Adeyemi family provided the leadership of the Islamic community in Ilaro. This story of quiet and successful revival of Islam in Ilaro by refugees from places in the northern Oyo country was replicated in many towns – Saki, Osogbo, Iwo, Ogbomoso, Ede, as well as towns in Ife, Ijesa, Egba, Egbado and Ijebu. In general, the Muslims among the northern Oyo refugees were more knowledgeable than the Muslim natives of the towns further to the south, and they therefore usually supplied the drive and the leadership for the revival of Islam. Many of them were products of the effusive evangelism of the first two decades of the century but, by and large, they and their disciples adjusted their activities to the changed circumstances of the later years of the century, conducted their religious activities calmly, and therefore accomplished much for the propagation of their faith.

In Abeokuta, the few Muslims among the Owu and Egba refugees formed the foundation of an Islamic community that gradually became quite considerable and influential in the second half of the nineteenth century. Many refugees who were Muslims had flocked to Iseyin from destroyed Oyo towns and villages during the wars, attracted there by the information that there were many Muslims among the indigenes of Iseyin. In the second half of the century, therefore, Iseyin became a very strong center for Islam. There were many Muslims among the crowd of Oyo refugees who had participated in the founding of Ibadan in the 1820s. Because of the wars and the general hostility towards Ilorin, these were compelled to practice their faith unobtrusively and privately. After some time, however, they formed an Islamic community; but they went too far when they proceeded to build a mosque. The government of Ibadan, under the Basorun Oluyole, ordered the mosque demolished immediately. In the changed atmosphere of the 1840s, however, the Muslim community won the patronage of some influential citizens, the most notable of whom was Opeagbe who was Osi Balogun in the 1840s and later rose to the position of Baale of Ibadan. With the protection and assistance of such patrons, the Muslim community was at last able to build a small mosque at Oja-Iba. Thereafter, the Muslim community in Ibadan experienced much success and, as a result, Islam grew rapidly in the city. In fact, many persons (free Ibadan residents and freed slaves) returning from Ibadan to their homes in various parts of Yorubaland became carriers of Islamic influence. The small town of Epe on the Ijebu coast received a sudden influx of Muslims in 1851 when political conflicts in the Lagos kingdom forced many leading citizens of Lagos to migrate to Epe. The cosmopolitan society of Lagos contained many Muslims (some of them of Nupe origin), and therefore some of the immigrants to Epe were Muslims. Epe thus suddenly became a strong Islamic town on the Ijebu coast.

The general growth of Islam in the second half of the century appears to have affected all parts of Yorubaland. In Ijesa, some growth of Islam began in Ilesa in the 1860s with the return of some converted Ijesa men from Ibadan and various other parts of the country. The leader and organizer of the Muslim community here was a certain Sedu Ogun. With some patronage from Ogedemgbe, they built two mosques in Ilesa before the end of the century. In Ekiti, hostility towards Islam took longer to disappear, largely because of popular memories about the Ilorin invasions of Ekiti in the late 1840s and the continued Ilorin pretensions in Igbomina after 1887. As late as 1894, Bishop Charles Phillips noted that "the Ekitis were influenced by resentful feeling against Islam."[6] In Ijero, Muslim converts, including an Ajero, renounced Islam. The Ewi of Ado, Ali Atewogboye (who reigned from 1836 to 1885) had been converted to Islam before he came to the throne, but as king, he played his role as patron of all traditional cults, and Islam experienced no expansion in his kingdom. Nevertheless, there were small Islamic groups in a few places in Ekiti. Among Oyo immigrants in Ado and Ikere, for instance, a few were Muslims and they courageously kept their faith alive. In the 1880s, some converted Ado citizens returned to Ado from Ibadan and slowly started a Muslim community going. In most of the rest of Ekiti, Islam did not show much growth until the early twentieth century.

From the 1870s, largely because of the opening of the route to Lagos through Ode-Ondo, an Islamic group began to emerge in Ode-Ondo. The first persons in the group were from Lagos, some of them emigrants; others were from Ilorin as well as persons returning home from Ibadan. During the reign of the Osemowe Jimekan (1881–94) the group was finally strong enough to form a community and appoint an Imam (spiritual leader). Similar circumstances as in Ondo, especially trade between the southern and northern parts of the country (particularly Ilorin) accounted for the growth of Islam in places like Akure, Owo and Ijebu in the last decades of the nineteenth century.

Lagos became the home of one of the fastest growing Muslim communities in the second half of the century. In addition to the converts already part of Lagos society by the middle of the century, Lagos came to receive Muslims from various sources – Muslims among the emigrants from the Americas and Sierra Leone, and Muslims among traders and slaves from the Yoruba interior. By 1862, the number of Muslims in Lagos was estimated at 800 out of a population of about 30,000; by 1871, the number had jumped to 10,600 out of a population of 60,200 and continued to rise throughout the rest of the century. As the number of Muslims rose, mosques sprang up in various locations in Lagos.

As would already be obvious from the above, most of the spreading of Islam in Yorubaland in the late nineteenth century was the work of indigenous Yoruba converts. Communities of Hausa and Nupe Muslims continued to exist, but it was the Yoruba converts who took Islam to the compounds and homes of their people. Most of the early leaders, in the 1840s and 1850s, were persons of northern Oyo origin. Later, however, locally born persons returning home from slavery (or from free sojourn) in Ibadan played increasingly important roles. From the 1870s when the Ondo route was opened, the influence of Ilorin citizens contributed increasingly to the propagation of Islam in eastern and southern Yorubaland. Besides that, the large Yoruba Muslim population of Ilorin served as encouragement and motivation to Muslim activists in all parts of Yorubaland. After all wars ended in the 1890s, Ilorin became a school of Islam for Muslims ambitious for leadership roles in the Muslim communities in many parts of Yorubaland.

In general also, the mode of Islamic growth in the second half of the nineteenth century was such as to ensure success. Paying careful respect to Yoruba indigenous culture, Yoruba converts to Islam steadily became very good at weaving their religion into the fabric of Yoruba society and culture. Some of the leaders of Islamic communities became a new elite, literate in Arabic, well informed about the outside world of Islam – some of them men and women of very high levels of learning in Arabic. Everywhere, the Yoruba king, as father of all his subjects (even though not a Muslim), was successfully wooed into becoming the patron of the Muslim community in his kingdom, a patron to whom crowds of Muslim converts went to pay their respects on the Islamic festivals – in imitation of the traditional practice whereby all cults took their celebrations to the king in the palace. In summary, then, by the end of the nineteenth century, Islam had become a powerful and well accepted civilizing influence among Yoruba people, considerably well integrated into Yoruba society.

Changes in Overseas Trade and Relations

Throughout the sixteenth, seventeenth and eighteenth centuries, the contacts of the Yoruba people with Europeans had been limited entirely to trade with European traders along the coast. Moreover, that trade had increasingly featured, throughout the three centuries, the trade in slaves. When wars broke out in the Oyo homeland and then in the rest of Yorubaland early in the nineteenth century, the prevailing character of the trade was greatly intensified, and Yoruba people became, for some years, the largest single nationality among slaves being exported from West Africa. However, even as the Yoruba wars were intensifying and the volume of Yoruba slave exports was skyrocketing, change was beginning. In the first decade of the century, the official attitude of Britain (the largest slave-trading country) to the slave trade changed. This is no place for a full discussion of the reasons for this. Suffice it to say that very important changes in the economy of Britain (consequent mostly on the coming of the Industrial Revolution), the growth of humanitarian opposition to the traffic in human beings, and other factors, caused Britain to want to end the slave trade and substitute for it trade in the products of tropical Africa – trade that came to be known as "legitimate trade."

In 1807, therefore, the British government passed a law that made it illegal for British citizens to participate in the slave trade, and in 1833, another law abolishing slavery in Britain and all British territorial possessions. Britain then embarked upon efforts to bring the slave trade to an end. The British navy began to intercept slave-carrying ships on the high seas and to set free the slaves being conveyed on them. Many of such persons set free on captured ships were resettled in a settlement which the British established in Sierra Leone. As more and more European countries abolished the slave trade and slavery, the number of ships coming to the West African coast for slaves dwindled gradually, until it finally ceased during the late 1860s.

For Yorubaland, the immediate and far-reaching consequence of these developments was a change in the nature of trade with the outside world, a change that set Yorubaland on the path to a new economy. As would be remembered from the previous chapter, as the opportunities available for exporting slaves gradually dwindled, more and more of the captives in the wars stayed in the country, employed by their captors or buyers in various productive enterprises – especially farming, the production of palm oil and other palm produce, and commerce. The implication of this is that, instead of draining labor from Yorubaland, the enslavement of war captives tended increasingly to result in accumulations of servile labor under certain masters for productive enterprises. The massive increase in the production of palm oil in Yorubaland in the late nineteenth century, the widening instances of large farming enterprises, and the great increases in the observable sizes of trading caravans – all these were largely the result. In Ibadan, many chiefs and prominent citizens raised larger and larger farms, worked largely by enslaved war captives. The tradition of large farming enterprises had been established by the early leaders of the Ibadan republic. Oluyole, the first Basorun of Ibadan, is said to have been "fond of husbandry" and to have had "extensive plantations of okra, beans, vegetables, corn and yams, on separate farms for each."[7] That practice increased steadily among leading Ibadan citizens throughout the century. Anna Hinderer (David Hinderer's wife), wrote that all substantial citizens of Ibadan had "extensive farms which are cultivated by their slaves, whom they sometimes number by hundreds".[8] In the late 1870s, a rich woman trader, the Iyalode Efunseyitan Aniwura, had more than 2000 workers employed on her farms. In fact, according to Anna Hinderer, every citizen of Ibadan was a farmer "whatever other calling he follows", and in the seasons when farms were being cultivated or harvested, almost the entire population was engaged on the farms. In one such season in 1858, David Hinderer wanted to erect a church building, but he found that he could not procure labor for the purpose "either for love or money – all because everybody is wanted in the farms." The picture was the same in other parts of the country. All the notable war chiefs of the country were owners of large-scale farms. Below their level, owners of any number of slaves farmed varying acreages. During his tours beyond Ibadan to places like Ife and Ilesa, Hinderer passed by many large farms owned by people who had chosen not to be involved in warfare and who had made themselves rich by farming.

More and more of the labor was also devoted to an enterprise traditionally ancillary to farming, namely palm oil production. Of the crops native to Yorubaland, the one most in demand for export, and demanded in ever-increasing volumes in the growing legitimate trade, was palm oil. Cultivation of palm tree plantations was rare; but the palm tree grew naturally abundantly on farmlands in virtually all parts of Yorubaland. The Industrial Revolution in Europe demanded more and more of the palm oil for lubricants and soap manufactures, and by the last decades of the nineteenth century, the ancient occupation of palm oil production had become a very large income earner for Yoruba people. Cotton also slowly increased in the exports as more and more farmers ventured into cotton farming, some of it on a large scale. And in the last years of the century, more and more farmers established kolanut plantations, to produce the type of kolanuts known as *gooro* (*Cola nitida*) for export to the countries north of the Niger. The 1880s also witnessed the first cocoa plantations in Yorubaland.

By the 1850s Lagos had become the main port for exporting from and importing into Yorubaland. Both the imports and exports through Lagos grew more or less steadily from the 1850s until the end of the century – with occasional declines due to disturbances of trade routes by the wars going on in the interior. The new economy, of which legitimate trade with the outside world was the main pillar, grew fairly steadily throughout the second half of the nineteenth century, generating bigger and bigger volumes of economic activity. Trade expanded, resulting in increases in the number and sizes of traders' caravans and in the volumes of merchandise, as well as in the number of persons who made large fortunes from commerce. On a journey to Ibadan in 1853, David Hinderer traveled with a caravan of traders and carriers "consisting of not less than 4000 people." The missionary, William H. Clarke, has left this full description of the picture of trade in Yorubaland in the 1850s. He wrote:

> The trade in native produce and art keeps up continual intercommunication between the several adjacent towns, the one interchanging its abundance of one article for that of another. Thus on those smaller routes may be seen caravans of fifties passing almost daily from one town to another, acting as the great reservoirs of trade … (On the long-distance routes) a network of trade is carried to a distance of hundreds of miles, and with an energy and perseverance scarcely compatible with a tropical people … Hundreds and thousands of people are thus engaged in the carrying trade … Not infrequently, the articles from the Mediterranean and Western (European) coast may be seen in close proximity, and the productions of the four quarters of the globe within a circumference whose diameter may be measured by a few yards. In the disturbed state of the country, when several caravans are thrown together for the purpose of defence, a correct idea of the extent of trade may be found in the imposing numbers that stretch over several miles in length.[9]

Much of what Clarke described in this passage would, of course, have been true of Yorubaland in the eighteenth century or perhaps even earlier – with the difference that the caravans would usually have been smaller in the eighteenth century. The important point to note here is that, even in spite of the "disturbed state of the country", Yorubaland remained a country of great trade, and Yoruba people benefited quite strongly from, and advanced, the economic transformation and progress of their country.

A rich merchant class arose in Lagos, and also in Ibadan and probably most other Yoruba cities. Wealthy merchants based in Ilesa in the late nineteenth century became the chief sponsors of *osomaalo* traders doing itinerant trading all over Yorubaland, while as early as the 1880s merchants in Ode-Ondo formed a Chamber of Commerce. Of the richest Yoruba people of the second half of the century, the two most celebrated in popular Yoruba traditions are Madam

Tinubu of Lagos and the Iyalode Efunseyitan Aniwura of Ibadan, both of them women. Lagos, of course, came to have many people who were much richer in the last decades of the century than Madam Tinubu had been earlier in the century. One Lagos merchant of the late nineteenth century, Chief Taiwo Olowo, even had a shipping line of his own. It is not unlikely that Efunseyitan was the richest person in the whole of the Yoruba interior in about the late 1870s. All these developments meant that the economy of Yorubaland was expanding quite rapidly in the nineteenth century.

European Exploration of the Yoruba Interior

The above changes were destined to affect Yorubaland in many other ways. Very importantly, they brought the Yoruba interior into its first direct contact with Europeans. From the beginning of the nineteenth century, the need especially to know the interior in the interest of the legitimate trade brought European explorers, traders and others into the Yoruba interior. The first to come was the Clapperton expedition of 1825–6 through parts of western Yorubaland from Badagry to Oyo-Ile, their purpose being to discover the course of the River Niger. From Oyo-Ile, the expedition proceeded north to the countries of the Bariba and Nupe on the Niger and then to Hausaland. Four years later, Clapperton's assistant, Richard Lander, returned with his brother John, and traversed the same part of Yorubaland traveled by the earlier expedition. Thereafter, especially from the 1850s, various Europeans and Americans penetrated more widely into Yorubaland, going as far east as Igbomina and Ekiti. Some note has earlier been made of these men – especially the English commercial traveler Daniel May, the American Baptist missionary T. J. Bowen, and William H. Clarke. We owe to these travelers our earliest written direct information about the Yoruba interior. No matter what their motives for coming into the interior, the explorers, as representatives of European culture, came face to face for the first time in history with the deep seats of Yoruba culture and with the centers of Yoruba power and government – first with rulers subordinate to the Alaafin, then with the Alaafin himself (ruler of the then greatest state in the West African forests), and then with the other kingdoms and states of the Yoruba people. As strangers in the land, the explorers lived under the authority of the host governments, obeyed the laws of the land, and respected the culture of their hosts. Their coming was historically significant. It began to introduce in depth two peoples who had known each other only peripherally for centuries. For both, it represented a step in the worldwide evolution of what has come to be generally known as the "modern world."

The Return of the Emigrants

Another important promoter of change in nineteenth century Yorubaland was the return from the Americas and other places, in gradually increasing numbers, of persons of Yoruba origin who had won their freedom from slavery abroad. From early in the century, some of these persons (especially from Cuba and Brazil) took the step of returning home to their own country. As the Atlantic slave trade slowly wound down during the century, the number of the returnees, better known as emigrants, increased. Furthermore, recaptives who were resettled in Sierra Leone had among them many Yoruba, representing most subgroups (Oyo, Egba, Ijebu, Ife, Ijesa, Ekiti, etc.), and these also desired to return home to Yorubaland. In the Americas or in Sierra Leone, these returning ex-slaves had obtained some Western education and varying levels of various types of new skills – as carpenters, masons, farmers, traders, etc. Many had been converted to Christianity, but there were also many who were Muslims – either Muslims before they were enslaved, or converted to Islam by fellow slaves abroad.

From early in the century until the end of it, the emigrants kept arriving from Sierra Leone, Brazil and Cuba. Their total number is not known, but it most probably belonged in the range of tens of thousands. In 1851, a British naval officer, on a visit to Abeokuta, estimated that there were as many as 3000 emigrants in Abeokuta, and another navel officer that there were "hundreds" in Badagry. By the same date, there were very many others in Lagos, Ibadan, Ijaye, and in many towns and villages further up country in Iwo, Ede, Osogbo, Ilesa, Ejigbo, Iragbiji, even Ilorin. By the 1880s and 1890s, many had settled as far inland as some towns in Ekiti. With the opening of the route through Ode-Ondo in the 1870s, some came and settled in the Ilaje, Ikale and Ondo towns and villages. After Lagos became a British colony in 1861, more of the arriving emigrants chose to live in Lagos. By the last quarter of the century, Lagos had the largest population of emigrants in Yorubaland.[10]

The return of these people was to contribute enormously to making the nineteenth century an era of great and important changes in Yoruba history. They were the first Yoruba people to have some Western education, and the first to be Christians. Working under the auspices of the Christian organizations, they served as pioneers of the Christian religion in almost all parts of Yorubaland. Throughout the history of Christianity in Yorubaland in the nineteenth century, the majority of Christian missionaries were Yoruba people.

One of the Christianized emigrants, the man who later became famous as Bishop Samuel Ajayi Crowther, deserves a brief special note. Ajayi was fifteen years old when he was seized from his small home town of Osogun near Iseyin in the dry season of late 1821. As a captive, he was sold to a woman trader in the Egba town of Ijaye, and from there he was sold from trader to trader until he reached Lagos where he was sold to a Portuguese slaving ship, the *Esperanza Felix*, on April 7, 1822. That same evening, while still in the vicinity of Lagos, the *Esperanza Felix* was captured by British naval ships. The slaves on the *Esperanza Felix* were liberated and taken to Sierra Leone. Ajayi arrived in Sierra Leone in June 1822 as a freed youth – one of the earliest Yoruba recaptives to arrive in the settlement. In Sierra Leone he was baptized as Samuel Ajayi Crowther. Intelligent, industrious and humble, he won the affection of the Christian missionaries who then taught him to read and write and took him to England in 1826, where he attended school for a few months. By the time he returned to Sierra Leone in 1827, the school that was later to become Fourah Bay College was being established, and he was enrolled as its first student. Trained there as a teacher, he went on to teach in various schools. In 1841, when the missionaries in Sierra Leone decided to send an expedition to Badagry on the Yoruba coast, Samuel Crowther at last returned to the land of his fathers as a missionary of the Church Missionary Society (CMS) of the Church of England (the Anglican Church). From then on, he served at various mission stations in Yorubaland and rose steadily in the service of the CMS. By the 1860s, the missionary enterprise had extended to the Niger country – comprising the Nupe territory and the area south of it to the Niger Delta. In 1864, Samuel Ajayi Crowther was consecrated Bishop of the growing Niger Mission – thus becoming the first Black African to rise to that position in Africa.

While the Christians among the emigrants thus expanded the influence of Christianity in Yorubaland, the Muslims among them also assisted the growth of Islam in various parts of the country. In Lagos in particular, they became leaders of Muslim communities, and contributed immensely to the growth of Islam as a major religious influence.

Of very great importance in Yoruba history also was the contribution of the emigrants to the expansion of Western education. They were the first schoolteachers in most communities in Yorubaland – the native advance guard of a revolutionary movement that would ultimately, in the next century, make the Yoruba people one of the most literate in Africa. Equally important, the emigrants themselves invested heavily in Western education for their children. In many new schools, the first students were emigrants' children. Many of the sons and daughters of the Lagos emigrants especially were sent to various universities and other educational institutions in England, and began to return in the last years of the nineteenth century and the first years of the twentieth as the first generation of lawyers, doctors, journalists, accountants, men of letters, in the territory that was by then being constituted to become the British

27. Bishop Samuel Ajayi Crowther (c.1809–91).

Colony and Protectorate of Nigeria. They and other Yoruba men and women educated like them provided the new country of Nigeria with its first crop of indigenous civil servants and professionals.

A very important aspect of the development of literacy in Yorubaland was the rendering of the Yoruba language in writing, and in this also the Yoruba emigrants played a significant role. Increased European contacts with the interior of Yorubaland from the 1820s generated a desire to write the language down. In the appendix to his journal of his 1825–6 travels in Yorubaland, Clapperton made a list of a few Yoruba words. But it was the Christian missions, and missionaries of various denominations and various European nationalities, that pushed forward the effort to create a generally acceptable orthography for the writing of the Yoruba language – in their desire to make the Bible, Christian worship manuals, hymnals, and other Christian literature available to Yoruba people. Samuel Ajayi Crowther took a leading part in all this from the beginning. The CMS began in 1843 to conduct services in Yoruba in the Sierra Leone settlement. Crowther did the first Yoruba translation of some texts from the New Testament, conducted the first Yoruba language services, and preached the first sermons in Yoruba. Other mission groups followed suit.

However, the creation of a generally accepted Yoruba orthography did not come easily. This grew gradually over the next three decades as a result of the work of language experts and Christian mission leaders of various European nationalities. The emigrant Yoruba employees of the various mission bodies were widely involved in the search for answers in the making of the orthography, and led the way in increasingly employing Yoruba translations and writings in their daily Christian work in their mission stations. Throughout, Crowther stayed in the forefront of the emigrant contributions to this historic development and, among other things, ultimately wrote a dictionary of the Yoruba language.

By 1875, it was possible at last to hold a general conference of all concerned (mission leaders and language experts called to the task by the mission bodies), in order to finalize the decades-long discussions and arguments on the details of a common orthography. The conference was held in the CMS Mission House, St. Peter's, Faji, Lagos, on January 28 and 29, 1875. Rev. (by then Bishop) Samuel Ajayi Crowther was Chairman, assisted by Rev. Adolphus Mann (a German) as Vice-Chairman, and Rev. J. B. Wood (an Englishman) as Secretary. The orthography as agreed upon in this conference has remained substantially the accepted Yoruba orthography till the end of the twentieth century – a fact which, according to Ade Ajayi, constitutes "the greatest tribute to the excellence and the thoroughness of the work" of the pioneers from many lands. This was one of the greatest gifts of the nineteenth century to Yoruba civilization. With that task so excellently accomplished, the foundation was laid, according to the Rev.

Henry Johnson (brother of Samuel Johnson, author of *The History of the Yorubas*), "for progress to any extent" for the Yoruba nation.[11]

Of the emigrants settled in Lagos, very many ventured into trade, as agents of the growing legitimate trade, mostly as factors or subsidiaries of the European merchant companies. Because they were Yoruba, easily reintegrating into the native culture and speaking the language, and even discovering and reestablishing lost family ties, they became the ideal organizers of trading caravans that took imported goods for distribution in the interior and brought export goods back. Some grew to become significant merchants and built up considerable fortunes from trade.

The desire of the original sponsors of the emigrants from Sierra Leone was that they would, on return to their country, go into farming and spread the Christian message. Some did go into farming, but their success in that venture was very limited. The most significant contribution of emigrants to the development of agriculture in Yorubaland was their introduction of some new crops.[12] Of the crops from the Americas, the most important was cocoa, which was to become, in the twentieth century, the greatest cash crop of Yoruba farmers and for decades the foremost foreign exchange earner for Nigeria. Another crop was cassava. Cassava was known in some places in West Africa (for instance in Dahomey) before the nineteenth century, but it was in the late nineteenth century that it spread into Yorubaland. The emigrants, especially those from Brazil, are believed to have been responsible for the propagation of cassava as a common crop of Yoruba farmers. Yet another crop was rice. Rice was grown before the nineteenth century in the region of West Africa to which Sierra Leone belongs, as well as in Allada, and it was from Sierra Leone that the emigrants brought it to Yorubaland. In the course of the twentieth century, all these crops were to become very important in the economic life of Yoruba people.

As the emigrants settled in Lagos, their attention was gripped by the wars going on in Yorubaland. In general, they passionately desired that the wars should end so that the homeland could return to peace and order. After the British seized the kingdom of Lagos as a British colony in 1861, the emigrants, as well as Christian missions and foreign traders in Lagos, began to pressurize the British government of the colony to intervene for peace in the Yoruba interior. When the Kiriji War started in 1877–8, it generated some division in the ranks of the emigrants in Lagos. Those of them who were of Ijesa and Ekiti origin believed that the revolt of the Ekiti and Ijesa against Ibadan was justified and that the Ekitiparapo was the underdog in the Kiriji War. Therefore, as would be remembered, they organized to give assistance to the Ekitiparapo. In spite of that, however, the emigrant community as a whole never relented in its pressure on the Lagos government for intervention in the wars – until it finally intervened in 1886. From then on, the Lagos government remained involved in the tortuous quest for peace until all the major wars were brought to an end in1893.

In summary then, when the persons later known as emigrants first left their homeland, they left it as slaves – and therefore as losses to their families, communities, and country. Most of those who left in this way never returned but became assets to the lands where they had been taken in the Americas. However, the few who returned became blessings in many ways, and served as agents of progress to their native land. In them and through them, the Yoruba country and people received significant compensation for the heavy losses occasioned by the century-long wars in Yorubaland.

The Coming of Christianity[13]

The first batch of Christian missionaries landed at Badagry in 1842, preceded there by some emigrants from Sierra Leone. The intention of the missionaries was to establish in Badagry their base for sending missions to the interior, but they quickly found the town unsuitable. Badagry's formerly thriving trade in slaves had fallen, because the British naval patrols had frightened the slaving ships away, and legitimate trade had not yet picked up. The town was dull and depressed, and the people were in no mood to cooperate with the missionaries. Consequently, they decided to move further inland to Abeokuta, a new and vibrant city. At first, the Abeokuta chiefs, led by Sodeke, hesitated to welcome the missionaries, but later reconsidered the matter, hoping that they would be helpful to the city in its political maneuvers with Ibadan, Ijebu, Lagos and other enemies. Abeokuta thus became the first Christian missionary base in Yorubaland, and quickly became known in Christian circles in Britain as the "Sunrise within the Tropics." Soon after, mission stations were established in Badagry and Lagos. Emigrants served in leading positions in all these missions from the beginning. Samuel Ajayi Crowther was a leading missionary in the Anglican mission in Abeokuta. From 1849 to 1859, the Methodist mission in Abeokuta was led by an emigrant of Egba origin, Edward Bickersteth.

From the 1850s, Christian missions expanded rapidly into other parts of Yorubaland. In 1853, a mission was established in Ibadan, which later became a center from which missionary agents were sent to many places in the further interior. Another center was established in Ijaye in the same year. From Lagos, mission stations were set up at Igbesa, Ikorodu and Sagamu, but Ijebu-Ode refused permission for a mission station at the time. Between 1853 and 1858, leaders of the Abeokuta missions toured the country intensively – north to Oyo, Awaye, Iseyin, Saki and Ogbomoso, and west to Ibara, Isaga, Ilaro and

Ketu, at most of which places mission stations, manned by emigrants, were soon set up. In Ilorin, the Emir received the missionaries well but withheld permission for a mission station. The leader of the Anglican mission in Ibadan, David Hinderer, toured the country east of Ibadan, and agents were placed as a result in Ilesa, Ife and Modakeke. Political developments in the Ife–Modakeke area stunted the development of the Ife and Modakeke stations, and both soon died out. After the opening of the route through Ondo in 1872, a strong Anglican mission station was established at Ode-Ondo, and smaller ones at Itebu in the Ilaje creeks and Aiyesan in the Ondo southern forests. The Ode-Ondo mission then became the center for missionary expansion northeastwards and eastwards into Ife, Ijesa and Ekiti. Before the end of the century, mission stations had sprung up in Modakeke, Ife, Ado, Ijero, Aiyede, Ise, Akure, Ikere, and missionary activity was to expand from these places to other Ekiti towns and to Akoko and Owo. By 1900 indeed, virtually all towns and villages of the Yoruba people housed Christian missions, sponsored by various Christian denominations – Anglicans, Methodists, Baptists, and Roman Catholics.

In a little over fifty years, then, Christian missions started and spread over all parts of Yorubaland. That rapid development benefited much from the civilization of the country – its cities and towns, its age-old road networks, its tradition of acceptance and protection of strangers, its general toleration of religious differences, its respect (even in war time) for the trader and the peaceful traveler. Everywhere, missionaries in charge of outflung mission stations knew that they lived in a society of law, among law-respecting neighbors, and under the protection of kings and subordinate kings who, by the ancient lore of the land, were protectors and patrons of the stranger. It also helped greatly that most of the mission agents were emigrants from the Americas and Sierra Leone – that is Yoruba indigenes who had gone far away and learnt new things and were returning home to teach those new things to their people.

In many places, the new religion and the native religion of the Yoruba people brushed against each other. When David Hinderer preached the Christian message for the first time to an audience in the Ooni's palace in Ife, the chiefs welcomed him warmly but assured him that Ife was the springhead of all religion and that what he had preached to them was, in effect, nothing new. In the early days of the mission in Abeokuta, some native converts were arrested by the chiefs for some unacceptable behavior. When the leaders of the mission (including Crowther) went to intercede with the chiefs on behalf of the people under arrest, the head chief of Itoku, reported Crowther,

> said he had no quarrel with us, neither with the Sierra Leonean emigrants in his town; they might come to church and do as they pleased, but he checked his

people from doing so because they must do as their forefathers used to do, and they have no business with us (missionaries) ... he said moreover, that we never gave them any person to make Ogboni, nor to worship Ifa, nor Sango, etc. Moreover, that one of us called the worship of their deceased forefathers a lie.

In Ado in Ekiti in around 1899, because some Christian converts made a habit of ridiculing the *egungun* cult, whip-carrying *egungun* mask bearers targeted Christian Sunday services for some weeks, until the Ewi had to intervene to bring the attacks to an end and make peace between the Christian converts and the leaders of the *egungun* cult. Local incidents such as the above were probably common. As would be obvious from most of the instances here, the problem was usually not with the religion of Christianity as such, but with unacceptable or provocative behavior by Christian converts.

It was in Abeokuta ("Sunrise within the Tropics"), ironically, that the Christian missions encountered the greatest conflict. The root of the problem was not religious; it sprang from the fact that the white missionaries were perceived as agents of the British government. Until about 1860 that perception suited both Abeokuta and the Christian mission work beautifully. When, for instance, Dahomey brought a large army to attack Abeokuta in 1851, the missionaries did not only join in the defense of the city, they also influenced British authorities along the coast to send help. The Dahomey army, commanded by their king, Gezo, marched all the way to the walls of Abeokuta, but they were defeated there and pushed back. So far, then, Sodeke's original hope that the missionaries might become helpful to Abeokuta was wonderfully realized – and the missionaries therefore became the more acceptable to the Abeokuta authorities. Thereafter, however, developments gradually changed the tone of Abeokuta's relationship with the Christian missions. The year 1861 was the turning point. From the time Lagos was annexed, the British colonial administration began to take steps aimed at keeping the roads to the interior open and free, in their attempts to promote trade. The hostilities between Ibadan and Abeokuta frequently threatened the roads. Since Ibadan and the British were agreed in the desire to have the roads open and free, Abeokuta authorities came to perceive British policies as favoring Ibadan at their expense. Inevitably, the missionaries, who were seen as agents of the British, lost favor with the Abeokuta authorities. The culmination of all this came in 1867 when the Lagos colonial government's virtual annexation of Ebute-Metta (over which Abeokuta claimed ownership) left Abeokuta feeling very threatened. Led by Akodu, the Seriki of the Egba, and Solanke, the Jagunna of Igbein, crowds of enraged warboys and members of the public went on a rampage and destroyed the houses of the missionaries and most of the valuables of the churches. All the European missionaries, as well as some emigrants and converts, fled to Lagos. This incident became known as the *ifole* – that is, "housebreaking."

However, when the dust from the *ifole* settled, it became clear that Abeokuta people were not after the converts or emigrants, they were after the white missionaries – that is, British people. The *ifole* thus left the affairs of the missions in the interior entirely in the hands of the emigrant missionaries and prominent converts. The white missionaries would not be able to return until the 1880s. A very important consequence of this development was that the Christian venture by all missions in the Yoruba hinterland became effectively indigenous in its personnel and management.

Christian missionary efforts had also penetrated to the Niger, also largely through the agency of Yoruba emigrants. In June 1864, Samuel Crowther was consecrated in England as Bishop of the CMS Niger Mission. Crowther's Niger Mission extended from the Nupe country on the Middle Niger, through Lokoja and Onitsha, south to the small states of the Niger Delta. In addition, although he was not explicitly named over the CMS Yoruba Mission, he had considerable authority over the Yoruba Mission also. Traveling from end to end in this vast territory to supervise and establish mission stations, Crowther became the most important officer of Christianity in West Africa. His usual annual agenda saw him in Lagos in the dry season (from November or December to February or March) visiting nearby mission stations and writing his dispatches and reports; from Lagos he would go by ship to the Delta (Bonny, Kalabari, Brass, etc.); then in June he would proceed northwards to Onitsha, Lokoja, Egga, Bida; in October he would return to the Delta and, from there, to Lagos in November or December. What all this meant was that the Christian enterprise in the interior of the country that was later to be known as Nigeria was given a taste of indigenous independence and control quite early in its history, with Yoruba clergy as the leaders.

Rivalry Between Islam and Christianity

As would be expected, the paths of Christianity and Islam began to cross in Yorubaland from about the middle of the century. Conversions to Christianity picked up only slowly, whereas conversions to Islam grew quite fast in many parts of Yorubaland in the late nineteenth century. Consequently, the leaders of the Christian missions began to be concerned about the success of Islam. The Christian group that responded the most vigorously to the Islamic challenge was the Anglican, whose Church Missionary Society was the largest and most active of all the mission agencies. In 1875, one of their leaders, Reverend James Johnson, put forth a plan for confronting Islam. His plan laid down many directives for Christian workers: first, that local church ministers should serve more as missionaries (and spend more time in evangelizing) than as administrative pastors; secondly, that local ministers should learn Arabic so as to be better able to combat Islamic scholars and preachers; thirdly, that Christian tracts should be produced in Yoruba and Arabic for the benefit of Muslims; and finally, that Muslim children coming to Christian schools should be given as much Christianity as possible. This plan became the basic guideline of Christianity's response to the challenge of Islam in Yorubaland.

A large crop of Anglican ministers emerged, dedicated to the struggle against Islam – among the older ministers Samuel Crowther and James Johnson; and among the younger, enterprising and tireless fighters like R. S. Oyebode, G. B. Foster and A. W. Smith. In written tracts and debates, these men combated Muslims everywhere. By the 1890s a very elevated and energetic rivalry was alive between Christians and Muslims in Yorubaland, as the activism of the Christian ministers energized some of the most informed Muslims. And the tradition of the rivalry continued into the twentieth century. On the whole, in terms of conversion of the general population of "unbelievers," the rivalry benefited both Christianity and Islam very bountifully, even though the hold of the traditional religion on Yoruba political and social customs remained quite strong.

The Coming of Western Education

From the very beginning of Christian missionary work in Yorubaland in the 1840s, every mission station, as soon as it opened, started a school and went out to urge parents to enroll their children.[14] Samuel Crowther was a strong advocate of mission schools, believing that it was an inexpensive and effective way of penetrating the indigenous population. In probably every mission station, the missionaries encountered an initial resistance to their efforts to attract the children to school. For instance, the leader of the Ode-Ondo mission, Charles Phillips, found that when he visited parents and urged them to send their children to school, they would readily promise to do so, but that such promises were usually not fulfilled. As a result, he had to visit the same parents over and over again. This was an initial period in the life of every mission school, a period when parents did not know what schools were about and hesitated to hand their children over to strangers. In most new mission schools, therefore, the first students were children of the missionaries themselves plus children and dependants of prominent citizens like chiefs. Even after children had enrolled, mission schools tended generally to face the problems posed by irregular attendance, as well as premature withdrawal of children from schools for work on the farms. Missionaries discovered that the best solution to these problems was to persuade parents to allow their children to be brought up by missionaries in the mission house. In this way the institution of boarding school became a regular feature of the mission house and school.

In spite of these and other problems, however, schools spread out in Yorubaland and the number of children enrolled in, and graduating from, mission schools rose gradually. The areas with the earliest missions (like Abeokuta and Ibadan) became the providers of school teachers for the newer mission centers in eastern Yorubaland. As the nineteenth century rolled towards an end, the impact of the mission schools was beginning to be felt substantially among Yoruba people. A new class was emerging, marked by its literacy, its ability to speak the English language (or the French language in the far western region of Yorubaland), its knowledge of the outside world, and its possession of new skills and professions – as clerks, Christian church workers, interpreters, teachers, lawyers, doctors, journalists, accountants, etc., pillars of a new Yoruba society that was beginning to evolve.

Of course, Lagos, where the emigrants were most concentrated, led the way in the growth of Western education. Finding that Western education created access to opportunities in the service of the colonial government and the European merchant companies, Lagos people soon went far ahead of the rest of Yorubaland in educating their offspring. As would be remembered, long before the end of the century, Lagos youths educated in colleges and universities in England were already providing Yorubaland with its first crop of doctors, lawyers, men of letters and other highly educated professionals.

Beginnings of Modern Yoruba Nationalism

A very important outcome of the growing literacy in Yorubaland during the nineteenth century was the marked emphasis it brought upon Yoruba national consciousness and unity. As is obvious from previous chapters, the Yoruba had been, from ancient times, intensely conscious of their identity and cultural unity as one people. The strong commonalities in Yoruba culture, the powerful myths of common origin, the widespread and very influential myths and traditions around Ife and the name of Oduduwa, the common pantheon of gods and spirits, the common political culture and practices and the universal belief in the common ancestry of Yoruba ruling dynasties – all these were components of a strong consciousness of national identity and unity. The Yoruba lived in their many kingdoms and ethnic subgroups, but consciousness of the larger ethnic group ran through their lives, their politics, their rituals and worship, their economic institutions and practices, and their total worldview. Even in the considerable disruption by wars in the nineteenth century, the consciousness of oneness as a people remained strong. The rulers of the strong city of Ibadan urged the Ooni-elect of Ife to remember that he was father of "all our tribes" and the giver of the war banners of all the kingdoms of "all our people".

Whether or not a common group name was part of this whole picture of group consciousness from early times, we do not know. By the beginning of the nineteenth century, no such common group name seemed to be acknowledged by all Yoruba people. An ancient name, the name Yoruba, circulated among them and had for centuries been used by their neighbors in the Western Sudan to identify them;[15] but the first persons to be addressed as Yoruba among Yoruba recaptives in Sierra Leone in the early nineteenth century rejected the name and insisted on being identified by their subgroup names (Ijebu, Ijesa, etc.). Yet, within only a few years, the Yoruba community in Sierra Leone had generally adopted the name Yoruba. And as the influence of the literate emigrants and other Western educated Yoruba grew in the course of the nineteenth century, and as Western education expanded in Yorubaland, the fundamental common ethnic consciousness in Yoruba people became powerfully stimulated and, during the second half of the century, the name Yoruba became rapidly universally embraced as the common name for the whole Yoruba nation. The consequent upsurge of Yoruba cultural nationalism was to stimulate national unity and solidarity. Rapidly in the years after 1893, the divisive passions of the era of wars were superseded by Yoruba "national" consciousness – a major factor in the making of Yoruba political strength and influence, and in Yoruba economic and social successes, in the twentieth century, especially in the context of Nigeria. The belief in common descent from Oduduwa, a belief that had for many centuries been a strong factor of Yoruba consciousness and life, served as the readily available rallying symbol for this national movement. In the course of the twentieth century, the name of Oduduwa was to become perhaps the most visible rallying banner of any one African nationality.[16]

One very important aspect, and booster, of this growth of Yoruba cultural nationalism was the beginning of writings by literate Yoruba about the Yoruba people, their history, and their institutions. The men of Yoruba origin employed in the Christian missions, and the growing number of literate people in various parts of the country, were attracted to the fascinating traditions of the past preserved in every Yoruba community, and began to write about them, as well as about current happenings in Yorubaland. John Augustus Otunba Payne of Lagos became the leading person among the early writers, with his *Lagos and West African Almanack* published annually from 1874. As will be seen later, in the chapter on the twentieth century, writing on Yoruba history and institutions was to grow very richly during the last decade of the nineteenth century and to become even richer in the twentieth century. The reduction of the language into writing during the nineteenth century, and the emergence of a common Yoruba orthography, enabled some of the writers to produce their works in the Yoruba language – and this was to become a very significant cultural development during the twentieth century.

Imposition of European Rule

The closing act of the nineteenth century (the century of great changes and transformations), was the imposition of British rule on most of Yorubaland – and of French and German rule on the rest. As the twentieth century opened, all Yoruba people, like all other peoples of tropical Africa, were subjects of European imperialist overlords.[17]

The coastal kingdom of Lagos was the first part of Yorubaland to become a British possession. The British first interfered in the politics of the Lagos government in 1851. A contest for the throne of Lagos resulted in that year in one prince, Kosoko, seizing the throne from his rival, Akitoye. Claiming that their motive was to put an end to the slave trade in Lagos, the British intervened, bombarded the island, forced out Kosoko (who was said to be a "slave trader"), and helped Akitoye (who was said to be opposed to the slave trade) to regain the throne. The immediate consequence of the British action was to install the British, rather than Akitoye, as the controllers of Lagos. Before then, the British had been more or less shut out of the trade of Lagos by the Portuguese and Brazilians. From 1851, the British became dominant in the trade of Lagos and of Yorubaland.

Lagos thus gave the British a strong foothold on the Yoruba coast. The wars going on in the interior, and the British interest to promote the trade of Lagos, combined to increase British interest in the Yoruba hinterland. In 1861, the British bombarded the port town of Ajase (Porto Novo). Moreover, seeing the British as the formidable power on the Yoruba coast, some towns of the Egbado country (Ipokia, Oke-Odan and Ado), under constant military pressure from Dahomey and Abeokuta, applied to the British government of Lagos for protection. Meanwhile, however, the French were active in the Aja country, and intended to expand from there eastwards into western Yorubaland – especially to create a French corridor through Egbado and Egba territory to the Middle Niger. Consequently, a rivalry developed between the British and the French over western Yorubaland. In order to prevent British expansion towards the west and to create a coastal base for their own expansion eastwards, the French declared a protectorate over Porto Novo in 1862.

During the 1880s, the Anglo-French rivalry became more and more intense. At last, however, in 1889 the two reached an agreement establishing a boundary that placed the Egbado kingdoms of Ilaro, Ipokia, Ado, Oke-Odan, Ajilete, Igbesa, the Awori kingdom of Badagry, and parts of the kingdoms of Ketu, Sabe and Ifonyin, under the British. In 1891, the British proclaimed a protectorate over those territories. The 1889 Anglo-French Agreement thus settled the rivalry and ended French interest east of Porto Novo. In the end, all that the French acquired in Yorubaland comprised Itakete, Ohori-Ije, Ipobo, and parts of the kingdoms of Ketu, Ifonyin and Sabe. Of these kingdoms, the French acquired the royal towns and the metropolitan provinces, while many of their subordinate towns and villages fell into the British area of influence. In 1892, the French invaded and conquered the kingdom of Dahomey. The Dahomey kingdom (by then comprising all the Aja territories), together with the French Yoruba acquisitions, became the French Protectorate of Dahomey. To the west, French Dahomey shared a boundary with Germany's territory of Togo, and that boundary placed a small part of Yorubaland, especially the western Ife, under German rule in Togo – until 1918 when Togo also came under the French as a mandated territory.

European imperialism thus divided Yorubaland between three different countries – the greater part in British Nigeria, a much smaller part in French Dahomey, and a still smaller part in German (later French) Togo. For the Yoruba people of the subgroups and kingdoms of western Yorubaland, there thus arose two international boundaries splitting kingdoms, communities and families, and demanding to be observed and respected – as against the people's family, kinship, ethnic, cultural, political and historical bonds of unity.

In 1892 also, the British invaded the Ijebu country. The Ijebu-Ode government under Aboki (Fidepote's successor), while allowing the people of Ibadan to come and trade in the northern Ijebu towns, had resolutely continued to refuse free traffic between Lagos and Ibadan through Ijebu territory. Since British diplomacy failed to change the situation, the British resorted to force. On the pretext that the Ijebu-Ode authorities had insulted the British queen during a Lagos official's visit, the British commenced a military expedition into Ijebu, whose people prepared to defend their country. The final encounter took place at Magbon. The Ijebu forces fought gallantly, but in the end they had no answer for the British artillery pieces. The British therefore occupied and annexed the Ijebu-Ode kingdom and the rest of the Ijebu country.

In the further Yoruba interior, the success of the British government of Lagos in persuading Ibadan and the Ekitiparapo to sign a peace treaty in 1886 had immensely boosted their image. As the years dragged on after 1886 and the Yoruba themselves showed no ability to move the peace process forward, all

Yorubaland in the Nineteenth Century: Other Agencies 361

eyes turned to the British for help. In addition to the missionaries, the Lagos traders, the Lagos emigrant community, and significant Yoruba kings (especially the Alaafin) appealed to the Lagos administration to intervene and bring the wars to an end. Therefore, in 1888, the British signed a treaty with the Alaafin, and in 1893, treaties with the Alaafin and Ibadan separately. By 1893, therefore, the ground was prepared for a final resolution of the deadlock on the Kiriji War front as well as of other difficulties. Therefore, a high-powered commission of the Lagos government accompanied by a small unit of troops proceeded into the interior and saw to the departure of the Ibadan and Ekitiparapo armies from the Kiriji front. With that, the greatest war in the Yoruba interior finally came to an end. At a ceremony on the River Otin, the Ibadan–Ilorin hostilities were also brought to an end.

British intervention had the historic consequence of giving to the British a wonderful opportunity to pursue their own imperial interests in the interior of Yorubaland. In the treaties signed with Yoruba rulers after 1886, the British included harmless-looking clauses which provided for, or implied, British protection and sovereignty. The most important of such treaties was the one with Ibadan. Its Clause Four provided for the stationing in Ibadan of a British Resident, whose duty it would be to ensure that wars would not be resumed. With the first Resident, Capt. R. L. Bower, in Ibadan, it very quickly became clear that the British, as represented by the British administration of Lagos, had taken over the whole of the Yoruba interior – with the exception of Ilorin and an indefinite boundary area in the southeast (comprising the Owo kingdom). From then on, the assertion of British sovereignty, and the details of the administration of a British protectorate, with its headquarters in Ibadan, proceeded apace.

In 1897, two other agencies of British imperialism took possession of the rest of Yorubaland north and east of Ibadan. Forces of the Royal Niger Company, conquering the lands of the Niger valley and the territories north of the Niger, established control over the distant northeastern Yoruba territories (the homelands of the Yagba, Jumu, Bunu, Owe and Oworo, and parts of Igbomina), and conquered Ilorin. In the same year, forces of the Niger Coast Protectorate invaded and conquered the kingdom of Benin and proceeded to treat the Owo kingdom as part of the area under its control. In the years that followed, Owo found its proper place in Yorubaland in the administrative unit that became known as the Protectorate of Southern Nigeria. Ilorin and the other Yoruba territories initially controlled or claimed by the Royal Niger Company, as well as most of Igbomina and parts of northern Ekiti, were, however, included in the Protectorate of Northern Nigeria. Other than the conquest of these northern Yoruba territories by the agency of the Royal Niger Company (which had also conquered much of Northern Nigeria), there was no real justification for including them in Northern Nigeria, separate from their people in Southern Nigeria. Thus European imperial overlordship commenced, for the Yoruba people, with the fragmentation of Yorubaland: first between three different countries (Nigeria, Dahomey and Togo), and then, in Nigeria, into two parts (with two different British imperial administrations). In 1914, the Protectorate of Northern Nigeria and the Colony and Protectorate of Southern Nigeria were amalgamated as one country, the Colony and Protectorate of Nigeria, while remaining two separate administrations of that country. In spite of the obvious historical and ethnic irrationality of their territorial arrangement that had split Yorubaland into two in Nigeria, the British preserved that split throughout their overlordship over Nigeria.

A Nineteenth Century Overview

We must conclude this and the previous chapter together then with the statement that the nineteenth century was, for Yoruba people, a great century of change, transformation and progress. Because the Yoruba wars of the century were extensive, tumultuous and had a great impact, one can be tempted to view the nineteenth century in Yoruba history as "a century of wars." But such a characterization would be wrong. It was a century of a whole complex of huge and many-sided movements of change. Yorubaland and Yoruba society were very different by 1900 from what they had been in 1800. Cities, states and centers of population and power non-existent in 1800 dominated the geography and politics of Yorubaland by the 1890s, replacing many of the great centers of power dominant in 1800. The impact of Islam, Christianity and Western education, as well as significant economic changes had, by 1900, transformed Yoruba society far beyond what it had been in 1800.

Of course, there were innumerable and fundamental continuities. For instance, the Yoruba language was, by 1900, still itself (with its many dialects); but a "standard Yoruba" was evolving – the standard for all written communication in Yoruba, and the language taught in the schools. Born out of efforts to translate the Bible and other Christian literature, the "standard Yoruba" language, a creative amalgam of various Yoruba dialects, was already formalized with an alphabet and poised to become the preeminent common dialect. The *babalawo*, the *onisegun*, and the priests of the ancient Yoruba gods were still the notables of spiritual leadership, but they were beginning to have in their lineages the Islamic priest and the Christian priest, both of whom were making a strong bid to redirect the spiritual consciousness of all Yoruba people. Increasingly, the calendar of religious festivities in every community came to include days of Islamic, Christian, and traditional rituals and festivals. As new tools were coming into the service of old professions and pastimes, new ones were making their appearance. The Oba was still the "lieutenant of the gods," but new elites (products of the wars, of Islam, of Christianity, of Western education, of commerce and other economic enterprise) had, by the 1890s, appeared confidently on the scene. By 1895, the Yoruba people were very much a people advancing upon new frontiers.

One other important point needs to be made. The Ibadan-based attempt to unify, with the force of arms, all of Yorubaland into one single state, though fairly successful until about 1877, never had much of a chance in some parts of the country, and ultimately ran into widespread resistance. But besides that, other strong unifying developments entered upon the scene – the emergence and growth of a literate elite that became gradually, and then aggressively, pan-Yoruba in consciousness, the upsurge of Yoruba cultural nationalism (with its many ramifications), the making of a common orthography for writing the Yoruba language, the gradual evolution of a modern economy, the emergence of a business and professional class, etc. All of these combined to point to great possibilities for the future of the Yoruba as one people. In fact, the chances looked good that, if the advancing trends had been allowed to continue in their native strength, the outcome could have been the emergence of a modern Yoruba nation state in West Africa – similar to how the Japanese unified their country about the same time and rapidly became a powerful modern nation state in Asia. The imposition of European rule over Yorubaland cut off the possibility of a progression to such an outcome for the Yoruba people.

28. Followers of Orisha Yemaya at Havana's harbour during the celebration of the Yemaya Day. *Photo: A. Roque, 2009, AFP Photo.*

16

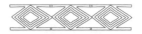

The Yoruba Diaspora

The Atlantic slave trade was not the first agency that established elements of the Yoruba as settlers beyond the homeland. As earlier pointed out, trade had, before then, resulted in Yoruba settler colonies in many distant places on the African continent. Before, and during, the centuries of the Atlantic slave trade, colonies of Yoruba traders lived in Nupe, Hausa and Kanuri towns in the north, in Benin in the southeast, in probably every sizeable Aja town in the west, and probably in as far away places as the valley of the Senegal in the west and the valley of the Congo in the east. To these must be added those Yoruba who ended up as slaves in Dahomey in the nineteenth century. Together, all these amounted to a very sizeable Yoruba diaspora unrelated to the transatlantic slave trade. Moreover, there are fairly clear indications of the impact of Yoruba culture in at least some of these distant lands – for instance, the impact of Yoruba political culture and language among the Edo and the Aja, the widespread influence of Yoruba trading practices, and the influence of Yoruba religion among various peoples in West Africa. What the Atlantic slave trade did was to lengthen the reach of the Yoruba diaspora beyond Africa to the Americas (as well as to Sierra Leone), and to create extracted and mixed African communities within which the Yoruba culture came to offer very significant cultural contributions.

Yoruba people were latecomers to the enforced transplantation of Africans as slaves across the Atlantic Ocean to the Americas. The Atlantic slave trade started in the sixteenth century, but hardly any Yoruba were recorded in the trade until the seventeenth century, and these were very few. From about 1750, starting with the beginning of the troubles in the Oyo Empire, the number of Yoruba slaves on the slave ships began to increase. It then increased rapidly as the nineteenth century opened, reaching a peak in about 1826, and remaining more or less at that peak until 1850. From about 1850, the number declined and continued to dwindle until about 1867 when the transatlantic shipment of Africans as slaves finally ceased.

The total number of Yoruba taken to the Americas as slaves (from the first in about the late sixteenth century to the last ones in about 1867) has been estimated to be about 1.12 million, representing a little less than 9 percent of all Africans taken to the Americas as slaves during the three centuries of the trade. Of this number, nearly 80 percent were taken away in the century between 1750 and 1850.[1]

Yoruba slaves were taken to most regions of the Americas – from the area of Chesapeake Bay in North America to that of Rio de la Plata in South America, as well as to many of the islands of the West Indies. Various sizes of Yoruba slave groups emerged in Virginia, North Carolina, South Carolina, Georgia and Florida in North America; some of the countries of Central America – Costa Rica, Nicaragua, Panama, and others; Guyana, Surinam, Venezuela and Brazil in South America; and Cuba, Saint-Domingue (Haiti), Jamaica, Trinidad, Tobago, Barbados, Guadeloupe, Martinique, St. Lucia, etc. in the West Indies.

In only three of these destinations – namely, Saint-Domingue, the large island of Cuba, and the province of Bahia in Brazil – did Yoruba slaves constitute sizeable percentages of the total numbers of African slaves. Estimates of Yoruba arrivals in these three destinations vary. According to recent estimates, a total of 700,000 African slaves were received into Saint-Domingue, of whom about 173,000 originated from ports on the Bight of Benin (that is, the coasts of modern western Nigeria and of the Republics of Benin and Togo). Of the 173,000, about 25 percent to 30 percent – or 43,000–57,000 – were Yoruba. An estimated total of about 564,000 African slaves were taken to Cuba, about 85 percent of them during the nineteenth century alone. Since for some years of the nineteenth century, the Yoruba constituted the largest single ethnic group being exported from the coasts of West Africa, slave imports into Cuba contained large numbers of persons of Yoruba origin. It is estimated that about 12 percent of Cuba's African slave imports were of Yoruba origin – that is, roughly 68,000. The Portuguese colonies in South America, which by 1822 became together the independent country of Brazil, were the destination of some 3.5 million African slaves, imported from about 1550 to about 1850 to various parts of the country. Of these, about 25 percent (that is, about 850,000) originated from West African ports; the rest from West-Central Africa (the area of the Congo and Angola). The coast of West Africa was known among Portuguese slave traders as Mina coast, and therefore, all slaves coming from West Africa were called the Mina in most parts of Brazil. It was not until the last quarter of the eighteenth century that Yoruba slaves began to be significant in Brazilian slave imports. From 1800 to 1850, the total number of Yoruba arriving in various provinces of Brazil rose much higher than before, and from then on the group name Mina came to be applied specifically to the Yoruba slaves in most parts of Brazil – except in the province of Bahia where they were called Nago. The name Nago is believed to be derived from Anago, a common name by which Yoruba people were known among Dahomey and other Aja people, from among whom many slaves came to the Americas in general, and to Brazil, long before the arrival of the earliest Yoruba slaves. In spite of the considerable increase in Yoruba arrivals, Yoruba slaves continued to be minorities among African slaves in most parts of the country – with the exception of the province of Bahia. In the province of Bahia, the Yoruba became the largest group of arriving slaves from about 1800, because Bahian slave carriers came to concentrate much of their traffic on the ports of the Yoruba coast. It has been estimated that a total of 439,000 Yoruba slaves were taken to Bahia from about 1675 to about 1850, and that about 292,000 of these were taken there during the fifty years 1800–1850. The total Yoruba imports of 439,000 represented about 40 percent of all African slaves received by Bahia throughout the era of the Atlantic slave trade.

In no other area of the Americas did the Yoruba as a group have the level of numerical strength in the African slave community (and freed African community) that they had in the above three destinations. But, as will be seen below, even though they were numerically small in most places, their cultural influence and impact was considerable almost everywhere they were taken.

In all destinations to which the African slaves were taken in the Americas, their lives came to exhibit certain common features. First, they were imported and purchased to supply labor – on plantations (of sugar cane, tobacco, cotton, etc.), in other agricultural pursuits, in processing enterprises (like sugar processing), in the mines, in the ports, in various trades, in commerce, as carriers of goods, and as domestic hands for their masters. Their lives as slaves were tied to these enterprises and to activities ancillary to such, and their quality of life (in shelter, food and other provisions) depended on the particular conditions of their servitude. Secondly, even if any African slaves were shipped to the Americas in boats containing mostly or even only slaves from their own ethnic group or nationality, they invariably were thrown together, in the Americas, with slaves from other African ethnic and cultural groups. Each slave community was thus confronted with the challenge of forging and inventing new bonds of association and identity, drawing on the realities of their situation – but, as most studies of the African diaspora would now confirm, every such creating, inventing and forging was informed by the African cultural heritages that the slaves had brought with them. Thus were produced the many variations of "African-American" cultures, or Creole cultures, now existing as very significant contributions to the civilizations of the New World.

Of the contributions of the cultural heritage of the Yoruba people to these processes, a fair amount is known today. And the overall assessment seems to be that the cultural impact of the Yoruba people on the evolution of

African-American or Creole cultures was great – greater than the numbers of the Yoruba slaves could justify. In a recent study, David Eltis writes:

> Within coerced African migration, the Yoruba were among the latest to arrive but were neither the most numerous nor the least scattered over the Americas. Reasonably precise estimates for other groups will eventually become available; but it is probable that Igbo and some West-Central African peoples were larger and more heavily concentrated than the Yoruba – the Igbo in parts of the British Caribbean and some of what have been termed Congo groups in southeast Brazil. Yet the impact of the Yoruba speakers on Creole societies that emerged in many parts of the Americas appears to modern scholars to have been strong and, in the light of the evidence presented here, out of proportion to the relative size of Yoruba arrivals.[2]

In comparison, that is, with other African groups, they contributed considerably more to Creole or African-American civilization in "oral traditions, especially as expressed in songs, religious rituals, stories, proverbs, and so on,"[3] as well as in various modes of family and societal structures.

The main explanation for this is to be found in the strength of the civilization from which the Yoruba of the New World were extracted and taken away into slavery – its strong family and settlement traditions, its urban orientation, its social and associational traditions, its innumerable cooperative, collaborative and support institutions, its highly developed artistic culture as expressed in the visual arts and folklore, and its strong religion. The view of the Yoruba voiced by Louis Antoine Aimé de Verteuil in 1858 is similar to views expressed by many other foreign observers in that century. He wrote that they were:

> guided in marked degree by the sense of association; … the principle of combination for the common weal has been fully sustained wherever they have settled in any numbers; in fact the whole Yoruba race may be said to form a sort of social league for mutual support and protection.[4]

An additional explanation was the widespread cultural influence which the Yoruba established over much of West Africa before and during the centuries of the slave trade. To the east and west of Yorubaland, Yoruba traditions and myths of origin, and Yoruba ideas of the importance of Ife, early influenced the Edo and Aja. As states and trade grew in these places, the Yoruba language, as would be remembered, developed into a sort of common language, especially for commercial purposes – no doubt a product of the widespread impact of Yoruba trade. The expansion of Yoruba cultural influence reached its climax in the era of the greatness of the Oyo Empire, Oyo being, not only an empire-builder and trader, but a mighty carrier of Yoruba culture far and wide. Founded and led by a mixture of Yoruba and Aja elements, the kingdom of Dahomey minutely mirrored Yoruba cultural institutions and traditions, all of which were later reinforced by Oyo conquest and overlordship. In particular through the Dahomey and other Aja people taken as slaves across the Atlantic, the influence of Yoruba culture was already significant in a number of places, for instance, Saint-Domingue (Haiti), long before the arrival of Yoruba slaves, and considerably assisted the growth of Yoruba cultural influence after that point.

The Nagos of Bahia[5]

Bahia province was one of the richest sugar plantation areas of Brazil, beginning from the sixteenth century. Most of its sugar plantations were established in the area of soft marshy soil known as Recôncavo lying east of Salvador, the capital city of Bahia. Bahia was also important for another cash crop – tobacco. Manioc, or cassava, grown extensively in the province, was the main food for the masses of slaves, freed persons and the poor.

Practically every one of the many African ethnic groups of Bahia organized for itself some sort of collective association or *parente* (the Portuguese word for 'relative'), but the available evidence indicates that the Nago group was the most cohesive, strongest and most influential.

Nago *parentes* groups existed on the plantations, in the remote villages, as well as in the city of Salvador. Many factors contributed to the building of the Nago identity. Of these, the foremost, of course, was the common Yoruba language. Then there were the common religion, Yoruba facial marks, surviving Yoruba personal names, belief in common descent from Oduduwa, and belief in Ife as a common, sacred, ancestral home. Religion gave the whole package a very powerful binder. On the whole, local and lineage deities and spirits common back home in Yorubaland tended to fade away in the slave community in Bahia, giving way and prominence to the pan-Yoruba gods – like the supreme deity Olorun (ruler of heaven), Obatala, Ogun, Sango, Ifa, Olokun, Yemoja, etc. The worship of these *orisas* of Yoruba civilization became known in Bahia as Candomblé. Inevitably, other non-Yoruba elements in the general African society of Bahia contributed some features to Candomblé, but, essentially, in its ultimate form, Candomblé was Yoruba – and a significant gift to the civilization of Bahia and Brazil. Rituals, festivals and the forms of art in the worship of the Yoruba gods have continued vibrantly in Brazil, spreading beyond Bahia to Rio de Janeiro and other parts of the country. In fact, in more recent times, descendants of non-Yoruba African peoples of Brazil have increasingly embraced Candomblé and Yoruba forms of art as a means of asserting an African heritage and identity. Even significant parts of the white Brazilian population have become attracted into the culture represented by Candomblé.

In nineteenth century Bahia, Candomblé served to reinforce Yoruba ethnic identity by bringing adherents together frequently in rituals, divinations, sacrifices, feasts and festivals, usually including loud music with drums as well as dancing. At the beginning, some of the Nagos were excluded from Candomblé because of their adherence to other religions (especially to Islam and to Roman Catholicism, the religion of the Portuguese slave masters). Some of the Yoruba taken as slaves to Bahia were Muslims, while interaction with the Portuguese resulted in the emergence of some Nago Roman Catholic converts and brotherhoods. Over time, however, the exclusion of the Nago Muslims and Roman Catholics was overcome in a uniquely Nago fashion. While in Yoruba religion the *orisas* are worshipped separately, each with his or her own shrine and rituals, Roman Catholicism's many saints are venerated in the same church building. The Nagos came to adopt for Candomblé this Roman Catholic practice – so that all Yoruba gods and goddesses came to be worshipped under the same roof. This simplified Candomblé for all Nagos; it also resulted ultimately in the convergence, for the Nagos, of the idioms of Candomblé and Roman Catholicism. The Nagos thus invented a Yoruba Catholicism, making it possible for each individual Nago to belong to both the religious systems of the *orisas* and the Catholic saints, to have patron saints and patron *orisas*, and to be free to choose to offer sacrifices to the *orisas* and the saints. As for Islam, the Yoruba Muslims in Bahia had formed themselves into local groups early in the century and their leaders had in fact taken over the leadership of Islam in Bahia from other Muslim peoples like the Hausa. During the second half of the century, however, the Muslim groups and Islam in general declined, so that, gradually, virtually all Nagos flowed into the general spiritual spectrum of Candomblé. Within Candomblé, therefore, Nago ethnic identity and solidarity became strongly expressed in spiritual and ritualistic terms.

In terms of work and the workplace, there were many differences between the Nagos who lived and worked on the plantations and the rural villages and those who lived and worked in the city of Salvador. For both, however, Candomblé's rituals and celebrations, as well as other expressions and institutions of Nago ethnic solidarity, were very important pillars of life. They did not only knit together Nagos of particular plantations and villages, they created links between Nago groups in distant plantations and villages, and between these and the Nagos of the city. Official records of various localities of Bahia contain accounts of Nago celebrations in villages and plantations, some of them at the workplace, and some bringing together large numbers of Nagos from many villages and plantations, especially on public holidays.

In the city, Nagos worked either as domestic hands or in the streets. Some of those who worked in the streets worked as cooks, tailors, seamstresses, washerwomen, bricklayers, carpenters, porters, traders, etc. Of the men, some worked in the ports, loading and unloading ships and carrying heavy loads of cargo for delivery to merchants' warehouses or to homes. Some of the men also worked as sedan-chair carriers to convey rich clients through the streets. For the women who sold cooked food in the streets, and for men and women who sold other goods, life was very similar to life in typical Yoruba towns where, in addition to the mass trading in the marketplaces, petty traders went from street to street offering things for sale. Slaves usually lived in quarters provided by their masters, but they were free to go out and work in the streets. (In very few cases, masters allowed their slaves to live in houses rented by the slaves themselves.)

Among the Nago slaves working in the streets, a practice arose whereby workers in the same trades were organized into groups called *cantos* – each of which was modeled after the Yoruba farming institutions of *aaro* or *owe*, within which, as would be remembered, members collaborated to give voluntary services to one another on their farms. Other ethnic groups among the slaves had *cantos* also, organized along lines of their own cultures. Each Nago *canto* appointed one of its members as its captain, whose function it was to work out the details of job contracts with clients, to allocate tasks in the job, to receive payment from clients and distribute it to members. Within each *canto*, members usually rendered small, uniquely Yoruba, services to one another: the Ifa diviner performed divinations for the rest, the herbalist or healer prescribed herbal preparations and treatments.

Almost all the above work by slaves in the streets was governed by a system called *ganho* or 'hire-out'. Under the system, a slave entered into an agreement with his master to go and work in the streets and bring home to the master daily or weekly a given sum of money, and keep the rest of his earnings to himself. The city slave could thus have some independent income, and if he was hard-working and prudent in handling his money, he could build up some savings. In the plantations and villages, a slave was usually allowed to raise a small garden, where he grew manioc and vegetables, part of the harvest of which he could sell in the slave community. Usually he would process the manioc into flour for sale. Like the city slave, the village or plantation slave could thus build up some savings.

The most important thing that a slave usually used his savings for was to buy his freedom. It was part of the Bahian system that a slave could offer money to his master as payment for freedom. Many masters would accept such payment and set their slaves free. However, a master was not obliged to do so; he could refuse – but a master's refusal in such a situation usually led to troubles between the master and his slave. Quite often, it resulted in slaves running away to secure their freedom – usually a very risky step, since fugitive slaves were usually likely to be recaptured and severely punished. In 1871, a law was made to correct this situation; the law laid it down that if a slave offered a fair price for his freedom, his master must accept and set him free. In some cases, masters chose on their own to set free, without any payment, slaves who had very good records of service. The way that this mostly happened was that an old slave master would include in his will a grant of freedom to the favored slave.

From as early as the first decade of the nineteenth century, therefore, there were some freed men and women in the Nago community. In most cases, freed persons simply continued to work the same trades as they had been doing before their manumission, and remained as members of the *cantos* to which they had belonged. Some of the most enterprising established fairly successful trading businesses, became fairly rich and came to own slaves. Mostly, they would take merchandise from the city for sale to rural communities, and bring from the rural areas livestock like chickens and pigs as well as farm produce and manioc flour for sale in the city. Some even became international traders, traveling as passengers on the slave ships and buying goods (especially homespun Yoruba cloth) on the West African coast for sale in the Nago community in Bahia.

Candomblé's rituals and celebrations, and various other Nago networks, served as powerful agencies of mutual help and support. For instance, the Nago slave struggling to obtain his freedom, while slowly saving money for the purpose, also had some support to lean on in the Nago community – help through manumission societies known as *juntas de alfornia*. These were credit organizations which provided funds (in the form of rotational loans) to assist individuals to buy their freedom – a sort of Nago version of the Yoruba system of *esusu*. The individual would borrow money from the group to supplement his personal savings, and buy freedom for himself. When he became free, he would pay the loan back in instalments into the fund. For the Nago slave who was compelled by circumstances to choose to run away from his master, help was usually available also, not only from close family and friends, but, more importantly, from the extended Nago networks – especially if other members of the Nago community were convinced that running away was, in the particular case, justified.

Moreover, more substantial forms of resistance to slavery, such as large-scale revolts, were quite common among the Nagos. In fact, the Nagos revolted more frequently, and exhibited much better organization in revolt, than any other African group in Bahia – proof of their more sophisticated networking. In other provinces of Brazil, the Nagos of Bahia became widely known for their revolts, and yet, on the whole, the slavery system and the conditions of the Nagos in Bahia do not appear to have been any more oppressive than one would find among other African slaves in Bahia or in any other part of Brazil. The frequent and massive revolts by the Nagos were therefore apparently a function of their native culture. The typical political life in a Yoruba kingdom and community tended, on the whole, to nurture confidence and a spirit of freedom; and it is significant that many of the young Yoruba men taken into slavery in the early nineteenth century had taken part in wars in their country, and therefore had come to Bahia with some military training, skills and experience.

The first major Nago rebellion on record occurred in 1814, when large numbers of Nagos joined with other ethnic groups (mostly Hausas) in a wide-ranging armed action that attacked parts of the port areas and headed for the main plantation areas, before they were stopped and overcome by troops. Other similar revolts, in which the Nagos allied with other groups, followed. The 1820s witnessed more than twelve violent revolts in which the Nagos provided the leadership and most, or sometimes all, of the activists. Some of these resulted in the burning of sugar cane plantations and plantation headquarters; one in September 1827 burnt ten plantations before it was suppressed.

Between 1828 and 1830, the Bahian authorities set up a plan whereby military units were stationed in the plantations, thus protecting them against the Nago revolts. That, however, did not put an end to the revolts; it only shifted them into the city of Salvador itself. In April 1830, a major Nago revolt shook the city. Supplied early in the morning with swords and knives looted from some hardware warehouses, a large crowd of Nagos gathered. Newly imported Yoruba slaves were roused and asked to join; many did, and the few who refused to join were killed. The large army of rebels then attacked a garrison or police establishment, but they did not have the kinds of weapons that might have enabled them to overcome its defenders. As the fighting raged, more troops arrived, and the revolt was brutally put down. Five years later, in January 1835, the most serious revolt in Salvador followed. The Nago slaves put much careful planning into this revolt, assisted by some Nago freed men. Their intention was to strike on Sunday, January 25. Unfortunately for them, however, their plans leaked to the authorities. As they were putting finishing touches to their plans on the evening of Saturday, in the home of a Nago freed man, law enforcement authorities burst upon them. The plotters resisted arrest, and the fighting between them and their assailants spread to the streets, where large numbers of African slaves (overwhelmingly Nagos) responded to the call of the rebel leaders, and a massive crowd surged through the streets, shouting the battle cry, "*Viva Nago*" (meaning, "Long live the Nagos"). Attacks on police stations, military barracks and other institutions of government followed. Unable to take any of these (because they did not have guns), they then made a bid to reach the region of the plantations, where Nago plantation slaves were waiting, according to arrangement, to join them. But before they could get far, the militia intercepted them. Fighting the well-armed troops as best as they could, the rebels were finally scattered and suppressed.

The Nagos numbered only about 30 percent of the African population of Bahia in 1835, but their numerical participation in this large revolt of early 1835 has been estimated to have been in excess of 70 percent; and their share in the organized leadership of it was nearly 100 percent. In the trials that followed the revolt, almost all the dozens of the ringleaders found guilty and convicted were Nagos (three were Hausas). Of its foremost leaders, four (all Nagos) were executed.

Most of these revolts were led by city slaves, but the Nago networks made it easy for plantation and village slaves to be quickly involved. Some of the freed persons among the Nagos secretly or openly assisted the revolts. In some of the revolts, run-away slave communities known as *quilimbos*, hidden in the woods, played significant roles. In such places Candomblé usually had a strong presence, and contributed much to the spirit and promotion of revolt. In the 1835 revolt, many of the Nago revolt planners were Muslims, but all of them did what they did as members of the "Nago nation" and not in the service of religion. By the time of the revolt, the Nagos had become dominant in Islamic leadership in Bahia. Following the suppression of the revolt, Islam and its influence declined among the Nagos as well as in Bahia in general.

The 1835 revolt was the last major slave revolt in Bahia, but it did not mark the end of militant resistance by the Nagos to unjust constraints. Concerning the slave trade and slavery, the situation was changing in the world in general – changes pointing to the end of both. The Nagos gradually changed with the changing prospects, focusing their acts of resistance on specific acts of oppression. When in 1836–7 the government decided to abolish the *cantos* and substitute for them government-created work groups, the Nagos (slaves and freed persons alike) resisted so emphatically that all work in the city nearly ground to a halt – forcing the business owners to speak up in support of the *cantos*, thus forcing the government to give up. This kind of confrontation resurfaced in the 1850s, when the municipal government of Salvador made a law in 1857 demanding that porters in the city be registered, pay an annual tax, and display identity badges on their persons. Led by the Nagos, who constituted a majority of porters, the porters went on strike for a whole week – the first such strike in the history of Brazil – paralyzing business in the city. Again, the business owners, whose businesses were threatened with destruction, brought pressure to bear on the government, forcing it to give up the tax (though not the identity badges).

The end finally came to the slave trade in Bahia and all of Brazil – and ultimately to slavery also. The slave trade was abolished in Brazil in 1850, causing any further importation of slaves to Bahia to cease. From the 1860s slavery became the hottest issue in Brazilian politics. Powerful interests resisted the abolition of slavery, even as all other countries in the Americas abolished it. Finally, however, slavery was abolished in Brazil too in 1888.

The Lucumis of Cuba[6]

It is probable that some of the earliest few Yoruba people to be involved in the Atlantic slave trade were taken by Spanish traders to Cuba and Saint-Domingue in the sixteenth century. Cuban records of the 1570s mention some Lucumi slaves. As in other places in the Americas, however, it was not until the late eighteenth century that the Yoruba began to appear in considerable numbers among slaves arriving in Cuba. Then, from the beginning of the nineteenth century, with the wars going on in Yorubaland, and with Cuba needing many slaves for its expanding sugar cane plantations, the number of Yoruba arriving in Cuba rose very sharply. As earlier pointed out, these increases raised the total number of Yoruba slaves imported to Cuba throughout the centuries of the slave trade to about 12 percent of all African slaves imported to the island. This means that, even in spite of the high numbers of Yoruba arrivals in the early nineteenth century, persons of Yoruba descent were always a small minority among persons of African descent in Cuba.

Yoruba slaves (and also, later, Yoruba freed persons) were called Lucumis in Cuba – and in many other places in the Americas. In Cuba, however, that name appears to have been more intensively and more persistently used. Concerning the origin of the name, there has been considerable debate among scholars. We may discard the suggestion that it came from the name of a Yoruba kingdom called Ulkomi or Ulkami, because we know that no Yoruba kingdom ever bore such a name (even though Olfert Dapper mentioned a "kingdom of Ulkami" in 1668). There has been speculation that it might have arisen from the Yoruba phrase, *Oluku mi* ("my friend"), with which Yoruba slaves probably identified and greeted one another in the strange and oppressive environment of New World slavery. Whatever its origin, the name Lucumi stuck to Yoruba people in most parts of the New World; and it has been most often employed for the Yoruba people of Cuba. In the earliest years of their presence in Cuba in the late sixteenth and early seventeenth century, the Yoruba slaves seem to have been identified by the appending of the names of their subgroups – thus, Lucumi-Yabu (Ijebu), Lucumi-Euba (Egba), Lucumi-Io (Oyo), etc.

From the beginning of slavery in Cuba, the African slaves became organized into fraternities known as *cabildos de nación*, each of which brought together Africans of the same ethnic origin. Approved of, and encouraged by, the Spanish rulers of the island, each *cabildo de nación* served as a forum within which Africans of the same ethnic group interacted together to practice and preserve their cultural heritage, their language, their native rituals, art, music, dance, chants, folklore, etc. Later, when, through manumission, a number of Africans became freed persons, they joined the *cabildos de nación* of their respective ethnic groups in all parts of the country. In general, these associations became very powerful instruments of mutual help and support in the social and economic lives of their members, providing various kinds of assistance, contact, and recreation. Typically, each was led by a *capital* (king or captain) and a *matrona* (queen), who not only provided leadership in the internal affairs of their association, but also managed its relationships with the colonial and local authorities.

For the Lucumis in Cuba, the *cabildos de nación* proved an invaluable organization within which they developed a Yoruba-Cuban cultural heritage, based on Yoruba social, religious, ritualistic, musical, dance, artistic and aesthetic values, and drawing richly and meaningfully on the Spanish and inter-African heritages of the Cuban milieu. In the process, in spite of their comparative smallness in the over-all African population of Cuba, in spite of their comparative lateness to come in sizeable numbers to Cuba, and in spite of contributions by cultures of the Aja and the Congo, the Lucumis came to contribute, during the nineteenth century, more than any other African ethnic group to the development and definition of an Afro-Cuban identity and culture. In fact, for the *cabildos de nación* of the capital city, Havana, Yoruba cultural roots provided ultimately the major part of the African foundation upon which growth was attained in aesthetics, music, dance, rituals, literature, etc. In the course of the 1920s and 1930s, African identity and consciousness created, from the nineteenth century roots, the Afrocubanismo movement which strongly defined and highlighted African contributions to the cultural development of Cuba. According to Eltis, many aspects of Afro-Cuban culture may not be instantly recognizable to Yoruba people in West Africa, "but it would be difficult to find many of its roots in non-Yoruba Africa."[7]

One of the most important gifts of the Lucumis to Afro-Cuban culture was the religion known as Santería. Like the Bahian Candomblé, Santería received some inputs from various African cultural heritages in Cuba, but its African foundation and ultimate form were based on Yoruba religion and the Yoruba worship of the *orisas*. Santería was developed from a syncretization of the Yoruba worship of the *orisas* with Roman Catholic practices. What resulted was neither an African nor Roman Catholic religion, but a peculiar Cuban spiritual and ritual system mostly based on Yoruba religious and ritual systems. "Santería" means both "the way of the saints" (that is, the saints of the Roman Catholic faith) and *La regla de Ocha* ("the rule of the *orisas*"). The central doctrine of Santería is that every human being has a guiding and protector spirit – that is, an *orisa* or saint – who is like a parent to the person (for which reason adherents of Santería often say that they are sons or daughters of their guiding saints or *orisas*). Each of the spiritual beings in this arrangement is associated with a force of nature and some aspect of human life (a central belief in Yoruba religion). For instance, Chango (also known as Saint Barbara) is the *orisa* or saint that controls lightning, thunder and fire, giver of power over difficulties, symbol of passion and strength. Yemaja (also known as the Virgin of Regla) is the *orisa* or saint of the sea and symbol of motherhood. Tens of saints and *orisas* were thus given attributes and symbolisms in this complex religious system. The god of divination, Ifa or Orunmila, is very important in Santería, as the giver of hidden knowledge or wisdom to help individuals through the vicissitudes of their lives. For this reason, diviners, called *babalawo*, are important persons in the whole spiritual system.

Although Santería developed in the *cabildos de nación* which, as would be remembered, had the approval of the Spanish colonial authorities, its profoundly syncretic nature made it largely unacceptable to them. However, with the emergence of the Afrocubanismo movement in independent Cuba in the 1920s, Santería's stature as a major African contribution to Afro-Cuban culture and Cuban civilization at last became firmly established. Santería remains today a major spiritual influence among Cubans of African descent (blacks and persons of mixed blood), who constitute an estimated 32 percent of the population.

Resistance to slavery was not as pronounced or as successful in Cuba as in Bahia, but the Lucumis appear to have been in the forefront of almost all of the serious plots conceived by African slaves and freed Africans in the nineteenth century to revolt and abolish slavery and Spanish rule on the island – one in 1812, another in 1835, and yet another in 1844. Leading Lucumis, slave and free, were among the persons arrested, tried and punished for these plots. One Jose Antonio Aponte, described as an influential freed man among the Lucumis and a member of the Ogboni secret society, was the brain behind the 1812 plot. Tried and found guilty, he was executed with his accomplices, some of whom were leading members of his *cabildo*. After the 1835 plot was exposed, it was called the Lucumi Conspiracy, because its planners were prominent Lucumis. Of the hundreds of conspirators arrested for the plot known as the Conspiracy of La Escalera in 1844, many were Lucumis. Here as in Bahia, the Yoruba love of freedom pushed many leading men and women of Yoruba descent to engage in plots to end slavery and Spanish rule even though, as is evident in the outcome of each plot, the government of the island was very vigilant.

The Revolutionaries of Haiti[8]

The earliest Yoruba slaves brought to the large island of Hispaniola, also known as Saint-Domingue, of which the western half (now known as Haiti) belonged to France, and the eastern half (now known as the Dominican Republic) belonged to Spain, probably came in the sixteenth century. However, it was not until the seventeenth century that Yoruba slave imports became important in Saint-Domingue. During the 1780s, demand for slaves by the plantations of Saint-Domingue reached great heights, resulting in the importation of very many slaves from the West African region. Most of such West African slaves were of Aja (Dahomey) and Yoruba origin. From 1790, great developments commenced on the island, leading to a massive and determined slave revolt that destroyed the French government and resulted in the emergence of an independent country with the name Haiti in 1804. The French planters fled the island, some of them with their slaves, and scattered to various destinations in the Americas, some ultimately coming to settle in Louisiana and South Carolina in the southern United States, as well as on the island of Jamaica. Further importations of slaves to Haiti ceased, and this new country of slaves who had fought and freed themselves became the first country in the world to abolish slavery.

The history of the Haitian Revolution, 1791–1804, is filled with stories of great courage and heroism by the rebelling slaves. In the face of some of Europe's best armies, sent by the Emperor Napoleon Bonaparte from France to suppress the rebellion, the slaves produced great leaders of men and won incredible victories in battles. Of the many leaders who emerged among them in the course of the revolution, two in particular, Toussaint L'Ouverture and Jean-Jacques Dessalines, both of them ex-slaves, earned immortality for their bravery and high quality of command in battle as well as for their leadership qualities.

Of the many battles won by the poorly equipped slave armies against vastly superior French forces, the one that was fought on November 16, 1803 remains perhaps the most memorable because it was one of the decisive final battles in the Revolution. Randall Robinson describes that battle thus:

> Reports on the famous battle were that, under blistering fire from the French muskets and heavy-gauge artillery pieces, Capois Death, a black officer leading a column of ex-slave soldiers, shouted above the concussive blasts, "En avant!

En avant!" Forward! Forward! as, mounted, he hurled himself and his men against the French line of fire, in an assault on the blockhouses of Breda and Champlin. Demonstrating the bravery that gave him his *nom de guerre*, Death, he then rode at full gallop toward the French fort at Vertières. When his horse was shot from under him, he rose and charged afoot toward the thick walls of the fort, pointing his sword in the direction of the French guns mounted behind the parapet, crying out anew to his men, "En avant! En avant!" His hat was then shot from his head. Again, he charged the French guns that exploded the ground around him. Men fell gut-shot, blood all about. The sounds, sight, and smell of the awful deaths mixed with peals of thundering ordnance. "En avant! En avant!" Death screamed, afoot still, never slowing. It was the battle that turned the war and handed victory to an army of ex-slaves who had soundly defeated three of the very best of Europe's armies.[9]

The revolt lasted twelve and a half years. Of the black slave and ex-slave population of about 465,000 in Saint-Domingue, about 150,000 died fighting for freedom and human dignity. Decades later, a Frenchman wrote in his memoirs:

> But what men these blacks are! How they fight, and how they die! One has to make war against them to know their reckless courage in braving danger … I have seen a solid column, torn by grape-shot from four pieces of cannon, advance without making a retrograde step. The more they fell, the greater seemed to be the courage of the rest.[10]

How much the Yoruba slaves and ex-slaves of Saint-Domingue contributed to this Revolution it is not easy to assess definitively from the records. Positive ethnic identification of the revolutionaries is made difficult by many factors. On arrival on the slave ships, the slaves were immediately given French names by their masters. And then, they had to learn the French language quickly – and so largely forgot their native tongues. If any children were born to them, these grew up speaking only French. Finally, Saint-Domingue was notorious as the place where slaves received the most brutal, the most dehumanizing, treatment in the Americas – a situation that, among other things, very rapidly wiped out distinctive ethnic identities. The Yoruba accounted for about 20 percent of Haiti's slave arrivals, and the Aja about 7 percent. As would be remembered, Aja culture and religion were very strongly influenced by Yoruba culture and religion, and there were therefore very profound cultural similarities between the two peoples. In the context of Saint-Domingue, where the African population originated from more than a dozen ethnic sources, the combined influence of the Yoruba and the Aja produced the most significant African cultural and political impact. The hideous maltreatment of slaves by the plantation owners in Saint-Domingue regularly resulted in large numbers of deaths among the slaves. Such heavy losses in labor were regularly made up for by more and more importations of new slaves – the largest volumes coming in the late eighteenth century. One important consequence of this was that, of the generation of Saint-Domingue's slaves which started the revolts in 1791, a very large proportion consisted of men recently brought from Africa, men whose memories of their African homes were still comparatively fresh. It was these men, many of whom had had some military training and experience in wars in their African homelands before ending up on slave ships, that constituted the core of the slave rebellions in Saint-Domingue. According to John Thornton:

> A majority of St. Domingue's slaves, especially those who fought steadily in the revolution, were born in Africa … In fact … a great many had served in African armies prior to their enslavement and arrival in Haiti … Sixty to seventy percent of the adult slaves listed on (St. Domingue's) inventories in the late 1780s and 1790s were African born. Where the African military background of the slaves counted most was in those areas, especially in the north (of St. Domingue) where slaves themselves led the revolution both politically and militarily … These areas … threw up the powerful armies of Toussaint L'Ouverture and Dessalines and eventually carried the revolution.[11]

Now, the second half of the eighteenth century was the period when the Yoruba began to enter in rapidly increasing numbers into the transportation of slaves from Africa (as a result of the Oyo wars of expansion, and then the growth of political instability in Oyo). And that too was the period of the largest volumes of slave imports from West Africa to Saint-Domingue, a major part of which imports consisted of Yoruba people. Therefore, Aja and Yoruba slaves constituted, by 1790, a very substantial part of Saint-Domingue's slaves born and raised in Africa and distinguished by the qualities and the skills that they had brought from their African homes – the ones who, as Thornton puts it, "carried the revolution." It seems certain therefore that the Yoruba contribution to the making of the Haitian Revolution was very great, and that many of the outstanding men in the Revolution were of Yoruba (and Aja) descent. Here, as in Bahia, we are almost certainly witnessing the Yoruba spirit of freedom (and the military capabilities of many of the Yoruba slaves) serving as a major contributor to the rebellion of enslaved African peoples against the horrific oppression characteristic of slavery in Saint-Domingue.

In the course of the nineteenth century, independent Haiti evolved its own Creole culture, drawing upon many African heritages, of which the Yoruba and Aja cultures were prominent. A major feature of the Haitian Creole culture was the unique language. While a small minority of Haitians (mostly the dwellers in the few urban centers) continued to speak French, the overwhelming majority evolved Haiti's national Creole language, which was different from (less French and more African than) the Creole spoken in the other French-owned islands of the West Indies. Today, about 90 percent of Haitians speak Creole, and about 20 percent speak both Creole and French.

It is in the area of religion, however, that Yoruba impact has been most measurable. Starting from the eighteenth century, the polyglot African community on the island, seeking to mitigate the vicious harshness of the slave environment, had started to evolve a new religious system, drawing on its various African heritages and, to some extent, on the Roman Catholic religion of the French planters. The new religion came to be known as Vodou. "Vodou" was derived from the Aja word for "spirit," and the form and substance of the religion were adapted largely from the Yoruba and Aja systems of religion – especially the Yoruba worship of *orisas*, belief in the efficacy of spiritually imbued charms, formularies and incantations, and various types of African sacred music and dance. In independent Haiti during the nineteenth century, the influence of Vodou increased greatly, bringing its impact to bear on Haitian culture generally – in art, music, dance, etc. – a significant contribution of Yoruba–Aja culture to one of the main Creole cultures of the New World. During the century also, the religious and other aspects of Haiti's culture, taken with them by slaves removed from Haiti at the time of the revolution, were carried to many places in the West Indies and the Gulf of Mexico and other parts of the southern United States.

Towards the end of the nineteenth century, the more educated Haitians, as well as the government of Haiti, began to show hostility towards Vodou on the grounds that, in their view, it prevented Haiti from growing as a modern civilized country. As it turned out, such attitudes did not diminish the influence of Vodou, because it was far too well entrenched among the broad masses of Haitians. In fact, during the first decades of the twentieth century, a change occurred and most Haitian intellectuals came to accept Vodou as a significant feature of the national heritage of their country, and that has remained the predominant attitude of the country's educated elite.

Trinidad

The island of Trinidad was a Spanish possession until the 1790s when the British took it from the Spaniards. By then the island was home to diverse groups of people – French and Spanish settlers (with their Roman Catholic religious tradition), free persons of mostly African descent, Hindus imported as indentured servants from India. With the coming of the British in the 1790s, larger sugar plantations were introduced, and African slaves were imported to work them, thus adding African slaves of various ethnic origins to deepen the cultural complexity of the island. It was in these years of the close of the seventeenth and beginning of the eighteenth centuries that Yoruba slaves became a factor in Trinidad, representing a minority of the slightly over 20,000 slaves imported there. In 1807, about one decade after taking over Trinidad, Britain abolished the slave trade, thus cutting off further importation of slaves to the island. Then, with the abolition of slavery in all British possessions in 1833, all Africans in Trinidad became free. From the 1840s, considerable numbers of Africans (many of them Yoruba) who were liberated from slaving ships were brought to Trinidad as indentured servants.

In short, Trinidad was different from most countries of the Americas in many respects: its ethnic composition was complex; slavery existed there for only a short time; and, even in that short time, the laws prohibited the practice of African religions. Yet, Yoruba culture did come to have a strong impact on the culture that developed there in the nineteenth century. In the years of slavery under the British, 1797–1833, the African slaves had to practice their religions in secret. In the circumstances of their hidden spiritual interactions, they evolved a syncretic religion incorporating elements from various African religious systems, from Catholicism, from Protestant Christianity, and even from Hinduism. For its gods, this religion chose the *orisas* of Yoruba religion and gave each *orisa* two names – a Yoruba name and a Catholic name. Thus, Obatala, the most senior of the Yoruba *orisas*, became known as St. Benedict, Yemoja became St. Anne, Ogun became St. Michael, Sango became St. John, to mention just a few. The religion was named Orisha Religion and employed typically Yoruba shrines, rituals and sacrifices. Each shrine (like a church) and its spiritual leader, called *mongba* (priest) or *iya* (priestess), had to register with the authorities to be able to operate and perform its *ebo* (rituals and sacrifices). Its use of the names of Catholic saints mollified official opposition, and over time, Orisha Religion developed relationships with some Protestant Christian sects (e.g. the Spiritual Baptists) and even with Hinduism.

The Yoruba among the indentured servants imported from the 1840s became particularly instrumental in boosting the influence of Yoruba culture and religion in Trinidad. The evolution of the Yoruba religious system as the main stem of Trinidad's Orisha Religion was also accompanied by the spread of Yoruba influence upon Trinidad's culture in many other dimensions – art, music, dance, costumes, etc. A great festival known as the Carnival evolved, putting all these influences on parade annually. The Trinidad Carnival, still celebrated every year by a broad spectrum of Trinidadians, features festive music, dancing, costumes and personal adornments of West African (mostly Yoruba) ritual and ceremonial traditions, and attracts many tourists from all over the world.

The Akus of Sierra Leone and Those Who Returned

From probably as early as the seventeenth century, some of the Africans forcibly taken away to slavery in the Americas found their way back to places on the West African coast, having bought their freedom, or become otherwise free, in the Americas. Some of such returnees became slave traders themselves on the West African coast, or worked in the service of slave traders or of West African rulers engaged in the slave trade on the coast. From the descriptions of their facial marks, some of these might have been Yoruba, but the evidence on that is inconclusive. However, the number of returnees, better known as emigrants, increased substantially from the early nineteenth century, and since the Yoruba were among the largest ethnic groups being exported to slavery in the Americas at that time, the Yoruba also came to be a large group among the emigrants. Also, as would be remembered, from the 1820s, the British navy seized illegal slave ships on the high seas, liberated the slaves being carried on them, and resettled the freed persons in Sierra Leone. Again, the Yoruba, known as Akus in Sierra Leone (because of the regular occurrence of *aku* in their greetings) came to be a significant part of the population of the Sierra Leone settlement.

The first Aku expedition from Sierra Leone to their Yoruba homeland took place in April 1839. After that, more followed (many under the auspices of Christian missionary organizations), resulting in a gradual increase in the number of Akus returning home. As would also be remembered, they came to accumulate mostly in Lagos from the 1850s, and there they became known as the Saros (people from Sierra Leone). Even before the Akus from Sierra Leone, many emigrants had started to return to Yorubaland from the Americas during the century – especially from Bahia, the rest of Brazil, and Cuba, and some from the islands of the West Indies. It was much more difficult for slaves to obtain their freedom in the United States, and, therefore, emigrants from there were very few. In Lagos, emigrants from any part of the Americas were known as the Amaros (people from the Americas).

Much has been said in earlier chapters about the emigrants, their return to various parts of Yorubaland, and their importance in the late nineteenth century history of Yorubaland. Here, we will limit ourselves to a brief description of an important aspect of the life of the Aku society in Sierra Leone.

The Akus were just one out of many African ethnic groups in Sierra Leone, but most of the content of the Krio culture that developed there came from Yoruba cultural origins – in language, folklore, music, food traditions, and way of life in general. Though the number of the Akus was one reason for such a strong cultural impact, number alone does not explain it. The most important factor was that the Akus, better than any other African group, had a strong tradition of keeping close together and evolving common institutions for their common good – even though they were partly Christians, partly Muslims, and partly worshippers of Yoruba traditional gods, and even though they originated from different Yoruba sub-groups. The Akus actually evolved into a distinct community, with their own internal constitution and laws. By as early as the late 1820s, they had elected a Yoruba king for themselves, and established laws binding on all members of their group – with serious group sanctions for the infringement of such laws. The colonial authorities were happy to have such an excellent organization among an African group, and gladly accorded the Aku king official recognition. In true Yoruba fashion, the Akus established the tradition of gathering in large numbers for important occasions (such as funerals and weddings) in the lives of members. The Akus also became well known for their spirit of enterprise. Akus joined together to start businesses, especially as traders, and the unity within their group usually gave their businesses a great advantage over other rivals. In the process, many of the leading Akus became quite rich. As a result of all this, the Akus became dominant in Sierra Leone – economically, socially and culturally.

Summary

In general, then, Yoruba culture provided many of the answers to the quests of enslaved African peoples in the New World for identity, and for spiritual and cultural survival and expression in the hostile world of slavery. In particular, Yoruba cosmology and the well ordered pantheon of gods in the Yoruba system of religion became, for Africans in many parts of the Americas, the readily available framework upon which to build spiritual experimentation and invention. As Wole Soyinka has put it, the *orisas* "travel well."[12] The Yoruba worship of the *orisas*, and the Roman Catholic veneration of the saints, exhibited strong similarities, facilitating an interpenetration of the one with the other wherever both met in the New World. And everywhere, the spiritual genius of the African recognized and seized upon the similarity to accomplish various needs – in some places to dissemble what they were really doing, in other places to include and mobilize among themselves, everywhere to fashion structures harmonious with their African spiritual intensity and appropriate to the realities of their current existence. Everywhere also, Yoruba and other African sacred art, emblems, music, drums, chants, songs and dance, proffered service to the new inventions, and brought in their train other art idioms that were secular. After the disappearance of institutional slavery, these new creations flowered into assertive Afro-Americanisms that today constitute icons in the civilizations of the New World.

Some of the main centers of the experimentation and invention (Bahia, Cuba, Haiti and Trinidad) have been surveyed above, but there was hardly any part of the Americas without some touch of Yoruba cultural influence. In the southern and eastern states of the United States, for instance, as well as in many countries of Central America, South America and the West Indies, there are to be encountered, inside the broad strokes of African cultural influence, various specific manifestations of Yoruba religious and artistic influence – in *orisa* worship groups, art groups, festivals and ceremonies. One such emphatic manifestation named Oyotunji Village, on the coast of South Carolina, has in recent years attracted considerable attention.[13] Oyotunji (meaning "Oyo resurrected"), founded about 1959, is a bold creation of a traditional Yoruba town, complete with an Oba and chiefs, Ogboni Society, priests and priestesses, shrines and rituals of the *orisas*, sacrifices, seasonal and annual festivals, Yoruba music and music groups. In the years after Nigeria's independence, chiefs of Surinam in South America took steps to establish contacts with the palace of Ife, the place universally known as the ancestral source of the Yoruba people and Yoruba civilization. Some scholars have traced survivals of Yoruba influence on the art, music and speech patterns of African-Americans of the southern states of the United States – for instance, in certain types of houses common in African-American culture in places like Alabama, South Carolina and other parts of the Deep South, the contemporary popularity of Yoruba clothing styles (*agbada, dasiki, buba, iro, gele, fila*) among African-Americans, the African-American Juba Dance, the influence of Sango sacred music and drums on African-American music, the common occurrence of adapted Yoruba folktales in African-American folklore, and many others.

Conclusion

The Yoruba part of the African diaspora, then, represents, culturally, its most vital, most measurable, part. In a recent study of Yoruba civilization and the powerful and widespread influence of the Yoruba diaspora in the Americas, Augustine Agwuele states:

> According to Matory, since the nineteenth century the Yoruba nation has risen above all other Afro-Latin nations; "It is preeminent in size, wealth, grandeur, and international prestige; it is studied, written about, and imitated far more than any other, not only by believers but by anthropologists, art historians, novelists, and literary critics."[14]

Agwuele adds that the Yoruba distinguished themselves in the diaspora by their "unity and personal traits as a distinct ethnic and cultural group"; and then he quotes Dr. de Verteuil who wrote in the nineteenth century that "the Yorubas deserve particular notice … they are a fine race … their houses neat, comfortable and kept in perfect order within. In character, they are generally honest, and in disposition proud, and even haughty."

Manifestations and expressions of Yoruba cultural heritage in the African diaspora, then, have received increasing attention since the late twentieth century, just as studies of Yoruba civilization at home in West Africa have intensified. What all this seems to point to is an advancing transatlantic development of major significance in the history of black people.

17

The Politics of the Twentieth Century

The Yoruba people entered the twentieth century as subjects of alien European powers – some in the French protectorate of Dahomey, a very small part in German (later French) Heligoland (Togo), and the rest in the British Colony and Protectorate of Nigeria. The parts which went to Dahomey (later the Republic of Benin) and Togo amounted, together, to only a small slice of Yoruba territory and population. We will first examine the history of the Yoruba people outside Nigeria in the twentieth century.

Yoruba Kingdoms under French Rule[1]

First, the Nigeria–Dahomey boundary through Yorubaland was a constant source of vexation and trouble, especially to the Yoruba in Dahomey, almost throughout the colonial era. Not only did the boundary separate these people from their kinsfolk in Nigeria, more importantly, it placed many of the subordinate towns and villages of their kingdoms beyond the border in Nigeria. This created the situation that whenever any of these split kingdoms tried to act like a kingdom together, their action contravened the international boundary. For instance, in important traditional functions, like the appointment and installation of their local rulers and chiefs, towns and villages on the Nigerian side of the border expected, and asked, their king beyond the border to perform his traditional role, and the king just had to act accordingly. Sometimes also, the towns and villages wanted to send their traditional dues or gifts to their king beyond the border.

On the whole the local British officials on the Nigerian side proved to be quite understanding in these matters. In fact, when confronted with succession disputes in communities on the Nigerian side, British officials sometimes sought the opinion and advice of the appropriate king beyond the border. In contrast, the French officials in Dahomey were usually very hostile in these situations, especially in the years after 1900. Hence the fact that Yoruba kings in Dahomey were frequently arrested, charged with treason, convicted, and imprisoned or banished into exile.

Second, French colonial policy proved, in general, much more destructive of Yoruba traditional political institutions than British policy was. In the first few years of French rule up to 1900, French local officials (called residents) were ideally supposed to relate to the Yoruba kingdoms as "protectorates," and to address and treat their kings as indeed kings of their people. In those years, French repressive vigilance was reserved for the Dahomey kingdom, while the situation in the Yoruba kingdoms could be described as one of "indirect rule." But from 1900, as the abiding character of French colonial policy evolved, their handling of the Yoruba kingdoms changed. Between 1900 and 1914, the French moved decisively for direct administration. The position of residents was abolished and replaced with that of "commandants," and the number of local French officials was considerably increased as the whole area was broken into smaller administrative units called *cantons*. The kings ceased to be *rois* (kings) and became *chefs de canton*, in which position they were merely administrative auxiliaries to the French administrators.. The *canton* over which each king was *chef* was usually a small part of his traditional kingdom, and over it his duties were strictly stated and circumscribed. In theory, he could hold a court, but real judicial authority lay in the hands of the French administrator. The king's principal functions in his *canton* were to transmit the administrator's orders to his people, and to assist in the recruitment of labor, the collection of taxes, and conscription to armed service – duties which progressively made him unpopular with his people.

These conditions led to resentment and reactions, which then produced almost constant conflicts between the French administration and the Yoruba traditional authorities. The French response was to withhold confidence more and more from the Yoruba rulers and to vest it in chiefs of their own creation – lowly citizens whose only claim to such political elevation was their known loyalty to the French. The increasing use of such persons only added to the resentment, the reactions and the conflicts. Of course, the Yoruba kings and those loyal to them were always the losers in these conflicts. The consequences were, first, a great instability in the position of the traditional rulers as many of them went to prison, to banishment, or to self-exile abroad. Some of the traditional thrones were then left vacant for long periods of time. The second consequence was the steady decline in the influence and prestige of all traditional political institutions. When French rule over their Dahomey protectorate finally ended in 1960, most of the Yoruba communities in the new Republic of Dahomey entered into the independence era with their traditional political institutions in, according to Anthony Asiwaju, "a state of collapse." In 1994, some citizens of the Benin Republic initiated the founding of a *Conseil des Rois* (Council of Kings), for the purpose of creating a forum through which the traditional rulers of the country could begin to influence the country's development. Of the Yoruba Obas of the Benin Republic, the Alaketu of Ketu played a prominent role in the founding of this body. Though the political, social or economic role of this *Conseil des Rois* did not become clear as the twentieth century came to an end, its creation was nevertheless some sign that the traditional rulers, largely suppressed under French colonial rule, might yet revive and play significant roles in the modern history of the Benin Republic.

Yoruba Traditional Rulers in Nigeria in the Twentieth Century[2]

The political leadership of Yoruba people in the last decade of British rule and in independent Nigeria was provided by the new class of Western-educated men and women. That was the common experience of all tropical African peoples in the twentieth century. After the kings had lost control over their kingdoms to the British overlord, the task of organizing and leading the Yoruba people and of confronting the agencies of British rule fell completely into the hands of the Western-educated, most of them primarily the products of the Christian mission schools. And when the British finally bowed out, it was to the class of the Western-educated that they handed the instruments of government in the country of Nigeria to which the Yoruba then belonged. However, traditional Yoruba political institutions only stepped down from center stage; they did not, at least in Nigeria, cease to exist – indeed, as far as the broad masses of Yoruba people in Nigeria were concerned, the king and the palace continued to represent deep-seated traditions and values that the modern government of elected politicians and bureaucrats could not.

First then, we will look at the fortunes of the Yoruba traditional rulers under British rule, and then in independent Nigeria. The dealings of the British officials with the Yoruba centers of power were very rough in the first years of British rule in Nigeria. Their first concern was about the many war chiefs who commanded large followings, had arsenals of weapons, and wielded enormous influence in almost all parts of Yorubaland. British local officials in various parts of the country made it a priority to show these men that the era of wars had ended, as had their power. First, the British officials asked the war chiefs to disband their crowds of clients and war boys. From the compounds and military bases of many warriors, streams of people issued forth and flowed to all parts of the country. Though probably most of the followers of the Ibadan war-chiefs chose to continue to live in Ibadan, the crowds that arrived from

Ibadan in Ekiti, Ijesa, Akoko, the country of the Okun Yoruba, Igbomina and the towns and villages of the Osun Valley were still considerable. From the fact that many of the Ekiti, Ijesa and Akoko among them had picked up Oyo dialect in Ibadan, they became known, in Ekiti and Akoko, as the Atoyobo (the arrivals from Oyo). Most of those who left from Ogedemgbe's group in Ilesa or from Aduloju in Imesi-Lasigidi headed towards Akoko and the country of the Okun Yoruba. In late 1894 or early 1895, Aduloju at last returned home from Imesi-Lasigidi to Ado, accompanied by a "family" that numbered in the hundreds, and established a sprawling compound.

Most of the breaking up of the war-chiefs' large followings went peacefully, making it unnecessary for British officials to employ a show of force. When, however, some of the chiefs were asked to send away even their close circle of trusted attendants, and to surrender or destroy their arsenals, some resistance surfaced. And such resistance provoked the arrest and incarceration of some chiefs – including some of the Ibadan chiefs who were believed to be unwilling to give up the career of warfare, Ogedemgbe, who was arrested and exiled to Iwo in 1894 and was not allowed to return home to Ilesa until 1896, and Aduloju, Fabunmi and Oso Akerele (a young veteran of the Akoko wars, by then the Egbedi of Ado in Ekiti), all of whom were taken to the British outpost at Oke-Imo near Ilesa, detained for some time, warned and released. Ogedemgbe's arrest did not go without physical resistance: a few of his closest men drew their swords to defend their chief, but Ogedemgbe commanded them to put their swords away. He was then arrested, and some quantity of arms and ammunition was taken away from his compound.

By 1900, the power of the war chiefs had been eliminated. They remained men of considerable fame and influence, to be sure, but the kind of independent authority enjoyed by them until about 1893 was gone. In Ibadan, the division between a civil and a military line of chiefs vanished, and Ibadan became a typical Yoruba monarchical state, with the Baale (later Olubadan) as head. In Ilorin, the titles of the war Baloguns became subsumed under the general chieftaincy system, under the king or Emir. In Abeokuta, the kind of preeminence enjoyed by the chiefs over affairs disappeared. Direct British defeat of the Ijebu army in 1892 had eliminated the military as an important factor in Ijebu affairs; after that, whatever military title remained was absorbed into the traditional chieftaincy system or became honorary. Many of the Ologuns of eastern Yorubaland accepted the traditional chieftaincy titles of their ancestors. For instance, Ogedemgbe became the Obanla of Ilesa; Aduloju was invested with the title of the Edemo (the title of his forebears) on his deathbed. Fajembola of Egosi in the Oye kingdom had taken the traditional title of Olugbosun even while the Kiriji War was on. In Ado (Ekiti), Oso Akerele was made the Egbedi (traditional second-in-command of the Ewi's army), and Faparusi returned from his camp to be honored with his father's traditional title of Osolo. The people of the old kingdom of Imesi-Ile invited prince Fabunmi and crowned him their king.

In effect, what the fate of the war chiefs in the first years of British rule represented was a resuscitation of the old monarchical system of the Yoruba people in its pre-nineteenth century purity – but now under British overlordship. The traditional rulers, the Obas and the subordinate Baales, and, below them, the various cadres of traditional chiefs, stood forth again as the undisputed indigenous leaders of Yoruba communities. For the British local officials, this represented a simplification of the political field; to implement the policies of British overlordship, all they had to do was to deal with the Obas.

In such dealings, during the first few years of British rule, the British Traveling Commissioners and their soldiers, policemen and clerks, paid little respect to the kings and chiefs, but generally tended to terrorize and bully them. The stated objective was to restore and maintain peace in a country that had been long torn by wars. The most violent of these acts of repression was perpetrated in Oyo town in 1895 by Captain Bower, the Resident of Ibadan and Traveling Commissioner. Captain Bower's action against the Alaafin Adeyemi and his town had no legal justification whatsoever; it was an arbitrary demonstration of British military power, the objective of which was to intimidate and suppress the Alaafin, even though he showed friendliness to British officials and contravened no clause of his treaty with them. After the Alaafin's palace had tried and punished two offenders (both of them subjects of the Alaafin), Bower queried the Alaafin and demanded that he should surrender the two men to him. Since Bower had no legal authority for such demands, the Alaafin and his chiefs refused. Bower then escalated his demands, going so far as to require the Alaafin to surrender the palace official who had carried out the punishments on the two offenders – and even that the Alaafin should prostrate to him. Early in the morning of November 12, Bower mounted the seven-pounder at the gate of Oyo and ordered a wholesale bombardment of the town. The palace and many of the houses of Oyo were destroyed, the Alaafin himself was wounded, uncounted Oyo citizens were killed, and the ancient government of Oyo was completely subjugated. No other Yoruba ruler or town saw a comparable scale of violent repression and unlawful use of power, but to the traditional rulers of the rest of Yorubaland, this act of terror at Oyo became an intimidating object lesson.

From the beginning of the twentieth century, however, changes began slowly to appear. In the years after 1914 especially, the Lugardian system of Indirect Rule, evolved by the British in the emirates of Northern Nigeria, was introduced in Yorubaland also. During the 1920s and 1930s, the system matured. In general, it meant at the local government level the official recognition of the Yoruba Oba as a Native Authority, with a native police force, a native court, and a native treasury. The local British official was the District Officer. The districts were grouped into provinces, each province under an official called the Resident. In Southern Nigeria there thus arose four Yoruba provinces – Ijebu Province, Abeokuta Province, Oyo Province, and Ondo Province, and in Northern Nigeria Ilorin Province and Kabba Province, each of these two having some non-Yoruba components. The Yoruba provinces of Southern Nigeria, together with the neighboring Benin Province and Delta Province, were constituted into the Western Provinces of Nigeria under a Lieutenant Governor based in the city of Ibadan. The kingdom of Lagos, being legally a crown colony (while the rest of Nigeria's Yoruba people were part of the Protectorate of Nigeria), was given a pattern of administration outside of, and somewhat different from, the one outlined above. Nonetheless, there was no real difference in the positions of the Lagos and other Yoruba kings under British rule.

On the whole, under Indirect Rule, the Yoruba traditional ruler in Nigeria enjoyed a certain level of respect and influence, as well as a certain amount of authority, which his brethren in Dahomey never enjoyed under French rule after 1900. Of course, it must not be forgotten that the reality of Indirect Rule was frequently different from its ideal. For instance, the District Officer was, ideally, supposed to be an adviser to the Native Authority; but, in fact, he was often more like a supervisor. Also, Indirect Rule was easier to implement in districts where one paramount ruler was easy to identify – like the Alaafin in Oyo or the Owa of Ilesa in Ijesa, or the Awujale of Ijebu-Ode in Ijebu. In any district where there was a plurality of equal traditional rulers, however, distortions crept in. The attempt by the British officials to simplify the situation by enforcing a paramount ruler of their own creation was, ultimately, an attempt to create illegitimate authority. For instance, the attempt to elevate one of the many Ekiti kings to a position of paramountcy over the rest led to protests in the 1930s, protests so serious that the attempt had to be abandoned. A worse case occurred in Egbado where a commoner, Seriki Abbas, was elevated to a position of paramount chief of the Western District in 1913, and Senior Chief of Ilaro Division in 1914–19. When all this has been said, however, it still remains true that Indirect Rule under the British tended, on the whole, to preserve some of the prestige and dignity of the Yoruba kings, whereas French rule resulted in almost total destruction of Yoruba traditional political institutions. The Native Court system under Indirect Rule was particularly acceptable to Yoruba people, because it seemed to them to be proof that their kings were still in control, and most people would rather take their cases to the palace and the Native Court than to the alternative (and foreign) courts of magistrates and lawyers.

On the whole, therefore, the Yoruba kings in Nigeria continued to be hailed as "lieutenants of the gods" by their subjects. A conference of the Ekiti kings, called "Pelupelu" (or gathering of the kings), met from time to time to consider matters placed before it concerning Ekiti. Each conference became a highly glorified festival in which the Ekiti kings competed in the show of traditional grandeur – shimmering, beaded, high-domed, Oduduwa crowns with dangling frills over the wearers' faces, flowing garments of richest texture, beaded shoes and scepters, all complete with buglers or trumpeters proclaiming the arrival of each king. For the people of Ado-Ekiti (where most of the conferences were held), and for other Ekiti people who could make the journey there, each conference was a celebration, a time to fill the air with loud proclamations of the ancient *oriki* for their kings.³ Variations of such royal grandeur were enacted in all parts of Yorubaland, perhaps the highest and most glistering often belonging to the Alaafin in Oyo. One Alaafin of the time, Siyanbola Ladigbolu, had a uniquely exalted hold on the grandeur of those times. In his masterful hands, the relationship between the king and the British Resident, Captain William A. Ross (Resident in Oyo from 1906 to 1933), so evolved that Ladigbolu became known among his subjects as "*Oba t' o npe oyinbo ran n' ise*" ("the king who sends white officials on errands").⁴ In fact, Ross regarded the Alaafin Ladigbolu as friend and was single-mindedly dedicated to boosting the Alaafin's authority and influence over Oyo Province – especially over the city of Ibadan.

The British were, of course, the rulers of the land. Ultimate authority belonged to them. The District Officer's court was superior to the Native Court, and served as a sort of court of appeal to it. The British had the last voice in the approval of any person selected for appointment as king. They also had the last voice in the removal of a king – as Ado-Ekiti people were to discover to their shock when they tried to remove their king, Ewi Aladesanmi II, in 1942. Unable to employ, under the British, the traditional Yoruba means of removing a king, Ado chiefs and people resorted to civil commotion to achieve their purpose. Enraged by the Ewi's show of disrespect to certain traditions, masses of Ado people, backed by their chiefs, poured into the streets, and a large stone-throwing mob besieged the palace. The Ewi escaped from the palace and from the town. The traditional chiefs and priests responsible for such matters then declared him dead, had royal funeral rights performed for him, and proceeded to select and install another prince as Ewi. The British government of Nigeria intervened, and ordered an investigation into the situation. The investigation came to the determination that, though Aladesanmi had infringed some traditions of his people, he had not broken any law of British Nigeria, and should be restored to his throne. On the day that he was to be brought back, some leading chiefs who could have considered plans for resistance were rounded up and brutally crushed by the police who had been drafted massively to the town. (The Ewi Aladesanmi settled down after this, made his peace with his subjects, and ruled for nearly five decades, deeply beloved by his people.) Thus ultimately British rule was absolute, upheld by police and military force. Even the Alaafin Ladigbolu came to experience the absolute character of British rule from 1934 on, as Ross's successor, H. L. Ward-Price, in implementation of changed British policies, rapidly demolished the extended authority and influence which the Alaafin had enjoyed over Ibadan up to 1933 – while he watched in helpless alarm. Even so, Yoruba kings found ways to hold their heads high under the system – and, occasionally, with impressive doses of traditional royal pomp and ceremony.

In these years also, the Yoruba Obas stood forth as the traditional wing of the Yoruba national movement of solidarity and unity. Fortunately in this regard, the British administration instituted a periodic conference of the leading traditional rulers of the Western Provinces, including the Oba of Benin. The first of these very exalted conferences was held in 1937. In the years that followed, they became proud exhibitions of the grandeur of the traditional political system of the Yoruba nation. The climax was reached in about 1949–50 with the founding of the prestigious association named Egbe Omo Oduduwa (Association of Oduduwa's Descendants). Comprising the rising political elite of the Yoruba people and the Obas, this association gave the Yoruba people, for over one decade, a solid, confident and glowing leadership in Nigeria. It was from its ranks that the politically active elite founded the first Yoruba-based political party, the Action Group, in 1950–51.

Meanwhile, beginning from as early as the 1920s, the new leadership of Nigeria by the literate elite had been evolving and confronting the British overlord. With the grant of limited self-government to Nigeria in 1949–51, the Yoruba among the new elite emerged as essentially the rulers of the predominantly Yoruba Western Provinces (by then the Western Region) of Nigeria – through elected legislatures, cabinet ministers, and local councils, all served by career civil servants. And with Nigeria's independence in 1960, the creation of the new dispensation was complete. Essentially, the new governments participated in by the Yoruba literate elite in Nigeria from 1952 represented a direct continuation of the imperial government of the British – over and above the traditional governments of the Obas, and related to the Obas exactly as the British imperial government had used to relate to them. The Yoruba cabinet minister or Premier of the Western Region was an embodiment of a Yoruba government higher in every respect than any Yoruba monarch, and the Western

House of Assembly in Ibadan (and the federal parliament in Lagos) made laws that every Oba, like every other citizen, must obey. If a Yoruba Cabinet Minister came from Ibadan or Lagos to visit an Oba's domain, the Oba must receive him with all the respect with which he had used to receive the British Resident or Governor. The essence of the new dispensation was demonstrated most sharply in the mid-1950s when the elected government of the Western Region, as part of its settlement of some political problems in Oyo, deposed one Alaafin and exiled him from his royal town.

For the Yoruba people in the new dispensation, therefore, there arose a conflict between two important realities: the new system of power and government on the one hand, and, on the other, the powerful traditional hold of the Obas, and of the great traditions that they represent. For an accommodation to be found between the two, it would have to be found and effected by the men and women controlling the new instruments of power — the people in the local, regional and Federal Governments. These people showed little understanding of the moment's need in this regard, and, on the whole, did little that was of abiding fundamental significance about it. Yoruba makers of the new Nigerian constitutions saw to the inclusion of a House of Chiefs in the constitution of the Western Region, starting from 1952, and the Western Region provided in the 1950s that Obas be presidents of the Local Councils in their domains. A president of a Local Council had no function other than to declare its meetings ceremonially open, and the position imperceptibly died out over time. The House of Chiefs existed until 1966, when the military seized control of all state governments in Nigeria. When elected governments returned in 1979, no mention was made of a House of Chiefs in any of the Yoruba populated states in Nigeria, and no provision was made for it anywhere. As the twentieth century rolled to an end, no consideration was given by the Yoruba elite to the issue of an appropriate role for the Obas in the new society and government of their people. Considerable respect for the Obas was shown by the first generation of Yoruba political leaders (of 1952–62); but from then on, a slow decline in the level of respect was the rule. In subsequent years, most politicians tended to see the Obas and Baales in either of two lights — as a very influential institution to woo for electoral support, or as a very influential political obstacle to rage and rant against.

Yet, as the twentieth century closed, there was no sign that the Yoruba institution of monarchy, and the deep-rooted traditions around it, were dying or even weakening. In fact, on the contrary, Yoruba monarchy seemed to be reinventing itself and to be enhancing its influence anew. In all parts of Yorubaland, chiefs on the traditional Committees of Kingmakers showed an increasing preference for well educated princes for selection as Obas. At the same time, more and more of such princes were not only willing to accept selection but were ambitious to seek it, and to give up highly paid, and otherwise prestigious, jobs in order to ascend the thrones of their forefathers. Some of the princes who were selected as kings in the late twentieth century were even wealthy businessmen and owners of businesses, and such usually brought their businesses with them to the throne. Also, below the level of Obas and Baales, more and more of the best paid men and women in the land were seeking to take on the traditional chieftaincies of their lineages. In fact, for the most successful, most educated, and wealthiest, Yoruba men and women, a chieftaincy title (even if only honorary) had, by the end of the century, become a most highly sought status symbol. Without doubt, the traditional aura surrounding Yoruba political institutions appeared to be entering upon a new era of importance in modern Yoruba society. As yet, until the end of the century, the Yoruba attitude to having a rich businessman (owning and still running his businesses) on the throne was ambivalent. While probably most people regarded owning and running businesses as inappropriate for a Yoruba king, most nevertheless welcomed the enhanced ability of an educated and personally rich king to enlarge and glamorize the traditional dignity of the monarchy. What all these developments would ultimately translate to in the life of the Yoruba people in the modern world was not yet possible to tell as the twentieth century came to an end

The Yoruba in Nigeria's Politics[5]

The above then is a brief account of the evolution of Yoruba traditional political institutions in Nigeria in the twentieth century. That part of twentieth century Yoruba history occupied a lesser level of importance than the experiences of the Yoruba people in the overall politics of the Federal Republic of Nigeria. It is in the evolution of Nigeria's political life that we see the overarching and most important developments affecting the Yoruba people of Nigeria in the course of the twentieth century. Whatever, and how much, they accomplished in economic and social development in the course of the century was strongly impacted by the inter-relationships and political interactions within Nigeria, and, for that reason, a slightly longer attention will here be given to twentieth century Nigerian politics as it affected the Yoruba people.

As is common with all African peoples, the twentieth century political history of the Yoruba of Nigeria divides into two periods – the colonial period, and the period after independence. British rule over Yorubaland was consolidated in stages between 1893 and 1914 (that is, if we exclude the Lagos kingdom which had become a British colony as early as 1861). By 1906, what later became the country of Nigeria was ruled under two separate British administrations: the

Colony and Protectorate of Southern Nigeria, and the Protectorate of Northern Nigeria. Most of Yorubaland was in the Colony and Protectorate of Southern Nigeria. The Yoruba city of Ilorin, most of Igbomina, the territories of the Okun Yoruba, and a thin slice of Ekiti (consisting of Moba and Obo kingdoms) were, as earlier stated, included in the Protectorate of Northern Nigeria. In 1914, the two protectorates were amalgamated, thus becoming two different components of the Colony and Protectorate of Nigeria. The whole country was then, as would be remembered, divided into provinces, of which the Lagos Colony, Ijebu Province, Abeokuta Province, Oyo Province and Ondo Provine in Southern Nigeria were wholly Yoruba provinces, and the Ilorin Province and Kabba Province in Northern Nigeria were partly Yoruba provinces.

The Northern Yoruba in Northern Nigeria Under British Rule

The internal boundary between Northern Nigeria and Southern Nigeria continued, then, to consign to Northern Nigeria the following parts of northern Yorubaland – Ilorin, most of Igbomina, part of the Ibolo, the Okun Yoruba, the northernmost Ekiti, and most of Akoko. Of these, after they instituted their system of Indirect Rule in Northern Nigeria, the British administration consigned much of Igbomina, Ibolo and northern Ekiti to the Ilorin Emirate, and the rest of Igbomina to the Lafiaji Emirate – later, all were included in a new province named Ilorin Province. Further to the northeast, the territories of the Okun Yoruba and the Akoko were organized together with their closest non-Yoruba neighbors (the Kakanda and the Nupe Kupa and Egan) to form a province – Kabba Province, with its headquarters in the Owe town of Kabba. Within this province, the Akoko and most of the Okun Yoruba (with the exception of the Oworo) were constituted into an emirate (the Kabba Emirate) under the Obaro of Kabba; and the Oworo, the Kakanda and the Nupe Kupa and Egan were constituted into another emirate (Agbaja Emirate) with Agbaja as headquarters and under the Olu of Oworo. Since neither the Obaro of Kabba nor the Olu of Oworo was a Muslim, neither could be titled Emir; each was given the title of "paramount chief."

The emirate experiment in the Yoruba northeast quickly failed. In general, the Yoruba of these places viewed the emirate as a foreign Fulani system, and suspected that it represented a British attempt to extend Fulani influence over them. In the Agbaja Emirate, the Nupe and Kakanda, who were predominantly Muslim and non-Yoruba, immediately rejected their being put under a Yoruba chief who was not a Muslim. As for the Olu himself, he showed no interest in the position of paramount chief over peoples who were so culturally different from his own Oworo people, and he took no step to exercise the powers of the position. In consequence, the Agbaja Emirate experiment fizzled out. In the Kabba Emirate, the Akoko protested so vigorously that they were removed from the emirate and re-assigned to Southern Nigeria in 1919. Meanwhile, the Jumu and other Okun Yoruba set up intense protests against the paramountcy of the Owe chief, the Obaro – with the result that the Kabba Emirate eventually broke up.

In Ilorin Province, in contrast, the emirate system under Indirect Rule came to acquire the characteristics of the typical Fulani emirates of Northern Nigeria beyond the Niger. As the British system of Indirect Rule evolved, they accorded the highest prestige to the Northern Nigerian Fulani emirate system among all of Nigeria's indigenous political systems, and allowed the Emirs considerable latitude in the administration of their emirates. Consequently, the British thus created the setting whereby the Emirs of Ilorin could at last attempt to accomplish what had been impossible for them in the nineteenth century – namely, the imposition of a typical, thorough-going, Fulani emirate system on Ilorin and Igbomina, Ibolo and northern Ekiti in the new Ilorin Emirate. This immediately generated protests. In the conferences of the Ekiti kings, for instance, requests were repeatedly made to the British administration to return the northern Ekiti kingdoms of Moba and Obo to the Ekiti District of Ondo Province in Southern Nigeria.

As the British system of Indirect Rule matured, the protests intensified, because most of the Yoruba in Ilorin Province found the system as it operated in the emirates of Northern Nigeria harsh and repressive. Not only did the system of taxation and tax collection in these emirates cause resentment, so did the operation of the native court system. The Emir of Ilorin levied taxes on the farm harvests of Igbomina and Ibolo farmers, and appointed officials (called Babakekere) to whom various Igbomina and Ibolo communities were made subject – a revival, more or less, of pre-British Ajele systems. These agents controlled the administration of all parts of the emirate, arbitrarily levied taxes, employed harsh and repressive (and sometimes even disruptive) methods to collect taxes, frequently demanded gifts from the communities subject to their authority, and abused the powers of the courts. The native courts were supposed to administer native law but, in fact, they were made to administer Islamic law, even though the populations of these places were predominantly non-Muslim. The Emir also demanded of the Igbomina and Ibolo Obas that they should cease wearing traditional Yoruba crowns and wear *lawani* (the Arab head-scarf used by Muslims). The Emirs of Lafiaji operated in more or less the same ways. In short, in the emirates of Ilorin Province, the British provided for the subjection of substantial parts of Yoruba people to the humiliation of indigenous cultural imperialisms.

The resulting protests only gave the Emirs (with the support of the local British officials) opportunities to exercise the rigor of their new powers – over Yoruba Obas and commoners alike. The protests therefore came to feature many popular communal revolts, especially in the Igbomina towns. By the 1930s, the protests began to include protest migrations of many Igbomina (and also some of the Okun Yoruba) to parts of Yorubaland in Southern Nigeria – particularly to places like Ogbomoso, Osogbo, Ibadan, Ife, and Lagos. In many of these places, the Igbomina immigrants quickly established themselves as very capable actors in the modern retail trade business. In Lagos in particular, where they usually started in menial jobs, their commercial skills and their prudence ultimately elevated many of them to rich traders and substantial owners of real estate properties. In the rich forestlands south of Ile-Ife, Igbomina farmers and plantation owners came to account for a major part of the expanding cocoa plantation industry.

In spite of the various manifestations of protest, the British administration preserved intact its imposed splitting of Yorubaland into two in Nigeria – with the exception, as would be remembered, of the reassignment of Akoko to Southern Nigeria in 1919, and of a small part of the Ekiti kingdom of Moba (especially the town of Otun) to the Ekiti District of Southern Nigeria in 1936.

This heritage of subordination of parts of the Yoruba people to the dominant Hausa-Fulani people of Northern Nigeria was to continue throughout British rule and into the years after independence. And the heritage of Yoruba protests against it was to continue in the politics of Nigeria throughout all the constitutional exercises that gradually prepared Nigeria for independence in the 1950s, and also in the years after independence in 1960. Since size and population became, from the early 1950s, the determinant of a region's influence in the affairs of Nigeria, the Hausa-Fulani leaders of the Northern Region were determined not to lose the Yoruba part of their region, and the British consistently supported them in that resolve. It was not until Nigeria was broken into smaller states in 1967 (with the Yoruba of Northern Nigeria becoming the dominant ethnic component of a new Kwara State) that this thorny matter was finally laid to some rest.

Western Region and Nigerian Politics

In 1939, the Yoruba provinces of Southern Nigeria plus the Benin and Delta provinces to the southeast were constituted as the Western Region. By 1952, British concessions to Nigerian nationalist demands resulted in the predominantly Yoruba Western Region being granted some measure of indigenous participation in its own administration. This led to the formation of political parties, to elections, and the appointment of Yoruba politicians as cabinet ministers in the government of the Western Region, under the supervision of British officials. In 1956, the measure of indigenous participation in the government of the Western Region was increased. Under this arrangement, called self government, the indigenous regional administration, with its legislature, cabinet and premier, exercised nearly full control over all matters, with the British Regional Governor occupying the position of regional representative of the British crown. In 1960, the whole of Nigeria attained full independence.

The years after independence witnessed a steady growth of political crisis in Nigeria. In response to the important fact that Nigeria comprises many nationalities, the British makers of constitutions for Nigeria in the years before independence had structured the country as a federation of three regions: a Northern Region, a Western Region, and an Eastern Region. The Northern Region was made territorially coterminous with the former Protectorate of Northern Nigeria, consisting of the vast territory spreading from Nigeria's borders on the edge of the Sahara Desert to a line south of the two great rivers (Niger and Benue) and still including the Yoruba territories of Ilorin, most of Igbomina, the Okun Yoruba, and part of Ekiti. The Eastern and Western Regions

Map 5. Nigeria's regional structure, 1955

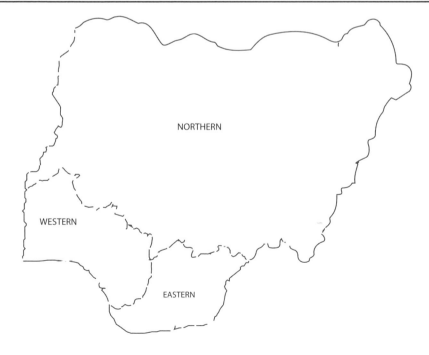

represented a splitting of the former Protectorate of Southern Nigeria, which had been smaller territorially than the Protectorate of Northern Nigeria, into two, with the Lower Niger as the dividing line. Territorially, the Northern Region amounted to over 60 percent of Nigeria's land area — a federal structure not justified or necessitated by any ethnic, cultural, historical or geographic considerations; a deliberate imbalance that was destined to bedevil Nigeria's internal relations and politics.

Each of these regions was dominated by one of the three largest nationalities of Nigeria — the Hausa-Fulani in the Northern Region, the Yoruba in the Western Region, and the Igbo in the Eastern Region. The dominant (or majority) nationality of each region shared it with many smaller (or minority) nationalities. Each majority nationality controlled the government of its region, with minor places given to the minority nationalities. During the decade preceding independence, three major political parties had emerged in the country, one from each region, essentially the political mouthpiece of the majority nationality: the Northern Peoples Congress (NPC) of the Hausa-Fulani, the Action Group (AG) of the Yoruba, and the National Council of Nigerian Citizens (NCNC) of the Igbo. The NPC made no effort to have any presence beyond the Northern Region, but the AG and NCNC sought to become nationwide and managed to establish some presence in the regions outside their bases. Elections held in 1959 produced the outcome that each party held the government of its region, while an alliance of the NPC and NCNC held the Federal Government, with the NPC as the larger of the two, and with the AG as official opposition, in the federal parliament.

The Yoruba people shared the Western Region with their historically and culturally close neighbors, the Edo and Edo-related peoples of Benin Province, as well as with a cluster of smaller nationalities (Urhobo, Isoko, Ika Igbo, Ijaw, and others) of Delta Province. The Yoruba kingdom of Lagos, made the capital city of Nigeria by the British in 1914, continued to serve as the capital and the seat of the Federal Government of Nigeria into independence. The Yoruba people of the Ilorin kingdom, many of the Igbomina kingdoms, the Ekiti kingdom of Obo, part of the Ekiti kingdom of Moba, and all of the Yoruba Owe, Oworo, Jumu, Ikiri, Yagba, Gbede, Bunu of Kabba Province, formed the southwestern provinces of the Northern Region with its regional capital city in Kaduna, north of the Middle Niger. With these Yoruba groups absorbed into the evolving systems and politics of the Northern Region, the Yoruba of the Western Region (consisting of the kingdoms of the Ijebu, Egba and Owu, Oyo, Ife, Ijesa, Ekiti, Ondo, Owo, Akoko, Itsekiri), plus the Yoruba of the Awori kingdoms (of the federal capital territory of Lagos), became the distinct representatives and voice of the Yoruba people in the political and social history of Nigeria.

The earliest flicker of Nigerian nationalist agitation against British rule was lighted by the Western-educated people of the Yoruba island kingdom of Lagos, to which place, being the capital of Nigeria, many literate persons from other parts of Nigeria were increasingly attracted. Nationalism had started, as will be seen in the next chapter, as Yoruba cultural nationalism in the last decade of the nineteenth century. Before 1920 it had developed political goals. When in 1923 the British granted to the Lagos Colony a constitution providing for an elected council, the politics of political parties, elections, newspapers, and mass rallies began in Lagos and provided a strong stimulus for nationalist agitation in Nigeria. Nationalist agitation soon spread to Ibadan, the highest center of British administration in the Yoruba interior, the largest city in Black Africa, and later to become the capital city of the Western Region. By the 1940s, nationalist politics had been introduced from Lagos to more parts of the Western Region as well as to the Eastern and Northern Regions, and political parties comprising prominent Nigerians of various ethnic origins competed with one another to win the support of Lagos people and to extend their influence to the rest of Nigeria. In 1947, the most prominent of the Lagos politicians, Herbert Macaulay (grandson of Bishop Ajayi Crowther), at the head of his political party (the National Council of Nigeria and the Cameroons, NCNC), embarked on a well publicized tour of Nigeria for these purposes, but he died before completing it. His place as leader of the NCNC was then taken by a Lagos politician of Igbo origin, Dr. Nnamdi Azikiwe. Under the leadership of Dr. Azikiwe, the NCNC (with its name changed to 'National Council of Nigerian Citizens' after the Southern Cameroons, which had been added to Nigeria in 1918 as a British-administered League of Nations Mandated Territory, voted to be separated from Nigeria in the 1950s) established branches in many towns of the Western and Eastern Regions. With the the granting of elected legislatures to the Nigerian federation and the three Regions by the 1949 Constitution, the other political parties earlier mentioned emerged – the NPC in the Northern Region, and the Action Group in the Western Region, as well as a number of smaller political parties in various parts of Nigeria. Dr. Azikiwe moved in 1952–3 to head the government of the Eastern Region, and the effective base of the NCNC thereafter shifted to the Eastern Region.

The years from the 1920s also witnessed the founding, by Western-educated Yoruba men and women, of local organizations named Progressive Unions or Development Associations – Ijebu Progressive Association, Ekiti Progressive Union, etc. These brought the rising literate elite of the Yoruba people together in sub-ethnic and other types of local groupings in order to consider ways to improve the quality of life of their people. Typically, the first priority of these associations was to encourage parents to send their children to school, in order to extend the benefits of education to all Yoruba people. For this important purpose, they raised funds among themselves, created scholarship programs, and organized enlightenment rallies, all of which, together, contributed considerably to giving the Yoruba people of the Western Region and Lagos a head start in education among the peoples of the African continent.

In 1949–50, a cultural organization of the educated Yoruba elite was founded (as would be remembered) with the name Egbe Omo Oduduwa (Association of Oduduwa's Descendants), to bring together educated Yorubas of all subgroups – a deliberately higher and more encompassing association of all the Yoruba elite than the progressive unions. Made up of traditional rulers and prominent Yorubas from all callings, Egbe Omo Oduduwa pursued policies and activities aimed at elevating the consciousness of a common origin and common heritage among Yoruba people.

In response to the creation of the Western Region, and a new constitution in 1949, the political party named the Action Group was founded by a large cross-section of the educated Yoruba elite – lawyers, doctors, teachers, pastors, journalists, business people, traditional rulers and chiefs – all under the leadership of an Ibadan-based lawyer named Obafemi Awolowo, from the small Ijebu town of Ikenne. The Action Group won the elections for the first elected government of the Western Region in 1952, and thus produced the first elected rulers of a Yoruba state in modern times. Many significant Yoruba persons continued to be members of the NCNC, however, and the Yoruba love of freedom of choice made the Western Region a bone of contention between the Action Group and the NCNC in the elections of most of the 1950s. However, slowly and laboriously, the Action Group won more and more support than the NCNC. In this, the great weapon of the Action Group leadership was its capacity to conceive, plan and execute programs of development and modernization, and to offer a very respectable government. More will be said about development later; suffice it to say here that as the Western Region became clearly the development pace-setter among the regions of Nigeria, and as the Yoruba people became more and more proud of their region, the Action Group's hold on Yoruba support became gradually unassailable, and Obafemi Awolowo as Premier became a modern-day idol of many Yoruba people.

When the federal election of 1959 came, the Action Group leadership, desirous of taking its vision and development capability to the management of the Federal Government, put up Awolowo for election to the position of Prime Minister of Nigeria. Another lawyer, Samuel Ladoke Akintola, an experienced parliamentarian (from Ogbomoso) in the federal legislature, came back home and replaced Awolowo as Premier of the Western Region. As things happened, especially since the majority of the House of Representatives belonged to the

Northern Region, Awolowo's party did not win enough to make him Prime Minister of Nigeria, in spite of its running a noteworthy campaign. Awolowo became Leader of the Official Opposition in the federal parliament.

Meanwhile, Ladoke Akintola brought many qualities to the position of Premier of the Western Region. Endowed with impressive people skills, witty and articulate, and gifted with an extensive mastery of the Yoruba language, Akintola quickly raised the electoral successes of the Action Group in the Western Region to new heights. He also sustained with considerable credit the economic and social development programs of the Regional Government, in spite of some weakening of the region's revenue base owing to declines in prices of its cocoa exports in the world market.

In Nigeria as a whole, however, the developing political picture was far from prosperous or happy. As the country had moved gradually towards independence during the 1950s, discordance had become an obvious fact of national life. The British, by giving Nigeria a federal structure which conferred virtually all political power on one of its three regions, had prepared the ground for conflicts and turmoil. Even as the country celebrated independence on October 1, 1960, some omen of impending crisis was inescapable. Differences in the political traditions of Nigeria's many nationalities were painfully obvious, and so were differences in their expectations and desires. Powerful undercurrents of rivalry and suspicion shaped the relationship between the major nationalities (not excluding the relationship between the Hausa-Fulani and the Igbo who were, meanwhile, allies in the Federal Government), while the minority nationalities fretted about being dominated by the majority nationalities in the regions. In the Western and Eastern Regions, there were grave resentments caused by fears that the Hausa-Fulani leadership of the Northern Region appeared bent at all costs on keeping total and perpetual hold on the Federal Government, with the surreptitious encouragement and assistance of the British.

The fundamental roots of the Nigerian problem are to be found in the composition of the country, and the nature of the structure that the British had bestowed on it. Nigeria arrived at independence as a country of very many nationalities, each with its own culture, homeland territory, history, political traditions that had evolved over millennia, and its own type of responses to the demands and challenges of life and development in the modern world. For Nigeria to move forward with some measure of stability and coherence, the leaderships of its various peoples needed to seek, together, arrangements that were meaningful in the circumstances – seeking carefully and with deliberate deference to the nature, the traditions, the predilections, the peculiar needs, and the pride of all its nationalities (large and small). Unfortunately, in the country that the British created for Nigerians, such modes of proceeding were impossible to arrive at. The underlying principles of inter-relationships in Nigeria, as they had been guided by the British before independence, were absolutely informed by ethnic power quests, dreams of ethnic dominance and brash power contests. In such a bruising atmosphere of power contests and of mutual distrust and fears, the one nationality which found itself with a chance to exercise dominance over the rest grabbed the chance and proceeded to expand it, and the rest, while swinging punches at one another, chaotically fought to resist the growing reality of domination by that one nationality. Over the years, the trend developed into a destructive tradition and took over the management of Nigeria's affairs, making a clear-sighted Nigerian leadership impossible, spawning a whole array of misguided "solutions," and enthroning crookedness and corruption over Nigeria's public life as a country.

One immediately touchy point in the months after independence was differences in attitudes to the obvious intention of the British to continue to mastermind Nigeria's affairs. Actions of the Federal Government quickly fomented a crisis from this. The Hausa-Fulani leadership of Northern Nigeria trusted the British more than it trusted the Igbo and Yoruba leaderships of Eastern and Western Nigeria. Through a series of acts (e.g. the appointment of British officials to sensitive national positions, and a military pact authorizing the establishment of British military bases on Nigerian soil), the Federal Government (or, more correctly, the NPC senior partner in the NPC–NCNC alliance) seemed intent on entrenching British influence over the management of Nigeria's affairs. This generated a wave of nationalist agitation, promoted by students and organized labor, endorsed by the Action Group opposition in the federal parliament, and enjoying considerable support especially among the literate people of the predominantly Yoruba Western Region and Lagos. In a major step aimed at suppressing the growing movement, the two parties in power in the Federal Government (led by politicians from the Northern and Eastern Regions) employed the weight of the Federal Government to strike with force at the Action Group federal opposition and at the Western Region where the Action Group was in control. Though the Eastern Region's Igbo leadership of the NCNC strongly suspected the NPC's every intention, they joined in the attack on the Action Group and the Western Region, because they calculated that their party would, with the destruction of the Action Group, at last have a chance to take over the government of the Western Region.

It was very unfortunate for the Yoruba people that, at the very time when a potent threat was thus developing against the Western Region, sharp disagreements arose among its leading citizens – the leaders of the Action Group. After this disagreement blew into the open, many explanations and conjectures appeared in the news media as to the cause of it. There were many small

29. Obafemi Awolowo (1909–87), Premier of Western Region, Nigeria (1952–59). *Photo: E. Elisofon, c. 1960, Getty Images.*

30. Samuel Ladoke Akintola (1910–66), Premier of Western Region, Nigeria (1959–66). *Photo: E. Elisofon, c. 1960, Getty Images.*

contributing factors – personal dislikes between some persons in the outgoing Awolowo administration and the incoming Akintola administration, resentment generated by the fact that the leading crop of Yoruba intellectuals, who had come to like working closely with and advising Awolowo as Premier, continued to remain close to him rather than to the new Premier, disagreements as to the influence of the party over the regional government, etc. However, a careful sifting would seem to reveal conclusively that the central factor was a growing divergence of opinions in the Action Group leadership about how to relate to, and handle, the Nigerian situation. The British, as earlier pointed out, had so ordered the political structure of Nigeria that the Northern Region enjoyed a strong hold on the Federal Government. Political leaders of Southern Nigeria were dissatisfied with this, but they never seemed to be able to find unity in dealing with the threat of Northern domination. The Action Group had started off very confidently, assured of its ability to make and keep the Western Region at the cutting edge of development and progress, in spite of the preponderance of federal power that the British had allocated to the Northern Region's political leadership. And the Action Group government of the Western Region had recorded, and was recording, great achievements in development and progress.

However, some leaders of the party gradually came to feel that, in spite of the serious objections to the Northern leaders' approach to Nigerian affairs, the Western Region needed to work with the Northern leadership, in order to avoid being marginalised in the affairs of Nigeria – in order, as it was commonly put, to ensure that the Western Region would get its fair share of Nigeria's "national cake." These leaders could point to the fact that the Igbo leadership of Eastern Nigeria had been doing just that, and therefore enjoying the benefits of participation in the Federal Government. Such a view, however, seemed to most Action Group leaders to represent a rejection of the high visions and ethos of the Action Group (the vision and ethos that had come to make it very popular with the Yoruba people). Most Action Group leaders, including Awolowo, strongly believed that to work with the NPC on the NPC's terms, and without any prospect that the NPC would modify its position in any way, was unacceptable surrender to Northern domination – a surrender that would only encourage the Northern leadership to dig further in in defence of Northern interest, a situation that would only provoke more resentment and ultimate instability in Nigeria. Many of the leaders who thought in this way would rather that the mainstream Yoruba leadership should work with the Igbo leadership of Eastern Nigeria, in order to bring some equity into Nigeria's affairs.

Given this growing cleavage in the Action Group, the decision to have Awolowo give up the governance of the Western Region and seek federal office in 1959 was a serious mistake. Following the failure of the Action Group in that 1959 federal election, the cleavage widened rapidly – with Akintola as Premier emerging as the most important leader among those promoting what looked more and more like the dissident opinion. The group around Akintola (including Ayo Rosiji, National Secretary of the Action Group) was displeased with the party's top leadership for not making a serious effort to work with the NPC after the 1959 election, and for negotiating with the NCNC at all since, in their view, the NCNC national leadership had always been unreliable. On the other hand, most leading members of the Action Group felt outraged by the fact that certain leaders in Akintola's circle had, without any authority from the party, taken the step of going behind the party to hold secret negotiations with leaders of the NPC after the 1959 election. The growing disenchantment between the supporters of the opposing views led ultimately in May 1962 to a major conflict, as a result of which the majority of the party's leadership in a top meeting asked Akintola to step down from the position of Premier, to be replaced by Dauda Adegbenro (a legislator from Abeokuta). With Akintola refusing to step down, his opponents took the battle to the House of Assembly, where they intended to remove him through a resolution of the legislature.

Akintola's supporters were determined that there would be no resolution. The outcome was a rowdy and noisy clash on the floor of the House of Assembly.[6]

All this played into the hands of the NPC–NCNC controllers of the Federal Government, making it possible for them to step in, to declare that all law and order had broken down in the Western Region, to establish a state of emergency over it, to suspend its elected government, to incarcerate its foremost politicians, and to institute over it a federally appointed emergency administration led by a Yoruba federal civil servant, Koye Majekodunmi, and to use their new strong positon to ensure that the division in the leadership of the Yoruba people would grow deeper and become permanent. Split from the main body of the Action Group, Akintola formed a new party of his own (first the United People's Party – UPP, and then the Nigerian National Democratic Party – NNDP). Akintola then took his party into an alliance with the NPC. Awolowo and the rest of the Action Group then became, openly, the principal target of the federal attack on the Western Region. An investigation (executed by a Commission of Enquiry chaired by a certain Justice G. B. Coker), was instituted into the management of the Western Region, covering only the years under Awolowo's premiership. While that was still going on, the Federal Government indicted Awolowo with treasonable felony charges – an action which most Yoruba people believed to be groundless and to be motivated only by politics. Then followed a court trial in which Awolowo was denied legal defense of his choice, and in which the federal authorities seemed bent on manipulating the outcome. At the expiration of the emergency administration in January 1963, large numbers of citizens of the Western Region urged the Federal Government to order new elections, so that they might elect a new representative government for their region. The Federal Government ignored this outcry and simply reinstalled Akintola as Premier. And then the criminal case against Awolowo was concluded, and he was convicted and imprisoned. And then also, the Federal Government separated the Benin and Delta provinces from the Western Region and constituted them into a new region named the Midwestern Region – an action which made the Western Region an exclusively Yoruba region, and which most Yoruba people saw as having the objective of reducing their weight and influence in the affairs of Nigeria. The vast majority of the Yoruba citizens of the Western Region took these federal actions as an affront on the Yoruba nation, and a mighty crisis developed.

The elections that came in 1964 and 1965 finally brought the crisis to a violent outcome. In the federal election of 1964 (with Akintola's party, the NNDP, in alliance with the NPC), the Yoruba people of the Western Region encountered, for the first time in their history of participation in modern democratic elections, the use of governmental powers to distort the processes and results of an election – in order to give the NPC–NNDP alliance victory in the Western Region. Most Yoruba people attributed this to the influence of the NPC, and the anger generated by it prepared the ground for the Western Regional elections due in October 1965. When, in the 1965 election, the same manipulations of 1964 were replicated on a bigger and more blatant scale to give the NNDP victory over the Action Group, the crisis in the region exploded into a great conflagration. For three months, violent protests ravaged the Western Region and parts of the federal territory of Lagos, resulting in the killing of countless persons and the burning of countless houses – of members of Akintola's party and of officials believed to have taken part in rigging the election. In the process, the authority of the regional and Federal Governments disintegrated in many parts of the Western Region. In desperation, the Federal Government increasingly brought the Nigerian armed forces into the maintenance of law and order, thus unwittingly inviting the armed forces into intervention in the politics of the country. Ultimately, early in the morning of January 16, 1966, the Nigerian armed forces struck, and seized control of the Federal Government and all the regional governments of Nigeria. In the bloody process of military seizure of power, Ladoke Akintola lost his life.[7]

The Yoruba, acting through a sizeable majority, had thus made their point and, as they saw it, upheld their dignity as a nation. But they had done it at a cost – in lost lives and lost properties, and, more importantly, in an unmistakable loss of Yoruba political unity. In spite of the participation of the Yoruba political elite in different political parties from 1951 to 1962, the general spirit of Yoruba national political solidarity developing from the late nineteenth century, and the focus of Yoruba leadership on the development and progress of Yoruba society, had, on the whole, stayed alive and well. In 1962–66, however, all of that suffered a serious setback. While that setback was engineered by the forces at work in Nigerian politics, most observers were nevertheless surprised by the ease with which the modern Yoruba leadership succumbed and allowed itself to fall apart in 1962–66. The political hangover from that crisis continued, till the end of the century, to becloud the behavior and image of the Yoruba in the politics of Nigeria and to dilute the influence that they deserved to have in Nigeria's affairs. On the whole, the Yoruba West in Nigeria ceased being the place to emulate in matters of political order and stability and in matters of socio-economic development, and became one of the constant centers of the truculence and violence that increasingly came to characterize Nigeria's politics and national life as the twentieth century ended and the twenty-first opened. At the turn of the century, the political leaders of the Yoruba people showed no serious signs of being able to ameliorate this political climate of their homeland, but increasingly seemed vulnerable to the negative forces at work in Nigerian politics.

After his release from prison in August 1966, Awolowo emerged from the 1962–66 crisis as the hero of most Yoruba people. To most, the years of his premiership of the Western Region (1952–59) came to be seen as the golden age of modern Yoruba history. More and more for the rest of the twentieth century, Yoruba people, especially the highly educated elite, hailed his 1952–59 management of the affairs of the Western Region as a faithful synthesis and demonstration of Yoruba character and political principles – usually stated as the principles of respect for the people's sovereignty and for the law, a dedication to democracy and to accountability, seriousness and exalted conduct in the running of public affairs, and dedication of government policies and actions to the improvement of the people's quality of life. After he was released from prison, Awolowo became far and away the most influential Yoruba in the affairs of Nigeria and one of the most revered political figures in Nigeria. Most Yoruba people harbored the expectation that whenever Nigeria returned to civilian rule, Awolowo would at last have the chance to bring the high principles that he represented into the governance of Nigeria. However, there were significant and influential pockets of opposition to Awolowo, as would be seen later. The old inter-ethnic rivalries and animosities were still very much alive – which meant that, when the time came for civilian politics, Awolowo would be powerfully resisted by the Hausa-Fulani leadership of Northern Nigeria and the Igbo leadership of Eastern Nigeria. But more importantly, mostly as a consequence of the 1962–66 Western Region crisis, there were some prominent and influential Yoruba persons who were strongly (even bitterly) opposed to Awolowo.

As for Nigeria as a country, the national crisis that thus started in 1962 never cleared throughout the rest of the twentieth century. The military ruled for thirteen years, until 1979. The first four years of military rule saw the national crisis escalate to its very worst. Not long after coming to power in January 1966, the Federal Military Government, led by a military officer of Igbo origin, General Johnson Aguiyi Ironsi, adopted some measures that denuded the regions of their powers and seemed to threaten the establishment of unitary rule over the country. Leading politicians and citizens of the Northern Region especially had good reason to fear that some of these measures were aimed specifically at their region. In particular, Ironsi's decree unifying the top levels of the civil service of the regional governments of Nigeria seemed clearly to threaten the takeover of the civil service of the Northern Region by the more academically qualified civil servants from Southern Nigeria. In the circumstance, the fact that the leaders of the January coup had been mostly Igbo, and that the coup had eliminated the most important Hausa-Fulani leader (Sir Ahmadu Bello, Premier of the Northern Region) and a major Yoruba leader (Chief Akintola) and not a single Igbo leader, came to be seen in the North as proof that the coup was an Igbo coup. Massive protests arose in the Northern Region – resulting in a widespread massacre of Igbo citizens of the Eastern Region living in the Northern Region.

A group of soldiers of Northern Region origin then overthrew the Ironsi regime in July 1966, and pushed aside the Yoruba military officer (Brigadier Babafemi Ogundipe) who was next in rank to Ironsi. In fact, Ogundipe faced threats to his life at the hands of the Northern coup makers and had to flee into exile. The Northern officers then installed one of their men, a comparatively junior officer named Yakubu Gowon (then a Lieutenant Colonel), in Ironsi's place. Even with the Northern Region's military men in control of the Federal Government, more massacres of Igbos erupted in the Northern Region. From the Northern Region, and then from the other regions, members of the Igbo nationality fled to their region, creating a big refugee crisis there. Under such painful pressures, the leadership of the Eastern Region slowly came to the conclusion that their people could never again find safety in Nigeria. In May 1967 therefore, they announced to the world that the Eastern Region was seceding from Nigeria and taking its place in the world as an autonomous country with the name Biafra. The Federal Military Government immediately responded with two actions: first, an announcement dividing Nigeria into twelve states (three in the Eastern Region, three in the old Western Region and Lagos, and six in the Northern Region – obviously for the purpose of weakening the hold of the Igbo leadership on the non-Igbo peoples of the Eastern Region), and, secondly, an invasion of the Eastern Region. Nigeria thus plunged into civil war, a war that was destined to continue until January 1970.

As the war started, the new Yoruba Western and Lagos States found themselves in a precarious position. For one thing, although there were many Yoruba in the officer ranks of the Nigerian army, there were almost none in the lower combat ranks – because Yoruba people had generally avoided seeking service at those lower levels of the military. As a result, Yorubaland found itself at the mercy of tens of thousands of troops of Northern origin, deployed to police and defend the Western and Lagos States. Moreover, most Yoruba people believed that, in spite of Nigeria's obvious downsides, the country was worth preserving; that if properly and decently managed (as the Western Region had been until the outbreak of the 1962 crisis), it had the capabilities to develop into a great power in the world and a land of opportunity for all its citizens. Also, Yoruba feelings were revolted by the brutalities and killings that Igbo people had been subjected to in the Northern Region. As crowds of wounded and traumatized

Igbo men, women and children, fleeing from the Northern Region, had come through parts of the Western Region on their way to the Eastern Region, relief teams had sprung up in Yoruba towns to offer them help and food, and to dress their wounds. In the months before the declaration of Biafra and the outbreak of war, the Military Governor of the Western Region, Brigadier (later General) Adeyinka Adebayo, had spoken fervently for reconciliation and peace in federal councils; at home in the Western Region, he had urged his people against any violence against the Igbo in Yoruba towns and villages. And Obafemi Awolowo, recently released from prison, had added his voice to that of the Military Governor. As a result, Igbo people had been safe in the Western Region and Lagos; those who had fled from there had done so only out of fear of soldiers of Northern Region origin still deployed in Yorubaland. To change that situation, representatives of the Eastern, Western and Midwestern States got the Federal Military Council to take the decision to redeploy all Nigerian soldiers to their regions of origin. Also, prominent Yoruba citizens of all political persuasions, acting together in their gathering known as Yoruba Leaders of Thought (under Awolowo's chairmanship) urged the Federal Military Government of Yakubu Gowon to redeploy all Northern soldiers from the West and Lagos to their own region, and to authorize the recruitment of Yorubas to the army to police the Western Region and Lagos. Though Gowon's responses to these demands

Map 6. Nigeria's state structure, 1967

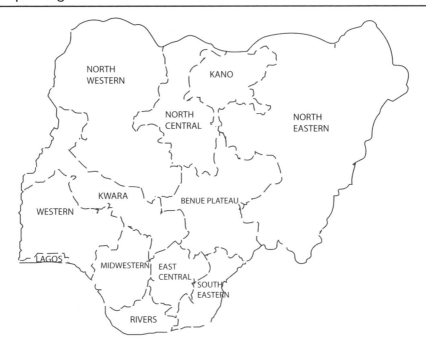

were always positive, he never took the actions demanded. His failure in this matter contributed greatly to Yoruba feelings that his Federal Government was an agent of the Northern leadership, and the feelings of the Igbo leadership that their people could never hope to be safe in the rest of Nigeria. And these fears of the Igbo people were destined ultimately to lead to secession – and to civil war. In general, as the civil war began, the Gowon government, under the influence of advisers who feared that Yoruba support for the federal cause was doubtful, operated in suspicion and fear of the broad generality of Yoruba people, and sustained the hold of the Northern soldiers on the Western and Lagos States – a situation which Awolowo categorized as reducing Yorubaland to a "protectorate" in independent Nigeria.

All of that, however, was soon to change. In July 1967, Midwestern military officers sympathetic to the Biafran cause overthrew the military government of the Midwest State, and elements of the Biafran army poured over the Onitsha bridge across the lower Niger, occupied the Midwest, and penetrated some distance into the southern parts of the Western State (Ilaje, Ikale and the southern Ondo forests). That, for the Yoruba people, created a totally unexpected situation. As the war had started, Biafra had stridently called on Yoruba people to revolt and declare their secession from Nigeria. Suddenly, however, with the Biafran occupation of the Midwest and thrust into Yorubaland, it seemed to Yoruba people in general that the Western and Lagos States, and the federal capital city of Lagos itself, would be occupied by Biafra too – and nobody could be sure what the Igbo leadership of Biafra would do to Yorubaland from that position of strength. Consequently, the Yoruba people of the Western and Lagos States became gripped by a feverish resolve to defend their territory. The Federal Military Government also changed course immediately and, among other things, ordered a general mobilization, thus opening the door to recruitment of Yoruba people into the army. In towns and villages all over the Western and Lagos States, Yoruba youths formed long lines at recruitment centers, eager to enlist for the defence of their homeland. They proved to be what the desperate federal situation needed. Products of the Western Region's Free Primary Education Program (about which more will be said later), they were easy to train quickly and deploy, and their coming rolled the Nigerian army forward. Thrusts from various directions were then made into the Eastern Region, many of which thrusts were commanded by Yoruba officers – of whom some (like Lt. Col. Benjamin Adekunle, Lt. Col. Ayo Ariyo, Col. Olufemi Olutoye and Col. Olusegun Obasanjo) became household names throughout the country on account of their accomplishments in the war.

Also, very importantly, in order to generate popular support for the federal war effort, Gowon (by then, General Gowon) invited some prominent civilians to join his war cabinet, and appointed Awolowo to the highest position in it as Commissioner for Finance and Vice-Chairman of the Supreme Military Council. With the appointment of Chief Awolowo, the management of the war finances came into the hands of the man acclaimed by many in his own lifetime and after his death as a masterful statesman, visionary and administrator in the twentieth century history of Nigeria. With prominent civilians in the military administration, the Federal Government's management of the war changed greatly for the better. Much of that was, according to all reports, due to Chief Awolowo's leadership qualities and to the unity of purpose exhibited by the civilian leaders in the war cabinet. The people of Eastern Nigeria, acquitting themselves very creditably against the overwhelming resources of the Federal Government, kept fighting for over two more years. When the war finally ended, Obasanjo received their surrender in the field, and the pieces of the shattered country began to come slowly together again. As soon as the war ended, Awolowo, saying that he was satisfied that the objective of the inclusion of civilians in the war cabinet had been fulfilled, offered his resignation from the Gowon administration.

For the Yoruba people, perhaps the most important developments of the civil war period were, first, the emergence of two states that were fully Yoruba out of the twelve states of the federation (namely, Lagos State and the Western State), and secondly, the presence of Yoruba citizens in the armed forces in numbers almost commensurate with their numerical strength in Nigeria. A third state, Kwara, with headquarters at Ilorin, was a predominantly Yoruba state. In the years that followed, this creation of states by Gowon came to convince most Nigerians that splitting the country into smaller states was good for economic development and political stability. Therefore, more states came to be later created; by the year 2000, the Nigerian federation consisted of thirty-six states. Of these, six were fully Yoruba states – namely, Lagos (with its capital at Ikeja), Ogun (with its capital at Abeokuta), Oyo (with its capital at Ibadan), Osun (with its capital at Osogbo), Ondo (with its capital at Akure), and Ekiti (with its capital at Ado-Ekiti). One other state, Kwara State (with its capital at Ilorin), was predominantly Yoruba. Another state, Kogi State (with its capital at Lokoja), had a strong Yoruba component, while Delta State had a small Yoruba component (namely, the Itsekiri).

As soon as the war ended, Gowon promised to embark on steps that would lead to a new constitution, and the return to democratically elected government. However, year followed year and Gowon showed hardly any sign of bringing an end to military rule. As a result, he lost all credibility and popularity, and therefore, five years after the war, another group of military officers overthrew him on July 29, 1975. The new administration, led by another Northern officer,

Lt. Col. Murtala Mohammed, won immediate and widespread admiration by promising an end to the sordid corruption that had become the mark of the post-war military administration, and by offering a program of return to democratic civilian government. Less than one year later, on February 13, 1976, Murtala Mohammed was assassinated by another group of mostly Northern military officers trying to take over. The takeover attempt failed, and Murtala's deputy, Olusegun Obasanjo, a Yoruba officer, assumed leadership of the country, promising to implement the Murtala program of return to civilian rule.

Since Northern military officers continued to be the most influential block in the Nigerian army, people have wondered why Obasanjo was allowed to assume leadership of the country in 1976. One probability is that, because he had been the most prominent Nigerian military officer in the last stages of the war against Biafra, the officer who had received the Biafran surrender in the field, he commanded some respect in the army. Some other observers have also suggested that military people close to him perceived him as a man with little or no emotional attachment to his ethnic roots – a sort of "detribalized" Nigerian – and that that image made him acceptable. But some have added that he was not only perceived as detribalized, but actually as one of the Yoruba strongly hostile to Awolowo – and therefore, a man who could be relied upon not to promote any Awolowo or Yoruba agenda in Nigerian affairs. In support of this latter, it is usually pointed out that Obasanjo, in and out of office, never openly (in writing and other ways) evinced any measurable warmth towards Yoruba group aspirations or interests.

In 1979, with Obasanjo as military ruler of Nigeria, elections were held for a civilian government under a new constitution modeled after the American presidential system. In the 1979 elections, the political party founded and led by Awolowo, the Unity Party of Nigeria (UPN) was one of the five political parties registered under the electoral law. It soon became clear that two of these, the UPN and the National Party of Nigeria (NPN, founded and led by the Hausa-Fulani leadership of Northern Nigeria) stood high above the other three. The UPN swept the then four Yoruba states of Western Nigeria (as well as the Midwestern region then known as Bendel State) – winning all the governorships, virtually all the membership of some of the state legislatures, and nearly all legislative seats in the federal National Assembly, and giving Awolowo very massive majorities in the presidential election. This was an unprecedented demonstration of Yoruba political unity in modern times, but it narrowly failed to give Awolowo a decisive victory in the race for the presidency of Nigeria, since his votes in the other parts of Nigeria did not sufficiently help.

Of the five candidates for the presidency, neither of the two front-runners (Shehu Shagari from Northern Nigeria and Obafemi Awolowo from Western

Nigeria) won decisively, and, in accordance with the electoral law, a run-off between the two became necessary. As things stood, and with the alliances emerging after the presidential votes were all announced, Awolowo seemed likely to win a run-off election. However, the military administration under Obasanjo intervened with a novel, and very questionable, reinterpretation of the electoral law in order to prevent a run-off election. The electoral law had stipulated that a number of issues would be decided if supported by two-thirds of the then nineteen states of Nigeria. From the Constituent Assembly which had created the constitution and the electoral laws, through the preparation for elections, and throughout the process of the elections, two-thirds of nineteen states had been universally and pointedly interpreted as thirteen states. The electoral law provided that, to be validly elected as Nigeria's president, a candidate must win not less than one-fourth of the votes cast in at least two-thirds of the nineteen states. Shagari, the NPN candidate, won the required one-fourth in twelve states, with Awolowo coming close behind. For two days, the Electoral Commission appeared to be preparing for the announcement for a run-off election – and all parties began to prepare for one. Suddenly, officials of Shagari's party (notably Richard Akinjide, legal adviser to the NPN) came up with the proposal that two-thirds of nineteen states was no longer thirteen states, but twelve states plus two-thirds of one state – and that since Shagari had won one-fourth of the votes cast in twelve states and one-fourth of two-thirds of the votes cast in a thirteenth state, he should be deemed as elected. To the shock of most Nigerians, Obasanjo accepted this truncated interpretation and had Shagari proclaimed as elected – drawing violent denunciations from all the other political parties.

In the context of Yoruba history, it is significant that the two persons most responsible for this manipulation of the electoral law in 1979 were Yoruba: General Obasanjo, and Richard Akinjide. Akinjide was one of Nigeria's most senior legal practitioners. He had belonged to the NCNC in the 1950s, and had later joined Akintola's NNDP in 1963. A man of outstanding intellect, Akinjide was one of Nigeria's best lawyers; for some years he was President of the Nigerian Bar Association. In the 1979 elections, he had stood as NPN candidate for the governorship of Oyo State, and had lost heavily to another first-rate lawyer, Bola Ige, candidate for Awolowo's party, the UPN. Thus the elections of 1979 clearly exhibited the two contrasting realities in Yoruba political life in Nigeria: first, a very solid unity of the generality of Yoruba people (a unity around strongly held principles and expectations), and second, a stubborn, and often hostile, strain of dissidence in sections of the very top of modern Yoruba political leadership – most of it a carry-over from the 1962–66 Western Region situation. Admirers of the modern Yoruba people have often expressed surprise that this cohesive and high-achieving people has somehow seemed to lack the capacity to deal with serious internal divisions that happen to arise – a weakness that has often hurt their interests in the affairs of multinational Nigeria, and that has repeatedly compromised their success in doing what they have been demonstrably best at doing: namely, developing and enriching their society.

The politics of the Shagari presidency proceeded to work against the Yoruba parts of Nigeria. Belonging to a party that was the leading rival of Shagari's party, the governments of the Yoruba states encountered serious difficulties, especially with inadequate funding for the programs that their people cherished. Nevertheless, each of the four governors (Lateef Jakande in Lagos State, Bisi Onabanjo in Ogun State, Bola Ige in Oyo State, and Adekunle Ajasin in Ondo State) doggedly pursued policies that sustained, and even expanded the scope of, free education, improved the quality of health care delivery and of the transportation systems. Jakande, who became known as "Action Governor," performed a near miracle with the Lagos schools system – providing temporary facilities that enabled the state to bring immediately to an end the confusing double-stream practice whereby some Lagos children had gone to school in the morning and the rest in the afternoon – a practice which had meant that neither stream had been able to learn effectively. Jakande also created housing estates, and considered a tram system as a solution to the chronic traffic jams that had long plagued Lagos. He was not able to carry the tram project to conclusion. However, he founded a university for his state, and so too did the other three state governors for their states. Again, the mood characteristic of the 1952–62 Western Region began to reappear in these four states – the mood of confidence in leadership, achievements and orderly progress.

But it was all destined to be very brief. With the NPN Federal Government and NPN party operatives always pointedly posing a threat to the four Yoruba state governments, some persons in two of the state governments (Oyo and Ondo), ambitious for election as governors come 1983, were encouraged to become excessive and even disruptive in pushing their ambitions against their governors. Assured that the NPN would use its federal powers to rig elections for its candidates, every one of these persons ultimately decamped and became NPN candidates or NPN strategists when the 1983 elections came. All these things developed in a country-wide political atmosphere in which all other political parties were raising alarms about the NPN's use of the Nigerian Police and other institutions of the Federal Government to rig elections. In the end, the election manipulations were successfully pushed through in gubernatorial elections in both Oyo State and Ondo State, provoking some popular commotions in both states. The commotion in Ondo State proved particularly cataclysmic, resulting, in one single morning, in the killing of tens of persons believed to be implicated in the rigging of the election, the burning of their houses, and the death of many young demonstrators in clashes with the police in the streets. The courts of law later reversed the result of the gubernatorial election in Ondo State, but not in Oyo State. But neither of these had any real significance ultimately. In response to the sullen mood pervading most of the country, the Nigerian military stepped in again on December 30, 1983, and seized control of the federal and state governments.

The new military government, led by Muhammadu Buhari from the North, with Tunde Idiagbon (a Yoruba officer from Kwara State) as his deputy, lasted only about nineteen months. In August 1985, it was overthrown by another group of military officers led by Ibrahim Babangida, also from the North. The Babangida administration ordered the writing of yet another constitution – and general elections to be held in 1990–93. The elections to the Local Governments and the State Governments were conducted in 1990–92, and the election of the President of Nigeria came on June 12, 1993. Of the two political parties, the National Republican Convention (NRC) and the Social Democratic Party (SDP), which confronted each other in the presidential election, the NRC put forward Bashir Tofa (a Northerner) as its candidate, and the SDP, M. K.O. Abiola (a Yoruba from the West).

As the results of the election came to be released in various parts of the country in the course of the days following June 12, Abiola quickly emerged as the overwhelming winner, even in the North and the East. This, for a Yoruba man, was a political feat of historic proportions – something that no Yoruba person had ever achieved. Many factors worked in Abiola's favor. First, he was a very rich man with enormous personal funds to draw upon. Secondly, being an open-handed person by nature, he had given to a lot of causes and persons in most parts of the country, and was widely regarded as a philanthropist. Thirdly, he had a very thick web of social relationships spanning most parts of the country. As a prominent leader in the Muslim community in Nigeria, he had developed strong friendships in the predominantly Muslim North, while the fact that one of his wives was of Igbo descent gave him family relationships in the East. But all of these were not as important as two other factors. The first was the very solid support that he enjoyed at home in the West. Abiola had been alienated from the mainstream Yoruba political elite led by Chief Awolowo in the 1970s, because he had been a leading member of the NPN and had very noticeably worked against Awolowo's 1979 presidential candidacy. By 1991, however, he had managed to make his peace with the very powerful mainstream Yoruba elite and its Awolowo heritage. After the SDP nominated him as presidential candidate in 1992, the party rolled out their powerful political machine in his support all over the country – and that meant, among other things, that the masses of the Yoruba people, who were mainly SDP, went out and voted overwhelmingly for him. The other very important factor was that the Northern, Hausa-Fulani, political elite mostly continued to see Abiola as what he had always been – a Muslim friend and ally. Therefore, even though they supported Tofa's candidacy, they did not show any marked hostility towards Abiola's. By the time most of the electoral results were published, Abiola's overwhelming victory was beyond doubt. Abiola was the first Nigerian politician ever to receive such strong electoral support in all parts of the country.

In the opinion of virtually all Nigerians, and of foreign observers who came from many countries and international agencies, many at the invitation of the Nigerian government, the presidential election of June 12, 1993 was free and fair, and without disturbances or violence. Yet, a few days later, the authorities of the Federal Military Government announced cancellation of the election – without giving any clear reason other than some criticism of Abiola as a person. Protests and demonstrations followed in many parts of the country, and a pro-democracy movement emerged with the name National Democratic Coalition, with strong units all over the country, but with Lagos and many Yoruba cities as its most determined base. By winning the presidential election and becoming the first Yoruba man to perform such a feat, Abiola became an icon of Yoruba political success in the context of Nigeria – and the Yoruba political elite, strongly backed by the masses of Yoruba people, showed in every way that they would not let themselves be denied or robbed once again.

Unable to continue in such circumstances, Babangida stepped down and, in a move calculated to appease the Yoruba elite, handed over to an interim administration led by a non-partisan Yoruba civilian, Ernest Shonekan, a highly respected businessman who had served with distinction as Chief Executive Officer of the UAC group, one of the largest companies in Nigeria and also as chairman of the Federal Economic Advisory Board under Babangida. Three months later, however, General Sani Abacha, yet another Northern officer, Babangida's former Chief of Staff and a member of the Shonekan Interim Government, stepped forward, seized control, dissolved the Interim Government, and proclaimed himself president.

To suppress the pro-democracy movement which then became very formidable, Abacha instituted a reign of terror – detaining many prominent citizens without trial, and charging many more with high crimes. Many military officers were accused of attempting to overthrow Abacha's regime, and were tried and executed, or imprisoned, some of the latter dying in prison. Assassination squads went after leading citizens, some of whom fell to their bullets. Abiola was arrested and detained in prison for continuing to claim victory in the election. Thousands of the Nigerian intellectual and political elite (most of them

Yoruba), fled the country. It looked as if the country would not survive the Abacha terror, as talk of secession or dissolution began to be heard from various quarters. Leading Yoruba citizens who were still able to stay in the country started to meet to consider the future of the Yoruba people, and founded various Yoruba organizations – notably, Afenifere (a name culled from Awolowo's 1951 political party, Action Group, known in Yoruba as Egbe Afenifere – "the group that seeks the welfare of all"). Obafemi Awolowo had died in 1987; one of his old associates, Michael Adekunle Ajasin (from Owo), former governor of Ondo State, became leader of Afenifere. A group of Yoruba youths, led by Dr. Frederick Faseun, formed a militant organization and called it Odua People's Congress, for the defense of Yoruba interests. In many countries of the world, Yoruba residents held meetings and formed associations of descendants of Oduduwa to respond to the situation in Nigeria. As the heat rose, however, Abacha died suddenly on June 8, 1998, probably from a heart attack.

Abacha's sudden death saved Nigeria from dissolution or another civil war, but it did not change the fundamental trends of Nigeria's political life. M.K.O. Abiola died too – while still in prison. The military officer who took over after Abacha, General Abdulsalam Abubakar (also a Northerner), organized another presidential election in 1999.

General Abubakar was the last military ruler of Nigeria in the twentieth century; but General Abacha's violent regime marked the climax of the military impact on the country's political history. All in all, the heritage of the military was a serious distortion of the direction of Nigeria's political development. Military rule destroyed the intrinsic essence of Nigeria's federalism by gradually vesting virtually all effective authority in the Federal Government and relegating the component states of the federation to a lowly subordinate status. The popularly welcomed act of creation of more states was usually seized upon by military rulers as an occasion to weaken the resulting states, arrogate more authority to the federal center, and take over assets created and owned by the regions or the states. The fact that the revenue accruing to Nigeria from the rents and commissions on the petroleum industry must first be collected by the federal authority before distribution among the governments of the federation became a powerful tool in the hands of the Federal Government for holding on to a grossly disproportionate share of the national revenue, and often reducing the states to beggar members of the federation. As a result, while the Federal Government operated in enormous excess, waste and corruption, the states regularly suffered drastic inadequacy of funds for their essential services. The first military governors of the regions after the first military takeover of government in January 1966 were citizens of the regions to which they were posted – persons who belonged to the culture of the regions they were asked to rule, who could relate to the needs of their regions and respond to the expectations of the people they ruled. After this first generation of military governors, the military gradually saw to it that military governors were foreigners to the states to which they were posted – hence, the frequent appointment of governors with little or no understanding of the states they were supposed to rule and with little loyalty to the people they ruled. As a result, the governors became hardly better than federal agents in the states. By the time of Abacha, Nigeria was a federation only in name. An ill-conceived process of national unification or integration was in progress, resulting in the virtual death of the loyalty, passion, and accountability that had moved the regions forward in the years 1952–65, and the emergence of a political leadership with no firm roots among, and very little loyalty to, the governed.

Partly because of this, and partly from other circumstances, public corruption became a very pronounced feature of the heritage of military rule. This development began to show up in the post-war years of the Gowon regime, although Gowon himself is generally believed to have been personally above corruption. Military officers holding political offices increasingly brushed aside established civil service rules and controls, and dipped hands into the public coffers to enrich themselves. Although Chief Awolowo never explicitly said so, informed Nigerians believed that the growth of this trend in government was the key reason why he quickly resigned from the Gowon administration. It happened that the post-war years were the time when income from the exploitation of Nigeria's petroleum resources began to make a marked impact on the country. The Gowon administration came to command far more financial resources than Nigeria had ever seen before and, by and large, proceeded to lead the country along paths that were to prove disastrous. As the military men enriched themselves, they also opened doors to huge unearned wealth for their civilian friends. Gradually, it became obvious to the informed and ambitious that associating with government and government functionaries in order to get access to public money was more productive of financial success than engaging in truly productive and legitimate enterprises. This led to a new era of daringly fraudulent handling of public money, of public contracts designed not so much to build public assets as to enrich the contractors and the public officials, of sudden millionaires and billionaires whose wealth had no ascertainable source. In the brief period under General Murtala Mohammed, it seemed as if the trend would cease, but with his death its growth resumed. In the four-year civilian administration of President Shagari (1979–83), the trend matured considerably, and then in the hands of General Babangida, it became Nigeria's deliberate system of government – to be continued under his Chief of Staff and successor, General Abacha (and also in the civilian regime that succeeded

Abacha and Abubakar). Some of Nigeria's military rulers joined the ranks of the richest people in the world, with some of their civilian friends and collaborators coming close behind, and these became the role model for most public officials and most of Nigeria's politically ambitious, from the level of the federal center to that of the lowliest local government.

The combined effect of the above developments was that Nigeria was very firmly diverted from the path of developing a democratic political culture. As gaining access to public money became the principal objective of participation in politics, elections became desperately violent and bloody exercises, and victory at elections came to be won mostly by fraud and by criminal brigandage. Ultimately, assassinations became a major instrument in the politics of Nigeria.

The great crisis consequent on the cancellation of the 1993 June election of M. K. O. Abiola, the Abacha terror (which had targeted mostly the Yoruba elite), and the seething Yoruba discontentment, resulted in the circumstance whereby the presidency of Nigeria was more or less conceded to the Yoruba political

31. Moshood Kashimawo Abiola (1937–98), voting in the presidential elections on June 12, 1993, Lagos, Nigeria. *Photo: F. Rojon, AFP.*

32. Olusegun Obasanjo (1937–), Nigerian Head of State from 1976–79 and President 1999–2007. *Photo: M. Ngan, 2006, AFP.*

leadership in 1999. Two Yoruba candidates for the Nigerian presidency therefore emerged – retired General Olusegun Obasanjo, and Chief Olu Falae, a retired civil servant. The leadership of the party to which Obasanjo belonged, the People's Democratic Party (PDP), consisted mostly of retired wealthy military officers and their rich civilian allies, and seemed to be set on continuing the tradition of public life that had evolved under the military regimes – the tradition of corruption and disrespect for the law. Moreover, most Yoruba people saw the PDP as another Northern or Hausa-Fulani party. The party to which Olu Falae belonged, the Alliance for Democracy (AD), consisted, at the top, of many persons known to have been formerly associated with Chief Awolowo, and seemed to most Yoruba people to hold the promise of a return to the Awolowo tradition of disciplined service, responsible leadership, and dedication to development and progress. An additional, and very important, factor in the Yoruba choices in this election was the almost universal perception of Obasanjo among the Yoruba. As earlier pointed out, Obasanjo had never seemed, in the opinion of some sections of the Yoruba elite, to be concerned for Yoruba interests. Many could not forgive him for what was, in their view, his unfairly robbing Awolowo of victory in the 1979 presidential election. Many also sadly remembered that while most Yoruba leaders had been fighting for the reinstatement of Abiola's electoral victory after the cancellation of the June 12, 1993 election, Obasanjo had kept aloof and had been reported as saying that there was no reason to regard Abiola as a messiah. An overwhelming majority of Yoruba voters therefore rejected Obasanjo at the polls and voted for Falae. At the gubernatorial elections, all the (by then) six mainly Yoruba states also rejected the candidates of the PDP and voted for those of the AD. Obasanjo won the presidency, however, because the rest of Nigeria voted strongly for him and his party. And so, as the twentieth century came to an end, a Yoruba politician held the post of President of Nigeria – and was to hold that position until 2007.

A full account and assessment of the Obasanjo presidency is beyond the scope of this book. Suffice it to note the following points. Many informed observers at home and abroad acclaim Obasanjo for doing a number of things beneficial to the upper levels of the economy. First, his presidency ended the chaos into which the banking system had fallen under his predecessors, and therefore made Nigeria considerably more attractive to foreign investment. Secondly, he greatly advanced the much-needed privatization of Nigeria's publicly owned businesses which had always been a stinkpot of corruption – even though the process of privatization turned out to be very corrupt and to benefit mostly favored persons. Thirdly, he evolved policy that would attract private investment into the financing of some of Nigeria's infrastructures. Finally, of Prime Ministers or Presidents since independence, Obasanjo was the most open to the outside world; and this paid a great dividend when some part of Nigeria's foreign debt was cancelled by its creditors.

However, since most ordinary citizens were, by the nature of things, ignorant of, and mostly untouched by, these achievements, it was Obasanjo's failings in many other things that appeared to dominate the public assessment of him as he stepped down from the presidency in mid-2007. The general perception by most informed Nigerians opposed to Obasanjo was that while the government of Nigeria controlled much more revenue in the Obasanjo years than at any other comparable period since independence, yet Nigeria seemed to experience more neglect of the country's infrastructure than probably ever before – assets such as the highways, electricity, the important port and business city of Lagos. Education, it is said, was hard hit, and the universities in particular suffered very damaging neglect and deprivation. Teachers' wages were irregularly paid – in many states, teachers did not receive wages for months. Strikes by university lecturers and schoolteachers, and protests by students, repeatedly closed down schools and universities and paralyzed the educational system. Again and again, shortages of gasoline and sharp increases in gasoline prices provoked widespread strikes that lasted days. Unemployment among Nigerian educated youths (a good part of them Yoruba) reached the highest level ever,

Map 7. Nigeria's state structure, 1995

and so did flight by educated citizens (also many of them Yoruba) to other lands. Violent crimes drastically reduced security in virtually all parts of the country. Since independence, Nigeria had faced a rebellion in the Niger Delta (the source of almost all of its petroleum), because the indigenes of that area, whose livelihood had been severely damaged by petroleum exploitation activities, were aggrieved as a result of what they saw as inadequate federal planning and action towards their welfare. During the Obasanjo presidency, the rebellion became bigger, more confidently violent, and more sophisticated in resources and methods – which was all blamed on Obasanjo by many people. Above all, incidents of corruption in public life, and of sordid electoral fraud, dominated the news and the worldwide image of Nigeria, and so did news of political assassinations, for almost none of which the perpetrators were ever successfully investigated or prosecuted – and again, all this has been commonly debited to Obasanjo's account. As against all this, however, it needs to be pointed out that other informed observers urge the view that most of the said failings were not Obasanjo's *per se*, but were well established trends in the development of Nigeria's national life – trends that pre-existed Obasanjo's election and that had become powerful and unstoppable before his presidency.

The Yoruba Recoil

In the face of the prevailing and intensifying trends of corruption, fraud, rejection of accountability, and disrespect for law, by the general political leadership of Nigeria since independence, some Yoruba intellectuals began to speak up in order to articulate what they identified as Yoruba principles of political life, society, and governance. By the end of the century, articulating these principles had become a significant movement among a segment of Yoruba intelligentsia. In a 'Yoruba Retreat' (a symposium of leading Yoruba) held in Ibadan in October 2007, a political scientist, Wale Adebanwi, presented a paper titled "The Yoruba Vision" in which he outlined the development and essence of the movement. According to Adebanwi, the principles enunciated by the movement are distilled from the norms, philosophy and practice of Yoruba societal and political life from very early in, and throughout, Yoruba history – norms, philosophy and practice that became strongly exemplified in modern times in the Awolowo type of leadership in the affairs of the Western Region and of Nigeria.[8] Adebanwi supplies many quotations from recent statements of Yoruba thinkers who have offered details of the contents of this "Yoruba Vision." One such view from Segun Gbadegesin, professor of Philosophy at Howard University, Washington DC, states as follows:

Faithful to the vision of the founding fathers and founding mothers of the Yoruba nation, who dream of a prosperous community of men and women, and worked hard to actualize their dreams at various stages in the life of the nation, we envision a nation that sustains the principles of welfare liberalism, the rule of law and its democratic values, a nation which memorializes its vibrant culture and promotes its values in the homeland and the diaspora, a prosperous economy that exploits its natural resources through the instrumentality of its human resources that have been fully developed in the crucible of an educational system that caters for all children and adults.

The simple answer to the question "what do the Yoruba want" is this: The Yoruba want a Nigerian State which respects its multinational character and gives adequate recognition to the inviolability of its federating nationalities, no matter how small or big, a Nigerian State that promotes equal justice for all its citizens and makes a sacred commitment to the secularity of its character … The Yoruba have always wanted a Nigeria that practices and is committed to the principles of true federalism.[8]

Another quotation from Dr. Lateef Adegbite, Secretary-general of the Nigerian Supreme Council of Islamic Affairs, runs as follows: "The Yoruba have always demanded the highest standards of governance from their rulers since the ancient times and have also insisted that justice, due process, equity, non-discrimination, integrity, transparency, loyalty and humaneness be adhered to by those who run the government."[9]

Adebanwi also quotes from others, including Cornelius Adebayo (former Nigerian senator and former governor of Kwara State), and from the Yoruba Position Paper presented to a National Political Reform Conference called by the Obasanjo government in 2005. In summary, the proposition of all these statements goes as follows: that from ancient times, the Yoruba people created a political culture based on recognition of, and respect for, human rights and the sovereignty of the people; that throughout their history, the Yoruba have demanded from their rulers accountability, integrity, equity, social justice and enlightened leadership; and that in modern times, the Yoruba people, as a component of Nigeria, have sought to have those principles enshrined in their governance as a people and in the governance of the larger country to which they belong, and have also sought for Nigeria a truly federal structure based upon a careful respect for every nation, big or small, that forms part of Nigeria.

Even before these voices, there had arisen the voices of countless Yoruba entertainers, playwrights, singers, poets, and bards, employing their art to proclaim daringly sharp denunciations of the deterioration of Nigeria's politics and public morality. A 1962 production by a drama company, the Ogunde Theatre Group, with the title of *Yoruba Ronu*, profoundly shook the Yoruba parts of Nigeria in the 1960s. At the same time, in the intellectual society of the University of Ibadan, the playwright Wole Soyinka (later to become famous as Africa's first Nobel Prize winner for Literature), created a theater group named Orisun Theater and staged with it a series of (according to Soyinka himself) "pugnacious" political satires on the deterioration of public morality in Nigeria.[10] However, the poets and bards (called *akewi*) attracted perhaps the most attention with their recorded audio productions, rendered typically in torrential Yoruba poetry. As far as is known, a youth named Olanrewaju Adepoju started the *akewi* movement in the political life of Nigeria in the 1970s. After him, there followed many, of whom one of the most daring by the beginning of the twenty-first century was one *akewi* named Kunle Ologundudu who, as a result of official persecution, had to flee into exile abroad, from where he vigorously continued his risky art. Springing, as they have done, from deep roots in Yoruba artistic and political traditions, the *akewi* voices have represented the agonized folk voices of the Yoruba people, and their popularity with the Yoruba masses has guaranteed their survival and prosperity, even through difficult times of official reaction and persecution.

In effect, then, many members of the Yoruba intelligentsia in Nigeria, as well as representatives of other strata of Yoruba society, were beginning, as the twentieth century ended and the twenty-first began, to distance the Yoruba as a people from the prevalent political and moral condition of Nigeria. As is clear in Adebanwi's paper and the spoken poetry of the *akewi*, these voices did not deny that some among the Yoruba political leadership have shared part of the responsibility for the making of Nigeria's moral and political situation (in fact, some of the *akewis'* most vitriolic condemnations were reserved for some among the Yoruba political leadership). However, their claim has been that the essential character of Yoruba political, societal, economic and moral norms and standards of life, to which the generality of the Yoruba have remained attached, is radically different from the ones that have developed, and that prevail, in Nigeria. Secondly, the intellectuals affirm that some significant parts of the mainstream Yoruba political leadership have always striven to establish these principles of the Yoruba Vision in the management of the Yoruba part of Nigeria, and attempted determinedly to get them accepted into the management of Nigeria's affairs. In effect, members of the Yoruba intelligentsia are proposing the Yoruba Vision as a political and developmental agenda of the modern Yoruba people – an agenda distilled from their history, traditions and culture. Whether the principles being thus enunciated will acquire influence in the context of Nigeria, and what shape the Yoruba response to the Nigerian situation will ultimately take, all remain to be seen as this account of Yoruba history comes to an end at the end of the turn of the twenty-first century.

33. A street in Lagos. *Photo: R. Mauny, 1949, IFAN.*

34. A square in Lagos. *Photo: R. Mauny, 1949, IFAN.*

18

The Social Transformations in the Twentieth Century

In this chapter, we will survey the social and economic developments and accomplishments of the Yoruba people in Nigeria in the twentieth century.[1] In the course of the century, the two imported religions, Christianity and Islam, grew widely among the Yoruba, and so did Western education, all of which brought significant formative influences into their lives. British imperialism, the growing impact of the world economy, the introduction of new tools, new methods of production, and new occupations, and the rise of a new class of literate Yoruba professionals, political leaders, artisans, artists, and religious leaders – all interconnected to contribute to the emergence of a transformed Yoruba society. In the general African struggle for socio-economic development and modernization in the century, Yoruba society in Western Nigeria established itself as a pacesetter – even, as would be remembered, in spite of the limitations imposed by the structural and political problems of a Nigeria of many nationalities.

It is important to note that most of what follows here on educational and economic development refers to the Yoruba of the Western Region of Nigeria. The Yoruba of the Northern Region came to lag considerably behind those in the Western Region in education and most other fields of socio-economic development, because of the Northern Region's slower pace of development and modernization. Even so, they supplied a substantial share of the most educated persons in the public service of that Region. Also, for most of the era of European rule in Africa, the French protectorate of Dahomey (now Benin Republic) was a key source of civil servants in the French administrative structure in West Africa, and the Yoruba of that country were always a major part of these.

Growth and Impact of Western Education

The first decades of the century saw the Christian mission primary schools spread into all corners of Yorubaland. By the 1920s, the missions were advancing their educational programs to the level of secondary schools and teacher-training institutions. By the 1950s, at which time the British admitted Yoruba politicians into limited participation in the government of their people, purely government schools were few and far between, most schools being Christian mission schools. As a result, most Yoruba recipients of Western education in the century were products of Christian mission schools. No other single factor impacted twentieth century Yoruba society as much as this.

In the development of education, indigenous Yoruba participation was important from the beginning. Even before the Lagos kingdom became a British colony in 1861, the people of Lagos had started to show interest in Western education. After 1861, that interest grew tremendously, as the influence of the Christian missions and the emigrants grew. The main initial incentive was that Western education provided sure access to high-level jobs in the services of the colonial government and the merchant firms. The same attitudes were later evinced in the rest of Yorubaland, barring a brief initial resistance by kings and other prominent people in virtually every community. It was the indigenous converts that the churches mobilized to build the mission schools which mushroomed all over Yorubaland. Everywhere, from about the 1930s, important societal organs employed their influence to persuade parents to send their children to school. From the late 1920s, as earlier pointed out, the few literate persons in every community began to form themselves into Development Associations or Progressive Unions, their favorite agenda being the encouragement of parents to send children to school. When the constitutional changes of 1949–51 brought these literate Yoruba into the government of their Western Region in the 1950s, they immediately made educational development the highest priority. Among other things, the Regional Government encouraged and assisted each sizeable community to build a secondary school of its own, and each administrative division to establish a teacher-training institution. Then it embarked upon the ambitious program of Free Primary Education, thus making the Yoruba people the first African people to institute a program of free education.

As children began to graduate from the elementary schools, secondary schools sprang up to receive them. Almost all such were community schools or schools founded by Christian churches or Muslim communities. Since the beginning of the century, Yoruba Muslim communities had increasingly contributed to the growing movement of Western education, both at the elementary and secondary school levels. As T. Gbadamosi has shown in his study of the growth of Islam in Yorubaland,[2] Yoruba Muslims, like Muslims all over the world, had reservations about Western education. In fact, as Christian mission schools had started and grown in Lagos in the late nineteenth century, Lagos Muslims had kept their children away from such schools – until during the 1890s when the British colonial government of Lagos had taken steps expressly encouraging Muslim participation in the growing educational movement. Thereafter, although the Muslims continued to have reservations about Western education, they increasingly sent their children to the schools that were available, while building some schools of their own. By the late 1950s, the contribution of Yoruba Muslim communities and organizations to the establishment of schools had become very considerable, and some large secondary schools in the Western Region and Lagos were products of their efforts. In addition, a whole class of entrepreneurs emerged who invested in the establishment of private secondary schools.

The massive increases in secondary school enrollment necessitated, in turn, more and more institutions of higher learning. In 1948, the British government of Nigeria had established Nigeria's first university, the University College, Ibadan, in the heart of Yorubaland. In 1962, two years after Nigeria's independence, the government of the Western Region established a regional university, the University of Ife, Ile-Ife (later, Obafemi Awolowo University). With the constitutional internal restructuring of the Nigerian Federation into smaller component states after independence, newly created Yoruba states founded universities of their own – Ogun State University, Lagos State University, Oyo State University, Ladoke Akintola University in Osun State, University of Ado-Ekiti in Ekiti State, Adekunle Ajasin University in Ondo State, and a number of private universities and polytechnics, all in the 1980s, the 1990s and the first years of the twenty-first century. In 1979–83, too, the Yoruba states expanded free education to the secondary school level.

Economic Growth

Economically, the Yoruba part of Nigeria experienced tremendous transformation during the twentieth century. One of the immediate effects of the cessation of wars in the 1890s was the freeing of the country for a great deal of travel and trade, stimulating general economic growth and progress.

Responding to the expansion in the volume and types of export goods, Yoruba farmers began to invest heavily in kolanut and cocoa plantations early in the twentieth century. They also multiplied the production of palm oil and palm kernels. In commerce, there quickly emerged an energetic class of retailers to distribute the imported merchandise. The greatly improved transportation resulting from the coming of railways and the motor highways sped the commercial development on. The first part of the Nigerian railway system, the line from Lagos to the Niger and from there to Kano in Northern Nigeria, was built in 1895 to 1912. At the same time, road transportation expanded steadily, also from Lagos. On the whole, the highway and motor vehicles helped the growth of the new internal trade in Yorubaland more than the railway. The impact of the railway was most pronounced along its corridor from Lagos to the North. In contrast, the motor road steadily fanned out, connecting town to town all over Yorubaland. By the 1920s, it had started to open up even the far eastern Yoruba areas like Ekiti and Akoko. The usually strong competition among the European firms tended to ensure good profits for the retailers; it also ensured very good prices for the export produce.

Meanwhile, long-distance trade between Yorubaland and the other parts of Nigeria, especially Northern Nigeria, grew. In this, the railway was particularly influential. The ancient kolanut route connecting Gonja in northern Ghana to Bussa on the Niger River was gradually abandoned as kolanuts from Ghana were shipped increasingly by sea to Lagos and then taken by rail to Northern Nigeria. This stimulated the establishment of kolanut plantations in the southern Yoruba forests, so that Yoruba kolanuts ultimately replaced the Ghanaian kolanuts. The corollary to this was the expansion of the old Hausa trade in cattle with Yorubaland. These commercial developments set in motion increasingly large migrations of people between Hausaland and Yorubaland.

The general economic advancements of the colonial era were somewhat disrupted by three events emanating from Europe in the first half of the twentieth century: the First World War, the Great Depression, and the Second World War. Recruitment for armed service in the two wars, especially the Second World War, took large numbers of able-bodied men away from economic activities at home. The First World War led to the elimination of the German firms. Since these had had the most liberal credit policies of all the European firms, their elimination adversely affected the retailers and prices. Also, the First World War drastically reduced the flow of investment capital from Europe; it never fully recovered after 1918. The Great Depression and the Second World War again dealt serious blows at the flow of investment capital and also at British government-sponsored capital development. The Second World War also caused a serious shortage of goods. For some time, for instance, the whole of Yorubaland suffered terribly from the shortage of such a basic commodity as salt. The last years of the war also witnessed a major famine caused by drought and consequent shortfalls in food crop harvests.

All these were, however, only interruptions in a generally upward moving economic picture. Technological improvements, such as in transportation and communication, were irreversibly improving the economic development capacity of Yorubaland. The end of the Second World War, the relaxation of wartime constraints and controls, a certain new increase in government-sponsored capital investment, the recovery of trade, and the innate virility of the Yoruba people themselves, all combined to produce a postwar economic boom in Yorubaland. In spite of the continuing deductions by the Marketing Boards, the income from produce soared, bringing an upsurge of wealth to the cash-crop farmers and produce buyers, and making a lot of money available for buying goods from retailers. The building of more and more roads, and the government-sponsored supply of insecticides and fungicides, especially to cocoa farmers, helped the boom. More and more forest land was opened up for new cocoa farms. Industrialization began, especially around the port city of Lagos and the inland city of Ibadan. In the immediate hinterland of Lagos Island, at a place called Ikeja, a new industrial city began to grow.

Perhaps the two most visible effects of the economic progress of the colonial era were the growth of education and the improvement of housing. The long strides taken in education have been described above. Suffice it to say here, therefore, that much of the wealth made by Yoruba families was expended on the education of their children and in the building of educational institutions.

By 1910 the traditional thatched roofs had mostly disappeared in Lagos and largely in Abeokuta, while Ibadan was still a city of thatched roofs. Soon thereafter, Ibadan and other cities began to get the new metal roofs. By the late 1920s, the development was already reaching Ekiti and Akoko in the far east. The coming of metal roofs represented a major improvement in the quality of housing then. It also induced most who had the money for metal roofs to opt out of the old family compounds and build their own individual houses. This led to the beginning of the breaking up of the old sprawling family compounds into smaller houses; it also started the extension of Yoruba towns beyond their old town walls.

From the moment that Yoruba political leaders were admitted into the government of the Western Region in 1952, an era of very rapid economic and social development began. In education, as well as in many other areas of development, the Western Region became a pacesetter for the Nigerian Federation. Indeed, there was considerable euphoria caused among Yoruba people by the popular claim that, in most development endeavors, the Western Region was "first in Africa."

The Yoruba cocoa farmers led the way. Their export produce became the main provider of funds for the development of the Western Region and the biggest foreign exchange earner for Nigeria. As cocoa farming and cocoa trading became the richest sources of personal income, investments poured briskly into expanding cocoa plantations, and cocoa production volumes soared. The Regional Government aided the growth with many support programs – research, the supply of improved cocoa seedlings, subsidized supply of insecticides, establishment of a Cocoa Marketing Board, the promotion of a cocoa cooperative movement, etc. These developments correspondingly stimulated all other areas of the economy.

The Regional Government also invested heavily in encouraging private industries, as well as in government-sponsored industries. Ikeja on the outskirts of Lagos became a place with one of the heaviest concentrations of industry on the African continent. The government sponsored Western Region Development Corporation, a holding corporation with many industrial, commercial, and service companies, had by the 1960s one of the largest accumulations of capital in Africa.

The boom in the Western Region continued until the early 1960s. In the mid 1960s, the regional economy began to weaken – partly as a result of the slump in the world price of cocoa, but more particularly because of the political crisis in the Western Region which disrupted orderly growth for four years, 1962–66. The Nigerian Federal Government made the regional situation much worse by taking over the functions of the regional Cocoa Board. The result of this federal action was a sharp decline in the quality of government attention to the cocoa industry. In the late 1960s, petroleum from the Niger Delta area emerged as Nigeria's principal foreign exchange earner. As cocoa farming lost virtually all governmental support and much of its profitability, farmers abandoned their cocoa plantations, and by the mid 1980s, Nigeria's cocoa export was a small fraction of what it had been in the late 1950s. A small part of the decline was due to the fact that traders began to smuggle cocoa to the neighboring Republic of Benin, where cocoa exports and smuggling earned better prices.

The 1962–66 crisis, then, more or less effectively pulled the Yoruba down from the high level of socio-economic progress that they had attained in the 1950s. As the twentieth century came to a close, the Yoruba West in Nigeria had not returned to the brisk economic growth of the late 1950s, even though the momentum of the 1950s continued somewhat to sustain it in a leading place in Nigeria. The tradition of orderly, focused and disciplined promotion of development by the Yoruba leadership, characteristic of the Western Region in the decade 1952–62, and disrupted in 1962–66, was never revived. The Yoruba achievements in literacy and higher education continued more or less to uphold general modernization in the Yoruba West in Nigeria. But government-led development of economic and social infrastructures (roads, water installations, etc.), though showing some increases, slackened noticeably. Businesses and entrepreneurship continued to grow, but even in this, the great promise of the 1950s and the first two years of the 1960s largely waned. Perhaps most importantly, the confidence in leadership, in direction and in progress, so strongly evident in the Western Region in 1952–62, largely disappeared. In summary, the great expectations that Yoruba unity and collective dedication to modernization and socio-economic progress would continue to produce great attainments declined considerably in the decades after 1962.

In 1986, the Nigerian Federal Government deregulated the export trade in cocoa – as part of a national movement towards a free market economy. This meant that cocoa producers were freed to sell directly in the world market, unfettered by the government's bureaucratic controls. As a result, cocoa exporters showed renewed interest in the Yoruba West, thus bringing back to Yoruba cocoa farmers a little bit of the income levels of the 1950s. Cocoa farmers resumed care of their abandoned cocoa plantations, and Nigeria's cocoa exports began to rise again as the twentieth century came to an end. This infused new funds into the economy of the Yoruba West, and added a little to the widening of economic transformation – in the growth of indigenous businesses, the rise of a business and entrepreneurial class, the growth of industry and commerce, and the growing strength of financial institutions and of technology.

Changes in Family, Home and Community

For all African peoples, the twentieth century was an era of great cultural transformations. For a people with such a rich cultural heritage as the Yoruba, it is impossible to do more in a book of this nature than give a very brief outline of the massive cultural transformations of the century.

The dissolution of the *agbo-ile* or lineage compound was, without doubt, one of the greatest and most profound transformations of Yoruba society in the twentieth century. The process of the dissolution has not yet, as at this writing, received any focused study. However, it is fairly well known from family traditions, court records, and published accounts in various media, that the process was rocky in many places. Emotional attachment to the ancestral compound usually resulted in the circumstance that persons with financial resources for building new homes often sought to take a piece of the old compound, tear it down and build the new house in its place. Not infrequently, this produced conflicts of claims – and disputes and feuds among lineage members. By about the last quarter of the century, the dissolution was virtually complete for most compounds, and the volume of fratricidal strife petered out. The fact that the dissolution was effected, in most cases, piece by piece over a long time and without any coordination, resulted in considerable deterioration of the physical structure of the old Yoruba cities and towns – houses built in disorder on the sites of once beautiful compounds, large quarters impossible to provide with paved roads, serious problems of hygiene arising from lack of sewage and trash disposal arrangements. By the last decades of the century, persons desiring to build new houses tended mostly to go beyond the old town walls – to land that used to be farmland. As a result, by, say, the year 2000, every sizeable Yoruba town had two segments – the old town within the old town walls, and then the new town beyond them. The latter, being usually a place of land layouts and building plans approved by the Local Governments, was normally much more orderly and attractive than the former.

The effects of the dissolution of the *agbo-ile* on lineages and on society in general were quite complex. A dispersal of most of each *agbo-ile's* lineage followed. However, a core of the lineage members of each *agbo-ile* continued to inhabit its old site in their new types of houses – thus constituting a strong pull on dispersed members. Even in the growing new town beyond the town walls, the members of each lineage tended also to build homes close together – since each lineage gave land to its members on land that had used to be its farmland, although it also usually sold plots to non-members. Moreover, the old lineage functions (funerals of departed members, naming ceremonies for newly born members, engagement ceremonies and weddings, contests over the selection of chiefs, chieftaincy installation rituals and ceremonies, annual and seasonal lineage rituals, sacrifices and festivals), continued – also a strong force pulling members together. And the old obligations for the welfare of members remained indestructible, so that even the farthest dispersed members of a lineage still accepted and bore responsibilities for the welfare of other members. Consequently, although the *agbo-ile* disintegrated, the social and psycho-spiritual bonds uniting its lineage survived quite strongly. At the end of the twentieth century, the lineage factor continued to be a very major factor in Yoruba society. It is important to note, in conclusion, that all that has been said here about the *agbo-ile* and lineage is applicable to Yoruba people, not only in Nigeria, but also in Benin and Togo Republics.

Religious Transformation

In the course of the twentieth century, the two imported religions, Islam and Christianity, exerted very profound influences on Yoruba culture. Their various levels of contribution to the growth of Western education and literacy have been briefly described. But their influences were much more encompassing than that. In fact, they accounted for a very significant part of the changes in Yoruba society in the century.

As incoming and growing influences, both Islam and Christianity ultimately attained high levels of integration into Yoruba society, but their paths to that end differed considerably. As Gbadamosi has shown, Islam, while basically regarding Yoruba religious norms and practices, as well as much of Yoruba social ways, as unacceptable, consistently sought inclusion into Yoruba society as a way to promote the kind of changes that Islamic tenets preach.[3] For instance, Yoruba Muslims generally made a point (from as early as the late nineteenth century) of using, and promoting pride in, the varied styles of Yoruba traditional clothes and costumes for special occasions, thereby contributing greatly to the refinement and beauty that these acquired in the course of the twentieth century. Yoruba traditional investiture of chiefs-elect into chieftaincy positions, and the traditional functions of chiefs, continued to be rooted in traditional religious practices. If a Muslim was made a chief, therefore, the Muslim community could not approve of the religious ramifications of his position; but they developed the tradition of going about this matter cautiously and establishing relationships with the chief that harnessed his political influence for the benefit of Islam in the community. Since Islam does not preach monogamy, Yoruba Muslims had no problem with the polygamy in the Yoruba family system. Moreover, Muslim communities in every town cultivated linkages with the traditional political system – until, in most towns, the point was reached that persons appointed leaders in the Muslim communities were usually turbaned in the Obas' palaces (just as the investiture of traditional chiefs was done in the palaces). Unlike Muslim communities in many parts of the world, Yoruba Muslim communities, in deference to the very significant influence that women had traditionally exercised in Yoruba society, accepted them fully into participation in prayers in mosques, as well as into leadership positions. There were, of course, always some Muslims who rejected these tendencies in Yoruba Islam and preached fervently against them as unacceptable compromises. However, such radicals were always few – and, without doubt, mainstream Yoruba Islam gained much acceptance and strength by pursuing the path of inclusion and by being respectful of Yoruba cultural norms. The expansion and establishment of Islam resulting from all this received, from time to time, big boosts from indigenous, mainstream preachers who traveled over Yorubaland, preaching Islam, gathering in converts, and establishing or strengthening Muslim communities.

Islam became more or less a popular Yoruba religion, and Yoruba Muslims imported into Islamic festivals and activities the Yoruba love of ceremony, glamour, music and dance. For instance, setting off for, or arriving back from, the pilgrimage to Mecca, became a glamorous and festive ceremony, and so did the ordinary act of admission to Islam through a baptism-like rite known as *wonka*. Alhaji (for men) and Alhaja (for women), the titles for persons who had performed the pilgrimage, became proud and fashionable titles in Yorubaland. Not surprisingly, although Islam was not as strong as in Hausaland in the Northern Region, the government of the Western Region under Awolowo's premiership was the first government in Nigerian history to establish a Pilgrims Welfare

Board, whose function was to help and care for Muslims on the pilgrimage to Mecca.

With Christianity, the path was different.[4] The various Christian missions started in the mid-nineteenth century with European missionaries in charge and Yoruba emigrant (and ultimately other Yoruba) clergy serving as their assistants. The optimistic projection at this early stage was that, as each mission station matured, the Yoruba clergy would take over, and the white missionary would move on to start another station. As time went on, however, the white missionaries became unwilling to move on to new stations – unwilling to start again the pioneering work and the raising of support from backers in Europe. More importantly, the European imperialist agents began, in the 1890s, to take over Yorubaland (and all of Africa) – and with that, anthropological theories claiming intellectual and moral inferiority of the black race gained ground among Europeans in general. The European Christian missions largely became influenced by these theories and the attitudes they engendered, and members of the Yoruba clergy began to suffer discrimination in the service of the missionary bodies. In the context of these new ideas and behavior, even the pioneer work done on the Niger Mission by Bishop Ajayi Crowther and many Yoruba clergymen came to be treated as undeserving of honorable reward, and many of those clergymen were disgraced from their ministerial jobs. In Yorubaland, the most important consequence of these developments was the growth of a cleavage between the European and Yoruba clergy, and the rise of an African Church Movement.

The African Church Movement was pioneered by the seceding Yoruba clergy from the various Protestant mission churches. It resulted in the emergence of an African (or Native) Anglican, Baptist and Methodist Church. Its central thrust was the indigenization of Christian evangelism and worship, while keeping faithful to the message of salvation through faith in Jesus Christ. It introduced indigenous Yoruba music (with a lot of drumming) into church services and became prodigious in the writing of hymns and publishing of hymnals. The mission churches had rejected the Yoruba institution of polygamy; the African churches accepted the believing polygamist into full membership of the church. The African churches emphasized evangelism and charged all church members, clergy and lay alike, with the duty of evangelizing in the wider Yoruba society. They also endorsed the Ogboni cult, which had been very influential in the political life of Yoruba communities and, as will be seen below, even created a Christian version of Ogboni. In the course of the early twentieth century, the Christian Ogboni Fraternity or Society, (sometimes also called Reformed Ogboni) became a broad association of the Yoruba political, social and religious elite, promoting unity in their ranks and in Yorubaland in general. Thus, on the whole, the African Church Movement may be regarded as one of the first major expressions of African nationalism in Nigeria.

By the second decade of the twentieth century, then, there were three broad streams in Yoruba Christianity – the Protestant mission churches, the Roman Catholic churches, and the African churches. For all three, schools remained a major tool for winning people to Christianity. To the schools, another type of institution was added in the course of the first half of the century – church hospitals and maternity centers. In addition, as the efficacy of the methods (especially the use of Yoruba music and drums) employed by the African churches became self-evident, the mission churches, and to a lesser extent the Roman Catholic churches, gradually adopted them too. In the Protestant mission churches and the Roman Catholic churches, Yoruba clergy gradually took over. Yoruba popular culture (like dressing styles and colorful ceremonies) came gradually to be firmly established in the lives of all church congregations.

From the 1920s, a powerful new movement spread in Yoruba Christianity – namely, the Aladura Movement.[5] Aladura means "the ones who pray" or "the praying people" – and the churches of the Aladura Movement were characterized by very strong belief in the power of prayer. In Yoruba traditional religion, supplications, sacrifices and rituals to gods and spirits were believed to attract intervention by those gods and spirits into the daily lives and affairs of the supplicants – for the healing of sickness, for the removal of life's difficulties, for the increase of success, for deliverance from oppression by hostile spirits, etc. Of the two imported religions, Islam featured a tradition of praying for divine assistance in life's travails, and of special supplications, but Christianity as spread by the European missions did not – that is, the mission churches focused only on eternal salvation but could not offer their members spiritual healing from sickness, deliverance and protection from evil spirits, divine guidance, and success. In order to fill this gap in Christianity, some Yoruba clergy of the mission and African churches moved out and started the Aladura Movement in 1918.

The Aladura churches represented a conscious step towards integrating Yoruba culture and the Christian faith, and they rapidly became very popular. As the Aladura churches offered many earthly benefits to their members through powerful prayers, fasting, observances, and rituals that seemed, in some ways, not too dissimilar from traditional Yoruba rituals, large numbers flocked into their congregations. Not surprisingly, foreigners and leaders of the mission churches strongly criticized the new movement as not being true Christianity but a new Yoruba religion, or an imperfect hybrid religion, but criticisms did not do anything to slow down its growth.

Ultimately, four major branches of the Aladura Movement developed – the Apostolic Church, the Cherubim and Seraphim Church, the Church of the

Lord, and the Celestial Church of Christ, all founded and led by Yoruba clergymen. Each of these developed its own unique spiritual emphasis, but in general they worked through prayers, the scriptures, fasting, blessed water, blessed oil, candles, various rituals, visions and dreams, and prophesying. Unlike members of the mission, Roman Catholic and African churches, members of most of the branches of the Aladura churches early started to wear special clothing for church and church activities – usually a white robe, with trimmings or sashes of other colors for ministers and other church officials. All the Aladura churches laid a strong emphasis on evangelism and demanded it of every member, and some developed the practice of proclaiming the Christian message, with bell and bible in hand, through the streets. All rejected Yoruba traditional religion, as well as the use of medicine, modern or traditional. Unlike the Protestant mission churches, the Roman Catholic churches and the African churches, the Aladura churches contributed only minimally to the establishment of schools and hospitals. Every branch of the Aladura Movement emphasized in its services and practices the use of Yoruba music, drums and songs, and festive dancing. Congregations of Aladura churches sprang up in every Yoruba town and village. The Aladura Movement was a product of Yoruba creativity – a unique Yoruba contribution to the history of Christianity. Soon, the Yoruba were exporting the movement to the rest of West Africa, and even to Yoruba and other African people resident in various places in Europe and America.

In the course of the first half of the century, yet another movement entered into the world of Christianity in Yorubaland – namely, the Pentecostal Movement (also known as the Charismatic Movement).[6] The Pentecostal Movement started in the United States early in the century. Its central doctrine was the belief in the ready availability of the power of God (or the Holy Spirit) to the Christian, for miraculous outcomes – such as miraculous healing, deliverance from demonic possession or oppression, miraculous protection from danger, miraculous supply of needs. This movement was, thus, close to the Aladura Movement in its basic belief. Like the Aladura Movement also, it believed in the power of prayer and fasting, but unlike the Aladura Movement, it rejected all forms of rituals and sacrifices and formularies, as well as such tools as holy water and special robes. In contrast, it emphasized knowledge of, and intense familiarity with, scriptures as (together with prayers and fasting and faith) the means of accessing and imploring the power of the Holy Spirit for intervention in earthly events and circumstances. It also preached a higher spiritual experience known as "Holy Ghost Baptism," the outward manifestation of which could include the ability to speak in strange tongues. The Aladura Movement appealed mostly to the illiterate and less educated among the Yoruba; the Pentecostal Movement, on the other hand, appealed mostly to the more educated

— to high school and university students and graduates and their like. It employed a lot of music and song and dancing (just like the Aladura Movement), but its type of music was close to American gospel choruses and American popular music, and its lyrics were mostly in English, usually accompanied with guitar, band set, and amplifiers. The Pentecostal movement produced a very great number of songs and choruses in English and Yoruba, and it also borrowed richly from Pentecostal songs and choruses composed in the languages of other southern Nigerian peoples, among whom Pentecostalism was also very strong. Its clergy, dressed simply in Western business suits, were the most fiery gospel preachers in twentieth century Yoruba Christianity.

From about the late 1960s, the Pentecostal Movement swept the schools and colleges and universities, as well as the ranks of educated people, throughout Yorubaland. The earliest groups in this movement were from America (notably the Assemblies of God, and Four Square Gospel Church), but by the 1970s, more American groups had come, and indigenous groups, founded and led by highly educated Yoruba persons (some of them university professors who gave up their academic careers for the Christian ministry) were springing up. By the 1990s, some of these home-grown groups (like the Redeemed Christian Church of God founded by Josiah Akindayomi, Deeper Life Bible Fellowship founded by William Folorunso Kumuyi, Winners Chapel by David Oyedepo, etc.) counted their members in the millions and boasted some of the largest Christian congregations and church buildings in the world.

Some of the Yoruba Pentecostal churches and members developed global visions too — a commitment to a reverse missions program aimed at taking the gospel message to Europe and America in order to revive Christianity there. By the last years of the century, their usually large congregations (made up of persons of all races, and founded and led by Yoruba clergy) were to be found all over Western and Eastern Europe, North America, and many countries of Africa and Asia. In the first years of the twenty-first century, perhaps one of the most famous of these Yoruba missionaries abroad is Pastor Sunday Adelaja, whose Christian mission is based in the city of Kiev in the Ukraine. Nurtured in the Pentecostal tradition in Nigeria, Adelaja arrived in 1986 as a young college student in Belarus, then part of communist Soviet Union, and started a small underground Pentecostal church — an action that was to cause him repeated troubles with the police. In the early 1990s, Adelaja moved to Ukraine a few years after it broke away from the Soviet Union and founded his church, which quickly attracted many influential Ukrainians. By the year 2007, the congregation of the Embassy of the Blessed Kingdom of God, more commonly known as God's Embassy, in Kiev numbered more than 25,000 members (virtually all of them Ukrainians). By that date also, his church had spread to most countries of

Europe and become, according to one writer on the subject, "Europe's largest church" – with an estimated two million members in more than six hundred congregations, located in more than twenty countries, most of them in Europe, and some as far afield as India and the United States of America.[7]

As a result of these developments in Islam and Christianity among the Yoruba, most Yoruba were professed Muslims or Christians by the end (or even as early as the middle) of the twentieth century, and only a small and dwindling minority continued to adhere explicitly to the traditional religion and ways of worship. Consequently, resources and talent moved away from the old shrines, and many shrines became poor or even dilapidated – or even perished. However, all this did not mean that the influence of the traditional beliefs and spiritual practices disappeared. On the contrary, the influence of the traditional religion and some of its institutions remained quite strong. Yoruba monarchical and chieftaincy systems remained more or less firmly based on their ancient religious and spiritual roots. The influence of the *babalawo* and *adahunse* remained, and so did their traditional services (in divination and the provision of spiritual protection, success and power through charms, sacrifices and formularies). And in every Yoruba community, certain seasonal and annual rituals and festivals, for many centuries pillars of the political and social system, continued – and continued to rally the citizens, including even the Islamized or Christianized; and the lineages that had traditionally held the priesthoods for them continued to do so, in spite of losses of their members to the new religions. One incident in Ado-Ekiti in the 1940s illustrates these trends very poignantly. Once every new yam season from an unknown antiquity, the Oitado festival of the deity known as Elefon had rallied the citizens of Ado-Ekiti in large festive gatherings at the Ewi's palace and in the streets, as well as in the cooking and sharing of the most cherished foods. Sometime in the 1940s, the young man who was the then high priest for the festival became converted to Christianity by the Roman Catholics, and his new Christian friends then spirited him out of Ado-Ekiti and into hiding. For two years, although the lower priests of Oitado kept the festival going, the absence of the high priest was like a torment to the whole town (even though most Ado-Ekiti people were by then professed Muslims or Christians). When the festival approached in the third year, the young high priest told his hosts at his place of hiding that he just had to return home and to his priesthood, because he knew that he was hurting his community far too much. And his return made the Oitado festival of that year one of the largest and loudest in the modern history of Ado-Ekiti.

In short, some festivals, some observances, were too integral to the essence of community in every Yoruba town or village to be given up yet in the twentieth century – no matter how Islamized or Christianized the Yoruba people had become. And some lineages, traditionally priests and leaders in community festivals and observances, continued doggedly to serve their communities in their ancient roles. In most Yoruba communities, there developed the tendency to relate to and handle traditional community festivals in ways that downplayed their religious and spiritual connotations while emphasizing and promoting their purely social and community-rallying importance – and this tended to guarantee the survival and continuance of many a traditional community festival in all parts of Yorubaland.

Side by side with the above picture, however, the influence of both Islam and Christianity continues to deepen significantly among the Yoruba at the turn of the century. Generally better educated than the generation of their parents, the younger generation of Yoruba people tend to adhere more to the fundamentals of their Islamic or Christian faith, thereby distancing themselves from the spiritual ramifications of their indigenous culture. Many (especially the Pentecostal Christians, also known as born-again Christians) now commonly drop or modify family names that are perceived by them to honor traditional Yoruba deities – or "idols". While planning for the funerals of departed parents or grandparents, families tend to be split on account of religious differences – with the younger and more ardent Muslims or Christians refusing to approve of traditional funeral practices that they regard as "pagan". More and more Yoruba kings who are of Islamic or Christian faith are daring to move away from the traditional spiritual roots of Yoruba monarchy and boldly inculcating their own religion into the spiritual life of their palaces. Spiritually, as in many other respects, the Yoruba society of the beginning of the twenty-first century is a very dynamic society.

Changes in Occupations

Increasingly throughout the twentieth century, the growing changes in the economy and in the way of life produced great changes in occupations. Peasant farming with the traditional tools (mostly hoes and machetes or cutlasses) continued even till the end of the twentieth century to be the way of life of most Yoruba people employed in the traditional economy. However, education had drawn most of the younger generation away from the land – resulting in much loss of talent to farming (and increasing dependence on food from other parts of Nigeria or imported from abroad). From early in the century, plantation farming (in cocoa and kolanuts and, to a lesser extent, in palm trees and rubber) gradually increased, mostly in the forest areas of Yorubaland. The establishment of the plantations was accomplished mostly with the traditional hoes and machetes, but plantation owners gradually became familiar with the use of new tools like pesticides and some crop dryers and crop processing machinery. The old occupation of palm oil and palm kernel production continued to enjoy a boost, to produce for home consumption and for export – and it slowly incorporated new processing equipment (such as mechanical oil presses and kernel crackers). The old cloth industry (yarn spinning on spindles, dyeing, weaving, and sewing) went through many changes. With the introduction of factory-produced cotton yarn, silk yarn and synthetic yarn, traditional spinning on spindles gradually declined. Cloth weaving and dyeing became very creative, resulting in large varieties of colorful fabrics called *aso-ofi* (cloth woven on traditional looms), and the introduction of new (factory-produced) colors into traditional fabrics. Production of the type of Yoruba cloth called tie-and-dye (*adire*) became a popular occupation – and, indeed, spread to many parts of the world.

Much of the family treasuries of old beads survived and continued to be preferred over newly imported beads, for important uses such as status accessories for kings and chiefs, ceremonial adornment at funerals, traditional rituals, weddings, etc. New beads came only from imports, and never matched old beads in prestige. As far as is known, the old occupation of bead production disappeared. Gold came increasingly to supplement beads as jewelry, and a new class of goldsmiths emerged. As far as is known, the old occupation of brass jewelry making (producing brass neck bands, bangles, wristlets and anklets) died out. And so, gradually, did the use of the heavy brass jewelry. A whole large class of modern garment designers and tailors (male and female) emerged, employing imported sewing machines, and creatively using *aso-ofi*, as well as many varieties of imported fabrics (lace, damask, silk, synthetics, etc), to produce Yoruba clothes – *agbada, dasiki, gbariye, sokoto* and others for men, and *iro, buba, gele, iborun* for women. The occupation of the *babalawo* (the diviner) continued to enjoy great influence, and so did that of the *onisegun* (the herbalist), in spite of the growing popularity of European medicine and hospitals. In fact, in the course of the century, many pharmacopeias and other books on Yoruba traditional medicine were published, and some effort was made to standardize the preparation of Yoruba herbal medications and to streamline their prescription and administration. Research was also undertaken in some universities into particular Yoruba herbs. Blacksmiths continued to produce iron goods for the market, but their importance in the economy was gradually wiped out by factory-produced and imported iron goods. Side by side with these and other traditional occupations, education and the growth of the new economy were spawning a large array of practitioners of new local occupations – furniture makers using the new mechanical tools, sawyers, letter-writers, printers and book-binders, bicycle and motor mechanics, barbers and hairdressers, various artisans connected with the housebuilding trade: masons, brick makers and bricklayers, concrete mixers, carpenters, plumbers, electricians, house painters, etc. In commerce, the marketplaces in Yoruba towns continued to be the almost exclusive province of women traders, while men engaged in the retail trade tended to set up shop in the front rooms of dwelling houses along town streets, to sell mostly imported goods. Bringing their traditional commercial expertise and enterprise into the new economy, Yoruba women commanded substantial shares of the new import and export commerce. Yoruba women importers of foreign fabrics usually went to far-away countries (various parts of Europe, as well as countries such as Hong Kong, Taiwan and South Korea in Asia) in order to guide manufacturers to produce the designs acceptable in the Yoruba market in Nigeria. The evolving modern government and economy gave rise to professional civil servants, teachers, pastors, lawyers, judges, industrialists and industrial workers, owners of, and workers in, large mercantile businesses, transportation companies, civil engineering companies engaged in large public and private construction projects, import and export companies. In short, in response to the demands of the evolving new society, the occupational activities of Yoruba people saw a great deal of transformation – resulting in the emergence of countless new occupations, the disappearance of some old occupations, the modification and strengthening of some old occupations, and steady improvements in people's productive and earning capacity.

Cultural Nationalism and Cultural Growth

From the last years of the nineteenth century, Yorubaland experienced a strong and growing movement of cultural nationalism, championed mostly by the growing literate elite.[8] In tropical Africa in general, European conquest and rule (beginning in the last years of the nineteenth century) reinforced, and fed on, the race theories increasingly prevalent among Europeans, theories asserting an intellectual, moral and cultural inferiority of the black race. In Yorubaland, therefore, British conquest and rule (proudly called "Pax Britannica") came to assume for itself the mission of "civilizing" the Yoruba. The Christian missions, as earlier pointed out, increasingly endorsed those theories, and, therefore, Christian evangelism and Western education came to mean, for them, a two-pronged mission for winning the Yoruba from the supposed "barbarism" of their culture. In this context, the Christianized and the Western educated Yoruba were projected as the advance guard of a new Yoruba people, as much as possible European in culture, manners and dress. In the mission schools, students were taught that a renunciation of the culture of their society – customs, indigenous names, clothing, and language – was essential to attaining their new status of civilized people. A contemporary described sarcastically in these words what the missionaries were trying to achieve: "That which distinguishes a heathen from a Christian is not moral character or allegiance to Christ, but outward dress. The stove-pipe hat, the feathered bonnet, the high-heeled shoes, the gloved hands, and all these under the burning tropical heat, make a man a Christian gentleman."[9]

To begin with, the Western educated, the emigrants, and many of the Christian converts did make efforts to become like Europeans – in the hope that that would earn them acceptance into the European community as equal members. In dress, in language, in personal names, and in various other details of life, many of the Western educated generally tried hard to meet the expectations of their European teachers and mentors. In Lagos in particular, the emigrants came to command such social influence, wealth and power as to constitute a distinct and prestigious elite which built and promoted schools and academies (mostly under church sponsorship), and proudly promoted a European way of life. A strong culture of European music and opera even made its appearance in Lagos. In extreme cases, some members of the Lagos emigrant elite, born and raised in Lagos and sent abroad for higher education, were known, on returning home as graduates of British schools or universities, to claim ignorance of the Yoruba language.

Inevitably, many voices came to be raised against these trends. Of these the most prominent were the Anglican bishop, James Johnson, the West Indian intellectual, Edward Wilmot Blyden, and D. B. Vincent, a pastor of the Native Baptist Church. Both Johnson and Blyden spent all their lives championing the cause of African culture – Blyden through his writings, and James Johnson in his activities in the church. Neither, however, went as far as D. B. Vincent in actually adopting an indigenous Yoruba way of life. In 1894, D. B. Vincent changed his name to Mojola Agbebi. Thereafter, he toured Britain and America giving lectures on African culture, and he made a life-long decision to wear Yoruba clothes. Not even the winter cold in Britain or America was strong enough to make him put off his Yoruba *agbada*.

Ultimately, a very powerful movement of cultural nationalism emerged among the emigrants, the Western educated, and the Christian converts. Those who had avidly adopted European ways had gradually become disappointed about the outcome. Not only were they not being accepted by Europeans as equals, they were, in fact, increasingly ridiculed by Europeans as caricatures of Europeans and as inferior to the authentic native African. Those who were merchants found their businesses seriously threatened, or even destroyed, by the monopolistic practices of the European merchant companies, assisted by the policies of the colonial government. Those who worked in the civil service of the British administration of Lagos were discriminated against in every aspect of the service and treated as inferior. For all these people, therefore, there was no other option than to return to their own native civilization.

As E. A. Ayandele has shown, the consequent Yoruba attacks on European cultural imperialism came from various sources at the same time. Western educated Lagosians began to attack the Christian missions as promoters of cultural imperialism, and these attacks grew increasingly trenchant in the Lagos newspapers as the twentieth century opened. Some of the Lagosians employed in the Civil Service of the British administration of Lagos, rather than continue to endure the racial discrimination in the service, resigned and became self-employed citizens, and even founded churches of their own, churches completely free of European missionary influence. Meanwhile, the rapid increases in the number of Christian converts at the turn of the century in many parts of Yorubaland made control by the European missionaries gradually impossible even in the mission churches. More and more, Yoruba clergy assumed control, and by as early as 1900, Anglican, Wesleyan and Baptist mission churches in places like Abeokuta, Ijebu-Ode and Ibadan had a Yoruba majority on their clergy and on their church councils.[10]

The grand outcome of all this was a mighty upswell of Yoruba cultural nationalism, among the emigrants, Western educated, and Christian converts – and ultimately in the general population. Regretting the readiness with which they had earlier accepted European foreign customs, the emigrants and Western educated turned around and began to proclaim and promote intense pride in their native culture, customs, and institutions. European cultural imperialism, they said, "threatens to extinguish us as a race," and one Lagos newspaper wrote, "We are Negroes first and Christians afterwards."[11] By 1914, the new movement was so vehement in the Lagos press that both the European missionaries and the British administration were alarmed.

The movement manifested in many areas of the life of its champions and the rest of Yoruba society. Perhaps its most important institutional product was the revival of the ancient institution of Ogboni. The British and the missionaries had been very hostile to Ogboni, regarding it as an influential threat to both Christianity and British pacification of Yorubaland. The British had destroyed its council chamber in Ijebu-Ode in 1892, and also later suppressed its influence in the government of Abeokuta. Ogboni as an institution looked as if it was on the way to disappearing. In response, the champions of cultural nationalism acted to save Ogboni and convert it to a Christian society for the benefit of the Yoruba people. Under the leadership of Reverend T. A. J. Ogunbiyi, a senior pastor in the African Church Movement, a Christian Ogboni Society was founded. The new Ogboni Society was the ancient Ogboni itself in most details – but remodeled as a Christian institution, structured as a prestigious association of the modern Yoruba elite for the preservation of Yoruba civilization and integrity (within the culture of Christianity), and claiming its power from the God of the Christian faith. It enshrined a copy of the bible in each of its council houses, consecrated the ancient paraphernalia of the Ogboni as instruments of God's power, limited its membership only to Christians, and substituted Christian oaths for the ancient Yoruba oaths. Altogether, the creation of the Christian Ogboni Society was an important step in integrating Christianity into Yoruba political culture at its highest level, and in making Christianity powerfully relevant to the political life of the Yoruba nation. It was also a major contribution to the movement of Yoruba national unity. The Christian Ogboni Society (more commonly known as the Reformed Ogboni Society) was later to occupy a central place in Egbe Omo Oduduwa (Association of Descendants of Oduduwa).

Cultural nationalism also produced effects at more ordinary levels of the culture. Many who bore English last names renounced them and took Yoruba names. A great pride in Yoruba clothing and fashions developed. Traditional rulers had never wavered from upholding pride in indigenous Yoruba clothing and ceremonial dress, and the generality of the Yoruba people had never been touched by the desire to look like Europeans. Moreover, as earlier pointed out, Yoruba Muslims, among the general population, had generally given deliberate emphasis to traditional clothes. The emigrants, Western educated and Christians now joined in the crusade to use, and popularize pride in, indigenous Yoruba clothes. Yoruba politicians soon followed. By the time of the first Yoruba government of the Western Region in the 1950s, pride in indigenous dress had completely won the day. Yoruba clothing entered upon a colorful revolution in refinement and beautification – featuring creative uses of indigenous and foreign fabrics, a reinvention of the old art of embroidery, experimentation with new styles of couture, and adaptation of old, new, and exotic accessories. Yoruba women (historically the leaders in fashion) led in this wave of experimentation and style. By the end of the century, Yoruba clothing and styles of dressing were being widely adopted in most parts of Nigeria, some parts of West Africa, and even in African-American societies in the Americas.

Yoruba cultural nationalism also generated an outpouring of writing on the Yoruba people, especially on their origin and history. As would be remembered, the earliest literate Yoruba had started to write about Yoruba history and institutions as early as the middle of the nineteenth century. In the atmosphere created by Yoruba cultural nationalism from the 1890s, there arose a great desire among literate Yoruba to find out about the history and institutions of their nation and to put their findings into writing. As written knowledge from Yoruba oral traditions accumulated, Lagosians asked the British administration of the colony to add Yoruba history to the school curriculum. J. A. Otunba Payne continued to be a leading writer on Yoruba history, publishing in 1894 his *Table of Principal Events in Yoruba History*. In Ode-Ondo, Bishop Charles Phillips recorded in writing some of the traditions of the Ondo kingdom. Other significant publications of the time included *Historical Notes on the Yoruba Country and its Tribes* by J. O. George, and a series of articles published in the newspaper, the *Weekly Record*, in June and July 1901 under the title "A Short History of the Ijeshas and other Hinterland Tribes" by H. Atundaolu. Meanwhile, the most comprehensive of the books on Yoruba history of the time was being compiled by the Reverend Samuel Johnson from oral traditions collected by him in various places in Yorubaland. Titled *The History of the Yorubas*, this book was completed in 1897, but was not published until 1921.

Following the publication of Johnson's book, the twentieth century developed into a great century of Yoruba historical studies. In practically all parts of Yorubaland during the first half of the century, literate people wrote the histories of their kingdoms or communities, using the information from the oral traditions. Toyin Falola has, in a recent book,[12] highlighted the historical work of a few of these tens of local historians – M. C. Adeyemi, the historian of Oyo, Oba Isaac Babalola Akinyele and Kemi Morgan, historians of Ibadan, Chief Samuel Ojo Bada, the historian of Ilorin, Chief Theophilus Olabode Avoseh, the historian of Badagry and Epe, and others (like P. O. Dada, J. O. A. Ogundeji and others), who wrote on the history of parts of Igbomina. Of the many others who are not examined im Falola's book, among the best known are Rev. Father Anthony Oguntuyi, the historian of Ado-Ekiti, Chief M. B. Ashara, the historian of Owo, J. D. Abiola, the historian of Ilesa, and Chief Isola Fabunmi, the historian of Ife. Many of these local historians wrote in English, but many others wrote in the Yoruba language.

From the 1950s, the study of Yoruba history advanced to another level, with many studies and books by academic historians (most of whom were Yoruba), from various universities. The publication of two books in the 1950s and 1960s (one by Saburi Biobaku on Egba history, the other by J. F. Ade Ajayi on the coming of the Christian missions), inaugurated the new era of academic historians. In addition to historians, academics in other disciplines soon joined in Yoruba studies – archaeologists, art historians, scholars of linguistics, etc., again very many of them Yoruba. The result was a large and growing number of important studies and books on Yoruba history and other areas of Yoruba studies as the twentieth century came to an end and the twenty-first commenced.

The twentieth century era of Yoruba literacy and cultural ferment also nurtured a rich outflow of literary work in fiction, myths, legends, folktales, poetry, music and theater. Most of such writing derived its materials from the Yoruba culture's enormous wealth of folklore. Again, many of these Yoruba literary men and women of the century wrote in English while many others wrote in Yoruba. Of the writings of this nature in Yoruba, the preeminent work was that of D. O. Fagunwa, who wrote a series of great legends that became acknowledged as classics of the Yoruba language and literature. His most famous work, *Ogboju Ode Ninu Igbo Irunmole*, was translated into English and became a very significant educational tool. Yoruba literature in English attained its highest peak in the work of Wole Soyinka, who acquired much renown worldwide for his plays, novels, poetry and other writings, became the first African to win the Nobel Prize for Literature, and traveled the world extensively teaching African literature and culture.

The Yoruba tradition of the itinerant entertainer (*alarinjo*) blossomed during the twentieth century into a rich indigenous traveling theater movement which borrowed creatively from European drama traditions, employed modern technology (like motorized transport, modern lighting, costumery, and even cinema technology), and nurtured many traveling theater groups producing operatic works for popular entertainment. The movement started from Yoruba church music and opera, and its earliest practitioners were former school teachers and church organists who had produced music and opera in their churches and Christian schools. The mission churches had started in the nineteenth century by prohibiting the use of Yoruba indigenous music in church services, because such music was regarded as carrying "pagan" connotations. One of the effects of Yoruba cultural nationalism in the churches in general was the increasingly assertive use of Yoruba music and dancing in services and other church activities by the beginning of the twentieth century. Among Yoruba clergy and teachers, there arose many (like Mojola Agbebi, A. K Ajisafe, I. O. Kuti), who became very active in adapting or creating Yoruba songs for church organs and other Western musical instruments. Since these composers worked basically with the church organ, many of their compositions tended to have a syncretic character – that is, Yoruba songs with typically European tones, a type of production which became known as Native Airs.

These early Native-Air operas produced in churches and schools came to serve as the modern root for the growth of the new Yoruba opera. Some of the men who led in the production of the church Native-Air operas went out of the Christian church and school system, and began to create works in the Yoruba language, works that were based on purely traditional models, especially the model of the *alarinjo* entertainment groups, and derived their plots, themes, songs, music and musical instruments, cultural character, dance systems, etc., from the enormous wealth of Yoruba culture, folklore, traditions, religion, philosophy, festivals and rituals. Of the opera groups that thus arose, the most famous of the earliest ones were Hubert Ogunde Theatre, Kola Ogunmola

Theater, and Duro Ladipo Theatre. The traveling theater was a very important and unique part of the outstanding Yoruba contributions (in music, dance and various types of entertainment) to the popular culture of modern Nigeria and Africa in the twentieth century.

In the course of the second half of the twentieth century, the Yoruba people also began to produce many notable playwrights whose works belonged to Western drama and theater traditions. This important cultural development had its roots in the emerging universities in Nigeria as well as universities abroad. Like the people of the traveling opera groups, these playwrights derived their plots in general from Yoruba history, folklore, and traditions. Unlike the traveling opera groups, however, they wrote in the English language. By the last years of the century, there were many of these playwrights, the most notable ones being Wole Soyinka, Ola Rotimi, Wale Ogunyemi, and Femi Osofisan. Wole Soyinka was the leader in this cultural development, and became recognized worldwide as one of the greatest playwrights in the English language in the twentieth century.

As the twentieth century drew to a close, a modern cinema or movie industry emerged among the Yoruba. As early as the 1970s, some of the traveling theater groups had started to improve the distribution of their productions by recording them on film, with which they then traveled the country – a development in which the Ogunde Theater served as pioneer. From this root, independent movie groups and companies soon began to emerge – usually producing movies from themes of Yoruba history and folklore. By the beginning of the twenty-first century, there were many of these movie companies, and some of their productions (much of which was still rudimentary in technology and sophistication) were already entering into the world movie market and featuring in international movie festivals and contests.

Conclusion

Chapters Seventeen and Eighteen have presented an overview of the twentieth century history of the Yoruba people. The Yoruba passed from a century of great transformations (the nineteenth century) to another one of even greater transformations. As the nineteenth century closed, the Yoruba were losing their independence to alien European conquerors; by 1960, they entered the world as citizens, with other peoples, in three independent countries – Nigeria, Benin and Togo.

In all three countries, shared citizenship with other nationalities has posed tough challenges – and those challenges have been toughest in Nigeria, the largest country. While the economic advantages of living in the large country of

Nigeria might seem obvious, for instance, that country's multi-ethnic state experiment has produced, since independence, serious disruptive difficulties and troubles – inter-ethnic conflicts, conflicting ethnic ambitions and expectations, rigged and violently disputed elections, violent overthrows of governments, much publicized corruption in public life, a full-scale civil war, and unambiguous signs of disintegration of ethical and cultural values. All these have generally interfered with, slowed down, and distorted, efforts at socio-economic development and progress. For instance, the economic situation in Nigeria, disrupted by frequently recurring political troubles and by other problems, has set in motion a large exodus of Yoruba educated men and women to all parts of the world, resulting in a substantial and growing modern Yoruba diaspora in many countries. This has robbed the homeland of much of the expected return on the massive Yoruba investment in education since the late nineteenth century. Moreover, significant sections of the contemporary Yoruba social, religious, political and intellectual leadership see the disruptions of 1962–66 in the Western Region of Nigeria, as well as the escalation of public corruption, electoral fraud, and political violence and assassinations, among a substantial part of the Yoruba political elite in the years of the Obasanjo eight-year presidency, as signs of the impact of Nigeria on Yoruba people, and symptoms of the Yoruba share of the degeneration of peoples' traditional and ethical values in Nigeria. Yoruba achievements of the century – in social and economic development, in education, in businesses and the professions, in scholarship, in the literary and entertainment arts, etc. – acquire a surprising stature when viewed against this dismal political backdrop. The conclusion at the present point in the history of the Yoruba people can only be that the full measure of what the evolution of the multi-ethnic, multi-nation country holds in store for the Yoruba people in the modern world, and the fullness of Yoruba responses thereto, remain to be seen.

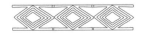

Notes

Chapter 1

1. David Hinderer: "Diaries," Ibadan, Christian Mission Society (CMS), quoted in I. A. Akinjogbin, ed., *The Cradle of a Race: Ile-Ife from the Beginning to 1980*, Port Harcourt, Sunray Publications, 1992, xi.
2. CMS (Yoruba) 1/7/5. Johnson to Griffith, Jan. 23, 1882.
3. "Report of the Special Commissioners to the Lagos Interior, 1886," Enclosures in Higgins to Colonial Secretary, Jan. 1887, Parliamentary Papers 1887, C.4957.
4. For the archaeological data for the following, see: Thurstan Shaw: "Prehistory," in Obaro Ikime, ed., *Groundwork of Nigerian History*, Ibadan, Historical Society of Nigeria, 1980, 30–35 ; T. Shaw: "Prehistory of West Africa," in J. K. Zerbo, ed., *General History of Africa: Methodology and Prehistory*, Paris, UNESCO, 1981, 611–33; T. Shaw and S. G. Daniels: "Excavations at Iwo-Eleru, Ondo State of Nigeria," *West African Journal of Archaeology*, 14, 1984, ix-xiv; A. K. Fatunsin: "Ifetedo: A Late Stone Age Site in the Forest Region of Southwestern Nigeria," *West African Journal of Archaeology*, 26, 1996, 71–87; for a good synthesis of the archaeological data, see, Raphael A. Alabi: "Late Stone Age Technologies and Agricultural Beginnings," in Akinwumi Ogundiran, ed., *Precolonial Nigeria: Essays in Honor of Toyin Falola*, Trenton, Africa World Press, 2005, 87–104. For dates, Alabi's article and some of the other archaeological literature use the formulations YBP (Years Before the Present) and BC (Before Christ) side by side. To avoid the confusion that this can constitute for the general reader, I stick in this book to the older, better known, BC.
5. Bassey W. Andah: "Agricultural Beginnings and Early Farming Communities in West and Central Africa," *West African Journal of Archaeology*, 17, 1987, 171–204; Alabi: "Late Stone Age Technologies."
6. Ade Obayemi: "The Yoruba and Edo-speaking Peoples and their Neighbors before 1600," in J. F. A. Ajayi and Michael Crowder, eds., *History of West Africa*, Vol.1, Third Edition, London, Longman, 1985, 196–263.
7. Shaw and Daniels: "Excavations at Iwo-Eleru."
8. I. A. Akinjogbin: "The Expansion of Oyo and the Rise of Dahomey, 1600–1800," in Ajayi and Crowder, eds., *History of West Africa*, Vol.1, 373–412.

9. Ulli Beier: "Before Oduduwa," *Odu: Journal of Yoruba and Related Studies*, 3, 1956, 25–32.
10. See Akinjogbin, ed., *The Cradle of a Race*, chapters by Ade Obayemi: "The Phenomenon of Oduduwa in Ife History," 62–76; Biodun Adediran: "The Early Beginnings of the Ife State," 77–95; and Isola Olomola: "Ife before Oduduwa," 51–61.
11. Paul Ozanne: "A Preliminary Report of an Archaeological Survey of Ife"; also "A New Archaeological Survey of Ife," *Odu*, new series, 1, 1969, 131–48.
12. Adediran: "The Early Beginnings of the Ife State," in Akinjogbin, ed., *The Cradle of a Race*, 80.

Chapter 2

1. For a summary of recent scholarship on the development of metal technology in Nigeria and Yorubaland and its economic, social and political implications (as well as for a helpful list of publications on the subject), see David Aremu: "Change and Continuity in Metallurgical Traditions: Origins, Technology and Social Implications," in Ogundiran: *Precolonial Nigeria*, 133–55; see also Bassey W. Andah: "Iron Age Beginnings in West Africa: Reflections and Suggestions," *West African Journal of Archaeology*, 9, 1979, 135–50; David Adeniji: *Iron Smelting at Isundunrin*, Ibadan Institute of African Studies Occasional Publications, no. 34, 1979; David Aremu: "The Archaeology of Northeast Yorubaland, Kwara State, with Emphasis on Early Techniques of Metal Working," Ph.D. thesis, Ibadan, University of Ibadan, 1990.
2. For the accounts that follow on population growth, state formation and the elaboration of group culture, see Ade Obayemi: "The Yoruba and Edo-speaking Peoples," in Ajayi and Crowder: *History of West Africa*, vol. 1, 196–263; Oladipo Olugbadehan: "Owo, A Frontier Yoruba Kingdom," PhD thesis, Union Institute and University, Cincinnati, Ohio, 2006, chaps. 3 and 4 on early state formation in Owo; I. Olomola: "Ife before Oduduwa," in Akinjogbin: *The Cradle of a Race*, 51–61, on early state formation in Ife. See also N. A. Fadipe: *The Sociology of the Yorubas*, Ibadan, University of Ibadan Press, 1970. My visits and interviews in many parts of Yorubaland from the Department of History, at the then Ondo State University, Ado-Ekiti, in 1985, also helped the synthesis and analysis in this chapter considerably.
3. Fadipe, *The Sociology of the Yorubas*; Emmanuel Babatunde: "Traditional Marriage and Family," in Nike Lawal, Matthew Sadiku and P. A. Dopemu, eds., Understanding Yoruba Life and Culture, Trenton, Africa World Press, 2004, 217–236.
4. A. O. Banwo and H. O. Danmole: "The Traditional Economy," 299–312; and Olagbemi Moloye: "Apprenticeship System," 333–40, in Lawal et al., *Understanding Yoruba Life and Culture*.
5. Adeagbo Akinjogbin: "The Expansion of Oyo and the Rise of Dahomey," in Ajayi and Crowder: *History of West Africa*, vol. 1, 374–412; Toyin Falola and A. G. Adebayo:

Culture, Politics and Money Among the Yoruba, New Brunswick: Transactions/Rutgers University, 2000.

6. Ade Obayemi: "Yoruba and Edo-speaking Peoples," in Ajayi and Crowder: *History of West Africa*, vol. 1; also my interviews on early Yoruba government, Yoruba crowns and the role of women in early Yoruba government, with Chief Isola Fabunmi, the Odole Atunobase of Ife, at the Institute of African Studies, Obafemi Awolowo University, June 1975, and with Oba Aladesanmi II, the Ewi of Ado-Ekiti, in the Ado-Ekiti Palace, about Yoruba crowns, in June 1975.

7. P. A. Dopamu: "Traditional Medicine and Health Care Delivery," in Lawal et al., *Understanding Yoruba Life and Culture*, 427–42; Fadipe: *Sociology of the Yorubas*; Akintunde Oyetade: "The Born-To-Die," in Lawal et al., *Understanding Yoruba Life and Culture*, 97–112.

8. Studies in Yoruba religion are many. For a selection, see: Bolaji Idowu: *African Traditional Religion: A Definition*, London, SCM Press, 1973; *Olodumare: God in Yoruba Belief*, London, Longman, 1977; J. O. Awolalu and P. Dopamu: *West African Traditional Religions*, Ibadan, Onibonoje Press, 1979; O. E. Alana: "Elements of Yoruba Religion," in Lawal et al., *Understanding Yoruba Life and Culture*, 65–80.

9. For instances of the confusion of the names Odudu and Oduduwa in some studies, see, e.g., Idowu: *Olodumare*, 27; A. B. Ellis: *The Yoruba Speaking Peoples of the Slave Coast of West Africa*, London, Chapman & Hall, 1894, 40.

10. Wande Abimbola: *Ifa: An Exposition of Ifa Literary Corpus*, Ibadan, Oxford University Press, 1976, and *Sixteen Great Poems of Ifa*, Niamey, UNESCO, 1975.

11. Frank Willett: "On the Funeral Effigies in Owo and Benin and the Interpretation of the Life-size Bronze Heads from Ife," *Man*, n.s. 1, 1966, 34–45; Rowland Abiodun: "A Reconstruction of the Function of Ako, Second Burial Effigy, in Owo," *Africa: Journal of the International African Institute*, 46, 1, 1976, 4–20.

12. Saburi Biobaku: *The Egba and Their Neighbors, 1842–1872*, Oxford, Oxford University Press, 1957, 2.

13. Robin Horton: "Ancient Ife: A Reassessment," *Journal of Historical Society of Nigeria*, 6, 4, 1976, 69–185.

14. For the village group in Ife, see Olomola: "Ife before Oduduwa," in Akinjogbin: *The Cradle of a Race*, 51–61.

Chapter 3

1. Olomola: ibid.
2. Horton: "Ancient Ife."
3. Ekpo Eyo: "Recent Excavations at Ife and Owo and their Implications for Ife, Owo and Benin Studies," Ph.D. thesis, University of Ibadan, 1974; Frank Willett: *Ife in the History of West African Sculpture*, London, Thames & Hudson, 1967.
4. Cited in Horton: "Ancient Ife."

5. Toyin Falola and Tunde Lawuyi: "Not just a Currency: The Cowry in Nigerian Culture," in D. Henige and T. C. McCaskie, eds., *West African Economic and Social History: Studies in Memory of Marion Johnson*, Madison, African Studies Program, 1990.
6. P. Garlake: "Excavations at Obalara's Land, Ife, Nigeria," *West African Journal of Archaeology*, 4, 111–48; Ozanne: "A New Archaeological Survey of Ife."
7. Henry Drewal, John Pemberton and Rowland Abiodun: *Yoruba: Nine Centuries of African Art and Thought*, New York, Center for African Art in association with Harry Abrams Publishers, 1990, 46.
8. Details of the alliance and its outcome in Adediran: "The Early Beginnings of the Ife State," in Akinjogbin: *The Cradle of a Race*, 77–95.

Chapter 4

1. M. R. Doortmont: "Samuel Johnson: Missionary, Diplomat and Historian," in Toyin Falola, ed., *Yoruba Historiography*, Madison, University of Wisconsin African Studies Program, 1991, 167–82.
2. For the account that follows, see the following chapters in Akinjogbin: *The Cradle of a Race*: Adediran: "The Early Beginnings of the Ife State," 77–95; Obayemi: "The Phenomenon of Oduduwa in Ife History," 62–76.
3. David Aremu: "Change and Continuity in Metallurgical Traditions: Origins, Technology and Social Implications," in Ogundiran: *Precolonial Nigeria*, 147; Peter Morton-Williams: "The Yoruba Ogboni Cult in Oyo," *Africa*, 30, 4, 1960, 364–73.
4. On early Ile-Ife walls, see Babatunde Agbaje-Williams: "Yoruba Urbanism: The Archaeology and Historical Ethnography of Ile-Ife and Old Oyo," in Ogundiran: *Precolonial Nigeria*, 215–40; Ozanne: "A New Archaeological Survey of Ife."
5. Ibid.; Adeagbo Akinjogbin: "The Growth of Ife from Oduduwa to 1800" in Akinjogbin: *The Cradle of a Race*, 96–122; Horton: "Ancient Ife."
6. Ibid.; O. Eluyemi: "The Technology of the Ife Glass Beads: Evidence from the Igbo Olokun," *Odu: Journal of Yoruba and Related Studies*, new series, 32, 1987, 200–216.
7. Ibid.; Willett: *Ife in the History of West African Sculpture*; Ekpo Eyo: *Two Thousand Years of Nigerian Art*, Lagos, Federal Department of Antiquities, 1977.

Chapter 5

1. Adeagbo Akinjogbin: "The Growth of Ife," in Akinjogbin: *The Cradle of a Race*; Horton: "Ancient Ife"; Willett: *Ife in the History of West African Sculpture*; R. S. Smith: *Kingdoms of the Yoruba*, London, Methuen, 1969, 16–31; see also Akinwumi Ogundiran: "Chronology, Material Culture, and Pathways to the Cultural History of Yoruba Edo Region, Nigeria, 500BC–1800AD," in Toyin Falola and Christian

Jennings, eds., *Sources and Methods in African History: Spoken, Written, Unearthed*, Rochester, University of Rochester Press, 2003; O. Eluyemi: "The Role of Oral Traditions in the Archaeological Investigation of the History of Ife," in Wande Abimbola, ed., *Yoruba Oral Traditions: Proceedings of the Conference on Yoruba Oral Traditions*, University of Ife, Department of African Languages and Literature, 1975.
2. Interview with Chief Fabunmi, the Odole Atunobase of Ife, 1975.
3. Akinwumi Ogundiran: *Archaeology and History in Ilare District, Central Yorubaland, Nigeria, 1200–1900*, London, Cambridge Monograph in African Archaeology, No. 55, 2002, 20.
4. Frank Willett: "Ife and its Archaeology," *Journal of African History*, 6, 1960, 231–48.
5. Leo Frobenius, quoted in Eyo: *Two Thousand Years*, 100.
6. Ibid.
7. See note 1 above, especially Akinjogbin: "The Growth of Ife," *The Cradle of a Race*.

Chapter 6

1. Of such written collections (usually employed in historical analysis), there are many. See the following: Samuel Johnson: *The History of the Yorubas from the Earliest Times to the Beginning of the British Protectorate*, Lagos, CMS, 1921, 15–25; Ade Obayemi: "The Yoruba and Edo-speaking peoples," in Ajayi and Crowder, *History of West Africa*; Smith: *Kingdoms of the Yoruba*; Funso Afolayan: "The Early Yoruba Kingdoms," in Lawal et al., *Understanding Yoruba Life and Culture*, 31–49; Akinjogbin: "The Expansion of Oyo," in Ajayi and Crowder, *History of West Africa*, vol. 1, 374–80; G. Parrinder: "Yoruba-speaking Peoples in Dahomey," *Africa*, 17, 2, 1947, 122–9; R. C. C. Law: "The Heritage of Oduduwa: Traditional History and Political Propaganda among the Yoruba," *Journal of African History*, 14, 2, 1973, 207–22, etc. There are also tens of written local histories and chronicles, each a collection of local traditions.
2. Johnson: *History*, 7–12.
3. Parrinder: "Yoruba-speaking Peoples in Dahomey"; Adediran: "The Early Beginnings of the Ife State," in Akinjogbin: *The Cradle of a Race*, 83.
4. Akinjogbin: "The Growth of Ife," *The Cradle of a Race*, 101–2.
5. See S. A. Akintoye: "The Northeastern Yoruba Districts and the Benin Kingdom," *Journal of the Historical Society of Nigeria*, 4, 4, 1969, 539–53; Olugbadehan: "Owo".
6. Smith: *Kingdoms of the Yoruba*, 98–9.

Chapter 7

1. See ch. 6 note 1 above; also, E. A. Kenyo: *Yoruba Natural Rulers and their Origins*, Ibadan, 1964.
2. J. D. E. Abiola, J. A. Babafemi and S. O. S. Ataiyero: *Iwe Itan Ilesha*, Lagos, CMS Press, 1932.
3. A. Oguntuyi: *History of Ekiti from the Beginning to 1939*, Ibadan, Caxton Press, 1979; Isola Olomola: *A Thousand Years of Ado History and Culture*, Ado-Ekiti, Omolayo Press, 1984.
4. M. B. Ashara: *The History of Owo*, Owo, 1952; Olugbadehan: "Owo," 41–90.
5. Benjamin Okpevra: "Ijo–Itshekiri Relations, 1500–1800," in Ogundiran: *Precolonial Nigeria*, 395–410.
6. J. U. Egharevba: *A Short History of Benin*, Ibadan, Ibadan University Press, 1960.
7. Obaro Ikime: "The Peoples and Kingdoms of the Delta Province," in Ikime, ed.: *Groundwork of Nigerian History*, 89–108.
8. M. C. Adeyemi: *Ondo Kingdom: Its History and Culture*, Ibadan, Bounty Press, 1993; J. K. Olupona: *Kingship, Religion and Rituals in a Nigerian Community*, Stockholm, Almqvist and Wiksell, 1991; Bada of Saki: *Iwe Itan Ondo,* Ondo, 1940.
9. Apena B. M. Okubote: *Iwe Itan Ikereku ati Ijebu,* Ibadan, 1937; Femi Ayantuga: "Ijebu and its Neighbors, 1851–1914," Ph.D. thesis, University of London, 1965.
10. J. B. Losi: *History of Lagos*, Lagos, Tika Tare Press, 1914.
11. S. Biobaku: *The Egba and their Neighbors*.
12. E. G. Parrinder: *The Story of Ketu, an Ancient Yoruba Kingdom*, Ibadan, Ibadan University Press, 1967.
13. Ade Obayemi: "The Yoruba and Edo-speaking Peoples," in Ajayi and Crowder: *History of West Africa*, vol. 1, 196–263.
14. J. Pemberton and F. Afolayan: *Yoruba Sacred Kingship: A Power like that of the Gods*, Washington, D.C., Smithsonian Institute Press, 1996.
15. R. C. C. Law: *The Oyo Empire c. 1600–1836: A West African Imperialism in the Era of the Atlantic Slave Trade*, Oxford, Oxford University Press, 1991.

Chapter 8

1. See Fadipe: *Sociology of the Yoruba*; P. C. Lloyd: "Sacred Kingship and Government among the Yoruba," *Africa*, 30, 1960, 221–37; P. C. Lloyd: *Yoruba Land Law*, London, Oxford University Press, 1962; Pemberton and Afolayan: *Yoruba Sacred Kingship*.
2. See Pemberton and Afolayan, *Yoruba Sacred Kingship*; Karen Barber: *I Could Speak until Tomorrow: Oriki, Women and the Past in a Yoruba Town*, Washington, DC, Smithsonian Institution Press, 1991; Local History subheading in Bibliography below.

3. For the place (or absence) of Ogboni in Oyo-Ile, see J. A. Atanda: "The Yoruba Ogboni Cult: Did it Exist in Old Oyo?" *Journal of the Historical Society of Nigeria*, 6, 4, 1973, 365–71.
4. Pemberton and Afolayan: *Yoruba Sacred Kingship*, 89–94.
5. William Clarke: *Travels and Explorations in Yorubaland, 1854–1858*, ed. J. A. Atanda, Ibadan, Ibadan University Press, 1972.
6. Duarte Pacheco Pereira: *Esmeraldo de Situ Orbis*, quoted in Smith: *Kingdoms of the Yoruba*, 75.
7. Smith: *Kingdoms of the Yoruba*, 79; CMS CA2/049: Account of David Hinderer's Journey to Ijebu-Ode, Dec. 1855 to Jan. 1856.
8. Clarke: *Travels and Explorations*.
9. David Hinderer's Report of his tour, CMS, CAO/049.
10. Ade Obayemi: "Yoruba and Edo-speaking Peoples," in Ajayi and Crowder: *History of West Africa*, vol. 1, 255.
11. J. De Barros: *Da Asia*, Lisbon, 1552, quoted in A. F. C. Ryder: "A Reconsideration of the Ife–Benin Relationship," *Journal of African History*, 6, 1, 1965, 26–7.
12. Ryder: ibid.
13. Willett: *Ife in the History of West African Sculpture*; also Eyo: "Recent Excavations."
14. For instance, see David Hinderer's account of his visit to Ile-Ife in the 1850s, in ch. 3 above.
15. See Olugbadehan: "Owo," 91–102.
16. Smith: *Kingdoms of the Yoruba*, 22.
17. Akinjogbin: "The Growth of Ife," in Akinjogbin: *The Cradle of a Race*, 96–121.
18. I. E. Babamboni: *Itan Ewi, Elekole ati Ajero*, Ado-Ekiti, n.d.
19. Barber: *I Could Speak Until Tomorrow*.
20. Olugbadehan: "Owo."
21. E. A. Ayandele: "The Changing Position of the Awujales of Ijebuland under Colonial Rule," in M. Crowder and O. Ikime, eds., *West African Chiefs: Their Changing Status under Colonial Rule and Independence*, Ife, 1970, 231–54.
22. See Funso S. Afolayan: "External Relations and Socio-Political Transformation in Precolonial Igbomina," Ph.D. Thesis, Obafemi Awolowo University, Ile-Ife, Nigeria, 1991.
23. Obayemi: "Yoruba and Edo-speaking Peoples," in Ajayi and Crowder: *History of West Africa*.
24. The subject of internal migrations and folk movements in the Yoruba homeland is a large and important one. It is to be hoped that some day someone will give us an in-depth study of it.

Chapter 9

1. Richard Lander: *Records of Capt. Clapperton's Last Expedition to Africa*, London, Henry Colborn & Richard Bentley, 1830, vol. 1, 95–100, vol. 2, 211.

2. Eva Krapf-Askari: *Yoruba Towns and Cities*, Oxford, Clarendon Press, 1969, 39.
3. Hence the song, *Osogbo n' ile aro* (Osogbo is the home of dyes).
4. Hence the fact that most of the oldest mosques in Yorubaland are to be found on the edge of kings' market places, close to palaces.
5. Interview with the Orangun of Ila and Ila chiefs, September, 1963.
6. Akintoye: "The Northeastern Yoruba Districts and the Benin Kingdom."
7. Captain Hugh Clapperton: *Journal of a Second Expedition into the Interior of Africa from the Bight of Benin to Soccatoo*, London, John Murray, 1829, 59.
8. Adeagbo Akinjogbin: "The Economic Foundations of the Oyo Empire in the 18th Century," in I. A. Akinjogbin and S. O. Osoba, eds., *Topics in Nigerian Economic and Social History*, Ife, University of Ife Press, 1980, 35–54.
9. Quoted in ibid., 39–40.
10. Clapperton: *Journal of a Second Expedition*, 12.
11. T. J. Bowen: *Adventures and Missionary Labours in Several Countries in the Interior of Africa, 1849–1856*, Charleston, Southern Baptist Society, 1857.
12. Lander: *Records*, vol. 1, 52–101.
13. Hinderer's Journey to Ijebu, CMS, CA2/049.
14. Daniel J. May: "Journey in the Yoruba and Nupe Countries in 1858," *Journal of the Royal Geographical Society*, 30, 1860, 212–33.
15. See Akinjogbin: "Economic Foundations of Old Oyo," in Akinjogbin and Osoba, eds., *Topics in Nigerian Economic and Social History*, 37–9.
16. Dapper, quoted in Akinjogbin: ibid., 38.
17. Ibid.
18. Ibid.; also Falola and Adebayo: *Culture, Politics and Money among the Yoruba*.
19. Pereira, *Esmeraldo de Situ Orbis*, quoted in Smith: *Kingdoms of the Yoruba*, 75.
20. Lander: *Records*, vol. 2, 217.
21. Walter Rodney: *A History of the Upper Guinea Coast, 1545–1800*, Oxford, Clarendon Press, 1970.
22. Olugbadehan: "Owo," 103–58.
23. Interviews with Chief Isola Fabunmi, the Odole Atunobase of Ife, 1978.
24. Lander: *Records*, vol. 1, 298–300.
25. Ibid.

Chapter 10

1. Toyin Falola: "The Yoruba Toll System," *Journal of African History*, 30, 1, 1989, 41–63; R. C. C. Law: "Slaves, Trade and Taxes: The Material Basis of Political Power in Pre-colonial West Africa," *Research in Economic Anthropology*, 1, 1978, 37–52.
2. A. O. Banwo and H. O. Danmole: "The Traditional Economy" in Lawal et al., *Understanding Yoruba Life and Culture*, 299–312.
3. Toyin Falola: "The Yoruba Caravan System in the 19th Century," *The International Journal of African Historical Studies*, 24, 1, 1991, 111–32.

4. S. A. Akintoye: "The Ondo Road, Eastwards of Lagos," *Journal of African History*, 10, 4, 1969, 581–98.
5. A. O. Banwo: "Women in the Traditional Economy," in Lawal et al., *Understanding Yoruba Life and Culture*, 313–22.
6. See Falola and Adebayo: *Culture, Politics and Money*, 127–46.
7. Ibid.
8. Johnson, *History*, 119.
9. William R. Bascom: "The Esusu: A Credit Institution of the Yoruba," *Journal of the Royal Anthropological Institute*, 82, 1, 1952, 63–9.
10. Falola and Adebayo: *Culture, Politics and Money*, 151–67.
11. Johnson: *History*.
12. Falola and Adebayo: *Culture, Politics and Money*, 158–59.
13. Adeagbo Akinjogbin: "Wars in Yorubaland, 1793–1893: An Analytical Categorization," in I. A. Akinjogbin, ed., *War and Peace in Yorubaland, 1793–1893*, Heinemann, Ibadan, 1998, 34–7.
14. Lander: *Records*, vol. 1, 45–105.
15. Ibid., vol. 2, 195.
16. Ibid., vol. 1, 101–2.
17. Drewal et al.: *Yoruba: Nine Centuries of African Art and Thought*, 1.

Chapter 11

1. For the development of Yoruba–Aja relations, see I. A. Akinjogbin: "The Expansion of Oyo and the Rise of Dahomey," in Ajayi and Crowder: *History of West Africa*, vol. 1, 374–412.
2. For one recent account of Yoruba–Nupe relations in history, see Idris Sha'aba Jimada: *The Nupe and the Origins and Evolution of the Yoruba, c. 1275–1897*, Zaria, Abdullahi Smith Center for Historical Research, 2005.
3. Aribidesi Usman: "Crisis and Catastrophe: Warfare in Precolonial Northern Yoruba," in Ogundiran: *Precolonial Nigeria*, 361–84.
4. Ibid., p. 366; also Michael Mason: "Jihad in the South: An Outline of the 19th Century Nupe Hegemony in Northeastern Yorubaland and Afenmai," in *Journal of the Historical Society of Nigeria*, 5, 2, 1970, 195.
5. Akintoye: "The Northeastern Yoruba Districts and the Benin Kingdom."
6. Ibid.; also Olugbadehan: "Owo"; Ashara: *The History of Owo*.
7. Oguntuyi: *History of Ado*; Olomola: *A Thousand Years of Ado History*.
8. Oguntuyi: ibid.
9. The Oore had been given a copy of my 1971 article ("The Northeastern Yoruba Districts and the Benin Kingdom") by Dr. N. F. Aina (of the Faculty of Education, Ife), and had sent for me in order, as he put it, "to correct mistakes" in my article. Two interviews at the Otun palace resulted.
10. Olfert Dapper, quoted in Akintoye: "The Northeastern Yoruba," 549–50.

11. J. Barbot: *A Description of the Coast of North and South Guinea*, London, 1732, quoted in Akintoye: ibid., 550.
12. Capt. H. L. Galway, quoted in Akintoye, ibid., 550.
13. Akintoye, ibid.
14. Ben. Dist. 3/1/1 (National Archives, Ibadan), Akure Chiefs to Roupell, April 15, 1897.
15. Oba Adegoriola, the Ogoga of Ikere: "A Note on the Administration of Ikere before the Advent of the British," *Odu: Journal of Yoruba and Related Studies*, 3, 19–24.
16. Akintoye: "Northeastern Yoruba Districts"; also, my interviews with the chiefs of Ara, Ogotun, Ilawe and Igbara-Odo, in 1974–5.
17. Smith: *Kingdoms of the Yoruba*, 89–94; Losi: *The History of Lagos*.
18. Obayemi: "Yoruba and Edo-speaking Peoples," in Ajayi and Crowder: *History of West Africa*, vol. 1, 252.
19. For the paragraphs that follow, see Olugbadehan: "Owo," chs. 6 and 7, 103–54.
20. Ibid.
21. Ibid.
22. Ibid.
23. Ibid., 144–8.

Chapter 12

1. Lander: *Records*, vol. 1, 105–6.
2. Johnson: *History*.
3. Law: *The Oyo Empire*.
4. Ibid, 39–42, offers, for the revival of the Oyo-Ile kingdom, a hypothesis that rejects the popular traditions and the common conclusions from them.
5. Lander: *Records*, vol. 2, 222.
6. Johnson: *History*, 73.
7. Ibid.
8. Adeagbo Akinjogbin: "The Expansion of Oyo," in Ajayi and Crowder: *History of West Africa*, vol. 1, 387–9.
9. Ibid. 385–9.
10. Johnson: *History*, 174.
11. Akinjogbin: "The Expansion of Oyo," in Ajayi and Crowder: *History of West Africa*, vol. 1, 410.
12. See Law: *The Oyo Empire*, 225–8.
13. Archibald Dalzel: *History of Dahomey*, London, Blackwells, 1793.
14. Ibid., 196.
15. Lander: *Records*, vol. 2, 227.
16. Ibid., 197–200.
17. Ibid., 115–21.

Chapter 13

1. For most of the accounts that follow, we are indebted to Johnson's collection of Oyo traditions in his *History of the Yorubas*, 178–82; also, Law: *The Oyo Empire*, 245–99.
2. Johnson: *History*, 177.
3. Ibid., 174.
4. Ibid., 176.
5. Adeagbo Akinjogbin: "The Prelude to the Yoruba Civil Wars of the Nineteenth Century," *Odu*, 2nd series, 1965, 24–46; also Akinjogbin: "The Expansion of Oyo," in Ajayi and Crowder: *History of West Africa*, vol. 1, 407–8.
6. Ibid., 410.
7. Biobaku: *The Egba and Their Neighbors*, 10.
8. Lander: *Records*, vol. 2, 227.
9. Richard and John Lander: *Journal of an Expedition to Explore the Course and Termination of the Niger*, London, Thomas Tegg & Sons, 1832.

Chapter 14

1. The literature on this subject is considerable; see, Johnson: *History*; J. F. Ade Ajayi and R. S. Smith: *Yoruba Warfare in the Nineteenth Century*, Cambridge, Cambridge University Press, 1964; Adeagbo Akinjogbin: "The Prelude"; Bolanle Awe: "The Rise of Ibadan," D.Phil. thesis, Oxford, 1964; S. A. Akintoye: *Revolution and Power Politics in Yorubaland: Ibadan Expansion and the Rise of the Ekitiparapo, 1840–1893*, London, Longman, 1971; J. F. Ade Ajayi: "The Aftermath of the Fall of Old Oyo," in Ajayi and Crowder: *History of West Africa*, vol. 2; a gold mine of in-depth chapters in Akinjogbin, *War and Peace in Yorubaland*.
2. Johnson: *History*.
3. In addition to materials in note 1 above, see A. Mabogunje and J. D. Omer-Cooper: *Owu In Yoruba History*, Ibadan, Ibadan University Press, 1971; R. C. C. Law: "The Owu War in Yoruba History," *Journal of the Historical Society of Nigeria*, 7, 1, 1973, 141–7.
4. Biobaku: *The Egba and their Neighbors*.
5. S. A. Akintoye: "Ife's Sad Century: The 19th Century in the History of Ife," *Nigeria Magazine*, 104, 1970.
6. Toyin Falola: *The Political Economy of a Precolonial African State: Ibadan, 1830–1900*, Ife, University of Ife Press, 1984; "The Yoruba Caravan System in the Nineteenth Century"; S. A. Akintoye: "The Economic Foundations of Ibadan's Power in the Nineteenth Century," in Akinjogbin and Osoba: *Topics in Nigerian Economic and Social History*, 55–65.
7. Ajayi and Smith: *Yoruba Warfare*.

8. Isola Olomola: "The War Generals of Eastern Yorubaland," in Akinjogbin: *War and Peace,* 181–8.
9. Akintoye: "The Ondo Road," 581–98.
10. Jimada: *The Nupe*, 99–106.
11. Olugbadehan: "Owo," 159–78.
12. Akintoye: "The Northeastern Yoruba Districts."
13. Akintoye: *Revolution and Power Politics*, 76–212.
14. Z. O. Apata: "The Nupe Imperialism and the Ogidi Grand Alliance, 1894–1897," in Akinjogbin: *War and Peace*, 431–42; Jimada: *The Nupe*, 137–9.
15. *The Lagos Observer*, June 5, 1884.
16. CMS CA.2/049: David Hinderer: "Account of a Journey to Ibadan," June 4, 1851.
17. Clarke: *Travels and Explorations in Yorubaland*, 153–63.

Chapter 15

1. T. G. O. Gbadamosi: *The Growth of Islam among the Yoruba, 1841–1908*, New York: Humanities Press, 1978.
2. Lander: *Records*, vol. 1, 277–81.
3. Ibid.
4. Gbadamosi: *The Growth of Islam*, 12.
5. Ibid, 22–39.
6. "Bishop C. Phillips's Report of a Tour to Ekiti, June 1894," quoted in Gbadamosi: *The Growth of Islam*, 87.
7. Johnson: *History*, 306.
8. Anna Hinderer: *Seventeen Years in the Yoruba Country: Memorials of Anna Hinderer, Wife of David Hinderer, CMS Missionary in West Africa*, London, 1872, 59–62; "David Hinderer's Annual Letter, 1858," quoted in S. A. Akintoye: "The Economic Foundations of Ibadan's Power in the Nineteenth Century," in Akinjogbin and Osoba, eds.: *Topics in Economic and Social History*, 57; Falola: "The Yoruba Caravan System in the Nineteenth Century"; *The Political Economy of a Precolonial African State*.
9. Clarke: *Travels and Explorations in Yorubaland*, 263–5.
10. J. H. Kopytoff: *A Preface to Modern Nigeria: The "Sierra Leonians" in Yoruba, 1830–1880*, Madison, Wisconsin University Press, 1965.
11. For the account of the beginning of Yoruba language in writing, see J. F. Ade Ajayi: "How Yoruba was Reduced to Writing," in *Odu: Journal of Yoruba and Related Studies*, 8, 1960, 49–58.
12. S. A. Agboola: "Agricultural Changes in Western Nigeria, 1850–1910," in Akinjogbin and Osoba: *Topics in Nigeria Economic and Social History*, 128–45.
13. J. F. Ade Ajayi: *Christian Missions in Nigeria, 1841–1891*, London, Longman, 1965; E. A. Ayandele: *The Missionary Impact on Modern Nigeria, 1842–1914*, London, Longman, 1966.

14. Ibid.
15. By the Songhai scholar, Ahmed Baba, in Timbuktu in 1615.
16. See Law: "The Heritage of Oduduwa."
17. J. A. Atanda: "The Wars and Imperial Conquests of Yorubaland," in Akinjogbin: *War and Peace*, 307–20; A. I. Asiwaju: "The Western Provinces under Colonial Rule," in Ikime, ed.: *Groundwork of Nigerian History*, 429–46.

Chapter 16

1. Atlantic Slave Trade numerical data in these pages rely mostly on David Eltis, Stephen Behrendt, David Richardson, and Herbert Klein: *The Trans-Atlantic Slave Trade: A Database on CD-ROM*, Cambridge University Press, 1999; also Philip Curtin: *The Atlantic Slave Trade: A Census*, Madison, University of Wisconsin Press, 1969.
2. David Eltis: "The Diaspora of Yoruba Speakers, 1650–1865: Dimensions and Implications," in Toyin Falola and Matt Childs: *The Yoruba Diaspora in the Atlantic World*, Indiana University Press, 2004, 33.
3. Ibid.
4. Louis Antoine Aimé de Verteuil: *Three Essays on the Cultivation of Sugar Cane in Trinidad*, Port of Spain, 1858, quoted in Eltis: "The Diaspora," 34.
5. For a fuller account of slavery and society in Bahia, see Stuart B. Schwartz: *Sugar Plantations in the Formation of Brazilian Society*, Bahia, Cambridge University Press, 1985; João Jose Reis and Beatriz Galotti Mamigonian: "Nago and Mina: The Yoruba Diaspora in Brazil," in Falola and Childs: *The Yoruba Diaspora*, 77–110.
6. Pedro Perez Sarduy and Jean Stubbs, eds., *Afro-Cuban Voices: On Race and Identity in Contemporary Cuba*, Gainesville, University of Florida Press, 2000; Michele Reid: "The Yoruba in Cuba: Origins, Identities and Transformations," in Falola and Childs: *The Yoruba Diaspora*, 111–29.
7. Eltis: "The Diaspora," in Falola and Childs: *The Yoruba Diaspora*, 34.
8. Carolyn Fick: *The Making of Haiti: The St. Domingue Revolution from Below*, University of Tennessee Press, 1990; also, Kevin Roberts: "The Influential Yoruba Past in Haiti," in Falola and Childs: *The Yoruba Diaspora*, 177–84.
9. Randall Robinson: *An Unbroken Agony: Haiti from Revolution to the Kidnapping of a President*, New York, Civitas Books, 2007, 10–11.
10. Ibid., 11.
11. From John K. Thornton: *African Soldiers in the Haitian Revolution*, quoted in Robinson: *An Unbroken Agony*, 10.
12. Wole Soyinka: *Myth, Literature and the African World*, Cambridge, Cambridge University Press, 1962, 1.
13. See e.g., Kamari M. Clarke: *Mapping Yoruba Networks: Power and Agency in the Making of Transitional Communities*, Durham, Duke University Press, 2004.

14. Augustine Agwuele: "Yorubaisms in African-American Speech Patterns," in Falola and Childs: *The Yoruba Diaspora*, 326–7; quotations from Lorand Matory: "The English Professors of Brazil: On the Diasporic Roots of the Yoruba Nation," in *Comparative Studies in Society and History*, 41, 1, 1999, 76; Verteuil: *Three Essays*, 175.

Chapter 17

1. A. I. Asiwaju: *Western Yorubaland under European Rule, 1889–1945*, London, Longman, 1976.
2. S. A. Akintoye: "Yoruba History from Early Times to the 20th Century," in Lawal et al.: *Understanding Yoruba Life and Culture*, 15–18; A. I. Asiwaju: "The Western Provinces under Colonial Rule," in Ikime: *Groundwork of Nigerian History*, 439–46; G. Olusanya: "Constitutional Developments, 1861–1960," in ibid., 513–44.
3. S. A. Akintoye: "Obas of the Ekiti Confederacy since the Advent of the British," in Crowder and Ikime: *West African Chiefs*, 255–71.
4. J. A. Atanda: *The New Oyo Empire*, London, 1973; for a general account of this period in the history of Yoruba traditional institutions in Nigeria, see also, I. F. Nicolson: *The Administration of Nigeria, 1900–1960: Men, Methods and Myths*, Oxford, Clarendon Press, 1969; Ayandele: "The Changing Position of the Awujales of Ijebuland," in Crowder and Ikime: *West African Chiefs*.
5. For in-depth studies in the political history of the Nigerian federation, see Paul Beckett and Crawford Young, eds.: *Dilemmas of Democracy in Nigeria*, Rochester, University of Rochester Press, 1997.
6. See Funso Afolayan: "Colonial Rule and Anti-Fulani Revolts among the Igbomina," *Odu: Journal of Yoruba and Related Studies*, 36, 1989, 24–42; also chapters in O. Ayodeji, Z. O. Apata, and O. Akinwumi, eds.: *Northeast Yorubaland: Studies in the History and Culture of a Frontier Zone*, Ibadan, Rex Charles Publication, 2003.
7. For a good study of Yoruba politics in Akintola's time, see: Akinjide Osuntokun: *Chief S. Ladoke Akintola: His Life and Times*, London, Frank Cass, 1984.
8. Ibid.
9. Wale Adebanwi: "Yoruba Vision," paper presented at the Yoruba Retreat, Ibadan, October 26–29, 2007.
10. Soyinka, Wole: *You Must Set Forth at Dawn*, New York, Random House, 2007, 57.

Chapter 18

1. R. J. Gavin and Wale Ogunmakinde: "Economic Development in Nigeria since 1800," in Ikime: *Groundwork*, 492–512; S. O. Osoba and A. Fajana: "Educational and Social Development," in ibid., 570–600.
2. Gbadamosi: *The Growth of Islam*, 159–213.
3. Ibid., 197–213.

4. Ayandele: *The Missionary Impact*.
5. M. N. O. Sadiku: "The Practice of Christianity," in Lawal et al.: *Understanding Yoruba Life and Culture*, 125–36.
6. Ibid.
7. Valerie G. Lowe: "The Unlikely Ambassador," *Charisma*, 33, 3, October 2007.
8. Ayandele: *The Missionary Impact*, 243–78.
9. Quoted in Ayandele: ibid.
10. Ibid.
11. Ibid.
12. Toyin Falola: *Yoruba Gurus: Indigenous Production of Knowledge in Africa*, Trenton, Africa World Press, 1999.

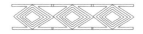

Bibliography

Selected Material at the National Archives, Ibadan, Nigeria

1. British Parliamentary Papers:
    1862, Papers Relating to the Occupation of Lagos, C.2982.
    1887, Correspondence Respecting the War between Native Tribes in the Interior and the Negotiations for Peace conducted by the Government of Lagos, C.4957.
    1887, Further Correspondence Respecting the War between Native Tribes in the Interior and the Negotiations for Peace conducted by the Government of Lagos, C. 5144.
    1893, Despatch from Sir Gilbert Carter furnishing a General Report on the Lagos Interior Expedition, C.7227.
2. Ben. Dist. 3/1/1, Akure Chiefs to Roupell, April 15, 1897.
3. Intelligence Reports:
    A collection of Intelligence Reports, written in the 1920s and 1930s, on various Districts of Yorubaland. (Copies also available in some Local Government offices in Nigeria).
4. Printed Government Reports:
    Colonial Reports – Annual, *Lagos*, 1888–1902
    Colonial Reports – Annual, *Southern Nigeria*, 1899–1909.
5. Christian Mission Records.
    Church Missionary Society (Y) 1/5-4/1.
    Wesleyan Methodist Mission Records (W.M.M.R.).
    Some other Christian Mission Records are available in the Ibadan University Library in microfilm: CA2: Yoruba Mission, 1842–1880; CMS CA2/049: Account of David Hinderer's Journey to Ijebu-Ode, Dec. 1855 to Jan. 1856; G3 A2: Yoruba Mission, 1880–1914.

Books

Abimbola, W.: *Sixteen Great Poems of Ifa*, Niamey, UNESCO, 1975.
Abimbola, W., ed.: *Yoruba Oral Traditions*, *Proceedings of the Conference on Yoruba Oral Traditions,* Ife, University of Ife Press, 1975.

Bibliography

Abimbola, W.: *Ifa: An Exposition of Ifa Literary Corpus*, Ibadan, Oxford University Press, 1976.

Adams, Captain J.: *Remarks on the Country Extending from Cape Palmas to the River Congo*, (London, 1823), Frank Cass, 1966.

Adediran, A. A.: *The Frontier States of Western Yorubaland, 1600–1889*, Ibadan, French Institute for Research in Africa, 1994.

Adeniji, D.: *Iron Smelting at Isundunrin*, Ibadan Institute of African Studies Occasional Publications, no. 34, 1979.

Ajayi, J. F. A.: *Christian Missions in Nigeria, 1841–1891*, London, Longman, 1965.

Ajayi, J. F. A. and Crowder, M. eds.: *History of West Africa*, vol. 1, Third Edition, London, Longman, 1985.

Ajayi, J. F. A. and Smith, R. S.: *Yoruba Warfare in the Nineteenth Century*, Cambridge, Cambridge University Press, 1964.

Ajisafe, A. K.: *Laws and Customs of the Yoruba People*, London, Routledge, 1924.

Akindele, A. and Aguessy, C.: *Dahomey*, Paris, Éditions Maritimes et Coloniales, 1955.

Akinjogbin, I. A.: *Dahomey and Its Neighbors, 1708–1818*, Cambridge, Cambridge University Press, 1967.

Akinjogbin, I. A. ed.: *War and Peace in Yorubaland, 1793–1893*, Ibadan, Heinemann, 1983.

Akinjogbin, I. A. ed.: *The Cradle of a Race: Ile-Ife from the Beginning to 1980*, Port Harcourt: Sunray Publications, 1992.

Akinjogbin, I. A. and Osoba, S. O. eds.: *Topics in Nigerian Economic and Social History*, Ile-Ife, University of Ife Press, 1980.

Akintoye, S. A.: *Revolution and Power Politics in Yorubaland: Ibadan Expansion and the Rise of the Ekitiparapo, 1840–1893*, London, Longman, 1971.

Akintoye, S. A.: *Ten Years of the University of Ife, 1962–72*, Ife, Ife University Press, 1973.

Alagoa, E. J.: *A History of the Niger Delta: An Historical Interpretation of the Oral Tradition*, Ibadan, Ibadan University Press, 1972.

Asiwaju, A. T.: *Western Yorubaland under European Rule, 1889–1945*, London, Longman, 1976.

Atanda, J. A.: *The New Oyo Empire*, London, Longman, 1973.

Atanda, J. A.: *An Introduction to Yoruba History*, Ibadan, Ibadan University Press, 1980.

Awolalu, J. O.: *Yoruba Beliefs and Sacrificial Rites*, London, Longman, 1979.

Awolalu, J. O. and Dopamu, P.: *West African Traditional Religions*, Ibadan, Onibonoje Press, 1979.

Ayandele, E. A.: *The Missionary Impact on Modern Nigeria 1842–1914*, London, Longman, 1966.

Ayandele, E. A.: *Holy Johnson: Pioneer of African Nationalism, 1856–1917*, London, Frank Cass, 1970.

Ayodeji, O., Apata, Z. O. and Akinwumi, O. eds.: *Northeast Yorubaland: Studies in the History and Culture of a Frontier Zone*, Ibadan, Rex Charles Publication, 2003.

Balogun, K.: *Government in Old Oyo Empire*, Lagos, Africana Publishers, 1985.

Barber, K.: *I Could Speak until Tomorrow: Oriki, Women and the Past in a Yoruba Town*, Washington, DC, Smithsonian Institution, 1991.

Bascom, W. R.: *Ifa Divination: Communication between Gods and Men in West Africa*, Bloomington, Indiana University Press, 1969.

Bascom, W. R.: *The Yoruba of South Western Nigeria*, Prospect Heights, Waveland Press, 1969.

Beckett, P. and Young, C. eds.: *Dilemmas of Democracy in Nigeria*. Rochester, University of Rochester Press, 1997.

Beier, U.: *Yoruba Poetry: An Anthology of Traditional Poems,* Cambridge University Press, 1970.

Beier, U.: *Yoruba Myths,* Cambridge University Press, 1980.

Biobaku, S. O.: *The Egba and Their Neighbors, 1842–1872*, Oxford, Oxford University Press, 1957.

Biobaku, S. O.: *The Origin of the Yoruba,* Lugard Lectures, Lagos, Government Printer, 1956.

Biobaku, S. O. ed.: *Sources of Yoruba History,* Oxford, Clarendon Press, 1973.

Bowen, Rev. T. J.: *Adventures and Missionary Labours in Several Countries in the Interior of Africa, 1849–1856*, Charleston, Southern Baptist Publication Society, 1857.

Burton, R.F.: *Abeokuta and the Cameroon Mountains*, London, Tinsley, 1863.

Campbell, R.: *A Pilgrimage to my Motherland: An Account of a Journey among the Egbas and Yorubas of Central Africa in 1859–1860*, New York, Thomas Hamilton, 1861.

Clapperton, Captain H.: *Journal of a Second Expedition into the Interior of Africa from the Bight of Benin to Soccatoo*, London, John Murray, 1829.

Clarke, K. M.: *Mapping Yoruba Networks: Power and Agency in the Making of Transitional Communities*, Durham, Duke University Press, 2004.

Clarke, W. H.: *Travels and Explorations in Yorubaland, 1854–1858,* ed. J. A. Atanda, Ibadan, Ibadan University Press, 1972.

Connah, G.: *African Civilizations: Precolonial Cities and States in Tropical Africa: An Archaeological Perspective*, Cambridge, Cambridge University Press, 2001.

Crowder, M. and Ikime, O. eds.: *West African Chiefs: Their Changing Status under Colonial Rule and Independence*, Ife, Ife University Press, 1970.

Crowther, Rev. S. A.: *A Grammar and Vocabulary of the Yoruba Language*, London, Seeleys, 1852.

Curtin, P.: *The Atlantic Slave Trade: A Census*, Madison, University of Wisconsin Press, 1969.

Dalzel, A.: *History of Dahomey*, Oxford, Blackwell Publishers, 1793.

Delano, I.O.: *The Soul of Nigeria*, New York, AMS Press, 1978.

Drewal, H., Pemberton, J. and Abiodun, R.: *Yoruba: Nine Centuries of African Art and Thought*, New York, Center for African Art, 1990.

Eades, J. E.: *The Yoruba Today*, Cambridge, Cambridge University Press, 1980.

Ellis, A. B.: *The Yoruba-speaking Peoples of the Slave Coast of West Africa*, London, Chapman and Hall, 1894.

Bibliography

Eltis, D.: *The Rise of African Slavery in the Americas,* Cambridge, Cambridge University Press, 1999.

Eltis, D., Richardson, D., Behrendt, S. and Klein, H.: *The Trans-Atlantic Slave Trade: A Database on CD-ROM,* Cambridge, Cambridge University Press, 1999.

Eyo, E.: *Two Thousand Years of Nigerian Art,* Lagos, Federal Department of Antiquities, 1977.

Fadipe, N. A.: *The Sociology of the Yoruba,* ed. R. D. and R. O. Okediji, Ibadan, Ibadan University Press, 1970.

Fage, J. D.: *An Atlas of African History,* London, Edward Arnold, 1970.

Falola, T.: *The Political Economy of a Precolonial African State: Ibadan, 1830–1900,* Ile-Ife, Ife University Press, 1984.

Falola, T., ed.: *Yoruba Historiography,* Madison, University of Wisconsin African Studies Program, 1991.

Falola, T.: *Yoruba Gurus: Indigenous Production of Knowledge in Africa,* Trenton, Africa World Press, 1999.

Falola, T.: *A Mouth Sweeter than Salt: An African Memoir,* Ann Arbor, University of Michigan Press, 2004.

Falola, T.: *Politics and Economy in Ibadan 1893–1945,* Lagos, Modelor Press, 1989.

Falola, T. and Adebayo, A. G.: *Culture, Politics and Money Among the Yoruba,* Somerset, Transaction/University of Rutgers, 2000.

Falola, T. and Childs, M. eds.: *The Yoruba Diaspora in the Atlantic World,* Bloomington, Indiana University Press, 2004.

Falola, T. and Jennings, C. eds.: *Sources and Methods in African History: Spoken, Written, Unearthed,* Rochester, Rochester University Press, 2003.

Fick, C.: *The Making of Haiti: The St. Domingue Revolution from Below,* Knoxville, University of Tennessee Press, 1990.

Forde, D.: *The Yoruba-speaking Peoples of Southwestern Nigeria,* London, International African Institute, 1951.

Fyfe, C. H.: *A History of Sierra Leone,* London, Oxford University Press, 1962.

Gbadamosi, T. G. O.: *The Growth of Islam among the Yoruba, 1841–1908,* New York, Humanities Press, 1978.

Henige, D. and McCaskie, T. C. eds., *West African Economic and Social History: Studies in Memory of Marion Johnson,* Madison, African Studies Program, 1990.

Hinderer, A.: *Seventeen Years in the Yoruba Country: Memorials of Anna Hinderer, Wife of David Hinderer, CMS Missionary in West Africa,* London, Seeley, Jackson & Halliday, 1872.

Hopkins, A.G.: *An Economic History of West Africa,* London, Longman, 1973.

Idowu, B.: *Olodumare: God in Yoruba Belief,* London, Longman, 1962.

Idowu, B.: *African Traditional Religion: A Definition,* London, SCM Press, 1973.

Ikime, O. ed.: *Groundwork of Nigerian History,* Ibadan, Historical Society of Nigeria, 1980.

Ikime, O. *Niger Delta Rivalry: Itsekiri–Urhobo Relations and the European Presence, 1884–1936,* London, Longman, 1977.

Inikori, J., and Engermann, S., ed.: *The Atlantic Slave Trade: Effects on Economies, Societies and Peoples,* Durham, Duke University Press, 1992.

Jimada, I. S.: *The Nupe and the Origins and Evolution of the Yoruba, c. 1275–1897,* Zaria, Abdullahi Smith Center for Historical Research, 2005.

Johnson, S.: *The History of the Yorubas from the Earliest Times to the Beginning of the British Protectorate,* Lagos, CMS (Nigeria), 1921.

Johnston, H.H.: *The Negro in the New World,* London, Methuen, 1910.

Kenyo, A.: *Founder of the Yoruba Nation,* Ibadan, Yoruba Historical Research Scheme, 1959.

Koelle, S.W.: *Polyglotta Africana,* Christian Mission Society, 1856.

Kopytoff, J. H.: *A Preface to Modern Nigeria: The "Sierra Leoneans" in Yoruba, 1830–1880,* Madison, Wisconsin University Press, 1965.

Kopytoff, I., ed.: *The African Frontier: The Reproduction of Traditional African Societies,* Bloomington, Indiana Univ. Press, 1987.

Krapf-Askari, E.: *Yoruba Towns and Cities,* Oxford, Clarendon Press, 1969.

Lander, R.: *Records of Captain Clapperton's Last Expedition to Africa,* vols. 1 and 2, London, Henry Colburn & Richard Bentley, 1830.

Lander, R. and Lander, J.: *Journal of an Expedition to Explore the Course and Termination of the Niger, with a Narrative of a Voyage Down the River,* London, Thomas Tegg & Son, 1832.

Law, R. C. C.: *The Oyo Empire, 1600–1836: A West African Imperialism in the Era of the Atlantic Slave Trade,* Oxford, Clarendon Press, 1977.

Law, R. C. C. ed.: *From Slavery to Legitimate Commerce: The Commercial Transition in Nineteenth Century West Africa,* Cambridge, Cambridge University Press, 1995.

Law, R.C.C., and Strickrod, S.: *Ports of the Slave Trade (Bights of Benin and Biafra): Papers from a Conference of the Center of Commonwealth Studies, University of Stirling, June, 1998,* Stirling, University of Stirling Center of Commonwealth Studies, 1999.

Lawal, N., Sadiku, M. and Dopemu, P. A.: *Understanding Yoruba Life and Culture,* Trenton NJ, Africa World Press, 2004.

Lloyd, P. C.: *Yoruba Land Law,* Ibadan, Oxford University Press, 1962.

Lloyd, P. C., Mabogunje, A.L., and Awe, B. eds.: *The City of Ibadan,* Cambridge, Cambridge University Press, 1967.

Lovejoy, Paul, and Falola, T.: *Pawnship, Slavery and Colonialism in Africa,* Trenton, Africa World Press, 2003.

Lucas, J.O.: *The Religion of the Yorubas,* Lagos, Christian Mission Society, 1948.

Lynch, H.R.: *Black Spokesman: Select Published Writings of H.W.Blyden,* London, Frank Cass, 1971.

Mabogunje, A.L.: *Yoruba Towns,* Ibadan, Ibadan University Press, 1962.

Mabogunje, A.L.: *Urbanization in Nigeria,* London, University of London Press, 1968.

Mabogunje, A. and Omer-Cooper, J. D.: *Owu in Yoruba History,* Ibadan, Ibadan University Press, 1971.

Moore, W.: *History of Itsekiri,* London, Stockwell Ltd., 1936.

Bibliography

Nadel, S.F.: *A Black Byzantium: The Kingdom of Nupe,* London, International African Institute, 1942.

Newbury, C.W.: *The Western Slave Coast and Its Rulers,* Oxford, Clarendon Press, 1961.

Nicolson, I. F.: *The Administration of Nigeria, 1900–1960: Men, Methods and Myths*, Oxford, Clarendon Press, 1969.

Ogundiran, A.: *Archaeology and History in Ilare District, Central Yorubaland, Nigeria, 1200–1900*, London, Cambridge Monograph in African Archaeology, No. 55, 2002.

Ogundiran, A., ed.: *Precolonial Nigeria: Essays in Honor of Toyin Falola*, Trenton, Africa World Press, 2005.

Ojo, G.J.A.: *Yoruba Culture: A Geographical Analysis,* London, University of London Press, 1967.

Ojo, G.J.A.: *Yoruba Palaces,* London, London University Press, 1966.

Olupona, J. K.: *Kingship, Religion and Rituals in a Nigerian Community: A Phenomenological Study of Ondo Yoruba Festivals*, Stockholm, Almqvist and Wiksell, 1991.

Osuntokun, A.: *Chief S. Ladoke Akintola: His Life and Times*, London, Frank Cass, 1984.

Oyebade, A. ed.: *The Foundations of Nigeria: Essays in Honor of Toyin Falola*, Trenton, Africa World Press, 2003.

Parrinder, E. G.: *The Story of Ketu. An Ancient Yoruba Kingdom*, Ibadan, Ibadan University Press, 1956.

Payne, J. A. O.: *Table of Principal Events in Yoruba History, with certain other Matters of General Interest, Compiled Principally for Use in the Courts of Lagos,* Lagos, The Author, 1893.

Peel, J. D.Y.: *Aladura: A Religious Movement among the Yoruba*, London, Oxford University Press, 1968.

Peel, J. D.Y.: *The Ijeshas and Nigerians: The Incorporation of a Yoruba Kingdom, 1890s–1970s,* Cambridge, Cambridge University Press, 1983.

Peel, J. D.Y.: *Religious Encounter and the Making of the Yoruba,* Bloomington, Indiana University Press, 2000.

Pemberton, J. and Afolayan, F.: *Yoruba Sacred Kingship: A Power like that of the Gods*, Washington, DC, Smithsonian Institution Press, 1996.

Pereira, D. P.: *Esmeraldo de Situ Orbis*, trans. G. H.T. Kimble, London, 1937.

Phillips, T. ed.: *Africa: The Art of a Continent,* London, Prestel Verlag, 1999.

Robinson, R.: *An Unbroken Agony: Haiti from Revolution to the Kidnapping of a President*, New York, Civitas Books, 2007.

Rodney, W.: *A History of the Upper Guinea Coast, 1545–1800*, Oxford, Clarendon Press, 1970.

Sarduy, P. P. and Stubbs, J. eds.: *Afro-Cuban Voices: On Race and Identity in Contemporary Cuba*, Gainesville, University of Florida Press, 2000.

Schwartz, S. B.: *Sugar Plantations in the Formation of Brazilian Society*, Bahia, Cambridge University Press, 1985.

Shaw, T.: *Lectures on Nigerian Prehistory and Archaeology*, Ibadan, University of Ibadan Press, 1975.

Shaw, T.: *Nigeria: Its Archaeology and Early History*, London, Thames & Hudson, 1978.

Shinnie, P.: *The African Iron Age,* Oxford, Clarendon Press, 1971.

Smith, R. S.: *Kingdoms of the Yoruba*, London, Methuen, 1969.

Smith, R. S.: *Warfare and Diplomacy in Precolonial West Africa,* London, James Currey, 1989.

Soyinka, W.: *Myth, Literature and the African World*, Cambridge, Cambridge University Press, 1962.

Soyinka, W.: *You Must Set Forth at Dawn*, New York, Random House, 2007.

Stevens, P.: *The Stone Images of Esie,* New York, Africana Publishing, 1978.

Thornton, J.: *Africa and Africans in the Making of the Atlantic World, 1400–1680,* Cambridge, Cambridge University Press, 1992.

Trager, L.: *Yoruba Hometowns: Community, Identity and Development in Nigeria*, Boulder, Lynne Reinner Publishers, 2001.

Usman, A.: *State–Periphery Relations and Socio-political Development in Igbominaland, Nigeria,* BAR International Series, (Hedges Ltd and Archaeopress, 2001).

Vansina, J., Mauny, R., and Thomas, L.: *The Historian in Tropical Africa*, Oxford, Published for the International African Institute by Oxford University Press, 1964.

Walker, Sheila S.: *African Roots/American Culture: Africa in the Creation of the Americas,* New York, Rowman & Littlefield, 2001.

Webster, J. B.: *African Churches among the Yoruba, 1888–1922*, Oxford, Clarendon Press, 1964.

Wesler, K.: *Historical Archaeology in Nigeria,* Trenton, Africa World Press, 1998.

Willett, F.: *Ife in the History of West African Sculpture*, London, Thames & Hudson, 1967.

Zerbo, J. K. ed.: *General History of Africa 1: Methodology and Prehistory*, Paris, UNESCO, 1981.

Local History

Abiola, J. D. E., Babafemi, J. A. and Ataiyero, S. O. S.: *Iwe Itan Ilesa*, Lagos, CMS Press, 1932.

Adeleke, W.: *Iwe Itan Ilu Iseyin*, Iseyin, 1962.

Ademakinwa, J. A.: *Ife, Cradle of the Yoruba*, Lagos, 1958.

Adeyemi, M. C.: *Ondo Kingdom: Its History and Culture*, Ibadan, Bounty Press, 1993.

Aguda, Chief: *A Brief History of the Central Mosque, Lagos*, Lagos, n.d.

Ajisafe, A. K.: *History of Abeokuta*, London, Richard Clay, 1924.

Aluko-Oluokun, N.: *Ondo Kingdom, Its History and Culture,* Ibadan, 1993.

Akindoju, S. A. and Olagundoye, D. O.: *History of Idanre*, Ibadan, 1952.

Akinyele, I. B.: *Iwe Itan Ibadan*, Ibadan, 1911.

Apena M. B. Okubote: *Iwe Ikekuru ti Itan Ijebu*, Ibadan, 1937.

Asabia, D. O. and Adegbesan, J. O.: *Idoani Past and Present*, Ibadan, 1979.

Ashara, M. B.: *The History of Owo*, Owo, 1952.

Avoseh, T. O.: *A Sort History of Epe*, Epe, 1960.

Avoseh, T. O.: *The History of Badagry*, Badagry, 1960.

Bada of Saki, Ojo, S.O.: *Iwe Itan Ondo*, Ondo, 1940.
Babamboni, I. E.: *Itan Ewi, Elekole ati Ajero*, Ado-Ekiti, n.d.
Dada, P. O. A.: *A Brief History of Igbomina*, Ilorin, Matanmi Press, 1985.
Egharevba, J. U.: *A Short History of Benin*, Ibadan, Ibadan University Press, 1960.
Epega, Rev. D. O.: *Iwe Itan Ijebu ati awon Ilu Miran*, Lagos, 1934.
Kenyo, E. A.: *Yoruba Natural Rulers and their Origin*, Ibadan, Yoruba Historical Research Company, 1964.
Laotan, A. B.: *The Torch Bearers or Old Brazilian Colony in Lagos*, Lagos, 1943.
Leigh, J. A.: *History of Ondo*, Ondo, 1917.
Losi, J. B. O.: *The History of Lagos*, Lagos, Tika Tore Press, 1914.
Ogundeji, J. O. A.: *Itan Ilu Iwo*, Kano, n.d.
Oguntuyi, A.: *A Short History of Ado-Ekiti*, Akure, The Author, 1957.
Oguntuyi, A.: *History of Ekiti from the Beginning to 1939*, Ibadan, Caxton Press, 1979.
Ojo, S.O.: *A Short History of Ilorin*, Oyo, 1957.
Olomola, I.: *A Thousand Years of Ado History and Culture*, Ado-Ekiti, Omolayo Press, 1984.
Oyerinde, N. D.: *Iwe Itan Ogbomosho*, Jos, 1934.

Journal Articles

Abiodun, R.: "A Reconstruction of the Function of Ako, Second Burial Effigy, in Owo," *Africa: Journal of the International African Institute*, 46, 1, 1976, 4–20.
Oba Adegoriola, the Ogoga of Ikere: "A Note on the Administration of Ikere before the Advent of the British," *Odu: Journal of Yoruba and Related Studies*, 3, 19–24.
Adepegba, C.: "Ife Art: An Enquiry into the Surface Patterns and the Continuity of Art Tradition among the Northern Yoruba," *West African Journal of Archaeology*, 12, 1982, 95–109.
Afolayan, F.: "Colonial Rule and Anti-Fulani Revolts among the Igbomina," *Odu: Journal of Yoruba and Related Studies*, 36, 1989, 24–42.
Agbaje-Williams, B.: "The Discovery of Koso, an Ancient Oyo Settlement," *The Nigerian Field*, 54, 1989, 123–127.
Agbaje-Williams, B.: "Oyo Ruins of NW Yorubaland," *Journal of Field Archaeology*, 17, 3, 1990, 367–373.
Agbaje-Williams, B.: "Potsherd Pavements and Early Urban Centers in Yorubaland," *The Nigerian Field*, 66, 2001, 92–104.
Agbaje-Williams, B.: "Estimating the Population of Old Oyo," *Odu*, New Series, 30, 1986, 3–24.
Ajayi, J. F. A.: "How Yoruba Was Reduced to Writing," *Odu: Journal of Yoruba and Related Studies*, 8, 1960, 49–58.
Ajayi, J. F. A.: "Samuel Johnson, Historian of the Yoruba," *Nigeria Magazine*, 81, 1964, 141–6.
Akinjogbin, I. A.: "The Prelude to the Yoruba Civil Wars of the Nineteenth Century," *Odu: Journal of Yoruba and Related Studies*, 1, 2, 1965, 24–46.

Akinjogbin, I. A.: "A Chronology of Yoruba History, 1789–1840," *Odu: Journal of Yoruba and Related Studies,* 2, 2, 1966, 81–111.

Akinjogbin, I. A.: "The Oyo Empire in the 18th Century: A Reassessment," *Journal of Historical Society of Nigeria,* 3, 3, 1966, 449–60.

Akintoye, S. A.: "Ife's Sad Century: The Nineteenth Century in the History of Ife," *Nigeria Magazine,* 104, 1970.

Akintoye, S. A.: "The Ondo Road, Eastwards of Lagos, 1870–1895," *Journal of African History,* 10, 4, 1969, 581–598.

Akintoye, S. A.: "The Northeastern Yoruba Districts and the Benin Kingdom," *Journal of the Historical Society of Nigeria,* 4, 4, 1969, 539–53.

Alabi, R. A.: "Environment and Subsistence of the Early Inhabitants of the Badagry Area of Southwestern Nigeria," *African Archaeological Review,* 19, 4, 2002, 183–201.

Alagoa, E. J.: "Long Distance Trade and States in the Niger Delta," *Journal of African History,* 11, 3, 1970, 319–29.

Andah, B. W.: "Iron Age Beginnings in West Africa: Reflections and Suggestions," *West African Journal of Archaeology,* 9, 1979, 135–50.

Andah, B. W.: "Agricultural Beginnings and Early Farming Communities in West and Central Africa," *West African Journal of Archaeology,* 17, 1987, 171–204.

Apata, Z. O.: "British rule and Protest Movements in Northern Nigeria, 1900–01," *Trans-African Journal of History,* 25, 1996, 225–50.

Apata, Z. O.: "Administrative Integration and Conflict in Nigeria, 1840–1940: The Case of Northeast Yorubaland," *Trans-African Journal of History,* 24, 1995, 106–22.

Arkell, A. J., Fagan, B., and Summers, R.: "The Iron Age in Sub-Saharan Africa," *Current Anthropology,* 7, 1966, 1–9.

Atanda, J. A.: "The Yoruba Ogboni Cult: Did It Exist in Old Oyo?" *Journal of the Historical Society of Nigeria,* 6, 4, 1973, 365–71.

Babayemi, S. O.: The Oyo, Ife and Benin Relationship Reconsidered," *African Notes,* 8, 2, 1981, 15–26.

Bascom, W. R.: "The Esusu: A Credit Institution of the Yoruba," *Journal of the Royal Anthropological Institute,* 82, 1, 1952, 63–9.

Beier, U.: "Before Oduduwa," *Odu: Journal of Yoruba and Related Studies,* 3, 1956, 25–32.

Eluyemi, O: "The Technology of the Ife Glass Beads: Evidence from the Igbo Olokun," *Odu: Journal of Yoruba and Related Studies,* new series, 32, 1987, 200–216.

Falola, T.: "The Yoruba Toll System," *Journal of African History,* 30, 1, 1989, 41–63.

Falola, T.: "The Yoruba Caravan System in the 19th Century," *The International Journal of African Historical Studies,* 24, 1, 1991, 111–32.

Falola, T.: "Migrant Settlers in Ife Society, 1830-1960," *The Calabar Historical Journal,* 3, 1, 1985, 18–35.

Falola, T.: The Foreign Policy of Ibadan in the Nineteenth Century," *Odu,* 22, 1982, 91–108.

Fatunsin, A. K.: "Ifetedo: A Late Stone Age Site in the Forest Region of Southwestern Nigeria," *West African Journal of Archaeology,* 26, 1996, 71–87.

Garlake, P.: "Excavations at Obalara's Land, Ife, Nigeria," *West African Journal of Archaeology*, 4, 1974, 111–48.

Garlake, P.: "Excavations on the Woye Asiri Family Land in Ife, Western Nigeria," *West African Journal of Archaeology*, 7, 1977, 57–95.

Hopkins, A. G.: "Economic Imperialism in West Africa: Lagos, 1880–92," *The Economic History Review*, New Series, 21, 3, 1968, 580–606.

Horton, R.: "Ancient Ife: A Reassessment," *Journal of Historical Society of Nigeria*, 6, 4, 1976, 69–185.

Iliffe, J.: "Poverty in 19th Century Yorubaland," *Journal of African History*, 25, 1984, 43–57.

Law, R. C. C.: "The Heritage of Oduduwa: Traditional History and Political Propaganda among the Yoruba," *Journal of African History*, 14, 2, 1973, 207–22.

Law, R. C. C.: "The Owu War in Yoruba History," *Journal of the Historical Society of Nigeria*, 7, 1, 1973, 141–7.

Law, R. C. C.: "Slaves, Trade and Taxes: The Material Basis of Political Power in Precolonial West Africa," *Research in Economic Anthropology*, 1, 1978, 37–52.

Law, R. C. C.: "Trade and Politics Behind the Slave Coast: The Lagoon Traffic and the Rise of Lagos, 1500-1800," *Journal of African History*, 24, 1989, 343–48.

Lloyd, P. C.: "The Yoruba Lineage," *Africa*, 25, 1955, 235–51.

Lloyd, P. C.: "Sacred Kingship and Government among the Yoruba," *Africa*, 30, 1960, 231–7.

Lowe, V. G.: "The Unlikely Ambassador," *Charisma*, Sept. 30, 2007, Cover story.

Manning, P.: "Contours of Slavery and Social Change in Africa," *American Historical Review*, 88, 4, 1983, 834–57.

Mason, M.: "Jihad in the South: An Outline of the 19th Century Nupe Hegemony in Northeastern Yorubaland and Afenmai," in *Journal of the Historical Society of Nigeria*, 5, 2, 1970, 195.

Matory, L.: "The English Professors of Brazil: On the Diasporic Roots of the Yoruba Nation," *Comparative Studies in Society and History*, 41, 1, 1999, 72–103.

May, D. J.: "Journey in the Yoruba and Nupe Countries in 1858," *Journal of the Royal Geographical Society*, 30, 1860, 212–33.

Morton-Williams, P.: "The Yoruba Ogboni Cult in Oyo," *Africa*, 30, 4, 1960, 364–73.

Ogundiran, A.: "Filling a Gap in Ife–Benin Interaction Field (AD 13th–16th Centuries): Excavations and Material Culture in Iloyi Settlement, Ijeshaland," *African Archaeological Review*, 19, 1, 2002, 27–60.

Ogundiran, A.: "Of Small Things Remembered: Beads, Cowries and Cultural Translations of the Atlantic Experience in Yorubaland," *International Journal of African Historical Studies*, 35, 2–3, 2002, 427–57.

Oyelaran, P. A.: "Early Settlement and Archaeological Sequence of Northeast Yorubaland," *African Archaeological Review*, 15, 1998, 65–79.

Ozanne, P.: "A New Archaeological Survey of Ife," *Odu: Journal of Yoruba and Related Studies*, new series, 1, 1969.

Parrinder, G.: "Yoruba-speaking Peoples in Dahomey," *Africa*, 17, 2, 1947, 122–9.

Ryder, A. F. C.: "A Reconsideration of the Ife–Benin Relationship," *Journal of African History*, 6, 1, 1965, 25–37.
Shaw, T. and Daniels, S. G. H.: "Excavations at Iwo Eleru, Ondo State of Nigeria," *West African Journal of Archaeology*, 14, 1984, ix-xiv.
Smith, R. S.: "Yoruba Armament," *Journal of African History*, 8, 1, 1967, 87–106.
Soper, R. and Darling, P.: "The Walls of Old Oyo," *West African Journal of Archaeology*, 10, 1980, 61-81.
Sowunmi, M. A.: "The Significance of the Oil Palm in the Late Holocene Environment of West and Westcentral Africa: Further Consideration," *Vegetation History and Archaeology*, 8, 1999, 199–210.
Tylecote, R.: "Iron Smelting at Taruga, Nigeria," *Journal of Historical Metallurgy Society*, 9, 1975, 49–56.
Usman, A.: "A View from the Periphery: Northern Yoruba Villages during the Old Oyo Empire," *Journal of Field Archaeology*, 27, 1, 2000, 43–61.
Willett, F.: "Investigations at old Oyo, 1956–57: An Interim Report," *Journal of Historical Society of Nigeria*, 2, 1, 1960, 59–77.
Willett, F.: "Ife and its Archaeology," *Journal of African History*, 6, 1960, 231–48.
Willett, F.: "On the Funeral Effigies in Owo and Benin and the Interpretation of the Life-size Bronze Heads from Ife," *Man*, n.s., 1, 1966, 34–45.

Unpublished Material

Adebanwi, W.: "Yoruba Vision," paper presented in the Yoruba Retreat, Ibadan, October 26–29, 2007.
Afolayan, F. S.: "External Relations and Socio-Political Transformation in Precolonial Igbomina," Ph.D. Thesis, Obafemi Awolowo University, Ile-Ife, Nigeria, 1991.
Aremu, D.: "The Archaeology of Northeast Yorubaland, Kwara State, with Emphasis on Early Techniques of Metal Working," Ph.D. thesis, University of Ibadan, 1990.
Awe, B.: "The Rise of Ibadan," D.Phil. thesis, University of Oxford, 1964.
Ayantuga, F.: "Ijebu and Its Neighbors, 1851–1914," Ph.D. thesis, University of London, 1965.
Eyo, E.: "Recent Excavations at Ife and Owo and their Implications for Ife, Owo and Benin Studies," Ph.D. thesis, University of Ibadan, 1974.
Olugbadehan, O.: "Owo, A Frontier Yoruba Kingdom," PhD thesis, Union Institute and University, Cincinnati, Ohio, 2006.

Index

A

aaro, owe 182, 190, 274, 371
aba 157
Abacha, Sani 419–422
Abbas, Seriki 392
Abeokuta 56, 228, 294, 297, 300, 304, 319, 326, 340, 354, 447
  Ibadan–Abeokuta battles 300
abiku 30,
Abilagba 123
Abiodun, Alaafin 152, 237–238, 254, 297
Abiodun, Rowland 52, 204
Abiola, J. D. 449
Abiola, M. K. O. 418–421, 423
Abipa, Alaafin of Oyo 5–6, 12, 19, 36, 158, 237
Abodi 107
abolition of slavery 291, 378, 382
Abomey 246
Abubakar, Abdulsalam 420–422
abule 89, 157, 168
Action Group (AG) 394, 401–409, 419
adahunse 20, 35–36, 73, 152, 272–274, 442
Ade Ajayi, J. F. A 5, 33, 350, 449
Adebanwi, Wale 425–426
Adebayo, Adeyinka 412
Adebayo, Cornelius 426
Adebo, Alaafin 275
Adediran, Abiodun 53, 89
Adegbenro, Dauda 408
Adegbite, Lateef 426
Adekunle, Benjamin 413
Adelaja, Sunday 441

Ademiyewo Fidipote, Awujale of Ijebu 150, 168, 315, 318
Adepoju, Olanrewaju 427
Adeyemi, M. C. 449
adire 444
Ado Kingdom 88, 99, 120, 126, 138–139, 145, 147–148, 184, 196, 214, 244, 309, 312
Ado–Ikere feud 143
Aduloju, Ado Ekiti 310–317, 331, 390
Afenmai 10, 101, 143, 164, 210–212, 222, 322
Afolayan, Funso 151
Afonja of Ilorin 101, 171, 185, 198–199, 205–206, 213–214, 221–222, 229, 231–232, 240, 245–246, 272, 296, 301, 325, 337
Afonja's death and the Ilorin Emirate 171, 282–284
African-American cultures 367–368
African-Americans 248, 254, 367–368, 385, 448
African Church Movement 438–439, 447
African Studies 20, 72, 99, 255, 261
Afrocubanismo 376–377
Agbaakin 72, 243
Agbebi, Mojola (D. B. Vincent) 446, 450
agbo-ile 20–25, 36–40, 45, 47, 51–52, 69, 70, 172, 187, 298, 334, 435–436
Agboluaje, Alaafin 262
Agboniregun 35, 69
age-grade associations 35–37, 127–128, 187, 190, 311
Agemo 49, 233

Agiri, Babatunde 49, 88
Agirilogbon 109
Ago-Iwoye 6
Agricultural Revolution 5
agriculture 165–169, 306, 344, 351
　new crops from the Americas 351
Aguiyi Ironsi, Johnson 410–411
Agwuele, Augustine 385–386
Ahori 107
Airo 107–108
Aiyede, Ekiti 303
Aja 108, 123, 171, 246, 321, 359–360, 365–369, 376–381
Ajagbo, Alaafin 162, 241, 274
Ajaka, Alaafin 84
Ajase (Porto Novo) 77, 155, 253
Ajasin, Adekunle Michael 416, 419, 431
Ajayi Jegede (Ogboriefon), Balogun 316–317
Ajele 252, 302, 304–306, 316
Ajiboyede, Alaafin 251
Ajisafe, A. K. 450
ajo, akojo 187
Akalako 109
Akarigbo 112
Ake 109, 323
akewi 427
Akija 8
Akindayomi, Josiah 441
Akindein, Basorun 242
Akinjide, Richard 416
Akinjogbin, Adeagbo 84, 88, 268
Akintola, Samuel Ladoke 403–409, 411, 416, 431
Akitoye, Oba of Lagos 359
ako 77
Akodu, Seriki of Egba 354
akojo 187
Akoko 109–110, 150, 168, 187, 322, 311, 314
Akoko wars 390
akoro 111
Akran 111
Aksum 17, 48

Akure 4, 7, 14–15, 99, 101, 120, 133, 138–139, 146, 152, 158, 162, 164, 414
Akus 383–385
Alaafin of Oyo 15, 118
Alabama 385
Alade-Ife, Agbolawoluowe, Alaketu 386
Aladesanmi II, Ewi of Ado-Ekiti 393–394
Aladura Movement 439–441
　Apostolic Church 439
　Celestial Church of Christ 440
　Cherubim and Seraphim Church 439
　Church of the Lord 439
Alagoa, E. J. 48, 105,
alajapa 159
alajo 9
Alaka-aiye 73, 187
Alake of Egbaland 112, 249, 297, 329
　emergence of Alake seniority 329
Alaketu 88, 96, 113, 386, 389
Alale 15, 67
Alana, Olu 32
Alapini 250
alarinjo 159, 167, 187, 190, 194
alarobo 159, 167, 187, 191
Alayemore, Obalufon 49
Alimi 278–280, 282–285, 335–338
Allada 171, 246, 278
Alliance for Democracy (AD) 422–423
Amaros 383
Americas 326, 342, 365, 383
Amodo, Alaafin 171
Anago 366
Anglican Mission 271, 348, 352–356, 438, 446, 447
Anglo-French Agreement 360
Anglo-French rivalry 359
Angola 150, 366
Anosin 29–30
apebi 28
are 63
Apomu 142, 295, 296
Aponte, Jose Antonio 377
Ara 69, 309
Ara War 142–143

Index

archaeology 2, 4–6, 8, 14, 15, 17, 51–52, 67, 449
  Igbo-ukwu 21, 52–53
  Itaogbolu 4
  Iwo Eleru 4, 7
  Obalara 50
  Taruga 17, 18
Aremo 161, 308
Are Ona Kakanfo 50, 243, 299–300, 307–309, 314
Ariyo, Ayo 413
arms and ammunition 242, 296, 304, 310–318, 320, 373–379, 390
Aro (of Ilaro) 8
art 83, 368, 452
  funeral 146
  murals 110–111
  periods in Yoruba art 20–25, 52–56, 78–79, 198–201, 204, 326–327, 345–346, 369–370, 376–377, 381–386, 426–428, 448–450
  sculptural art 24–25
ase 274
Ashamu, Basorun 229
Ashanti 222
Ashara, M. B. 222, 449
Asheru, Benin chief 249
Asipa 243
Asipa, king of Lagos 222
Asiri, Woye 50
Asiwaju, Anthony 388
aso-ofi 444
Asunlola Ojugbelu, Omolaghaye 266
Atiba, Alaafin 299, 308
Atewogboye 310
Atundaolu, H. 449
Audu Bida 322
Avoseh, Theophilus Olabode 449
Awole, Alaafin 295
Awolowo, Obafemi 403–425, 431, 437
  emergence as leader 410
  treason trials 408
Awori 8, 300–301, 305, 327, 360, 402
Awujale of Ijebu-Ode 295, 315, 318–319, 392
Ayandele, E.A. 447

Ayorinde, Chief 304, 313, 331
Azikiwe, Nnamdi 402

B

Baale of Igbogun 273–277
Baba-kekere 398
babalawo 10, 33–34, 73 110–111, 161, 167, 362, 377, 442, 444
Babangida, Ibrahim 418, 419, 421
Babylon 56
Badagry 4, 10, 169, 113, 116–117, 144, 164, 171, 172, 176, 327, 334–335, 346–348, 352, 360, 449
Bada of Saki 274
Bada, Samuel Ojo 449
Bahia 366–367, 369–375, 377, 380, 383, 385
balekale 219
Baptist Mission 166, 218, 346, 353, 438, 446, 447
Barbados 366
Barber, Karin 121, 243
Barbot, J. 217
Bariba 3, 11, 259, 288, 338, 346
Basorun 242, 298
Bata music 257
beaded products 153
beads 51, 68, 76, 77, 84, 187, 444
Bebe 249
Before Oduduwa 11, 43–54
Beier, Ulli 11, 100
beliefs 33
  afterlife 34, 35
  babalawo 33
  epade 34
  ere 13
  erele 13
  Igboere 13
  ipade 31
  Ogunladin 8, 56
  ore 39
  witchcraft 31, 74, 113, 171
Belarus 441
Bello, Ahmadu 411
Benin kingdom 48–49, 66, 75, 80–81, 88, 90, 100, 102–107, 110, 117,

141–147, 152, 160–168, 170–171, 196–197, 210–332
Benin and Akure linkages 146
Benin and Oduduwa linkages 117
Benin and Owo linkages 212–213
Benin–Lagos linkages 222–223
Benin Republic 2, 10, 112, 366, 386–389, 429, 434, 451
Biafra 411–414
  Civil War 413–414
  Midwest occupation 413
Bickersteth, Edward 352
Bight of Benin 153, 161, 171, 229, 366, 473
Bight of Biafra 171
Biobaku, Saburi 39, 172, 245, 275, 449
blacksmiths 25, 40, 50, 444
Black Studies 231
Blyden, Edward Wilmot 446
body tattoo 153
Bonny 171, 355
Borgu 48, 113, 229
Bornu 333
Bowen, T. J. 346
Bower, R. L. 361, 391
Brazil 347, 351, 366–375, 383
British 303, 312–313, 318, 320–323, 328–331, 343, 347–348, 351–352, 354–355, 359–362, 368, 381–383, 387–402, 404–407, 429–432, 445–448
  amalgamation of Nigeria 397
  annexation of Lagos 312, 347, 351, 354, 359, 430
  attack on Oyo 391
  invasion of Benin 361
  military expedition into Ijebu 360
  colonial rule in Nigeria 389
brass 49, 52, 64, 69, 77–79, 141–142, 171, 197, 204, 256, 444
bronze 17–18, 52–53, 69, 77–79, 126, 142, 197–198, 204, 211, 223, 256
Buhari–Idiagbon coup 418
Buhari, Muhammadu 418

C

cabildos de nación 376–377
Candomblé 369–376
cantos 371–374
Carthage 17
cavalry 15, 37, 210, 288, 292, 301–302, 322, 337
Central Africa 171
Central America 4, 385
Central Kingdoms 97
central West Africa 230
central Yorubaland 37, 49
Chango 377
checks and balances 266
Chesapeake Bay 366
Chief Osagwe 220
chieftaincy 56, 121–129, 312, 330, 390, 396, 436–437, 442
chieftaincy installation 1
Christian evangelism 445
"Christian gentleman" 446
Christianity 55, 291, 326, 333, 347–348, 354–356, 362–363, 382, 384, 429, 436–443, 447–448
  coming of Christianity 332, 352–359
Christian missions 55, 169, 291, 332, 351, 353–354, 383, 429, 438, 445, 447
Christian mission schools 5, 389, 430
Christian Ogboni Society (Fraternity) 438, 447–448
Church Missionary Society (CMS) 320, 324, 348, 350, 355
cities 256
city kingdoms
  government 121, 1
  seniority 121
  Ilu-alade, royal city 119
  urban-dwelling 119–120
city walls 134–136
  adena 204
  bode 135
  Onibode 135
  yara (*odi*) 135
Clapperton, Hugh 163, 334, 338, 346, 350
Clarke, William H. 136, 324, 345–346
clothing 385, 444, 446, 448
clothing industry 61, 444
cocoa 404

Cocoa Marketing Board 434
Coker, G. B. 408
Cola acuminata (obi abata) 5, 46–47, 49, 157
Cola garcinia (orogbo) 46–47, 49, 157
Cola nitida (gooro) 5, 49, 344
Colony and Protectorate of Nigeria 397
commerce 51, 159, 183, 298, 345
   alajapa, long distance traders 169–170
   commercial advantages 169
   the rise of Yoruba coastal towns 162
commodity associations 138, 166, 187
conflict of "201" years 61
Congo 159, 171, 365–366, 368, 376
Conspiracy of La Escalera 377
Copper 17–18, 53, 69, 77, 183, 214, 256
Copper/Bronze Age 17
cosmology 1, 31, 34, 384
   aye 31
   orun 31, 78
Costa Rica 366
cotton 25–28, 37, 156–157, 159, 165, 186, 190, 198–199, 265, 344, 367, 444
cowry 26, 50, 170–171
Creole cultures 367–368, 380–381
Creole language 380–381
crown 28, 68, 74–77, 82–84, 112, 123, 142, 153–154, 186, 195, 197, 236, 393, 398
Crowther, Samuel Ajayi 209, 347–350, 352–356, 402, 438
Cuba 347, 366, 375–377, 383, 385, 364
cultural nationalism 358, 363, 402, 445–451, 446–448, 450
culture 1, 3–5, 298, 325–327, 330, 335, 339, 342, 346, 351, 357, 365, 368–369, 373, 376–385, 404, 420, 421, 425–427, 436, 439, 443–451

D

Dada, P. O. 449
Dado 293, 294, 299
Dahomey 112, 170, 247, 295, 301, 320, 321, 325, 327, 328, 351, 354, 359, 360, 362, 365–369, 378, 387–388, 392, 429
Dahomey revolt 286

Dalzel, Archibald 255, 217
Dapper, Olfert 169–170, 217–218, 375
dasiki 385, 444
decline of the Alaafinate 271
Deji Osupa, Akure 216–220
Delta Province 401
Dessalines, Jean-Jacques 378
de Verteuil, Louis Antoine Aimé 368, 386
dialects 6, 8, 10–11, 92, 104, 110, 125, 169, 211, 362
Diascoria latifolia (yam) 5
Diaspora 30, 365–386
District Officer 392–393
divinations 30, 370–371
domestic slavery 174, 176, 328
   eru system 176
   iwofa system 176
Dominican Republic 366
Drewal, Henry 52
Drewal, Pemberton and Abiodun 52, 204
Dutch 111, 171

E

early settlements
   Iloran 14, 44
   Okeoja, Odin, Ideta, Iloromu, Iwinrin, Oke-Awo, Ijugbe, Iraye, Imojubi, and Ido, Ita Yemoo, Ilara, Orun, Oba Ado, Idio 44
   Omologun 44
   Parakin 14, 44, 63
Early Stone Age 4
early Yoruba society 17–41
Eastern Region 400
ebi 70
Ebira 6, 322
ebo 382
Ebumawe 109
Ebute-Metta 110, 354
economic development 37, 155–178, 409, 414, 429, 432, 452
   commerce 51, 158, 159, 186, 190, 298, 326, 343, 345, 363, 367, 431, 435, 445
   dye industry 29, 37, 47, 444
   eighteenth century 179–203

European coastal trade 155
farm types 157–158
impact of the Atlantic Slave Trade 170–175
indigo 157
livestock 157
manufactures 158
palm oil 8, 9, 11, 33, 25, 155–157,
palm wine 25, 37, 47, 156, 182, 186
patterns in internal trade 162, 3
role of agriculture 155, 179–181
role of market tolls and taxes 179
royal finances 179, 9
salt industry 156, 35
topography 156
edan 64
Ede 58, 59, 90, 110–112, 300, 326, 340, 347
Edegi, Tsoede, Nupe 209, 237
Edo 3, 6, 8, 10, 33, 50, 75, 80, 90, 93, 103, 107, 141–142, 147, 160, 170, 211–224, 314, 365, 368, 401
education 333, 396, 413, 429
Efunseyitan Aniwura 298, 344, 346
Egba 8, 9, 11, 108, 111–114, 139, 144, 157, 162, 177, 197, 204, 269, 275, 293, 294, 296, 297, 300, 312, 315, 323, 325–327, 329, 339–340, 347–348, 352, 354, 359, 375, 401, 449
  Egba Agura (Gbagura), Egba Oke-Ona, Egba Agbeyin 111, 82
  Egba Agbeyin 28
  Egba Olorogun 274
Egbado 8, 9, 90, 110–112, 177, 206, 221, 245, 252, 286, 298, 300–301, 315, 320, 325–329, 335, 338, 340, 359, 392
  Erinja, Ilobi, Ilaro, Ijana, Ketu, Sabe, Popo 112
Egba revolt 274–275
Egbe Afenifere 419
Egbedi 390
Egbe Omo Oduduwa 394, 403, 448
Egharevba, Jacob 103, 107, 221
Egun 11

Egungun 12, 128, 152–153, 173, 354
egun, *eguru* 14
Egypt 56, 79
eighteenth century 107, 140, 155–203
Ejigimogun, Obalufon 81–83
Ekiti 12, 99, 100, 140, 298, 302–307, 309–322, 325–328, 334–335, 339, 341, 346, 347, 351, 353–354, 361, 390, 392–393, 397–399, 401–402, 414, 431–433, 442, 449
  Ado, Ikere, Ise, Emure, Akure, Ogotun, Efon, Ara, Ijero, Otun, Ido, Ikole, Ishan, Oye, Itaji, Aiyede, Obo, Omuo 99–100
Ekitiparapo Association 318
Ekitiparapo Confederacy 316–322, 331, 351, 360–361
Eko 110, 111, 161, 221
eku 25, 29
Eku Apa 115
Ekun Osi 252, 299, 307
Ekun Otun 252, 299, 307
Ekusi Hill 226
Elefene 28
Elempe 232
Elesun 82
eleventh century 17
Eltis, David 368, 376
elu, erele, ore 12–20, 26, 34, 39–41, 44, 52, 54, 60, 62, 87, 91–92, 99, 121
Eluyemi, Omotoso 10
emigration 297, 383
emirate system 330, 391, 398
Emure 99, 148, 213
eni orisa 239
entertainers 70, 152, 153, 173, 259, 261, 426
Epe 107, 109, 149, 162, 341, 449
epidemics 12, 58, 59, 286
Epo (Osun) 280
Eredo 135
ereko 140, 180
erele 13
eru 174–176, 215
Eruwa 112
Esie 115, 204, 303

Esinminrin Stream 58, 61
esisun 82
"esoteric sciences" 74
Eso 238, 242–243, 251
Esperanza Felix 348
Esu 32
Esugbayibi 169, 303, 310, 311, 312, 327, 331
esusu 184, 187, 189–191, 372
Ethiopia 17,
Etsu Jibrilu 263
Etsu Majiya I 263
eunuchs 251
European exploration of the Yoruba interior 346
European imperialism 359–362
European territorial scramble 321
European trade 10, 50, 51, 156, 160–163, 194, 222, 296
Ewi Aladesanmi, Ado-Ekiti 154
Ewi Amonaola 144
Ewuare, Oba of Benin
 Oduduwa lineage 117
ewura 5
export trade 161, 171, 327, 435
Eyemode 145, 147

F

Fabunmi, Isola 74, 152, 175, 315, 317, 319, 449
facial marks 153, 173, 369, 383
Fagunwa, D. O. 450
Fajembola, Egosi 311, 312, 390
Falae, Olu 422
Falola, Toyin 449
Faseun, Frederick 419
Father Columbin of Nantes 46, 259
Federal Government of Nigeria 401–413, 417, 420, 434–435
festivals 46, 369
 Alile 167
 Ayan 167
 Bebe 249, 259, 262
 Egungun 128, 167
 Idiroko 145
 Oitado festival 442

fifteenth century 111
First World War 432
Florida 366
folklore 3, 19, 22, 25, 31, 33, 35, 37, 43, 66, 74, 90, 114, 145, 152, 203, 224, 368, 376, 383, 385, 449–451.
folktales 29–30, 37, 368, 385, 449
Fon 9, 112, 205, 319, 321
Foster, G. B. 356
Fourah Bay College 348
fourteenth century 14, 75, 85, 119, 148, 174, 207, 212, 333
fraternities 376
Free Primary Education Program 413, 417, 430, 431
French 79, 159, 165, 169–171, 321, 325, 328, 357, 359, 360, 378–381, 387–389, 392, 429
French administration 325, 328, 357, 359, 388, 429
Frobenius, Leo 79, 234
frontier effect 205–228
 Benin effect and invasions 211–224
 Eastern frontier 210–224
 Northern frontier 206–210
 Southern frontier 221–225
 Western frontier 205–206
Fulani 201, 299
Fulani jihadists 285
funerals 34, 46, 77, 129, 182, 187, 192, 235, 384, 393, 443

G

Gabu 217, 218
Gaha, Basorun 254, 261–271, 274, 278
Galway, H. L. 217–218
ganho 371
Gao 48
Garlake, P. 50
Gbadamosi, T. 339, 430, 436
Gbadegesin, Segun 425
gbagede 134
Gbagura 11, 29
Gbagyi 6, 227, 287
gbariye 444
Gbe 10

Gbedegi 209
gbedu drums 195, 227, 287
Geebuu 135
gender
  Anosin 29, 33
  Osin 29
gender authority 29, 30, 47, 70, 81, 126, 128
  female chieftaincy 126
  Olokun 70
  obirin-ile 128
  titled wife 128
  titled wife of the king 126
  women rulers 126
gender economy
  idi-aro 158
  women porters 183–184
George, J. O. 449
Georgia 366
German 56, 222, 350, 359–360, 387, 432
Ghana 49, 161, 196
girls 22, 145, 166, 184, 203
glass 51, 68, 77, 186, 202
gobi 257
goddess 31–32, 68, 73, 105
  Aiyelala 105–106
  Olokun 68, 369
  Yemoja 363
gods 18, 40, 362, 384
  Elefon 442
  Ifa 32–36, 41, 59, 67, 73–74, 88, 98–99, 102, 115, 131, 141, 144, 189, 206, 329, 354, 369, 371, 377
  Ogun 131
  Orisateko 47, 81–82
  Osin-mole 31
  Sango 73, 131, 233, 235, 238, 251, 257, 265–266, 354, 369, 382, 385
God's Embassy 441
Goldsworthy, Roger 313
"go to sleep" 124, 129, 250, 265–266, 279–280
Gowon, Yakubu 411–414, 421
Grand Popo 10
Great Depression 432
Greece 56, 79

Guadeloupe 366
Gumso, Muhammad Dan Haja 335–336
Gun (Igun) 10
Guyana 366

H

Haiti 366, 369, 378–381, 385
Haitian Revolution 378, 380
Hausa 160, 176, 231, 326, 333, 373
Hausa Balogun 330
Hausa-Fulani 399, 401, 404–405, 410–411, 415, 418, 422
Hausa kingdoms 333, 335
Hausaland 49, 56, 231, 254, 285, 330, 333–334, 346, 432, 437
Hausa trading communities 160, 334
Heligoland 387
Higgins, Henry 2
Hinderer, David 1–2, 135–136, 168, 324, 344–345, 353
Hinduism 382
Hindus 381
Hispaniola 366, 378
Holy Ghost Baptism 440
horses 233, See also cavalry
Horton, Robin 40, 47, 48
House of Chiefs 395
hunting 22

I

Ibadan 2, 18, 23, 55–56, 111, 135–137, 168–169, 221, 232, 294, 297–354, 357, 360–361, 363, 389–395, 399, 402–403, 414, 425–426, 431, 433, 447, 449
  emergence 297–299
  provincial administration 327
  Ibadan–Ijebu alliance 300
  republican system 298, 331, 344
  territorial expansion 302–307
Iba Magaji, Basorun 242
Ibarapa 8–9, 111–113, 241, 244, 252, 274, 305
Ibariba 33
Ibikunle, Balogun of Ibadan 307

Index

Ibolo 204, 242
Idanre 108
Idanre Hill 11, 13, 107
Idasin 15
Idassa 9, 114
Ideta-Oko 58–59
Idiagbon, Tunde 418
idi-aro 158, 159, 190
Idoma 6
Idowa 109
Ifa 32–36, 41, 59, 67, 73–74, 88, 98, 99, 102, 115, 131, 141, 144, 189, 206, 329, 354, 369, 371, 377
Ifa oracle 329
Ife (Ana) 8
Ife 1, 2, 4, 8, 11, 14–16, 18, 25, 33, 40–117, 120, 126, 139–143, 149, 152, 156–158, 160, 162–164, 169, 172, 175, 197–198, 204–205, 207, 209, 211–212, 222–223, 229, 232–234, 249, 252, 270, 272, 276, 295–307, 311–328, 331, 339–340, 344, 347, 353, 357–358, 360, 368–369, 385–386, 399, 401, 431, 449
  decline 143–145
  eleventh to fifteenth century 71–80
  Ife in the ninth to tenth century 43–56
  political influence of Ife in Yorubaland 144
  primacy in the eleventh to fifteenth century 71–83
  revolution in Ife 55–66
Ife–Benin route 103
"Ife bowl" 15, 44, 45, 53, 63
Ife–Ijebu alliance 295–296
Ife-Modakeke 326
Ife–Ondo disputes 312
Ifetedo 4, 7, 163
Ifewara 94
ifole, 'housebreaking' 354–355
Igala 6, 7, 115
Igbara-Odo 221
Igbara-Oke 213
"Igbo" (Ife settlements) 46
Igbo 6, 368, 401, 410–411, 418
Igbodo Nla 67

Igboho 117, 120, 237–240, 251–252, 276, 334
Igbo-Igbo 59, 63, 66, 84–85, 89, 143
Igbomina 7, 115, 151, 178, 203, 302–303, 397, 401
Igbomina (Igboona)
  Ila, Ajase, Isanlu, Omu, Aran, Oro, Igbaja, Iwo, Esie, Eku Apa, Ora, Oba, Idofian, Oro-Ago 115–116
Igbomina–Oyo-Ile alliance 151
igbo-orunkoja 134
Ige, Bola 416–417
Ighare chiefs, Owo 225
Igogo 224
Igun 111
Igunu 153
Ihare 122
Ihumbo 113, 168, 201
Ijanna 256
Ijaye, emergence 299
Ijaye War 306–307, 309, 311
Ijebu 2, 8–11, 14–15, 39, 48, 50–51, 67, 75, 79, 177, 223
  Ijebu-Ode, Ofin, Makun, Epe, Idowa, Ikija, Ago-Iwoye, Ijebu-Igbo, Ijebu-Ife 109–110
Ijebu-Ife 109
Ijebu-Igbo 109
Ijebu-Ode 48, 295, 300, 315, 352, 360, 392, 447
Ijesa 8, 97–98, 297–298, 300, 302–307, 309–311, 315–319, 321, 325–328, 334, 335, 339–341, 347, 351, 353, 358, 390, 392, 401
  Ilesa, Imesi-Ile, Esa, Ipetu, Otan, and Igbajo 148
Ijesa Wars 148
Ijo 48, 50, 104–106, 110
Ijo-Arogbo 106
Ijugbe 8, 14, 44, 46, 47
Ikale 8, 9, 11, 32, 106, 107
Ika-Odan 293
Ikenne 403
Ikere 104
Ikime, Obaro 104, 223
Ilaje 8, 9, 11, 50

Ila kingdom 121, 132, 204, 229
  Pemberton and Afolayan 121, 132
ilari 110, 146, 251, 286
Ilawe 221
iledi 64
Ile-Ife 2, 42–45, 59–60, 62–63, 65–81, 84, 87–89, 92–98, 117, 119, 140–144, 169, 204, 211, 232–234, 300–305, 318, 320, 323, 326, 331, 399, 431
Ile Iyagba 313
Ilesa 44, 49, 67, 72, 74, 88, 90, 98, 120, 126, 133–136, 138–140, 143, 146, 148–149, 152, 158, 160, 163, 177, 196, 209, 236, 239, 241, 244, 303, 309, 341, 345, 345, 390, 392
ileto 158
Ilorin 18, 277, 286–289, 332–340, 277
Ilorin, emergence 286–289
Ilorin vs Oyo wars 286–289
Iloromu 14
Ilu-alade 119
Imesi-Lasigidi 312–317, 390
Imojubi 14
imole 32
Imole cult 69
incantations 30, 35, 381
indentured servants 382
India 381, 442
Indian Ocean 50, 161
indigo 26, 157, 159, 192
Indirect Rule 391–392, 397–398
Industrial Revolution 343–344
infant mortality 30
installation rituals 99, 130, 226, 436
internal feuds 147–149
Ipole-Ijesa 48
iron 204
Iron Age 17
iron production 15, 17–20, 22, 25–26, 29, 32, 39–40, 50–52, 66, 68, 73, 78–79
  Meroe 85
  Taruga 85
iron tools 157, 184
iru 157, 184
irugba 157, 283

Irving, Dr 168
Ise 213
Ise–Emure feud 148
Iseri 110
Iseyin 117
Ishan 212
Islam 55–56, 278–279, 284, 287, 291, 326, 330, 333–335, 337–342, 347–348, 355–356, 362–363, 370, 374, 429–431, 436–437, 442–443
  Spread 291, 333–343
Islam and Christianity rivalry 355–356
Islamic emirate in Ilorin 296
Islamic law 398
Islamic movement in Yorubaland 279
Isoya 2
Isundunrin 18
Ita-Ijero 67
Itaogbolu 4
Itapa, the great conflict 59
Itsekiri 8, 9, 50, 102–106, 110, 156, 161, 162, 184, 185, 213–214, 222, 402, 414
Iwere 117, 252, 273, 276
iwofa 176, 185, 191, 192
iwope 21, 69
Iyalaje 166
Iyalode 298
iyere okin 195

J

Jakande, Lateef 417–418
Jakuta 73
Jamaa 280–286, 296, 337, 338
Jamaica 366, 378
January 1966 coup 410, 420
Japan 363
Johnson, Henry 350
Johnson, James 355, 356, 446
Johnson, Samuel 2, 11, 26, 32–33, 39, 43, 47, 49–51, 55–63, 65–76, 78, 80–84, 87–88, 91–92, 108–109, 113, 146, 167, 188, 193, 232, 235, 237, 241, 243, 249, 264, 265, 351, 355, 449
judicial and penal authority 38, 65, 175

Jumu 7, 8, 14, 18, 114–115, 305, 313, 322, 327, 329, 330, 361, 398, 401
June 12, 1993 418–423
juntas de alfornia 372

K

Kabba Emirate 398
Kakanda 6, 10, 115, 210, 254, 397
Kanla War 287
Kanuri 365
Katunga 229–230
Ketu 8, 9, 89–90, 113, 198, 229, 245, 386
Kingdoms of the Yoruba, Robert Smith 222
kingdoms of Yorubaland 97–154
    Ita Ijero oath 140
    One Band of Brothers 140–144
    Oyo Kingdoms: Oyo-Ile, Ogboro, Adikun, Iresa, Igbon, Ijeru, Iganna, Iwere, Asia, Okeho, Igijan, Saki, Igboho, Ibode, Ipapo, Kisi, Iseyin, Ilobu, Ifeodan, Iwo, Idese, Ede, Ogbomoso 116–118
    Central Kingdoms: Ife, Ifewara, Owu, Ilesa 97–99
    Eastern Kingdoms: Ekiti, Akoko 99–102
    Extreme Northeastern Subgroups: Owe, Ikiri, Abunu, Oworo, Yagba, Gbede and Jumu 114
    Northern Kingdoms: Igbomina
        Ila, Ajase, Isanlu, Omu, Aran, Oro, Igbaja, Iwo, Esie, Eku, Apa, Ora, Oba, Idofian, and Oro-Ago 115–117
    Southern Kingdoms: Owo, Itsekiri, Ilaje, Ikale, Ondo, Ijebu and Awori 102–111
    Subordinate towns and villages 138–141
    Western Kingdoms: Egba, Ibarapa, Egbado, Ketu, Sabe, Idasa, Ahori 111
kingmakers 94, 123–124, 127, 129, 130, 276, 395
King's Council (Inner Council) 121
King's Marketplace 137
King's Palace 133–135
kinship system 21–22
Kiriji War 320–322, 331, 351, 361, 390

knowledge 5, 15, 17–19, 22, 26, 30, 33, 35, 39, 44, 56, 57, 64, 74, 75, 92, 152, 176, 222, 266, 314, 340, 357, 377, 440, 448
Kobalede, Council of chiefs, Ketu 198
Kogbaye 239
Koiwo 44
kolanut 5, 47, 49, 66, 67, 157, 186, 191, 192, 275, 344, 431, 432, 443
Koran 301, 338
Kori, Alaafin 241
Kosoko 359
Kpengla, king of Dahomey 271
Krapf-Askari, Eva 158
Krio 383
Kumasi 49
Kumuyi, William Folorunso 441
Kurunmi 293, 294, 297, 299, 300, 306–308, 325, 331
    emergence 293
Kuti, I. O. 450
Kwara State 399, 414, 417, 426
Kwa subfamily 6, 9

L

labor 22, 26, 29, 36, 47, 181–185, 343, 367
    alagbawun 183
    influence of polygamy 181
    mutual labor pool 182
Laderin, Baale of Ilorin 276
Ladigbolu, Alaafin 393, 394
Ladipo, Duro 451
Lagos 56, 110, 135, 139, 161, 162, 221–223, 231, 254–255, 270, 298, 300–301, 306, 312, 313, 315, 318, 320–323, 326–328, 335, 341, 342, 345–348, 350–352, 354–355, 357–361, 383, 392, 395–397, 399, 401–403, 405, 409, 411–417, 419, 423, 428, 430–434, 446, 447
    origins 222–223
Lagos State 231
Lajamisan, Ooni 83–84
Lake Chad 159, 333
land 19, 29
    land ownership 29

Lander, Richard 157, 173, 176, 198–204, 230, 242, 254, 256–259, 285, 336, 338
language 3–4, 8–9, 110, 170, 357, 368, 445
  Kwa sub-group 6, 9
  Ode-Itsekiri 104
language and literature 362, 450
La regla de Ocha 377
Late Stone Age 5
Latoosa, Momoh Obadoke 309–311, 314, 315, 317–318, 320
lawani 398
Law, Robin 234
leadership 28, 38
Licomin 170
Lijadu, L. M. 233
lineage compound 52, 78, 153, 190, 199, 204, 283, 290, 435
lineage systems 11–90
  age grade 35
  ebi 38, 70, 85
  family 3, 20–21, 27, 34–39, 63, 77, 80–83
Lisabi 274–275
literacy 350, 357
Little Popo 10
livestock 372
loans and credit systems 191–194
  usufruct loans 192
Lokoja 217, 218, 355, 414
Louisiana 378
L'Ouverture, Toussaint 378, 380
Lower Niger 210, 218, 401
Lucumis of Cuba 375–378

M

Macaulay, Herbert 402
Mahi 8, 9, 271
Majekodunmi, Koye 408
Majeogbe, Alaafin 262
Majotu, Alaafin 202, 271, 276, 281, 285, 286, 287, 335, 336
Makun 109
Mali 333
Mann, A. C. 169
Mann, Adolphus 350

market days/cycle 41, 163–164, 188
Marketing Boards 433
marketplace 26, 40, 45, 46, 67, 137–138
markets 26, 37, 41, 47, 50, 53, 67–68, 84, 163–165, 167, 253, 325
market system 164–167
marriage systems 21, 22, 38, 46, 67, 146, 185, 233–234, 248, 437
Martinique 366
May, Daniel 169, 303, 346
Medieval Europe 51
Mediterranean 17, 75, 160, 231
Mejiro 4
Meko, Ketu 198
meritocracy 327
Meroe 17–18
metallurgy 18
Methodist Mission 352–353
Mewe 111
Middle East 55–56, 160, 232
Middle Niger 4, 6–8, 206, 209, 230, 231, 240, 355, 359, 401
migration 7, 56, 88, 89, 103, 151, 327, 452
  alarinjo, traveling entertainers 152–153
  causes 88–96
  distinguished migrants 152–153
  egungun entertainers 151–153
  kingdom creation 151–153
  meeting of "wise men" 152
  Oyo-Ile emigration 290
military power 269
military roles and leaders 251
Mina 161, 366
Moba 138, 302, 397, 398, 399, 401
Moba, Ekiti 302, 397
Modakeke 44, 300, 304, 305, 318, 320, 326, 328, 331, 353
Mohammed, Murtala 414–415, 421
monarchical government 84, 264, 328
  checks and balances 265
Moremi 66
Morgan, Kemi 449
Mugbamugba War 283
murals 21, 24, 45–46, 52, 69, 131, 257

music 25, 70, 167, 195, 197, 201–202, 257, 261, 370, 376, 381–385, 437–441, 446, 449–451
myths 1, 3, 13, 56
myths of creation 1

N

Nago 366, 369–374
Nago revolts 372
Napoleon Bonaparte 378
national consciousness 39, 153, 357, 358, 362–363, 376, 403
  influence of the eleventh to eighteenth century 153
National Council of Nigeria and the Cameroons (NCNC) 402
National Council of Nigerian Citizens (NCNC) 401–405, 407
National Democratic Coalition (NADECO) 419
nationalist agitation 402
National Party of Nigeria (NPN) 415–418
National Political Reform Conference 426
National Republican Convention (NRC) 418
Native Airs 450
Native Authority 392
Native Baptist Church 446
Native Court system 392, 393
New Calabar 171
newspapers 56, 402, 447
New World 367, 368, 381, 384
Nicaragua 366
Niger–Benue confluence 6–8, 114–115, 218, 299, 305
  Owe, Ikiri, Abunu, Oworo, Yagba, Gbede and Jumu 114–115
Niger Coast Protectorate 221, 361
Niger-Congo family 9
Niger Delta 424
Nigeria 4, 5, 70, 95, 112, 332, 350, 351, 355, 358, 360–362, 366, 385, 387, 389, 391–429, 431–436, 439, 441, 443, 445, 448, 451, 452
Nigerian Bar Association 416
Nigerian civil war 411–414

Nigerian independence 394, 400
Nigerian National Democratic Party (NNDP) 408, 409, 416
Nigerian railway system 431
Nile Valley 7
nineteenth century revolutions 291–363
ninth to tenth century 39, 40, 43, 47, 48, 50, 52, 53, 60–62
North Carolina 366
northeastern Yoruba 7, 204
Northern Africa 4, 7
Northern Peoples Congress (NPC) 401–402, 405, 407–409
Nupe 3, 6, 7, 10, 33, 51, 90, 101–102, 115–117, 143–144, 151, 153, 159, 160, 162–164, 171–178, 185, 197, 206–209, 210, 218, 229–242, 295, 303, 312–342, 346, 348, 355, 365, 397
Nupe–Bariba frontier 265
Nupe influences 206–209
Nupe raids 203
Nupe trading communities 160

O

Obafemi Awolowo University 44
Oba Isaac Babalola Akinyele 449
Obajio 28
Obajio of Ijio 28
Obalara 50
Obalokun, Alaafin 241–245, 265
Obalufon 66
Obalufon II 16
Obameri 58, 60
Obasanjo, Olusegun 413–416, 422–426, 452
Oba settlement 15
Obatala 1–3, 47, 54, 58–62, 72–73, 89 369
Obawinrin 89
Obayemi, Ade 139, 152, 223
Obo, Ekiti 79, 99, 184, 302, 397, 398, 401
Obokun 49, 88, 98
Ode-Itsekiri 103–105, 161–162
Ode-Ondo 204
Ode-Ondo mission 356
odi 135, 150

Odua People's Congress 419
Oduduwa 1–3, 11, 26, 32–33, 39, 43, 47, 49–51, 55–73, 75–76, 78, 80–84, 87, 89, 91–94, 97–99, 102, 107, 108, 113, 115, 117, 121, 130–131, 146, 151, 187, 195, 197, 232, 234, 357–358, 369, 393–394, 403, 419, 448
Oduduwa Constitution 63
Odu Ifa 33, 34, 49, 59, 67, 74, 88, 99, 102
Offa 90, 116, 242, 321
Ofin 109
ofo 74
Ofinran, Alaafin 237, 238, 241
Ogbogbodinrin, Obalufon 81, 82
Ogbomoso 117, 169
Ogbomudu, Benin 215
Ogboni 64–65, 98, 124, 126, 150, 207, 354, 377, 385, 438, 447, 448
  origins 64–65
Ogborogan 109
Ogedemgbe 309–314, 316–317, 331, 341, 390
Ogho 15
ogede 74
Ogidi Alliance 322–323, 330
Ogiso 117
Ogoga 100, 148
Ogotun 101, 213, 221
Ogo Were 280
Ogun 18–19, 31–32, 66, 73–74, 81, 83, 99, 131, 184, 195, 215, 233, 299, 369, 382, 414, 416
Ogunbiyi, T. A. J. 447
Ogunde, Hubert 426, 450–451
Ogundipe, Babafemi 411
Ogundiran, Akin 61, 76
Ogunfunminire 110
Ogun Jalumi 317
Ogunmola, Balogun 308–309, 450
Ogunmola, Kola 450
Ogun Oluponakusupona, Benin–Ado war 215–216
Ogun River 110, 112–113, 161, 274
Ogunsigun, Seriki of Ijebu 2, 319
Oguntuyi, Anthony 148, 196, 216, 449

Ogun Wokuti 311
Ogunyemi, Wale 451
oil palm 6, 52, 156
Oja Igbomoko 46
Ojigi 241, 242, 248, 249, 265
Ojo Agunbambaru 278
Ojoko of Kesi 112, 139, 150
Ojumu 58, 61, 225
Ojumu peace 61
Okemesi, Imesi-Igboodo 315
Okeoja 14, 44, 46, 63
Oke Suna 278, 282, 284, 337
oko egan 199
Okuku kingdom 116, 121
Okunade, the Maye of Ife 297
Okun Yoruba 7–8, 26, 114–115, 156, 163, 164, 169, 173, 177–178, 210–211, 218, 248, 254, 299, 313–314, 322, 325, 330, 390, 397–399, 401
Olaleetan 310
Oloba 15
Olodumare 1, 31–32, 71
Olofa of Offa 320
Olofin 111
Ologundudu, Kunle 427
oloja 67
Olokun 68, 70, 73, 77, 187, 369
Olomola, Isola 44, 46
Olomu of Omu 151
olori-ebi 38
Olori-Marun 122
Olorogun chiefs 329
Olorun 1, 31, 32, 369
Olosunta 220
Olosunta Hill 13, 100
Olota Rock 13–15, 100, 120, 136
Olotu-Ado 218
Olotu Ekirun 213
Olowagbon (of Igbon) 28
Olowo Adedipe 226
Olu 28
Olua, Oba of Benin 103
Oluewu, Alaafin 271, 287–289, 299, 330, 338
Olugbadehan, Oladipo 121, 147, 174, 224–226

Olukere 220
Olupo of Ajase Ipo 151
Olupopo of Popo 88, 113
Olusin 210, 329, 330
Oluwa 32
Oluwa River 105
Oluyole, Basorun of Ibadan 307, 344
Omologun 14, 44, 63
Omu 103, 115, 151, 255, 311
Onabanjo, Bisi 417
Ona River 111
ondaiye 43
Ondo 8, 9, 11, 14, 32, 44, 107, 108
Onibode 135, 179, 252
Onigbogi, Alaafin of Oyo 237
Onikoyi 251, 252, 255, 263, 273, 281, 284, 285, 285, 295
Onire of Ire 154
Oni River 72
onisegun 30, 41, 73, 444
onisegun aremo 30
Onishile, Alaafin 265
Oore of Otun 216
opa akun 142
opa ileke 142
Opa Oranmiyan 42, 79, 204
oral traditions 3, 11, 14, 19, 29–30, 48, 66, 368, 385, 448–449
Oranfe, ruler of Ora 54
Orangun of Ila 154, 324
Oranmiyan 42, 56, 79, 81–82, 88, 94, 100–101, 104, 113, 117, 142, 204, 232–236, 250
Oreluere 57, 59, 60
Orhogbua, Oba of Benin 222
ori aiye 261
origins 1, 7, 8, 11
   Johnsonian "Middle Eastern" hypothesis 55–57
   Oranmiyan 56
oriki 21, 49, 84, 125, 145, 182, 195, 393
orirun 43, 140
Orisa 31–32
orisa 32, 204, 369, 381, 384
Orisanla 32, 73, 95
Orisateko 47, 81, 82

Orisha Religion 382
Orisha Yemaya 364
oro 68
Oronna 44
Orosun Hill 11, 13, 107, 216
Orungberuwa 107
Orunmila 70, 73, 74, 99, 102, 377
Oseganderuku, Ooni 84
Osemowe 88, 108, 138, 149, 319, 341
Osi (Ekiti) 48
Osin 28–31
Osin, king 28–29
Osin-mole 31
Oso Akerele 390
Osofisan, Femi 451
Osogbo 90, 140, 164, 169, 300–301, 339, 414
Osogboye 133, 136, 197, 214–215, 218, 224–226
osomaalo 194, 231, 345
Osun River 231, 249–255, 281
Osun Valley 11, 184, 300–302, 316
Otta 74, 110–111, 153, 238, 301, 327
Owamuaran, Oba of Benin 160
Owiwi Stream 300
Owo 4, 8–9, 13, 15, 32–34, 48, 75, 79, 88, 102–103, 120–121, 133, 135–136, 138, 142, 147–149, 152, 156, 158, 160, 162–164, 167, 174, 177, 185, 197–198, 211–216, 218–219, 221, 223–227, 261–288, 298, 304–305, 308, 313–314, 319, 327, 328, 342, 353, 361, 402, 419, 449
owo eyo 50, *See* cowry
Owu 88, 96–97, 108, 111, 116, 157, 160, 164, 139, 144, 146, 149, 197, 205, 207, 229–230, 233, 236, 238, 245, 269, 280, 293–297, 321, 323–328, 400, 401
Owu-Ipole siege 296
Owu War 356
Oyebode, R. S. 356
Oyedepo, David 441
Oyo 2, 4, 8–11, 26, 29, 56, 71–73, 75, 116
Oyo Empire 56, 229–292, 296, 299, 302, 334, 365, 368

administration 249–255
culture 256–259
decline and revival of Oyo-Ile 237–239
defence and war tactics 242–245
early beginnings 232–236
fall of Oyo Empire 261–288, 292
growth and power 240–243
influences 292
provinces 252
slaves, source and trade 254–256
territorial expansion 244–249
Oyo-Ile 4, 71–73, 75, 88, 90, 104, 108, 110, 117, 119–120, 123, 126, 131, 135, 140, 144, 147, 149, 151, 157, 160, 162–164, 167, 173, 176, 180, 197, 198, 201, 203, 206–207, 209, 216, 229–242, 244, 245, 246, 249–254, 256–290, 297, 299–300, 323, 326, 334–336, 338, 340, 346
Oyotunji Village 385
Ozanne, Paul 14–15, 47, 50, 67
Ozolua, Oba of Benin 107

P

palm oil 25, 343, 444
palm wine 25, 37, 47, 156, 161, 182, 186
Panama 366
pan-Yoruba 74, 363
pan-Yoruba gods 31, 32, 73, 369
Parakin 14, 44
paramount chief 392, 397
participatory meritocracy 328
patterns in trade
    decline of the south-central parts of Yorubaland 163
pawning 185
Pax Britannica 445
Payne, John Augustus O. 358, 448
peace agreement 58–59
Peace Treaty 1886 331
"Pelupelu" ('gathering of the kings') 393
Pemberton, John 52, 79, 121, 132, 204
Pentecostal Movement 440–441
    Assemblies of God 441
    Deeper Life Bible Fellowship 441
    Four Square Gospel Church 441

Redeemed Christian Church of God 441
    Winners Chapel 441
People's Democratic Party (PDP) 422–423
peregun 147
"permanent existence" 58
Perreira, Duarte Pacheco 135, 171
pharmacopeia 24, 30, 39, 52, 444
Phillips, Charles 341, 356, 449
philosophy 33
Pilgrims Welfare Board 437
plantations 157, 168, 171, 199, 344, 367, 369–371, 373, 375, 378, 381, 431–435, 443
poetry 3, 21, 33, 84
Pole War 302
political systems 172, 328
politics of kingdom rule
    Abilagba, Ewi of Ado-Ekiti's first son 123
    Aremo, Alaafin's first son 80, 123, 224, 250
    Baale 124
    chieftaincy 124–126
    Committee of high chiefs 123–124
    Council of Kingmakers 123–125
    foundational model 121
    "go to sleep", royal deposition 124, 129, 250, 265
    hereditary principles 124–125, 129–130, 250–251, 265–266
    Ihare 122
    installation rituals 130
    King-in-Council 122–123
    King's Council (Inner Council) 121–122
    monarchical system 55, 80, 107, 126, 130, 179–181, 215, 264–265, 328, 391
    Olori-Marun 122
    Oyo Mesi 122, 243, 250–251, 266, 267, 270, 276, 285
    primogeniture 80, 123, 224, 250
    quarter chief 12, 45, 64, 64, 120–122, 127, 192
    sources of royal income 179–181
    the king as 'god': *Ekeji Orisa, Alase, Alaye, Agbogbomoja-ekun, Baba-yeye* 125–126
    Prime Minister 122

Index

town crier 122
weaknesses 129–130
women rulers 126
politics of the twentieth century 387–424
  Agbaja Emirate 397–398
  British Colony and Protectorate
    of Nigeria 387
  chefs de canton 388
  Conseil des Rois (Council of Kings) 389
  Northern Yoruba under British
    rule 397–398
  Yoruba in Nigeria's politics 396
  Yoruba kingdoms under
    French rule 387–389
  Yoruba traditional rulers in Nigeria
    389–396
polygamy 437–438
Popo 8–10, 88, 113–114, 246, 249
population 11, 20, 47, 51, 53, 60, 75, 91, 105, 107–108, 112, 119–120, 136, 144, 157, 160, 167, 199, 206, 211, 222, 231, 235, 245, 261, 284, 287, 292–294, 297–300, 306, 310, 323, 326–328, 333, 342, 344, 347, 356, 362, 369, 374, 376, 377, 379, 383, 387, 399, 447, 448
Port Novo. See Ajase
Portuguese 50, 135, 141–142, 160–161, 171, 247, 348, 359, 366, 369–370
pre-Oduduwa 33, 60, 63, 65–66, 69–72, 80–82, 89, 108, 113, 121
professional guilds and trade associations 22, 127
Progressive Unions, Development Associations 402, 430
Protectorate of Nigeria 392
Protectorate of Northern Nigeria 361
Protectorate of Southern Nigeria 361
protector spirit 13, 15, 41, 100, 377
Protestant Christian 382
provincial administration 255, 302, 311, 316, 327
Pupupu 107

Q

quilimbos 374

R

race theories 445, 447
Raffia vinifera, *oguro* 46, 47, 156
Recôncavo, Bahia 369
Red Sea 17
refugees 294, 296–297, 326
refugee settlements 322, 324
Regional Government 404, 430–434
religion 1, 3, 6, 9, 31–35, 45, 55, 63, 73, 334, 368–369, 381
religion and the state 130–133
  "companion of the gods" 130
religious rituals 368
religious transformation 436–442
Renaissance Europe 79
Renrengenjen, Olowo of Owo 224–226
Rift Valley 4
Rio de la Plata 366
rituals 3, 6, 11, 13, 19, 22, 27–28, 30–32, 35–38, 40–41, 45, 56, 59, 66, 77–78, 82, 382, 442
  installation rituals 130
ritual suicide, "go to sleep" 250
River Mono 261
River Moshi 240, 244, 249, 261
River Niger 40, 159, 169, 231, 235, 249, 251, 346, 432
Robinson, Randall 378
Rodney, Walter 174
Roman Catholicism 353, 370, 376, 381–382, 384, 439
Rome 56, 79
Rosiji, Ayo 407
Ross, William A. 393
Rotimi, Ola 451
Royal Niger Company 323, 330, 361
Ryder, A.F.C. 141–142

S

Sabe 8–9, 88, 113–114, 120, 249, 360
sacrifices 442
Sagamu 329
Sahara Desert 4, 40, 401
Saint-Domingue 366, 369, 375, 378–380
salt 39, 50, 156, 184, 432

Salubi 113
Salvador 369
Sango 73, 131, 233, 235, 238, 251, 257, 265–266, 354, 369, 382, 385
Santería 376–377
Saros 383
satiric festival 128
Savi 205, 246
savings and capital formation 187–192
  alajo 188
  esusu 188
  usufruct loans 192
sculptural art 24–25, 34, 48–49, 52, 59, 69, 77–79, 186, 195, 197–198, 200, 204, 256–257
Second Republic 415–418
  two-thirds debate 416
Second World War 432
seized crowns 236
sekere 265
self government 400
seniority 121, 151
Sha 8, 114
Shagari, Shehu 415–417, 421
Shaki 199, 202
Shonekan, Ernest 419
shrines 257
Sierra Leone 2, 55, 318, 326, 342–343, 347–348, 350–353, 358, 365, 383–384
sixteenth century 155–178
slavery 312, 322, 326–327, 343, 366
slave trade 170–178, 205, 209, 246, 253, 254, 267–269, 277, 291, 306, 325, 327, 343, 347, 359, 365, 367–368, 374, 375, 382, 383
Smith, A. W. 356
Smith, Robert 92, 108, 135, 142, 222
Social Democratic Party (SDP) 418
Sodeke 329, 352, 354
sokoto 444
Solagberu 228, 337
Solanke, the Jagunna of Igbein 354
Songhai Empire 48
Sopasan 113
source of Yoruba Kingdoms 140–142

South Carolina 366, 378, 385
southern Yorubaland 16
Soyinka, Wole 384, 427, 450–451
Spanish settlers 171, 366, 376, 378, 381
Spiritual Baptists 382
standard Yoruba 362
St. Lucia 366
Stone Age 17
  Late Stone Age 4–6
  Middle Stone Age 4
stone carvings 204
strangers' area 60, 62
subgroups 8, 384
  Ahori 8
  Akoko 8
  Awori 8
  Bunu 7
  Egba 8,
  Egbado 8
  Ekiti 7
  Gbede 8
  Ibarapa 8
  Idasa 8
  Ife 7
  Ife (Ana) 8
  Ifonyin 7
  Igbomina 8
  Ijebu 8
  Ijesa 8
  Ikiri 7
  Itsekiri 8
  Itsha (Sha) 8
  Jumu 250
Sultan Bello 56, 254
Surinam 366, 385
Supreme Being 31–32

T

talking drums 257
Taruga 17–18, 85
tenth century 11–12, 14, 26, 31–32, 40–47, 52–53, 55, 162
theatre 258
the great conflict 59–62
The History of the Yorubas 55–56, 87, 351, 449
Third Republic 418–420

tie-and-dye 444
Tobago 366
Tofa, Bashir 418
Togbesu 248
Togo 8–11, 113–114, 169, 196, 229, 231, 249, 360, 362, 366, 387, 436, 451
town crier 122
Toyeje, Baale of Ogbomoso 278, 282–283, 295
trade 3, 26, 39–40, 47–53, 60, 66–69, 72, 75, 85, 306, 432
tradition 10, 21, 28, 33, 47, 62–63, 66–68, 79, 82, 89, 93, 104, 107–108, 110, 113, 128, 146, 181, 190, 193–194, 204, 212, 226, 233–234, 237, 241–242, 249, 258, 266, 273, 298, 331, 333, 336, 344, 381, 384, 405, 422, 434, 437, 439, 441, 450
traditions of kingdom founders 87–96
   Alaketu, Ketu 88
   Awamaro, Ado Ekiti 88
   Badagry 111
   chieftaincy contests and disputes 89, 129
   Imesi Igbodo 90
   Ita Ijero oath 140
   migrations 88–89, 151
   Obanta, Ijebu-Ode 88
   Ojugbelu, Owo 88
   Olojo Agbele, Ifewara 89
   Olowu, Owu-Ipole 88
   Onisabe, Sabe 88
   Oranmiyan, Benin 88, 141
   Sopasan, Ketu 89
   ways and means 92
transatlantic slave trade 171–175, 365. *See also* slave trade
transportation 432
trans-Saharan trade 40, 48, 50–51, 53, 75, 160
Trinidad 366, 381, 381–382, 385
Trinidad Carnival 382
Tuaregs 160
twelfth century 50, 102, 126, 148, 212
twentieth century 4, 20, 39, 55, 70, 79, 99, 103, 126, 135–136, 188, 191, 194–195, 224, 226, 299, 326, 328, 341, 350, 351, 356, 358–359, 381, 386, 387, 389, 391, 395, 396, 410, 413, 420, 423, 427, 429–439, 441–443, 447, 449, 450–451
   social transformations 429–449
      communal changes 435–436
      economic growth 431–434
      occupations 443–445
twins 31, 38, 107, 108

U

Ugbo 106
Ughoton (Gwarto), Benin port 161
Ulkami, Ulkomi, or Alkamy 217, 218, 375
Ulsheimer, Andreas Joshua 222
umale 104
United People's Party 408
United States 378, 381, 383, 385, 440, 442
Unity Party of Nigeria (UPN) 415, 416
University College, Ibadan 431
Upper Ogun 299, 305, 307–309, 320, 325
urban citizens 119–121
urban communities 120, 193
urban dwellers 158
urbanism 157–158
Urhobo 104
Usman, Aribidesi 207, 234, 235
Usman dan Fodio 335
usufruct loans 192

V

Venezuela 366
village groups 12
Virginia 366
visual artists 153
Vodou 381

W

war (warrior) chiefs 64, 125, 174, 242, 251, 261–268, 273, 274, 304, 310, 313, 315–316, 320, 329–330, 344, 389–391
Ward-Price, H. L. 394
wars of change 291–331
   1886 Peace Treaty 320, 331

anti-Ibadan resistance 314–322
  British intervention 312, 320
  causes 291–295
  decade of minor wars 308–314
  effects of the wars 323–330
  emergence of cosmopolitan Lagos 326
  fall of Bida 323
  Ibadan–Abeokuta battles 300
  Jabara War 300
  new centers of population 326
  newly consolidated states 297–303
  Ogidi Alliance 322–323
  Owu War 295–301
  seige of Owu-Ipole 296
weave 25
wedding 37, 46, 384
Weme 205, 246, 255
Wesleyan Mission 447
West Africa 2–7, 14, 16–19, 48–51, 53, 77, 117, 135, 159–160, 169–171, 186, 187, 209, 229–231, 242, 259, 260, 318, 343, 351, 355, 361, 366, 368, 372, 380, 386, 429, 446, 448
Western education 292, 333, 347, 356–357, 363, 389, 429–431, 445
Western Ife 8–9
Western Nigeria 366
Western Region 394, 395, 401, 434
Western Region crisis 403–408, 452
  effect on Yoruba solidarity 409
Western Region Development Corporation 434
Western Region in Nigerian politics 399–420
Western Yoruba 9–10
West Indies 171, 366, 381, 383, 385
Whydah 161, 165, 171, 205, 246–247
Willet, Frank 142
Williams, Joseph 221
witchcraft 31, 74, 113, 171
women 18, 21, 22, 25, 29–31, 35, 37, 38, 45, 69–70, 73–74, 437, 437
women in the economy 186–187, 445
women rulers
  Adetinrin, founder of Ila 115, 126, 142
  Luwo Gbagada, Ooni of Ife 142
  Owa Ori (Yeye Wari) 126
  Yeye Loreowu, Ado 126
wonka 437
Wood, J. B. 350

Y

yadi, 'break out' 90
Yagba 14
yam festivals 19
yams 5, 6, 12, 19, 46–47, 83
Yau Yamba, Basorun 242, 247–248, 261
Yegbata 83
Yemoja 363
Yemoja, Yemaja 363, 369, 377, 382
Yoruba Akoko 218
Yoruba Baloguns 330
Yoruba Catholicism 370
Yoruba consciousness 153, 358
Yoruba Diaspora 365–385
  Akus 383
  Nagos of Bahia 369–373
  Revolutionaries of Haiti 378–381
Yoruba Itsha 229
Yorubaland in the nineteenth century 291–354
  advent of "legitimate trade" 343
  changes in overseas trade and relations 343–347
  coming of Christianity 332, 352–359
  European exploration of the interior 346
  Lagos and intercontinental trade 345
  return from the Americas 347–351
  return of the emigrants 347
  the new "family" 298
Yoruba nationalism 357–359
Yoruba orthography 350–351
Yoruba Vision 425–427